ARNOLD BENNETT:
THE CRITICAL HERITAGE

THE CRITICAL HERITAGE SERIES

GENERAL EDITOR: B. C. SOUTHAM, M.A., B.LITT. (OXON.)
Formerly Department of English, Westfield College, University of London

For a list of books in the series see the back end paper

ARNOLD BENNETT

THE CRITICAL HERITAGE

Edited by
JAMES HEPBURN
Dana Professor of English
Bates College
Lewiston, Maine

ROUTLEDGE & KEGAN PAUL
LONDON, BOSTON AND HENLEY

First published in 1981
by Routledge & Kegan Paul Ltd
39 Store Street, London WC1E 7DD,
9 Park Street, Boston, Mass. 02108, USA, and
Broadway House, Newtown Road,
Henley-on-Thames, Oxon RG9 1EN
Printed in Great Britain by
Redwood Burn Ltd, Trowbridge & Esher
Compilation, introduction, notes, bibliography and index
Copyright © James Hepburn 1981

British Library Cataloguing in Publication Data

Arnold, Bennett. – (Critical heritage series)

1. Bennett, Arnold – Criticism and interpretation –
Addresses, essays, lectures
I. Hepburn, James   II. Series
823'.9'12   PR6003.E6Z/   80–41525

ISBN 0–7100–0512–1

General Editor's Preface

The reception given to a writer by his contemporaries and near-contemporaries is evidence of considerable value to the student of literature. On one side we learn a great deal about the state of criticism at large and in particular about the development of critical attitudes towards a single writer; at the same time, through private comments in letters, journals or marginalia, we gain an insight upon the tastes and literary thought of individual readers of the period. Evidence of this kind helps us to understand the writer's historical situation, the nature of his immediate reading-public, and his response to these pressures.

The separate volumes in the *Critical Heritage Series* present a record of this early criticism. Clearly, for many of the highly productive and lengthily reviewed nineteenth- and twentieth-century writers, there exists an enormous body of material; and in these cases the volume editors have made a selection of the most important views, significant for their intrinsic critical worth or for their representative quality—perhaps even registering incomprehension!

For earlier writers, notably pre-eighteenth century, the materials are much scarcer and the historical period has been extended, sometimes far beyond the writer's lifetime, in order to show the inception and growth of critical views which were initially slow to appear.

In each volume the documents are headed by an Introduction, discussing the material assembled and relating the early stages of the author's reception to what we have come to identify as the critical tradition. The volumes will make available much material which would otherwise be difficult of access and it is hoped that the modern reader will be thereby helped towards an informed understanding of the ways in which literature has been read and judged.

B.C.S.

TO MY WIFE

CONTENTS

'Hilda Lessways' (1911)

General Views: 1910–12

'The Regent' (1913)

'The Price of Love' (1914)

'These Twain' (1916)

'The Lion's Share' (1916)

General Views: 1913–16

I have been a reviewer myself. I once reviewed one
thousand books in three years. The first article I
insinuated into a London daily was a review. And it
appears to me that I am still (in a manner) reviewing.
I have even reviewed for the 'Manchester Guardian'!
Glorious day! For in the matter of reviewing the
'Manchester Guardian' is a twin summit with the 'Times
Literary Supplement'. So that I know about reviewing.
And although I have suffered from reviewers, I would
always defend them against the charges of the laity.

The wonder is not that book reviews are as dull as
they usually are, but that they are as bright as they
usually are. For you will kindly remember that during
a large part of their time reviewers have to occupy
themselves with dull books. What can you say about a
dull book except that it is dull?

Further, during a large part of their time reviewers must con books of which the authors have all been
consciously or unconsciously engaged in imitating one
another. Think of the terrible narcotic effect on reviewers. Talk about reviewers being unwilling to
recognise originality! Why, no hart ever panted after
a water-brook as a reviewer yearns for originality in
a book. There are crises in a reviewer's career when
the advent of an original work may save him from the
madhouse.

    Arnold Bennett, writing in the 'Evening
    Standard', 1927

Can't something be done to buck up the 'Lit. Suppl.'?
It is getting duller & duller, though it always contains 1 or 2 good articles.

    Arnold Bennett, writing to F.S.A. Lowndes,
    who was on the staff of 'The Times', 1920

The Review in the 'Daily Mail' is kind enough but it is execrably written and shows no comprehension of the book whatever. I do not see how any quotation from it would persuade anybody with any experience of other novels or reviews to buy the book. Further, no one who is interested in books cares a fig what the 'Daily Mail' thinks about a novel. (I know I am exaggerating a little but you understand what I mean.)

Further, I hope you will not imitate the extraordinary stupidity of publishers' advertisements (which are notoriously the most futile in the world) and quote the same reviews in all the papers in which you advertise. Extracts which might please the readers of the 'Evening Standard' for example, would leave quite cold the readers of the 'Nation', 'New Statesman', 'Literary Supplement', 'Observer', or 'Sunday Times'. No publisher within my experience has apparently ever thought of this obvious truth.

> Arnold Bennett, writing to a member of the staff of Methuen, who had just published 'Mr. Prohack', 1922

Preface

I have restricted this collection to criticism of twenty-four of Arnold Bennett's novels and one volume of short stories. In the Introduction I have sketched the critical reception of all of his books. Discussion of plays, librettos, and film stories is in a section separate from the other material. The criticism is arranged chronologically. I have given special attention to reviews in the 'Staffordshire Sentinel' and the 'Manchester Guardian'. All reviews have been reprinted from their original sources, with typographical errors silently corrected. Long quotations from the novels or long summaries of plots in the reviews have been omitted, with the omissions indicated.

I have given a fairly full account of editions without attempting to be exhaustive. I have not noted translations or editions in English other than English and American. Tauchnitz in Leipzig did issue twenty-seven volumes of Bennett's works in the years 1902-21. George Doran, the American publisher, tried several times to arrange for a collected edition, but Bennett had so many English publishers that it was not feasible. Uniform editions of several novels were issued in 1926 (in the Minerva Edition of Modern Authors) and again in 1949-51. The Arno Press in New York recently issued a facsimile edition of ninety volumes of Bennett's works.

Acknowledgments

My chief debt is to my wife, who helped with searching for
reviews and preparing the manuscript. I am also obliged
to Nicholas Redman for lending me his file of clippings
on Bennett from the 'Daily Express' and other newspapers.
Anita Miller kindly gave me information on many reviews,
Patrick Quinn gave me reviews of short story collections,
and John Ford gave me advice. I am indebted to the late
Dr LaFayette Butler and to Charles Tolhurst Butler for
repeated helpfulness. Most of the information on sales
and contracts derives from Dr Butler's collection of
Bennett material. I am also very much obliged to Norman
Emery, Deputy Area Librarian, Central Library, Hanley,
Stoke-on-Trent, and to Ian H.C. Fraser, Archivist, Uni-
versity of Keele Library, for providing information and
other help. Mrs Lola Szladits, Curator of the Berg
Collection, New York Public Library, and the Librarian
of the Chichester Library kindly provided information.
I relied upon Norman Emery's 'Arnold Bennett, A Biblio-
graphy' and Anita Miller's 'Arnold Bennett, An Annotated
Bibliography' for many details. Louis Tillier's 'Arnold
Bennett et ses romans réalistes' and Margaret Locherbie-
Goff's 'La Jeunesse d'Arnold Bennett' were also helpful.
Most of my research was done at the British Library in
Colindale, and I would like to express my appreciation to
the people there. I am similarly obliged to people at the
British Library in Bloomsbury, the Central Library,
Hanley, Stoke-on-Trent, and the Manchester Central
Library. Several newspapers and publishers kindly pro-
vided information: the 'Guardian', the 'Evening Sentinel',
Penguin Books, Eyre Methuen, Cassell, Hamish Hamilton,
Chatto & Windus, and J.M. Dent. Peter Moore and Joline
Goulet provided able secretarial assistance. Lastly
I would like to thank the administrators of Bates College
for a grant in support of the work.

Forty-nine of the 136 reviews and other items originally appeared in the 'Manchester Guardian', the 'Staffordshire Sentinel', the 'Spectator', and the 'Times Literary
Supplement', and I am especially obliged to the editors of
the 'Guardian', the 'Evening Sentinel', the 'Spectator',
and the 'Times Literary Supplement' for their generosity.
Acknowledgments are due to the 'Atlantic Monthly' for No.
58 (Copyright © by The Atlantic Monthly Company, Boston,
Mass., reprinted by permission); to the Trustees of the
Joseph Conrad Estate for No. 6; to the 'Contemporary
Review' for No. 88; to the 'Daily Express' for Nos 81,
103, and 130; to the 'Sunday Express' for Nos 102 and 104;
to Associated Newspapers Group Ltd for Nos 44, 74, 85, 98,
121, and 127, from the 'Daily Mail', 'Daily News', 'Daily
Chronicle', and 'News Chronicle'; to the 'Daily Telegraph' for No. 91; to Frank Swinnerton and the 'Evening
News' for Nos 128 and 135; to the 'Evening Sentinel'
(Staffordshire) for Nos 11, 20, 25, 26, 33, 37, 52, 63,
78, 92, 96, and 134; to the 'Guardian' for Nos 5, 15, 21,
28, 32, 38, 49, 53, 60, 65, 75, 76, 79, 89, 94, 99, 105,
114, 123, 126, and 133; to 'Harper's' for No. 73 (Copyright © 1911 by 'Harper's Magazine', all rights reserved,
reprinted from the March 1911 issue by special permission); to the 'Nation' (New York) for Nos 59, 67, and 87
(Copyright 1911 and 1915 The Nation Associates); to the
'New Statesman' for Nos 41, 48, 54, 66, 72, 77, 83, 100,
108, 110, 118, and 124, from the 'New Statesman', the
'Nation and Athenaeum', the 'Nation', and the 'Athenaeum';
to the 'New Republic' for Nos 84, 93, and 95; to the 'New
York Times' for Nos 17, 55, and 111 (© 1902/10/23 by The
New York Times Company, reprinted by permission); to
Oxford University Press for Nos 10, 12, 19, 24, 27, 41,
42, 103, and 121; to J.B. Priestley for No. 112 (reprinted
by permission of A.D. Peters & Co. Ltd); to V.S. Pritchett
for No. 131 (reprinted by permission of A.D. Peters & Co.
Ltd); to 'Punch' for Nos 101, 106, and 119; to the 'Scotsman' for No. 22; to the 'Spectator' for Nos 9, 14, 34, 69,
86, 109, 115, and 131; to Times Newspapers Ltd for Nos 122
and 129 from the 'Sunday Times'; to the 'Times Literary
Supplement' for Nos 8, 16, 39, 50, 61, 64, 82, and 117;
to A.P. Watt Ltd and the Executors of the Estate of H.G.
Wells for Nos 10, 19, 27, 40, and 125; to A.P. Watt Ltd
and the Executors of the Estate of Dorothy Cheston
Bennett for Nos 1, 10, 12, 19, 24, 27, 36, 40, 41, 42,
103, and 121, and for miscellaneous passages from Bennett's 'Journals' and other writings; to Rebecca West for
No. 85 (reprinted by permission of A.D. Peters & Co. Ltd);
to the Wilmer House Museum, Farnham, Surrey, for No. 12;
to The Hogarth Press and Harcourt Brace Jovanovich, Inc.,

for No. 113 (from 'The Captain's Death Bed and Other
Essays' by Virginia Woolf, copyright 1950, 1978 by Harcourt Brace Jovanovich, Inc., reprinted by permission of
the Author's Literary Estate and the publishers).

I am also grateful to the Staffordshire County Library
for permission to quote from a letter from Bennett to
Amphilis Carter, and to the Henry W. and Albert A. Berg
Collection, the New York Public Library, Astor, Lenox
and Tilden Foundations, for permission to quote from
Bennett's manuscript Some Impressions.

Abbreviations

ABM   Mrs Arnold Bennett, 'Arnold Bennett', London, 1925

ABP   Dorothy Cheston Bennett, 'Arnold Bennett: A Portrait Done at Home', London, 1935

DHL   'Collected Letters of D.H. Lawrence', ed. Harry T. Moore, London, 1962

FH   'Frank Harris to Arnold Bennett: Fifty-Eight Letters', Merion Station, Pa, 1936

HGW   'Arnold Bennett and H.G. Wells', ed. Harris Wilson, London, 1960

'Journal' 'The Journals of Arnold Bennett', ed. Newman Flower, 3 vols, London, 1932-3. Passages are identified by date rather than by page. Bennett kept a variety of journals, and much of the material is unpublished, or published elsewhere. Such material is suitably identified in context or by L&L explained below

LAB   'Letters of Arnold Bennett', ed. James Hepburn, 3 vols, London, 1966, 1968, 1970

L&L   'Life and Letters' - issues of this magazine, January and February 1929, containing extracts from Bennett's journals

L&LC   G. Jean-Aubry, 'Joseph Conrad: Life and Letters', London, 1927

LB   Manuscript held by the late Dr LaFayette Butler

LN   'Arnold Bennett's Letters to His Nephew', London,
         1936

RP   Reginald Pound, 'Arnold Bennett', London, 1952

SI   Some Impressions, manuscript held at the Berg
         Collection, New York Public Library

SOT   Material held at the Central Library, Hanley,
         Stoke-on-Trent

SSAB   Louis Tillier, 'Studies in the Sources of
         Arnold Bennett's Novels', Paris, 1969

TA   Arnold Bennett, 'The Truth About an Author',
         London, 1903

TTHIM   Arnold Bennett, 'Things That Have Interested Me',
         London, 1921

In the Introduction I allude to reviews of which I have
seen only extracts in publishers' advertisements. I have
indicated the publication of such reviews as precisely as
I can: 'b. 26 November' means that the review appeared
before 26 November in the journal named, in the year
named.

Introduction

I

In the twentieth-century volume of the revised 'Cambridge
Bibliography of English Literature' (CBEL), Arnold Bennett
is listed among the seven major novelists of the first half
of the century. The others are Joyce, Conrad, Lawrence,
Woolf, Forster, and Wells. It is a curious list and
reflects the curious condition of the novel in twentieth-
century England. Two of the novelists, Joyce and Conrad,
are outsiders; another two, Woolf and Forster, are notably
lacking in the fecundity usually associated with major
authorship; and Wells is author of no single novel that
many people have claimed to be of the first rank - his
importance depending in part on transparently extra-
literary virtues as social philosopher-historian. But it
must be said of Joyce, Conrad, Lawrence, Woolf, and Forster
as novelists that they have grown in stature and reputation
in the course of the century. It is in this respect that
Bennett is the curiosity among curiosities. His fame as a
novelist declined drastically with his death - had declined
beforehand - and nothing since has provided occasion for
general reconsideration: not the rare sympathetic review of
his work by people such as Angus Wilson and John Wain, not
a successful filming of 'The Card' in the 1950s nor the
television dramatisation of 'Clayhanger' in the mid-1970s,
not the biography by Margaret Drabble in 1974, not the fact
that in England the reading public still read him regularly. The inclusion of Bennett among the major novelists
in CBEL was in fact a matter for deliberation. Yet the
reasons why he belongs among them are obvious: the single
most substantial novel in the realistic tradition in England

is probably 'The Old Wives' Tale'; his series of novels on
the Five Towns probably stand next to Hardy's novels in
merit in the depiction of a specific provincial life; he
did undoubtedly seem the major English author of his time
to English and American critics alike in the years 1909-18,
and he was a formidable figure for a quarter of a century;
and he was prolific and successful also as playwright,
essayist, and literary critic.

It is remarkable, then, and understandable, that the
present volume is the first substantial gathering of
criticism of Bennett's work. No accumulating weight of
attention, interpretation, and controversy in the half-
century since his death has brought into being another
volume. The characteristic issues of modern criticism -
of form, symbol, myth, imagery, irony, and the like - have
rarely been turned upon him. It has seemed to be too
obviously the case that he could not bear the sort of
scrutiny that Joyce withstands every day. Even now, when
modern criticism itself is in some disarray, there has
emerged no suggestion that Bennett has been seen unjustly.
Thus a collection of criticism of Bennett's contemporaries
is the most appropriate and the most useful to his case.
It remains the freshest and most serious attention he has
received, being written by critics for whom he was a living
force.

II

How accurately does the present culling of reviews
represent the critical reception of Bennett? In a broad
way the story of his reputation has long been known, and
it will be modified only in detail here. He made a lucky
start with his first novel, 'A Man from the North', in
1898, and then four years elapsed before his next serious
work, 'Anna of the Five Towns', appeared in 1902, and it
too had lucky reviews. In the meantime he worked hard at
light fiction and other things, and in 1901 had a notable
success with the serial publication of 'The Grand Babylon
Hotel'. Thereafter he continued to work hard, producing
two, three, four, and sometimes more books a year of
several sorts. Yet not until 'The Old Wives' Tale'
appeared in 1908 did he receive general acclaim. Thence-
forward he was a major figure on the literary scene until
his death in 1931. It seemed to one critic or another in
the intervening years that 'Clayhanger' (1910) or 'These
Twain' (1916) or 'Riceyman Steps' (1923) or 'Lord Raingo'
(1926) or 'Imperial Palace' (1930) was almost as good as
or even better than 'The Old Wives' Tale', and it also

seemed to other critics that 'The Old Wives' Tale' was the
high point, that his powers were more or less sustained
for another decade and then appeared only fitfully or in
grotesque distortion.

This is the general picture, and the more one learns
the less one knows. There are, for example, a dozen
reviews of 'A Man from the North' that I have seen. From
them can be assessed the critical reception of that novel.
But Bennett says in 'The Truth About an Author' (1903) - a
book that has proved in the main to be the truth - that he
counted forty-one notices of it and that he very likely
missed several others. It is doubtful whether many more
beyond the known dozen will ever be recovered, and thus
the assessment is based upon one-quarter or so of the
total number of reviews. Luckily Bennett provides an
assessment of the forty-one notices he knew; but unluckily
he was a partial judge. (Later, with 'The Old Wives'
Tale', he was to prove to have a faulty memory about
reviews.) It is a fact that two of the reviews were
written by himself and his brother Frank, a third was by
friend Eden Phillpotts, and at least two others were
written by other friends and acquaintances in literary
London. It is also a fact that though Phillpotts's review
was very kind, the review in the 'Academy' was scathing -
and yet Bennett had been a regular contributor to that
journal for more than a year and was well known to the
staff.

Similar problems exist with all the novels. As Bennett
became better known, he was reviewed more widely, and the
greater mass of readily available reviews became then the
tip of an iceberg. It is very probable that the reviews
relied upon for assessing 'Imperial Palace' represent less
than one-twentieth of the reviews of that novel. It is
also the case that most of the reviewers of 'Imperial
Palace' in London either knew Bennett personally or knew
people who knew him or worked on journals whose proprietors were beholden to him or friends of his, and so
on and so forth. Again it is a fact that one of the most
scathing reviews of Bennett's works appeared in the 'New
Statesman', a journal of which Bennett was a director and
to which he had contributed free a large body of
journalism.

All such complications tell us that the reception that
appears on paper is not necessarily the same one that the
work receives in the critic's heart of hearts, and that we
will never add up either paper or hearts. There is
another aspect of the problem. One of the expected facts
that emerged in the preparation of this collection was
that as Bennett arose from obscurity into importance the

reviews of his novels became more lengthy and were given
more prominence. This was by no means an unwavering progress, and there were reasons why and doubtless accidents
why. Consider the work which in retrospect has become his
major work. 'The Old Wives' Tale' came unheralded upon
the scene and the review of it in the 'Times Literary
Supplement' (like other reviews) does not give it pride of
place as the most important piece of English fiction of
the autumn of 1908. It follows in third place in Fiction
of the Day after 'A Prince of Dreamers', by Flora Annie
Steel, and 'Mr. Beke, of the Blacks', by John Ayscough.
The review gets to the heart of the novel, and it shows
awareness of the magnitude of aim and effect of the author.
What more could one want except for the reviewer to say
that it is streets beyond the two preceding books under
review? And this he does not do, very possibly because he
does not know what the preceding books are, or possibly
because invidious comparisons ill become the weekly
reviewer. There is the responsibility that a reviewer
does well to heed to examine the individual work for its
own merits, without trying consciously or conspicuously
to judge it under the aspect of either a season or
eternity. Furthermore, he knows that any author who has
produced a book has laboured over it, and that the labour
must to some degree be a labour of love. He knows that
young authors of talent need to be encouraged rather than
discouraged, and that old authors ought to be treated
decently on account of previous services. Thus, for
whatever reasons, 'A Prince of Dreamers' is treated
respectfully, and the reviewer concludes that though it
may be 'caviar to the vulgar', it is 'both fascinating and
lifelike'. Similarly 'Mr. Beke, of the Blacks' is
'a quiet but thorough study of a fairly common type of
character'. And thus the discerning praise of 'The Old
Wives' Tale' (which the reviewer persists in calling 'An
Old Wives' Tale') may seem less discerning than it is, or
be less than it seems. If we look at the whole page of
the 'Time Literary Supplement' we seem to see that 'The
Old Wives' Tale' is merely a cut above the other novels -
and might as easily drop into limbo with the passing year.
Of course, the aspect of eternity is a longer aspect than
the seventy years that have passed since 'The Old Wives'
Tale' was published. Under the aspect of eternity it may
get lost too; or if someone in the year 5000 resurrects
it along with the other two works, their differences in
quality may not seem significant. In the eye of a truly
god-like reviewer, would not all human endeavour seem
equal and equally small? It is merely a rash assumption
that because 'A Prince of Dreamers' and 'Mr. Beke, of the

Blacks' have already gone to limbo they are unworthy of
our attention. Will someone someday rediscover 'A Prince
of Dreamers' and rediscover the discerning review of it in
the 'Times Literary Supplement'?

In any event, the review of 'The Old Wives' Tale' in
the 'Times Literary Supplement' occupies little more space
than, and approximately the same position as, the reviews
of 'Leonora' and 'Anna of the Five Towns' five and six
years earlier. A year later Bennett is in first place
under Fiction in the review of 'The Glimpse', and though
the reviewer does not like the novel he knows Bennett's
importance and makes an allusion to 'that masterly and
admirable novel "An Old Wives' Tale"'. If it was the same
reviewer making the same mistake in the title, why had he
not said 'masterly' the preceding year? Thereafter in the
'Times Literary Supplement' Bennett's novels usually come
first or second under Fiction or New Novels. The review
of 'The Price of Love (1914) is longer than the review of
'The Pretty Lady' (1918), and the longest review of all -
twice as long as many of the others - goes unaccountably
to 'The Roll-Call' (1919).

III

Critical reception is not necessarily the same thing as
popular reception, and in Bennett the clash and the con-
sonance of the two were notable aspects of his career. It
is apparent that he had a natural gift for popular writing.
In Stoke-on-Trent in his youth, before he came to London
at the age of twenty-one, he wrote items of local gossip
for the 'Staffordshire Knot', in 1888-9, and they quickly
gained prominence in the paper. A few years later in
London he entered literary contests in the popular magazine 'Tit-Bits', and won them (1891, 1893). In 1894 he
became assistant editor of 'Woman', and his book reviews
in that journal soon had publishers deluging him with
books. Presently Lewis Hind, editor of the high-class
'Academy', wanted his services, and from 1897 to 1902 he
was one of their leading critics and essayists. By the
latter year 'The Grand Babylon Hotel' had had its dazzling
success. Bennett's popular reputation was now considerable. It increased during the rest of his life; it merged
with and then to some degree separated from his critical
reputation; and in the half-century since his death it has
endured in England in spite of the decline of the other.

This popular reputation had several elements, and in
each of them the reputation was not merely - sometimes not
mainly - popular in the sense of mass appeal; it was

popular according to the sort of audience it met. His
book reviews for the 'Academy' were fairly highbrow, and
so were his later reviews for the 'New Age' (1908-11) and
to a lesser extent those for the 'Evening Standard'
(1927-31). Among people interested in books the latter
two series were commonly reckoned to be among the most
widely read and influential of their time. The journals
themselves indicate the range of popular appeal that
Bennett commanded: the 'Academy' was highbrow literary,
the 'New Age' was liberal political, the 'Evening Standard'
was mass daily (although presumably not everyone who read
the 'Evening Standard' read Bennett's column). Probably
no other author of his time moved as freely as did Bennett
among a variety of literary audiences. At the one end of
the literary spectrum at the turn of the century were the
mass papers the 'Golden Penny' and the 'Sun', at the other
extreme was the elegant 'Yellow Book', and in between
ranged 'Tit-Bits', 'Hearth and Home', 'T.P.'s Weekly', the
'Strand Magazine', the 'Windsor Magazine', the 'Daily
Chronicle', and the 'Academy', and Bennett pleased them
all. At the one end in the 1920s was the 'Sunday
Pictorial', at the other end was the 'Criterion', and in
between were the 'Daily Mail', 'John Bull', and the
'London Mercury', and they all wanted Bennett.

Bennett's essays on the conduct of life were doubtless
his most popular writing with the ordinary public. In
1902 and 1903 he published anonymously a series of Savoir-
Faire Papers in 'T.P.'s Weekly'. They provided comment
and advice on a host of topics such as clothes, holidays,
foreign travel, reading habits. Their popularity was
measurable in part by letters to the editor about them.
As Bennett remarked to his literary agent a year later:
'Anyone who wants to know what sort of effect these things
have on a solid regular public of 150,000 a week has only
got to enquire at the editorial department of "T.P.'s W"'
(LAB I, 46). Some of the correspondents wanted to see the
papers republished in book form, and so did Bennett, but
his literary agent was not enthusiastic. In 1927 in the
Explanation to 'The Savour of Life' Bennett remarked upon
another series of such essays that he wrote for the
'Evening News' in 1907:

> When I proposed to republish them in book form I was
> most strongly urged not to do so, and terrible pro-
> phecies were made to me of the sinister consequences
> to my reputation if I did. I republished them. 'How
> to Live on Twenty-Four Hours a Day' sold very well from
> the start; it still has a steady sale, and it has
> brought me more letters of appreciation than all my

other books put together. I followed it up with a
dozen or more books in a similar vein. And I do not
suppose that my reputation would have been any less
dreadful than it is if I had never published a line
for plain people about the management of daily
experience.

Bennett's aggrieved tone reflects the fact that his literary agent's qualms had been justified and in some highbrow
quarters Bennett's reputation had indeed become dreadful.
    Most of Bennett's journalism for the ordinary public
was less serious (with a light touch) than the pocket
philosophies, and some of it was more. Most notable was
the long series of political articles he wrote for the
'Daily News' during the First World War. He wrote rather
more than a hundred of these articles, and matched them
with a slighter set of Observations for the 'New Statesman' in the latter two years of the war. These were
widely read too, and again they contributed to the suspicion among some people that Bennett was less a novelist
than a journalist, or that the novelist's strengths were
being dissipated in ephemeral enterprises.
    Then there were his plays. In the years 1912-14 he had
two major hits on the London stage, and these and several
other plays were played round the provinces. Bennett
thought well of these plays, and so did most of the
critics, but no one suggested that he was primarily a
playwright, and again it appeared that in pursuing
theatrical fame he was wasting himself. In later years
he failed to please the theatre-going public, and his
last play, 'The Return Journey' (1928), was a disaster,
and there seemed all the more reason to believe that he
was debasing his energies or giving them to the wrong
thing.
    The word that expressed the incongruities of popular
and critical reputation was 'pot-boiling'. Bennett
responded to the charge on several occasions, but nowhere
more succinctly than in the Explanation of 'The Savour of
Life':

    There remains the charge of pot-boiling. I have never
    expressed opinions that I do not hold; nor have I ever
    been asked to express such opinions. Life for me has
    many savours, which I relish keenly. Therefore many
    subjects interest me. I never write on a subject which
    does not interest me, and I always write as well as
    heaven permits. Nevertheless, journalists who are not
    novelists accuse me about once a week of pot-boiling.
    The argument is not stated very clearly; but it seems

to amount to this: first, that a man who has written
long, realistic novels which have met with approval
ought not, if he is a serious artist, to write anything
but long realistic novels; second, that a man who can
make a livelihood out of writing novels ought to confine himself to novels, because if he goes outside
them he will make more money. Personally, I cannot
see that a writer ought not to write what he wants to
write simply because the result of his doing so would
be to increase his income. I write for money. I write
for as much money as I can get. Shakespeare and Balzac
did the same. I might of course give my articles to
newspapers gratis. (I sometimes do.) But why should
I? And are reviews of books pot-boilers, or are they
not?

Bennett had a talent for pot-boiling, and his progress
in it meant an income in the 1920s of £20,000 a year. But
the beginning was slow. Despite his youthful success in
provincial journalism (which was unpaid), he went to
London in 1889 to become a clerk in a law office, and he
remained a clerk for four and a half years, eventually
earning £200 a year. He abandoned that job to become
assistant editor of 'Woman', beginning at £150 a year,
and he remained there for six years. Until 1892 (when
he was twenty-five) he had published merely a handful of
trivial, short pieces in the popular press, and written
nothing of another kind. He says in 'The Truth About an
Author' that he earned about threepence an hour at such
spare-time labour which would amount full-time to less
than £40 a year). In the course of the next few years he
grew bored with being an editor, and saw the possibility
of earning his living with his pen. Until he finished
'The Statue' in 1907 (written in collaboration with Eden
Phillpotts), he conceived and wrote many things primarily
for a commercial purpose. He apparently enjoyed this
writing, and sometimes was embarrassed by it afterwards.
Most of his early plays were conceived in such a spirit,
and so were the so-called sensational novels. The fact
that he failed to get the early plays produced is beside
the point. On 12 September 1897 he wrote in his 'Journal':

I have decided very seriously to take up fiction for a
livelihood. A certain chronic poverty had forced upon
me the fact that I was giving no attention to money-
making, beyond my editorship, and so the resolution
came about. Till the end of 1899 I propose to give
myself absolutely to writing the sort of fiction that
sells itself. My serious novel 'Anna Tellwright'

['Anna of the Five Towns'], with which I had made some
progress, is put aside indefinitely.

A year and a half later he wrote to his friend George
Sturt: 'You may say that writing popular fiction is poor
work. It is, absolutely, but it is a damn sight better
fun than going to an office & editing a ladies' paper,
& pays much better' (LAB, II, 115).
    Luckily Bennett had not only desire and talent but also
a developing ability to produce in quantity. It was very
likely this last quality that made the charge of pot-
boiling stick to him long after he was writing solely
because he wanted to write. In the same letter to George
Sturt he noted a great increase in his facility in writing,
and added: 'I believe I could fart sensational fiction
now.' The record of his facility is indeed extraordinary -
100 books in about thirty-three years, 300,000 to 400,000
words a year, the whole 160,000 words of 'Clayhanger' in
five months of writing, 1,700 words of 'The Old Wives'
Tale' in two and a half hours and another 1,000 words of
an article later the same day. In 1908 he wrote three-
quarters of 'The Old Wives' Tale' (150,000 words of it),
the novel 'Buried Alive' (60,000 words), a full-length
play 'What the Public Wants' (27,000 words), half a dozen
short stories, 'The Human Machine' (a guide to living,
25,000 words), and 'Literary Taste' (a guide to literature, 25,000 words). By and large Bennett's critics were
amazed by his productivity before they became annoyd by
it.
    They were not the only ones. His literary agent and
his publishers were sometimes alarmed. They thought he
would glut the market, and they wanted to slow him down.
A number of letters between him and his agent argue the
matter. Bennett tells Pinker that an author is not like
a Bradford mill to be shut down for the sake of profit;
he reminds him that certain classic authors wrote faster
than himself; he says that he is not even working hard:

You would be under a false impression if you imagined
that I am working at pressure. I am not. I could do lots
more. I have vast leisure. When I think that I wrote
the 'Grand Babylon Hotel' in less than a month & that
I am taking over 3 months with 'Hugo', I ask myself,
Why? You don't yet realise what an engine for the
production of fiction you have in me. I could take
long holidays & still produce as much as you would
require from me, but the fact is I am never content
unless I am turning out the stuff. I have much the
same objection to holidays that you have. I ruined

my summer last year by 3 months idleness. You must
accustom yourself to these facts & do what you can
to meet them. (LAB I, 50)

One seems to see from all this that Bennett could
hardly help boiling the pot fast and furiously. Yet for
several years he earned a fairly modest living by his pen,
and had he limited himself to serious fiction he might
have earned a poor living. His first novel, 'A Man from
the North', earned him virtually nothing, and ten years
later 'The Old Wives' Tale' earned him an advance of £150
(for eight months' labour), did not sell well, and was
allowed to go out of print after a year or so. His income
from all sorts of writing in the years 1906-9 averaged
less than £500 a year. The transformation of his income
came in 1911 when he had the luck that other English
authors before and after him have had - the opening up of
the American market to him. That happened in the first
instance because the wife of the American publisher George
Doran read 'The Old Wives' Tale' and liked it, and it
happened in the second because that mass market *par
excellence* was ready and waiting for 'How to Live on
Twenty-Four Hours a Day'.
In the popular and critical acclaim that Bennett
achieved, the serious novels have an ambiguous role. In
the main they sold badly or modestly or moderately well.
Yet they were the basis of his national and international
reputation. His other work gave him popularity among
various groups, and his serious novels gave that popularity importance. For a while popular and critical acclaim
united, and the notorious and distinguished author who
visited America in 1911 and who was co-author of the
major hit on the London stage in 1912 held the world in
thrall rather in the manner of Charles Dickens - except
that not until 'Imperial Palace' at the end of his career
did Bennett have anything like a best seller among his
serious novels. 'Imperial Palace' was a special case in
that it alone among the serious novels dealt with a
subject - glittering hotel life - that might be presumed
to appeal to the mass market. And none of the other
serious novels so thoroughly divided reputable critics.
Some thought highly of it, and some thought it was a
public disgrace. In any event its popularity was short
lived, overtaken by Vicki Baum's 'Grand Hotel' which was
published at the same time.
With his death Bennett disappeared from the press and
from attention in high literary/academic circles. Today
it is surprising to realise that for a score of years in
London he was a public figure, a man whose presence

at art galleries and at first nights was reported in morning newspapers and whose dress and appearance were
favoured subjects of cartoonists. His fame helped only
somewhat to sell his serious books, and it gained him
certain animosities, and then it washed away.

IV

Bennett had a high ideal of the novelist's calling.
'Essential characteristic of the really great novelist:
a Christ-like, all-embracing compassion', he wrote in his
'Journal' on 15 October 1896. He emulated such compassion
in his own novels, and his compassion ran him into trouble
with critics, who sometimes saw that his sympathies for
unpleasant characters were misplaced admiration. At the
same time, the high ideal made Bennett a severe self-
critic. In 1894, when he had written a quantity of
frivolous work and also his first serious story, he wrote
to George Sturt: 'I may say that I have no inward assurance that I could ever do anything more than mediocre
viewed strictly as art - very mediocre.' And in the same
letter he expressed confidence that he could 'turn out
things which would be read with zest, & about which the
man in the street would say to friends "Have you read so
& so in the What-is-it?"' (LAB II, 12). Six and a half
years later he wrote again to Sturt:

> Although I am 33 & I have not made a name, I infallibly
> know that I *shall* make a name, & that soon. But I
> should like to be a legend. I think I have settled in
> my own mind that my work will never be better than
> third rate, judged by the high standards, but I shall
> be cunning enough to make it impose on my contempor-
> aries. (LAB II, 151)

In another seven and a half years the writing of 'The Old
Wives' Tale' enlarged his views, and he could write to
Frank Harris about himself as 'a fully equipped artist'
(LAB II, 239). The emphasis here upon technical ability
was characteristic, and his considered praise for his own
work in later years was customarily expressed in such
terms. He did not especially care for 'The Card', but
he thought that it was 'well invented, and done up to the
knocker, technically, right through' ('Journal', 2 March
1909), and he thought 'The Pretty Lady' and 'Riceyman
Steps' were 'jolly well constructed' ('Journal', 16 February 1929).
    Technique was not everything, though, and in 'The

Author's Craft' (1915) he wrote:

> I am obliged to say that, as the years pass, I attach
> less and less importance to good technique in fiction.
> I love it, and I have fought for a better recognition
> of its importance in England, but I now have to admit
> that the ... greatest novelists of the world, according
> to my own standards, have either ignored technique or
> have failed to understand it.... I begin to think that
> great writers of fiction are by the mysterious nature
> of their art ordained to be amateurs.

The greatest masters for him were the Russians, Dostoevsky,
Tolstoy, and others, the first of whom he had done much to
introduce to the English public some years earlier. In
1925 he was reading 'Anna Karenina', 'which is so much
superior to any novel I could write' (ABP, 277).
    In a way Bennett was always diffident about his writing.
He was least so about his journalism. In some notes he
made about himself in 1926 he said:

> I have not had a clear & fixed ambition. I began to
> write novels because my friends said that I could. The
> same for plays. But I always had a feeling for journal-
> ism, which feeling is as strong today as ever it was....
> I don't analyse or realise the characteristics of my
> novels. They seem sometimes to me to be so simple &
> obvious that I wonder anybody can feel any interest in
> them at all. (SI, 29 August 1926)

In another way Bennett cared very much about his writing,
and did not care about either his readers or his reviewers. The most eloquent expression of his attitude came in
an address to himself at the end of 'The Truth About an
Author', an end that his publisher wanted him to change:

> 'You may be richer or you may be poorer; you may live
> in greater pomp or luxury, or in less. The point is
> that you will always be, essentially, what you are now.
> You have no real satisfaction to look forward to except
> the satisfaction of continually inventing, fancying,
> imagining, scribbling. Say another thirty years of
> these emotional ingenuities, these interminable varia-
> tions on the theme of beauty. Is it good enough?'
>   And I answered: Yes.
>   But who knows? Who can preclude the regrets of the
> dying couch?

THE BOOKS

In the year 1893 Bennett began to take himself seriously
as an author. Behind him were the columns of local gossip
for the 'Staffordshire Knot' and also a few items for the
London press. In addition he had published in 1891 'A
Century of Books for Bibliophiles', a list of rare and
unusual books he was offering for sale. He had become a
collector of books under the guidance of a fellow clerk at
the law office. He issued a second list bearing the same
title, probably in 1892. In 1893 he published at least
four stories and several other items in London papers.
More importantly he sat down one day that year with a high
artistic aim in view, namely to write a serious story. He
says in 'The Truth About an Author' that he sent the story,
A Letter Home, to a popular weekly magazine, where it was
refused, and then he sent it to the 'Yellow Book', where
it was accepted. It was published in 1895 and was reprinted in 1905 in 'Tales of the Five Towns'. It was an
uncommonly good story for a beginner, and customarily was
praised by Bennett's critics in later years. In his
column in the 'Daily Express' on 10 September 1938 James
Agate said that he thought it was the best story in the
English language. It certainly gave Bennett the impetus
to go on in a serious vein.

'A Man from the North' (1898)

Published on 23 February. Bennett began writing the novel
in the middle of April 1895, about six months after an
attempt to write a purely commercial novel. 'A Man from
the North' proceeded by fits and starts, with a good deal
of rewriting necessitated because of improving style.
Bennett found novel-writing 'the damnedest, nerve shattering experience as ever was' (LAB II, 25). He finished the
novel on 15 May 1896 and submitted it directly to John
Lane, who published the 'Yellow Book' and who was known to
Bennett also in connection with 'Woman'. Lane's reader
for the novel was the young John Buchan (later author of
'The Thirty-Nine Steps'). Buchan reported that the novel
showed 'great knowledge and a good deal of insight' and
that the characterisation showed 'a succession of rare
and subtle touches' (LAB II, 54n). Buchan and Bennett met
in Lane's office, and Buchan told Bennett his style was
'excellent'. Reporting on this to George Sturt, Bennett
said, 'as to the style, I doubt it may be a little exotic'
(LAB II, 55). Lane accepted the book and offered a 5 per
cent royalty on the first 1,000 copies, 10 per cent on the

next 1,000, and 15 per cent thereafter. There were long
delays before a contract was signed and the book published,
and the actual royalty turned out to be 5 per cent on the
first 2,000, 10 per cent to 5,000, and 15 per cent thereafter. According to Bennett in 'The Truth About an
Author', both he and Lane knew that the matter of royalty
was academic, and in three years the book earned one
sovereign more than the amount it had cost to have the
manuscript typed.

The reception of the novel is described in some detail
in 'The Truth About an Author'. There was, first of all,
the reaction in Stoke-on-Trent and among Bennett's family
- a reaction perhaps idealised in remembrance:

> For months I hesitated to visit the town which had the
> foresight to bear me, and which is going to be famous
> on that score. I was castigated in the local paper.
> My nearest and dearest played nervously with their
> bread when my novel was mentioned at dinner. A rela-
> tive in a distant continent troubled himself to inform
> me that the book was fragmentary and absolutely worth-
> less.

(Many years later, in his essay The Making of Me, Bennett
said that his favourite aunt 'burnt my ... book in
Wesleyan horror'.) Of the forty-one reviews that Bennett
collected, some of them from America where Lane also
issued the book, he reported the following division:
four unfavourable, eleven mixed and twenty-six favourable.

> All the principal organs were surprisingly appreciative.
> And the majority of reviewers agreed that my knowledge
> of human nature was exceptionally good, that my style
> was exceptionally good, that I had in me the makings of
> a novelist, and that my present subject was weak. My
> subject was not weak; but let that pass.

He noted that the reviewer for 'Vanity Fair' was a friend,
who slanged the book, and that the reviewer for one of the
morning papers - unknown - was also a friend, who was
tepid about it. He quoted one review - unknown - that
pleased him most: 'What our hero's fate was let those who
care to know find out, but let me assure them that in its
discovery they will read of London life and labour as it
is, not as the bulk of romances paint it.' He was so
pleased generally that he could afford to smile at the
condescension of the 'New York Observer', 'the story and
characters are commonplace in the extreme', and the moral
concern of a seaport paper (perhaps in Liverpool), 'We do

not consider the book a healthy one'. He made no allusion
to the reviews by himself and his brother.

A couple of these reviews and others are reprinted here
(Nos 1-5). In addition the 'Pall Mall Gazette' took a
slight and unfavourable glance at it prior to publication
(12 February). The 'Athenaeum' (19 March) deplored in it
'not the romance of the commonplace, but the veriest
commonplace of the commonplace'. The 'Academy' (26 March,
with an earlier mention 26 February) found it 'the kind of
worthlessly clever book which neither touches nor moves
the reader'. The 'Glasgow Herald' (31 March) found it a
faithful account of a rather dull life, somewhat lacking
in narrative force. The 'Bookman' (April, reprinted in
the American 'Bookman' in June) wondered whether a dull
life such as Richard Larch's was not too dispiriting to
be a proper subject for fiction. 'The Times' apparently
took notice of the novel, but no reference could be found.
There was also, some while later, a letter from an appreciative reader, Joseph Conrad (No. 6). Despite Bennett's
mention of such a review, none could be found in the
'Staffordshire Sentinel'.

Bennett's own opinion of the novel modified itself
over the years. He informed George Sturt in January 1897
that all his novels would have purposes. 'The purpose of
"A Man from the North" is to "expose" a few of the hardships and evils of the life of the young celibate clerk
in London. Of course I use "expose" in the French sense'
(LAB II, 75). He wrote to H.G. Wells in 1900: 'There is
much in it that is not authentic, merely fanciful, and
quasi-sentimental - I can see now. But I seriously meant
all of it at the time' (LAB II, 136). He gave several
pages of 'The Truth About an Author' to a sardonic account
of the stylistic elegance and clinical realism that the
novel was meant to have - in the manner of Flaubert and
the Goncourt brothers - and only fitfully achieved. In
1910 when his fame made a new edition possible, he remarked
to his literary agent: 'For twelve years I have consis-
tently stuck up for this book, as having a quality which
none of my other books has' (LAB I, 139). There was a new
American edition in 1911 and a new English one in 1912.
The English edition achieved a third printing as early as
March in that year. A sixth impression appeared in 1924.
Hamish Hamilton issued a small edition of the novel in
1973 with an introduction by Frank Swinnerton.

'Journalism for Women' (1898)

Published in March. On 5 October 1896 Bennett published
an article on journalism in 'Woman' as part of a series
on How Women May Make Money. The notion of turning the
article into a book came to him later in the year, and in
December he made a tentative arrangement with John Lane
for publication. The writing followed. According to Mrs
C.S. Peel, a contributor to 'Woman' and later editor of
it, Bennett had severe views on women journalists. She
brought him an article one day, and he scanned it and
said, 'Why do you not learn to write?' He offered to
teach her, and then decided not to. He told her 'that
women were idle and would not take the trouble to learn
their jobs'. (See LAB I, 15.) He intended the book to
be 'a practical guide, with aesthetic reflections on the
art which has, say, raised the "Daily Mail" to 250,000
circulation & the position of first *newspaper* pure &
simple in this great country' (LAB II, 73). The book
was finished by early December 1897. On 15 December
Bennett noted in his 'Journal' that the book 'lashed with
scorpions' the typical female journalist.
  He submitted it to Lane with the understanding that if
Lane liked it he would publish it within three months.
Bennett wrote to George Sturt on 13 January: 'Lane is
desperately excited about my little journalism book, his
readers report being positively panegyric. He is going to
publish it in 3 weeks; gave me a 15% royalty, & made me
sign the contract at once' (LAB II, 101). On 28 March he
wrote to Sturt: 'My journalism book is being rarely
reviewed. It has had no less than 4 articles of over
a column each' (LAB II, 108). Of the several known
reviews, two are more than a column long. The 'Pall Mall
Gazette' noticed the book before publication (12 February),
and expressed concern that it would encourage would-be
journalists rather than discourage them. The woman who
reviewed it in 'Woman' (15 March) was surprised at how
well written and useful it was, and suspected that the
author must be associated with 'the office of some popular
and progressive daily'. Bennett's attitude towards women
journalists was not condescending: 'in fact, he believes
in us, and is determined to make us better'. The 'Manchester Guardian' (25 March) regarded the cover of the
book as 'gaudy' and 'delirious' (it showed a Lautrec-
Beardsley figure in red against a stylised landscape of
green and blue, and was a superior example of book-making
at the turn of the century), but found the inside very
commonsensical. The reviewer thought that Bennett was
hard on women journalists and deservedly so: 'Anyone

desiring to test the accuracy of Mr. Bennett's remarks on
this head may refer with advantage to a "Symposium" on
their profession by a number of women journalists in a
recent magazine.' 'To-Day' (26 March) repeated and
elaborated upon some of the good advice of the book but
objected at length to Bennett's recommendation of Roget's
'Thesaurus'. 'Vanity Fair' (31 March) offered 'blessings
on Mr. Bennett's head if he succeeds ever so little in his
good intent!'. The 'Academy' (14 May) said that 'this
clever little brochure is destined to teach woman how to
be a journalist instead of a woman-journalist'. The
'Critic' in America (September) said that to judge from
the vapid advice of the book, the British female journalist must be antediluvian. American women needed no such
advice. The book was worthless, and therefore 'the price
of this book is above rubies'. No later edition of the
book is known.

'Fame and Fiction' (1901)

Published in September. The book was drawn from a series
of articles on fiction that Bennett wrote for the 'Academy'
beginning in July 1899. It included extended discussions
of Moore, Gissing, and Turgenev, and analyses of popular
authors such as Silas Hocking and Charlotte Yonge.
Bennett wrote of the essays to Sturt in 1900 that they
were really studies in the psychology of readers. 'They
much please Lewis Hind [editor of the "Academy"]....
I myself think these articles are very good, and distinctly original, too' (LAB II, 130). He described the
article on Gissing to Sturt as 'a real bit of ME' (LAB II,
128). He was equally enthusiastic about the piece on
Moore. The material of the book represents Bennett's most
systematic and serious literary criticism. At this time
and later he gave thought to writing a history of English
literature. He seems to have had difficulty finding a
publisher for the collection, but ultimately it was taken
by Grant Richards, who 'has got as far as expressing his
delight in the book & asking the lowest terms' (LAB II,
148). Bennett expected the book to raise a rumpus in so
far as 'I have expressed my candid views in it on about
15 living English writers.... I shall probably have to
retire to Boulogne till the scandal blows over' (LAB II,
148). He expected advertisement for him from the book
rather than sales, and acquiesced to a 10 per cent royalty
rather than 15 per cent. The difference would mean £6 to
him, assuming sales of 500 copies, and he could earn £6 a
day writing fiction. He found the reviews of the book

'amazingly appreciative' (LAB II, 162).

A notice in the 'Academy' (7 September) before publication remarked upon the fact that the essays had been first
published in the 'Academy' and spoke of their 'vigour and
originality'. The 'Pall Mall Gazette' (25 September) took
issue with certain of Bennett's strictures on individual
popular novelists, and thought he overestimated the literary taste of 'the novel-reading proletariat', but otherwise found the criticism 'luminous'. The 'Manchester
Guardian' devoted a long leader to the book (30 September),
arguing with Bennett's contention that the moralistic and
melodramatic elements of popular fiction are allied to the
qualities of great literature, but nevertheless finding
the book 'always interesting'. The 'Morning Leader'
(b. 12 October) thought that 'his extremely readable
essays should help both those who agree with him and those
who disagree to a clearer understanding'. The 'Morning
Post' (b. 12 October) was enthusiastic: the book 'justifies a hope of newer and better methods in discussing the
art of fiction', and it avoids the 'jaded jog-trot and
indifference alike to good or bad' of much journalistic
criticism. Some notice of the book was taken in the
'British Weekly' (see 'Journal', 8 January 1909).
H.G. Wells wrote to Bennett deploring Bennett's failure
to discuss him in the book and denouncing Bennett's
opinions. Bennett replied that he needed to study Wells
for twenty-five years first and that Wells's opinions of
his opinions left him cold. (See HGW, 58-62.) Sales of
the book were apparently about what Bennett estimated.
No further edition is known. Some of the material is
republished in 'The Author's Craft and Other Critical
Writings of Arnold Bennett', edited by Samuel Hynes,
1968.

'The Grand Babylon Hotel' (1902)

Published on 9 January. Bennett wrote a serial story when
he was a young man in the Potteries, and the editor who
refused it saw enough talent there to invite Bennett to
write the items of local gossip that appeared in the
'Staffordshire Knot' in 1888-9. Bennett's first serial
story written in London was 'The Ghost' (see below,
pp. 34-5). 'The Grand Babylon Hotel' followed, and it
was intended to be a glittering serial story to end all
such. Bennett wrote the several instalments in fifteen
days sometime during 1900, and he sold the entire rights
to the tale to the Tillotson syndicate apparently for
£100. Bennett realised he was being done the moment he

named his price, and the agent for Tillotson, Philip Gibbs, did so too. (See LAB II, 167n, 168n.) First serial rights went to the 'Golden Penny' in London, where the story began appearing on 2 February 1901. Afterwards, says Bennett in 'The Truth About an Author', 'it overran the provincial press like a locust-swarm'. It appeared in the 'Staffordshire Sentinel' in 1902. Bennett was fairly delirious with pleasure over a circular that was issued describing the tale as 'the most original, amusing, and thrilling' serial of the decade ('Journal', 18 January 1901), and it was advertised in railway stations up and down the land. Tillotson sold the world book rights to Chatto & Windus for £80, and they promised Chatto a good review in their syndicated column Five Minutes at a Bookshelf.

In the front pages of the first edition of 'Leonora', issued by Chatto in 1903, are reproduced extracts from twenty-three sometimes ecstatic reviews describing the book's 'magic', 'cunning', and 'brilliant ingenuity'; it was 'a tale out of the "Arabian Nights"'. Bennett says in 'The Truth about an Author':

> It was the first of my books that the 'Times' [Literary Supplement] ever condescended to review; the 'Spectator' took it seriously in a column and a quarter; and my friends took it seriously. I even received cables from foreign lands with offers to buy translation rights. I became known as the author of that serial. And all this, save for an insignificant trifle, to the profit of an exceedingly astute syndicate!

The book went into a second printing immediately. It was reprinted frequently, was serialised in the 'Evening Standard' in 1930 (beginning 26 April), and was issued in paperback by Penguin in 1954 with an introduction by Frank Swinnerton. It remains in print today in a Penguin edition. Bennett himself was not keen on the book in later years. In an uncollected passage in his 'Journal' in 1907 (L&L, February 1929) he referred to its 'mechanical ingenuities', 'surface glitter', and lack of theme. When George Doran was preparing a uniform edition of earlier novels in 1911, Bennett wanted 'The Grand Babylon Hotel' issued separately and with a slightly apologetic note. First American publication came in 1902 with the title 'T. Racksole and Daughter'. For three reviews, see Nos 7-9.

'Anna of the Five Towns' (1902)

Published about 15 September. Bennett began thinking
about the novel in February 1896 or before, and intended
to make it much better than 'A Man from the North'. He
began writing in September 1896, but assumed full editorship of 'Woman' shortly thereafter and had to abandon it.
Subsequent writing proceeded by fits and starts, including
breaks for the writing of 'The Ghost' and 'The Gates of
Wrath'. He completed a draft in 1899 and rewrote it
largely or wholly in 1900-1, finishing it on 17 May 'at
2:45 A.M., after 17 hours' continuous work, save for
meals, on the last 5,000 words. I was very pleased with
it' ('Journal', 17 May). In May 1896 Bennett reviewed
George Moore's 'A Mummer's Wife' in 'Woman'. Twenty-four
years later he wrote to Moore:

> I wish also to tell you that it was the first chapters
> of 'A Mummer's Wife' which opened my eyes to the roman-
> tic nature of the district that I had blindly inhabited
> for over twenty years. You are indeed the father of
> all my Five Towns books. (LAB III, 139)

In January 1897 he wrote to Sturt of the novel that 'if it
is not a sermon against parental authority, then I say it
is naught' (LAB II, 75). In the following autumn he made
a trip to the Five Towns, and on 10 September he recorded
in the 'Journal' that during the visit 'the grim and
original beauty of certain aspects of the Potteries, to
which I have referred in the introduction to "Anna Tellwright" ["Anna of the Five Towns"], has fully revealed
itself for the first time'. Just before finishing the
novel he referred to it as his 'serious, melancholy, &
fine novel of Staffordshire life' (LAB II, 154), and just
after he finished it he was reading Wordsworth's 'Michael'
for the first time and took lines from the opening as an
epigraph: 'Therefore, although it be a history / Homely
and rude, I will relate the same / For the delight of a
few natural hearts'. Recollecting the writing of the book
some years later, he recalled 'being drunk with my own
creative emotion' (L&L, February 1929, printing a passage
from the 'Journal', 1907).
  Bennett had difficulty in finding a publisher. The
book was refused by several English firms. Duckworth made
an offer on the recommendation of Edward Garnett, and
Garnett wrote to Bennett that both he and his wife had
enjoyed the novel greatly but that he thought Willie
Price's suicide at the end was irrelevant and ought to be
eliminated. (Bennett later agreed about Willie Price, and

made the change when he dramatised the novel as 'Cupid and
Commonsense'; see below, p. 123.) Bennett wanted a
higher royalty than Duckworth offered, and the book was
finally taken by Chatto. In America Harper's refused it,
and the publisher who did take it, McClure Phillips, did
so with trepidation. The contract with Chatto involved
not only 'Anna of the Five Towns' but also 'The Gates of
Wrath', 'Teresa of Watling Street', and 'The Ghost', for
all of which Bennett received £250 for book rights in the
United Kingdom and Colonies and Possessions.

The book was very favourably received. The front page
of the first edition of 'Leonora' quotes thirteen reviews
and the end pages of the first edition of 'Tales of the
Five Towns' add several more. Bennett records in his
'Journal' on 16 June 1904 receiving a lot of 'very favourable' American reviews, including one from the 'Omaha
Daily Bee': 'the "Bee" was not flattering, but gorgeously
condescending'. A flattering American review that Bennett
succumbed to was W.L. Alden's in the 'New York Times',
which reviewed the English edition. Bennett wrote to his
literary agent: 'He says it is the best novel of the sort
since "Esther Waters". (It is.)' (LAB I, 34) For this
and other reviews see Nos 11 and 13-18. Among reviews not
reprinted here, the 'Athenaeum' (4 October) found both
characterisation and description admirable, the whole book
being 'a very able study of life among the potteries', and
the 'Bookman' (October) in a brief notice thought that the
book was 'good, clever, and boldly written, with an unexpected pathos which is very genuine'.

Bennett wrote to a Five Towns friend that the novel was
misunderstood in the Five Towns, but he did not explain
why. He also thought that the French appreciated it more
than the English, perhaps partly because serial publication of it was thinkable there. (It began to appear
serially in 'Echo de Paris' on 18 April 1907.) He had
an appreciative letter from Conrad, who regarded it
as a considerable advance over 'A Man from the North',
'fine, very fine' (L&LC I, 305-7). George Sturt's
and H.G. Wells's reactions are given below (Nos 10 and
12). In 1904 Bennett expressed confidence that the novel
would be read and respected twenty years later. It had a
fourth printing in 1912, and D.H. Lawrence read it then,
and wrote to a friend:

I have read 'Anna of the Five Towns' today, because it
is stormy weather. For five months I have scarcely
seen a word of English print, and to read it makes me
feel fearfully queer. I don't know where I am. I am
so used to the people going by outside, talking or

singing some foreign language, always Italian now: but
today, to be in Hanley, to read almost my own dialect,
makes me feel quite ill. I hate England and its hopelessness. I hate Bennett's resignation. Tragedy ought
really to be a great kick at misery. But 'Anna of the
Five Towns' seems like an acceptance - so does all the
modern stuff since Flaubert. (DHL I, 150)

Lawrence began writing 'The Lost Girl' in 1912 in reaction
against 'Anna of the Five Towns'. Penguin issued it in
paperback in 1954, with an introduction by Frank Swinnerton. It is currently in print in Penguin and Methuen
editions.

'The Gates of Wrath' (1903)

Published in February. Bennett wrote the novel perhaps
entirely in July-August 1899 for serial publication in
'Myra's Journal', where it began appearing on 1 October.
He revised and extended it for book publication, and 'much
improved it' (LAB I, 53). (On the contract for it see
above, p. 21.) On 8 January 1904 Bennett wrote in his
'Journal' after glancing through the novel: 'Its smartness
and clarity prevent me from being quite honestly ashamed
of it.' Excerpts from seven reviews appeared in the front
pages of the first edition of 'Leonora'. The reviewers
found it 'racy', 'delightful', and 'absorbing', and the
reviewer for 'Vanity Fair' said, 'I am not ashamed of
liking it.' The 'Manchester Guardian' (4 February) saw
the book as a lively example of a sort 'which has grown
by very intelligible causes out of the conditions of
modern life'. The 'Academy' (7 February) thought that of
its sort it was all right, 'but since it comes from
Mr. Bennett, it is disappointing melodrama'. The
'Athenaeum' (28 February) thought that it should have
been left unpublished. There were several editions in
later years, including a cheap edition by Newnes in 1912
and one by Methuen in 1914.

'The Truth About an Author' (1903)

Published in July. In his Preface to a later edition of
this work Bennett said that the idea for it came from
Lewis Hind, editor of the 'Academy', but a letter to Sturt
of 11 May 1898 suggests that a similar idea was floating
in Bennett's head then, and he said to Sturt that 'I certainly am shameless and brutal enough to make it candid &

therefore a true human document' (LAB II, 111). Bennett
said in the Preface that he wrote the book in his spare
time in much less than three months, presumably late 1901
and possibly early 1902. Serial publication in the
'Academy' began on 3 May. Publication there and in book
form was anonymous, partly, said Bennett, from discretion
and partly to stir conjecture. 'The success of the serial
was terrific', said Bennett, 'among about a hundred
people', and he said the same was the case with the book.
He found the publisher Andrew Chatto tearing out the pages
of the serial from the 'Academy', yet Chatto told him that
as a book it would never sell. It was offered to several
publishers before Constable took it. 'The reviews', said
Bennett, 'varied from the flaccid indifferent to the fero-
cious. No other book of mine ever had such a bad press',
and the 'number of copies sold ... was the smallest in my
experience'. But after it was remaindered the Times Book
Club picked up copies and sold them, using Bennett's name
without his permission, and Bennett reckoned (in 1910 or
1911) that of all his books it was most often quoted from
in the press, particularly in the United States.

    Known reviews of the book are mainly flattering.
'To-Day' (12 August) thought that it was 'a delightful
satire' and supposed that the author was a more serious
artist than he made himself out to be. 'T.P.'s Weekly'
(14 August) offered two long excerpts, from beginning and
end, with a brief comment on its 'strong and vivid picture' and 'the deeper note which runs throughout'. The
'Manchester Guardian' (20 August) was impressed by its
truthfulness, especially with regard to reviewing and
reading for publishers. The 'Daily News' (b. 29 August)
called it 'a most entertaining volume'. 'Hearth and Home'
(1 October) thought it was 'one of the most interesting
books of the year': 'and I could hazard a guess as to the
author's name'. The 'Author' (October) called it 'an
admirable piece of invective'. When it was published in
America in 1911, with the Preface, it had some excellent
reviews and was widely excerpted. The 'Dial' (1 November)
thought that the book was 'as strikingly original ... as
anything its author has yet produced'. The 'Nation'
(16 November) questioned the good taste of publishing such
an account and thought the book, like all his writing,
displayed 'a lack of deep feeling'. 'Current Literature'
(January 1912) summarised at length and found it an
'astonishing little book'. The book was not reissued in
England until 1914, but in the endpapers of 'Tales of the
Five Towns' in 1905 it was listed among Bennett's works.
Bennett tried to arrange a reissue in England in 1910 and
failed. In 1911 the Books and Bookmen column in the

'Manchester Guardian' expressed the hope that it would be
reissued (1 April). In 1912 the editor of 'Everyman'
published an article on Bennett in which he asserted that
Bennett had chosen to suppress the book because of its
indiscretions. Bennett was furious and exacted an
apology. (See LAB II, 316-18.) When Methuen issued the
book, with the Preface, in March 1914, they ran a double-
column advertisement on the front page of the 'Times
Literary Supplement' saying 'THE TRUTH ABOUT AN AUTHOR
Q. - What author? A. - Arnold Bennett.'

'How to Become an Author' (1903)

Published in September. The rise of popular journalism in
the last decades of the previous century itself gave rise
to numerous books of advice to aspiring authors. Bennett
finished the book by December 1902. There are few known
reviews. 'T.P.'s Weekly' (2 October) published extracts
from 'this very sound informing book'; the 'Saturday
Review' (3 October) was appalled at the sort of journalistic trivia that the book suggested an aspiring author
might think about writing; 'Hearth and Home' (5 November)
found the book readable and useful; the 'Manchester
Guardian' (7 November) devoted a long leader to summaris-
ing the book, and said of the author, 'he is neither a
prig nor a Philistine, and he knows very well what he is
talking about'. H.G. Wells wrote to Bennett: 'It's quite
the best book in its way and it's a orrible way. It will,
thank God! be not of the slightest use to any human being'
(HGW, 98). The book was used by a literary correspondence
college in 1906. A second edition appeared in 1908.
Chatto & Windus planned to issue an edition in 1920 and
then did not. Bennett said at the time that he was constantly getting inquiries about the book.

'Leonora' (1903)

Published on 1 October. Bennett wrote most of 'Leonora'
between 1 April and 30 June 1903; he wrote some of it in
1902. In the 'Journal' on 27 January 1909 he recalled
that 'when I was writing "Leonora" at the Hôtel du Quai
Voltaire I used to go out into the Rue de Rivoli (towards
the end of the book) with a sensation as if the top of my
head would come off'. He wrote to a friend from Paris on
18 June, 'It is quite different from "Anna", &, I hope,
much better' (LAB II, 177). Bennett's contract for the
novel with Chatto & Windus called for a royalty of 16.6

per cent on the first 5,000 copies in the six shilling
edition, and 20 per cent thereafter, with £75 advance on
the day of publication. Cheaper editions in the colonies
and elsewhere paid 10 per cent.

The novel had a very mixed reception. The 'Times
Literary Supplement' (9 October) thought the characterisation remarkable, the narrative defective, and the dialogue
unnatural. The 'Morning Leader' (b. 28 October) admired
the original psychological perception. The 'Glasgow
Herald' (28 October) liked its sense of actuality, its
characterisation, its narrative strength. The 'Athenaeum'
(31 October) thought it was a good piece of work all
round. The 'Daily Chronicle' (4 November) gave the novel
a longer review than most of the other journals, but spent
much of its space on general comment on Bennett and on
summary. The reviewer was not inclined to credit Bennett's
account of the sensations of love of a forty-year-old
woman. The 'Academy' (7 November) thought it would take
more than Bennett's undoubted ability to make the trivial
matter of the novel interesting. The 'Spectator'
(21 November) was offended almost to the point of nausea
by reading about a woman of forty in love, and reckoned
that Bennett would do better to stick to sensational fiction. The 'Daily Mirror' (b. 28 November) said that the
book was 'a remarkable addition to this year's novels ...,
a remarkable study of provincial life'. The 'Sketch'
(b. 1 December) found the book fascinating. See also the
reviews reprinted below, Nos 20-3.

On 28 September 1903 Bennett recorded in his 'Journal'
the opinion of his friend Marcel Schwob: 'You have got
hold of the greatest of all themes, the agony of the older
generation in watching the rise of the younger.' Conrad
wrote Bennett an appreciative letter suggesting that there
was perhaps not enough of Leonora herself in an otherwise
fine book. (L&LC I, 320-1.) Wells's reaction and the
reaction of another friend are given below, Nos 19 and 24.
On 21 October Bennett wrote in his 'Journal':

In the reviews of 'Leonora' what strikes me most is the
inability of the reviewers to perceive that the life
therein described (with its 'meat teas' - which they
always fasten on to) is no more vulgar than any other
sort of life. The 'Scotsman' says, 'The smug prosperity of the home, with its six-o-clock "meat-teas" and
its subservient attitude to the blustering head of the
house.' As if that kind of thing was not tremendously
prevalent everywhere in England and Scotland. No, what
really abrades them is not the life described but what
the 'Scotsman' calls 'the fearless strength of description of it.

On 22 October Bennett wrote to his literary agent: 'The
reviews of "Leonora" in "Athenaeum", "Sketch", & "T.P.'s
Weekly" have much pleased me. The swine in the "Chronicle"
hadn't read the book, & refrained from saying anything very
definite' (LAB I, 41). He wrote to Sturt in June the
following year, 'I have not yet seen the faults of
"Leonora", at least not the faults which some people say
are obvious' (LAB II, 190). Later editions of the book
appeared in 1914, 1918, and 1925.

'A Great Man' (1904)

Published on 19 May. Bennett began writing the novel in
December 1903 and finished it on 13 March, with an interruption of five weeks. He wrote in his 'Journal' on the
13th: 'I began it with an intention merely humorous, but
the thing has developed into a rather profound satire.'
The next day he was overcome 'by a grave fear of its being
dull and not funny after all'. The contract with Chatto
was the same as for 'Leonora'. On the whole the novel had
a good press, with assistance from Bennett. The 'Pall
Mall Gazette' gave it a brief notice on 28 May following
eight other brief reviews. The notice misrepresented the
novel, and Bennett wrote to the editor to complain, with
the result that the 'Gazette' printed a much longer review
on 13 June praising 'Mr. Bennett's gentle sarcasm against
the fiction-reading public' in the novel. 'The Times'
(b. 4 June) found the book 'capital reading'. 'Outlook'
(b. 4 June) thought it 'an exceptionally smart piece of
satire'. The 'Athenaeum' (4 June) found it 'distinctly
amusing and entertaining, like most of the author's work,
but as with some of his other writing, a vein of essential
vulgarity runs through it'. The 'Court Circular' (b. 11
June) thought the book 'one of the most delightfully smart
and witty books I have read'. The 'Academy' (18 June) was
amused, and liked the book rather more than 'Leonora'.
'Hearth and Home' (23 June) enjoyed it. The 'Illustrated
London News' (2 July) found the book 'admirable fooling'
but doubted that it would amuse the great public. On
8 July the book review column in 'T.P.'s Weekly' began:
'Readers of this journal who have so constantly testified
to their appreciation of the author of the "Savoir Faire
Papers" and "A Novelist's Log-Book" will welcome the
appearance of "A Great Man", by Arnold Bennett.'
On 26 May Bennett wrote in his 'Journal': 'Wells,
Whitten, and Marriott think that "A Great Man" is my best
book. And Phillpotts is enchanted with it.' (On Whitten
see p. 175; Frederick Marriott was a personal friend.)

On the following day Bennett wrote:

> Today I am 37. I have lived longer than I shall live.
> My new series [the stories for 'The Loot of Cities']
> begins to appear today in the 'Windsor'. My name is
> not on the cover. Anthony Hope's stands there alone.
> And I am 37. Comment is needless.

Wells's praise for the novel was barbed. He liked it, and
thought it had more distinction than 'Leonora', but he
also thought it could be better, and he did not think it
would be popular. Bennett agreed that it could be better,
especially towards the end. (See HGW, 109-10.) In 1908
Bennett recommended the novel to Edward Garnett, and
Garnett replied: 'with all its justness & clever satire
there is some element lacking in it: I think the detailed
atmosphere is *generalised* instead of being particularised?'
Bennett agreed. (See LAB II, 232-5.) In later years
Bennett preferred 'A Great Man' to 'The Card' (see p. 42).
On 2 January 1905 Bennett described the novel as a 'commercial failure' in the 'Journal'. Methuen issued an edition in 1915, of which there was an eleventh printing in
1925.

'Teresa of Watling Street' (1904)

Published in October. Bennett finished writing this serial
story by or before August 1901, and it ran in the 'Golden
Penny' beginning 4 July 1903. They paid £45 for it. By
the time the serial had finished its run, Bennett was
hoping that Chatto would never publish the book, which
was already under contract, and he tried and failed to
negotiate an exchange of other work for it. Chatto
published the book with eight illustrations. (On the
contract see p. 21.) On 30 October Bennett wrote to his
literary agent: 'The reviews of "Teresa" have been better
than I expected, much better. And I could not honestly
quarrel with even the severe ones' (LAB I, 58). 'To-Day'
(19 October) thoroughly recommended it as a pleasurable
mystery story. 'Black and White' (b. 5 November) thought
it was 'excellent', 'well and vividly written'. The
'Academy' (5 November) described Bennett's mind as 'strata
of earth rich with mineral deposits all varying in nature',
sometimes gold, sometimes

> almost valueless ore. In 'Anna of the Five Towns'
> Mr. Bennett showed himself at his best; in 'Teresa
> of Watling Street' he shows himself at his worst.

It is a farrago of improbable detective adventure that
the merest tiro might write.... We hope Mr. Bennett
will not give us another surprise like this.

The 'Manchester Guardian' (7 November) thought it was
'readable trash'. Bennett asked one or another friend
to ignore the book. He wrote to E.V. Lucas in 1924:
'I always regard "Teresa" as the world's worst novel'
(LAB III, 228); he was trying to discourage Methuen from
issuing a uniform edition of several novels including it.
Methuen issued its sixth printing of the novel in 1920.
An edition was published in 1962 in Birmingham.

'Tales of the Five Towns' (1905)

Published on 10 January. Bennett began thinking of a
collection of such tales in 1900 or before, and in 1900
he wrote to George Sturt to express pleasure in those he
was currently engaged in writing. One of the two sections
of the collection does not concern the Five Towns.
A Letter Home (see p. 13) appears with a note explaining
that it was written many years earlier. Most of the
stories appeared serially between 1900 and 1904. There
was some revising. Bennett regarded the story Tiddy-fol-
lol as a 'perfect & delicate trifle' (LAB II, 133). His
Worship the Goosedriver was also a favourite. Bennett
wanted publication in 1904, but Chatto & Windus were concerned about what was to them too rapid publication of his
books. The contract was the same as for 'Leonora' except
that there was no advance.
    Although reception of the collection was mixed, there
was fairly general awareness among the reviewers - it
would seem for the first time - that they were dealing
with an important author. The opinion of the reviewer
in the 'Staffordshire Sentinel' (No. 25) that Bennett 'has
taken his place amongst the leading writers of English
fiction' was merely expressing with provincial pride what
other reviewers were acknowledging. The 'Pall Mall
Gazette' (14 January) had only a slight favourable notice.
'To-Day' (18 January) thought that Bennett was 'one of the
cleverest of those of our writers who have not quite
"arrived"'; it was unfortunate, therefore, to see 'the
originality and excellence of his ideas' marred by careless writing. The 'Manchester Guardian' (25 January) had
similar praise and reservations. The 'Academy' (28 January) was more severe: 'one expects more in a book from him
than a few good paragraphs'. The 'Speaker' (28 January),
like one or two other journals, contrasted the collection

unfavourably with 'Anna of the Five Towns'; 'nevertheless, the "Tales" are distinctly worth reading', 'his pages contain really valuable documents of provincial life'. The 'St. James's Gazette' (b. 11 February) found the collection 'admirably clever work', and the 'Daily Express' (b. 11 February) expressed itself similarly. The 'World' (b. 25 February) said that he 'handles his materials with as much confidence as Mr. Hardy and Mr. Phillpotts do'. 'Vanity Fair' (b. 25 February) said that 'there are not many passages in the true literature of the English people that are finer'. The 'Spectator' (b. 25 February) said that 'Mr. Bennett has not his equal in the description of the upper strata of the great middle class'. The 'Morning Post' (b. 25 February) thought the stories 'almost worthy of Daudet'. The 'Daily Chronicle' (b. 25 February) said that 'if this volume proves unlucky, then verily the public does not know a good collection of stories when it sees it'. The collection was reprinted several times. An edition by Chatto in 1964 was expanded to include 'The Grim Smile of the Five Towns'.

'The Loot of Cities' (1905)

Published in June. The six stories in this collection were written for the 'Windsor Magazine'. They were written mainly in October-November 1903. Bennett wrote in his 'Journal' on 27 November 1903 that he had 'learnt a lot about the technique of construction while writing them', and four days later he wrote that they were 'all good on their plane'; but he also remarked on the 27th that at times while writing them he had been vastly bored. He reckoned to make £200 to £250 all told on them. They began appearing in the 'Windsor' in June 1904. The book was published by Alston Rivers. An edition published by Thomas Nelson in 1917 had additional stories. Three brief reviews are known, and they all said that the collection was entertaining: the 'Glasgow Herald' (28 June), 'To-Day' (5 July), and the 'Academy' (30 September).

'Sacred and Profane Love' (1905)

Published on 21 September. In thinking about the novel in March 1904, Bennett saw it forming an informal trilogy with 'Anna of the Five Towns' and 'Leonora'. It was his third serious novel in a row to have a woman as its chief character. All three novels prepared the way for 'The Old Wives' Tale'. The idea, Bennett told Sturt in

June 1904, had been in his head for three years. It was a
bawdy subject in spite of the fact that he was not a bawdy
man, '& I am gradually perceiving that it will be rather
fine' (LAB II, 190). Just before he began writing, he
noted in the 'Journal' - 22 November 1904 - that the first
part would be 'entirely magnificent'. He began writing
about 24 November, interrupting the writing in the following spring to write 'The City of Pleasure', and finished
on 16 July. The contract with Chatto was the same as for
'Leonora'.

Of all Bennett's serious novels, 'Sacred and Profane
Love' has been the one that later critics have least been
able to take seriously. The immediate reception was mixed,
but some of the critics who found fault with it did so for
reasons of taste and propriety that are not troublesome
today. The 'Times Literary Supplement' (22 September) in
a brief notice said that 'the promise of the somewhat awe-
inspiring title ... is hardly fulfilled'. The 'Daily
Chronicle' (26 September) was exultant: 'fierce, brilliant,
brutal'. The 'Scotsman' (b. 7 October) found the book 'a
record which none but the strong may read - throbbing
passionate pages'. The 'Glasgow Herald' (b. 14 October)
found it 'vivid', 'compelling', and 'bold', and the
'Morning Leader' found it 'remarkable'. The 'Evening
News' (b. 20 October) said that Bennett was 'so ingenious
that he has made us read his absurd story through to the
end'. The 'Athenaeum' (21 October) said: 'What Mr. Bennett
means, if he means anything, it is hard to discover. His
tale reads like a parody of a French novel, and at times
is positively grotesque.' See also the reviews printed
below, where H.G. Wells's opinion is also printed, along
with Bennett's response, Nos 26-31. Bennett's views
changed. In 1908 he wrote to Edward Garnett: 'I don't
regard "Sacred and Profane Love" as anything more than a
tour de force' (LAB II, 255). In 1910 Bennett wrote a
Preface for the American edition (which was called 'The
Book of Carlotta'), and discussed briefly the style and
viewpoint of the novel and also its position in the trilogy. George Doran reported to him that he had sold 5,000
copies before publication there. In England the book went
into a second printing within about four months, but then
it faded. Royalties for six months to the end of December
1907 were £2. 13s. 3d. Bennett dramatised the novel in
1916 (see p. 127).

'Hugo' (1906)

Published 18 January. A 'Journal' entry in March 1904

indicates that Bennett gave more imaginative attention to
'Hugo' than to any other of his sensational books. He
wrote to his literary agent on 18 April:

> I am happy to say that I have begun a sensational serial
> compared to which the 'Grand Babylon Hotel' is nothing.
> Its title is simply & majestically
>
> 'HUGO'
>
> It will be immense. (LAB I, 48)

The writing was accomplished between 19 April and 16 July.
It was rejected by 'T.P.'s Weekly', presumably on the
grounds of sexual suggestiveness, but Bennett suspected
T.P. O'Connor's personal animus. Nevertheless he made
minor alterations, and the story was taken by 'To-Day',
where it began appearing on 3 May 1905. 'To-Day' paid
less than Bennett had hoped to get; he had expected to
earn £300 altogether. His contract with Chatto was the
same as for 'Leonora'.

Known reviews were mixed. The 'Pall Mall Gazette'
(20 January) assumed that the book would have a certain
popularity, but 'as an artistic performance or a picture
of life it does not exist'. A.N. Monkhouse, whose own
writing Bennett had reviewed favourably, said in the
'Manchester Guardian' (24 January) that the book was
'exuberant and extravagant and brilliant'; 'of course it
is outside humanity, but it is capital sport and a good
diversion for a very able writer who is not compelled to
be serious all the time'. The 'Speaker' (27 January)
recited the thrilling plot with just a slight note of
sarcasm. The 'Academy' (27 January) recited it without
sarcasm, and thought that 'Mr. Bennett has surpassed himself in his latest fantasia'. The 'Spectator' (27 January) found the book uninteresting, and barely credible
on its own terms; the reviewer longed for another 'A Great
Man'. The 'Morning Leader' (b. 10 February) found the
book 'amazingly exciting', and the 'Academy' (b. 10 February) 'breathlessly exciting'; moreover the 'Morning Leader'
thought that Bennett had raised the sensational novel 'to
the level of an artistic achievement'. The 'Tribune'
(b. 21 February) was very favourable. Bennett's own estimation of reviews at the time was that they were 'exceptionally favourable' (LAB I, 68). The book was published
in America at the same time by Buckles. It had mixed
reviews in both the 'New York Times' (5 January) and the
'Nation' (17 January). The 'Nation' thought that Bennett
showed a certain condescension towards his material.

H.G. Wells professed to enjoy the novel: 'glittering and absurd and we like it no end' (HGW, 131). Violet Hunt did not like it. She was living in Paris at this time, and became acquainted with Bennett there. Bennett wrote to her: 'I distinctly warned you not to read "Hugo"....
It is astonishing that I cannot keep my friends from reading the *un*-literature which I write solely in order to be in a position to offer myself a few luxuries' (LAB II, 205). 'Hugo' did not provide many luxuries. Bennett quarrelled with Chatto over what he thought was lack of advertising of it, and the first four months of sales seem to have brought £75 in royalties, presumably merely earning the advance. In the first half of the following year it earned £1. 8*s*. 11*d*. A sixpenny edition was issued in 1911.

'Whom God Hath Joined' (1906)

Published at the end of October. The novel, and its subject of divorce, were specially commissioned by the publisher Alfred Nutt. Bennett was very much interested in the subject, and told Nutt that he could make it 'very striking & documentary' (LAB I, 60). He began writing on 8 November 1905 and finished in early July 1906, with an interruption mainly in February-March to write 'The Sinews of War' with Eden Phillpotts. In the 'Journal' on 16 November 1905 Bennett wrote that the first chapter seemed 'rather original and rather good, and quite unlike anything I had done before'. Eventually he became irritated with the book, no doubt in part because his private life had become complicated. In June 1906 he became engaged to an American girl, Eleanor Green, whom he had met not many months before. Little is known of the relationship except that it was a troubled one, and was broken off in early August, about three weeks after the novel was finished. Bennett wrote to his brother Frank on 9 July:

> So nice and cheerful to read aloud your most secret and unsentimental thoughts on the relations of the sexes, and particularly on divorce, to your betrothed during the first month of your engagement! No wonder the tragical parts drew tears, whether of sorrow or fury God knows. (RP, 162)

The contract called for an advance of £125, with a royalty of 20 per cent on the six shilling edition and 8.3 per cent on the two shilling Colonial edition.
      The 'Times Literary Supplement' (2 November) in a short

notice approved of the 'touch of the affidavit' with which Bennett treated his inflammatory subject. In another brief notice in the 'Daily Express' (6 November) Sidney Dark thought that the story showed 'a cleverness beyond the ordinary'. The 'Academy' (3 November) admitted that the book was clever and truthful, but the story it told was 'disgusting, sordid, utterly vile', and readers ought to read Arthur Quiller-Couch's more edifying tale 'Sir John Constantine'. The 'Tribune' (b. 24 November) thought it was a work of 'consummate skill'. In two other brief notices the 'Speaker' (1 December) thought that the book was carefully done and depressing, and the 'Athenaeum' (8 December) said it was 'a thoughtful novel, but it is not at all a work of art'. For other reviews see Nos 32 and 33. Nutt was unhappy with the reviews and wanted Bennett to respond to the one in the 'Academy'. In March 1907 Nutt wrote to say that sales had amounted to 1,404 all told, with an earned royalty amounting to £27. He thought that Bennett's detached treatment was responsible, and he wanted to issue a cheap edition with a 10 per cent royalty to try to recoup his loss. Bennett agreed to the cheap edition, which was issued in May, and he reminded Nutt of the fact that sometimes works that do not make a profit in the short run make one in the long. Bennett wrote in his 'Journal' on 24 July 1907 that the 'lofty nobility' he was aiming for in 'The Old Wives' Tale' he had achieved only 'now and then' in the earlier novel. In 1910 he found the opening chapters compulsive reading. Methuen issued an edition in 1915, and Sidney Dark reviewed it again in the 'Daily Express' (11 March), this time finding it rather thin. A seventh impression appeared in 1935. A new edition was issued by Methuen in 1951 with an introduction by Desmond MacCarthy, who noted that the reprinting came at the urging of readers rather than of critics.

'The Sinews of War', with Eden Phillpotts (1906)

Published on 31 October. Phillpotts was the better known novelist, and his proposal of collaboration on a serial flattered Bennett. (On their collaboration on plays see pp. 121-3.) Phillpotts's name came first, and he received an equal share of royalties, but he merely provided the scenario (estimated by Bennett to be the labour of four days) and Bennett did the writing, except for a couple of descriptions. Bennett began writing on 26 January 1906 and finished on 7 April. The serial was sold to 'T.P.'s Weekly' for £450, and began appearing there on 2 March.

It was an immediate success. The book was issued by
T. Werner Laurie. The terms with Laurie are unknown but
probably the advance was £300-400. A.N. Monkhouse in the
'Manchester Guardian' (31 October) supposed that the best
parts were written by Bennett; overall it was 'a stunning
piece of rather frantic adventure'; he hoped that it gave
the authors 'zest for their real work'. The 'Pall Mall
Gazette' (31 October) was vastly amused, and imagined
each author trying to outdo the other in his share of the
writing. The 'Academy' (17 November) found it sometimes
dull and never thrilling. The 'Tribune' (b. 1 December)
reckoned it to be 'one of the best murder mysteries' in
recent years. The 'Scotsman' (b. 1 December) found it
'wholly entertaining'. The 'Evening Standard' (b. 1 December), the 'Morning Leader' (b. 1 December), and the
'Birmingham Post' (b. 1 December) praised it similarly.
The 'Athenaeum' (1 December) was bored. The 'Bookman'
(December) found it 'a gorgeous medley of triumphant and
audacious absurdities'. Laurie reported six months later
that he had lost £150 on the book. A Readers Library
paperback edition appeared in 1931 (with Bennett's name
first), and was in its thirty-second thousand about
fifteen years later.

'Things That Interested Me' (1906)

Privately printed in Burslem and presented at Christmas to
friends. This was a slender volume of extracts from
Bennett's journal, which he had been keeping since 1896.
According to George Sturt, who provided an introduction to
the extracts, 'there were to be no vapourings or rhapso-
dies; introspection was barred out; speculation on the
riddle of the universe was discountenanced'. A letter
from Bennett to Sturt in 1901 expressed dissatisfaction
with the result: 'the fact is I am too ignorant of everything to observe the phenomena with any fineness....
I haven't got down a single thing of importance, though
naturally I have found some drolleries' (LAB II, 144-5).

'The Ghost' (1907)

Published on 24 January. Bennett wrote a series of seven
stories about the occult for 'Woman' in 1894, but the
immediate origin of 'The Ghost' was the fact (as described
in 'The Truth About an Author') that as editor of 'Woman'
he paid out sums of money to literary syndicates for work
that he saw he himself could do. He told the agent of a

syndicate that he was writing a serial. The agent was interested, and Bennett thereupon sat down to his task, in late October 1898.

> As an editor, I knew the qualities that a serial ought to possess. And I knew specially that what most serials lacked was a large, central, unifying, vivifying idea. I was very fortunate in lighting upon such an idea for my first serial. There are no original themes; probably no writer ever did invent an original theme; but my theme was a brilliant imposture of originality. It had, too, grandeur and passion, and fantasy, and it was inimical to none of the prejudices of the serial reader. In truth it was a theme worthy of much better treatment than I accorded to it.

Bennett says that he wrote the twelve instalments in twenty four days, composing in his head as he walked to work in the morning, and writing 2,500 words when he came home in the evening. A letter to Sturt in November 1898 says that at first the writing went slowly, and he had to rewrite, but then the knack of it came, and 'I can do it now at the rate of 700 words an hour, on my head, so to speak' (LAB II, 113). He 'put in generous quantities of wealth, luxury, feminine beauty, surprise, catastrophe, and genial incurable optimism' (The Truth About an Author'). He finished on 23 January 1899, well pleased with the result, and wrote in the 'Journal' the following day: 'It is, of the kind, good stuff, well written and well contrived, and some of the later chapters are really imagined and, in a way, lyrical.' He obtained £75 from the syndicate, and it appeared under the title 'Love and Life' in 'Hearth and Home' (of which Bennett was an editor and to which he contributed regularly) beginning 17 May 1900. In February 1902 he contracted with Chatto & Windus for publication in book form (see p. 21 on the contract); but a year and a half later he was hoping to suppress both it and 'Teresa of Watling Street'. When Chatto insisted, Bennett decided to rewrite the novel, believing that he could now make it 'very striking & thrilling indeed, & at the same time good' (LAB I, 52). He did the rewriting in October-November 1906.

A.N. Monkhouse in the 'Manchester Guardian' (31 January) wanted to be kind, but he did not find in the novel the zestful spirit of 'The Sinews of War' and 'Hugo'. The 'beginning was almost brilliant', but interest waned, and 'mysteries are poor affairs when we come to close quarters with them'. The 'Times Literary Supplement' in a brief notice (1 February) thought it was well told and

unconvincing. The 'Scotsman' (b. 9 February) found itself
in a 'delightfully impossible world'. The 'Academy'
(9 February) acknowledged 'amazing cleverness and astonishing verisimilitude' but wondered whether 'it would seem
impertinent to wish that he would think a little more and
write a little less'. The 'Staffordshire Sentinel'
(4 April) found it gripping holiday reading. The 'Bookman' (September) found it poor stuff compared with 'The
Grand Babylon Hotel': mechanical, almost ridiculous. The
book was published in America by Herbert Turner in Boston.
The 'New York Times' (15 June) reviewed it among Best
Books for Summer Reading and said that some authorities
reckoned it to be the best ghost story since Bulwer
Lytton's 'House of the Braln'.

   The book did not sell well. Chatto reported at the
beginning of March that they had sold 2,500 copies.
Bennett thought they should have sold 5,000, and he
suspected - wrongly - that the figures were inaccurate.
Not until 1910 did total sales rise above 3,000.
Bennett's relations with Chatto were never easy. He
objected to their manner of advertising; he did not like
the company he kept on their list; and he was unable to
get a starting royalty of 20 per cent out of them. He
may have noticed that the advertisement for 'The Ghost'
in the 'Academy' on 30 March called it 'The Goths' and
on 13 April called it 'The Ghosts'. He had been angry
some years earlier when their advertisements for 'Leonora'
said it was 'by the author of "The Grand Babylon Hotel"'.
He wanted to be published by Methuen, and he went there
via Chapman & Hall, but when he got there he was not keen
on Methuen, and presently went to Cassell. Chatto was his
publisher in later years for some of his non-fiction and
most of his plays. Later editions of 'The Ghost' appeared
in 1922, 1933, and 1940.

'The Reasonable Life' (1907)

Published about 20 March. 'The Reasonable Life' was the
first of Bennett's so-called pocket philosophies. To his
friends, Bennett's best qualities were his kindliness and
his commonsense. It was these qualities that inspired the
pocket philosophies, along with an ability to write for
ordinary people without condescension and with humour.
His first extended effort in this direction was the
'Savoir-Faire Papers', published in 'T.P.'s Weekly' in
1902-3. Despite the interest of readers of that journal
in seeing these essays published in book form, they were
not (see p. 6), but the succeeding series in the same

vein, the 'Savoir-Vivre Papers', published in the same
place from 1 December 1905 to 28 September 1906, became
'The Reasonable Life' after some revision. The book
was published by A.C. Fifield. Only two English
reviews are known. The 'New Age' (28 March) thought
that Hazlitt, Lamb, and Stevenson on similar subjects
were better, but understood that 'Mr. Bennett is a
popular writer' and found the essays 'pleasant' and
'wholesome'. The 'Manchester Guardian' (4 April) found
'a good deal of sound sense and even a philosophy that
seems sincere and workable'. The book was later
revised and enlarged and published under the title
'Mental Efficiency'. Publication in America in 1911
under the latter title brought several favourable
reviews, an especially flattering one appearing in the
'Literary Digest' (2 September 1911): 'every page glows
with brilliant thought'.

'The Grim Smile of the Five Towns' (1907)

Published in June. This second serious collection of
stories contains work that was published serially during
1906-7 and other previously unpublished stories. Bennett
wrote of them to his literary agent in April 1907:
'I attach much importance to the publication of the short
stories in the summer. They are artistic work, some of my
best, & they must come between a potboiler like "Ghost",
& another potboiler like "City of Pleasure" (LAB I, 87).
The collection was offered to Chatto & Windus for £100
outright for seven years - terms that Bennett rightly
assumed Chatto would not accept. Bennett wanted Methuen,
but his agent advised him that Methuen was not keen, and
the collection went to Chapman & Hall, who paid Bennett
20 per cent royalty, with an advance of £50.
  The few reviews known are short and mixed. That in
the 'Staffordshire Sentinel' (18 June) is longest, but
consists largely of summary and quotation. It finds the
stories clever, and one of them, In a New Bottle, nasty;
part of the pleasure in reading them is in penetrating the
thin disguises of fiction. The 'Manchester Guardian'
(19 June) liked The Death of Simon Fuge but thought that
otherwise the stories were slight. The 'Academy' (27 July)
saw a similar division between serious and slight, but
overall was much more favourably impressed: 'The characters are natural, human and intensely alive'. The 'Bookman' (August) was mainly full of praise, but thought In
a New Bottle 'grotesque' and The Death of Simon Fuge too
long. H.G. Wells wrote to Bennett: '"The Grim Smile" is

I think your high watermark so far. I've read it and
admire and envy a pen so wonderfully under control and now
astonishingly expert' (HGW, 143). Bennett himself described The Death of Simon Fuge in 1911 as 'still one of
the best things I have done' (LAB I, 152), an opinion
shared by most of his later critics. The collection seems
not to have sold well, and a year and a half after publication Bennett was complaining of inadequate advertising
by Chapman & Hall. The book has been reprinted occasionally. Penguin issued their first edition in 1946. Their
most recent edition, 1971, remains in print.

'The City of Pleasure' (1907)

Published in October. Bennett had the notion for the
novel in 1903, at which time he referred to it as 'my *big*
book..., the whole of which moves in the hotel-restaurant-
Covent Garden ball atmosphere' (LAB I, 37), and perhaps he
was thinking of writing something on a larger scale than
'The City of Pleasure' proved to be. By July 1904 it had
become 'an exciting yarn "round" an Exhibition like Earl's
Court' (LAB I, 54), and he knew that the Tillotson syndicate would find it irresistible. He wrote it from about
1 April to 30 May 1905, and the Tillotson syndicate
apparently paid £87 for it and did not like it. They
wrote to Bennett's agent:

> We should like to publish further work by Mr. Bennett's
> pen, but naturally it must be such work as we can sell.
> 'The Grand Babylon Hotel' hit the mark with our clients,
> but 'The City of Pleasure' was unacceptable to them,
> and we have lost considerably on the story, while the
> majority of those who did publish it say they will not
> publish another from the same pen. (LAB I, 55)

The novel appeared in the 'Staffordshire Sentinel' and in
four other papers beginning 6 January 1906. In the course
of the year it appeared in at least nine other papers.
Chatto & Windus paid £200 for it rather than lose it. The
'Times Literary Supplement' (17 October) found it 'not
quite farcical enough to amuse, and not quite real enough
to move the feelings'. The 'Academy' (19 October) was
thoroughly entertained: 'Mr. Bennett writes with absolute
gusto', the book is full of 'splendidly impossible things',
'the workmanship ... is quite brilliant'. The 'Manchester
Guardian' (30 October) was mildly amused. The 'Athenaeum'
(9 November) was dismayed: 'to be readable, this should be
a very funny book; but unfortunately it is not that; it is

only grotesquely unreal, and exhibits the author's faulty
taste'. The book was published in America in 1915, and
received some long reviews. The 'New York Times'
(25 April) recounted the plot at length, and thought it
made excellent light reading. The 'Nation' (13 May) found
it to be 'in Mr. Bennett's lightest and most high-spirited
vein' and wondered 'whether in following the fashion of
glum realism a fine romantic writer had been spoiled'.
The 'New Republic' (22 May) offered one of the very few
considered discussions the novel has ever had, exemplify-
ing in brief detail two central assertions:

> In the first place, we have Mr. Bennett the observer.
> He has walked this world with his eyes open. He has
> looked at it partly because he takes, as he has himself
> said, 'a malicious and frigid pleasure' in seeing and
> 'setting down facts which are opposed to accepted
> sentimental falsities'.... His chapter called The Heart
> of the City is almost a piece of self-portraiture. It
> reveals his joy in the defeat of expectations by life.
> It reveals that busy interest in the concrete working
> of things which is one with his busy interest in the
> concrete working of men's and women's heads and hearts.

The book sold badly. It required sales of 10,000 copies
to cover the advance, and not until 1919 did it sell even
2,500. Nevertheless Dent issued an edition in 1914. Late
in life, after seeing a film version, Bennett recalled
that 'the book was full of humour' (LN, 253). Further
editions appeared in 1914 and 1938.

'Things Which Have Interested Me, Second Series' (1907)

Privately printed in Burslem and presented at Christmas to
friends. It consisted of further extracts from the journal. Bennett wrote to Sturt beforehand:

> My journal is still kept up (seventh volume is just
> being finished), but I doubt if it is really any good.
> Arthur Hooley has written the preface for this year's
> Xmas selection, & I have had it printed in Burslem in
> rather a classy style in black and red. (LAB II, 220;
> on Arthur Hooley see p. 121)

Wells wrote to Bennett that 'the book of "Things" this
year is better than ever' (HGW, 146). One hundred num-
bered copies were printed.

'The Statue', with Eden Phillpotts (1908)

Published in March. This book was apparently produced in
the same way as 'The Sinews of War'. Phillpotts was so
pleased with Bennett's first instalments of the earlier
novel that he immediately proposed to do another, and sent
a rough outline in March 1906. By June the novel was completely planned. Bennett probably did the writing of it
in five weeks during the first three months of 1907.
There then ensued an unpleasantness between the authors in
the negotiations for publication. Phillpotts seems to
have distrusted Bennett's agent, and he seems to have
assumed without warrant that he could obtain in excess of
£300 for serial rights and at least £600 for book rights.
The work was apparently not serialised in any major
papers, but it did appear in the 'Staffordshire Sentinel'
beginning on 19 March 1908. Cassell paid £350 for the
book. Bennett and Phillpotts had already begun a third
serial, but never finished it; they wrote a play together
in the autumn of 1907; then their friendship lapsed for
many years. When Bennett received his copies of the novel
from Cassell, he wrote in his 'Journal', on 28 March: 'I
hope I have now done with sensational work.' Six months
earlier he had written to his agent about both the serials
on which he collaborated with Phillpotts: 'on their plane,
they are thoroughly sound & conscientious work, of which
nobody need be ashamed' (LAB I, 93). Two reviews are
known. The 'Times Literary Supplement' in a very brief
notice (26 March) found it 'an enthralling narrative,
which, however, moves sometimes a little uneasily, as if
the strands of the two authors' threads were not quite
evenly twisted together'. A.N. Monkhouse in the 'Manchester Guardian' (1 April) was concerned: 'one feels a little
doubtful whether the more natural and refined work of the
authors may not suffer from such exercises as this'; the
novel was 'sound and fury signifying nothing'. The book
was issued in America in the same year. A cheap edition
appeared in England in 1910.

'Buried Alive' (1908)

Published on 3 June. Bennett wrote the novel in an interlude in the writing of 'The Old Wives' Tale', apparently
in part because he needed money. He had married in July.
He owed his literary agent £1,000. He conceived the idea
of the novel on 10 December 1907 and did the writing between 1 January and 27 February. He gave some thought to
it as a serial at first, but his agent told him that the

market for serials was not good, and he thereafter wrote
it solely with the book in mind. He wrote in his
'Journal' on 29 February: 'Except one chapter, which I
thought would be the best in the book, it is all pretty
good.' The advance from Chapman & Hall was £150. Bennett
suggested using a sandwich man to advertise the book outside Mudie's on the day of publication, but Mudie's
objected, and the man marched up and down Oxford Street
instead.

   'The reviews have been excellent', Bennett wrote to his
agent a month later (LAB I, 105). Most of the known ones
are brief, and they mainly summarise the plot. The 'Times
Literary Supplement' in a very brief notice (4 June)
described the book as 'an agreeable extravaganza'. The
'Daily Chronicle' (17 June) called it 'the most amusing -
and permanently amusing - book that the present reviewer
has encountered for many years', and the 'Birmingham Daily
Post' (24 June) said the same. The 'Academy' (4 July) was
very pleased, and thought that 'had Mr. Bernard Shaw
written this book it would have been hailed as a masterpiece, but happily, Mr. Bennett is not sufficiently well
advertised yet to rob the critics of their commonsense'.
The 'Morning Post' (of unknown date) said: 'He who would
laugh at the humorous excesses of modern life and the
eternal absurdities of human character, and would at the
same time enjoy the excitement of a surprising narrative
should read this book.' The book was issued two years
later in America, first by Brentano's and then by George
Doran, and Bennett wrote to his agent that the reviews
there 'have been quite remarkable' (LAB I, 139). No
remarkable reviews could be found. The 'Bookman' (August
1910) was moderately enthusiastic: the book was 'never
tedious, never vulgar'; it was an unusually honest piece
of humour. The 'Nation' (20 October) found it 'entertaining farce'. W.D. Howells in a general discussion of
Bennett in 'Harpers's' in March 1911 classified 'Buried
Alive', and also 'The Glimpse', in a lump with 'The Grand
Babylon Hotel', 'The Gates of Wrath', 'The Ghost', and
'Hugo' as false and bad books (see No. 73). His article
elicited a cordial letter from Bennett which remarked
incidentally 'that I consider "Buried Alive", though as
you say a farce, as a quite serious "criticism of life",
& that I mean to continue at intervals in this vein'
(LAB II, 274). For one English review and for a comment
from Frank Harris see Nos 34 and 35. Bennett regarded
'Buried Alive' as his best comic novel. He wrote in his
'Journal' on 9 November 1909: 'I began to read "Buried
Alive", and ... smiled the whole time. I don't think I
have ever read a funnier book than this.' In an

unpublished letter to a woman who wrote a master's thesis
on him in 1927 he said: '"Buried Alive" ... is far better
than "The Card". I am not very keen on "The Card" as a
whole. I prefer "A Great Man", but the latter two are
simply not on the same plane as "Buried Alive"' (SOT).

The book did not sell well, and failed to earn its
advance. Arthur Waugh, the head of Chapman & Hall, seems
to have taken the view that Bennett's account was therefore overdrawn, a view that Bennett thought was ludicrous.
Bennett wrote to him in February 1910, when a sixpenny
edition was being arranged with the Amalgamated Press (who
paid Bennett £75 and issued it in their 'Daily Mail'
series): 'You were good enough to express a high opinion
of "Buried Alive" & I think that the unsatisfactory sales
ought not to be laid at my door' (LAB II, 262). Bennett
wrote to his agent about Waugh at the same time:

> He is a born grumbler. The fact is, he is not a busi-
> ness man, but a second-rate artist by temperament with
> his emotions undisciplined. I like him, to talk to,
> but on business I am sick of him.... When he ...
> learns that we have gone to Methuens ..., Henrietta St.
> won't hold him! (LAB I, 131)

In a full column advertisement list by Chapman & Hall on
4 July 1908, two-thirds of the column advertised two
books, Vincent Brown's 'The Last Shore' and A.E. Copping's
'Gotty in Furrin' Parts'. The remaining third was given
chiefly to Ethel Mayne's 'The Fourth Ship', with the
remainder listing five other novels, one of which was
'Buried Alive'. Initial sales of the book in America
were good, and when the sixpenny edition appeared in
England Bennett noted, 'Extraordinary, how a really honest
book won't die. I've noticed it again and again' (RP,
108). Apparently sales continued to be poor in England
until Methuen took over the book in 1911. They had
issued seven impressions by 1914. Nelson issued an edition in 1916. Penguin issued a paperback edition in 1976.
A Methuen edition is currently in print as well.

'How to Live on Twenty-Four Hours a Day' (1908)

Published about 3 June. The record of Bennett's writing
during 1907 and the first quarter of 1908 is so full that
he must have found several days with forty-eight hours in
them to write this work and its companion-piece, 'The
Human Machine'. Presumably he wrote the essays for this
series at regular intervals during the first ten months

of 1907. He wrote to George Sturt on 4 November:

> I seem to be getting more and more 'earnest' every day.
> At the end of this year I shall have jolly near written
> 365,000 words in the year - much of which is nothing
> but Marcus Aurelius & Christ assimilated & excreted by
> me in suitable form. (LAB II, 220)

The series began in the 'Evening News' on 6 May 1908, and
ran for twelve instalments, ending on 13 June. Publication in book form had been arranged with A.R. Orage on
2 March. It is unknown why the publication of the book
should have preceded the completion of the serial run.
Orage's book list was small, and he apparently did not
advertise the book except in the pages of his journal,
the 'New Age'.

Bennett's opinion of the book and its popular and critical reception over the years are given on pp. 6-7. 'The
Times' (b. 11 July) noted briefly that 'Mr. Bennett writes
with his usual crispness, point and humour on 'the art of
making the best use of time'. The 'Bristol Daily Mercury'
(b. 11 July) reckoned that it was 'the cheapest shilling-
worth of practical wisdom now going in the book market'.
'Public Opinion' (b. 11 July) thought that 'it would be a
good thing if the book stalls and book shops were to fill
their counters with it and sell it instead of the magazines'. The 'Daily Chronicle' (of unknown date) said that
'if you are at all interested in your soul and the life
you live outside the money-making hours, take this book
very seriously'. The 'Literary World' (of unknown date)
said, 'This volume is a profound pocket book of commonsense.' Bennett reported receiving very many press cuttings about it from America before it was published there.
During his visit to America in 1911 he wrote to a friend
that he 'could have got scores & scores of engagements to
read extracts from "How to Live on 24 Hours a Day" at from
£75 to £100 a night' (LAB II, 293). A note in the 'Journal' in 1929 says that over the years it sold better than
any of his other books. In 1930 Henry Ford told him that
he had once bought 500 copies to give to his staff. The
book was taken over from the New Age Press in England by
Frank Palmer in 1910, and then taken over by Hodder &
Stoughton in 1912. Hodder & Stoughton issued a ninth
impression in 1914, and an eleventh impression in 1916
with a new preface. It was serialised in the 'Recorder'
in November-December 1951, and another edition was pub-
lised in 1960.

'The Old Wives' Tale' (1908)

Published on 30 October. The origin of the novel was
related by Bennett in his Preface to the American edition
of 1911. In 1903 he was living in Paris, and he often
dined at a restaurant where two waitresses engaged his
especial attention, the stout, middle-aged, and managing
one who customarily served him, and a beautiful young girl
who served in another area. One evening an old woman came
in who behaved grotesquely and who soon was being laughed
at by the two waitresses and by everyone else.

> I reflected concerning the grotesque diner: 'This woman
> was once young, slim, perhaps beautiful; certainly free
> from these ridiculous mannerisms. Very probably she is
> unconscious of her singularities. Her case is a tra-
> gedy. One ought to be able to make a heartrending
> novel out of the history of a woman such as she.'
> Every stout, ageing woman is not grotesque - far from
> it! - but there is an extreme pathos in the mere fact
> that every stout ageing woman was once a young girl
> with the unique charm of youth in her form and movement
> and in her mind. And the fact that the change from the
> young girl to the stout ageing woman is made up of an
> infinite number of infinitesimal changes, each unper-
> ceived by her, only intensifies the pathos.

Bennett decided to transform the old woman into a sympathetic and ordinary woman, and he determined to show two
such women instead of one. The difference between his
two waitresses was in part the difference between youth
and middle age; it became also the difference between
Constance and Sophia Baines, the one plain, the other
beautiful. The book intimidated him, Bennett said in the
Preface; he thought about it often, and he turned his
attention to smaller books for several years.

Bennett recorded the episode in the restaurant in the
'Journal' on 18 November 1903, with slightly different
detail and with more emphasis on the story to be made of
it - a story of 10,000-15,000 words. The story would
begin in the restaurant and then go back to the infancy
of the two heroines, who would be sisters. One of them
would live a prosaic life, the other would become a whore,
and they would live together again in old age. On 22
November he wrote to his agent of his 'really fine idea
... dramatic & powerful ..., as serious as "Leonora"'
(LAB I, 41). In February 1904 he was thinking of material
for it and hoping to make it his next serious book. He
abandoned it for 'Sacred and Profane Love' and then for

'Whom God Hath Joined'. In April 1907 he wrote to his
agent of 'the length, and general ambitiousness, & the
blend of tragedy & humour in the new novel, which will be
ready for publication next summer.... It is a great work'
(LAB I, 87). Several entries in the 'Journal' during July
and August 1907 concerned the conception of the novel. In
a prefatory note to some of them that were published in
'Life and Letters' in 1929, Bennett said that at this
time 'the idea of "The Old Wives' Tale" moved within me,
beneath everything else' (L&L, 16). Some of these entries
were probably self-conscious revisions and elaborations
made at a later date; in any event in one of them - 19
July - Bennett reported having seen on the night before
an aged French peasant woman harnessed to a dogcart along-
side a dog, and of being visited with a temptation to have
Sophia Baines end her days similarly. Another like entry
of 23 July mentioned 'fecundating an epic'. In an entry
in the 'Journal' on 1 August he expressed uncertainty
about the character of Constance's husband, and on 25
August he noted the idea of introducing a public execution
into the second part of the novel. A letter to his agent
on 9 September said that the novel would be 120,000 words:
'in every way it will be my largest work' (LAB I, 94).
Apparently in September Bennett began deliberate and
sustained work on the book, and he wrote in the 'Journal'
on 19 September: 'Today I finished the construction of the
first part of "The Old Wives' Tale".' Such construction
usually occurred in these years during walks in the forest
of Fontainebleau.
    Another preliminary to writing the novel was Bennett's
learning a fine calligraphic hand. From the time he wrote
'A Man from the North' he was interested in the look of
his manuscripts, but the revisions of both 'A Man from the
North' and 'Anna of the Five Towns' made a mess of them.
Only now was Bennett ready to try to unite the arts and
crafts of writing. In the 'Journal' on 23 July he wrote:

> I began to see yesterday how my 'fine writing' and
> illuminating must develop. I saw that I could only
> advance with any hope of continuing by uniting utility
> with beauty; that I must not therefore make fine manu-
> scripts for the sake of making them, but rather in
> connection with my own work; also that I must form a
> natural hand that could be written quickly. These
> principles having been arrived at, I began to practise
> a little.

The entry as given in 'Life and Letters' said also: 'I
have an idea that I can produce the most beautiful

original manuscript of a novel that a novelist ever did
produce' (L&L, 24). In his prefatory note to the facsimile edition of the manuscript, published in 1927,
Bennett described the conditions of writing a novel in
such a way:

> Of course if your manuscript is to have even the most
> modest pretensions to calligraphic decency, you must
> know all the time exactly what you are about to do.
> It will be noticed that now and then in the writing of
> 'The Old Wives' Tale' something rather like a regular
> mess did ensue, consequence of not having absolutely
> decided in advance just what I wanted to write, and in
> what order, and how. The reader, however, sees the
> worst of these messes; no page, so far as I remember,
> was destroyed and rewritten.

Bennett began writing on 8 October. In the very first
days the writing went slowly and uneasily, but in eighteen
days he produced 18,000 words, and he finished the first
section (48,000) by 3 December. He then went to London,
and tried to continue with the writing in a hotel there,
but he found London distracting, and he wrote 'Buried
Alive' instead. In early March he was ready to begin
again. On 12 March he wrote in the 'Journal': 'I have
read through first part of "Old Wives' Tale", and am
deeply persuaded of its excellence.' On 5 April he
wrote there:

> Habit of work growing on me. I could get into the way
> of going to my desk as a man goes to whiskey, or
> rather to chloral. Now that I have finished all my
> odd jobs and have nothing to do but 10,000 words of
> the novel a week and two articles a week, I feel quite
> lost, and at once begin to think, without effort, of
> ideas for a new novel. My instinct is to multiply
> books and articles and plays.

On 17 June he wrote to his agent: 'The serious novel is
proving terrific. It will be 200,000 words long' (LAB I,
102). On 26 June he wrote in the 'Journal': 'Seriously
disturbed by my novel. It is an immensely complicated
undertaking.' He finished writing on 30 August.
The 'Journal' entry of 5 April indicates something of
Bennett's general state of mind while writing the novel.
He had written to George Sturt the preceding November:

> The most curious thing that has happened to me is that
> I have practically lost all my ambition except the

ambition to be allowed to work quietly. This remarkable phenomenon coincides with my marriage, but I do not honestly think the two things are connected, as it has been 'coming on' for a year. (LAB II, 220)

On 1 April 1908 he wrote in the 'Journal': 'I expect I am as happy as I can be. I have learnt a lot, and am learning.' On 9 July he wrote to his literary agent, apropos of Arthur Waugh's uneasiness over paying £150 in advance on the novel (with a royalty of 20 per cent, rising to 25 per cent after the sale of 5,000 copies):

I will not disguise my opinion that I am one of the future great prizes of the publishing world. I did not form this opinion myself. It was forced on me by many people known and unknown. It is very widely held by very good judges. (LAB I, 105)

According to Bennett's wife, who was recalling the occasion at a distance of fifteen years and who was not the most reliable of witnesses, Bennett said to her on the day of publication: 'This day is the most important day of my life! I have done my very best.... I shall never be able to do better'; moreover: 'No, they will never understand! ... The book is too good, they can't possibly understand it' (ABM, 53). Bennett's account of the English reception in the Preface to 'The Old Wives' Tale' seems in some agreement. According to him the initial reaction was similar to that expressed by a friend: 'that the work was honest but dull, and that when it was not dull it had a regrettable tendency to facetiousness', and that only gradually did the reception become 'less frigid'. Letters to his agent at the time, on 29 November 1908 and 9 January 1909, expressed considerable pleasure in the reviews; they had been 'extraordinary' (LAB I, 110, 118). The gathering of English reviews here (Nos 37-9, 41, 43, and 44) suggests that 'The Old Wives' Tale' was more favourably received than any of Bennett's earlier books. The reviewers of 'Tales of the Five Towns' seemed to know that they had an important author on their hands, but they were not entirely pleased with the collection. Some of the reviewers of 'Buried Alive' reckoned that it was not merely a book of the season, but their reviews occupied small space. With 'The Old Wives' Tale' Bennett was generally accorded more space and more praise. Only the 'Manchester Guardian' was unenthusiastic - as though A.N. Monkhouse had become disheartened by 'The Sinews of War', 'The Ghost', and 'The Statue', and given Bennett up and assigned him to someone

else. Among other reviews, the 'Standard' (30 October)
garbled the plot but found it 'haunting', 'enthralling',
presented 'with a charity as broad and a humour as healing
as the rays of the sun'. The 'Daily Graphic' (b. 19 November) spoke of its 'sympathy, humour, observation, and
tragedy'. The 'Daily Mail' (b. 26 November) thought it
was 'a piece of real life such as novelists rarely give
us nowadays'. The 'Morning Post' (b. 26 November) found
it 'a very remarkable novel'. The 'Liverpool Post' (b.
26 November) described it as 'a human document of the
highest order'. The 'Dundee Advertiser' (b. 26 November)
thought that 'Mr. Bennett has achieved a masterpiece'.
The 'Spectator' (5 December) warned the reader that the
book was long, but found it 'exceedingly clever' and well
worth the time for readers who had time. The 'Graphic'
(2 January 1909) said that the novel described 'all conditions and all the elemental emotions with a mordant wit,
a wonderful insight, and a comprehension as wide as the
world'. Some months later, W. Robertson Nicoll took brief
notice of it in the 'British Weekly' (of unknown date):
'There is no book in the fiction of recent years that I
should rank as equal to it. The story is a masterpiece,
and it lacks only a touch of poetry to put it in the very
front rank.' When Hodder & Stoughton, who owned the
'British Weekly', took over 'The Old Wives' Tale', they
quoted Nicoll's first sentence on the cover. Bennett had
contempt for Nicoll as a critic, and had attacked him more
than once in his 'Jacob Tonson' reviews in the 'New Age'
(see p. 79). When he received copies of the Hodder &
Stoughton edition he wrote to his agent: 'Did you notice
they have engraved Nicoll's sickly praise on the actual
binding of the book itself. I do think this is a bit
thick!' (LAB I, 152).

In America the novel received similar praise. The 'New
York Times' (21 August 1909) said that Bennett was scarcely
known in America, but 'it will be strange and regrettable
if discriminating readers of fiction do not speedily discover his novel'. The reviewer summarised at length; he
found some parts tedious but overall thought the book 'a
remarkable illusion of life'. The 'Independent' (2 September) took brief, flattering, and somewhat confused
notice of it. The 'Nation' (14 October) summarised at
length; it found the novel 'a work of singular sincerity
and force'. The 'North American Review' (December) was
flattering and brief. For other American reviews see
Nos 45 and 46.

Bennett's friends and acquaintances were mainly astonished by 'The Old Wives' Tale'. They had not expected
such good work from him. The reactions of Wells and

Frank Harris are printed below (Nos 40 and 42). Eden
Phillpotts wrote to Bennett (as recounted by Bennett to
his agent) that 'though he regards our friendship as definitely broken, he feels he must tell me that "The Old
Wives' Tale" stands on a higher plane than any novel of
modern times' (LAB I, 106-7). F.M. Ford (again as
recorded by Bennett) told Bennett it was 'a great masterpiece' and he would have it reviewed in his 'English
Review' (LAB I, 106). The review never appeared, apparently in part because Ford was even keener on a novel by
Stephen Reynolds. Max Beerbohm wrote to express his
appreciation 'to the man who had laid so large an aesthetic debt on me' (RP, 207). When Somerset Maugham read
'The Old Wives' Tale' he 'was astounded to discover that
it was a great book.... I had never suspected that Arnold
was capable of writing anything of the sort' (L&L, June
1931). H.W. Massingham, editor of the 'Nation', wrote to
Bennett in November 1909 to invite him to write for them,
and said that 'he considered "The Old Wives'Tale" to be
one of the one or two really great novels of the last 30
years' ('Journal', 26 November). Bennett himself had
little to say about the novel after he had finished it.
In the 'Journal' on 17 March 1910 he wrote, 'I was
frightened by a lot of extraordinary praise of "The Old
Wives' Tale" that I have recently had.' On 1 August 1926
he noted without comment that some American critics
regarded 'Lord Raingo' as the equal of 'The Old Wives'
Tale'.
    Over the years 'The Old Wives' Tale' has probably been
Bennett's best selling novel, but it began modestly, and
Bennett wrote with some annoyance to his agent in November
1908 to say that Waugh was failing to send out review
copies and to advertise in appropriate places. He was
also incensed that Waugh's advertisements described the
novel as 'by the author of "The City of Pleasure"'. The
book had a second printing at the end of the year, and a
third in January 1909. The Amalgamated Press issued a
sixpenny edition in 1909 in their 'Daily Mail' series,
paying Bennett £100 for it. In 1910 Waugh allowed his
edition to go out of print. Methuen declined to take it
up, and Hodder & Stoughton took it. Over the years, to
the annoyance of Bennett, they occasionally advertised it
as 'An Old Wives' Tale'. In America the book was rejected
by several firms before George Doran took it up on the
recommendation of his wife. He was Hodder & Stoughton's
American representative, and was just going into business
on his own. He paid £274 in advance on it. His first
issue of the book was under the imprint of Hodder &
Stoughton, New York. Doran wrote to Bennett in October

1909 to say that he had sold out two printings of 1,000 copies each. He became Bennett's chief American publisher. In November 1910 he reported total sales of the novel as 12,000 copies. By 1924 the total was 60,000. There have been several notable editions over the years, including the facsimile edition of the manuscript, Benn, 1927; Oxford University Press (for the Limited Editions Club and with an introduction by Frank Swinnerton), 1941; Penguin Books (with an introduction by Frank Swinnerton), 1954; J.M. Dent in the Everyman Library, 1935; Harper in 1950 (with an introduction by J.B. Priestley); Signet Books in New York (with an introduction by John Wain), 1963; Pan Books (with an introduction by Alan Sillitoe), 1964. Editions by Dent and by Pan are in print today.

'The Human Machine' (1908)

Published in November. On the character and composition of of this pocket philosophy see pp. 42-3. Bennett wrote the essays week by week in the earlier months of 1908. They began to appear serially in 'T.P.'s Weekly' on 20 March 1908, and Bennett reported to his literary agent in June, when the articles were finishing: 'They have made a sensation among the readers which Whitten describes to me in a letter as *immense....* They are really quite striking, & they undoubtedly have startled a lot of people' (LAB I, 104). In the 'Journal' on 4 May 1908 Bennett recorded that the articles prompted one reader to write him an account of her life, including details of a suicide attempt. The New Age Press issued the book, once again without advertising except in the pages of the 'New Age'. Bennett believed that, properly advertised, it and 'How to Live on Twenty-Four Hours a Day' would sell immensely. The 'Manchester Guardian' (b. 28 January 1909) found it useful and admirable. The 'Westminster Gazette' (of unknown date) felt the same way. The 'Bristol Daily Mercury' (of unknown date) thought that it was 'full of the profoundest wisdom. Such a wealth of level-headed commonsense and practical guiding principles has rarely been gathered between two covers'. The review in the 'British Weekly' (7 January) was by John Adams, Professor of Education at the University of London, and it deserves to be quoted at length.

>   This is a remarkably freshly written little book....
>   If it is objected that the book is a metaphor that has
>   taken the bit between its teeth, the author cannot but
>   plead guilty, with the extenuating circumstance that it

has also carried the reader with it. Philosophers
and scientific men might have something to say against
one or two of the elements of the metaphor. But whatever quarrels Mr. Bennett may have brought upon himself
in connection with the relation between the brain and
the ego, or with the nature of unconscious cerebration,
he may successfully plead that the debatable nature of
these matters does not diminish the value of his essay
as a powerful and much needed stimulus. A hundred and
sixty years ago Julien Offray de Lamettrie published
two little books - 'Homme Machine' and 'Homme Plante'.
A year or two ago history repeated itself, and Luther
Burbank published his little pamphlet on 'The Human
Plant', and now Mr. Bennett comes along and completes
the parallel.... His book owes nothing to Lamettrie,
the main resemblance between the two being the freshness of the treatment. Lamettrie was frankly material-
istic, the nature of his speculation drove him into
this attitude. But things have advanced since his day.
We know more about mechanical reactions than he did.
Accordingly Mr. Bennett is under no compulsion to adopt
the materialist position.... In spite of his figure,
Mr. Bennett really treats his machine as an organism.
The metaphor suffers a technical shock.... From all
this you may imagine that you are invited to read a
psychological treatise. Nothing of the kind. The
psychology is there all right, but it is put in such an
attractive way that every man of intelligence will be
drawn to read it.

In America the book made much the same sort of appeal as
'How to Live on Twenty-Four Hours a Day', and Bennett
received very many press cuttings about it from America
before it was published there in 1911. The 'Nation'
(20 April 1911) praised its good sense. The 'Literary
Digest' (20 May) thought that 'every page is replete with
brilliantly expressed truths'. The 'New York Times'
(18 June) gave the book three half-columns of summary and
praise. Hodder & Stoughton took over the book in England,
and a ninth impression of their edition appeared in 1915.

'Things Which Have Interested Me, Third Series' (1908)

Privately printed in Burslem and presented at Christmas to
friends. This last of the privately printed series consisted of several essays, some of which were later printed
chiefly in 'Paris Nights' in 1913, and also very recently
in the collection 'Sketches for Autobiography' 1980. The

Preface was by the French music critic M.D. Calvocoressi.
H.G. Wells wrote to Bennett that '"Things" is very jolly,
but not quite so intimate as the older model' (HGW, 160).

'Literary Taste' (1909)

Published in July. The writing of this guide for the
ordinary man was finished by 13 December 1908, and probably begun the preceding September. The sixteen sections
of it were published in 'T.P.'s Weekly' from 2 October
1908 to 15 January 1909. The book was issued by the New
Age Press. The 'Manchester Guardian' (11 August) devoted
a leader to a sympathetic exposition of Bennett's advice
on how to form literary taste. The 'Globe' (b. 9 September) said:

> The book is quite excellent. There are many who wish
> to read good-class literature, yet who are without any
> reasonable idea of what constitutes that desirable com-
> modity. Let them consult Mr. Arnold Bennett. He will
> give them a list of books - 226 to be precise. This
> list is the first really satisfactory guide that we
> have seen; and many will be grateful to him for its
> compilation.

The 'Daily Express' (b. 9 September) hoped that the book
would have a wide circulation: 'its effect must be
altogether good'. The 'Scotsman' (b. 9 September) said
much the same. The book appeared in America in 1911.
The 'New York Times' (13 August) 'laid it down with
renewed admiration for its erudite and brilliant author.
It is a wise, helpful, and inspiring work, intensely
practical and delightfully lucid'. The 'Nation' (21 September) saw Bennett as 'the schoolmaster of the masses';
his message is simple and direct and moving'. The book
remained popular for many years. Frank Palmer took it
over from the New Age, and a third impression of his
edition appeared in 1911. In 1912 Hodder & Stoughton
issued their edition, which was in its eighth printing
in 1914. George Doran issued an edition in 1927 with
'an American library' added. Jonathan Cape issued the
book in 1937 with additions by Frank Swinnerton, and it
was reissued the following year by Penguin Books.

'The Glimpse' (1909)

Published on 7 October. The novel emerged from a story

Bennett wrote for 'Black and White' in May 1908. Bennett
wrote in his 'Journal' on 23 May that the story was 'much
too good, too spiritual', and 'Black and White' declined
to publish it because they knew their readers would not
like it. By mid-December Bennett decided to write the
novel, and he seemed 'to see something rather fine at the
end of the tunnel' (LAB II, 246). He began writing on 18
May 1909 and finished about mid-August. The contract
called for a reduced advance of £100 - a concession made
by Bennett in order to reduce Waugh's risk. The novel had
uneasy reviews. The 'Times Literary Supplement' (14 October) summarised at length, and concluded that it was
'superficial and only fleetingly impressive'. The review
in 'Vanity Fair' (3 November) was by Frank Harris, who had
written to Bennett privately in the same vein. All the
while the hero was having his vision of the next world,
Harris was wondering what the wife and the lover were
doing in this. Perhaps in another book Bennett would combine successfully 'all the realistic insight of "The Old
Wives' Tale" and all the poetic passion of "The Glimpse"'.
The 'Spectator' (20 November) took short and sceptical
note of the book, finding the visionary part unconvincing
and the worldly parts 'decidedly disagreeable in tone'.
For other English reviews see Nos 48 and 49. The book was
published in America by Appleton, who paid £100 in advance.
The 'New York Times' in a short notice (27 November 1909)
did not care for it and did not think it would please the
average reader. The 'Bookman' (December) was puzzled and
impressed: 'as a sheer bit of speculation, a brilliant
juggling with words, the episode refuses to be forgotten';
but on the whole one would hardly guess it was by the
author of 'The Old Wives' Tale'. Although Bennett had
some notion that the book would sell well in both England
and America, it sold badly or modestly. A second printing
came out within a month of publication, but apparently
that was all. A new edition appeared in 1916. Bennett
wrote to his sister Tertia and her husband when the book
was published, saying that 'I am sure that the 1st and 3rd
parts are as good as the best I can do' (RP, 109), but
most of his critics have thought otherwise. H.G. Wells
said after Bennett's death that the book was 'a glimpse
into an empty cavern in his mind' (LAB I, 151n).

'Helen with the High Hand' (1910)

Published in March. Bennett wrote the novel for serial
publication, finishing it in the middle of June 1907 and
writing a supplementary instalment in March 1908. He

'designed it to be something which would please the serial
public without giving the *serious* public a chance to
accuse me of "playing down" - as in "The City of Pleasure",
etc' (LAB I, 96). The National Press Association commissioned it, and paid £150 for serial rights, and seem
to have been not entirely pleased with the result.
Chapman & Hall gave an advance of £150. The serial ran
in the 'Star' under the title 'The Miser's Niece', beginning on 12 June 1909, in the 'Staffordshire Sentinel'
beginning on 1 July, and presumably elsewhere. Bennett
described reviews of the book to his agent as being 'without exception effusive' (LAB I, 133). In the 'Journal' on
22 March he wrote: 'the reviews ... are exceedingly polite
and kind, but they do not gloss over the slightness of the
thing'. The 'Daily Express' (15 March) described it as
sunny and slight. A.N. Monkhouse in the 'Manchester Guardian' (16 March) thought it was 'a delightful piece of
fun'. The 'Times Literary Supplement' (17 March) was
altogether pleased, and made thoughtful observations about
Bennett's work generally: 'he ... touches lightly but
surely on essential characteristics of man and of woman';
'though every new book by Mr. Bennett gives the impression
that it is an experiment, though he is one of the most
elusive and variable of modern novelists, he is also one
of the most safely trusted for good work'. The 'Spectator' (2 April) found 'plenty of amusement'. The 'Saturday
Review' (9 April) found it conventional good fun. The
'Athenaeum' (16 April) was always amused but a trifle dis-
dainful of its tendency towards farce. The book had similar reviews in America from the 'Dial' (16 November 1910,
see the last paragraphs of No. 56), the 'Nation' (17 November), and the 'New York Times' (26 November). See also
the brief mention in the review of 'Clayhanger' in the
'Atlantic Monthly', No. 58. Other editions appeared in
1915, 1928, and 1963.

'Clayhanger' (1910)

Published on 15 September. On 29 July 1907, before he
began writing 'The Old Wives' Tale' but when the character
and outline of the novel were clear, Bennett wrote to his
sister Tertia: 'I have got hold of a whole new aspect of
the Potteries which will result in prodigious books' (RP,
177). This was perhaps the first thought of the Clayhanger trilogy. In March 1909 Bennett was in the Potteries for a few days to see his mother and to make notes of
local matters. Very probably this visit marked the first
conscious work on 'Clayhanger' itself, which so far as is

known was conceived at the outset as the first volume of a
trilogy (completed with 'Hilda Lessways', 1911, and 'These
Twain', 1916).   In September he was reading 'When I was a
Child, By an Old Potter', and the use he made of the book
in the novel brought a charge of plagiarism some years
later (see LAB III, 8-11, and SSAB, 109-24).   In October
he wrote to his sister Tertia and her husband:

> I shall positively appear in the Five Towns early in
> December, and remain there at least 2 weeks.   I must
> have at least two weeks with Mr. Dawson.   My next
> hero's father is the Pater plus Mr. Beardmore; a steam-
> printer.   And the hero is a sort of Edward Harry Beard-
> more.   This novel has to be begun on January 1st. (RP,
> 209)

(Joseph Dawson, of Burslem, printed Bennett's three gift-
books of 1906-8.   The Beardmores were a local family,
related by the marriage of one of Bennett's sisters to
Frank Beardmore, younger brother of Edward Harry.)   On
19 November he recorded a walk in the forest at Fontainebleau during which he 'arranged most of the construction
of the first part of the novel'.   On 8 December he was in
the Potteries, where he recorded getting 'into an extraordinary vein of "second sight".   I perceived whole chapters'.   He wrote the novel from 5 January to 23 June,
partly in a hotel in Brighton, and with interruptions of
a week or so between each section.   He wrote in his
'Journal' on the first day: 'I felt less nervous and self-
conscious than usual in beginning a book.   And never
before have I made one-quarter so many preliminary notes
and investigations.'   On 21 January he wrote: 'I am trying
to lift the whole thing up to a great height, but I feel
sure that up to now it is nothing more than interesting in
a nice quiet way.'   On 24 April he advised his agent that
'there is nothing in it to shock prudes, as there was in
the "O.W.T." Not even a confinement.   It ends happily'
(LAB I, 125).   On 12 June he spent twelve hours writing
2,400 words, and noted in the 'Journal': 'I really doubt
whether, as a whole, this book is good.   It assuredly
isn't within 10 miles of Dostoevsky.'   When he read the
proof on 19 August he decided that 'a good deal of it is
as good as anything I've done'.
    With 'Clayhanger' Bennett moved to Methuen, not without
unease on the part of A.M.S. Methuen himself, who wanted
to bind Bennett to producing no more than one novel a year.
Bennett was annoyed, and wrote to his agent:

> Two months is my time for an ordinary novel.   I know I

am singular. But it is me that Methuen has to deal
with, not another man. I have a very great deal to
say, and I mean to say it. As for my work being taken
seriously, we shall see about that. Suppose I do a
novel in two months, & a play in one, what am I to do
with myself in the other nine? I write fast, but
Methuen ought to know that nearly all the classic
English & French novels have been written & published
at a greater rate even than I work. Even now Methuen
does not realise that in me he has to deal with someone
slightly out of the common. Anyhow, while quite sympathising with Methuen, I will not bind myself. The
mere idea of doing so strikes me as simply monstrous.
He must take me or leave me. (LAB I, 123)

Methuen offered £1,050 in advance on the trilogy: £300
for 'Clayhanger', £350 for 'Hilda Lessways', £400 for
'These Twain'.

Bennett wrote to his agent on 12 November 'that "Clayhanger" has been received better than I expected. After
all, a book like that *is* a stiff dose for the public'
(LAB I, 143). Most of the known English reviews were
fairly ecstatic, and only one of them was negative. See
Nos 50-4. The 'Glasgow Herald' (15 September) said: 'The
difference between "The Old Wives' Tale" and "Clayhanger"
is simply that in the latter the vision is at once more
impassioned and genial, more ironic and more tender.
Mr. Bennett is one of our great novelists.' E.S. Grew
in the 'Daily Graphic' (16 September) said: 'It is extraordinarily interesting. No living writer can do this as
he can. "Clayhanger", like "The Old Wives' Tale", will
find a permanent place on the bookshelves.' Sidney Dark
in the 'Daily Express' (21 September) objected to the bias
against Conservatism, and he thought that Bennett's understanding of life was not absolutely complete, but he
admitted to being bowled over by the novel. The 'British
Weekly' (29 September) wrote 'Mr. Bennett's "Clayhanger"'
large on the cover, and Claudius Clear (W. Robertson
Nicoll) described it as 'unquestionably a great and original achievement'. Nicoll thought it was a biography and a
history as much as a novel. He admired the decent qualities of the characters (clean, faithful, hardworking); he
knew that 'Mr. Bennett is too true an artist to bring in
filth where none exists'. The 'Spectator' (22 October)
expressed concern about the omission of sporting life in
the Five Towns, but excused it, and went on to summarise
this 'very long but deeply interesting novel about a multitude of people who are for the most part entirely undistinguished'. 'Punch' (26 October) was a trifle ironic

about the infinite detail and length, and about one or two
lapses into vulgar style, but was powerfully impressed.
'And I like his mind and his sense of humour and pathos
which help him to make a dramatic story out of such unpromising material as everyday life in Bursley.' The
'Morning Leader' and 'Morning Post' (of unknown dates)
said, '"Clayhanger" is a great book' and 'the literary
event of 1910'. Publication of 'Clayhanger' inspired
another general article on his work, in the 'Nation',
10 December (see No. 72).

In America publication was preceded by brief comment
on his life and work in the 'Bookman' (September 1910).
The book was issued by Dutton, with an advance of £250
and what Bennett described as a good royalty – presumably
20 per cent. The contract was arranged before George
Doran appeared on the scene. Reviews in America were
mixed, with one harsh one. See Nos 55-9. The 'Independent' (27 October) acknowledged Bennett's 'uncanny gift
of creeping inside the minds of his characters' and also
thought that he was 'working out a new theory of fiction:
that the life of a community should in these democratic
days, take the place of the life of one individual'.
The 'Chicago Tribune' (b. 29 October) described it as
'a rich drama of life'. The 'Philadelphia Press' (b.
29 October) found it 'marvelous in its minute detail,
singularly interesting in the gradual development of its
theme, and brilliant in the general effect made by its
execution'. The 'Nation' (17 November) recited the plot
('told so scrupulously') and warned readers that if they
had not liked 'The Old Wives' Tale', they would not like
'Clayhanger'. 'Outlook' (26 November) had little more to
say than to 'advise the reader who balks at the sluggish
writing to persevere'. Frederic Taber Cooper in a rather
diffuse discussion in the 'Bookman' (December) thought 'it
would be rather difficult to overpraise this study of the
unfolding and maturing of a single human character'. A
brief notice in the 'Review of Reviews' (January 1911)
praised it. A general article in the same place in April,
Arnold Bennett: A New Master in English Fiction, noted the
intense inner drama in a life of outward monotony, and the
focus on the community as well as on the individual - an
obligation of authors in the modern democratic world.
Other very favourable reviews appeared in the 'New York
Morning Telegraph' (b. 28 October) and the 'Boston Evening
Transcript' and the 'Chicago Evening Post' (both b. 11
November). All in all, Bennett must have been very
pleased with the press reaction. And John Galsworthy
wrote to him to say that although 'The Old Wives' Tale'
was better, 'Clayhanger' was nevertheless 'amazing' - but

privately Galsworthy was noting that it 'lacks selective power and temperamental poignancy'. And André Gide, who did not read English easily, did not think 'Clayhanger' worth the struggle (RP, 218).

In the 'Journal' on 19, 21, 22, and 25 September, and also on 28 October and 11 November, Bennett identified sixteen reviews, not all of which have been mentioned here. On 30 September he wrote in the 'Journal':

> I was put in a strange state yesterday by reading Methuen's advertisement in the 'Westminster Gazette'. My novel, having now been published a fortnight, had taken a place lower down their list - was indeed only one of a very mixed lot of novels. Lucas's 'Mr. Ingleside', being their latest published, was head of the list. They have just invented a new and striking dodge of indicating the number of editions printed of a work by putting a small elevated numeral after it (as if indicating a raised 'power'). Thus Lucas's was 'Mr. Ingleside'[3], and it has only been out a week. No number after 'Clayhanger'. A [2] after many of the other novels.

On 14 and 17 September on the front page of the 'Westminster', 'Clayhanger' was first among four new books joining Methuen's autumn list. On the 21st it assumed first place among the already published, with E.V. Lucas's novel coming in above among the just-published. On the 28th 'Mr. Ingleside' assumed first place among the already published, and 'Clayhanger' was fifth. But over the next two months other novels disappeared from the list, and Lucas and Bennett remained. On 23 November Bennett moved back up to second place with a third printing, and Lucas was in third place with a fifth printing. In a special Christmas advertisement that did not indicate printings, Bennett was in second place and Lucas third. A fourth impression of 'Clayhanger' appeared in December, and sales to mid-December were 5,800 copies in the six shilling edition and 700 in the Colonial. A ninth impression appeared by the end of 1911. To the end of 1915 it sold 11,000 in the English edition and 4,500 in the Colonial. In America it sold 7,000 copies to mid-March 1911, and 21,000 to the end of 1915. Editions by Methuen and Penguin are in print today.

'The Card' (1911)

Published on 23 February. Bennett began writing on

1 January 1909 and finished on 1 March. On 27 January he
wrote in the 'Journal' that the novel was 'probably too
good for a serial'; on 16 February he thought it was 'good
honest everyday work, vitiated by my constant thought of a
magazine public'; on 2 March he wrote, 'stodgy, no real
distinction of any sort, but well invented, and done up
to the knocker, technically, right through'. Serial publication was in 'The Times Weekly Edition', beginning 2
February 1910. 'The Times' paid £160 for it. Methuen and
Dutton each gave £250 in advance for it. The American
title was 'Denry the Audacious'.

Looking over the dozen or so reviews of the first two
days, Bennett said they were 'much too kind on the whole'
('Journal', 26 February). A brief review in the 'Daily
Express' (23 February) said it was 'excellently done in
its slighter manner'. The review – unsigned – was probably
by Sidney Dark, who many years later wrote affectionately
about the hero, 'that delightfully human comic character',
whom he supposed it would be impertinent to liken to
Arnold Bennett ('T.P.'s Weekly', 9 March 1929). Hubert
Bland in the 'Daily Chronicle' (23 February) thought the
series of events was improbable but diverting; he was
cheered up reading the book but decided he did not like
Denry. The 'Morning Post' (b. 2 March) said: 'Mr. Bennett
is in his liveliest form.... It is a true comedy of
character. He has created a type for eternal laughter.'
The 'Athenaeum' (11 March) was conscious of a certain
artificiality, but the book 'triumphantly holds the
reader' and Denry 'is a genuine creation'. 'Punch'
(22 March) was much amused by Denry, but 'he tails off
a little towards the end of his career'. The 'Spectator'
(25 March) admired the book as 'a most entertaining specimen of its author's particular type of humour', and suspected that a card in real life would not rest content to
be mayor of Bursley but would be looking for 'fresh woods
and pastures new'. For four other English reviews see Nos
60-3. In America the 'New York Times' (12 March), in the
only major notice given to the book among the American
journals mentioned here, reflected upon the attractiveness
of sin in literature, identified Denry as an 'inspira-
tional crook', and admired the 'facility' and 'cleverness'
with which Bennett depicted him. 'Outlook' (23 March)
expressed bewilderment at Bennett's variety, but nevertheless was interested; the novel was 'a glorification of the
unscrupulous'. The 'Nation' (30 March) made some comparisons, but without elaboration: 'as "Clayhanger" is a
soberly ironical study of the humdrum, "Denry the Audacious" is a blithely ironical study of the inspired';
'Mr. Bennett's versatility of mood is more remarkable than

his virtuosity of method'. The 'Literary Digest' (1 April)
found 'laughs and good, cheery episodes'. Frederic Taber
Cooper in the 'Bookman' (April) was cheered up by 'Denry
the Audacious' and depressed by 'The White Peacock'. The
'North American Review' (August) could not admire either
the unscrupulousness of the hero or the vulgarity of the
author who depicted him.

In England 'The Card' had an immediate commercial
success greater than that of any of the earlier novels,
and in March 1911 Bennett's debt to his literary agent
was finally cleared. By May 1911 'The Card' was in its
fourth printing, and by 1913 it had reached its tenth.
Sales of English and Colonial editions reached 37,000
by the end of 1915. In America sales reached 14,000 by
the same date. There were consequences of such improved
sales in England and of the publicity that now attended
Bennett and his work. Clement Shorter, editor of 'Sphere',
wanted Bennett to repudiate the portrait of the Duchess of
Sutherland in the novel. In the novel the Countess of
Chell is known as 'Interfering Iris' and in life Millicent
Duchess of Sutherland, was known as 'Meddlesome Millie'.
Bennett wrote to Shorter on 29 April:

> I see that you expect me 'to repudiate the picture of
> the Duchess of Sutherland' in 'The Card'. I absolutely
> repudiate it. I have never seen the Duchess of Suther-
> land in my life. If I have seen her portrait in the
> 'Sphere' I have forgotten the fact. My knowledge of
> the Duchess is that of the ordinary newspaper reader -
> rather less than more. There is only one portrait to
> be found in all my books - myself. (LAB II, 278)

Several weeks later Bennett was placed beside the duchess
at a dinner party, and she had it out with him - apparently
objecting in the main to the assertion that the Countess
of Chell was not punctual, whereas she herself was.
Bennett's formal reply to her in a letter afterwards said
that 'if there is resemblance between you and the young
woman in "The Card" it is simply because you are the sole
representative of that particular class in the Five Towns'.
Also, 'considering that the whole book is written in a
fiercely sarcastic vein, I think the Countess's portrait
is a sympathetic one' (LAB II, 284-5). Bennett ran into
more difficulty with 'Lord Raingo' fifteen years later.
See pp. 99-102, 461-83. The last sentence in the letter to
Shorter expressed one aspect of the matter that might have
surprised some people for whom Bennett was the realistic
author *par excellence*, but Bennett stated the view with
equal force in 'The Author's Craft' a couple of years

later: 'When the real intimate work of creation has to be
done - and it has to be done on every page - the novelist
can only look within for effective aid.' 'The Card' has
remained one of Bennett's most popular novels, and editions by Methuen and Penguin are in print. Methuen's
thirty-eighth printing came in 1965. Latter-day commentators usually have seen something of Bennett himself in
Denry, and if Bennett's views about writing are to be
believed, the commentators must be right. Bennett himself
never liked the book nearly as much as he liked 'Buried
Alive', and he even preferred 'A Great Man' (see p. 42).

'Hilda Lessways' (1911)

Published on 21 September. In so far as Bennett was
making notes for 'These Twain' in December 1909, his
thoughts about 'Hilda Lessways' must have been reasonably
far advanced by then. On 2 October 1910 he wrote in his
'Journal':

> Yesterday I had a goodish large notion for the Hilda
> book - of portraying the droves of the whole sex,
> instead of whole masculine droves. I think I can do
> something with this, showing the multitudinous activi-
> ties of the whole sex, the point of view of the whole
> sex, against a mere background of masculinity.

By December he was constructing the novel. He began
writing on 5 January, just a year after beginning 'Clay-
hanger', and finished on 13 June. It was 100,000 words.
There was some attempt to sell serial rights to the
'Saturday Evening Post' for £1,000, but it came to nothing.
Methuen paid £350 in advance, as arranged in 1909, and
Dutton £250.

Reviews were mixed. The novel invited comparison with
'Clayhanger', and reviewers approached it self-consciously
and sometimes sceptically. Sidney Dark in the 'Daily
Express' (26 September) thought that whereas 'Clayhanger'
was a 'masterpiece', 'Hilda Lessways' was 'melodramatic',
with conventional curtains. Nevertheless the character of
Hilda was admirably realised, and Bennett's skill was
'wonderful'. 'Punch' (4 October) had waited patiently for
a year for 'Hilda', and although the novel was enormously
clever, it was disappointing, and the reviewer felt the
same way a friend did: 'I feel as if all the characters
were my relations, and I didn't like them!' Yet in summa-
tion: 'its minute and laborious analysis of one character
must give "Hilda Lessways" a high place in the list of

Mr. Bennett's already amazing achievements'. The 'Academy'
(7 October) thought that Bennett's minute attention to the
thoughts of his characters might eventually turn him into
Henry James. The psychological portraiture of George
Cannon was perhaps deficient, the depiction of the
Orgreaves was masterly, the image of the Brighton boarding-
house was vivid enough to bring shivers. Overall it was a
depressing novel, and perhaps Mr Bennett should bring a
lighter, less introspective atmosphere into the third
novel. The 'Standard' and the 'Pall Mall Gazette' (b. 21
October) thought that 'the book is packed with cleverness', with 'artistry of a rare and excellent kind'.
'Bystander' (b. 21 October) thought that Bennett might be
on his way to producing one of the finest trilogies in all
literature. The 'Bookman' (November) found the book 'a
masterly essay in feminine psychology', 'presented ... with
a supreme and a singularly fascinating art'. The 'Daily
Chronicle' (of unknown date) described it as 'a fine book
in its truth, its comprehending sympathy, its courage'.
For other English reviews see Nos 64-6 and 68-70. The
review in the 'Staffordshire Sentinel' (4 October) was
unavailable.

In America the 'Independent' (12 Ocotber 1911) noted
the marvellous skill and the 'vivid sense of hidden drama'
in obscure lives; the absence of major and minor characters as attractive as those in 'Clayhanger' made it less
interesting. 'Outlook' (4 November) found it an impressive human document, less successful than 'The Old Wives'
Tale' and 'Clayhanger', with much distressing material in
it, some 'beyond the bounds of good taste'. The 'New York
Times' (3 December) saw 'something Hellenic in the development of his themes. There is always a Fate which contrives episodes and shapes personality from the beginning
to the end'. Margaret Sherwood in the 'Atlantic Monthly'
(May 1912) was disappointed: the style was newspaper
style, the characterisation was mechanical, uncoordinated,
unconvincing. For reviews in the 'Nation' and the 'Dial'
see Nos 67 and 71. Bennett was in America during October
and November 1911, and one or another of the reviewers
took notice of his presence. He recorded in his 'Journal'
on 30 November, as he was beginning the voyage home, that
he had received letters of farewell from several women,
'chiefly hating "Hilda Lessways", but nevertheless all
rustling with flattery'. In America sales of the novel
were 16,600 to December 1915. In England it had reached
a seventh printing by November 1911. Sales in England to
December 1915 were 12,500, Colonial sales 5,000. Bennett's
growing importance to Methuen was suggested by the advertisement for the novel in the 'Times Literary Supplement'.

On 21 September, given pride of place and one and a half inches, was Marie Corelli's 'The Life Everlasting', then in its third printing. Second place and three-quarters of an inch went to Anthony Hope's 'Mrs. Maxon Protests', published that day. Bennett came third with half an inch. Editions by Methuen and Penguin are currently in print.

'The Feast of St. Friend' (1911)

Published in October. In December 1910 Bennett arranged with George Doran to write 10,000 words on the subject of an agnostic celebration of Christmas, 'perfectly serious & in my best philosophic vein', payment to be £100 in advance on a royalty of 15 per cent. He began writing on 5 July 1911. Bennett was not keen on English publication, 'because the English public is liable to misunderstand a realistic novelist publishing booklets of a Christmas nature'. He was also not keen on the book being published by Hodder & Stoughton, Doran's English associate, 'because I don't fancy myself in Hodder & Stoughton's Christmas advertising' (LAB I, 146). The few known reviews were mainly kind. The 'Manchester Guardian' (3 November) took amused and sympathetic note of it in a leader. The 'Daily Express' and the 'Athenaeum' (both 9 December) liked it: 'an effective little homily', said the 'Athenaeum'. In America the 'New York Times' (3 December) thought it was 'uplifting', 'the right book at the right time'. The 'Review of Reviews' (January 1912) was pleased. In England the book sold badly - 1,500 copies in five months. Nevertheless Hodder & Stoughton were proud of it, and issued another edition, in 1914, under the title 'Friendship and Happiness'.

'The Matador of the Five Towns' (1912)

Published on 14 March. Bennett wrote the title story of the collection in 1908 for the 'English Review', where it appeared in April 1909. He described it to his agent as 'quite as good as Simon Fuge' (LAB I, 152). One of the stories had appeared serially as early as 1905; more than half of them had not been published serially. Bennett received £150 in advance for it from Methuen and also from Doran in America.
    Known reviews were mixed. The 'Athenaeum' (16 March) doubted whether Bennett had written 'forty pages more compact of life and imagination' than those of the title story. Other stories were charming and merry, and others

'clumsy, far-fetched, and jejune'. The 'Daily Express'
(21 March) did not think that the short story was
Bennett's métier. The 'Daily Chronicle' (b. 4 April)
found 'a wealth of observation, insight, and creative
power'. The 'Dundee Advertiser' (b. 4 April) found 'the
hand of the master', and the 'Liverpool Post' (b. 4 May)
'the work of a master hand'. The 'Spectator' in a short
notice (13 April) did not think the short story was
Bennett's métier, but did like The Glimpse, which was much
better than the novel of the same name, and some of the
other stories were amusing. The 'Glasgow Herald' (b. 4
May) found 'subtle variety', and the 'Evening Standard'
(b. 4 May) found 'graphic description, industrious character portrayal, and a wonderful atmosphere of invigoration
and rush'. The collection in America omitted several
stories that were in the English edition and added some
from 'Tales of the Five Towns' and 'The Grim Smile of the
Five Towns'. The 'New York Times' in a long review (17
March) wished that the dates of composition had been
given, so that it would be possible to assess the advance
or decline of Bennett's art; but in any event Bennett was
an author of 'prodigious importance', and his best stories
- The Death of Simon Fuge and The Matador of the Five
Towns - were very much superior to the best of his novels.
The reviewer was inclined to wish that Bennett had written
only short stories. The 'Nation' (11 April) found the
stories agreeable and light. 'Current Literature' (June)
limited itself to quoting extracts from favourable reviews
in the 'Academy', the London 'Outlook', and other English
journals. Margaret Sherwood in a brief notice in the
'Atlantic Monthly' (November) was bored, and singled out
'the imitative insincerities of The Death of Simon Fuge'
for rebuke. The collection seems to have been much less
successful than the earlier collections of Five Towns
stories. A second impression of the English edition was
called for in May 1912, but no further printings and no
further editions are known - aside from a translation
into Esperanto in 1919 and one into Spanish in 1921 -
until one by Chatto in 1972.

'Your United States' (1912)

Published in November in America. Bennett's visit to
America in October and November 1911 was a notable success.
He was fêted in several cities and at several universities,
he saw a large display of his books at Jordan Marsh's
department store in Boston, and he was told by doctors
that they prescribed 'How to Live on Twenty-Four Hours

a Day' and 'The Human Machine' to their patients. According to 'Harper's Weekly', underneath a full-page photograph of him, he was 'the most talked-of living novelist'
(21 October 1911). Harper's had reason for hoping they
were right, for they were paying him £800 for serial
rights to several articles on his impressions of America,
and they were contemplating paying him their highest ever
price for a serial novel - £3,000 for serial rights plus
another £1,000 in advance on the book. On 16 December a
special supplement to 'Harper's Weekly' appeared, A Tribute to Arnold Bennett, which described a dinner given for
Bennett at the St Regis Hotel in New York, with more than
a hundred celebrated and would-be celebrated people present. Bennett wrote the articles upon his return to
France. They ran in 'Harper's Magazine' from April to
November 1912. Harper's paid £100 in advance on book
royalties of 15 per cent rising to 20 after the sale of
5,000 copies. English publication was by Martin Secker
a month earlier, with the title amended to 'Those United
States'.

Reviews were very mixed. R.A. Scott-James in the 'Pall
Mall Gazette' (25 October) and Sidney Dark in the 'Daily
Express' (31 October) were full of praise, Scott-James
taking special note of the adroitness with which Bennett
criticised the Americans. The 'Athenaeum' (16 November)
was severe: 'Mr. Bennett is trifling with his art when he
writes a book of this sort'; 'he has written more about
American telephones than about American men, more about
the Capitol than about legislators'. The 'Spectator'
(16 November) found the book 'extraordinarily readable',
and noted - as did other reviews - that the book was
intended as a record of impressions rather than of truths.
Dixon Scott in the 'Manchester Guardian' (30 December) was
full of enthusiasm for Bennett's descriptions of dynamos
and the like. The 'Guardian' had taken some notice of
Bennett's visit a year earlier (18 November 1911).
H.I. Brock in the 'New York Times' (3 November) was
annoyed. How could Bennett pretend not to see the bustle
and rush of New York? How could he say that Broadway
lacked distinction? Bennett was a snob, and did not see
what he looked at. The 'Nation' (14 November, along with
an earlier notice of serial publication, 25 April) thought
that Bennett observed America with an almost American
freshness and enthusiasm and - perhaps - a touch of complacency. Edith Kellogg Dunton in the 'Dial' (1 December)
thought that Bennett's enthusiasm was mere literary pose.
He who was a 'seasoned resident of London and Paris' had
decided to play at being a 'provincial Englishman with
imagination'. She thought that the illustrations by Frank

Craig – which Bennett thought deplorable – were just as
slick and smart as the text. 'Outlook' in a brief notice
(7 December) said that 'if one judges by comments heard
and extracts printed, no magazine articles of the year
have been more widely read'; the book made 'agreeable and
often suggestive reading'. The 'Literary Digest' in
another short notice (14 December) found the book full of
'grace, kindliness, and ample appreciation'. The 'Bookman'
(December) discussed the book twice at length, in one
place defending Bennett against Brock and in the other
suggesting that in the main 'it is a book of first impressions politely curtailed out of decent regard for the
people who entertained him – an exceedingly decorous book
by a man whose real talent and individuality quite obviously are to be sought elsewhere'; the reviewer, C.M.
Francis, expressed pleasure in Bennett's caustic remarks
about Europeanised Americans. 'Current Literature'
(December) alluded with pleasure to the many flattering
things Bennett said about American culture in his
'delightful chronicle'. The 'North American Review'
(February) said that of course the book was not so much
a description of America as an 'account of the adventures
of a "Five Towns" mind'; it was 'brilliantly written'.
By the end of May 1912, 12,000 copies were sold in
America; by March 1915, 19,500 copies. No later editions
are known.

'The Regent' (1913)

Published on 4 September. Bennett began constructing this
sequel to 'The Card' in January 1912. The writing was
done from 14 February to 11 April. Bennett wrote to his
agent on 13 April: 'I have read nearly all of it aloud to
friends, with enormous success' (LAB I, 168). The
'American Magazine' seems to have paid £2,000 for serial
rights, and it began appearing there in December 1912, and
began a month earlier in the 'London Magazine'.
     The book was a popular and critical success in England,
and was in its third printing on the day of publication.
The 'Times Literary Supplement' (4 September) found it
glittering, clever, amusing, and just a trifle mechanical.
Sidney Dark in the 'Daily Express' (4 September) found it
'quite good fun'. The 'Daily Chronicle' (b. 11 September)
thought that 'mirth bubbles in the book like hot water in
a jogging kettle'. The 'Spectator' (13 September) doubted
'whether any of Mr. Bennett's books is likely to give more
unmitigated amusement'. 'Truth' (b. 9 October) thought
that 'Mr. Bennett is astonishingly clever ...; the dominant

characteristic of his mind is its amazing versatility'. The 'Times Literary Supplement' returned to it (30 October) as one of the best and also one of the most successful books of the season. The 'English Review' (October) found it 'a trifle boring'. For the 'Manchester Guardian' review see No. 75.

In America the book bore the title 'The Old Adam'. The 'Nation' (26 June 1913) was thoroughly amused, and so was 'Outlook' (5 July). The 'Independent' (31 July) thought it was slapdash farce. Frederic Taber Cooper in the 'Bookman' (August) was much amused but could not help thinking of the gulf between it and 'The Old Wives' Tale'. Sales to December 1915 were 11,000 copies in England, 6,600 in the colonies, and 12,500 in America. Other editions were published in England in 1937 and 1951.

'The Plain Man and His Wife' (1913)

Published in October. Bennett wrote this little book in the summer of 1912. It appeared serially in the 'Strand Magazine' beginning in December 1912, and two months earlier in the 'Metropolitan Magazine' in America. The serial title was 'The Case of the Plain Man'. The 'Strand' paid £200 for it, and at first were not too pleased by what they got, and the 'Metropolitan' paid £600 and were pleased, and then forgot they were pleased when some later work displeased them. The 'Metropolitan' permitted an American life insurance company to reprint a passage that seemed to flatter the notion of life insurance (ignoring another passage that did not flatter it). Bennett was much annoyed. (See LAB I, 196-7.) The few known reviews were mixed. Sidney Dark in the 'Daily Express' (4 October) said that 'Mr. Bennett is a hopelessly unreliable teacher of the art of living, because he is so complete and purblind a materialist'. The 'Manchester Guardian' (6 October) devoted a leader to his 'shrewed, practical hints'. The 'Times Literary Supplement' (9 October) thought that Bennett's view of the problems of life was outmoded, sometimes 'antediluvian'. The 'Athenaeum' (11 October) recommended the book to young people for its 'sound commonsense'. The 'Spectator' (11 October) wondered why Bennett wasted his time. In America the 'New York Times' (9 November) thought that it contained familiar wisdom 'cleverly and entertainingly' expressed. The book was later issued under the titles 'Married Life' and 'Marriage: The Plain Man and His Wife'. It seems not to have sold well. Hodder & Stoughton, who issued the English editions, wrote to Bennett in 1920 to

say they were losing money on it and asking him to accept
a reduced royalty.

'Paris Nights' (1913)

Published in October. The essays that made up the collection were written between 1904 and 1911. The earliest
ones appeared in 'Things Which Have Interested Me, Third
Series', in 1908. Some of the later ones were written for
the 'English Review' and for the 'Nation'. Bennett wrote
to his agent about the material for the 'English Review':

> It will take the form of descriptive sketches of the
> very newest & most spectacular manifestations of social
> life in London, & contrasting similar sketches of Paris.
> Something new; certainly dealing with matters not yet
> touched in the way of literature. (LAB I, 128)

The book was a handsome and fairly lavish example of book-
making - like the other travel books that followed it -
and the material inside was substantial in size and scope.
Nevertheless it seems to have attracted remarkably little
attention. The 'Times Literary Supplement' (30 October)
merely took note of its appearance. The 'Athenaeum' said
in a brief notice (18 October) that 'it forms the most
important volume of essays that has yet come from the pen
of Mr. Bennett', and in a longer review (8 November) that
'all the articles are good, and some will bear higher
praise'. Sidney Dark in the 'Daily Express' (20 November)
quoted at length and found it 'altogether a splendid
book'. In America the 'New York Times' (23 November)
admired the way Bennett could lend enchantment to the
commonplace, but found some of the latter part of the
volume hackneyed. Edith Kellogg Dunton expressed a
similar opinion in the 'Dial' (1 December). The 'Nation'
(4 December) had thought after 'Clayhanger' that Bennett
had the makings of greatness, but he was now 'settled down
to a workaday pace'. The best of the collection concerned
the Five Towns, the rest was readable. Charles Hessel-
grave took brief and favourable notice of it in the
'Independent' (11 December). Hodder & Stoughton, publishers of the book in England, brought out an edition
without illustrations in 1921. Several of the essays are
reprinted in the recent collection, 'Sketches for Autobiography', 1980.

'The Price of Love' (1914)

Published on 1 October. Bennett wrote this novel as a
serial for 'Harper's' in America. Aside from 'These
Twain', already conceived, it was the last of his Five
Towns novels. He began writing on 15 October 1912 and
finished on 29 September of the following year, with an
interruption of at least three months. He intended the
style to be different from his earlier style, 'a freer
style than before - a little more capricious and swinging'
('Journal', 6 November 1912). While writing it, he remarked in his 'Journal' on portions of it: 'sound, but not
brilliant', 'some things in it jolly good', and 'goodish'
(24 April, 2 July, and 31 August). Serial publication
began in 'Harper's' in December 1913 and in the 'Daily
News' on 4 August 1914. On 30 July in the 'Daily News'
an interview appeared with Bennett, an interview that he
wrote himself so that he would be quoted accurately. The
interview mainly concerned playwriting and the delay with
the third Clayhanger novel, but Bennett did say of 'The
Price of Love': 'It contains the sincerest realism and the
least crude psychology that I'm capable of; but it's a
serial, and if it hadn't been intended for a serial the
plan of the story would have been different.' On the same
page the 'News' announced a contest, with a first prize of
£25, for the best postcard criticism of the novel. On
3 August the 'Star', an associated newspaper, had a large
story on The Most Read Novelist, telling of the unfailing
popular success of Bennett's career and repeating some
material from the 'News' story. The 'Daily News' serialisation was interrupted on account of the paper shortage,
and was begun again on 5 January 1915. Harper's apparently did pay the record serial price of £3,000 for the
novel (see p. 65), and the 'Daily News' paid £400. Book
rights apparently went to Harper's for £1,000. The sum
from Methuen is unknown; it may have been affected by the
war.
    None of the English reviewers imagined that this was
Bennett's best novel, and one or two were caustic. The
'Times Literary Supplement' (1 October) admired his ability to 'make articulate for us instincts and processes'
in the minds of ordinary women. The 'Scotsman' (3 October) admired the 'clear insight into ... human hearts' and
the 'quietly cynical realistic' style. The 'Spectator'
(10 October) summarised and quoted at length, and described Bennett's attitude towards the Five Towns as
'loyalty tempered with detachment'. A very brief notice
in the 'Daily Express' (17 October) said it was 'very,
very clever. Perhaps that is the reason why I did not

like it at all'. 'Punch' (21 October) was 'grateful for
every word and incident of this enchanting chronicle and
for the portrait of Rachel in particular'. The 'Pall Mall
Gazette' (b. 22 October) spoke of 'vivacity, irony, and
humour, illuminating insight and fine characterisation'.
For three other English reviews see Nos 76-8. The book
was issued several months earlier in America. The 'New
York Times' (24 May) admired the characterisation and
found the novel 'mellower' than Bennett's earlier work.
'The Arnold Bennett "boom" is over - and this is good for
the world and better for Mr. Bennett. Now no longer does
he need to be ostentatiously, militantly a "realist."'
'Outlook' in a brief notice (13 June) thought it was
small-scale work of the same character as 'Clayhanger'.
The 'Nation' (2 July) admired the minute and true observation of character and the perception of beauty in the
ordinary. The 'Independent' in a brief notice (20 July)
thought it was a convincing portrait of unattractive
people. Frederic Taber Cooper in the 'Bookman' (August)
was disappointed: the story had possibilities that were
not realised, and some of the plotting was 'clap-trap'.
The 'Atlantic Monthly' in a brief notice (October) thought
it had more of the zest of 'The Old Wives' Tale' than
anything else Bennett had written since. W.D. Howells in
the 'North American Review' (December) thought there was
too much of the real, too little of the ideal, in the
book.

Henry James's opinion of the novel was reported to
Bennett by their mutual literary agent:

> 'I read it', he said, 'with great interest, rather
> wondering all the time why I *was* so interested in it.
> It is an example of Bennett's amazing talent. I do
> not quite see why he should want to do it, but for
> what it sets out to be it is excellent. He has, it
> seems to me, rather declined in it on too easy a style,
> but it is wonderfully interesting to see how he can,
> after apparently squeezing his own particular orange
> so dry, come back to his original inspiration, and find
> us something fresh.' (LAB I, 217)

It is interesting to compare this opinion with James's
comments on Bennett in the first of his two articles on
The Younger Generation in the 'Times Literary Supplement'
(19 March and 2 April 1914, and reprinted in 'Notes on
Novelists'). There he mainly talked about 'The Old Wives'
Tale' and 'Clayhanger' and he saw Bennett and Wells as
authors who 'squeeze out to the utmost the plump and more
or less juicy orange of a particular acquainted state and

let this affirmation of energy, however directed or un-
directed, constitute for them the "treatment" of the
theme'. (James had earlier described 'Hilda Lessways' as
'the slow wringing out of a dirty sponge'.) The same
article was notable for putting D.H. Lawrence a distant
third behind Hugh Walpole and Compton Mackenzie among the
youngest novelists. Bennett had had his say about James
some years earlier in the 'New Age': 'But on the debit
side: - He is tremendously lacking in emotional power.
Also his sense of beauty is over-sophisticated and wants
originality. Also his attitude towards the spectacle of
life is at bottom conventional, timid, and undecided.'
Bennett wrote to an American friend in November 1914:
'The best judges I know are of opinion that "The Price of
Love" is A1. This rather surprises me, but it relieves
me' (LAB II, 358). Sales of the novel to the beginning
of November were 6,700 in England and 3,500 Colonial.
By mid-December the figures were 8,000 and 3,600. To the
end of 1915, in which year a fourth impression was issued,
the figures were 8,900 and 3,800. In the first four
months of American publication 19,000 copies were reported
sold. At the end of 1915 the figure was nearly 21,000.
Other editions appeared in 1918, 1920 and 1962.

'Liberty' (1914)

Published in October. 'I am an Englishman', Bennett
wrote in 1911, 'and I grow daily more English'. (See
LAB I, 113.) In 1912 he returned to England to live,
and in the little essay Graphic Art in Paris he wrote,
'I suppose I have a grim passion for England. But I know
why France is the darling of nations' (TTHIM). He reacted
to the war with intense patriotism, and gave a great deal
of time to it in both paid and unpaid work. He wrote
'Liberty' for the 'Saturday Evening Post', where it
appeared on 17 October 1914. The 'Post' paid £200 for it.
Few reviews are known. The 'Times Literary Supplement'
took notice of it twice (22 October and 12 November),
saying on the latter occasion that it 'brilliantly and
forcibly' stated the case against the German 'challenge
to civilisation'. The 'New York Times' (8 November) and
'Outlook' (9 December) offered detached and brief summaries.

'From the Log of the Velsa' (1914)

Published in December in America. Yachting was a great

and longstanding pleasure in Bennett's life. He purchased the *Velsa* in 1912, and sailed in it to various
English and Continental cities. The articles were commissioned by W.W. Ellsworth, president of the Century
Company in America, who told Bennett's agent that he had
read every word Bennett had written. He paid £1,000 for
serial rights and possibly an additional sum for book
rights. Bennett wrote the articles in February-March
1914, apparently culling them from a yachting journal
of the preceding two years. They appeared in the 'Century
Magazine' beginning in June 1914 and in the 'Graphic'
(with significant differences) beginning 25 July. Because
of the war the book was not published in England until
1920, when Chatto & Windus issued it. Chatto paid £100
in advance on a royalty of 25 per cent on the published
price. The frontispiece of both American and English
editions was a water-colour by Bennett. Few reviews are
known. The 'Independent' in a brief notice (14 December
1914) described it as 'pleasant'. Edith Kellogg Dunton
in the 'Dial' (16 December) was pleased, and recounted
details at some length. The 'Boston Evening Transcript'
(16 December) found the volume 'extremely entertaining'.
Algernon Tassin in the 'Bookman' (December) found it 'in
the most smartly journalistic style of this Janus of
authors'. In England in 1920 the 'Daily Express' gave
it brief, favourable attention (15 June) and the 'London
Mercury' (September) thought that the book 'suffers from
the lack of that close observation of material' that one
usually finds in Bennett. The book sold 2,000 copies in
the first six months in America.

'The Author's Craft' (1915)

Published in October. Bennett wrote in the 'Journal' on
27 January 1909: 'On Monday and yesterday I wrote the
first chapter of a book about novel-writing and the
fiction-reading public, which will appear in pieces over
Jacob Tonson's name. I was most enthusiastic over it.'
That book was never written, but the first parts of it
appeared in the 'New Age' beginning on 4 February, under
Bennett's pseudonym there, and were reprinted in 'Books
and Persons' in 1917. These pieces themselves had their
origin in the essays that went into 'Fame and Fiction'
in 1903, and together they provided the ground for the
more general and reflective essay, Artist and Public,
that makes the fourth part of 'The Author's Craft'. For
the rest, as Bennett wrote in 1913, 'my idea was that the
larger public had never had any authoritative and honest

account of the inner craft of writing and that such
account would therefore be a novelty and arouse interest'
(LAB I, 184). Bennett's words were in response to the
editor of the 'Metropolitan Magazine' in America, who
found the first of the four essays unsuitable for his
half-million readers. He did not publish it, and the
series began there with the second essay in June 1913.
The 'Metropolitan' paid £600 for the material. The complete series ran in the 'English Review' beginning in
April 1913. It elicited argument from J.M. Murry in the
'Blue Review' in July. The English edition of the book,
issued by Hodder & Stoughton, and bearing the date 1914,
was held up on account of the war. Few reviews are known.
C.H. Herford gave it a long review in the 'Manchester
Guardian' (26 October), arguing with Bennett's view that
every author must see beauty in what he writes about,
agreeing with him that '"Naturalist" is merely an epithet
expressing self-satisfaction', and correcting him on some
points. He found the book 'illuminating' and written in
the same 'fresh and racy idiom of the novels'. The 'Times
Literary Supplement' in another long review (28 October)
took umbrage at Bennett's comments on critics, as did
Herford to a lesser extent, and gave most of the review
to arguing about Bennett's views on plotting.

In America the 'New York Times' (21 September 1914)
noted the 'characteristic iconoclasm of Mr. Bennett the
essayist' and recommended the volume to writers and
general public for both its 'entertainment' and its
'irritation'. The 'Dial' (1 November) found some of the
material trivial and 'futile' but noted 'a wealth of
illuminating comment' in the essay Writing Novels. The
'Independent' (9 November) remarked upon Bennett the
iconoclast, and saw the book as a 'curious blend of
wisdom and folly'. Calvin Winters in another brief
notice in the 'Bookman' (January 1915) thought that
Bennett's view of English literature was 'myopic' and
that Bennett's view of the unimportance of good technique
was amply illustrated in Bennett's own novels. The book
apparently did not sell well, and Hodder & Stoughton - who
along with Cassell in later years regarded it as an honour
to publish Bennett's books - wrote to him in 1920 to ask
him to accept a reduced royalty. No later edition of the
book is known until 1968, when Samuel Hynes put together
a collection of Bennett's essays on writing and criticism.

'Over There' (1915)

Published in November. Bennett was invited by the

Government in April to visit the Front, and he was there
from 21 June to 15 August. He was ill for a couple of
weeks after his return, but completed the 25,000 words
of the book on 25 August. The material appeared serially
in the 'Illustrated London News' and the 'Saturday Evening
Post' beginning on 21 August. The 'Illustrated London
News' paid £1,500 for it. The American price seems to
have been £600. Methuen issued the book in England,
Doran in America. Few notices of it are known. The
'Spectator' (8 January 1916) found in it 'more emotion
than we find as a rule in his cool, analytical method',
and expressed restrained pleasure in the result. The
'Pall Mall Gazette' in a brief notice (13 January) felt
rather the same way. In America the 'Springfield Republican' (20 November 1915) thought that Bennett 'writes
more entertainingly' than others who have described the
Front. The 'New York Times' (21 November) gave the book
prominent review, mainly to describe its contents and to
say that 'deep indignation gives unwonted color to Mr.
Bennett's descriptions and edge to his comments'. The
'Nation' (20 January 1916) thought that Bennett's patriotism got in the way of his observation.

'These Twain' (1916)

Published on 14 January. In the self-written interview
published in the 'Daily News' on 30 July 1914 Bennett
wrote:

> I am now writing the third and last volume of my
> Clayhanger series. I have been cursed by readers over
> the entire civilised world for not writing it sooner.
> I didn't know enough about life to write it any sooner.
> I had to spend a year or two in learning. Also I was
> ill.... It will be published next year if I'm alive.
> And I will tell you this – it will be the last volume
> I shall ever write about the Five Towns. I am going
> to write about London. I've published several novels
> about London, and I'm going to publish some more.
> London is a far better subject than the Five Towns.
> And also I'm going to write about the Continent – or,
> rather, about the English on the Continent. There's
> a rich subject for irony.

(In 1903 Bennett wrote to a Five Towns friend: 'I don't
comprehend your general objection to "provincial novels",
seeing that the majority of all the greatest novels in the
world are provincial'. See LAB II, 177.)

Bennett began writing on 25 May 1914 and finished on 12 February 1915. On 31 August 1913 he wrote in his 'Journal', 'the third Clayhanger must be quite different from "Clayhanger" and "Hilda"', and on 7 and 26 June 1914 he expressed pleasure there about the beginning of the writing. A few months later he wrote to an American friend, 'I can't spoil the simplicity of my novel by letting Edwin and Hilda procreate. They have young George, & he's quite enough for my purposes' (LAB II, 358). The novel was 128,000 words, and Bennett cut it to 100,000 for serial publication in 'Munsey's Magazine' in America, where it appeared in September and October 1915. Munsey paid £3,000 for it. George Doran apparently bought the book rights from Dutton for more than £1,000 and paid Bennett £1,000. Methuen paid £400, as contracted in 1909.

On 22 January Bennett wrote in the 'Journal':

Some rotten reviews. Apart from other things, the book is too jolly true for some people. They say it lacks the ideal, and mean that it refuses to be untruthful. Several of the best critics have noted this with satisfaction and laudation.

For some reviewers 'These Twain' marked the very summit of Bennett's achievement, and they headed their reviews A Great Novel, A Great Literary Achievement, and the like. For others the novel marked a sad decline or a confirmation that Bennett was second-rate. The 'Pall Mall Gazette' (14 January) said that on its own it was 'the very greatest literary achievement of recent years ...; it is a satire, merciless, but not malignant ...; it is a history of the manners of an epoch ...; it stands exalted and solitary as a work of art'. Mary Prendered in the 'Daily Chronicle' (14 January) thought that it 'has more vitality than "The Old Wives' Tale", more power and firmness than the first two books of the trilogy'; she found excessive analysis and external detail. J.C. Squire in the 'New Statesman' (15 January) saw much to admire in the individual parts, and the book was 'engrossing', but also 'it never more than mildly stirs', and he thought that the working out of the action was contrived to a purpose - Edwin in the earlier books seemed more intelligent than he now seemed, and Hilda less brutally selfish. 'Punch' (19 January) thought that the novel was perhaps too much of a good thing:

the study of both Edwin and Hilda is marvellously penetrating and minute almost to the point of

defeating its own end. I had, not for the first time
with Mr. Bennett's characters, a feeling that I knew
them too well to have complete belief in them. They
became not portraits but anatomical diagrams.

'Truth' (19 January) acknowledged that the novel was 'very
clever indeed', but thought that Bennett was 'rather tired
of Edwin and Hilda' and that the book was 'dull, deadly
dull'. The 'Staffordshire Sentinel' contented itself with
reproducing the reviews in the 'Times Literary Supplement'
(No. 82), the 'Nation' (No. 83), and 'Truth'. The 'Athenaeum' (February), acknowledging that Bennett was a 'consummate artist', was mainly concerned to discuss the novel
as a guide to middle-class values in marriage. The 'Free-
man's Journal' (b. 17 February) said, 'this book places
Mr. Bennett in the front rank of all English novelists of
whatever time'. F.G. Bettany in the 'Bookman' (March)
mainly emphasised the regional portrait in the trilogy,
'a picture of Five Towns society, manners and progress
ranging over a generation of time', a picture that Bettany
found very impressive. The 'Standard' (b. 16 March)
thought that the novel was 'Bennett at his best'. For
other English reviews see Nos 79-83.
    The novel was issued in November 1915 in America. The
'Boston Evening Transcript' (17 November) decided that
'compared with its two preceding novels "These Twain" is
a very slipshod, haphazard and lackadaisical performance'.
The 'New York Times' (21 November) found it 'the greatest
of the three ..., mainly by virtue of its own deep illumination of life and character'; it 'is at once a subtle
study of marriage and an amusing comedy of daily life'.
Edward E. Hale in the 'Dial' (9 December) wrestled at
length with the question of whether Bennett was propound-
ing a pocket philosophy of marriage in the book. He was
puzzled by omissions of material about religion, business,
and sex, but overall 'the book as well as the completed
trilogy is a great achievement'. Frederic Taber Cooper
in the 'Bookman' (January) found it tedious and repetitious. For another American review see No. 84.
    In 1925 Bennett wrote to L.G. Johnson, who had just
published a small book on him:

With regard to your criticism of 'These Twain', I will
only say that the restriction, the 'narrow-down', was
intentional and deliberate, and part of the scheme as
a whole. Compare the much more drastic narrowing down
into domestic life at the end of 'War and Peace'. I
cannot remember whether I read 'War and Peace' before
or after I planned 'Hilda Lessways', which I consider

to be quite inferior to 'These Twain'. Frank Swinnerton calls it a 'tour de force' and this is my view also. Whereas I have received the most *passionate* testimonies to the authenticity and force of 'These Twain'. (LAB III, 233)

Bennett was told by A.M.S. Methuen that sales in the first week were over 13,000, and Bennett reported to a friend that it was a great success in America as well. Later figures indicated English sales of 10,8000, Colonial of 6,700, and American of 17,2000 to mid-November 1916. These more modest figures still made 'These Twain' Bennett's best selling novel to date – in the short run. The three novels of the trilogy were published in a single volume, 'The Clayhanger Family', in 1925. Editions by Methuen and Penguin of 'These Twain' are in print today.

'The Lion's Share' (1916)

Published on 14 September. On 5 January 1915 Bennett wrote to his agent:

All I care to say now is that the action will be largely in modern Paris (the first time I have written of it in fiction), & that the tale will be light & humorous in character, but with decidedly more senti-ment, love, and advanced civilisation than there is in 'The Card' and 'The Regent'. (LAB I, 223)

He wrote the first part of the book between 2 April and 6 May 1915, and the second part between 22 September and 1 December. He described it in the 'Journal' on 10 April as 'light and of intent not deeply imagined, but it seems to me to be fairly good and interesting'. It was intended for serialisation in the 'Strand Magazine', but the 'Strand' people objected to it because it dealt with the suffra-gette movement. They did not want to offend either suf-fragettes or anti-suffragettes. Bennett was outraged. The 'Strand' refused to publish the novel, and it appeared in the 'Grand Magazine', beginning in March 1916. It ran in the 'Metropolitan Magazine' in America beginning in October 1915. The editors there liked it. The 'Metro-politan' paid £3,000 for serial rights. Doran and Cassell paid £1,000 each for book rights. Bennett went to Cassell on the advice of H.G. Wells, and Cassell published most of Bennett's novels thereafter. Bennett became a good friend of Newman Flower, who in the 1920s became head and then owner of the firm.

Not many of the known reviews approved of the novel.
Sidney Dark in the 'Daily Express' (14 September) found
it 'sunny, human, wise, and witty'. Gordon Phillips in
the 'Manchester Guardian' (14 September) was entertained
by parts of the narrative but thought that Bennett's view
of womankind was narrow and old-fashioned. The 'Athenaeum' (September) was annoyed that Bennett had taken a
serious subject and done nothing with it; his narrative
bore little relation to the actualities of the suffragette
movement. For Rebecca West's opinion and one other English review see Nos 85 and 86. In America the 'New York
Times' (12 November) recited the plot at length and found
it 'labored'; so much had happened on the suffragette
front in the past two years that the pre-war setting
seemed Victorian. A slight notice in the same place
(26 November) found the book 'exceedingly entertaining'.
The 'Independent' in a brief notice (27 November)
expressed distaste for Bennett's heroines - Hilda Lessways
as well as Audrey Moze. Edward E. Hale in the 'Dial' (30
November) liked the novel:

> there is the extravagant Bennett that tells of the most
> impossible things and shows them to be perfectly natu-
> ral and according to the great truths of life, and the
> commonplace Bennett who tells of the most ordinary
> things and shows them to be full of the most emotional
> adventure. People have rather settled down into the
> idea that the latter Bennett is the real one, and per-
> haps because they like best to have the drabs and grays
> of their average experience made golden-pink and tawny.
> But both kinds are real and both are very English.
> 'The Lion's Share' is of the latter kind, and an excel-
> lent example of it. It has exhilarating action, more
> indeed than most novels of its kind; but it has also
> those moments of vision, those utterances of great
> truths about life, and those flashes of insight that
> we associate with the serious Mr. Bennett.

The 'Nation' (25 January 1917) found it 'an amusing entertainment, with touches of seriousness'. The 'Bookman'
(January) believed that Bennett 'is always interested in
human nature not only as the main thing, but as a pretty
stable thing, fundamentally the same as the generations
pass'; his intention in the present novel was more to
please than to edify. To November 1916 the novel sold
8,500 copies in England and 3,000 in the Colonial edition.
No later editions are known, aside from a French edition
in English in 1917.

'Books and Persons' (1917)

Published in July. The articles in this collection
represent about one-third of the weekly articles that
Bennett wrote gratis for eighteen months and then for
a token fee of one guinea for the 'New Age' in 1908-11.
He had the idea for the articles on 12 March 1908 and
thereupon sat down and wrote the first one and sent it
off. He used as a pseudonym the name of the eighteenth-
century publisher, Jacob Tonson. Six days later he wrote
in the 'Journal': 'Last week I began a column of book
gossip for the "New Age". Pleasure in making it *rosse*.
Writing under a pseudonym, I seemed to think that as a
matter of fact it must be *rosse*. Strange!' Early the
following year he had some intention of making a book
out of a group of the articles, but it came to nothing
(see p. 72). In January 1917 Hugh Walpole read through
the series and urged Bennett to publish a selection.
Bennett wrote to a friend about the articles a few weeks
later: 'They are extremely rollicking & will infuriate
many while diverting the judicious (I hope)' (LAB III, 25).
Chatto & Windus paid £75 in advance on the book, with a
royalty of 20 per cent on the published price of five
shillings, rising to 25 per cent when 1,000 copies were
sold. Some 3,400 copies seem to have been sold in England
within five months of publication.

 The 'Times Literary Supplement' (5 July) said, 'Mr.
Arnold Bennett is one of the few who can catch their sayings before they are cold and enclose them all alive in
very readable prose'; all the same, 'we do not think this
is a book of first-rate criticism'. J.C. Squire in 'Land
and Water' (5 July) thought that few people other
than Bennett could have written the piece on the provincial book market, and the book as a whole was lively and
vigorous and inevitably of more topical than permanent
interest. C.H. Herford in a long review in the 'Manchester Guardian' (9 July) argued about Bennett's views on
critics; he found the articles very lively and often
wrongheaded. The 'Saturday Review' (21 September) was
mainly preoccupied with the wrongheadedness. The 'Spectator' (22 September) and the 'Athenaeum' (September) in
brief notices found the collection lively. American
reviewers were attracted or irritated and generally agreed
that the material was superficial. See the 'New Republic'
(20 October), the 'Dial' (22 November), 'Outlook' (5 December), and the 'Nation' (13 December). Chatto & Windus
issued a cheaper edition in 1919.

'The Pretty Lady' (1918)

Published on 28 March. This novel has more seriously
divided Bennett's critics than any other except perhaps
'Imperial Palace'. Writing in 'The Author's Craft' a
few years earlier, Bennett remarked upon the concessions
to public taste that he felt any artist perforce makes:

> For example, no first-class English novelist or drama-
> tist would dream of allowing to his pen the freedom
> in treating sexual phenomena which Continental writers
> enjoy as a matter of course. The British public is
> admittedly wrong on this important point – hypocritical,
> illogical and absurd. But what would you? You cannot
> defy it; you literally cannot. If you tried, you would
> not even get as far as print, to say nothing of library
> counters. You can only get round it by ingenuity and
> guile. You can only go a very little further than is
> quite safe. You can only do one man's modest share in
> the education of the public.

On Wednesday, 9 May 1917, Bennett wrote in his 'Journal':
'On Sunday I had an idea for a short novel about an episode in the life of a French *cocotte*. I thought I could
tell practically everything about her existence without
shocking the B.P.' 'Journal' entries of 11 September and
18 October 1915, 14 December 1917, and 2 July 1918 indicate some of the material that Bennett drew into the
novel. He wrote to Newman Flower about it on 19 May 1917:

> The next novel I write will be short, and will empha-
> tically be unfit for serial use. This you may take
> it from me as a fact, seeing that the principal person
> in it is a professional courtesan. It is a war-novel
> and I anticipate that it will startle the public.
> Please treat this item as confidential. (LAB III, 32)

Bennett began writing on 24 May 1917 and finished on
28 January 1918. On 16 October 1917 he recorded in the
'Journal' that he was 'fairly well pleased' thus far.
On 28 January he wrote that 'the close seemed to me to
be rather ingenious, well executed, and effective'. On
20 February when he was reading the proof, he wrote,
'I can now see things that I have left out of that novel.
Nevertheless the story held me.' Cassell paid £1,000 in
advance on it and Doran £1,470.
     Reactions ranged from high praise to abuse. Robert
Lynd in the 'Daily News' (28 March) regarded the novel
as 'not a great but a good example of his genius';

'Mr. Bennett does not see life passionately or poetically but he regards it with astonishment and in a very rare spirit of justice as well as of mercy.' Lynd's chief reservation was that the novel offered a very partial view of war-time London. The 'Globe' (b. 5 April) said, 'he has through "Pretty Lady", made himself an easy first among contemporary writers'. Arthur Machen in the 'Evening News' (9 April) gave it merely a few lines of scorn as a work more suitable for the 'flicker pictures' than for literature. 'Punch' (10 April) admired the 'fresh angle of vision' that Bennett invariably brought in his work; the novel had material of 'startling indecorum' in it that the reviewer did not like, but he objected still more to Bennett's failure to treat the material fully. The 'Times Literary Supplement' (11 April) felt several ways about the book: it was cynical; it was sometimes 'unpleasantly frank' and sometimes veiled and insinuating as though to titillate the naive reader more; it was 'brilliant, finished, easy'; it perhaps represented on Bennett's part 'the protest of a hurt mind against the blasphemy of war'; it was 'better entertainment than he has done for a long time'. The 'Saturday Review' (13 April) thought it was a clever satire of a particular world, but not observed with intimate knowledge. H.M. Richardson in the 'Sunday Chronicle' (14 April) said: '"The Pretty Lady" is a damnable book ..., decadent, ignoble and corrupting', containing 'hundreds of pages of pimpishness'. There were two adequate ways of dealing with vice, Balzac's cynical and witty approach and Zola's moral passion. Bennett merely made vice attractive, and he had the audacity to call his harlot Christine. 'This book ought to be banned under the Defence of the Realm Act as a work calculated to destroy the morals of the people. It is an abomination.' The 'Westminster Gazette' (b. 18 April) admired the 'keen and unerring' portrait, the 'humour and knowledge'. The 'Pall Mall Gazette' (b. 25 April) found it a 'remarkable, daring, and arresting novel'. 'Country Life' (b. 25 April) found it 'brilliant in its observation and its uncanny skill'. 'Truth' (b. 25 April) was fascinated by the characters. The 'Nation' (11 May) emphasised the detachment and irony of 'his extraordinarily acute power of vision'; the reviewer objected to the literal translation of Christine's French into English. Rebecca West in 'Outlook' (b. 16 May) thought that the book would not shock any adult reader and that it was 'brimful of beauty'. The 'New Statesman' (b. 16 May) thought it might be a corrective to naive views about the ennobling character of war. The 'Athenaeum' took notice of the book twice, once briefly (May)

to say that it was 'doubtless a faithful picture ... but
... not to our taste', and again (June) to admire 'passages of unsurpassable descriptive drama - the funeral
of Lord Roberts, the Zeppelin night, the meeting of the
war hospital committee, the visit to a night club' and
to suggest that the 'dominant motive of the story is
ironical satire'. The 'Daily Express' described it on
29 July as a description of a changing world: 'the old
order ... vanished ...; in its place came a life of high
and crude colours'; and Bennett's novel 'has about it
something of that disorder, as of a richly coloured night-
mare'. For other English reviews see Nos 89-92.

In America the 'New York Times' (26 May) was not
pleased that Bennett was trying to show the unchanging
quality of human nature, for that would put American boys
on a level with the Hun. The novel offered an uninspiring
view of war-time London. It was written in a style unlike
Bennett's other work, fragmented, impressionistic.
Lawrence Gilman in the 'North American Review' (July)
prefaced his long review with long comment on the lack
of plain and honest language in American journalism, and
he turned to Bennett as 'not only a literary artist of
positive and extraordinary excellence but a genuinely free
spirit'. Gilman would not want to praise Bennett as the
'moral standpatter' that Stuart Pratt Sherman saw in him
(see No. 87); he would praise 'The Pretty Lady' 'for its
flaring honesty, its witty candour and shrewdness', for
its depiction of the heroine 'with rare beauty and delicacy of comprehension: he has understood her perfect
pragmatism, her deep-seated goodness'. In sum Bennett
had 'helped to bring a little nearer that incredible day
when the only fear that will oppress a writer ... will be
the fear of reporting life dishonestly'. The 'Nation'
(13 July) said that Bennett's story was 'filthy and
untrue': an Englishman who did not care whether the woman
he loved sold herself nightly was a figment of Bennett's
imagination. The 'Independent' (31 August) gave the novel
six lines to say that it was unworthy of Bennett and of
the time. For another American review see No. 93.

Early in April 1918 Bennett wrote to Hugh Walpole:
'Most of the reviews of the "P.L." so far are specially
footling. Astonishing the number of critics who daren't
mention that the chief character is a whore!' (LAB III,
55) Later in the month he wrote to a friend in the Air
Force: 'My novel has made a hades of a racket in the
press, & also in what is known as the "West End". It
has several times been called "pornographic", "the last
word in decadence", "shameful", "abominable", etc; still
I survive' (LAB III, 57). In May he wrote to George Doran

to tell him the novel was selling well, and he added,

> Some of the good reviews have said ... that it gives
> an entirely ruthless picture of heartless people in
> London. This is not so, and I particularly want you
> to note that the war has a good effect on the three
> principal characters.... The book is emphatically
> not cynical. (LAB III, 58)

The book was boycotted by booksellers in Cambridge and
Bath. Boots refused to stock it in their lending library.
In May, W.H. Smith banned it from their stalls. Also in
May the Catholic Federation of the Archdiocese of West-
minster and the Catholic Truth Society protested to
Cassell. Bennett wrote to Newman Flower of the firm:

> It is surely unnecessary for me to point out, first,
> that in so far as the book deals with Catholicism it
> does so exclusively from the point of view of an
> ignorant and superstitious courtesan anxious to justify
> her own conduct to herself, and, secondly, that all
> the details given as to legends of the Virgin Mary
> can be found, with hundreds of others, in devout
> Catholic literature.
>   As to the detail that Christine goes out into the
> streets at the supposed call of the Virgin Mary, the
> story makes quite clear that she went out to find one
> particular man and to succour him, - really to save him
> from the consequences of his drunkenness. (LAB III, 59)

The result of all this was that 'The Pretty Lady' was
Bennett's best selling novel to date. In England sales
to 23 April were 18,000. Nine months later they were
34,000. In America sales were 15,000 by early July.
Doran seems to have issued a brochure advertising the
book, with reviews quoted, perhaps to blunt the attack
on the novel. In August, according to Doran, sales took
a terrible dip because two articles by Bennett published
in America in August were interpreted as pacifist.
Bennett at this time was director of British propaganda
in France. He had been appointed to the post by Lord
Beaverbrook, head of the Ministry of Information, who
had read 'The Pretty Lady' and decided that no one understood French psychology better than Bennett.
   Bennett reported in his 'Journal' on other opinions.
James Stephens told him '"The O.W. Tale" was "it", but
"The Pretty Lady" was "itter"', and he 'put it at the top
of all modern fiction' (31 August 1919). On 22 May 1921
Bennett invited George Moore to lunch:

He said that Christine was the finest *cocotte* in
literature, and that I must have lived with her, and
actually witnessed the Sunday afternoon kitchen scenes,
etc.   I don't think he believed my denial of this and
my statement that it was all invented, including Christine.   I didn't tell him that when I was hunting about
for a physique for Christine I saw Madame R. accompanying her husband at a concert, and immediately fastened
on her physique for Christine - sadness, puckering of
the brows, etc.

Bennett's own considered view of the novel seems to have
been that it was 'too brilliant.   No really first-class
book is ever glittering' (LAB III, 68) and that it was
jolly well constructed' ('Journal', 16 February 1924).
Cassell issued cheap editions in 1919 and 1932.   The
Richards Press issued an edition in 1950 with an introduction by Frank Swinnerton.

'Self and Self-Management' (1918)

Published in December.   The material for this little book
was commissioned in February 1917 by 'Cosmopolitan Magazine' in America, who paid £120 for each of six articles.
'Nash's and Pall Mall Magazine' paid £75 each for English
serial rights.   Publication began in 'Cosmopolitan' in
November 1917 and in 'Nash's' in January 1918.   Bennett
described the collection as 'a book of moral essays for
the young of both sexes' (LAB III, 63).   In England,
where Hodder & Stoughton issued it, 'The Times' (of unknown date) noticed it briefly as one of Bennett's 'series
of little books on life and letters, in which the novelist
buttonholes the public and gives it a good deal of shrewd,
stimulating and often amusing advice'.   In America some
journals found it useful: the 'Springfield Republican'
(11 February 1919) and 'Outlook' (12 February).   Others
found it trivial: the 'Nation' (15 March) and 'Catholic
World' (July).

'The Roll-Call' (1919)

Published on 16 January.   This novel was an informal
fourth part to the Clayhanger series, and treated the
maturity of Hilda Lessway's son, who had figured briefly
in the trilogy.   Bennett was thinking of writing it as
early as the autumn of 1910, when he mentioned it in a
letter to his friend E.A. Rickards, who was the model

for the hero (see LAB II, 266). He characteristically
referred to it as his 'London' novel. He began writing
on 16 October 1916 and finished on 30 April 1917. When
he was reading the proof he wrote to Hugh Walpole, 'Now
when I was writing this I didn't think much of it - from
30 to 16 months ago. But at the present moment it seems
to me to be quite all right, & very interesting' (LAB III,
55). The reason for delay in publication had to do with
complications over serial publication in America. Bennett
wanted it to precede publication of 'The Pretty Lady'
because it dealt with the earlier part of the war. But
he got into a row with the Munsey syndicate, who had contracted to pay $17,500 (£3,500) for serial rights in the
belief that they were getting something in the vein of
'Buried Alive'. Their memory of negotiations - which
dated back to 1914 - proved to be better than Bennett's
(see LAB I, 251 ff.). The quarrel was settled with their
paying £3,668 for 'The Roll-Call' and withdrawing from a
contract on a further serial for which they had intended
to pay $17,500 as well. 'The Roll-Call' appeared in
'Munsey's Magazine' beginning in April 1918. The book
was issued by Hutchinson in England, who paid £800 in
default on serialisation and apparently advanced £1,000
on the book. Hutchinson did not please Bennett. He wrote
to his agent upon receipt of his copies:

> They are odious in a very high degree. I do not com-
> plain of the quality of the paper, but I object to
> there being two half-titles, one before the title
> and the other after it! I object more strongly to
> the illustrated cover being passed without reference
> to the author and still more strongly to the descrip-
> tive matter not being submitted to the author. The
> description of the book inside the jacket: 'Can a man
> love two women is the theme of this book', is perfectly
> ridiculous and extremely misleading. Really Hutchin-
> sons ought to have more sense than to make fools of
> themselves and of me in this style. (LAB I, 271)

Reviews in England were generally restrained or hostile. S.P.B. Mais in the 'Evening News' (16 January)
remarked by the way that 'The Pretty Lady' was 'as poor
a "pot-boiler" as any famous man of letters has ever
produced'. 'The Roll-Call' in contrast was an interesting
book, with excellent description, leavened by the vulgarity often found in Bennett's work. Mais looked forward
to a sequel. Louis J. McQuilland in the 'Daily Express'
(16 January) saw the book as 'a great pageant of life,
with vast splashes of luxury', 'a revue rather than a

novel', and he was well pleased. The 'Times Literary
Supplement' (23 January) thought that the novel broke
off rather than ended, and looked forward to a sequel.
The book surpassed all Bennett's other books in a certain
personal quality – in letting the characters master their
worlds. The comic touches about army life were superb.
The 'British Weekly' (6 February) was deeply impressed:
'Bennett can understand and render a beautiful soul';
the book was worthy to rank with 'The Old Wives' Tale';
it was 'the best he has written for years'. The 'Saturday
Review' (8 February) wanted to box Bennett's ears for
writing books as trivial as 'The Pretty Lady' and 'The
Roll-Call'. The latter was not even a complete book,
but merely broke off at the end. The 'Spectator' (15
February) found much of the temper of 'The Card' in the
book and also thought that it was more spiritual than
Bennett's earlier books – material things no longer dominated the aspirations of his characters. The 'Athenaeum'
noticed the book twice, once (February) to say that it was
undistinguished, and again (March) to complain of the
ending and to admire the experience of life and the richness of characterisation that the novel displayed. For
two other English reviews see Nos 94 and 96.

In America reviews were equally mixed. The 'New York
Times' (26 January) thought that never had Bennett's
satire been 'so richly humorous'. The 'Nation' (8 February) recalled the vulgarity of Bennett's producing 'The
Pretty Lady' while the world was in torment, and recited
the plot of 'The Roll-Call' with some relief. 'Living
Age' (22 February) thought that the book exhibited less
care and less passion than the trilogy. 'Outlook' in a
brief notice (5 March) was lukewarm. The 'Independent'
(8 March) especially admired Bennett's ability to see with
the eyes of his characters. The 'Dial' (June) admired the
observation and detail but found the satire strident. For
two other American reviews see Nos 95 and 97.

In 1921 Bennett wrote in his yachting journal:

I finished reading 'The Roll-Call'. I could find less
fault with this book than with any of mine that I have
re-read. In fact I thought highly of it. It certainly
seemed to me to be the most accomplished. And the
race-course chapter and all the second part impressed
me as being genuinely the goods. (RP, 298)

No further editions of the book are known.

'Our Women' (1920)

Published on 23 September. In the 'Journal' on 8 July
1904 Bennett recorded saying to someone, 'Don't you think
women are the most interesting thing in the world?' At
that time he kept a private journal of observations on
women, and the pages of the regular journal contain plentiful comment on them. Women are the chief characters of
quite as many of his major novels as men are. He wrote
to a woman friend in America, 'I am partly a woman, à mes
heures' (LAB II, 295). He apparently arranged to write
the book in October 1918, and wrote then to his agent
'that there will necessarily be some plain speaking in
the book, & subjects must be dealt with that are not
usually dealt with' (LAB I, 267). He wrote the book between 1 March and 2 June 1919. On 30 May he described
it in his 'Journal' as 'damnable, pedestrian, fair-minded,
sagacious'. Two days later he wrote there, 'I haven't
come to any conclusion as to its value'. 'Cassell's
Magazine' and 'Cosmopolitan Magazine' began serialising
it in December 1919. Doran apparently advanced £500 for
book rights on a 20 per cent royalty, and Cassell
advanced £400.
    The 'Daily Mail' (23 September) excerpted bits for the
interested reader. A.N. Monkhouse in the 'Manchester
Guardian' (23 September) admired the general commonsense
and lucidity; he thought that Bennett failed entirely to
be fair to the woman in the staged quarrel at the end.
The 'Saturday Review' (2 October) mainly summarised; the
reviewer thought that for an avowed feminist, Bennett
made 'some damaging admissions against his fair client'.
The reviewer for the 'Times Literary Supplement' (23
October) thought that Bennett was too much preoccupied
with the differences between the sexes, but recommended
his book to all young women and their parents, and he
especially admired Bennett's approval of social and
psychological independence for women. In America the
'New York Times' (10 October) was glad to count Bennett
a feminist, if not a complete one, and summarised his
views at length. Dorothy Scarborough in the 'Bookman'
(December) thought that the author illustrated in his
writing the attributes he gave to women: 'it is delightful, provocative, and exasperatingly illogical'; she
believed American women were more independent than English
women and less in need of his recommendations on independence. The 'Nation' (19 January 1921) found the book a
combination of the 'platitudinous' and the 'delightful';
the reviewer could not take seriously Bennett's belief
in the superior imagination of men. Cassell issued
another edition in 1923.

'Things That Have Interested Me' (1921)

Published on 13 January. Bennett wrote to his agent in
February 1920:

> I enclose some items from a sort of journal of various
> lengths. I also enclose a copy of a description of a
> prize fight, also from a journal, which I gave to the
> 'New Statesman'.... These impressions deal with both
> life and the arts. They are certainly as interesting
> as 'Books & Persons'. But in the main they are not
> popular; nor intended to be so; they are *my* lark.
> (LAB I, 278)

Bennett wanted to arrange for a series with an American
magazine, but failed. Some of the journal material
appeared in two issues of the 'London Mercury' during the
year. The published book - issued by Chatto & Windus in
England - included the 'London Mercury' material and a
good deal of hitherto unpublished material, the most
notable portion of which consisted of reminiscences of his
life in Paris in the first years of the century. The contract called for an advance of £100, with a royalty of 20
per cent on the first 1,000 copies at a published price of
five shillings, and 25 per cent thereafter. The 'Manchester Guardian' (13 January) gave it as long a review as it
had given anything of Bennett's, mainly to excerpt passages for admiration, argument, and disparagement. Louis
J. McQuilland in the 'Daily Express' (13 January) admired
it. The 'Times Literary Supplement' (20 January) seemed
to find some of the material tedious but thought the
reminiscences 'fresh and bright'. James Douglas in the
'Sunday Express' (23 January) was highly enthusiastic.
John Middleton Murry in the 'Athenaeum' (28 January) was
scathing: 'Except for a few pages on his early experiences
in Paris it contains no evidence that Mr. Bennett ever had
a subtle thought or saw things with other eyes than the
auctioneer's.' In America the 'Boston Evening Transcript'
(13 April) found the collection 'varied' and 'shrewd' and
'full of charm and surprise'. The 'Nation' (1 June) was
inclined to call it a pot-boiler and was certain that no
publisher would have touched similar work by an unknown
author; nevertheless some of the material was vivid and
witty. The 'New York Times' (6 November) thought that it
was characteristic work: lucid and humorous and always
exhibiting 'the trained novelist's effective touch'.

'Mr. Prohack' (1922)

Published on 27 April. The years 1919 and 1920 were given mainly to the writing of four plays. Bennett began writing 'Mr. Prohack' on 11 October 1920 and finished on 16 June 1921, with an interruption of two months. See below, p. 111, for some material used in it. On 23 April he reviewed the first chapters, and wrote in his 'Journal': 'The hero seemed to me to be a new sort of character, and the story made me laugh again and again.' Two days later he wrote to his agent to express the same feeling in more restrained language. Bennett received £3,000 for serial rights in America, £1,250 in England. Serialising began in the 'Delineator' in September 1921 with cuts unauthorised by Bennett, and in the 'Westminster Gazette' on 7 November with approved cuts. Bennett was angry about the manner of the 'Delineator' cutting (see LAB I, 293). Methuen published the book in England, and their handling of it did not please Bennett (see p. xiv).

Reviewers were widely divided in their understanding of the book. Some liked its genial satire, others were mainly attracted by its sentiment, others were bored by its catalogue of wealth, others were affronted by its trivial spirit. S.P.B. Mais in the 'Daily Express' (27 April) was pleased to see a novel that, for a change, described a happy marriage. The book was 'Mr. Bennett at his very best'. Newman Flower in the 'Sunday Times' (30 April) thought that it was 'the first novel that has really adequately dealt with post-war social conditions'; it was 'a very brilliant piece of observation'. The 'Times Literary Supplement' (4 May) gave two long columns to distinguishing the particular sort of satire in which Bennett engaged - neither angry nor moralistic, but founded upon his joy in life and his sense of the absurd. Forrest Reid in the 'Nation and Athenaeum' (20 May) was delighted: 'a comedy ... worked out with a rare mastery of tone and atmosphere'. He preferred it to 'The Card' and 'The Regent'. The 'Saturday Review' (13 May) found it very amusing, and accurate psychologically, but rather brittle. The 'Spectator' (3 June) was much amused, and much taken with the figure of Prohack, but found Mrs Prohack a bore. Edward Shanks in the 'London Mercury' (June) felt the same way the 'Spectator' did. For other English reviews see Nos 98-102. In America Louise Maunsell Field in the 'New York Times' (26 February) was mildly amused by its 'conventional sarcasm'. A brief notice in the 'Dial' (April) offered moderate praise. Burton Rascoe in the 'Bookman' (April) described it as 'a charming story, tinged with authentic and

whimsical irony, rapidly told, brightened by suave humor
and tightened by good drama'. It was not, though, 'of the
first rank'. Percy Lubbock in the 'Independent' (10 June)
was disappointed that the novel did not genuinely deal
with the new and strange conditions of post-war life;
it was amusing, ingenious, long-winded, and unhelpful.
The 'New Republic' in a brief notice (23 August) thought
the novel was up-to-date.

A.M.S. Methuen wrote to Bennett on 22 April: 'I congratulate you on "Prohack". It is brilliant and I have
read it with intense admiration' (LAB I, 312). Bennett
himself wrote to André Gide on 28 May:

> You remember when I saw you I told you I was determined
> to write a novel with a (for me) new technique. Well,
> I couldn't do it! And yet now that it is published
> everybody says that it is quite different from any
> other novel I have written! Is not this rather queer
> and disturbing? The book is 'Mr. Prohack', and the
> unanimous enthusiasm with which it is being received
> makes me think that there must be something fundament-
> ally bad in it. (LAB III, 163)

The book sold well. Methuen paid royalties in December
of £544 and paid another £400 six months later. Other
editions appeared in 1931 and 1968. Bennett dramatised
it in collaboration with Edward Knoblock (see below,
p. 132).

'Lilian' (1922)

Published on 19 October. According to Frank Swinnerton,
Bennett wrote 'Lilian' to show Swinnerton what the appropriate end to Swinnerton's novel 'Coquette' should have
been. In the summer or autumn of 1921, when he was thinking about the novel, Bennett wrote in his yachting journal:

> Considerable melancholy owing to my too vivid concep-
> tion of a minor character for my next novel, a jealous
> and melancholy woman who longs ardently and ingenuously
> for 'the peace of my grave'.... The vividness of my
> realisation of the woman's feelings almost made me
> think I was going off my head. (RP, 299)

He began writing on 4 December 1921 and finished on 24
January 1922. The novel appeared serially in 'Cassell's
Magazine' in July and September 1922. Cassell probably
paid £900 for serial rights and advanced £1,000 on the

book, and Doran advanced £900 on the book. Cassell
requested Bennett to modify two sentences for serial
publication: 'I am going to have a baby' and 'I am seven
months gone'. Later there was dissatisfaction with the
ending, and change was wanted for book publication.
Bennett wrote to his agent:

> I'll write 1000 words, if the price is reasonable.
> But it must be understood that the end simply is that
> Lilian has the baby, looks after it, & runs the busi-
> ness. She may marry again - probably will marry the
> doctor. But she can't possibly *marry* him in the book.
> She may perceive how comfortable and loving & useful
> he is. (LAB I, 316)

The book received a worse press than any other Bennett
novel. The 'Times Literary Supplement' (19 October)
viewed it uneasily: the detached and accurate description
of materialists left the reader wanting more. A.N. Monkhouse in the 'Manchester Guardian' (20 October) admitted
that it was 'expert work' but he longed for 'Clayhanger'
and 'The Card', and 'Lilian' was the sort of book which
would make people believe Bennett was second-rate. James
Douglas in the 'Sunday Express' (22 October) said: 'I hate
Mr. Arnold Bennett's new novel.' He had hated 'The Pretty
Lady' too. 'Lilian' was 'a cynical tale, told with cynical brilliancy'. 'Affable Hawk' (Desmond MacCarthy) in
the 'New Statesman' (28 October) said that Bennett 'has
ceased to be a realist except in details': his books these
days are fairy tales in which his characters 'fill their
pockets' with 'everything that Mr. Bennett conceives as
making life worth living. The mediocrity of this conception, if you do not read his stories just as fairy stories,
is depressing'. The 'Spectator' (11 November) decided
that the novel was so deplorable it must be by a young man
named Bennett Arnold, who might improve with the years.
Gerald Gould in the 'Saturday Review' (11 November)
deplored it. 'Punch' (15 November) described it sardonic-
ally as the latest in Bennett's 'series of amoral guide-
books to the unconventional life'. Forrest Reid in the
'Nation and Athenaeum' (2 December) thought that it must
have been written 'in cold blood'. Edward Shanks in the
'London Mercury' (December), reviewing it after 'Jacob's
Room', said of Bennett: 'he finds the story of Lilian
trivial and vulgar, and trivial and vulgar he leaves it'.
The 'Daily Mail' (of unknown date) said that it treated
humanly of ordinary experience. The 'Daily Telegraph'
(of unknown date) found it 'full of wit, character and
worldly wisdom'. For one English review and Bennett's

response to it see No. 103. In America the 'New York
Times' (5 November) liked what it saw beneath the surface:
'one finds that it is in truth an illustration, and an
illustration replete with irony, of the position of the
vast majority of women even in this present day and
generation, when so much stress is laid upon their freedom'. The 'Independent' (31 January 1923) thought that
the book was rather bad. So did Joseph Wood Krutch in
the 'Nation' (31 January). As he had done on earlier
occasions Bennett complained to Cassell about lack of
advertising for 'Lilian', and also about the manner of
advertising. Newman Flower sent him a large batch of
advertising clippings. By 14 November the novel had sold
14,000 copies in England. By 31 March 1923 it had sold
15,000 in America. No further editions are known.

'Things That Have Interested Me, Second Series' (1923)

Published on 8 February. Like the collection in 1921 this
consisted largely of hitherto unpublished material along
with a number of items that had appeared serially. Chatto
& Windus were again the publishers, and made the same contract as on the first volume. S.P.B. Mais in the 'Daily
Express' admired the 'breadth of vision' and the vividness, and saw also 'a lack of depth'. The 'Times Literary
Supplement' (8 February) was scathing - the material was
superficial, facile, and confused. James Douglas in the
'Sunday Express' (11 February) was admiring: Bennett in
these pieces was every bit as good as Shaw. The 'Nation
and Athenaeum' (10 March) said:

> There are exacting critics who declare of these note-
> books by Mr. Bennett that the writing is cheap, the
> thought commonplace, and that Mr. Bennett is vulgar.
> Some of us, we may confess, wish we were so well able
> to obey the injunction to speak in the vulgar tongue
> that a greater multitude would attend to what we have
> to say on matters which we think of consequence. But
> we have not that great gift. Beyond Mr. Bennett's
> vulgarity ... he has a virtue which some fine writers
> would give a little of their delicate reputations to
> possess: he is interesting.

The 'English Review' (March) said: 'if he issues a third
volume as undistinguished in quality he will tick off himself as a creative force'. The 'Manchester Guardian' (28
March) found the essays 'refreshingly varied and liberal'
but deplored the attack on the critic A.B. Walkley. The

'New Statesman' (14 April) noted that Bennett had little
to say about the past or about scenery and that he was
never enraptured, but the best pages were 'vivid, precise
and informative'. In America the collection was admired
for its zest, readability, and variety by the 'New York
Times' (25 February), the 'Boston Evening Transcript'
(7 March), and the 'Bookman' (August).

'How to Make the Best of Life' (1923)

Published in May. Bennett proposed the series of articles
to the Newnes firm for the 'Strand Magazine', and told
them that 'the subject would be treated truthfully and
not sentimentally' (LAB I, 289). He described it to his
nephew Richard as 'a subject as to which I know 1/2 nothing, but a good subject' (LN, 65). He did the writing
between 22 August 1921 and 21 May 1922. The sum paid by
Newnes was at least £1,200. The articles ran in the
'Strand' beginning in May 1922, and in 'Pictorial Review'
in America beginning in June. Hodder & Stoughton and
George Doran each paid £400 in advance on the book. The
'Daily Express' (12 May) and S.P.B. Mais in the 'Sunday
Express' (13 May) offered little more than summaries. The
'Manchester Guardian' gave a fairly long leader to admiring its author: 'being ... able to write archangelically,
he can do the almost impossible - make moderation piquant,
compromise exciting, and the golden mean in all things
genuinely shiny'. The 'Evening Standard' (b. 17 May)
found it 'packed with everyday wisdom'. The 'Daily Mail'
(b. 17 May) found it 'charmingly persuasive and humorous'.
The 'Times Literary Supplement' (17 May) thought that
Bennett was 'a very human philosopher' who offered good
advice for ordinary people leading ordinary lives. The
'Spectator' (2 June) found 'nothing absolutely silly' and
'nothing memorable and wise'. David Garnett in the
'Nation and Athenaeum' (16 June) compared Bennett's observations with those of the philosopher Greville 200 years
earlier and almost saw signs of plagiarism, and offered
sardonic gratitude. In America the 'New York Times' (13
May) found the book dull, the 'Boston Evening Transcript'
(19 May) especially recommended the chapter on marriage
for its 'beneficial hints', and the 'Bookman' (September)
believed that a lot of people could 'profit pleasantly'
from it. No later edition is known.

'Riceyman Steps' (1923)

Published on 25 October. The 'Journal' on 20 October 1907
and 30 January 1913 records material that went into the
novel. The immediate origin was a visit to a bookshop
in Southampton in 1921, where Bennett conceived a story
about two misers. He returned there in the summer of
1922, and 'I had the idea that my projected story about
two misers would make a fine novel, and within about an
hour I had decided to make it a novel, and was much excited' (RP, 301). He transported the shop to Clerkenwell
in London, a district with which it is commonly said he
was unfamiliar; but in the 1890s he must have had some
acquaintance with it on account of his frequent excursions
along the Farringdon Road in search of books (see the
essay, Alone in London - II, in the collection, 'Sketches
for Autobiography'). He began writing on 10 October 1922
and finished on the following 17 March. A letter to his
nephew Richard on 6 November 1922 remarked upon taking
Harriet Cohen the pianist to the London district in which
the novel was set to show her 'what a romantic and curious
place Clerkenwell is and where my hero and heroine lived.
The chief heroine is a charwoman' (LN, 89). The same
letter expressed pleasure in the writing thus far. On 24
November he described the novel to his agent: 'The whole
movement of this book is slow, and must be slow. It is
in the same mood as "The Old Wives' Tale"' (LAB I, 319-20).
A later letter to his nephew, of 26 February 1923,
remarked that Winifred Nerney, his secretary, thought that
the novel was 'extremely fine, and she ought to know' (LN,
97). In May 1923 he described it to George Doran:

> I think that the story is exciting. It is, however,
> not in the least melodramatic. Also it has no showy
> personages, no material splendours, and no 'daring'
> sexualities. It might be put into the hands of the
> most young-ladyish young lady on the Atlantic coast.
> There are broadly speaking two themes - the miser
> theme and the love theme. (LAB III, 189)

In August Bennett gave proofs to the novelist Pauline
Smith to read:

> In a quarter of an hour she was weeping. 'Here!' said
> I, 'what are you crying for?' She said: 'It's beauti-
> ful.' Yet believe me it's the most sordid, shop-py
> story. (LAB III, 198)

Bennett had some hope of selling serial rights, especially

in America, where he failed. He sold them in England to
Cassell for £1,000, but Cassell had misunderstood the
nature of the book and would not publish it and did not
think - in the words of Newman Flower - that anyone in
England would buy the serial rights for fourpence.
Flower reported Bennett's reaction, in Bennett's characteristic stammer:

> This is a ... great novel.... Those editors who-who
> don't ... who don't w-want the ... the s-serial rights
> ... are fools. My dear Newman, they ... they are
> bloody fools.... But they are all God's creatures....
> I-I will repay you ... repay you a thousand pounds....
>   (LAB I, 329n)

Cassell's advance on the book was £1,000, Doran's was
£800.

The reviews of 'Riceyman Steps' were generally as ful-
some as those of 'Lilian' had been scathing. The 'Staffordshire Sentinel' seems to have taken less heed of it
than almost any other journal that reviewed it. The
notice there (23 October) was flattering and irrelevant,
describing the novel as a garden of delights, and was
tucked away in a small corner as though the proprietors
of the 'Sentinel' had decided to disown Bennett. (See
the Bibliography, p. 533, for derogatory local opinion
on Bennett in 1925 and 1926.) The 'Daily Express' (26
October) liked the book and summarised it. The 'Times
Literary Supplement' (1 November) admired 'Mr. Bennett's
remarkable instinct for reality' in the Clerkenwell setting, but thought that the narrative bore some air of
contrivance. Edward Shanks in 'T.P.'s Weekly' (3 November) thought that 'there are not many things in modern
fiction more beautiful than the scene in which Elsie ...
goes out to tell Joe that she cannot come with him that
night'. For the 'Daily Graphic' (b. 8 November) it was
'powerfully and brilliantly conceived and executed'.
J.D. Beresford in a brief notice in the 'Nation and
Athenaeum' (8 December) admired the 'master-craftsman'.
The 'Bookman' (December) said it was Bennett's best book
since the war but that it was not up to the level of 'The
Old Wives' Tale'. J.B. Priestley in the 'London Mercury'
(December) thought that not a word was wasted and that
some of the chapters were 'among the very finest things
in modern fiction'. For another review by Priestley and
other English reviews see Nos 104-10. The 'New York
Times' noticed the book twice (18 November - no. 111 -
and 2 December). The latter review said that the novel
belonged to 'that small but radiant company' of Bennett's
permanent books. His scene was 'as squalid as a Hogarth

print, and as vivid', and though he did not point a moral,
a moral was surely there.   Joseph Wood Krutch in the
'Nation' (19 December) admired the book and argued that
'Mr. Bennett has always made his best books out of his
most unpromising material'.   Mrs Cecil Chesterton in a
brief notice in the 'Independent' (22 December) did not
like 'the sense of futility' in the book.   A brief notice
in the 'Bookman' (January 1924) said that it was skilful,
fine, and full of grim humour.

On 21 December 1923 Bennett wrote to Frank Swinnerton:
'The reception of this book is staggering me.   And it's
all on account of Elsie!   What a way of appreciating a
book: good God!' (RP, 306)   On 25 February 1924 he wrote
to André Gide:

> I was undoubtedly, with H.G. Wells, falling under the
> whips of les jeunes.   In fact every book was the signal
> for a general attack (Wells suffered more than me).
> Also my bourgeois public was considerably disgusted
> by those very innocent works 'The Pretty Lady' and
> 'Lilian'.   So that I was being counted as a back number.
> 'Riceyman Steps' has altered all that, and I am suddenly
> the darling of the public - not because of the excel-
> lence of 'Riceyman Steps', but because the heroine
> thereof is a sympathetic, *good*, reliable, unselfish and
> chaste character!   She is a domestique, and all London
> and New York is wishing that it could find devoted ser-
> vants like her!   (LAB III, 213)

H.G. Wells wrote to Bennett that he thought 'Riceyman
Steps' might even be better than 'The Old Wives' Tale'
(HGW, 223).   Joseph Conrad wrote to him:

> As I closed the book at 7 in the morning after the
> shortest sleepless night of my experience, a thought
> passed through my head that I knew pretty well my
> 'Bennett militant' and that, not to be too complimen-
> tary, he was a pretty good hand at it; but that there
> I had 'Bennett triumphant' without any doubt whatever.
> A memorable night.   (L&LC, 330-1)

In the 'Journal' on 31 March 1924 Bennett reported that
George Moore told him that 'it was the only really objective novel ever written, and very original', and also that
'it has no form whatever, *no* form'.   Bennett added:
'Considering that in my opinion it is very well constructed...!'   In October 1924 the novel was awarded the James
Tait Black prize (£141) for the best novel of the preceding year, 'the first prize for a book I ever had', Bennett

noted in his 'Journal' on the 18th. The novel was
Bennett's best seller to date. By 8 November 1923 it was
in its sixteenth thousand in England; by early January
1924 it had sold 31,000. There were four impressions of
the Cassell edition in 1923. Cassell published a cheap
edition in 1925. Other editions were by Penguin in 1954,
Collins in 1956 (with the story Elsie and the Child and
with an introduction by Michael Sadleir), and Pan Books
in 1964 (with an introduction by Alan Sillitoe). The most
recent Cassell edition came in 1968.

'Elsie and the Child' (1924)

Published on 16 October. The idea for the title story
came from Newman Flower, who shared the general liking
for Elsie in 'Riceyman Steps'. Bennett wrote the story
between 15 January and 14 February 1924. Cassell paid
£500 for serial rights to the story, and the Century
Company paid £300. It was published in 'Story-Teller'
in September 1924 and in three instalments in the 'Century
Magazine' beginning in September. Most of the other
stories in the collection were published serially in
1921-4. When the collection was in proof, Cassell suggested that Bennett change the names of newspapers mentioned in the stories, apparently recommending that papers
owned by Cassell should be named. They had made the suggestion with 'Riceyman Steps' as well. Bennett was furious and told the firm that 'only my close friendship with
Mr. Newman Flower prevents me from bringing this matter
officially to the notice of the Society of Authors' (LAB
I, 342).
    Reviews generally assumed that the great public wanted
more of Elsie, one review assumed that Bennett himself
could not leave her alone, and another that the theme was
meant for a sequel to 'Riceyman Steps' but Bennett could
not get on with it and reduced it to a story. The 'Times
Literary Supplement' (16 October) emphasised the ordinari-
ness of Bennett's situations and the general kindliness
of his viewpoint. A.S. Wallace in the 'Manchester Guardian' (16 October) thought that Elsie was more a bulletin
than a story; the other stories were high-spirited.
Arthur Humphreys in the 'Daily Express' (17 October) was
pleased, and James Douglas in the 'Sunday Express' (26
October) was delighted. Con O'Leary in 'T.P.'s Weekly'
(1 November) emphasised Bennett's 'sympathetic power'.
The 'New Statesman' (8 November) was laudatory and
abstract: Bennett understood human relations and was true
to them. The 'Spectator' (8 November) thought that a lot

of the material was slight. Edwin Muir in the 'Nation and Athenaeum' (15 November) was disappointed, and certain that the short story form was not suitable to Bennett's talents. J.B. Priestley in the 'London Mercury' (December) liked Elsie but found the other stories trivial. In America the 'New York Times' (9 November) found the collection 'delightfully entertaining', and so did the 'Saturday Review of Literature' (29 November). The 'New Republic' (31 December) thought the stories were 'polished, inimitable, a little tired'. A limited edition was issued by Cassell in 1929, with drawings by E. McKnight Kauffer. In 1954 Collins issued Elsie and the Child and 'Riceyman Steps' in a single volume.

'Things That Have Interested Me, Third Series' (1926)

Published in February. Bennett had put together the collection in October 1925 from pieces published serially in the preceding years and from other unpublished material. Chatto & Windus published it on the same terms as for the two earlier volumes. Bennett noted in his 'Journal' on 22 February: 'The reviews I have had so far are quite favourable, some of them are very favourable. But the critics are all wrong. They say that this is the best of the three volumes. I think it is the worst.' The 'Daily Express' (11 February) enjoyed the collection and was satisfied even to find that 'Mr. Bennett is not above a few platitudes'. The 'Sunday Express' (14 February) enjoyed 'Mr. Bennett's pugnacity'. The 'Times Literary Supplement' (15 February) was slightly patronising but enjoyed the autobiographical material and the comments on literature. Edward Shanks in the 'Saturday Review' (20 February) admired the zest and freshness of Bennett's observations, and saw something of the Card in him. Robert Ellis Roberts in the 'New Statesman' (20 March) thought that only the churlish could fail to enjoy Bennett's enjoyment, but he was also a trifle annoyed that Bennett seemed to expect that everyone would be interested in what interested him, and he thought that on the subject of religion Bennett had nothing useful to say. The 'London Mercury' (June) was 'uninterested'. In America the 'Independent' (3 April) said that the volume was 'vulgar and banal', the 'New York Times' (18 April) said it was superficial and pleasing, and the 'Saturday Review of Literature' (24 April) said it was fascinating.

'Lord Raingo' (1926)

Published on 7 October. In so far as 'Lord Raingo' was
a novel about death, it represented the culmination of an
interest that was evident in Bennett's writing over the
previous twenty years. In so far as it was a novel about
politics, it reflected his involvement in politics during
the war and his friendship or acquaintance with numerous
political leaders then and later. The 200 articles that
he wrote on the war for the 'Daily News' and the 'New
Statesman' and other journals very often concerned the
political side of it. Nevertheless he wrote to a friend
in 1917: 'Like you, I have no first-rate interest in
politics' (LAB III, 42). The immediate origin of the
novel was an account by Lord Beaverbrook of the career
of Beaverbrook's father, recorded in the 'Journal' on
15-20 August 1919, with the final words, 'It is a great
subject for a novel.' By 9 March 1920 it had become a
novel about the elder Beaverbrook's old age: 'I read "Le
Curé de Campagne" for the death-bed scene at the end.
I shall have a great death-bed scene ... and I want to
stage it with the utmost magnificence'. Another 'Journal'
entry on 5 May recorded further details from Beaverbrook.
A letter to his agent in April said: 'I am thinking about
it very seriously indeed, and I am anxious to get on to
it.... You may take it from me that it is the best idea
I have had for a novel for years and years' (LAB I, 279-
80). The novel was never written but provided the basis
for Part II of 'Lord Raingo'. Part I was drawn to some
extent from the life of Lord Rhondda (D.A. Thomas, 1856-
1918), details of whose career were also provided by
Beaverbrook. Some details are recorded in the 'Journal'
on 23 and 28 January 1925. On 11 May Bennett recorded
getting general political material from Beaverbrook. He
began writing on 13 May and finished on 26 January 1926.
On 12 January he wrote in the 'Journal':

> I was rather depressed about the general 'feel' of the
> end of the book. I fear people (discerning persons)
> may ask: 'What is the book *about*?' and I mayn't be able
> to answer them. I don't know, articulately, what the
> 'idea' of the book is.

Bennett told his literary agent in June 1925 that he
doubted that the novel would do as a serial in the United
States because there was a mistress in it. Later the
'Saturday Evening Post' was interested. 'The "Sat Eve
Post" will buy it if they like the last part', Bennett
wrote to Frank Swinnerton, 'but I know they won't like

the last part.   £3-4,000 gone to pot through my damnable
artistic integrity' (LAB III, 262).   It did not appear
serially in America.   In England Cassell bought it
serially, probably paying £900.   Newman Flower himself
was keen on the novel, but it ended up serially in Beaverbrook's 'Evening Standard', beginning on 20 September.
Bennett wrote to Harriet Cohen about its changing hands:

> Which surprises me, for it is all compact of fornica-
> tory passages.   *I* didn't sell it to the 'Standard'.
> Cassells had bought the serial from me long ago, &
> paid for it, and they, shy of it, have unloaded it
> on to the 'E.S.'.   (LAB III, 256-7)

For two and a half weeks before serial publication the
'Evening Standard', the 'Daily Express', and the 'Sunday
Express' published items on it, mainly raising two questions: who was the original of Lord Raingo? and was it
right for a novelist to depict political figures alive
or dead?   The Rt. Hon. Charles Masterman, friend of
Bennett's and formerly a member of the Government,
wrote to the 'Daily Express' (17 September) to say that
Disraeli had used living political figures in his novels.
A 'reader' of the 'Evening Standard' (18 September) suggested that a prize might be offered for the right answer
to the identity of Raingo.   Other newspapers took up the
issue.   Bennett reported to Miss Cohen that Beaverbrook
was spending £5,000 on advertising, including posters put
about London with Bennett's portrait on them ('horribly
revolting', said Bennett, LAB III, 274) and with the
legend 'Who is "Lord Raingo"?'   For the book, Cassell
paid £1,000 in advance, and George Doran £950.
     Reviewers took extreme stands on the novel, with
regard both to its literary merits and to the issue of
depicting political figures.   Bennett wrote in his 'Journal' on 9 October, after seeing several reviews: 'Better
than I expected, for I had expected a bad press, as there
is no really "lovable" or "pure" character in the book.'
The 'Evening News' (7 October) was shocked by the unrelen-
tingly grim depiction of death and by the slanderous
depiction of political figures.   The 'Daily Mail' (7 October) thought that the disguises were thin, and that the
political part of the novel was the weaker part, sometimes
bordering on farce; the second part was a 'masterly' study
of a dying man.   The 'Westminster Gazette' (7 October)
remarked in a leader on Public Men in Fiction that 'Mr.
Bennett can never fail to tell a deft story' but that he
'has indulged in a naughty literary experiment, and we
hope, on behalf of both politics and fiction, that he will

return at once to the manner of his master - Flaubert'.
The 'Yorkshire Observer' (7 October) regarded the novel
as a 'literary triumph'. The 'Morning Post' (b. 14 October) thought it was 'an admirable study of chicanery alike
in private and in public life'. The 'Daily Mirror' (b. 14
October) found it 'devastatingly brilliant and amusing'.
The 'New Statesman' (16 October) did not think that the
two halves of the book had a genuine connection, and supposed that Bennett wanted to write about two things,
Whitehall from the inside and a man's dying, and made an
artificial link. The book was valuable historically,
although Bennett exaggerated the chicanery. The part on
Raingo's death was not altogether convincing. 'Taken as
a whole, it is not a very good book.' T.P. O'Connor in
'T.P.'s Weekly' (16 October) mainly summarised; he
believed that Bennett had never 'written pages more
poignant' than the ending. L.P. Hartley in the 'Saturday
Review' (16 October) thought that the 140 pages on Raingo's
death were harrowing, but he did not know whether they
were Art; he found the first part of the book trivial.
For other English reviews and for the exchanges between
Bennett and Lord Birkenhead see Nos 114-21. Other reviews
appeared in the 'Daily Despatch' and the 'Yorkshire Post'
(7 October), the 'Sunday Times' (10 October), the 'Glasgow
Evening News' (21 October), the 'Walsall Observer' (30
October), and the 'Bookman' (Christmas). The 'Staffordshire Sentinel' apparently took no notice of the novel
other than to reprint (24 November) Bennett's letter to
the 'Daily Mail' in response to Lord Birkenhead's attack
on him (see No. 121).

Bennett reported in the 'Journal' on 2 August that
George Doran had cabled that readers in America 'acclaim
"L.R." as the peer of the "O.W.T."'. The American dustjacket assured the reader that the novel had 'the scope
and vision of "The Old Wives' Tale"'. The 'Boston Evening
Transcript' (16 October) did not believe it: the novel was
disheartening, 'devoid of idealism', and a sad reflection
on twenty-eight years of authorship. Montgomery Belgion
in the 'Saturday Review of Literature' (16 October) was
somewhat disappointed in Part I but found Part II to be
'one of the remarkable passages in modern fiction, standing beside Mr. Bennett's own famous account of an execution in "The Old Wives' Tale"'. H.I. Brock in the 'New
York Times' (17 October) rejected the comparison with 'The
Old Wives' Tale': the book was merely an 'expert and
interesting record of war-time England as he knew it',
'closely observed and ruthlessly reproduced'. The
'Independent' (16 November) found the first part of the
book 'a wonderful piece of mockery' and the second part

a bit wearisome; but 'Bennett is a great novelist, perhaps
the greatest of his time'.

Newman Flower wrote to Bennett before publication:
'My dear Arnold, "Raingo" is *tremendous*. Unless my judge-
ment is all wrong this will be one of your best selling
novels. I am in raptures about it' (LB). Within ten days
of publication more than 18,400 copies had been sold -
slightly ahead of 'The Pretty Lady' - with 35,000 printed
(in three printings). By mid-June 1927, 30,000 copies
were sold - slightly behind 'The Pretty Lady'. In May
1927 Cassell sent a royalty cheque for £1,082. Sales in
America are unknown. Doran was apparently pessimistic
about sales, and Bennett wrote to him before publication:
'I am never surprised when my books do not sell and always
surprised when they do sell' (RP, 320). For some months
after publication there were efforts made by others to
dramatise the novel. Another edition was issued in 1929
in Cassell's pocket library series. It was also reprinted
in 1931 in 'The Arnold Bennett Omnibus Book' (along with
'Riceyman Steps', Elsie and the Child, and 'Accident'),
and was issued again separately by Cassell in 1968.

'The Woman Who Stole Everything' (1927)

Published on 9 June. Bennett wrote the title story
between 20 July and 11 August 1926. When he was reading
the proof, he recorded in the 'Journal', on 13 February
1927, that he thought the story was 'one of the best I
had ever done'. It appeared serially in 'Story-Teller'
in May 1927, and in 'College Humor' in America in March.
Cassell and 'College Humor' each paid £500 for serial
rights. The other stories in the collection appeared
serially from 1924 to 1927, and included a Five Towns
story, Death, Fire and Life. The 'Daily Express' review
(9 June), which was mainly summary, was headed Modern
Woman Pilloried. Ivor Brown in the 'Manchester Guardian'
(9 June) found most of the stories perfunctory, but Death,
Fire and Life was one of Bennett's very best stories.
The 'Sunday Express' (12 June) was generally enthusiastic,
and found the title story 'healthy satire'. The 'Times
Literary Supplement' (16 June) thought that the title
story was 'extremely interesting' and characteristic of
Bennett; the other stories were not so good. The 'Spectator' (18 June) was generally enthusiastic; the title
story was the best, and it was 'ruthless'. L.P. Hartley
in the 'Saturday Review' (25 June) found most of the
stories frivolous and repetitious. Edwin Muir in the
'Nation and Athenaeum' (July) tried to isolate the

realism-with-commentary that seemed to him to mark
Bennett's method: 'the economy, the selection, the power
of suggestion in these stories are remarkable ...; his
skill here is so extraordinary as to have all the appearance of nature.' In America the 'New York Times' (24
April) found pleasure in the stories: they represented
an ingenious, amusing, and up-to-date survivor; 'the
Bennett of "The Old Wives' Tale" and "Hilda Lessways"
is dead'. 'Outlook' in a brief notice (8 June) was
amused. The 'Saturday Review of Literature' (16 July)
found some of the stories dull, but other stories offered
'a flash of the real Bennett, the incomparable Bennett'.
The best story was Death, Fire and Life: 'no one with a
feeling for mankind will read it without being moved
toward tears'. Gerald Gould in the 'Living Age' (1 July)
gave most of his space to caustic comment on some aspects
of Bennett's method and material, including - it would
appear - an allusion to Bennett's marriage as a source
for the title story. But though the stories were slight,
'there is brilliance in the way they are told'. On 24
June - thirteen days after publication in England -
Bennett reported in his 'Journal' that Cassell had 'sold
548 copies last week - over 12,000 copies in all....
So that I was rather pleased'. No further edition is
known.

'The Strange Vanguard' (1928)

Published on 26 January. Bennett began writing on 8 February 1926. In a letter to his nephew Richard in February
he described the novel as 'sensational and yet sociological' (LN, 160). In a 'Journal' entry on 10 June he
expressed doubt that it was any better than 'The Ghost',
which he was re-reading. 'Neither of them is more than
a fantastic lark, nor pretends to be more'. The 'Journal'
on 8 July reads:

> I finished 'The Vanguard' today at 4:15, having written
> 5500 words of it in two days. I began the work on 8th
> February in Rome; it was very seriously interrupted by
> the birth of Virginia, and I wrote the 10 or 12,000
> words of it all over afresh, and I'm glad I did it.
> I wrote the last two-thirds of it here in Amberley
> in 44 days. I have never worked more easily than
> during the last six weeks.

It appeared serially in the 'Pall Mall Magazine' beginning
in May 1927, and in 'College Humor' beginning in October.

Cassell paid £900 for serial rights and £1,000 in advance
on the book. 'College Humor' paid £1,029 ($5,000), Doran
£944. Doran published his edition in the autumn of 1927.
The English book title was altered to 'The Strange Vanguard' because Allen & Unwin issued a novel called 'The
Vanguard' in the autumn.

The 'Daily Express' (26 January) regarded the book as
light entertainment, and not the best. The 'Times Literary Supplement' (26 January) was enthusiastic: superior
people might not approve of the book, but the majority
of Bennett's readers enjoyed his fantasias 'because they
are so unashamedly English, so definitely boyish, so
cheerfully middle-class and so magnificently ridiculous'.
A.S. Wallace in the 'Manchester Guardian' (27 January)
found 'dashes of acidity' that kept it 'from cloying to
the point of surfeit'. The 'New Statesman' (28 January)
found much in the novel that was 'adroit and lively',
'amusing and delightful', but was scathing about its
snobbism, superficiality, and the contempt of its author
for the popular audience to whom it was addressed. The
'Spectator' (28 January) found it 'a comedy that is full
of amusing situations, but is even more delightful for the
wit and incisiveness with which Mr. Bennett illuminates
the interplay of the masculine and feminine mind'.
Rebecca West in 'T.P.'s Weekly' (4 February) was indulgent
and sardonic in turn and at some length; the novel was
clever and amusing and satirical, and she wondered when
Bennett would get around to writing 'an authentic satire
on the Grand Babylon instead of a series of aimless
extravaganzas'; she thought Bennett wrote about women 'as
if he had last seen a woman in 1885'; as a fellow North-
erner she felt even stronger contempt than Bennett for
the decadent South. Edwin Muir in the 'Nation and Athenaeum' (4 February) was appalled by the general unbeliev-
ability of the material and by the indiscriminate admiration that Bennett seemed to have for the odd assortment
of characters. The 'Sunday Express' (5 February) thought
that it was a very merry satire on wealth and the wealthy.
Edward Shanks in the 'London Mercury' (March) thought that
the book was 'smoothly and intricately contrived' and
somewhat 'cloying'. In America Percy Hutchinson in the
'New York Times' (11 December) was pleased: it was
'shrewd, mellow, whimsical, humorous, witty'. The
'Nation' in the briefest of notices (14 December) said
that it was 'a tosh-tosh piece of hammock fiction. Mr.
Bennett is the man who once wrote a book called "The Old
Wives' Tale"'. Parker Tyler in a brief notice in the
'Bookman' (February 1928) called it 'fourth class entertainment'. The Literary Guild picked up the book in

America and paid £1,460 for it. Bennett wrote to his
second wife on 9 March 1928, when he was writing his play
'The Return Journey': 'I must say I can see nothing whatever against my writing things like "The Vanguard" quite
apart I mean from finance. I *will not* always be writing
grave and gloomy plays' (ABP, 326). No further editions
are known.

'The Savour of Life' (1928)

Published on 10 May. This collection of material was
of the same character as the three preceding 'Things
That Have Interested Me'. Bennett put it together in
July 1927. Cassell published it in England. The 'Daily
Express' (10 May) offered summary and praise. A.S. Wallace in the 'Manchester Guardian' (14 May) found the
pieces pleasant, lively, sometimes pugnacious. The
'Spectator' (12 May) said it was 'good journalism',
possessing 'wisdom' and 'good taste'. The 'New Statesman'
in a brief notice (19 May) was sardonic about the fascinating material and the assertive style. The 'Saturday
Review' (26 May) was scathing: the book almost convinced
one that Bennett was a philistine 'in spite of his dazzling achievements in creative literature'; moreover 'the
book is flung together'. The 'Times Literary Supplement'
(31 May) saw Bennett as a kindly schoolmaster in the book,
and was pleased. Rose Macaulay in 'T.P.'s Weekly' (2
June) recited some of the agreeable details. The 'London
Mercury' in a brief notice (July) liked the pieces by
Bennett the novelist (writing on Russian fiction) and did
not like those by Bennett the journalist (writing on discontented youth). Robert Blatchford in a column of book
gossip in 'T.P.'s Weekly' (22 September) quarrelled with
Bennett's view that new novels are more important than
old. In America the 'Boston Evening Transcript' (17
March) found the pieces interesting, candid, and light,
the 'New Republic' (18 April) was slightly bored, the
'Nation' (2 May) was bored to tears, and the 'New York
Times' (17 June) was agreeably entertained.

'Mediterranean Scenes' (1928)

Published in November. Bennett sailed in the Mediterranean on Otto Kahn's yacht in April and May 1927. The
trip came as an interlude in the writing of the novel
'Accident'. During the trip he wrote a portion of a private novel called 'Arthur' that has never been seen.

He wrote in the 'Journal' on 19 April: 'I decided the form
of my cruise articles, namely the disjointed note form –
rather like Taine's "Notes sur l'Angleterre".' He wrote
to his second wife on 10 May, describing his day's work:
'I have ... written 1300 words of my beautiful impressions
de voyage' (ABP, 309). The material began appearing in
the 'Sunday Express' on 24 July 1927. The 'Express'
apparently paid £500 for it. Cassell published the book
only in two limited editions, a special edition of twenty-
five copies and a limited edition of 1,000 copies. Very
likely the contract was for half-profit, as it was with
the limited edition of 'Elsie and the Child' that Cassell
issued in 1929. The book was not published in America,
where George Doran was merging his firm with Doubleday to
form Doubleday, Doran. Bennett wrote to his agent about
the rejection by Doubleday, Doran:

> I cannot understand it. I think that this is a pretty
> good book, and such is general informed opinion of it
> here. I have always been supposed to be rather good
> at travel stuff. At the worst the book is very read-
> able. It makes a volume pleasing to the eye, and
> Flower told me today that he fully expects to sell
> the edition out. (LAB I, 386)

The one known review, in the 'Times Literary Supplement'
(17 January 1929), was slight and caustic, and noted
errors of historical and geographical fact.

'Accident' (1929)

Published on 10 January. The origin of the novel lay with
an accident Bennett had on a train in France on 7 July
1911. The account is recorded in the 'Journal' the
following day and also in a letter to Jane Wells (LAB II,
285-6). The 'Journal' entry was reproduced fairly exactly
as Railway Accident at Mantes in the 'Cambridge Review' on
22 October 1920, and excited attention in the national
press, the 'Daily Express' on 25 October reporting Famous
Author's Escape. It was reprinted the following year in
'Things That Have Interested Me'. On 30 October 1926
Bennett wrote in the 'Journal':

> I began to think more seriously about the plan of my
> new novel. I had already got the moral background for
> it: the dissatisfaction of a successful and rich man
> with his own secret state of discontent and with the
> evils of the age. I wanted a frame. I walked about

three miles this morning, and about a mile after tea,
without getting a really satisfactory idea; then as I
was lolling in my 'easy' about 6:30, I suddenly thought
that I would extend the role of the *train de luxe*,
which I had thought of for the scene of the opening
of the story, to be the scene of the whole of the novel
- so that the entire time-space of the novel will only
be about thirty hours or so.

Bennett began writing on 26 November 1926 and finished on
19 July 1927, with an interruption of nearly two months
for his Mediterranean cruise. He wrote to his nephew
Richard on 3 January 1927: 'No one will read it, as it is
unlike any other novel I have written' (LN, 179). He
wrote in his 'Journal' on 9 March: 'It seemed to me to be
sound and interesting; of course, old-fashioned - at least
I suppose so.' On 8 June he reported being 'rather
pleased' with the second part of the novel. Beaverbrook
bought the serial rights from Cassell for £2,250, Cassell
having bought them from Bennett for £1,000. Bennett and
Cassell split the difference. The serial began in the
'Daily Express' on 16 July under the title 'Train de
Luxe'. In the course of serialisation about eight letters
from readers were published expressing pleasure in the
tale, and a couple expressing pain. Cassell advanced
£1,250 on the novel. Bennett's agent tried to get a
royalty rising to 30 per cent, but Bennett told him it
would not be fair. Doubleday, Doran advanced £950.

'Accident' seemed to provide occasion for more critics
than usual to dilate upon the varying quality of Bennett's
work. The 'Times Literary Supplement' (10 January)
offered a scathing summary of the novel. The 'Daily
Express' (10 January) admired one 'extraordinarily brilliant' description and 'three or four deeper things' but
warned the reader that it was not a masterpiece. Rachel
Annand Taylor in the 'Spectator' (12 January) found it
'facile', 'sentimental', and unbelievable; she resented
Bennett's millionaires, his spoiled girls, his preoccupation with luxury. The 'Sunday Express' (13 January) was 'faintly bored'. 'Punch' (16 January) called
the book a 'masterly trifle', finding the technique
'attractively archaic' ('a study of the conjugal relations
of three couples running quietly across its vehemence of
episode') but enjoying 'the merriment, vivacity and human
discernment'. Dilys Powell in 'T.P.'s Weekly' (19 January) thought that 'the whole point of the book is the
succession of moods and emotions brought by the circumstances of an adventurous journey to play upon this solid
yet sensitive mind'; 'the book is curiously slick and

direct; it makes diverting reading'. Lyn Ll. Irvin in the
'Nation and Athenaeum' (19 January) said: 'The guiding
imagination of Mr. Bennett fumbles.' An unusually large
advertisement in the 'Times Literary Supplement' on 24
January quoted admiration from the 'Daily Mail', the
'Evening Standard', the 'Daily Chronicle', the 'Morning
Post', the 'Daily News', the 'Dundee Courier', the 'Yorkshire Post', the 'Western Mail', and 'Country Life': 'on
every page there is something to arrest the attention';
'Mr. Bennett has a genius for being interesting'; 'there
is close and penetrating observation'; 'on almost every
page ... there is a surprise'; 'Mr. Bennett in one of his
joyous moods'; 'well calculated to keep the reader on
tiptoe with expectation'; 'infinitely rich in wit and
humanity'; 'a magnificent achievement'; 'a gem of a
book, a talisman against winter, tedium, worry, insomnia'.
The 'Bookman' (February) offered effusive praise. The
'London Mercury' (March) found the book 'not worthy of
Mr. Bennett even in his lighter mood', but singled out
for praise 'an exquisitely real and thrilling picture of
a night-journey, such as no one else could have made'.
For three other English reviews see Nos 122-4.
   In America the 'New York Times' (13 January) admired
the heroic English spirit of the old soldier Bennett still
marching on, but had to admit there would not be another
'Hilda Lessways'. 'Accident' was a good tale, told with
gusto. 'Outlook and Independent' (16 January) regarded
the novel as 'a delicate necklace of observation, keen,
witty, and tender'. The 'Saturday Review of Literature'
(16 February) was thoroughly entertained. Sales in
America to May 1929 were 17,800, and in September Doubleday, Doran paid royalties of £900. In September Cassell
paid royalties of £400. No later editions are known other
than its collection in 'The Arnold Bennett Omnibus Book'
in 1931.

'The Religious Interregnum' (1929)

Published in March. In 1925 Bennett wrote an article
What I Believe that initiated a series of such articles
by well-known authors. The series ran in the 'Daily
Express' and elicited a good deal of correspondence, some
of it very angry and most of directed at Bennett, who
began his essay by saying that Christian dogma did not
enter into his life at all or into the lives of most of
his friends and acquaintances. One of the temperate responses was by the Bishop of Liverpool. Two years later
the Bishop of Liverpool came to see Bennett. 'Wanted me

to contribute to a series of little books which will be
meant to show some sort of design, order, divine origin
in the world' ('Journal', 26 July 1927). Bennett wrote
the book between 16 September and 20 October 1928. In
a letter to his nephew Richard on 25 September he said:
'I know nothing about God or the Holy Ghost or anything.
This gives me a marked advantage over religious writers
and experts' (LN, 237). The book was issued by Ernest
Benn. It provoked a response from Dean Inge in the
'Evening Standard' (27 March), who wondered why Bennett
wrote the book: he himself had not offered to the world
his views on Bach and Beethoven. He also thought Bennett
need not have chosen to visit an ugly dissenting chapel
to obtain some notion of the present state of religious
worship. Bennett's reply (3 April) is reprinted in LAB
III, 322-3. The 'Times Literary Supplement' (25 April)
took brief notice of the book, mainly to summarise.
H.G. Wells wrote to Bennett on 6 May to say that he
liked the book but did not approve of the ethics of Jesus
as Bennett did.

'Piccadilly' (1929)

Published in March. There were attempts to film Bennett's
novels as early as 1913, and during the war films were
made of 'The Great Adventure', 'Milestones', and 'The
Grand Babylon Hotel'. In the 1920s Bennett did a considerable amount of writing for films (see pp. 134-6). The
most successful of it was 'Piccadilly'. The idea was
supplied in the first instance by British International
Pictures, and Bennett wrote two scripts, writing all day
on 14 April 1928 to produce the first one. He then wrote
the second, and from it or from them both composed a
17,000-word film story in two weeks, finishing on 24 May.
He wrote in his 'Journal' on that date: 'This has been the
most strenuous fortnight I've had for years.' Bennett
was paid £2,000. The film story was published serially
in 'Film Weekly' (beginning 22 October) who paid Bennett
£300. He did some work on the subtitles for the film,
which was silent. The first performance of the film,
which starred Anna May Wong, Gilda Grey, and Jameson
Thomas, was on 30 January 1929. For Bennett's comments
on the film see LAB I, 389-90; in a letter to Harriet
Cohen on 8 February he said that it was having 'a great
success at the Carlton Theatre' (LAB III, 320). The 'New
Statesman' (16 February) described the film as clever and
fast moving, with good subtitles. It was mentioned
favourably in Paul Rotha's 'The Film Till Now' (1930) and

James Agate's 'Around Cinema' (second series, 1948). No
reviews of the published book are known. It was issued
by the Readers Library.

'Journal, 1929' (1930)

Published in June. Bennett kept a regular journal from
1896 onwards, and also a variety of extra journals for
special subjects, purposes, and occasions. Material from
these journals appeared in the Christmas books, 1906-7,
in the three series of 'Things That Have Interested Me'
in the 1920s, in 'Methuen's Annual' and 'From the Log of
the *Velsa*', 1914, in the 'Bookman' (New York) and the
'Criterion', 1927-8, in 'Life and Letters', 1929, and
elsewhere. In 1928 an American named Crosby Gaige
negotiated with Bennett for a limited edition of a volume
of the journal, with a view to publishing further volumes,
but it fell through. On the basis of the material in
'Life and Letters', the 'Daily Telegraph' offered £1,000
for 40,000 words. Some of the material Bennett provided
came from the regular journal for 1928, but it had been
considerably changed in tone and character. The regular
journal for 1929 (unpublished as yet) bears little resemblance to 'Journal, 1929'. The 'Daily Telegraph' sold the
material to the 'Daily Mail', where it began appearing on
17 March 1930 as Arnold Bennett's Journal. Cassell paid
£400 in advance on book royalties of 20 per cent rising
to 25 after the sale of 3,500 copies. In America the book
was issued by Doubleday, Doran under the title 'Journal
of Things New and Old', a change made without Bennett's
permission and causing him some anger.
     Robert Ellis Roberts in the 'New Statesman' (14 June)
was sardonic about its superficiality. The 'Spectator'
(21 June) found in it the same immense interest in ordinary things that the reviewer had seen in one of the
Christmas gift-books many years earlier. The 'Times
Literary Supplement' (31 July) was caustic. George
Rylands in the 'Nation and Athenaeum' (9 August) found
the book slight but entertaining; it was not 'The Old
Wives' Tale', but the mark of 'the born novelist is on
every page'. In America the 'New York Times' (7 September) said: 'It is only when a man like Arnold Bennett
opens our eyes to the life-richness of small things that
we realise how persistently blind we mostly are'. H.W.
Boynton in the 'Saturday Review of Literature' (27 September) thought that Bennett was blind: 'when a man learns
to write twenty-four hours a day, he condemns himself to
be a sort of recording machine'. The 'Bookman' (October)

thought that the book was altogether too self-conscious,
superficial, and professional: 'the gifted amateur alone
can keep a good journal'.

'Imperial Palace' (1930)

Published on 9 October. 'Imperial Palace' has always
divided Bennett's critics. It devoted itself to a world
of wealth and idleness that many of his critics had
deplored in his work for a decade or more, but it did
so on a scale that implied more than the frivolities of
'Mr. Prohack' or 'The Strange Vanguard'. It was his
longest novel, a fifth again as long as 'The Old Wives'
Tale', it had some eighty characters in it, and it displayed a mass of consciously acquired information such
as no earlier novel had demanded of him. Over the years
the question of his genius took two forms: could he write
greatly about anything besides the Five Towns? could he
write greatly about the modern world as well as one past?
'The Pretty Lady' and 'Lord Raingo' established a certain
cleverness, perhaps brilliance, in dealing with aspects
of the modern world, and 'Riceyman Steps' offered a surprising example of his being able to take a corner of life
about which he was supposed to know little and make a fine
novel of it. But all the while he was getting older, and
the intimate life that was in his bones from the Five
Towns was slipping away, and young authors and critics
seemed increasingly to believe that his sense of the
modern world was narrow.
     The origins of the novel lay, nevertheless, with
Bennett's earliest writing. Gracie Savott, the advanced
woman of the novel, had many earlier incarnations, going
back to a story called The Advanced Woman published in
1893. The restaurant scenes of the novel similarly went
back to the story Restaurant Spooks of the same year. The
microcosm of the Imperial Palace went back to 'Hugo' and
'The Grand Babylon Hotel' and also to a projected novel
about hotel life referred to in a letter of 1914 (see LAB
I, 256). On 31 December 1920 Bennett had his New Year's
Eve dinner at the Savoy Hotel, and made notes about it for
use in 'Mr. Prohack', in which there is a dinner at the
Grand Babylon Hotel. A letter to his nephew Richard a few
days later said:
     The New Year's Eve dinner at the Savoy was the noisi-
     est, vulgarest, costliest thing of the sort I ever had
     anything to do with. I had scarcely imagined there
     were so many people in London with so much money and
     so little taste. However, I got all the material I

wanted, and I had 2 gifted young creatures to dance
with. (LN, 47)

In February 1924 he was shown over the Savoy by members of
the staff, one of whom, Richmond Temple, had been a friend
for some years. On 14 March 1927 Bennett wrote in his
'Journal':

> Lunch with Richmond Temple in a private room at the
> Savoy.... I wanted to get from Temple a few general
> ideas about hotel management here and on the continent,
> so that I could decide whether it would be practicable,
> artistically or otherwise, for me to write a 'big'
> novel with a hotel organism, or two hotel organisms,
> as environment, and probably a hotel manager as hero.
> Temple has imagination and he abounds in general ideas
> and in 90 minutes or less he gave me all the ideas I
> wanted, and I practically decided to write the book.

On 10 March a year later he wrote there:

> George Doran came to lunch, and after lunch in my
> study he began talking about the idea he had given me
> last year for a novel based on the tragic life of
> Ernest Hodder-Williams. I said I liked it, but
> couldn't handle it yet, as I was more attracted by
> a scheme for a realistic novel about a big luxury
> hotel. Then I saw that I might combine the two
> schemes and that one would strengthen the other.
> From that moment I seemed to see my next novel as
> a complete entity.

In September 1929 he stayed at the Savoy, inspecting it
and making extensive notes. He began writing on 25 September. He expected the novel would be 150,000 words,
and it proved to be 243,000. He finished on 5 July 1930.
An entry in 'Journal, 1929' dated 25 September', gave a
perhaps coloured view of his conception:

> I know the three chief characters, but by no means all
> the ins and outs of them. They won't alter - I would
> never allow any character to get the whiphand of me -
> but I shall fill them out. I know the 'feel' of the
> novel. That won't alter either.

Letters to his nephew Richard recorded the progress of
the work: at the end of October, 'it may be rotten'; in
late November he thought that the shareholders scene
might be something never done before, but he was not

certain it was interesting; in mid-December, 'it does not seem to me to be as good as it ought to be'; in the following April, 'I am now getting rather tired of writing about hotels' (LN, 277, 279, 281, 296). According to Reginald Pound, the unpublished journal for 1929-30 recorded unusual physical and domestic upsets in the course of the writing (RP, 337). Cassell advanced £1,187 or slightly more on the book, and Doubleday, Doran presumably advanced £950.

In August, before publication, Hugh Walpole wrote in the 'New York Herald Tribune' that the novel was about the Savoy. Bennett wrote to him:

> I shall ... be glad if you will recall your dread statement in your next article. It is quite true that I have obtained a very large part of my material from the Savoy people, who were all told that I wanted the stuff for a novel. But the novel is not about the Savoy. It is about a larger and a different hotel, situated in Birdcage Walk, a hotel with a history of its own: The Imperial Palace. (LAB III, 338)

Bennett also cabled to Doubleday, Doran to ask them to deny the assertion. Presently he wrote to the managing director of the Savoy to say that though there was of necessity a grill-room manager in the novel, members of the Savoy staff should not imagine that he was the grill-room manager of the Savoy, and so forth. A few days later Bennett was shown the dustjacket for the American edition, and on it was a picture of the Savoy. 'I was furious. I really was ...; it was absolutely monstrous', he wrote to George Doran, who apparently had suggested the dustjacket and then had left the firm before Bennett's cable to Doubleday arrived. (See LAB III, 338-41, and RP, 352-4, for all the correspondence.)

Bennett wrote in his journal that he was 'nervous about its reception' (RP, 352). He wrote to George Doran on the day of publication that a leading London bookseller 'has written to me out of the blue saying that he was immensely taken by it, and that it will be a great success. Well it may or may not' (RP, 354). Reviews ranged from ecstasy to amused scorn. The 'Times Literary Supplement' (9 October) was generally sardonic: Bennett aimed to capitalise on the present fashion for long novels, and his object seemed to be not to tell a story but to describe the workings of a hotel. The 'Evening Standard' (9 October) was very much of the same opinion, and thought that 'the book staggers under the weight of this mass of detail'. Robert Ellis Roberts in the 'New Statesman' (11 October)

was not certain that Bennett understood aright that love
and art are the only important things in life, but the
conflict between love and work in the novel was developed
in marvellous detail, with impressive characterisation.
Roberts thought that 'this book will take first place
among his novels as a feat of construction'. Gerald Gould
in the 'Observer' (12 October) said: 'The book is not the
one I should have chosen for Mr. Bennett to write; but
oddly, this author, in his wilful way, has kept for himself the choice of what books to write.' Gould did not
much care for the two heroines or for the millionaires.
'The real hero of the book is the hotel: its real qualities are the sustained descriptive brilliance, the
liveliness, the inexhaustible inquisitive interest, the
power of vision and stroke, which go to make the lesser
half of Mr. Bennett.' Gould also said in the 'Daily
Herald' (b. 16 October): 'What a vast achievement, at
once staggering and dazzling!' The 'Birmingham Post'
in a brief review (14 October) said: '"Imperial Palace"
is magnificent in conception, superb in construction, and
Mr. Bennett's greatest achievement. It holds the reader's
interest to the very end. What more can be said?' The
'Staffordshire Sentinel' (14 October) gave as much space
to its heading, 'Arnold Bennett's latest. Vivid characters', as it gave to the review, which described the book
in a few lines as long and impressive. Sheila Kaye-Smith
in the 'Sunday Express' (19 October) said she did not like
long books, but she liked this long book; in fact it was
'stupendous'. The 'Bystander' (b. 23 October) thought
that the book was 'as fresh and young as anything he has
written'. The 'Sunday Referee' (b. 23 October) regarded
it as 'one of the most enjoyable social documents of our
time'. Kathleen Tomlinson in the 'Nation and Athenaeum'
(1 November) was not inclined to be interested in the
world that the novel described, but she found herself
interested, and she professed to be awestruck by the
'magnitude' of the book. 'Punch' (12 November) found the
novel lively and entertaining and supposed that Arnold
Bennett could run a hotel as well as Evelyn Orcham. For
H.G. Wells's opinion and other English reviews see Nos
125-32.

In America several booksellers sent letters expressing
their enthusiasm to Bennett (see RP, 359). The reviews
were sometimes unkind. The 'New York Times' (23 November)
wondered why Bennett combined the study of a luxury hotel
with the study of a businessman in love, but thought the
result reasonably interesting. Henry Williamson in the
'Saturday Review of Literature' (6 December) said that
'"Imperial Palace" can justly rank itself in Mr. Bennett's

consciousness as the most balanced, most "human" thing he
has done.... "Imperial Palace" reveals the real Arnold
Bennett: benevolent, sensitive, understanding, and
lovable'. 'Outlook and Independent' (17 December) thought
that 'with "Imperial Palace" the Arnold Bennett of the
early Five Towns tales returns' and that it 'will fill
your evenings pleasantly for a fortnight'. George
Dangerfield in the 'Bookman' (February 1931) described the
book as a 'faultless piece of literary ingenuity with
scarcely any virtues at all'; '"Imperial Palace" proves
once and for all that Arnold Bennett neither was nor is
nor ever will be a great novelist'.

Counting English and American sales together, the novel
was Bennett's best seller. The first English printing was
21,000 copies, of which 14,000 were sold in the first two
weeks. (There was also a signed edition in two volumes,
limited to 100 sets.) In America, where it was published
at the end of October, sales reached 22,000 by Christmas,
and it was near the top of the best seller list briefly.
The Book of the Month Club arranged to take up the book
at the end of February and distribute 70,000 to 80,000
copies in connection with a subscription scheme, paying
Bennett and his agent ten cents on each copy. The novel
was occasionally in the news in London in later years.
In February 1939 the chief of the meat-buying department
at the Savoy celebrated his fiftieth wedding anniversary,
and the 'Sunday Express' (12 February) described him as
the original for Mr Craddock in the novel. On 29 May 1941
Sir George Reeves-Smith, managing director of the Savoy,
died, and his connection with Evelyn Orcham was noted.
When the novel was reissued by Cassell in 1962, Richard
Lister in the 'Evening Standard' (30 January) said that
'it rides buoyantly above time'. Cassell issued a ninth
edition in 1971.

'The Night Visitor' (1931)

Published in October. Bennett wrote the title story in
February 1929. Most of the others appeared serially in
1927-30. Among them was The Cornet-Player, written in
1925 and regarded by Bennett at the time as 'the most
original story I have ever written' ('Journal', 11 November 1925). The 'Times Literary Supplement' (15 October)
said: 'There is nobody who fills his particular vacancy,
nobody with his peculiar combination of knowingness, simplicity, whimsicality, matter-of-factness, sentiment and
disillusionment; nobody, in fine, who can write a story
such as The Cornet-Player.' The reviewer also singled

out The Wind for praise. The 'Daily Express' (16 October)
thought that the stories displayed Bennett's characteristic qualities: 'a craftsman of extraordinary competence
and a man whose zest for life was never extinguished by
the contemplation of its frequent triviality'. The
reviewer mentioned The Wind for its excellence. The 'New
Statesman and Nation' (7 November) thought that Bennett
did not understand cruelty or certain sides of the imaginative life: 'But how many things there were he did understand! How many people he saw happily, whimsically, with
that shrewd, personal critical intelligence that is shown
again and again in these tales.' J.B. Priestley in the
'Evening Standard' (16 June 1932) found the stories slight
but readable. In America the 'New York Times' (8 November
1931) thought that the stories showed Bennett's superficial knowledge of life, but they were workmanlike and
readable. The 'Saturday Review of Literature' (16 January
1932) found the stories rather bad, and yet to some degree
they testified 'to a great personality' who brought
'extraordinary warmth to life' and who had done 'more for
English fiction than almost any other half dozen writers
you could mention'.

'Dream of Destiny and Venus Rising from the Sea' (1932)

Published in June. Bennett wrote to his agent on 19 September 1930 about 'Dream of Destiny':

> I am already very keen on my next novel, and the scheme
> of it is complete. I shall begin it in December and it
> will be finished - I think - about May. It is based
> on the plot of the story The Dream.... If I had seen
> the possibilities of that plot earlier I should never
> have squandered it on a short story. (LAB I, 407)

He began the novel on 25 November and left off writing on
26 December to go to France for three weeks. There he
contracted the typhoid fever from which he died in March
1931. Dorothy Cheston Bennett wrote an account of the
novel for the 'Bookman' (New York, September 1932). Venus
Rising from the Sea was a long story written in April-May
1929. It appeared in 'Story-Teller' in November 1930,
and in the 'Woman's Home Companion' in three instalments
beginning in May 1931. It was issued separately by
Cassell in 1931 in a limited edition of 350 copies, with
drawings by E. McKnight Kauffer. Cassell paid 15 per cent
royalty on it. Terms of contract for the 1932 volume are
unknown. James Agate in the 'Daily Express' (16 June)

said that 'Dream of Destiny' was 'in Bennett's poorest
vein', and Venus Rising from the Sea was 'a lovely story'.
The 'Times Literary Supplement' (16 June) merely took
note of its appearance. L.A.G. Strong in the 'Spectator'
(18 June) recalled 'that greatly underrated novel "The
Pretty Lady"' and thought that 'Dream of Destiny' was of
the same character if not as good. 'The early chapters
have the old gusto and love of detail.' The 'New Statesman' in a brief notice said that 'Arnold Bennett's romanticism shines and is buoyant in this last book'; 'Dream
of Destiny' had 'a rare lightness and gaiety' and Venus
Rising from the Sea was 'charming'. In America the title
was 'Stroke of Luck and Dream of Destiny'. The 'New York
Times' (22 May) and the 'Saturday Review of Literature'
(11 June) regarded both pieces as light and agreeable
entertainment.

'The Journals of Arnold Bennett' (1932-3)

Published in three volumes, I, 1896-1910, May 1932; II,
1911-21, November 1932; III, 1921-8, May 1933. On the
origin, various kinds, and miscellaneous publication of
part of the journals, see pp. 34 and 110. The material
published in 1932-3 was presumably drawn entirely from
the regular journal, and constituted about one-third of
the whole of that journal. It included nothing from the
last years, 1929, 1930, and 1931, and nothing from a
volume covering a portion of 1906-7. Excerpts from the
1932-3 collection appeared serially in the 'Daily Express'
(18-30 November 1932) and in America in the 'Saturday
Review of Literature' (14 May 1932) and, with some differences, the 'Yale Review' (September 1932). Small differences occured between English and American editions,
mainly or wholly relating to the problems of libel. Each
volume as it appeared was widely reviewed on both sides of
the Atlantic. Some reviewers found the volumes trivial
and dull. Others found that Bennett had written another
great book. The excerpts below are from the three reviews
by E.F. Benson in the 'Spectator' (4 June and 25 November
1932 and 12 May 1933).

This record of his earlier years is far more interesting than the section he himself published in 1929. It
is fresher and hungrier, and whether he writes of the
conversation he had with an apparently idiotic yokel,
the dancing of Adeline Genée, the price of rooms at the
Strand Hotel, his own bilious attacks (indeed, his
description of a bilious attack is the most vivid piece

of writing in the book) he brings to them all his illimitable appetite. Of really intimate revelations there are almost none: his engagement, for instance, to Eleanor Green he tells us took place at five p.m. on June 15th, 1906, and it was broken off at eleven a.m. on August 3rd; but of the history of this engagement and of the cause of its termination there is nothing....

Life was a perpetual banquet to him, and for this feast he had the appetite of a *gourmand* and the appreciation of a *gourmet*, and out of the very multiplicity of these trivialities there emerges the figure of himself with a curiosity ever alert.... He had the same unappeasable gusto for life as Pepys, and though he gives us no intimate glimpses of himself we get to know him through his endless observation of other people. He never grew up. His appetite remained as capacious and as experimental as a boy's.

We know more about the general conduct of his days and the less intimate thoughts that occupied his mind than we know about those of any other man in the whole history of the world with the possible exception of Samuel Pepys.... It is all trivial, but the triviality is its importance; each detail is like a stitch on some immense tapestry, from the innumerable multitude of which the picture emerges, and shows us a man to whom nothing human was alien, and who had the supreme quality of enjoying himself enormously. Of just such quality was Pepys, who 'has chattered himself into the circle of the immortals' by means of it. Arnold Bennett was already the author of a masterpiece, 'Old Wives' Tale', but who shall say whether these jottings do not confirm his right there more than all the 365,000 words that he wrote every year...?

In 1954 Penguin issued a one-volume selection, with an introduction by Frank Swinnerton. A later edition by Penguin, 1971, which remains in print, had additions from the 1906-7 journal and the Florentine journal. In 1967 Chatto & Windus issued 'Florentine Journal', with illustrations by Bennett. Portions of this journal had been published in the 'Criterion', December 1927 and January and February 1928, and in the 'Bookman', November and December 1927.

THE PLAYS

For a few years early in the century Bennett was the very
model of a successful playwright. From 1908 to 1913 he
had five plays on the London stage. The first two, 'Cupid
and Commonsense' and 'What the Public Wants',were each a
succès d'estime; the third, 'The Honeymoon', had a fairly
good run; and the last two, 'Milestones' (written with
Edward Knoblock) and 'The Great Adventure', were commercial triumphs. Each of the latter two ran for more than
600 performances. Round the world in 1913 there were
2,700 performances of Bennett plays. Then came the war,
and although Bennett wrote one play just prior to it and
two plays during it, his work was not seen again in the
West End until 1918. Before his death he wrote nine more
full-length plays, and most of them were produced, but
only two were at all well received. His last play, written in 1929, remained unproduced and unpublished. All the
same, he could write to Lord Beaverbrook in 1925 that even
in a bad year he could expect 400 performances of his
plays somewhere.
    Bennett began his dramatic career as a theatre critic.
Writing in 1908 in his Preface to 'Cupid and Commonsense'
he recounted his beginnings:

> For five years I was dramatic critic for several London
> papers in turn, and in this capacity I attended nearly
> every first night from 1895 to 1900. I count several
> West End theatrical managers and leading actors among
> my friends, and I have talked at great length with
> them....

Such attention to theatre would seem preoccupation in anyone but Bennett, and only a somewhat lesser degree of
attention marked the rest of his life. It extended to
his marrying two women who themselves possessed considerable theatrical ambitions. He wrote about the theatre on
many occasions. The Preface to 'Cupid and Commonsense' is
a brief but serious review of contemporary conditions of
playwriting and play-producing in London. An interview in
the 'Standard' (3 October 1911) and a self-written interview in the 'Star' (30 July 1914) comment on his plays.
'The Author's Craft' (1915) devotes one of its four sections to Writing Plays. In 1921 he wrote a series of six
articles on the theatre for the 'Daily Express'. And
there are dozens of individual pieces of journalism over
the years that attest to his continuing interest and knowledge. Some of them are gathered in the several collections of his essays and reviews. Also important to note

was his co-directorship of the Lyric Hammersmith with
Nigel Playfair and Alistair Tayler in the last dozen years
of his life. He and Playfair were largely responsible for
the great success of that theatre in the 1920s, notably
with the productions there of Gay's 'Beggar's Opera'
(adapted by Bennett and running for three years), 'The
Cherry Orchard', and 'The Way of the World'.

Nevertheless it is apparent that the theatre was of
secondary importance to him both personally and profes-
sionally. In 'The Author's Craft' he observes that it is
easier to write plays than novels: 'On the average, one
may say that it takes six plays to make the matter of a
novel.' Such an assertion was intended to raise hackles,
and it did, in spite of the good sense with which it was
argued. Along with other comments there and elsewhere
that plays are less subtle than novels, that stage technique is crude, and that actors and actresses and managers
mainly behave like children, it established a certain condescension. What follows here is a bare outline of
Bennett's playwriting and of the reception of those plays
that were produced. All the plays that ran in the West
End were widely reviewed in the daily press, and most of
the plays so produced were published. Few reviews are
known of the plays as published. During Bennett's lifetime there were only the slightest attempts to review the
general body of his playwriting, notably by William Lyon
Phelps in the 'New York Times' (22 January 1921) and
Edward Shanks in 'Outlook' (see p. 126). Darton devoted
a few pages to the plays in his book on Bennett in 1915,
revised in 1924. Studies of Bennett since his death have
given scant attention to the plays. The best account of
them is by Georges Lafourcade, 'Arnold Bennett', 1939.

Most of Bennett's early writing for the theatre was
commercial in aim. He remarked later that not until he
gave up that aim and wrote a play to please himself
('Cupid and Commonsense') did he succeed in getting a
play produced. Most of the early work was done in collaboration. Options were taken on several of the early
plays, and Bennett earned a bit of money on them.

'The Music Lesson' (1899)

A one-act play. Bennett wrote it to celebrate the tenth
anniversary of his arrival in London. It was performed
on 2 March by friends at a party. The 'Journal' of that
date recorded 'intense and genuine enthusiasm and
applause'.

'The Arrival' (1899)

A one-act farce in composition on 18 April.

'Polite Farces' (1899)

Three one-act farces, 'A Good Woman' (also called 'Rivals
for Rosamund'), 'A Question of Sex', and 'The Stepmother'.
All three were written during the year, and published
together privately as 'Polite Farces' by Lamley in November, with the imprint 1900. The head of Lamley, the South
Kensington firm, was Charles Young, a friend of Bennett's.
Brief and favourable notices appeared in the 'Academy'
(9 December 1899) and in 'Hearth and Home' (b. January
1900). 'Rivals for Rosamund' was produced on 16 February
1914 at the Palace Theatre where it was 'received with
amiable indifference', as Bennett recorded in his 'Journal'
on the 18th. He added that it was 'no real good'. All
three plays were published separately by Gowans & Gray in
1929-30.

'The Post Mistress' (1900)

A curtain-raiser; written in February-March. It was pro-
visionally taken for the Haymarket Theatre, and then put
off.

'The Chancellor' (1900)

Written with Arthur Hooley, a teacher and friend. Bennett
said at the time that 'the thing (on its plane) is damn good'
(LAB II,130). It was taken by a producer but never put on.

'Children of the Mist' (1900)

Written with Eden Phillpotts and based upon Phillpotts's
novel. It was completed by 14 November, with Bennett
doing most of the work. Charles Frohman, the American
producer, apparently commissioned the play, but it was
never produced.

'A Wayward Duchess' (1900)

Written with Arthur Hooley. This too may have been

commissioned. It was accepted for production but never produced.

'Her Grace's Secret' (1901-2)

Adapted from Violet Tweedale's novel. Bennett may have written it soon after he moved to Trinity Hall Farm in October 1901. It was never produced.

'The Crime' (1902)

H.G. Wells was the intended collaborator. Bennett produced a scenario and some part of the rest of the script. Frederick Harrison of the Haymarket and Charles Frohman were interested in it. Harrison formally arranged with Bennett at this time for Bennett to adapt an old English comedy. Nothing came of either venture.

'The Ides of March' (1901-3)

A one-act play written with Fred Alcock. The surviving manuscript is in Bennett's hand. It was never produced but was published in 'One-Act Plays for Stage and Study, Eighth Series', 1934.

'The Duke's Sacrifice' (1902-3)

Two typescript drafts survive. It was never produced.

'Christina' (1904)

Written with Eden Phillpotts, also called 'A Credit to Human Nature'. Bennett described it as 'marketable footle' (LAB II, 188), but it was never produced.

'An Angel Unawares' (1904-5)

Written with Eden Phillpotts, and finished on 3 January 1905. Bennett noted in the 'Journal' on the 3rd that it was 'the most saleable thing I have ever done'. It was never produced.

'Que Faire?' (1905)

A two-act play, written in March. Bennett wrote it in
English, and his friend Henry Davray translated it into
French. According to a journal entry of 22 July 1907
(L&L, January 1929) it was intended for French production
and was relatively free in its sexual reference. Bennett
thought rather well of it. It was never produced.

'The Sole Survivors' (1907)

Written with Eden Phillpotts, and finished on 4 October.
Bennett was bored working on it, and he decided that he
would write no more plays until something was produced.
'The Sole Survivors' was never produced.

'Cupid and Commonsense' (1908)

Dramatised in the summer of 1907 from 'Anna of the Five
Towns' in response to the request from the Stage Society
for a play. In his 'Journal' on 12 August 1907 (L&L,
February 1929) Bennett said that he preferred the play to
the novel, especially in the ending. It was produced on
26 and 27 January at the Shaftesbury Theatre, where,
according to the 'Staffordshire Sentinel' (28 January),
it was 'cordially received'. Bennett was especially
pleased with E.F. Spence's review in the 'Westminster
Gazette'. There were productions in Glasgow in 1909, in
Manchester, Stoke-on-Trent, and Glasgow in 1910, and in
Hammersmith in 1912. It was published by the New Age
Press in 1909. Chatto & Windus issued an edition in 1925
and also published it in a collection of 'Three Plays' by
Bennett in 1931.

'The Snake Charmer' (1908)

A one-act play. It was written in March-April, on com-
mission, and was intended as a music hall sketch. It was
never produced. It was published in 1931 in 'One-Act
Plays for Stage and Study, Sixth Series'.

'What the Public Wants' (1909)

Written in the autumn of 1908. The immediate inspiration
for it was a libel case lost by Lord Northcliffe, recorded

by Bennett in the 'Journal' on 20 July 1907. It was produced by the Stage Society at the Aldwych Theatre on 2 May
1909. Several mainly favourable reviews were quoted at
length in the 'Staffordshire Sentinel' (4 May).
Max Beerbohm in the 'Saturday Review' (8 March) called it
'one of the best comedies of our time'. In the 'Journal'
on 13 May Bennett expressed some satisfaction with most of
the reviews. He especially liked E.F. Spence's review in
the 'Westminster Gazette'. A new production was mounted
on 27 May at the Royalty Theatre, where it ran for a
month. The new production apparently emasculated the
satire. It was produced again in Birmingham in 1917, in
New York in 1922, and elsewhere (see LN, 153). It was
published in the 'English Review' in a special supplement
in July 1909 and in 'McClure's Magazine' beginning in
January 1910. Duckworth issued it in book form in 1909,
and Frank Palmer and Chatto & Windus each issued it in
1910.

Play for ship use (1911)

A one-act play, constructed on 2 December while Bennett
was returning from America. It is not known whether the
play was written out and performed.

'The Honeymoon' (1911)

Written in the autumn of 1909. Bennett was very pleased
with it (LAB II, 252, 258). It opened at the Royalty
Theatre on 6 October, with Marie Tempest and Dion Boucicault in the leading roles, and ran for four months. It
had excellent reviews in the 'Manchester Guardian' and
the 'Daily Express'. There was also a review in the
'English Review'. Other reviewers thought it was a slight
work. Miss Tempest and Boucicault were generally much
admired. The play had occasional productions at London
theatres in 1912 and 1913, was revived at the 'Everyman'
in 1920 (having apparently been shown at Manchester and
Harrogate beforehand). There was another London production in September 1930. The play was published serially
by 'McClure's Magazine' in March and April 1911. Methuen
issued it in 1911, with a second edition to commemorate
the 100th performance. George Doran published it in 1910.

'Milestones' (1912)

Written with Edward Knoblock in August 1911. The scheme
was by Knoblock, and virtually all of the writing was by

Bennett, who at the time regarded it as 'extremely original, striking, dramatic and true to life' (LAB II, 289).
It opened at the Royalty on 5 March 1912 and ran for 609
nights. The cast included Dennis Eadie, Lionel Atwill,
Haidée Wright, and Gladys Cooper. Both the play and the
production were received with great enthusiasm. The
'Daily Express' (6 March) said that it was 'a play that
cries aloud for grateful superlatives'. 'Sphere' (23
March) called it 'the most remarkable play that has been
placed on the stage for a long period'. Bennett's net
income from the production was £60 a week. He earned
£5,000 from his plays in 1912 out of a total income of
£16,000, which income was more than he had earned in all
his previous years put together. He estimated that there
were more than 1,100 performances of his plays during the
year. 'Milestones' itself was produced by at least five
other English companies later in the year, at Hammersmith,
Holloway, and Kennington, and at Buxton and Southampton.
It was produced in New York in the autumn. It was also
produced at the Theatre Royal, Hanley, Stoke-on-Trent,
in the spring and again in the autumn of 1913. It was
revived briefly at the Royalty in the autumn of 1914,
and the end of that run on 30 November marked the end
of nearly three years of nightly performances of at least
one Bennett play in the West End. There were revivals at
the Royalty in 1920, with a provincial tour in the same
year; in Belfast and Glasgow in 1921; at the Criterion,
London, in 1930; in Glasgow again in 1931. Methuen and
Doran published the play in 1912, and it appeared in
'Munsey's Magazine' in October 1912. A ninth printing
of the Methuen edition appeared in 1920. Methuen issued
it with 'The Great Adventure' in 1926, and Dent published
it in their 'Modern Plays', 1937. It appeared elsewhere
in the 1920s and 1930s in anthologies of modern drama.

'The Great Adventure' (1913)

Dramatised from 'Buried Alive' in the autumn of 1910. It
was produced provincially in 1911. Granville Barker produced it at the Kingsway Theatre on 25 March 1913, with
Henry Ainley and Wish Wynne in the leading roles. It ran
for 673 nights. Some reviewers found the play too long,
but they also found it fresh, amusing, and original.
Honours characteristically went to the performances of
the two stars. It was produced at the Theatre Royal,
Hanley, Stoke-on-Trent, in the autumn, and the 'Staffordshire Sentinel' (4 November, also 5 November) thought that
it 'places Mr. Bennett amongst the leading playwrights of
his time'. It was also produced successfully in New York
in 1913. Bennett's income in 1913 was £17,000; this time

£9,000 came from the plays, of which there were 2,700 performances round the world. Frederick Harrison revived 'The Great Adventure' at the Haymarket in 1924, with Leslie Faber and Hilda Trevelyan. 'The Times' (6 June) thought that it was 'a happy revival', and the 'Daily Express' (6 June) thought that it was 'still the most delightful of Mr. Bennett's plays'. The revival occasioned a brief but interesting article by Edward Shanks in 'Outlook' (New York, 26 July), praising the play but wondering why it and 'Milestones' and the other plays were so much less substantial than the novels. Methuen and Doran published the play in 1913, and 'Hearst's Magazine' published it in abridged form in December 1913. Methuen reissued it with 'Milestones' in 1926, and Longman issued an edition in 1961 in their Essential English Library series.

'The Alarm' (1914)

A five-minute play. Bennett wrote it on 31 May for performance at the Actors' Orphanage Garden Party on 23 June.

War Play (1915)

A 'Journal' entry of 9 September indicated that Bennett was giving regular thought to the play. Whether it progressed beyond that stage is unknown.

'The Title' (1918)

Written in the spring. It opened at the Royalty on 20 July, with C. Aubrey Smith, Leslie Howard, Nigel Playfair, and Eva Moore in the leading roles. Bennett reported in his 'Journal' on the 23rd that 'the first night success had been really immense', an opinion that 'The Times' (22 July) agreed with while expressing its own more restrained enthusiasm. The 'Daily News' (22 July) regarded it as 'brilliant satire'. Desmond MacCarthy reviewed it at considerable length in the 'New Statesman' (27 July), finding the political satire dwindling into pleasant domestic comedy; he thought the play was a 'trifle' compared with Bennett's best work. It ran for 285 nights. A provincial tour began in February or March 1919. Chatto & Windus and Doran published it in 1918.

'Judith' (1919)

Written in January 1919 expressly for Lillah MacCarthy.
It opened at the Kingsway Theatre on 30 April. 'Journal'
entries of the next several days report on its reception:
'The press criticisms were without exception unfavourable';
'the news that Hardy was enthusiastic ... gave me more
satisfaction than anything that has happened to me for
a long time'; 'I know that there is too much psychological
realism ... to please a large section of the public'.
A review of the published play in the 'Daily Express'
(16 May) said: 'Mr. Bennett ... is not quite the type
of man to improve on the Apocrypha. He has a Handley
Page rather than a patriarchal mind.' Lillah MacCarthy's
altogether brief costume in Act II troubled several critics, for which circumstance Bennett himself was to blame
(see LAB I, 387-8). In an unpublished letter to J.C.
Squire on 14 May Bennett said: 'because of its originality
and fierce sarcasm ["Judith"] has had a press more rotten
than all the other rotten presses that I have had'.
Chatto & Windus and Doran published the play in 1919.

'Sacred and Profane Love' (1919)

Dramatised April-July 1916 from the novel. It was
intended for the American actress Doris Keane, but she
and Bennett quarrelled (see LAB I, 232 ff.). It opened
at the Aldwych Theatre on 10 November 1919, with Iris
Hooey and Franklyn Dyall as the lovers. A few reviewers
were enthusiastic, others were tepid or sardonic. The
most severe was W.J. Turner, himself a playwright, in a
brief notice in the 'London Mercury' (December). Turner
thought that the characters were puppets, that the subject
had nothing to do with love, and that Bennett was 'the
last person to expect us to take this play seriously'.
Bennett replied in a letter published the following
February, remarking of the quoted phrase, 'only a certain
ingenuousness prevents this remark from being outrageous'.
See also LAB III, 117-19, and see also below, p. 133. The
play came off after 100 performances. It was produced in
America by Charles Frohman early the following year, and
enjoyed considerable success in its tryouts in Philadelphia, Baltimore, and Washington, and then in New York.
'The receipts so far immensely surpass those of any other
play that I have ever had anything to do with', Bennett
reported to Hugh Walpole (LAB III, 123). He received
royalties from Frohman for £1,453, £1,300, and £600 in
March, April, and May 1920. He also sold film rights for

$1,500, and reckoned he should have been able to get much
more. The play was published by Chatto & Windus in 1919
and by Doran in 1920. Chatto & Windus issued another
edition in 1926, and also published it in 'Three Plays'
in 1931. An early provisional title for the play was 'Instinct'.

'The Love Match' (1922)

Written in July 1920. Bennett wrote to his nephew Richard
in January 1922 that the play was 'too good really to
succeed' (LN, 72). It opened at the Strand Theatre on
21 March 1922, with Arthur Bouchier and Kyrle Bellow in
the leading roles, and ran for just a month. According
to Bennett in an article about the play in the 'Sunday
Express' (2 April) the seventy to eighty reviews he saw
were, 'without exception, censorious. I doubt whether
any play of recent years has had a worse Press'. He
thought that had he made his heroine reform at the end,
he would have pleased his audience more; but women such
as he was depicting did not reform, and he thought that
his portrayal of the type - selfish, sensual, ruthless -
had been quite kind enough. Among all the reviews, four
were by Archibald Haddon, who reviewed the première at
Folkestone in the 'Daily Express' (31 January) and the
'Sunday Express' (5 February) and then again in the same
places (22 and 26 March) after the London opening. His
reviews which were mainly one review, said that the play
was 'witty and wise' but complained of the morally
unsatisfactory ending. On 30 March there was an exchange
of letters in the 'Daily Telegraph' between Bennett and
the producer, Frank Vernon (friend, and producer of four
of Bennett's plays, including 'Milestones' and 'The Great
Adventure'). Vernon said that he had received an extraordinary number of letters expressing dissatsifaction with
the ending, and he wondered whether Bennett could provide
an alternative ending without compromising himself.
Bennett replied, saying that the chief criticisms of the
play were twofold, firstly that it stopped rather than
ended, secondly that the character of the heroine did
not change. For him the character of the heroine was
unalterable, and so was the ending. He remarked incidentally that all his plays produced in the West End had
averaged 800 performances throughout the world. Vernon
wrote a second letter (31 March) to say that he did not
regard Bennett's answer as adequate: there was too strong
an opinion against it, including Vernon's own before the
play went on. In the 'Evening Standard' (8 April) Edith
Shackleton attacked Bennett's view of women in the play,

noting among other things the inability of the heroine
to make tea properly. Bennett replied (12 April) with
caustic comments on the moral, intellectual, and domestic
capabilities of many women, referring especially to his
heroine's inability to make a good cup of tea. In all
his life Bennett had not known ten women who knew how
to make tea, or twenty who cared whether the tea they
drank was good or bad. He then provided directions for
both Indian and China. (See LAB III, 157-60, and Egotism
in 'Things That Have Interested Me, Second Series' for
some of this material.) The play was published in 1922
by Chatto & Windus and Doran.

'Body and Soul' (1922)

Written in the summer and autumn of 1919. It opened on
11 September 1922 at the Euston Theatre of Varieties,
which for the occasion was renamed the Regent. Nan
Marriott Watson, Viola Tree, and Martin Walker took the
leading roles. Bennett wrote to his nephew Richard on
the opening day: 'a great sensation, seeing the name
"Regent" in vast gilt letters over the super-card's
theatre!' (LN, 85). Ten days later he had to write to
him, 'that play is a failure.... I don't know why.
No one does.' 'The Times' (12 September) was scathing
about both play and author: it was hardly a play, it was
frivolous and falsely modern, it was the product of a
provincial mind. Other reviews were equally severe. For
a few days in the 'Daily Express' there were items concerned with identifying the original of Lady Mab, but
neither they nor anything else saved the production, which
was withdrawn after a month. The play was published by
Chatto & Windus in 1922 and by Doran in 1921.

'Don Juan de Marana' (1923)

Written in December 1913 and January 1914, with a scenario
going back to September 1909 and thoughts about it to
April 1909. Bennett wrote to his literary agent in 1922,
'It is the best play I ever wrote, and will certainly one
day be produced' (LAB I, 319). Negotiations for production developed on several occasions from 1911 onwards,
with Granville Barker, Gilbert Miller, John Drinkwater,
John Barrymore, Matheson Lang, Leslie Faber, and others,
but it was never produced. Werner Laurie published it
in a limited edition in October 1923. It received a
favourable notice in the 'Westminster Gazette' (1 October)

and a neutral notice in the 'Daily Express' (6 October).
The 'Times Literary Supplement' (18 October) described
the play as 'a splendid, competent, and moving drama'.
Desmond MacCarthy in the 'New Statesman' (20 October)
did not think Bennett had 'felt his characters as living
people'; 'the subject is utterly unsuited to him'. John
Drinkwater in the 'Manchester Guardian' (25 October) said:

> Arnold Bennett ... has written two or three comedies
> of outstanding merit, and one, 'What the Public Wants',
> a masterpiece in his own piercingly ironic manner.
> But Mr. Bennett has also done more poor work in the
> theatre than anyone else in our time of anything like
> his intelligence and dramatic ability. He was at one
> time apt to treat the theatre rather cavalierly, and
> he must, perhaps, share the blame if the theatre has
> in turn become a little inhospitable to him. That,
> however, is a mere accident of his career and cannot
> interfere with our admiration of his work when it is
> good. And his newly-printed play 'Don Juan' is very
> good.... In view of Mr. Bennett's reputation, the
> quality of his work, and reflecting on the rubbish
> that so often fails in our theatres, it is an
> incredible thing if there is no management to take
> it.... Mr. Bennett does persuade us ... as to the
> reality and profound interest of the life that he
> is creating. This ... is fundamentally because the
> play has style. We are absorbed in Don Juan's pro-
> gress....

The 'Spectator' (17 November) thought that 'the characters
are not deeply conceived' and 'Mr. Bennett's interest in
his subject has been too visual, too rhetorical, too
"literary"';but 'the dialogue is good and often very
witty', and the play would make a 'charming entertainment' if produced.

'London Life' (1924)

Written with Edward Knoblock in April-June 1922. The play
was meant to be a spectacle, though not exactly of the
Drury Lane sort, and when it was accepted there both
Bennett and some portion of the management were dubious
about its prospects. The play inaugurated Basil Dean's
brief management there, and opened on 3 June 1924, with
Henry Ainley, Lillian Braithwaite, and Mary Jerrold in
the leading roles. A programme note by Bennett discussed
the aims of the play in relation to what he thought were

the characteristically more limited aims of the conventional Drury Lane production. The play was seen immediately to be a failure, and was withdrawn early in July.
Items in the 'Daily Express' (9 June and 3, 7, 8, and 9
July) discussed the problems of the play and its suit-
ability for Drury Lane. 'The Times' (4 June) saw precious
little difference between the play and conventional Drury
Lane plays. Ivor Brown in the 'Manchester Guardian'
(4 June) found some amusing bits but was mainly non-
commital. Horace Shipp in the 'English Review' (July)
considered both 'London Life' and Leslie Faber's revival
of 'The Great Adventure', and he deplored the one as much
as he admired the other: 'Drury Lane tempted all that was
bad in him.' Chatto & Windus and Doran published the
play in 1924.

'The Bright Island' (1925)

Written between January and April 1920, with some revision
in 1923. It was produced by the Stage Society at the
Aldwych for two performances on 15 and 16 February 1925,
with Felix Aylmer in the leading role. Bennett wrote in
the 'Journal' on the 24th:

> The play was coldly received on both Sunday and Monday.
> The points were not seen by that portion of the audi-
> ence which applauds. Yet the play had succeeded at
> rehearsals. Many people thought it amusing and true.
> I think that for one thing the audience was bewildered
> at the start by the strangeness of the scene, the
> 'Commedia dell arte' names of the characters, and the
> political quality of the plot. Also by the even-handed
> rigour dealt out to both parties. The Press, with the
> sole exception of 'Truth', who liked it and praised it
> and said it ought to be revived before a 'more intelli-
> gent audience', slanged it like anything. Not par-
> tially, but wholly. Some said that I ought to be
> stopped from writing such plays, a great mistake,
> deplorable, and so on. It was the worst Press any
> play of mine ever had.

P.P. Howe in 'Truth' (18 February) liked its 'malice and
wisdom', and called it 'a very superior and delightful
revue'. Hubert Griffith in the 'Observer' (22 February)
said it was 'the worst play written by a celebrated man
for a long time past'. See LAB III, 229 and 235-6, for
letters to G.B. Shaw and Griffith about their adverse
opinions. The Golden Cockerel Press published the play

in a limited edition in 1924. Doran issued it in 1925,
and Chatto & Windus in 1926. It was reprinted in 'Three
Plays' issued by Chatto & Windus in 1931.

'Flora' (1927)

Written between September and November 1924, and rewritten
in March 1925. The original title was 'Dance Club'.
Bennett wrote in his 'Journal' on 4 October 1924 that the
first act 'seems to me to contain more emotion in it than
anything dramatic that I have written for a long time'.
It was rejected by several West End managements and was
finally produced at the Rusholme Theatre in Manchester
on 17 October 1927. A.S. Wallace in the 'Manchester
Guardian' (18 October) found it trivial. 'The Times'
(18 October) said, 'it is just possible that a better
performance would have given the impression that Bennett
had written a better play'; it was 'a rather mechanical
and shoddy piece of theatricality'. The play was produced
again in October 1935 at the experimental theatre of the
Covent Garden Club, and 'The Times' (31 October) said,
'structurally unsound and weak in that it lacks tension
and drama, it is astonishingly successful in its revelation of character'. The play was published in 'Five Three
Act Plays' issued by Rich & Cowan in 1933.

'Mr. Prohack' (1927)

Dramatised from the novel in collaboration with Edward
Knoblock. Written and rewritten during the summer of
1923, the autumn of 1924, early 1925, and October 1927.
It was the second production in a three-month season at
the Court Theatre. It opened on 16 November, with Charles
Laughton in the title role. Laughton was made up to look
like Bennett, and there was comment in the press on it
(see the 'Westminster Gazette', 17 October, and the 'Daily
Express', 17 and 30 October; also the 'Daily Telegraph',
6 October 1938). The play had mixed reviews, but some of
them were very favourable, and it played to full houses
and helped to make Laughton's reputation. No other
theatre was available for transfer when the lease at the
Court ran out, and the play had to come off. 'The Times'
(17 November) thought that the play was dreary. Francis
Birrell in the 'Nation and Athenaeum' (26 November) said
that it was 'very, very good' and he 'was consumed with
mirth all through the evening'. Richard Jennings in the
'Spectator' (26 November) loved the character of

Mr Prohack. Dudley Carew in the 'London Mercury'
(January 1928) thought that it took Laughton to hold
together 'the ramshackle, untidy, amusing affair'. There
was a production in Manchester in February 1929. Chatto
& Windus and Doran published the play in 1927.

'The Return Journey' (1928)

Written from February to July 1928. It opened on 1 September 1928 at the St James's Theatre, with Gerald du
Maurier in the leading role. Bennett wrote to his nephew
Richard that the reception on the first night was luke-
warm; a week later he said that in the first week the
play did splendidly, and he added: 'But I don't count
too much on the piece. It is too original and unsparing
in plot and treatment for any London theatre public'
(LN, 235-6). On 4 September Bennett wrote to Max Beaverbrook: 'God knows whether the play is any good. I don't.
I merely know that nine critics out of ten have shown no
understanding of the play whatever. This is usual' (LAB
III, 310). Some critics found the play painful, and
W.J. Turner in the 'New Statesman' (22 September) was
outraged: 'How can one begin to discuss such rubbish...?
It reveals him as a man who if he ever did think, has now
ceased to think.' Bennett was annoyed by the review, but
after receiving a personal letter from Turner about it he
wrote to Turner to say that of the younger generation
Desmond MacCarthy was the only good critic and Turner
himself the only readable one (see LAB III, 311-13).
The play was taken off in November. Bennett declined
to have Chatto & Windus publish it immediately, and it
was never published.

Untitled play (1929)

Written between February and June 1929. An item in the
'Daily Express' (4 September 1929) said that it was being
sent that day to the Rusholme Theatre in Manchester. It
was never produced. On 18 June 1928, when he was finishing writing 'The Return Journey', Bennett wrote in the
'Journal': 'I really doubt whether I will ever do another.
Career as a dramatist closing!' On 4 September 1928, when
'The Return Journey' was being savaged by the critics, he
wrote to Max Beaverbrook: 'I hate the stage, but I cannot
help writing a play now and then.'

LIBRETTOS AND FILM STORIES

'Rosalys'

Bennett wrote the libretto of this 'musical play' in 1896-8 for music by James Brown. The work was produced at the Welsh Girls' School, Ashford, Middlesex, on 27 July 1898. It is printed in the Appendix of Margaret Locherbie-Goff's 'La Jeunesse d'Arnold Bennett', 1939.

'Deirdre'

A music drama in three acts. Bennett wrote some portion of this work in the late 1890s. The surviving manuscript shows only a portion of the first act to have been written.

'Antony and Cleopatra'

Bennett wrote the scenario of this 'operatic libretto' on 27-8 October 1907 for an unidentified French composer. It was never produced.

'The Beggar's Opera'

Bennett adapted Gay's work for the Lyric Hammersmith, where it was produced with great success in 1920, running for three years. It was produced there again in 1925. Bennett's enthusiasm for the work is recorded in detail in the 'Journal' on 24 June 1925.

'The Bandits'

Bennett and Eden Phillpotts wrote the libretto of this opera in 1925. The music was by Frederick Austin. It was never produced.

'Judith'

Bennett wrote the libretto (one act) on 16-17 August 1924, basing it on his play. Eugene Goossens wrote the music. It was produced at Covent Garden on 25 June 1929. The 'Evening Standard' (26 June) praised the libretto and

damned the music, the 'Manchester Guardian' (26 June)
thought that the libretto was all right and the music too
clever. J. and W. Chester published the opera in 1929.

'Don Juan'

Bennett wrote the libretto in September–October 1930,
basing it on his play. Eugene Goossens wrote the music.
It was produced at Covent Garden on 24 June 1937. The
'Evening Standard' (25 June) said nothing of the libretto
and thought that the music showed 'sterile brilliance'.
The 'Daily Express' (25 June) found the libretto 'fiery,
passionate, murderous stuff' and did not like the music.
For 'The Times' (25 June) 'the story keeps the hearer
hovering between mild interest and boredom'; the music
was better. F. Bonavia in the 'Daily Telegraph' (25 June)
thought that Bennett's hero failed to exhibit the idealism
that was attributed to him; the music was splendid.
A year before when J. and W. Chester published the libretto and piano score, Bonavia reviewed them in the 'Daily
Telegraph' (4 January), and on that occasion he admired
both libretto and score for their modernity. Of the libretto he said: 'here is something new and striking [in
opera], the apotheosis of a true sinner'.

'The Wedding Dress'

Bennett wrote the film story in November–December 1920.
It was 10,000 words long. It was never produced. In the
article In the Film World, in 'The Savour of Life', and in
LAB III, 298-302 and 322-3, are details of Bennett's
troubles with the film producer Jesse Lasky over the film.

'Faust'

Bennett wrote the English subtitles for this silent German
film in October 1926. The 'Spectator' (8 January 1927)
noted with some glee a mistake in grammar in the titles.

'Piccadilly'

See pp. 109-10.

'Punch and Judy'

Bennett worked on this film story during 1928-30. It was
never produced. For Bennett's difficulties with Alfred
Hitchcock and others over it see LAB III, *passim*.

Several of Bennett's novels and plays were filmed during
his lifetime. They included 'The Great Adventure' (1916,
1921), 'Milestones' (1916, 1920), 'The Grand Babylon
Hotel' (1917), 'Sacred and Profane Love' (1921/2), 'The
Old Wives' Tale' (1921), 'The Card' (1922), and 'The City
of Pleasure' (1929).

AFTER BENNETT'S DEATH

New books of Bennett's continued to be published after his
death, and the activity continues to this day. There were
the 'Journals', 'Florentine Journal', the 'Don Juan'
opera, and other items already mentioned. In addition
there were several volumes of letters: Dorothy Cheston
Bennett, 'Arnold Bennett: A Portrait Done at Home' (with
letters to her), 1935; 'Arnold Bennett's Letters to His
Nephew', 1936; 'Arnold Bennett and H.G. Wells', 1960;
'Correspondance André Gide - Arnold Bennett', 1962;
'Letters of Arnold Bennett', 1966, 1968, 1970, with a
final volume yet to appear; and 'Arnold Bennett in Love'
(with letters to Marguerite). In 1974 virtually all of
the 'Evening Standard' Books and Persons articles were
gathered into 'Arnold Bennett: The Evening Standard Years'.
And in 1980 appeared 'Sketches for Autobiography', which
included fourteen hitherto uncollected essays. With the
exception of the 'Journals' none of this publication
aroused great attention. It is fair to say, from the
standpoint of literary criticism, that with his death
Arnold Bennett became his detractors. There were occasional sympathetic books and articles on him - there was
Reginald Pound's lively biography in 1952 and Margaret
Drabble's in 1974; there was Angus Wilson's article in
the 'London Magazine' in October 1954, John Wain's appreciative study in 'Preliminary Essays' in 1957, and E.M.W.
Tillyard's discussion in 'The Epic Strain in the English
Novel' in 1958. Most astonishingly there was Frank
Swinnerton again with 'Arnold Bennett, A Last Word' in
1978. But neither these things nor a slow proliferation
of academic theses altered the fact of Bennett's decline
or the image of him that Ezra Pound and Virginia Woolf
imposed upon a ready literary world in the 1920s.
    But the literary world could not impose itself upon the

popular world, and it was here that Bennett survived, in England. His works remained in print, in diminished numbers, and were read. On 28 March 1951 the following item appeared in the 'Daily Express': 'Twenty years ago yesterday Arnold Bennett died. How many of his books are still read? A London bookseller tells me that nearly all are asked for now and then, with a steady demand from all ages.' In 1954 Penguin issued in paperback the following titles: 'The Old Wives' Tale', 'Clayhanger', 'Anna of the Five Towns', 'Riceyman Steps', 'The Grand Babylon Hotel', and the 'Journal'. Penguin reported in January 1958 that approximately 45,000 copies of each title had been sold. At the present time Penguin issue nine Bennett titles, and report the following average annual sales: 'Buried Alive', 2,500, 'Anna of the Five Towns', 8,000, 'The Card', 4,500, 'The Grand Babylon Hotel', 4,000, 'The Grim Smile of the Five Towns', 3,000, the 'Journal', 1,200, 'Clayhanger', 7,000, 'Hilda Lessways', 3,000, 'These Twain', 3,500. Such sales are modest from the publisher's standpoint, and they do not compare with the 40,000 annual sales of a novel like 'A Passage to India'. But what has to be allowed for in such a comparison is the influence of the academic world. Bennett's books are rarely set as texts in the schools and universities. They are bought by people who simply want to read them. In contrast, Forster, Lawrence, Woolf, Joyce, and Conrad provide many set texts, and hence many sales. How inflated and meaningless sales figures can be for a variety of reasons is indicated by the fact that at the time of the BBC television serial of the Clayhanger series, Penguin's sales of 'Clayhanger' rose to 200,000 in the year and of 'Hilda Lessways' and 'These Twain' to more than 100,000 each. Compare such figures also with the sales of 'Clayhanger' in 1910 (p. 58) when Bennett was the great novelist of the day and 'Clayhanger' itself was being acclaimed.

Perhaps a truer measure of popular reputation is to be had from library circulation. The public library of some size nearest my English home was asked about circulation of the following Bennett, Forster, and Woolf titles. The library replied:

'The Old Wives' Tale'	3 copies	all out on loan
'Clayhanger'	5 copies	each circulating on average once a month each
'Howards End'	4 copies	each circulating perhaps above once a month

'A Passage to India'	3 copies	each circulating perhaps once a month
'Mrs. Dalloway'	1 copy	out on loan
'To the Lighthouse'	1 copy	out on loan

By such means is preserved the best that has been known and thought!

Aside from Penguin's editions, the following works remain in print in England: with Eyre Methuen, 'Anna of the Five Towns', 'Buried Alive', 'The Card', 'Clayhanger', 'Hilda Lessways', 'These Twain'; with Dent and Pan, 'The Old Wives' Tale'. The record suggests the triumph of the Five Towns over the other novels, of the early years over the later.

No doubt Bennett would be glad his popular reputation survived his critical reputation rather than the reverse. He never took himself very seriously and had no wish to be taken very seriously. For him the savour of art mattered most for the savour of life in it. How else was one meant to respond to the words of the art-expert narrator in The Matador of the Five Towns (out of print in the volume of the same name) as he reflects upon the Five Towns scene?

I enjoyed all this. All this seemed to me to be fine, seemed to throw off the true, fine, romantic savour of life. I would have altered nothing in it. Mean, harsh, ugly, squalid, crude, barbaric, - yes, but what an intoxicating sense in it of the organised vitality of a vast community unconscious of itself!

'A Man from the North'

23 February 1898

1. 'SARAH VOLATILE', BOOKS AND AUTHORS, 'HEARTH AND HOME'

3 March 1898, 689

'Sarah Volatile' was E.A. Bennett himself in one of his
female impersonations in 'Hearth and Home' and 'Woman'.
Books and Authors was his regular column.

If Mr. Bennett had felt the need of a sub-title to his
book, he might have found a fitting one in his own pages:
'The Psychology of the Suburbs' - so was named the
masterpiece dreamt of by Richard Aked and by Richard
Larch, the hero. Dreamt of, not brought into being;
for Richard Aked died after he had instilled into Larch's
mind a dim conception of the truth that drama is of no
class, no place, no time, and Larch failed to realise the
dream. One of the most effective elements of this book
is the way in which is suggested the thorough sympathy
between these two, who met only half a dozen times, and
differed by forty or fifty years, yet were so close in
spirit that Aked's dying confession of faith is uttered
to Larch as the one best fitted to hear it.

When Richard Larch comes to London as shorthand clerk
in a solicitor's office, his knowledge of the world has
been gained from books and papers. Woman as a friend, as
companion, he had never known; his sister was many years
his elder. He revels in London and its meretricious
glories, taking no thought of the quiet eternal things.
His strivings for literary success were too crude, too

139

periodic to meet with success: and the old man Aked, 'who
had spoken to Carlyle,' seemed invested with a halo of
achievement. From him - a failure in life - Richard
learnt much; but the conflict between flesh and spirit
ever prevented him from using to their full end what
talents he had. The character is clearly drawn, and
interests the reader as true to nature: one might meet
Richard Larch on an omnibus top any morning of the year.
His weaknesses are those of our common humanity, and Mr.
Bennett has been pitiless in his delineation.

In Adeline Aked, the old man's niece, Richard's antithesis appears, and it is not wonderful that he refrained
from asking her to marry him. Adeline, whose strange
youth has an interest of which Mr. Bennett makes no
further use, is seen at first as a girl far beneath
Richard in Richard's own eyes: yet once she has free control of her uncle's money after his death, she grows
rapidly (too rapidly, almost, for verisimilitude), and
Richard thinks he loves her; but 'she had sharp limitations,' and he dimly divines that a *lover* is never so
metaphysical in his thoughts of the beloved. Her
independence grows, and, at last, she makes up her mind
to join her uncles in America. On the day of her departure she tells him she had so decided, weeks before he
knew, waiting to see if he and she cared for one another.
Her frankness is disconcerting, and Richard becomes
morally feeble after her departure, finally marrying a
restaurant cashier, an old acquaintance.

The book throughout is written with great strength -
the superfluous word occurs but seldom - and the minor
characters convince. Jenkins, the solicitor's clerk, is
portrayed with almost loving care, the scenes in the
British Museum, the Ottoman (I had almost written the
Alhambra), and elsewhere, are to the life; the London
that ennobles and crushes is the background to this drama
of a young man's career. If there is a fault, it is in
the absence of the better (spiritual, not mental) side of
the characters; but their humanity is so completely shown
that it suffices. The book does not depress, though
Richard fails to rise from his morass; and it is clean,
healthy, and powerful, a result achieved by the restraint
everywhere evident. Its construction is excellent; there
is no journalistic attempt to bring about 'good curtains'
at any hazard of veracity, or to write 'bright pages' at
the cost of true character-drawing. There is an air about
'A Man from the North' of a close study of men and things
that makes it presumptuous to say the author will go far.

He *has* gone far with his novel, and if I am sorry that he
exiled Adeline to America, I am sure he will, when he has
passed through the fiery furnace of Love, give the reading
public who care for good work many such charming pictures
of real women. 'A Man from the North' is a book that
needs no apologies, and I have every confidence in its
success.

2. 'FAITHFUL', FROM THE LITERARY LUCKY TUB, 'VANITY FAIR'

3 March 1898, 144

'Faithful' was an unknown friend of Bennett's. He dipped
in at the same time for 'Wild Life in South Seas', by
Louis Becke, 'The Sinner', by 'Rita', and 'The Princess
and the Butterfly', by A.W. Pinero.

Mr. E.A. Bennett seems to be a new novelist; at any rate,
he has all the young novelist's faults. It seems to me
that when he sat down to write his book he did so without
the least idea of a story to tell; and he has introduced
the ugly immoral unmeaningly, dragging it in by the hair.
These are glaring faults; for, given lack of interest, and
unpleasant scenes, how can a book be expected to be popular? But 'A Man from the North' is not to be dismissed
quite summarily. It has many points of cleverness - a
great many. It shows the result of deep observation of
men and things; it shows the writer to have the power of
giving us live characters; and it has the great merit of
being short. Mr. Bennett wants a plot, and he needs to
learn that unpleasant, almost dirty, scenes are neither
clever nor interesting unless they are exceedingly well
done. In this book of his he describes his hero, after
bidding good-bye, presumably for ever, to his lady-love,
strolling down Piccadilly, giving way to the importunities
inseparable from that region - a bit of writing that is
entirely irrelevant. One might forgive it were it necessary for the development of character, or were it cleverly
done; but it is neither. If Mr. Bennett will take advice,
he will try and write brightly, happily. He has a 'turn';
why does he not drive it in the proper - and the paying -
channel?

3. 'FRANCES', BOOK-CHAT, 'WOMAN'

8 March 1898, 8-9

'Frances' was Francis Clayton Bennett (1868-1938), a
younger brother, who came to London briefly in the 1890s.
Book-Chat was a regular column conducted mainly by Bennett
himself under the name of 'Barbara'. Frank Bennett undertook reviewing in 'Woman' just a few days before 'A Man
from the North' was published. Bennett wrote to George
Sturt at the time, 'Frank can write well enough, at any
rate on the drama. What he will do with books remains
to be seen' (LAB II, 103).

The argument of this book as the 'Pall Mall Gazette' has
very felicitously expressed it, is that there are men who
though born and bred in the country, are *de jure* of the
centre, men for whom there is only one place in the world,
and that place London. Richard Larch was one of these,
and like the rest of them he contrived before he was
twenty to 'come into his inheritance. London accepted him.
He was hers; she his; and nothing should part them.' He
was a clerk in a lawyer's office and had literary aspirations. At first he worked and studied, having occasional
fits of idleness in which he yielded to the glamour of
this fascinating city and tasted most of her pleasures.
In the office he made friends with Richard Aked, a middle-
aged, rather cynical, disappointed author, who vented
upon him all his theories of literary art, and in the
result did him no little good. But Larch was scarcely
the kind of man to progress rapidly. He lacked 'application.'

A further disturbing influence was very soon brought
into his life, woman to wit. First it was the cashier at
a restaurant; later a niece of Aked's. The latter began
almost at once to exercise considerable sway over him; so
much indeed that when, on the death of her uncle, she
was able to spend money upon herself, and give herself
that factitious attraction born of good clothes and
comfortable circumstances, Richard came very near to falling in love with her. But she was more penetrating than
he, and saw that his interest in her did not amount to
love, and, being of a very decided character, she suddenly
went off to America to live with two other uncles. At

first Richard was inconsolable, later he began to take an
interest in his dress, took a keen pleasure in wearing
smartly-cut clothes, frequented fashionable cafes and bars,
and then quite unexpectedly the literary fever returned,
and for a while he worked again. But it was no use, he
seemed unable to accomplish anything. He was still at the
lawyer's office, and his salary had risen. He was not
strong enough to resist the temptation to enjoy the comfort
he had for the sake of an intangible far-off ambition, and,
meeting the restaurant cashier again, he persuaded himself
that she was not uninteresting; and to end the frightful
solitude of his life asked her to marry him.

4. EDEN PHILLPOTTS IN 'BLACK AND WHITE'

12 March 1898, 372

Eden Phillpotts (1862-1960) was a new friend of Bennett's,
somewhat further along the road to success. He was on the
staff of 'Black and White'. He and Bennett became intimate friends for several years, and collaborated on two
novels and several plays. His career was remarkably like
Bennett's in some respects: he was very prolific, and his
strongest work was his series of Dartmoor novels.
Bennett wrote in his 'Journal' on 2 March 1898: 'Phillpotts was extremely enthusiastic about the merits of "A
Man from the North". It seemed strange and unreal to be
treated by this finely serious novelist as an artist of
the same calibre with himself.' Phillpotts's review was
unsigned.

If, as we have reason to believe, the author of this
remarkable book can point to it as his first sustained
effort, he and novel readers in general may be alike congratulated. There is freshness of thought and great
distinction of style in 'A Man from the North', for the
author is a conscientious artist with nice appreciation
of the force of words and a wide literary vocabulary. He
possesses further that rarest of gifts: self-restraint and
self-denial. There are a hundred fascinating scenes which
we can picture, and which he certainly must have pictured,
as possible in the story he tells; but he is content to

think them, and permits himself not a word or incident
which does not throw light on character or advance the
narrative. The treatment is almost austere, yet its
effect on the mind rings true, and we know with refreshing
certainty as we close the book that we are leaving the
presence of an artist. The spectacle of a young man from
the country entering London without a friend and setting
resolutely to his life's work must always prove fascinating. Richard Larch is such an one, and his creator
remorselessly turns the man inside out, dissects his
hopes and fears, ambitions and little vanities, exhibits
his mediocre intelligence, his lapses, and his renewed
struggles towards the light, with most finished psychology
and intuition. We doubt if a literary aspirant who wrote
so ill as Larch would have rated his own work with such
unerring judgment; but, on the other hand, he is represented as having some taste, and is not lacking in
pluck. The man is emphatically alive, and there are
lightning touches, as the tear in his eye when an author
is called on a first night, that show he had the true
stuff in him, though expression was denied. The erotic
side of Richard - which he confuses with a nobler instinct
- hurries him along, and his relations with the dual
heroines (if Mr. Bennett will allow us that old-fashioned
word) are intensely interesting; while the inner nature of
the man during his struggle has been wrought for us with
inspiration. Mr. Aked also furnishes a splendid study,
and we mourn his untimely demise. The women are not a
whit behind, and in Adeline the author gives us a beautiful piece of womanhood, natural in her limitations,
intensely human, and consequently fascinating. The study
of this girl reminds one forcibly of Turgenev, not only
in its artistic method of elaboration, but also in breadth
and sympathy. To sum up, Mr. Bennett has written a book
that will come to the jaded novel reader as a splendid
surprise. The piece abounds in felicities, and as a
Pennell pencil drawing makes us rub our eyes in doubt,
before we suddenly welcome some familiar scrap of town or
country in the new light the artist has thrown upon it, so
this artist finds unexpected beauties amid common things,
and transfigures in a phrase many well-known aspects of
London and Greater London. His glimpses of dawns and sunsets and the pearly curtains of rain glittering over some
mean concourse of suburban habitations, of Nature beheld
from the train window at dawn or gloaming - these and
such-like apparitions he touches with illuminating thought
and that expression we have before noted as amongst an
artist's most rare and precious gifts. No cultured reader
can well afford to miss 'A Man from the North', and for

ourselves we shall await with absolute impatience the
next expression of Mr. Bennett's remarkable art.

5. UNSIGNED REVIEW, 'MANCHESTER GUARDIAN'

15 March 1898, 4

There is a distinctly foreign note in 'A Man from the
North', by E.A. Bennett. The story is a careful and
really clever study of a middle-class clerk who is obviously intended to be typical or part of that respectable
but not very interesting body to which, as Mr. Arnold
said, we all belong. Our hero has literary aspirations,
but no literary industry. He desires to fall in love, but
lacks decision and the power to select. He is intensely
introspective, as perhaps even city clerks are becoming.
He abandons an attractive and clever girl because he is not
sure if he is really in love with her. He marries another,
who is neither clever nor attractive, mainly, we think, to
prove to himself that he is capable of falling in love
with somebody. Granting that such a character is worth
describing, it is well described. The writer is an uncompromising realist. He is master of all the little
sordid details, the little sordid ambitions and loves and
sorrows of lower middle-class existence; and he possesses
the art of drawing lifelike portraits with a few touches.
The subject is not a very attractive one, and the hero, it
must be confessed, is a cold fish at the best. We have
met him before in other walks of life. He has appeared in
'Hamlet' and 'Virgin Soil,' but the problems which palsied
the wills of the heroes of those tragedies were worth
solving. The difficulties of Richard Larch, we cannot but
feel, might have been removed by a touch of vice. An
English clerk, it is to be feared, would have solved them
in this way. Such obsessions of indecision are more
Russian than English.

6. JOSEPH CONRAD, IN A LETTER TO BENNETT

10 March 1902

Joseph Conrad (1857-1924) was well ahead of Bennett in
fame, having by now published 'The Nigger of the "Nar-
cissus"', 'Lord Jim', and 'Youth'. He and Bennett had
a common literary agent, J.B. Pinker, and a common friend,
H.G. Wells. Bennett's reply to Conrad is lost.

My dear Sir,
    The reading of the 'Man from the North' has inspired me
with the greatest respect for your artistic conscience.
I am profoundly impressed with the achievement of style.
The root of the matter - which is expression - is there,
and the sacred fire too. I hope you will give me the
credit for understanding what you have tried for there.
My dear Sir, I do envy you the power of coming so near
your desire.
    The thing as written is undeniable. To read it was to
me quite a new experience of the language; and the delight
was great enough to make me completely disregard the subject.
    This at first; but as you may suppose I've read the
book more than once. Unfortunately, I don't know how
to criticize; to discuss, however, I am ready. Now the
book (as a novel, not as a piece of writing) *is* disputable.
    Generally, however, I may say that the die has not been
struck hard enough. Here's a piece of pure metal scrupulously shaped, with a true - and more - a beautiful ring:
but the die has not been struck hard enough. I admit that
the outlines of the design are sharp enough. What it
wants is a more emphatic modelling; more relief. And one
could even quarrel with the design itself.
    Nothing would give me greater pleasure than to have
it out with you, the book there on the table, to be
thumped and caressed. I would quarrel not with the truth
of your conception but with the realism thereof. You stop
just short of being absolutely real because you are faithful to your dogmas of realism. Now realism in art will
never approach reality. And your art, your gift, should
be put to the service of a larger and freer faith.
                                        [Joseph Conrad]
    P.S. Of course I may have misunderstood your standpoint

utterly.   I want to hear what you have to say, if you think it worth while to say anything to me.   Only let it be *viva voce*.   Come when you can spare a day.   I won't be likely to have forgotten the book....

'The Grand Babylon Hotel'

9 January 1902

7. UNSIGNED REVIEW, 'ACADEMY'

18 January 1902, 54

This is a very amusing story of the *feuilleton* type. In
calling it a fantasia on modern themes Mr. Bennett shows
that he understands exactly what he has performed, and
the kind of pleasure his performance is likely to give to
discriminating readers. In plot and substance this story
of European intrigue, centred in the Grand Babylon Hotel
in the Strand, is like unto the scores of such stories
that pass before us. That is to say, the story, as a
story, grips while it lasts, and then all is over. But
whereas most novels of the same brand leave the reader
the innutritive memory of being gripped, this story leaves
also the memory of witty pages and situations. The pages
in which we know Jules simply as the head waiter, and
Rocco simply as the *chef*, and the Grand Babylon itself
simply as a modern Elysium, are in the end worth the many
in which these officials become conspirators and the
Grand Babylon a hot-bed of intrigue on behalf of the King
of Bosnia. Mr. Racksole's daughter Nella, with whom he
is travelling, is a girl of the costliest, wilfullest,
most adorable type; and when, in face of the most
recherché menu in Europe, she expresses a desire to dine
one evening on a steak for two and a bottle of Bass, her
multi-millionaire papa hesitates only a moment. Then the
order is given to the Napoleonic Jules:

> It was the bravest act of Theodore Racksole's life,
> and yet at more than one previous crisis a high courage
> had not been lacking to him.

148

> 'It's not in the menu, sir,' said Jules the imper-
> turbable.
> 'Never mind. Get it. We want it.'
> 'Very good, sir.'
> Jules walked to the service door, and, merely
> affecting to look behind, came immediately back again.
> 'Mr. Rocco's compliments, sir, and he regrets to be
> unable to serve steak and Bass to-night, sir.'
> 'Mr. Rocco?' questioned Racksole, lightly.
> 'Mr. Rocco,' repeated Jules, with firmness.
> 'And who is Mr. Rocco?'
> 'Mr. Rocco is our *chef*, sir.' Jules had the expres-
> sion of a man who is asked to explain who Shakespeare
> was.

Mr. Racksole begs his daughter to excuse him for two sec-
onds, leaves the room, and is absent for twenty minutes.
It had taken even Mr. Racksole that long to buy the greatest hotel in the world, lock, stock, and barrel.

Excellent in this mingling of farce and characterisation are the scenes in which Mr. Racksole picks up from
the sublime Félix Babylon, and from his own observations,
his first ideas of the art of running a vast hotel - populous with crowned heads, German princelings, financiers,
and cosmopolitans. For the business of the Grand Babylon
was enormous. It took him exactly half an hour to master
the details of the hotel laundry-work. In Félix Babylon's
opinion, from which there could be no appeal, Mr. Racksole
had missed his vocation. 'You would have been the greatest of all hotel-managers. You would have been greater
than me.' All this is vastly amusing and well done; so is
the melodrama that follows; yet we know what we like best
and shall remember.

8. UNSIGNED REVIEW, 'TIMES LITERARY SUPPLEMENT'

24 January 1902, 12

'The Grand Babylon Hotel,' by Arnold Bennett, derives
its name from a magnificent and exclusive establishment
on the Thames Embankment. Miss Nella Racksole, only
daughter of the third richest man in the United States,
is unable to find anything to her taste in the elaborate
menu provided in the *salle à manger*, and, as a birthday

treat, requests her father to order a filletted steak
and a bottle of Bass. The order is, of course, firmly
but courteously declined. In a quarter of an hour
Mr. Theodore Racksole has seen the proprietor and
purchased the hotel for £400,000. This is the prelude to
what the author describes as 'a fantasia on modern themes,'
which is performed during Mr. Racksole's tenure of the
hotel, and of which the *motif* is an international plot
woven round the person of the Hereditary Prince of Posen.
A Royal personage or two among the *dramatis personae* of
a story are sure to give it piquancy; but, if they are
European, their introduction is apt to suggest the *roman
à clef*. To obviate this difficulty the novelist has been
fortunate enough to discover the German principalities.
Mr. Anthony Hope was one of the first explorers in this
field, and he has had so many followers that the assiduous novel-reader doubtless regards these quiet little
German States as hotbeds of international intrigue.
This is no doubt unfair, but what are novelists, in an
exhausted world, to do? Mr. Bennett, at any rate, turns
the notion to excellent use, and the conspiracy against
the person of Prince Eugen which centres round the Grand
Babylon Hotel is unravelled with an amazing ingenuity of
incident. It is a story full of actuality, closely knit
together, and told with the cunning of a storyteller who
knows how to keep his readers' interest alive from the
first page to the last.

9. UNSIGNED REVIEW, 'SPECTATOR'

25 January 1902, 146

Since Miss Braddon abandoned the field of sensation so
diligently exploited by her for a quarter of a century
for the more tranquil domains of historical romance, no
successor of uncontested superiority has arisen to occupy
her throne. Miss Warden promised well, but her later
ventures have proved disappointing; Miss Adeline Sergeant
has paid a divided allegiance to serious character
analysis and lurid melodrama; and Mrs. Williamson has
thrown away quite a pretty talent for comedy on 'shockers'
which tax the credulity of the most omnivorous appetite.
That there is a demand for such books we have not the
slightest shadow of a doubt. One of the very ablest and

most hard-working Oxford philosophy dons that the writer
knew could never resist a 'yellow-back.' They may be
destitute in regard to detail of any correspondence
with the facts of life, utterly innocent of edification,
and yet capable of providing perfectly harmless entertainment. This result we take to be due to the fact that the
methods of sensationalism, as interpreted by most practi-
tioners, are, by their kaleidoscopic character and reli-
ance on a never-ceasing succession of incidents, incompatible with a deliberate insistence on morbid details
or the leisurely delineation of moral deterioration.
Sensationalism, again, in its essence makes for optimism,
since the conflict between the forces of good and evil,
if it is to be exciting, cannot be one-sided; and in
regard to the ultimate issue the Adelphi formula still
holds the field, which is, after all, only in keeping
with the statistics annually issued by the Chief Commis-
sioner of Police.

With these reservations we can extend a cordial welcome
to Mr. Arnold Bennett, whose 'Grand Babylon Hotel,'
described in its alternative title as 'a fantasia on
modern themes,' is a very favourable specimen of its
class. The author has discerned with no little shrewdness the opportunities for romantic crime furnished by
the temporary contact of that shifting cosmopolitan
society which frequents the modern fashionable monster
hotel, where the management asks no questions as to the
antecedents of the guests nor interferes with their freedom of action so long as they conform to a certain standard of living and pay their way. The story opens
excellently with a brilliant piece of extravagance on
the part of an American multi-millionaire. Foiled in
his request for a special American pick-me-up, and meeting unexpected difficulties in the way of gratifying his
capricious daughter's desire for a peculiarly homely
dinner, he carries his point by purchasing the hotel
'on the nail' for the modest sum of £400,000. The assumption of the cares of management at once brings him into
close quarters with a mysterious plot connected with the
visit of a German Grand Duke and his youthful uncle,
Prince Aribert of Posen, who while travelling *incognito*
the previous year had fallen in love with the millionaire's daughter. The aim of the conspirators – chief of
whom are the incomparable head-waiter Jules and the
unique *chef* Rocco – is to upset the financial negotiations
by which the Grand Duke proposes to regularise his position before being accepted as the suitor of an exalted
German Princess, since if he is unable to show a clean
bill of health, financially speaking, by a certain date,

the reversion of the Princess's hand falls to the King
of Bosnia, the contriver of the plot and paymaster of
Jules and Rocco. These two villains, who combine superb
urbanity of manner with diabolical unscrupulousness of
method, play the game of their patron with mediaeval
thoroughness backed by all the resources of modern
science. Toxicology, electricity, disguises, abduction, -
the whole armoury of the plutocratic criminal is employed
against the luckless Grand Duke, but at every turn the
artistic assassins are confronted by the indomitable
millionaire and his heroic daughter. To say any more
of the plot and its catastrophe would be to detract
from the pleasure of the reader, so we shall confine
ourselves to a quotation by way of illustrating Mr.
Bennett's gift for descriptive narrative. The scene in
question describes the attempt of the millionaire,
Theodore Racksole, to capture the villains by night
on the Thames:-

[Quotes ch. 25: 'That night, just after dark, Theodore
Racksole embarked' to 'that familiar substance comforted
him'.]

    Mr. Bennett, as we think the foregoing passage suf-
ficiently shows, has, by the artistic way in which he
diffuses an atmosphere of suspense and uneasy anticipation, shown himself capable of work on a higher level
than that of the melodrama - excellent of its kind -
which forms the staple of his present venture.

'Anna of the Five Towns'

About 15 September 1902

10. LETTERS BETWEEN H.G. WELLS AND ARNOLD BENNETT

9 and 20 September 1902

H.G. Wells (1866-1946), six months older than Bennett, established his reputation much earlier. Their long friendship began with a letter from Bennett in 1898 asking Wells what his connection was with the Potteries, there having been references to them in a couple of Wells's works.

My dear Bennett,
    'Anna' is very good indeed - a good picture of the Pottery culture (or want of it) full of incidental interest and interesting as a story. The characters strike me as real, consistent and individual, Mynors perhaps a little *hard* and flat, not quite modelled, a little touch of personal vanity - about the shape of his nose for example - would have rounded him off - but the rest all there. Your style is not of course my style and there's not three consecutive sentences I should let stand if I had the rewriting of it, but that is partly individual difference. Partly it isn't. Partly it is that - blessed thought! - you are not yet artistically adult, Gissing and George Moore and the impersonal school and a certain consciousness of good intentions are evident - it is not suggestive of the ease and gusto and mastery of your Potters with the clay for example, it isn't nearly so easy and engaging and *good* as the stuff you have been writing in the 'Academy' - so far as the style

goes. For example, down here you told a story about
'hanging about a chapel on the offchance of a service'
and you told it in just the note. It was enjoyed and
remembered. In your story that comes in inopportunely
with no sense of enjoyment. On the whole I should describe my impression as being that of a photograph a
little underdeveloped. It is most underdeveloped towards
the end. There you have arranged a series of very finely
planned and I (as an experienced workman) know, finely
imagined, emotional scenes. And they don't *tell* for a
quarter what they are worth. The visit of Anna and Mynors
to the Price home is cardinal. It ought to be charged
with emotion. It ought to be immense. It was worth
writing over and over again, it was worth sweating blood
to do well. Good lines of course in abundance - the last
on 341 for example [the last paragraph of the chapter At
the Priory] - but as a whole? You reach the top of the
book (and it's fairly high) in the Isle of Man. From
the death of Titus Price onward you are not all you will
someday be (D.V.) But the way you tip W.P. down the coal
shaft couldn't possibly be neater or better.

These are impressions. Don't take 'em to heart if they
don't please you.

Yours ever, H.G.

I like the book out of comparison with 'The G.B.H.' - a
mere lark that, as I said at the time.

My dear H.G.,
Knowing officially from you that for you 'no such thing
as excellence exists', I will not conceal my satisfaction
at your remarks about 'Anna'. I reckon no one in this
isle knows more about the *craft* of fiction than you,
except possibly me, & I am always struck by the shrewdness
of your criticisms of novels from that point of view.
But I think your notions about verbal style are fundamentally wrong, & nevertheless it just happens in this
instance that what you say about my style is, I think,
mainly correct. There *is* a 'certain consciousness of good
intentions' that has jolly well got to disappear. Also I
am inclined to agree that I am not yet artistically adult
(at 35!).
I don't think the book falls off *much* after the death
of old Price, & I think the emotional quality of the end
is as good as any. As to the under-developed photograph,
this is largely a matter of taste. But I trust you understand that the degree of development to which I have
brought the photograph, is what I think the proper degree.

It is Turgenev's degree, & Flaubert's. It is *not*
Balzac's. Anyhow it is the degree that comes natural
to me. I note the possibility of your having second
thoughts about the book.
  I have had no reviews worth mentioning yet....

                                        Yours, E.A.B.

11. UNSIGNED REVIEW, 'STAFFORDSHIRE SENTINEL'

15 September 1902, 2

'Anna of the Five Towns' is a novel by Mr. Arnold Bennett,
whose thrilling story, 'The Grand Babylon Hotel,'
recently appeared in the 'Sentinel,' and whose connection
with North Staffordshire is well known. The scene of
'Anna of the Five Towns' is for the most part laid in
Burslem, thinly disguised as Bursley. Anna - Anna
Tellwright - is a remarkable 'creation,' though the novel
not only contains a great deal of local colour, but perhaps a substratum of local history. However that may be,
it is, apart altogether from its relation to the Potteries, a powerful and absorbing novel. The 'plot' soon
seizes the attention and holds it, and some of the phases
of local life and the local colour are admirably portrayed and neatly hit off; but the real strength of the
book lies in its study of character. It is too much the
fashion amongst novel-writers nowadays to ring the changes
upon the impossible doings of an imaginary aristocracy or
the tiresome hysterics of objectionable women with a past.
All Mr. Bennett's characters move in a homely and limited
circle, yet the story of their lives supplies an abundance
of pathos, tragedy, and humour, and irresistibly compels
one to read on. The people to whom the reader is introduced possess a vivid personality. At least, their personality is vividly drawn. They stand out boldly against
the North Staffordshire background as might personal
acquaintances. It never crosses the mind that they are
not real people. The inhabitants of the Potteries are
shall we say notorious for the more or less kindly
interest that they display in their neighbours' affairs
- wherein they are antithetical to the dwellers in great
cities. Those to whom we are introduced in the novel are
essentially 'neighbours,' and everybody in North Stafford
ought to find the book one of the books of their lives.

But it appeals with scarcely any less power to the reading
public at large. For our own part, we have always had a
decided leaning towards George Eliot, and on more than one
occasion we have, we believe, expressed a hope that a
novel of the 'Mill on the Floss' type treating of the
Potteries might some day be forthcoming. We are very
well satisfied to regard 'Anna of the Five Towns' as
fulfilling that desire. We have read several novels in
which attempts have been made to work in the 'local
colour' of the Potteries. We have never been quite satisfied in that respect until we read 'Anna of the Five
Towns.' There is knowledge, and if not always sympathy,
there is a reserve that excludes mere caricature. We
found the novel so interesting, from many points of
view, that we were impelled to read it through at one
sitting, and the hold upon the attention never wavered.
We most heartily congratulate Mr. Bennett upon his latest
novel, which places him upon an infinitely higher plane
than he previously occupied, and the Potteries may very
well be proud of having produced so keen an observer, so
trenchant and effective a writer, and a novelist who is
gradually but, as we can scarcely doubt, surely winning
his way to a recognised position amongst the authors of
the day.

[The reviewer then summarises the action of much of the
novel, quoting liberally from it.]

Now, amongst the property that had come to Anna from her
grandfather was a tumble-down old factory that was occupied at a heavy rental by Titus Price, one of the superin-
tendents of the Wesleyan Sunday school. He has struggles
in his business, and cannot pay his rent, and old Tellwright, managing his daughter's affairs irrespective of
her wishes and knowledge, puts such pressure upon Price
that he forges and uses trust money to tide through his
difficulties, in the hope and belief that better days
would come so that he could redeem himself and nobody be
the worse for his makeshifts. But of course this prospect
is not realised, and Price hangs himself, and his son
Willie Price, also comes to a tragic end, though not
before Anna had, all too late, thrown off her father's
thraldom and tried unsuccessfully to save the Prices from
the results of the action which her father had taken in
her name. Willie Price is a simple, loveable soul, who
loves Anna. But for the story of how she returned his
love but dutifully married Mynors, we must refer our
readers to the book itself. The interest of this latter
portion of the novel is intense and almost heartrending.

One puts down the book with a feeling that the Tell-
wrights, the Prices, the Suttons, and Mynors have become
a part of one's intimate knowledge of the district, and
will always be associated with it. If there is a suspicion of a slight trace of priggishness about Mynors, and
if old Tellwright's harshness is somewhat difficult to
understand, such defects do not detract from the general
picture. Henry Mynors is the kind of man that carries
through great movements. No doubt, he would succeed in
business, make a fortune, become Mayor, and enter Parliament. The Potteries wants more of such men to-day.
Federation could be carried by a Henry Mynors. But at the
stage of his life at which we here leave him, he was still
a young man. Perhaps Mr. Bennett will some day write a
sequel to 'Anna of the Five Towns.' In the meantime, we
recommend the book to our readers as one they should not
miss reading.

In conclusion, we may refer to the local 'touches' and
characteristics with which the novel abounds. The 'Sentinel' is several times referred to under the title of the
'Staffordshire Signal,' and we are much obliged for the
implied compliment that the 'Sentinel' is one of the
permanent institutions of the Potteries. It will have
been gathered that the well-known local prominence of Non-
conformity is also indicated. During a revivalist mission at the 'Duck Bank' Wesleyan Church, Anna, who has no
theological enthusiasm, though she has an ardent desire
for 'more light,' attends an early morning meeting, and on
her way thither, noting the undisturbed demeanour of men
in the street as they go to their work, marvelled 'that
the potent revival in the Wesleyan Chapel had produced no
effect on these pre-occupied people. Bursley, then,
continued its dull and even course.' There is a very good
suggestion here of how little the public at large may be
affected by storms that sweep over individuals or groups
of individuals, which we mention as a sample of Mr.
Bennett's skill and insight. There is a hint as to the
power of a bank manager which is perhaps not untrue to
life. He 'was probably the most influential man in
Bursley. Every Saturday morning, he irrigated the whole
town with fertilising gold. By a single negative he
could have ruined scores of upright merchants and manufacturers. He had only to stop a man in the street and
murmur, "By the way, your overdraft -," in order to spread
discord and desolation through a refined and pious home.
His estimate of human nature was falsified by no common
illusions; he had the impassive and frosty gaze of a
criminal judge. Many men deemed they had cause to hate
him, but no one did hate him: all recognised that he was

set far above hatred.' When Anna first called at the
bank, 'His final glance said, half cynically, half in
pity: "You are naive and unspoilt now, but these eyes
will see you harder like the rest. Wretched victim of
gold, you are only one in a procession, after all."'
The troubles that came to Anna falsified the prediction
we may perhaps hope - by developing her sympathies. In
another place, alluding to Anna's investments, made for
her by her father, the author remarks, 'They were the
finest in the market, the aristocracy of investments,
based on commercial enterprises of which every business
man in the Five Towns knew the entire soundness. They
conferred distinction on the possessor, like a great
picture or a rare volume. They stifled all questions and
insinuations. Put before any jury of the Five Towns as
evidence of character, they would almost have exculpated
a murderer.' Can it be said that this is an altogether
unfounded suggestion of the attitude of some portions of
the community, at any rate, towards the subject of
money? It is possible that the curious and the imaginative reader might find more portraiture in the book than
is contained in the references to local industrial and
landscape and municipal features, but it is not our province to provide such an index. We need only say again
that it is a clever novel, displaying deep insight into
character, great analytical power, and the dramatic
faculty. It is smartly written throughout, and while
becoming an essential part of the literature of the
Potteries, should appeal strongly to those amongst the
ordinary reading public who like brains and character in
a book. It is a problem novel, and like the problem
play, makes one think and feel.

12. LETTERS BETWEEN GEORGE STURT AND BENNETT

15 September and 4 October 1902

George Sturt (1863-1927) was Bennett's chief friend for
several years. He was a wheelwright and author. Among
his best-known books are 'A Small Boy in the Sixties',
'The Bettesworth Book' and 'Memoirs of a Surrey Labourer'.

My dear Arnold;
      Well - I have read 'Anna'. And behold it is good, and
I strongly approve.
      Bear this in mind, for I have some faults to find, and
I don't want you to suppose that I think them damning. I
only want you to consider ... etc etc....
      My feeling is, that you haven't let yourself go suf-
ficiently. The stuff is absolutely convincing, so far as
it goes: only, it has partially failed to reach me, where
I expect first-class art to reach. The *people* do not come
close enough: I am not intimate with them. They are real
- no doubt at all about that - yet only with the reality
of people seen across the street, or overheard in a 'bus.
You have studied them as though they were animals at the
Zoo; and all you say about them is accurate, but you have
omitted to show the much more than that, which you obviously know and might have shown, if you had been so
minded.
      In other words, your people are not quite creations.
Instead of writing about them like the God who made them,
you write as if you were a recording angel. Consequently
your book is a sort of document - a scientific treatise.
      I wouldn't say this, if I hadn't an explanation to
offer: or several explanations.
      First: You refuse to be emotional yourself: you are
unimpassioned, will not take sides, and all that - which
is quite right. But, you seem unwilling to let the reader
be emotional. You refuse to ask him to sympathise: you
simply call upon him to observe. You ask him to say, Is
this accurate? Is the drawing correct? Not, Are these
living people, to like and dislike etc etc.
      Consequently, you rob yourself of that help which you
have a perfect right to demand from the reader - that
sympathy with the subject, which would go out to your art
and meet it half-way. You don't get at our imagination,
but only at our intellectual judgment.
      (If you say that this is the proper aim of Fiction, I
reply that in that case Fiction is distinct from all other
Fine Arts. For all the other Fine Arts exert the whole of
their technique in an appeal not to intellectual judgment,
but to *taste* and *feeling*. An appeal to the judgment of
the intellectual is an appeal to Science, not to Art.)
      The second explanation of why 'Anna' hasn't quite got
at me is perhaps the same as this first, only that it
touches more on the technique of the affair. I perceive
a resemblance to the French methods - like Flaubert - or
the Russian, like Tolstoy. Of course you intended this
and, though I don't know much about these chaps, I fancy
you have got the hang of the method extremely well. But

it leads you (like them in my view) into an elaboration
of the wrong things. You make an inventory of the furniture in Anna's kitchen: you even interrupt for that purpose an interview which obviously was of a most crucial
nature. But while you give three pages to the inventory,
you can spare less than a page to the interview, and when
it is over, the reader feels dished, because something
must have happened - some interchange of emotion between
Mynors and Anna - which you have said nothing about. Were
those trivial sentences which they exchanged really all?
Or if not, was it worth while to spend so much time in
describing the colour of the oak dresser that you had no
space left even for the colour of Anna's face or whatever
might manifest her feelings at the time?

I'm not complaining of details. They produce an
'atmosphere': but unless they produce the atmosphere
required, they are out place. In this case, the kitchen
details produce an atmosphere of hum-drum domestic life,
continuous through years - not an atmosphere of excitement
and thrill and impending change.

I find this sort of thing all through the book, with
the result (as already stated) that my acquaintance with
the people is distant - more distant than with their
possessions or environment. Towards the end of the revival meeting - a quarter way through the book - I didn't
know Anna well enough to judge whether she was going to
be converted or not.

Third Explanation. It may be that the tapping of a new
and rich vein of material has tempted you to overdo the
methods of Flaubert & Co. It seems to me that your plot
was seductive, because of the chances it gave for describing things unknown to outsiders. Remember, I like these
chapters - the Revival, the Pot-factory, the Guide to the
Isle of Man, the Sewing Party, etc etc: they are extremely
well done. Yet my feeling after one reading is, that you
have too willingly allowed yourself to be dragged from
your 'characters' to do these things, knowing how jolly
vivid you could make 'em. You rather wanted to show off
your 'properties'.

But when you do let yourself go, you can do it! In the
chapter called The Downfall there is some imaginative
writing that I won't try to put an epithet to, but that
I admire very greatly. So of course, in little bits, all
over the book. Crisp and vivid and strong.

And that doesn't make me any the less eager to see
you do, in the same way, the things that one wants: not
the tables and chairs, but the men and women.

The Society (apart from its individuals) - the Sect -

comes out life-like. I recognise that the fate of a
Society may be as enthralling a subject as that of a man
or a woman. But then, will you not (using Flaubert's
methods if you like) create the atmosphere of the Society
by giving the members of it in elaborate detail?

Of course one knows that to you personally a display of
sentiment may be a distasteful thing. At any rate if it
amounts to *gush*. But, as a realist, you ought to remember
that sentiment and passion and even gush are things quite
as real as - say the talk at a sewing party, or the morning mist over a harbour.

Still - when all is said - your book is of the true
genuine sort of Art. It's worthy of English Fiction, and
will stand by the same tests that apply to Jane Austen and
Thomas Hardy. For the real stuff is there.

Ever yours, George

My dear George,
I am glad to be able to praise your article in this
month's 'Cornhill' with less reserve than you praise my
novel....

Your explanations of the partial failure of my novel
are all wrong. The partial failure is not in the novel
but in yourself. (Of course I can tell you exactly what
I think.) If the characters do not seem real to you, not
intimate to you, they seem real & intimate to every other
person, expert or inexpert, who has taken the trouble to
say anything at all to me about the book. Nay, they seem
intensely real. I have been amazed at the extraordinary
enthusiasm of people about the reality, the conviction,
& the appeal of the book.

I have *not* studied the characters 'as though they were
animals at the Zoo'; I have studied them as though they
were human beings. When you say that I write about them
not like 'the God who made them', but like a 'recording
angel', I don't know what you mean, & I don't think you
know yourself. And when you say the book is a 'scientific
treatise', you are using an absolutely meaningless phrase
worn out long ago in the futile attacks on naturalistic
fiction. You must know that the book is not in the least
a scientific treatise.

But what astounds me most is your remark that I refuse
to be emotional, that I am unimpassioned. The book is
impassioned & emotional from beginning to end. Every
character (except perhaps a passing figure like the
coroner) is handled with intense sympathy. But you have
not perceived the emotion. Your note on the description
of Anna's dresser is a clear proof of this. The whole

thing, for some reason or other, has gone right past you.
You are looking for something which you will never get in
my fiction, or in any first-rate modern fiction - the
Dickens or Thackeray grossness. I 'let myself go' to
the full extent; but this does not mean that I shout and
weep all over the place. I might have been seriously
perturbed by your opinion on my novel (since I regard
you as, potentially, one of the most distinguished
writers now living), had I not remembered that you said
just the same things about Turgenev when you first read
him. It is a singular & surprising thing, but your taste
in imaginative work is crude & unreliable. I don't believe you have any genuine critical standard.

Things have fallen out so that I may be able to visit
your ancestral abode somewhat earlier than I expected:
which I shall look forward to doing.

Remember me to all your people.

Yours, E.A.B.

13. UNSIGNED REVIEW, 'ACADEMY'

20 September 1902, 287-8

The review was preceded by a short notice on 13 September
that described the novel as 'a powerful story of life in
the Potteries.... The characters are keenly observed,
and the background keeps its place in the picture'.

Mr. Bennett has given us in this story something very
different from his 'Grand Babylon Hotel.' In that 'fantasia,' as he rightly called it, we singled out for
praise those parts in which character was sketched. Here
character is not merely sketched, but portrayed, and that
throughout; while instead of a farcical-melodramatic
setting in the Strand we have the grey actualities of the
Staffordshire potteries. The Five Towns - here called
Turnhill, Bursley, Hanbridge, Knype, and Longshaw - are
the instantly recognisable centres of the pottery manufacture. Pottery and Wesleyanism constitute the atmosphere.

The outstanding merit of the story is its intimate and
not unpoetic understanding of the life of the Five Towns.
In a drama set under a smoke-pall, filled with portraiture

of petty chapel life, and dominated by the harsh and
miserly character of Ephraim Tellwright, it might be
supposed that, as a set-off, the course of love would be
allowed to run with smoothness, or, at least, with ultimate certainty. But this is not the case. Henry Mynors,
the most superior man in the town, who can do everything
well, from arranging and modernising his works to organising a revival, is without the power to stir the deep
waters of Anna Tellwright's heart. He can command her
boundless admiration, and waken the hunger or illusion
of love, but that is all.

The holier privilege is reserved - unfortunately it is
reserved rather too long - for Willie Price, the sheepish,
simple lad who develops a new manliness when his hypocritical father hangs himself for debt in his own slip-
house. It is the sudden postulation of futile love
between these two at the very end of the story that, to
our mind, is responsible for the reader's dissatisfaction
with the completed drama. For our part we think that Anna
did really feel for Willie Price the satisfying love which
she perceived only when she was bidding him farewell to
Australia. All her feeling toward the perfect Mynors
was weak compared with that which flowed unbidden into her
words, 'Yes, I shall always remember you - always.' She
had saved this lad from disaster by the boldest act of
her life, an act of opposition to her tyrannous father,
and she felt for him something of a mother's love - a
characterisation finely perceived by Mr. Bennett. A
woman's real love for a man has always in it a touch of
the mother, for her heart vibrates on a whole. 'As their
eyes met in an intense and painful gaze, to her, at least,
it was revealed that they were lovers.' What to do with
them on the last page but one? Mr. Bennett's solution
does not satisfy us. We do not think that Anna would have
done what she did, or that Willie Price would have done
what he did. At any rate neither act seems proved, and
we are led to wish that this complication had been introduced earlier in the story, had been of its stuff instead
of its selvage. But, as a whole, the story is a strikingly vivid presentment of life and character in the
Potteries: as such it is memorable for its courage and
intimacy.

14. UNSIGNED REVIEW, 'SPECTATOR'

20 September 1902, 407

The reviewer included notices on several novels.

...Here, too, we have tragedy, but it does not seem to
us quite genuine. Anna (the 'Five Towns' are the Pottery
towns) finds herself on her twenty-first birthday a woman
of property. Her father transfers to her some fifty
thousand pounds which he has been husbanding for her,
without intending, however, that she should really have
the control of it. The situation is interesting. How
long, we ask, will she put up with this servitude? Then
a lover declares himself. She has always admired him;
and, indeed, he is one of the most admirable beings in
modern fiction. He loves her for herself, though he
has a general notion that she will not have empty hands.
Everything seems to promise well, and we begin to ask -
Whence is the trouble to come? Will some flaw be found
in the faultless? - No. Will the wealth disappear? - It
is as safe as the Bank. Anna has used a debtor somewhat
hardly at her father's bidding, and he kills himself;
and the debtor has a son. Pity suddenly turns into an
overwhelming love, not, be it remembered, in an unoccu-
pied heart. We refuse to believe. The tragedy is not
according to nature, but according to art.

15. UNSIGNED REVIEW, 'MANCHESTER GUARDIAN'

26 September 1902, 3

'Anna of the Five Towns,' by Arnold Bennett, is the work
of a capable and conscientious artist, one who has here
recorded some life in the Potteries with unusual insight
and fidelity to nature. The book cannot be called cheerful, but it is deeply interesting both as a local and
general study of human nature. Anna, the heroine, is an
heiress who, possessing £50,000 and a cheque-book, is
unable to buy a new dress for a visit to the Isle of Man

until - but we will not tell tales. She who is so pas-
sively acquiescent in the dreary isolation brought about
by her father's want of human sympathies can be strong
and even daring where she feels opposition to him to be
her duty. She is cleverly contrasted with the other
young girl of the book, a volatile chatterbox, 'victim
of a temperament which had the childishness and the
impulsiveness of the artist without his higher and
sterner traits.' The greater womanliness of Anna compared
with the chattering Beatrice is felt continually, although
the author puts on no labels and uses no superfluous
adjectives. The same forcible reserve and careful word-
selection are used throughout, especially in the drawing
of the chief character, the gruesome miser-father of
Anna. A 'good Wesleyan,' he had for years expounded the
mystery of the Atonement in village conventicles and
grown 'garrulous with God' at prayer meetings. But his
two wives had died broken-hearted, and the days of his
children were embittered and those of his neighbours
darkened (in two cases to a suicidal ending) by his surly,
terrorising ferocity and by his parsimony. Never have the
hideous possibilities of entire discrepancy between
Christianity and a man's daily life been more clearly
drawn. Yet the joyous outcome of the glowing fervour
and real goodness of the pious Mrs. Sutton is also
depicted with skill and with almost as much enthusiasm.

16. UNSIGNED REVIEW, 'TIMES LITERARY SUPPLEMENT'

26 September 1902, 285

At the first page of Mr. Arnold Bennett's 'Anna of the
Five Towns' we make the acquaintance, just outside Sunday
school, of a child who, though she has little or nothing
to do with the story, should stand to the author's credit
for an excellently natural little-girl study. She serves
to convey us into the religious (Wesleyan-Methodistic) and
social (solid manufacturing) atmosphere of the five
(Staffordshire Pottery) towns, and also to introduce to
each other the young man and woman round whom the love
interest of the story centres. These passages in the
early womanhood of Agnes Tellwright's 'Big sister' Anna
deserve a cordial welcome. With generous capabilities
Anna has been 'born into a wrong environment.' She has

long had to keep niggardly house for her father, a rich
old skinflint of sinister and formidable individuality.
The psychological interest turns upon the effect likely
to result upon Anna from the sudden acquisition of £50,000
worth of property, every penny of which is, however,
tightly controlled by her father. While the gross result
of all this is incidentally tragic, the net result is
surprisingly small - many will think too small. But
there is good reading in the descriptions of life and
character in the populous manufacturing towns in mid-
England. Turnhill, Bursley, Hanbridge, Knype, and Longshaw are, more than one of them, thinly-veiled Staffordshire names, and Mr. Bennett appears to write from
considerable knowledge of the district. Its topography,
'sombre, hard-featured, uncouth,' is effectively given,
while there is an admirable description of the hideous new
town park - 'from its gilded gates to its smallest
geranium slips it was brand-new, and most of it was red.'
And the amenities of the holiday in the Isle of Man are
to the very life. The various characters are also, as
we have said, cleverly presented. These for the most
part must be left to the reader, but Mynors perhaps calls
for some comment. Conscious, probably, of a prejudice
against him, which we irresistibly share, and all the more
anxious on this account to do him full justice, Mr.
Bennett has delineated his paragon of a hero through the
eyes of those in whom he excites so much admiration. The
tale of his virtues is long, and had novels indices we
might read something like the following under the heading
'Mynors':-

> Mynors, Henry, Owner of Pottery works. Morning
> Superintendent of the Sunday School and Conductor of
> the Men's Bible Class. Sparkling vehemence of his
> eyes, 3; kindness, mysterious deliciousness, and the
> inexpressible something dwelling behind his eyes, 4;
> his beauty, complexion, accomplishments, and exemplary
> prospects, 14; his careful dressing; brilliance of his
> new red necktie; his gardenia, 69; addresses a revival
> meeting, 69; comparable to a god, 99.

He is indeed an excellent young man.

17. W.L. ALDEN, LONDON LETTER, 'NEW YORK TIMES'

4 October 1902, 662

William L. Alden (1837–1908) was a leader writer on various New York newspapers for many years. He was also a
novelist. In his later years he lived in London. For
Bennett's comment on his review see p. 21. The review
began with general comment on the book market in England.

...There is ... one book which was published a day or two
ago which ought to succeed, and I am anxious to see if the
public will perceive its remarkable merit.

   The book in question is Mr. Arnold Bennett's 'Anna of
the Five Towns.' Mr. Bennett I do not know, except as
author of 'The Great Babylon Hotel,' a book which was
published last Winter, and achieved a certain degree of
popularity. It was good of its kind. It began with
broad farce, which was amusing, and then developed into
a Russian Nihilist story of the usual sort. 'Anna of the
Five Towns' is a totally different sort of thing. It is
a study of life in a small, Nonconformist town, and it is
not in the least humorous, neither does it contain any
adventures worth mention. It is a study after the manner
of Zola, but without those peculiarities which make Zola's
books sometimes tedious and often unfitted for general
reading. The plot is a simple one, but it contains a
surprise that breaks on the reader in almost the last
paragraph. The characters are wonderfully true to life,
and are painted with the hand of a master.

   I have read every novel of importance that has been
published in England for the last ten years, and, of its
kind, 'Anna of the Five Towns' is certainly the best piece
of work since 'Esther Waters.' Mr. Bennett is an artist,
and how he could have been willing to write such an
amusing pot boiler as 'The Great Babylon Hotel' will seem
strange to the reader of his new book. One thing may be
safely prophesied. 'Anna of the Five Towns' will be
promptly recognized by those critics whose opinion is
worth something as the most thoroughly artistic story of
the year. Whether the public will care for it, remains
to be seen. I am inclined to think they will. Work so
good as that which Mr. Bennett has here done can hardly
fail of its reward. Besides, the book does not err on
the side of length. It does not tire one to read it

through at a single sitting.

Still, if the public does not see the merit of
Mr. Bennett's performance, he will at least have the
satisfaction of knowing that he has done work of which
any man might well be proud. We shall hear more of him
as time goes on. He has found his proper path, and he
has only to follow it with the same care which he has
shown in 'Anna of the Five Towns.'

I have spoken somewhat at length of Mr. Bennett's book,
for it came to me as a complete surprise. I took it up
expecting to find another amusing tale of the 'Great
Babylon Hotel' variety. I found instead a novel of which
nothing but praise can be said. I do not know if
Mr. Bennett is young or old – and in fact I know nothing
whatever of him, except that he is the author of the two
books which I have mentioned. But if he does not take
a high place among English novelists in the course of
the next ten years I shall be greatly surprised as well
as disappointed.

18. UNSIGNED REVIEW, 'CRITIC' (NEW YORK)

June 1903, 563

Its sincere simplicity makes this an unusual book. The
crude little English town, with its dual interests of
pottery and Methodism, is described with a realism that
is never dull and that is frequently leavened with an
almost sardonic humor. Though he does not make it too
obvious, the author is essentially a satirist. The
Methodist 'revival' is admirable. Anna herself is a
delightful and perfectly intelligible character, if one
except that timidity that is so strikingly frequent a
characteristic of contemporary English heroines. Perhaps
the satirical presentation of Henry Mynors is, alone, a
little overdone; it is plain that if the book had been
prolonged for a few more chapters, this blameless hero
would have been in danger of developing into a villain.
Like life, and like the master realists, Mr. Bennett
shows a fine scorn of plot and construction. His book
is free of artificiality and compromise.

'Leonora'

1 October 1903

19. LETTERS BETWEEN H.G. WELLS AND BENNETT

20 and 24 August 1903

My dear Bennett,
    'The Truth about an Author' is literature; 'Leonora' as
you will someday come to see is no more than a creditable
performance. In the former you are saturated in knowledge, and the result is altogether happy. The latter –
the latter is matter for discussion. The dreadful thing
is the death of the husband, I don't see how you can forgive yourself that, and the subsequent petering out of the
book. But anyhow you haven't wrung the guts of life
though ever and again you get astonishingly near the
illusion. One is impressed by the idea that the clever
Bennett is going to be a fearful job for the artist
Bennett to elude. 'The Dance' for example is astonishingly neat and near, but it's a fake. You've never been
there. You impress me as knowing everything about Leonora
except how it feels inside, and you've seen fit to write
the book from inside. One is continually sitting back and
saying Now *did* she do that? and deciding that it is not
improbable she did. But one doesn't do that with a
character that is really and truly *got*. With some of the
people of Thackeray and Dickens you say: 'How like Becky
(or whoever it is) to do that?' We aspire to exalted
levels my friend and in that spirit I write. You do all
sorts of subsidiary things in the book extraordinarily
well. The nice shallow daughters (not the examinee who's
not understood) (P.S. Jane says she is) the horrible
vulgar social atmosphere (though done without the complete
detachment one might like) David, the old uncle and his

inside window, the father (excellent in his secrecy)
many things like that couldn't be better. But Twemlow!
Look here! I think the trouble is this. You're afraid
of your principal characters. Twemlow hasn't modelling,
he hasn't the unexpected inevitable thing about him that
makes an individuality. He's all right everywhere – that
is to say he is all wrong. He might have been made by
combining all the virtues that get full votes in a committee on the upstanding manly commercial man of the
world, and excluding everything else. You never met him
Bennett. You'll say you've met him by the dozen perhaps.
Which is exactly what I'm after.

    Excuse my handwriting. I'm in bed with my beastly
kidney again, and believe me.

                                Yours ever, H.G.

My dear H.G.,

    Your letter robbed me of my afternoon's sleep today
(I only got it this morning). I think your criticisms
are usually tonic & wholesome for me. And you impress
me fearfully sometimes – it may be your matter or your
manner – I don't know which. I really do think you have
a power of finding fault with fiction which I have not
seen equalled. And yet I also feel that you are incapable
of learning what I *know*, critically, of fiction. Your
outlook is too narrow, & you haven't read enough.
You still cling to the Dickens-Thackeray standards, &
judge by them. As when you say: 'How like Becky Sharp!'
Would you say 'How like Eugénie Grandet, or Madame Bovary,
or Maisie?' The strongly marked character, the eccentric,
the sharply-defined type, is the easiest thing in the
world to do (you wouldn't believe how I despise my Meshach
Myatt as a creation) in such a manner that the reader can
recognise all *his* acts for *his*. But the less typical can
not, & ought not, to be done in this way, for the reason
that they are not so in life. It is in remarks like that
that I think you give yourself away, & impair the 'sanction' of what else you say. Far more important, have you
grasped the fact that what I aim at is the expression of
general moods, whether of a person or a whole scene, a
constant 'synthetising' of emotion, before the elucidation
of minor points of character? We should never be able to
agree about the death of the husband. I take it you
object to it because it is a *sort of coincidence* and
because it solves (anyhow apparently) the difficulty
of Leonora. I must talk to you sometime about coincidences in fiction & in life. The fact that this death

solves a difficulty is to me entirely beside the point.
It is a part of the inmost scheme of my book. I seem to
think that the novelists who would object to it that it
was too timely, are too proud to take the genuine material
of life as they find it. Or they are afraid to. Because
life is simply crammed full of such timelinesses. Personally, I think the stuff after the husband's death the best
part of the book.

Quite beyond argument, you are wrong about Rose. She
is dead right all through. I know the type as well as you
do. Whatever the 'dance' is, it is not fake. I have
emphatically *been* there, & the thing is quite genuine,
failure or not.

I fancy I shall make you a present of Twemlow, as I
don't know whether I believe in him or not myself. When
I began the book I didn't, but as I proceeded I gradually
believed in him. The plot demanded an Anglo-American, &
I simply invented him to meet the case exactly. I confess
I have never met him. My brother(who is [a] good judge)
said he was not convincing, but my sister (who is a better
judge) is quite satisfied with him.

I feel in spite of my judgment that most of what you
say is half true, in the annoying manner of half-truths.
And I am much obliged to you for your candour (no one else
will be so candid). I am conscious now of an intention to
make you get down unconditionally on to your knees yet, in
a future book. Of course I see you are dealing with the
thing at an extremely high level, & that is all right.
I do honestly wish, quite apart from this book, that I
could fill you with a sense of your artistic limitations.
No one, except Turgenev, ever had more technical skill
than you have. But your perception of beauty is deficient; at least it isn't sufficiently practised and
developed. However, go on & prosper -

'My confidence is unabated,' says Sir T. Lipton today.
So is mine. (This is rather fine humour, eh?) ...

Yours ever, E,A.B.

20. UNSIGNED REVIEW, 'STAFFORDSHIRE SENTINEL'

12 October 1903, 6

The first chapter of 'Leonora,' Mr. Arnold Bennett's new
novel, appeared, it will be remembered, in the Summer

Number of the 'Sentinel.' It constituted a complete local
sketch. But it decidedly whetted the appetite for more,
for there was every indication that the story would be
powerful both in its 'plot' and its study of character.
'Leonora' has now been published in volume form by
Messrs. Chatto and Windus, and it fully sustains all the
expectations that we had formed. There is a sufficiency
of incident. Mr. Bennett's 'The Grand Babylon Hotel'
proved his cleverness in that respect. But it is as a
study of character that 'Leonora' makes the greatest mark.
Leonora and her family and neighbours are as our own
familiar friends. We at once become absorbed in their
hopes and aspirations, fears and ambitions, their achievements and their failures, their inward longings and their
outward daily actions - how little the connection between
them is, in most people's lives! Leonora remains
throughout the central figure, however; and Mr. Bennett
accomplishes with great skill the difficult task of making
a woman no longer in the first bloom of youth, and with
grown-up daughters, the heroine of a romance which the
reader is bound to follow with the keenest interest. He
is gifted with insight into the beatings of the human
heart, and he has a remarkable talent for recording its
manifold emotions. Locally, the novel will prove addi-
tionally attractive because the theme is set in North
Staffordshire surroundings. The suburb in which Leonora
resides is easily recognisable as Porthill, and much of
the action takes place at 'Bursley,' which is but a thin
disguise for Burslem. The 'Bursley' Amateur Operatic
Society and the 'Tiger' Hotel are immediately identified.
We are again much obliged to Mr. Bennett for the kindness
of his references to the 'Daily Signal' - which we venture
to accept as a tribute to the position of the 'Sentinel'
as a local institution. But while 'local colour' has been
applied with a lavish hand, it would be unfair to seek to
establish any parallel or identification in particular
cases.

The mental atmosphere of the Potteries, Mr. Bennett
thoroughly understands and cleverly depicts. Life as it
is lived here may be intense, but it has a tendency to be
narrow in its outlook, and we do not know that Mr. Bennett
does any injustice to the district in this respect. It
would be well, perhaps, if the Potteries people could take
Mr. Bennett's novel to heart in the way of realising that
there are other fields beyond the boundaries of their own
particular hedges. The procession of the generations is
aptly indicated in the concluding sentences of the volume.
'The Myatt family had risen, flourished, and declined.
Some of its members were dead, in honour or in dishonour;

others were scattered now. Only Ethel and Fred remained;
and these two, in the house at Hillport (which Leonora
meant to give them), were beginning again the eternal
effort, and renewing the simple and austere traditions of
the Five Towns, where luxury was suspect and decadence
unknown.' But the novel would for the ordinary reader
have been just as telling if the family whose history is
related had been located in some other surroundings.
The setting it has received will give it a strong hold
upon the local reader; but its palpitating and even
thrilling interest, its minute study of the complexities
of a woman's heart, would have been just as impressive
if the novel had had no relation to the Potteries at all.
Leonora is the wife of a manufacturer who did not do the
square thing by his partner, now dead, and after many years
his late partner's son returns from America - a man of
position - and receives a hint that his father's affairs
even at this late hour would be worth investigation.
Leonora too receives a hint of the danger that threatens
her husband - her hard, narrow, overbearing husband,
between whom and herself there has apparently never been
any love of the tenderer sort. Fond mother and good
housewife that she is, she thinks to render the new-comer
a friend of the family, so as to ward off the danger to
the home which she vaguely feels his presence entails. The
kernel of the story is the love that springs up between
Leonora and the stranger, Arthur Twemlow. Leonora becomes
the centre of a three-cornered storm. The image of
Twemlow creeps into her heart, but it cannot exclude a
saving affection for her daughters and her home, and as
a good woman, she cannot ignore her duty to her husband -
the husband who even contemplates murder for the sake of
money, and finally commits suicide as a cowardly escape
from the troubles he has brought upon himself. Our readers may remember the description of Leonora:-

[Quotes ch. 1, 'She was a beautiful woman' to 'regretted
that she should have missed it'.]

Arthur Twemlow came later. The subsidiary characters
are well sketched. 'Leonora' is the best book that
Mr. Bennett has written. It is in some respects an epic
of a class. Altogether it is the most readable and telling novel that we have seen for some time. All Potteries
people should read 'Leonora' - it will interest them
immensely. But beyond all question of local connection,
it is an exceedingly clever book - an absorbing chapter of
life is recorded with rare faithfulness and literary
brilliance. We very warmly congratulate Mr. Bennett upon
'Leonora.'

21. UNSIGNED REVIEW, 'MANCHESTER GUARDIAN'

14 October 1903, 5

Mr. Arnold Bennett writes cleverly, but, like so many
clever and accomplished writers, Mr. Bennett makes too
brilliant a parade of his psychology, and his characters
are therefore more like mental abstractions than human
beings. His 'Leonora' is about a beautiful woman of forty
who is married to a pottery owner in a Staffordshire town.
Her husband, John Stanway, is a nervous, pompous, dishonest man, weak as water, who robbed his partner and
afterwards his partner's children. One of these, grown
to manhood, who has made money by a pottery in New York,
returns to England, and discovers through an aged relative
how John Stanway had robbed him in his youth. Leonora's
beauty and obvious dissatisfaction with the humdrum life
in her villa, attract this American strongly. He loves
her, and for love of her refrains from the exposure he had
planned. John Stanway contrives to lose money by speculation, and at last commits suicide with a hypodermic
syringe. After eighteen months the American returns.
Leonora accepts him, and the two are left together driving
home in a cab. Mr. Bennett might have made greater sacrifices to simplicity. Phrases and words such as 'gracile,'
'iterance,' 'aloof quiescence,' 'lenient flexure,' &c.
are finely calculated to irritate. The folk of the story
are too humdrum to possess emotions of such delicate web.
We think the book a disappointing one, by no means so good
as Mr. Bennett might have written or might write.

22. UNSIGNED REVIEW, 'SCOTSMAN'

16 October 1903, 7

There is a certain value always to be attached to a novel
which describes some phase of life or type of people
thoroughly well known to the author - so well known that
he himself perhaps hardly recognises what are the characteristic touches that will arrest the reader's attention.
Mr. Bennett has already proved himself familiar with life
at the potteries; and in the present volume he again

introduces a group of people whose lives are lived, and
whose interests are centred, in 'Five Towns.' At first
these people do not appeal to us, for though one is
struck by the truth and originality of making the heroine,
round whom all the romance weaves itself, a matron of
forty, with three grown-up daughters, yet her charm
hardly seems strong enough to counteract all the appalling vulgarity of these same pretty daughters, and the smug
prosperity of the home, with its six o'clock 'meat teas'
and its subservient attitude to the blustering head of the
house. But, as one turns the pages, all these characters
and lives become very convincing, very real, very interesting; and, in spite of the fact that detestable little
Milly and her sisters call their parents 'Pa' and 'Ma,'
and tweak young men joyously by the ears, and in spite
also of the boorish ways and words of Leonora's husband,
one finds oneself much concerned in all their fortunes;
and readily acknowledging a fearless strength of description that compels admiration. One or two of the scenes -
possibly suggested by actual happenings - remain pictures
in the memory; the scene, for instance, of the queer,
rough, old uncle lying unconscious on the bed in the
girls' room, to which he has been carried, and surrounded
by all the untidy and frivolous evidences of the occupants having dressed there for the ball. Or, again, the
funeral of the little spinster, and the pathetic interior
of her room. And there is one page - a comment on the
parental attitude of repression - that seems to point a
meaning as well as to adorn the tale.

23. WILFRED WHITTEN, A NOVEL OF THE WEEK, 'T.P.'s WEEKLY'

20 November 1903, 794

Wilfred Whitten (d. 1942) was editor of 'T.P.'s Weekly',
to which Bennett was a regular contributor at this time.
A Novel of the Week was itself a regular feature. Bennett
received a copy of Whitten's review on the 20th, and he
wrote in the 'Journal' on that date that the review
'pleased and excited me so much that I had some difficulty
in recommencing work in the evening'.

In the great mass of fiction professedly dealing with the complexities of modernity one finds occasionally a novelist who has really examined life for himself, who has formulated his own philosophy and adjusted his own perspective. Such a novelist is Mr. Arnold Bennett, as he shows himself in the pages of 'Leonora'.

First of all there is the place, with its own scheme of things, its own traditions, its own atmosphere. And from this place spring up men and women who are intimately associated with the deep-rooted convictions of this organic whole by which the individual unit is moulded until it has absorbed him. This author makes one know Hillport as one knows a familiar place, which one never dreams of criticising. He does it so easily and with so sensitive a flexibility of manner that one never for an instant imagines that the obtruding provincialities of a tiresome little town are being thrust upon us. His method with the human beings who belong to Hillport is equally unostentatious and equally certain. He holds no brief either for or against human nature as illustrated by Hillport, but he does make you at home with this or that individual. He does make you believe that these men and women really exist, that they are people with blood in their veins, expressing avarice, emotion, anything you will, except the exploited formulae of the theorist. They speak with their own voices, and one sees them as distinct from their artificer and from each other. I have laid great stress upon the distinctness of the individualities in this book, because all through it one is subconscious that these people are closed in, compressed, fashioned mentally, morally, almost physically, by the spirit of the Five Towns. Take as examples of this distinct drawing - always in intimate sympathy with the spirit of place - the admirable portraits of Meshach and his sister Hannah, the uncle and aunt by marriage of Leonora.

But just as there is in the spirit of the Five Towns something beyond the personality of the particular resident, so there is something beyond Hillport in the spirit of life. And it is Leonora herself, with the charm and the menace of her forty years, in whom the spirit of life throbs with a troubling persistence. It is Leonora, for whom the Five Towns is at once too much and too little, too stifling and too arid. She feels that one cannot think for ever in wedges, that one does not know life because one has become used to people, that there are feelings and emotions outside of the dominance of routine. Leonora, still beautiful in her perturbing femininity, feels all this acutely, just as Emma Bovary felt it; but, unlike Emma, she has the strength of austerity in her blood. None the less, love comes into her life and teaches her to view her home and children and husband with new eyes. In one strong scene this woman comes to know her husband, John Stanway, to the core. Old Meshach, from whom John has expectations in the event of his not surviving his sister Hannah, is taken ill in Leonora's home. He is absolutely at his nephew's mercy:

> And then Meshach impassively submitted to the hand-
> ling of his head and his mouth. He gurgled faintly in
> accepting the medicine, and soon his temples and the
> corners of his lips showed a very slight perspiration.
> But though the doses were repeated, and the fomenta-
> tions assiduously maintained, no further result
> occurred, save that Meshach's eyes, according to the
> shifting of his head, perused new portions of the
> ceiling.

Presently John Stanway is left alone with this pros-
trate bundle of matter who stands between him and the
money which he must have. If only this wretched remnant
of flesh would cease to cumber the earth in time! If
only the man could die before the woman! So ponders
John as he approaches the bed to peer into the expression-
less yellow face:

> He was alone with what remained of Uncle Meshach.
> He moved the blanket, and touched the cloth which lay
> on Meshach's heart. 'Not too hot, that,' he said
> aloud. Taking the cloth he walked to the fire, where
> was a large saucepan of nearly boiling water. He
> picked up the lid of the saucepan, dropped it, crossed
> over to the washstand with a brusque movement, and
> plunged the cloth into the cold water of the ewer.
> Holding it there, he turned and gazed in a sort of
> abstract meditation at Uncle Meshach, who steadily
> ignored him. He was possessed by a genuine feeling
> of righteous indignation against his uncle.... He
> drew the cloth from the ewer, squeezed it a little,
> and approached the bed again. And as he stood over
> Meshach with the cloth in his hand, he saw his wife
> in the doorway. He knew in an instant that his own
> face had frightened her, and prevented her from saying
> what she was about to say.
> 'How you startled me, Nora!' he exclaimed, with
> his surpassing genius for escaping from an apparently
> fatal situation,
> She ran up to the bed. 'Don't keep uncle uncovered

like that,' she said; 'put it on.' And she took the cloth from his hand.

'Why,' she cried, 'it's like ice! What on earth are you doing? Where's Rose?'

'I was just taking it off,' he replied. 'What about aunt?'

'I met the girls down the road,' she said. 'Your aunt is dead.'

So this is the man with whom this woman must live and die. She knows him now, but even now he is too much a habit for her to assume an attitude of detachment from which to judge him. There are no tears, no protests, no smothered outrage of the soul. The woman is simply, mentally, and physically, tired of it all; the shifty, tricky ways, the sham of their common lives, upon which love has cast its merciless searchlight. The restraint is as admirable as it is unlaboured. In his realism this author has gone to life itself for the answers to his enigmas. In his desire to create men and women he has not been put off with a show of puppets. His claim as an artist is drawn from the source of all art - life itself. And from the standpoint of art it is significant that one naturally refers this book, not to the fleeting fashions of the circulating library, but to the great standards themselves - to Tolstoy, to Flaubert, to Thomas Hardy.

24. BENNETT TO LUCIE SIMPSON

30 January 1904

Lucie Simpson (d. 1954) was a literary woman from the Potteries. Her letter to Bennett is lost. In her book 'Contacts, Literary and Political', 1952, she gives a brief account of a visit to Bennett in London some months before this letter was written.

Dear Miss Simpson,

Many thanks for your letter. 'I am going to be candid.' You are quite wrong about 'Leonora'. In every way it is a much better book than 'Anna'. What women of forty *ought* to concern themselves with is not the point. What they *do*

concern themselves with you will know, in your moments
of self-candour, when you reach that interesting age.
That women of forty, generally, do regret the past is an
undoubted fact. That they long to be young again is an
undoubted fact. That they are particularly, peculiarly,
& specially passionate & prone to sexual excitement is an
undoubted fact. It was the discovery of these piquant
truths which led me to write 'Leonora'. I didn't conceive
the idea, & then search round for confirmation. The reverse. I don't think 'love' is 'woman's whole existence'.
It was not Leonora's whole existence. She was extremely
addicted to the higher walks of housewifery. But I think
that 'love' is the major part of woman's existence. As it
is of man's. I think there are only two things in this
world really worth having - sexual love & the love of
children. The next thing I expect to hear about you is
that you are married. Over & over again, in a career
intimately mixed up with many & diverse women, I have
found that women with a tendency to 'sit on' love have
ended suddenly & swiftly with marriage & become even more
'domesticated' than their sisters. (I had a striking &
dramatic instance in Paris only two months ago. As you
read this letter you will think that you know a great deal
better than me, but there will come a time when you will
perceive the limitations of the attitude towards life
which abounds in the Writer's Club. How well I know it!)
I'm very glad you think the style of 'Leonora' more sympathetic than that of 'Anna'. And I need not say that it
ministers to my pride to have your appreciation.

Yes, I am The Novelist's Log-Book in 'T.P.'s Weekly'.
If you guessed it unaided, you showed the cleverness I
should have expected from you.

Don't be angry with this letter. There are various
forms of compliments & this letter is one....

Believe me,

Yours sincerely,

E.A. Bennett

'Tales of the Five Towns'

10 January 1905

25. UNSIGNED REVIEW, 'STAFFORDSHIRE SENTINEL'

13 January 1905, 2

Mr. Arnold Bennett's new book, 'Tales of the Five Towns',
comprises eight stories or sketches, the scene of which is
laid in the Potteries, and five others concerning occurrences and incidents in London in which people connected
with the Potteries are involved. If it were necessary
to search for an analogy, the 'Sketches by Boz' might be
recalled; but Mr. Bennett's stories are modern and possess
an individuality of their own. Mr. Bennett's books come
as a 'boon and a blessing' to the Potteries coteries who
frequent afternoon teas and evening parties - they provide
a new topic and provoke fresh discussions. 'Have you read
Arnold Bennett's book!' comes trippingly from the lips of
some who have read it and some who only pretend that they
have done so. It becomes almost a passport to social
salvation. Then the book and its author form the subject
of conversation that is more or less deep. It is said
that the English people distrust genius, but as an author
and a fellow-citizen, Mr. Bennett has 'pretty well of'
popularity in his native district; and if there are any
who have doubts as to his orthodoxy in the matter of convention, it is more than possible that their hesitation is
due to a limited range of mental vision on their own part
rather than to any defect in Mr. Bennett's capacity as
an author.
    But there are other people in the world - painful
though it may be to contemplate it - than the suburbanites

whose little lives Mr. Bennett can depict or satirise
with such remarkable smartness. There are the great
operative classes who monopolise the free libraries and
the votes, and there is the small class to whom insight
is vouchsafed - not always for their happiness, as happiness goes in this world. Mr. Bennett knows and understands all these sections of the community, and his latest
book, like most of his others, appeals to all alike, and
from all it may well meet with the keenest appreciation.
Those who buy books, especially those relating to the
district, will of course add this one to their shelves,
and if they are wise they will read it too - with infinite
pleasure; but the book ought to be obtainable at all the
local libraries, a hint which it would be well to act upon
promptly.

The Potteries people love the district in which they
live, strange as that fact may appear to supercilious outsiders, and Mr. Bennett's books 'hit off' the characteristics of the Potteries in a vivid, amusing, and sympathetic
manner that it is impossible not to appreciate.

North Staffordshire has, for its size and history, been
somewhat prolific in authors; but it is not too much to say
that success has come with the greatest emphasis to
Mr. Bennett. He has the gift of seeing how diversified
are the mental and moral attributes of humanity in these
parts as elsewhere, and how varied and with what comprehensiveness of pain and happiness are the beatings of the
human heart. He has a strong eye for local colour, and a
splendid capacity for grasping a story and presenting it
with telling and artistic success. Some people imitate
Nature and express their dreams on canvas or on ware.
Mr. Bennett is an artist with his pen, and as a seer and
an interpreter he excels most of his contemporaries. He
unites a genius for seeing and understanding the great
inner drama of life with an enviable faculty for reducing
his observations to a literary form which is not only
enjoyable to mere readers in search of entertainment but
is a revelation of a larger world to those with eyes to
see and ears to hear. The Potteries ought to be proud
of Mr. Bennett. He has taken his place amongst the leading writers of English fiction, and he is writing substantial, living literature - because he is interpreting life
as it is lived. In some senses, he is an historian. He
is placing on permanent record the characteristics of
the Potteries and of its people. What Barrie and Crockett
have done for Scotland, Quiller Couch for Cornwall, and
Baring-Gould for Devonshire, Mr. Bennett is doing for
North Stafford; and he is doing it with equal ability to
the others. North Staffordshire has a strongly-marked

individuality of its own, as becomes the principal seat
of the British china and earthenware industry; and
Mr. Bennett's local books sketch and develop that individuality to the life. His books are equally successful
and enjoyable when he goes elsewhere for his inspiration;
but there is special brilliance in his work as a delineator of the towns and their inhabitants amongst whom he was
born. His genius has not been of slow growth; it
developed early, and his London and Paris experiences,
so far from impairing the freshness of his work, have but
matured it and given it added zest. His early promise
is illustrated by one of the sketches in this volume,
A Letter Home, written in 1893. The accidents, the
chances, the irony, the heartbreaking disappointments,
and the mysteries of life are seized hold of in a wonderful way in this early sketch. It is interesting to compare it with The Hungarian Rhapsody, and to trace the
achievement of a much higher stage of understanding and
skill. Mr. Bennett shares the faculty of the dramatist
in placing light and shade, tragedy and comedy, in due
proportion and relief. He brings his reader to the brink
of heartbreak from the pathos of a story; and then
relieves the situation by a humorous side scene. He
has an astonishing power of perceiving and analysing the
hopes and fears and ambitions that underlie the sobriety
of the daily routine to which most people are condemned;
but he can also relate a quaint or rollicking tale in
inimitable style. It is ever a pleasure to receive
another of his books, and the volume under notice is
worthy of its predecessors and of the author's reputation.
In 'Anna of the Five Towns,' he gave us an elaborate study
of a woman's character which has won the cordial appreciation of literary critics and of the public both in
England and in America. In 'Tales of the Five Towns' he
has given us many shorter studies upon similar lines. The
book will be simply 'devoured' in the Potteries, because
it is so racy of the soil that the characters and characteristics cannot fail to be recognised as familiar
acquaintances - familiar as household words; but by the
larger audience of the general public, the book should be
even more heartily greeted. We read it here with the
peculiar pleasure of viewing accustomed scenes; but for
the outside reader, it should be no less fascinating.
In 'The Grand Babylon Hotel,' the author manifested his
capacity in the way of dashing and thrilling plot; but
Mr. Bennett has done his best work in interpreting character and in presenting the atmosphere and environment
amidst which his characters live and move and have their
being. Outside readers will be instructed and amused,

perhaps, by the setting of the Potteries amidst which the
people in the book exist; but the local colour can but
add to the pleasure of reading, which will also largely
rest upon experiences and events which could not but be
absorbing in whatever dressing they were presented. The
author is equally at home as a literary artist whether in
the Potteries or Paris or London.

Some of the stories and sketches in 'Tales of the Five
Towns' have appeared in the magazines, but others we have
not met with before. In any case, they make a delightful
volume. Most of them, we believe, have some foundation in
fact. His Worship the Goosedriver is the story of a Mayor
of Burslem who drove home a goose for a wager; it is a
screamingly funny yarn, with a dash of the pathetic.
Mr. Bennett is familiar with the antics of men; but he
sees right down into a woman's heart. The Dog relates to
a young man who brought down the wrath of his highly
decorous family upon his head by taking a 'Wakes girl'
for a drive. A Feud belongs to Hanley. The author, who
by his frequent mention of this journal in his stories
kindly places it in the category of an institution that
is interwoven with the history of the Potteries, says in
one place –

'Every business man in the Five Towns reads the
"Staffordshire Signal" from beginning to end every night.'

That is as it should be, of course.

'Sacred and Profane Love'

21 September 1905

26. REVIEW SIGNED A.J.G., 'STAFFORDSHIRE SENTINEL'

22 September 1905, 2

The reviewer is unidentified. He may have been a member
of the Greene family. Henry Barrett Greene was editor of
the 'Sentinel' from 1899 to 1927.

When a writer has made his mark it is generally observable
that he has also made his style. He has, as it were,
marked off his little plot of land in the district he has
chosen to make peculiarly his own, probed deep into the
quality of its soil, and after some mysterious processes
of cultivation, given of its produce to a waiting world.
After one or two specimens with similar characteristics,
one grows accustomed to the type, and learns to expect
it. There are many living novelists who adhere, in all
essentials, to their earliest ideals. The list is too
long, and the names are too well known, to require
recalling here. But here and there, with startling
suddenness, a writer takes a new departure, and produces
a book calculated to upset any previous theories that may
have been formed respecting him. And this is precisely
what Mr. Arnold Bennett has done. It is somewhat difficult to realise that the author of 'Leonora' and 'Anna
of the Five Towns' is also the author of 'Sacred and
Profane Love'. He has forsaken the paths of quiet
respectability, as represented by middle-class life in
the Potteries, and turned his attention to the limning
of the tortures of passion-driven souls on a background

of intellectual and artistic life. That he has done it
successfully, there cannot be a shadow of doubt; whether
there can be any desirable object to be achieved by the
doing of it, is open to question. It is emphatically an
extremely clever book. At the same time, it is a book
which is bound to provoke a considerable amount of unfavourable comment. To many minds, the first half of the
title may seem superfluous; yet we may credit the words
with a subtler meaning than appears on the surface, and
one which only a careful and thoughtful perusal of the
book may enable the reader to discern.

In each of the three 'episodes' into which the book
is divided, the scene changes. The story opens in the
Potteries, of which the heroine is a native; passes to
London; takes in incidentally Mentone and Monte Carlo; and
closes in Paris. And for his heroine Mr. Bennett has
selected a sample of womanhood less admirable than real.
A descendant of famous potters, of spotless course of
life, she is the curious anomaly sometimes met with in
families of puritanical tendencies. It is a perfectly
natural and painfully realistic presentment of a woman of
strong impulses and passions, with heart and mind largely
governed by the senses, and with whom instinct was
supreme. She transgressed without remorse and almost
without shame, for to her Nature was all-sufficient and
all-excusing. Her temperament was far removed from
grovelling sensualism, for she possessed genius, which
found its vent in literature and achieved for her world-
wide fame; and she likewise possessed the redeeming feature of unlicensed love - she knew how to eliminate self.
The hero who matches this heroine was also distinguished
in the arts. He was a world-renowned pianist, a kind of
Paderewski, in fact, wielding a magnetic influence over
vast crowds, capable of arousing his audience to the
wildest pitch of excitement, or moving them to the profoundest depths of emotion. He possessed an impressionable, yielding, generous, lovable nature - a very comprehensive study of the artistic temperament.

A girl reared on an indiscriminate course of Herbert
Spencer, Darwin, the Bible, and the plays and poems of
Shakespeare, capped by some French literature, may reasonably be supposed to possess some intellectual originality,
and even to be favourably predisposed towards emotional
situations. Such an one was Carlotta Peel, when, forced
by her combined passion for music and her desire to hear
the great pianist Diaz, she broke through the conventions
of her circumscribed life, and ventured along to 'Hanbridge,' to the pianoforte recital. And here are some
very beautiful passages, interpretative of the music of

Chopin, as played by Diaz.   They constitute some of the
most charming pages in the book.   Small wonder, it will
seem to the reader, that Carlotta Peel was powerfully
affected by such agitating music, and that some mesmeric
influence should draw together the eyes of the player and
his visibly fascinated listener.   So, under the spell of
the musician, the girl remained in her place till the
audience melted away, and she was joined by Diaz.   From
here events move with breathless rapidity.   She consented
to drive in his brougham to his hotel, to hear him play
in private, and from this point her self-control gradually
left her.   The novelty and excitement of her position,
the seductive music, the presence of the man for whom she
entertained an almost hysterical admiration, and the
stimulating influence of absinthe - all helped to under-
mine reason and restraint.   The last shred was cast aside
when, in a passion of inspiration and abandonment,
Carlotta began to play, in a duet with Diaz, the music of
'Tristan and Isolde.'   Mr. Bennett is not the first
novelist who has used Wagner's voluptuous music as an
incentive to passion.   In George Moore's 'Evelyn Innes'
there is the suggestion of this opera as a background to
a similar episode.   After these brief hours, came a violent reaction, emphasised by the fact that Carlotta's only
relative had died in her absence, and the girl passed out
of the musician's life as suddenly as she had entered it.
   In London, Carlotta's life, though for a space
oppressed by a haunting fear that was half a hope, grew
and widened; and her energies found an outlet in the
making of books.   For five years she had lived without
love, absolutely outside of its exactions and its penalties.   But at the age of twenty-six love dominated her
life again; and all she had won for herself - fame, social
position, riches - seemed as nothing beside the fact of
her passion for a man who was already married.   But for
the fact that a woman does sometimes in the course of a
life love two men who are diametrically opposite to each
other, it would seem impossible that the woman who had
loved Diaz could love such a pitiful craven as Frank
Ispenlove.   The tragedy of Mary Ispenlove's life was
infinitely sad, and is sketched with a master hand.   It
is very real, very true, and very convincing.   But the man
who indulged in almost maudlin sentimentality with Carlotta, who threatened to shoot himself if repulsed, who
was easily repulsed, who accepted the situation when circumstances threw them together again, and who finally,
before his last act of cowardice, revealed the old Adam
in his blame of the girl, arouses no feeling of sympathy.
It may be a faithful portraiture, but it is a repellent

and contemptible character.

The interest of the story culminates in the meeting of Diaz and Carlotta, after ten years. Carlotta found, on the Parisian boulevards, a travesty of the Diaz she had known. A prey to a restless desire to find Carlotta again, Diaz had fallen a victim to the insidious poison of absinthe. In the hour of his need, Carlotta succoured him, her disgust swallowed up in the maternal instinct which is an essential of every true woman's love. The alternate comedy and tragedy of Carlotta's reclamation of Diaz is very wonderful, and deeply interesting. Ultimately she was successful. Partly by force of her love, and partly by her genius, Diaz was completely reformed. Their period of idyllic love, and retirement in the forest of Fontainebleau, fitted him for the resumption of his career, and the writing of a libretto by Carlotta for his opera completed her triumph. If his fall had been due to her, she had at any rate raised him up again, strengthened him and inspired him, and fitted him for a magnificent re-entry into the musical world. With his public success, Carlotta's life-work was finished, though it ended without the realisation of some of her nearest and dearest hopes. There is just a touch of bathos in the 'appendicitis caused by pips of strawberries,' scarcely relieved by the subsequent 'obsequies.' It is one of those occasions upon which an author insists upon having actuality at all costs, though the poetic and artistic senses might have been allowed to triumph over realism for once.

From this slight sketch, it may be seen that Mr. Bennett has handled an absorbing theme with daring and originality. It is, without doubt, his most ambitious work, and can scarcely fail to be a popular success. It is not a book for ultra-sensitive minds, but for those who dare to look the facts of life in the face, it is a book of enthralling interest. In its breadth of treatment, its variety of subject, its wealth of detail, and above all, its masterly 'grip,' it is little short of marvellous. Perhaps the story loses something of its power in being related in the first person, but that is balanced by Mr. Bennett's obviously intimate acquaintance with what he calls 'feminine mentality.' Whatever imperfections exist in the portrait of Carlotta may be attributed to the necessarily oblique standpoint from which a man regards the feminine character. However deeply a man may study the intricacies of a woman's personality – and assuredly Mr. Bennett is amongst the few novelists who have come extraordinarily near the mark – there is bound to be a certain aloofness in his conclusions. It would require mental gymnastics beyond the power of a man to put himself

absolutely and perfectly in the place of any but the more
shallow of women.

If a book which is so entirely a sex novel can point a
moral it would be this - that no woman can, with impunity,
entirely defy convention. It is a deplorable fact that
the men who are the first to lead women astray are also
the first to despise them. To a true man his wife is
sacred, and - however contrary his actions may be - she
is in his heart of hearts on a pedestal infinitely above
any other to whom his fancy may turn. Carlotta realised
this in the 'strange and terrible emphasis' Frank Ispenlove put on the words 'My wife!' a few moments before her
death.

And here is a fragment of philosophy which carries a
lesson with it:

> The woman must husband herself, dole herself out,
> economise herself, so that she might be splendidly
> wasteful when need was. The woman must plan, scheme,
> devise, invent, reconnoitre, take precautions; and do
> all this sincerely and lovingly in the name and honour
> of love. A passion, for her, is a campaign; and her
> deadliest enemy is satiety.

27. LETTERS BETWEEN H.G. WELLS AND BENNETT

25 and 30 September 1905

Wells later referred to the novel as 'Sacred and Profane
Copulation'.

Dear Bennett,

It *is* good and it *is* bad, and it is most interesting
and readable. Ouida and the best French models and our
Bennett and a certain extraordinary and persistent cleverness take me in gusts. Your English though is much less
clear and simple than it was - stresses on the epithets,
and a surface of hard bright points. And I feel more than
ever the difference between our minds. You are always
taking surface values that I reject, hotels are not
luxurious, *trains de luxe* are full of coal grit, *chefs* and
pianists are not marvellous persons, dramatic triumphs are

silly uproars. But it isn't irony - you believe in these things. There never was a woman like your woman, but no end of women journalists and minor actresses have imagined themselves like her. For some unfathomable reason you don't penetrate. You are like George Moore. You have probably never been in love. I doubt if ever you weep. You have no passion for Justice. You prefer 'style' to beauty. You are not a poet, you are not a genius. But you are a dear delightful person and please let me know what time you come to England.

Yours ever, H.G.

My dear Wells
Amid the chorus ('a great book, a great book') which that glittering novel has naturally called forth from most of my friends, your letter, with its thin small handwriting, is like a grandma announcing that I have been having too much sugar in my tea & must be content with half a lump. My dear H.G. you move me to explain myself to you. I have not yet decided whether I am a genius, but I shall probably decide, with that astounding quality of self-criticism that I have, that I am not. I an probably too clever, and, what is more important, too infernally well-balanced. I am ready to agree with you that no such woman as Carlotta ever existed. No character in any novel is more than a hint at the real thing, & it is right it should be so. You can't honestly say that Mr. Lewisham ever existed. You know, we all know, that after all our satisfaction with Mr. Lewisham, he never lived & couldn't have lived. He is an arrangement to suit the necessities of a convention; & here & there he bears a resemblance to a man. I choose Mr. Lewisham because he is one of the least unreal characters I can recall at the moment. All I would claim for Carlotta is that now & then she does what a real woman would do, & that her stiff lay-figure movements are sometimes really not so very stiff. Again, I must agree with you as to the style. But incidentally you must remember that this is not my style, but Carlotta's style, & that it cost me a Hades of a lot of trouble. I am inclined to think however that as regards style the best book I ever wrote was 'A Man from the North.' The question of my style must really be looked into. I have never been in love. Sometimes the tears start to my eyes, but they never fall. These things are indubitable. I have no passion for Justice. That also is profoundly true. I recognise that progress is inevitable & that it can only be achieved

by a passion for justice. But I reckon I am above a
passion for justice. There we come to 'the difference
between our minds'. I look down from a height on the
show & contemplate a passion for justice much as I
contemplate the other ingredients. Whereas you are
simply a passion for justice incarnate. You aren't an
artist, except insofar as you disdainfully make use of
art for your reforming ends; you are simply a reformer –
with the classic qualities of the reformer. Hence your
amazing judgments on Balzac, Milton, etc. Like all great
reformers you are inhuman, and scornful of everything that
doesn't interest you. Hence the complaint of the anti-
Wellsites that in your 'scientific' novels, there is no
individual interest, that the characters don't exist indi-
vidually. A not unjust complaint. The pity is that these
persons cannot perceive the 'concerted' interest of your
'scientific' novels. You are not really interested in
individual humanity. And when you write a non-'scientific'
novel, you always recur to a variation of the same type of
hero, & you always will, because your curiosity about
individualities won't lead you further. You are concerned in big crowd-movements. Art, really, you hate.
It means to you what 'arty' means to me. You live in a
nice house, but you know perfectly well you wouldn't care
what sort of a house you lived in. When you say that a
great pianist is not a marvellous person, you give the
show away. For you he is not. The astounding human
interest of a dramatic triumph is for you a 'silly
uproar'. In these two instances you show clearly, as
regards art & as regards life, where your interests
stop. You won't have anything to do with 'surface values'
at all. You don't merely put them in a minor place; you
reject them. A couple of pages devoted to surface values
will irritate you. You will never see it, but in reject-
ing 'surface values' you are wrong. As a fact they are
just as important as other values. But reformers can't
perceive this. They are capable of classing chefs, pianists and *trains de luxe* all together & saying: 'Go to,
I am a serious person.' You are, you know. The same
spirit animates you as animated George Macdonald's grandmother, who objected to the violin as a profane instrument. And the mischief is that, though you will undoubtedly do a vast amount of good in the world, you will get
worse & worse, more & more specialised, more & more
scornful. All this is not an explanation of you; but an
explanation of me. It 'connotes' the difference between
our minds. I proposed writing to you to offer Mrs. Wells
and you the advantage of my presence for a night or so on
my way to England early in December. If this suits, I can

then respectfully listen to your defence. I am much too
vain to mind being called 'not a poet', and 'not a genius'.
But to be called a 'dear delightful person' rouses my
worst instincts. It makes me feel as if I was like
Marriott Watson or Pett Ridge, and I ain't, not really.

Hommages à Madame

Thine

E.A.B.

28. A.N. MONKHOUSE IN THE 'MANCHESTER GUARDIAN'

4 October 1905, 5

A.N. Monkhouse (1856-1936) was the literary editor of the
'Manchester Guardian'. He was also a novelist and playwright, and Bennett had reviewed his work in the 'Academy'
in 1898 and had then written to him to express sympathy
with his aims in the treatment of provincial life (see
LAB II, 113-14). In 1912 Bennett reviewed Monkhouse's
novel 'Dying Fires' in the 'Manchester Guardian'.

Mr. Arnold Bennett has written stories of various kinds,
and some of them need not be taken very seriously, but
his 'Sacred and Profane Love' is an imaginative study of
a temperament eloquently presented. It should be said
that the book, though written with insight and sincerity,
is not suitable for promiscuous circulation. The heroine,
Carlotta Peel, the offspring of placid, respectable folk,
her home a 'curious, compact organism' of middle-class
provincialism, flouts heredity in her vague, unbridled
aspirations, her 'illusion of spiritual woe,' her vigi-
lant discontent. She tells her own story, and her feelings suggest, in this sleepy home of the proprieties, the
fine analogy of an enchantment from which she must presently awake. To change the point of view, her 'corruption' begins with a book of Herbert Spencer's, is fostered
by 'The Origin of Species,' and - though it is hardly just
to Mr. Bennett to give the sequence so crudely - is completed by 'Mademoiselle de Maupin.' Her meeting with
Diaz, the world-famous pianist, brings her complete sub-
jection, and though the episode seems scientifically
untrue and the mysterious warning by her dying friend is a

dubious expedient, the influence of music on a temperament
extravagantly sensuous is remarkably described. The second
episode is a much weaker one, but it displays the woman's
tragic misconception of the terms of life and, in her
relation to the second lover, some saving elements of
capricious humanity. Disaster comes, and at last opportunity. The second meeting with Diaz, his rescue, and
the devotion to his service may be taken as a kind of
justification. There is no need for a logical conclusion
or for a moral severely pointed. The story ends with the
accident of death. It is a disturbing book that may be
misinterpreted, but if the passion is sometimes rather
florid it is not simulated. To write such a book from
the woman's point of view is no small feat. Some of the
descriptions are admirable, and the whole book is written
with brilliant facility.

29. UNSIGNED REVIEW, 'ACADEMY'

7 October 1905, 1032

Mr. Bennett appears before the public in a dual capacity,
as a writer of lucrative trash, and as an artist. We have
no concern with Mr. Bennett's artistic conscience. He
knows what he is about better than most men. In all he
does, that quality of assurance is manifest, and he does
nothing that is not good of its kind. His melodramas -
fantasias, he is clever enough to call them - could not
fail to satisfy the abandoned craving for sensation: his
criticism should be better known that it is - his essay on
George Moore in 'Fame and Fiction' expresses one point of
view with singular precision and some beauty: his 'A Great
Man' has wit. But his best, up till now, is undoubtedly
to be found in 'Anna of the Five Towns,' in 'Leonora,' and
in his latest book, which is now before us. We feel that
these are his work. The others are simply turned off for
amusement in leisure moments, safety-valves for his superfluous steam. In 'Sacred and Profane Love' Mr. Bennett
has set himself a great task: he narrates the three
experiences of passion that have come into the life of
a strong and beautiful woman - a character which any
imaginative writer might well be proud to have created.
Her name name is Carlotta: and she tells her own story. The
personal method of narration is in this case a necessity,

and is not the least of the many difficulties that have
beset Mr. Bennett's path and over which he has triumphed
by the power of his technique. The chief difficulty, however, is to make the theme noble: the least wavering or
uncertainty of grip in the author, and the theme of passion
infallibly and swiftly becomes ignoble and sordid. Here,
again, Mr. Bennett has succeeded: he has created feeling
that is intense enough and sincere enough to need no
apology: but here also, in our opinion, lies the weak point
of the book. He has not sufficiently trusted to his power
to ennoble the theme on its own merits. He has made use
of artifice which was not necessary for him. He has no
need to make the lover, Diaz, a world-famed pianist: by
so doing he weakens the essential by introducing an element
of improbability into the opening phase of the book: and
again, at the end, the emotional intensity is lowered and
not heightened to climax by the superficial pomp of Diaz's
triumph in the Paris opera-house. A weaker writer would
have had need for all the glitter and tinsel which he could
command. Mr. Bennett has not. Tinsel merely serves to
obscure the large humanity of his treatment, conspicuous
when Carlotta steals down into the hall of the hotel in
the early morning and buys the boat-shaped straw hat from
the servant girl, and comes in contact with the people
starting for their work on her journey home; conspicuous,
too, throughout the second part and especially in the
scene - splendidly dramatic - between Carlotta and Mrs.
Ispenlove, a weak, whimpering woman, who rouses all the
pity in the strong heart of Carlotta: conspicuous in the
character of the very old man, Lord Alcar. These are
touches of genius.

30. A CHARMING YOUNG PERSON, UNSIGNED REVIEW, 'PALL MALL
GAZETTE'

23 October 1905, 4

The title of Mr. Bennett's new novel is a triumph in the
art of misdescription. It suggests associations which
have no part at all in the crude and mundane story which he
has condescended to put on paper. We say 'condescended,'
because the book is not worthy of a serious novelist as
the writer can claim to be, but only of a certain notorious type of authoress which its readers will easily

identify. It is, in brief, a 'shocker.' Miss Carlotta
Peel is a young lady of talent who throws herself in the
way of a famous pianist and proves a ready accomplice in
her own seduction. Immediately afterwards she leaves the
Potteries for London, where she writes of 'startling realism' - something, we imagine, like 'Sacred and Profane
Love.' An intrigue with her publisher turns out badly,
because, on hearing that his wife's body has been found
in the Thames, the publisher shoots himself. Carlotta,
however, forgathers with her pianist, now a dipsomaniac,
and reclaims him. Here, the hasty reader will suppose, is
where the 'sacred love' comes in! But not at all; Diaz
(whose drunken pranks have been described in a spirit of
rollicking comedy) loses his sinister appetite as the
result of having taken six doses of sedative instead of
one. From that point he is quite ready to recover his
art, and the pair produce a brilliantly successful opera
on the subject of Louise de la Vallière. And a few days
later Miss Peel dies from appendicitis. There is no doubt
a market for such 'thrilling realism'; but one would
rather see it left to those who cannot produce anything
better.

31. UNSIGNED REVIEW, 'BOOKMAN'

November 1905, 90

In one way 'Sacred and Profane Love' seems to us a novelty
in English fiction. The heroine is a woman who errs
willingly - exultingly. Yet Mr. Arnold Bennett neither
excuses her, apologises for her, moralises over her, nor
punishes her. He lets her tell her own tale; leaves her
to the charity of his readers. She justifies her own
existence and the manner of it. Mr. Arnold Bennett's
technique is such that the rather melodramatic plot is
by no means necessary to sustain interest and provoke
us to read on. The writing itself is sufficient to do
that. 'Sacred and Profane Love' is a piece of bravura,
astonishing in its strength and rapidity, and, we may add,
in its directness, where most writers would go no further
than insinuation. Carlotta and Diaz dominate the story
of course, but we like as much some of the minor characters and less fateful scenes - Carlotta slinking home in
a train crowded with workpeople, her appreciation of her

dead aunt's calm, colourless life, Diaz practising, the
Parisian ladies with the *peignoirs*, Lord Alcar, and the
satirical sketch of Mrs. Sardis, 'that impeccable *doyenne*
of serious English fiction.' If we have a fault to find,
it is that the illumination cast on the characters is too
much of the stage. They move under a limelight which may
emphasise the acuteness, but as surely diminishes the
subtlety, of Mr. Arnold Bennett's psychology.

'Whom God Hath Joined'

Late October 1906

32. MRS H.M. SWANWICK, IN THE 'MANCHESTER GUARDIAN'

7 November 1906, 5

Helena Maria Swanwick (1864-1939) contributed regularly to
the 'Manchester Guardian'. She later wrote books on the
women's movement and the League of Nations.

Mr. Arnold Bennett has been playing with Mr. Eden Phillpotts, but he has been working by himself too. 'Whom God
Hath Joined' is a serious and delicate piece of work, for
Mr. Bennett is an artist with a conscience - the sort of
conscience which makes it impossible to write what is
meaningless or second-hand. This is what can alone make
a book interesting, this power of seeing and speaking in
a personal way and of refusing hearsay experiences. You
feel it in the very first pages of the book, which seize
your attention with nothing more exciting than a man
pounding up a hill on a highly geared bicycle. The region
Mr. Bennett describes, one of potteries and collieries,
is set before us with no fussy, disproportionate elaboration of description, but with those few pregnant words
which show that it has meant something to him. The book
is the story of two separate actions for divorce - the
one brought by a woman, the other by a man. Love in both
husbands is a purely animal passion, followed by a revul-
sion which makes them long to stamp into the mud, to
obliterate the woman who has beguiled them; they are, for
the time, almost erotic, homicidal maniacs. Several women
are realised with unusual completeness; we are shown the

wisdom and understanding of the injured wife, the bare
austerity of the girl, her daughter, animated by a white
fervour of righteousness and filial love, the insolent
self-will and defiance of the other wife, the guilty one.
The two husbands are well contrasted; the bookish, un-
practical man, fundamentally celibate, full of fretful
fury; the 'man of the world' full of greedy childishness
and vainglory. There is a biting humour in the picture
of the latter, of his incurable sentimentality and his
concern for decorum, his delicacy constantly shocked by
hearing acts put into words, and not least in the contemptuous pity that cannot be refused to a creature at once so
gross and so vulnerable. The scenes in the law courts are
not what is called sensational, yet they may well appal.
The male characters in the book at every crisis exclaim
of the incomprehensible and incalculable nature of women;
yet the law of partnership with this incomprehensible
creature, in which all her life and happiness are concerned, is made and administered by one partner only.
One feels that the problems of marriage will never be much
nearer solution until the other party to the contract, the
woman, is brought into consultation. Is this conclusion
formed in the author's mind? Whether or no, it emerges
from his powerful book.

33. UNSIGNED REVIEW, 'STAFFORDSHIRE SENTINEL'

8 November 1906, 4

For Bennett's letter to the 'Sentinel' that the review
alludes to, see LAB II, 183-6.

The publication of a new novel by Mr. Arnold Bennett always
creates considerable stir in local literary and social
circles, for he is a popular and gifted member of a well-
known Potteries family. Moreover, his themes are not only
invariably interesting in themselves, but generally introduce 'local colour.' In his latest book, 'Whom God Hath
Joined - ,' there is an abundance of 'local colour,' for
the 'scene' is laid in Burslem, Hanley, and Newcastle,
and the problem that is discussed - that of divorce - is
one of great possibilities. It is a more than usually

substantial volume, and Mr. Bennett has again proved
himself to be a literary artist of remarkable insight,
of singular facility of expression, of distinct construc-
tive skill, and of a wonderful descriptive faculty. With
equal daring and knowledge, he has set forth the lives of
individuals such as are to be found in the Potteries as
elsewhere, and the result is a vivid and powerful novel
of the realistic type - a novel that is sure to be eagerly
read and as certain to be vigorously criticised. None of
the 'locality' writers - Crockett, Q., and the rest of
them - has been more successful than Mr. Bennett in catch-
ing the colours of the skies, as it were, under which
their characters live and move and have their being.
While others have taken Cornwall, Devon, and the South
and North of Scotland for their domains, Mr. Bennett has
appropriated the Potteries, and he finds honour in his own
country as well as at the libraries everywhere. But while
the characters may be real enough, even in the Potteries,
the author of course does not intend to convey that life
as it is lived here is all of the same drab colour as is
thus depicted - a distinction which we hope may occur to
outside readers. It would have been better if one sentence with regard to the street-life of Hanley had been
omitted, as an inexcusable exaggeration. But Mr. Bennett
would very likely say that he is describing an average
town, and that we ought not to be too ready to say that
Hanbridge is Hanley, that Bursley is Burslem, or that
Bleakridge is Cobridge, urgent though the temptation be;
as a matter of fact, there are plenty of towns much smaller than Hanley - quiet market towns - where the social
evil is enormously more flaunting and rampant than it is
in Hanley. When Mr. Bennett argued in a letter to the
'Sentinel' during a late controversy that there are villages in which there are worse scandals than come to light
in the Potteries, he was saying that which is true.

'Whom God Hath Joined - ' is a sex novel, and it
graphically and absorbingly deals with the sex question.
Opinions will differ as to the desirability of collating,
as the central incidents of a novel, circumstances that
are more frequently confined to venturesome newspaper
reports of Divorce Court cases. But after all, life is
very complex, and it always seems a little hypocritical
and ridiculous to adopt towards some of its phases an
ostrich-like pretence that the truth is different from
what it really is. Assuming that the novelist, like the
Stage, must or may hold the mirror up to Nature - the
reflection is not the whole of Nature, but only an element
in it: and yet sex is the most far-reaching of all
instincts and motives - then it must be admitted that

Mr. Bennett paints with the hand of a master of his
craft. He is no doubt painting from life, and he gives a
true likeness of the matters that he has chosen to depict.
Unpleasant as the book is in some of its details, its
power and realism cannot be disputed. The theme may be
distasteful to some, but the gifts of the literary artist
cannot be gainsaid. It is not a mere record of the
Divorce Court, however, and the record as it stands is
not given in the language of passion or pruriency. It
is all the more striking because it is an almost matter-
of-fact narrative; but that only shows once more that
truth is stranger than fiction, and that a moving and
brilliant novel may be made out of a faithful chronicle
of the events of a few more or less obscure lives. In the
novel, we see less of the interior of the Divorce Court
itself than of the agony and the shame, the temptation
and the wantonness, the suffering and the punishment, that
may either lead up to a Divorce Court trial or result from
it. The veil is lifted from the surroundings of the
errors that eventuate in the Divorce Court. Men are not
the only tempters; but whoever is blameworthy, it is not
only the immediate actors in the drama who suffer - they
may suffer even less than those whom they are bound in
duty to consider. It might be supposed from the title
that the novel was a defence of the indissolubility of the
marriage tie; but nothing of the sort seems to be intended.
It is a fine title, and the author is to be congratulated
upon the dramatic instinct that prompted it - but it is
that and nothing more, unless the author means to inveigh
against conduct that might lead to divorce. Mr. Bennett
does not pronounce any opinion on the theological aspect
of matrimony. In one case, a woman who makes a marriage
of convenience with a man who might have been interesting
to the right woman is divorced; he divorces her as much
for her callous treatment of him as for her sin. In the
other case, a man who had sinned much more viciously is
finally taken back to the arms of his forgiving wife,
after a strange scene in the Divorce Court, in which a
daughter had flinched from giving evidence against the
father whom she had spied upon and denounced. On the
whole, Mr. Bennett sketches his men better in this novel
than he does the women. The men are more actual. The
women are a trifle intangible and unsympathetic - except
the French governess, who is cleverly drawn, and stands
out boldly - as, indeed, she seems generally to have done,
though in fairness to her be it said that she seems to
have been actuated more by a passing fancy and an access
of passion than by any ulterior motive of finance. The
scene in the Divorce Court is a stirring episode, and

dramatically written, though it is difficult to believe
that so businesslike a young woman as the daughter could
have been so ignorant as to the manner in which she would
be required to give her evidence. The fact that father
and daughter never met again, though she rather priggishly
often inquired after him when he had returned to her
mother, is natural enough. The daughter was placed in
a cruel position throughout by no fault of her own, and
perhaps she could not have acted otherwise than she did.
The story of Annunciata Fearns is one of the most terrible
indictments of immorality that could be conceived. The
agitation of the profligate husband when he found himself
likely to figure in the Divorce Court is well done, and
so is his unreasonable anger when he found that there was
a delay in getting rid of the French governess. The scene
upon which the daughter spied is unusual in profligacy, and
a wife would probably be granted a divorce for the adultery
of her husband under her roof, an aggravated circumstance
that might fairly be held to constitute legal cruelty.
Whether the daughter should have left the house before the
governess in the morning is an open question; but the
entire chapter is the most masterful in a book that is full
of vivid writing. If one looked for lessons in a novel
that only professes to be a mere record, one is that
divorce cases ought to be heard in private, or not
reported, and another is that the way of transgressors
is hard and that it is best after all to forego wanton
delights and live laborious days - best, that is, for
peace of mind and the fulfilment of duties and the avoidance of ultimate trouble. We need not here 'reconstruct'
the story of the two Hanley solicitors in the Cheapside
office, one of whom is the petitioner in one divorce case,
while the other is the respondent in the second case.
Our readers would doubtless prefer to study the cases for
themselves. They will find them presented in an alert and
graphic style, and we are very much mistaken if the novel
does not become something like a rage in the town in which
the 'Daily Signal' is published, as well as in Burslem,
where two of the families resided, and in Newcastle, where
lived the schoolmaster co-respondent who died before the
case in which he was involved could be heard. Local names
abound in the novel, and its publication is a first-class
sensation for the Potteries. It maintains Mr. Bennett's
high reputation as a writer, manifests his versatility, and
places him in the front rank of living realistic novelists.

'Buried Alive'

3 June 1908

34. UNSIGNED REVIEW, 'SPECTATOR'

4 July 1908, 25-6

The author of this very entertaining work is not the
Arnold Bennett who writes of 'The Grim Smile of the Five
Towns,' but rather the Arnold Bennett who delighted his
readers with that brilliant study, 'A Great Man.' The
present book - also a study of the character of a man --
does not equal 'A Great Man' in construction and plan,
but it perhaps contains an even cleverer strain of social
satire. Let it be at once granted that the story is
frankly impossible and extravagant, but as an ingenious
vehicle for satirising the social life of the twentieth
century it must be very highly praised. The hero is Mr.
Priam Farll, a painter with a command of his art very
difficult to match among contemporary artists. His
painting is that of a master, and his style individual
and original. So convincing, indeed, is Mr. Arnold
Bennett's description of the artist's powers that nothing
but his astounding choice of a subject for the picture
which made his fame will deter the most knowing connoisseur among Mr. Bennett's readers from believing for the
moment in the fame of his puppet. Mr. Farll, however, is
afflicted with terrible shyness, and lives as a recluse,
known to no one. So shy is he that when his valet, Henry
Leek, dies suddenly, and the doctor believes the dead man
to be Priam Farll, and the live man to be the valet, the
artist does not disabuse him. Mr. Arnold Bennett achieves
a 'palpable hit' at contemporary journalism in the following description of the reading by Priam Farll of the
accounts of his projected funeral in the daily papers:-

[Quotes ch. IV, A Scoop, 'The voice of England issued'
to 'newspapers expressed the same view'.]

The burial duly takes place in Westminster Abbey, though
the feelings of Priam Farll, who contrives to find his way
to the organ loft, are very nearly too much for him and
he makes a serious disturbance. The rest of the story
is extremely diverting. Priam Farll marries a woman best
described in the author's own words: 'She could have been
nothing but the widow of a builder in a small way of
business well known in Putney and also in Wandsworth.
She was every inch that.' With her Priam Farll lives a
perfectly contented life in Putney till the loss of her
money, by sending him again to the easel, makes him discover that his genius is not dead within him. He paints
for some years, while a noted connoisseur, who has
recognised his style but thinks it an imposture, makes a
fortune by buying his works through a small dealer at a low
price and retailing them in America as genuine 'Priam
Farlls.' The action brought by the American to discover
what he thinks is a fraud is described at full length,
and the refusal of Priam Farll through his obstinate shyness conclusively to prove his own identity is made absolutely convincing. The book is a brilliant example of the
author's skill in whimsical satire, and it may be safely
said that there is not a dull page in the whole volume.

35. A LETTER FROM FRANK HARRIS

12 November 1908

Frank Harris (1856-1931) was at this time editor of
'Vanity Fair'. He and Bennett had only recently met,
despite the fact that they had mutual acquaintances in
the literary world. Bennett had reviewed Harris's writing
favourably for some years. For a short while the two of
them became intimate friends.

My dear Bennett,
     ...All my last hours in Paris were taken up with reading
the book you gave my wife, 'Buried Alive'. I wanted to
shake you for it. It is admirably written and delightfully humorous; but why make the incidents improbable,

why rob yourself of the help which a real skeleton
affords? The humour would have been seen as clearly
in a true tale and would have been, I cannot but think,
more effective.   I know I have no business to say this,
I ought to talk of the story as it is; but just because
I admire the writing and the humour so infinitely I cannot
help wishing you had had a serious theme. I daresay this
is a fault in me. I can only say I read the book with
delight and thought it admirably done.

I cannot leave this book without speaking of your skit
on English law and the procedure of the English courts.
It is the best skit I think I have ever seen in print,
entirely true and convincing, with a perfect logical
reductio ad absurdum. I do not know what they would think
of you in England going about with a fool's bladder and
slapping one of their cherished institutions on the head
in this fashion - it is colossal. My god, sir, if you had
done it with reality behind you, if you had broidered this
laughter on to the stern face of fact, everyone in England
would have recognized you for the greatest living humour-
ist. No laughter in Dickens at all like it, not of the
same quality. It is more like Cervantes at his best. But
why did you not do it on a serious theme? Don Quixote did
attack the windmill, and his coming to utter grief is the
climax of the humour. I still want to shake you; but I
shook with you first....

Yours ever sincerely,
Frank Harris

'The Old Wives' Tale'

30 October 1908

36. BENNETT IN A LETTER TO THE KENNERLEYS

7 October 1908

Tertia Bennett (1872-1949), Bennett's youngest and favourite sister, married W.W. Kennerley (1870-1965) in 1903.
Kennerley worked for the Board of Education in London.

I have corrected the proofs of 'The Old Wives' Tale' -
678 pages. I am sure Tertia is wrong about those two
chapters. I deliberately lowered the tension in the last
part of the book, in obedience to a theory which objects
to violent climaxes as a close; and now I have done it
I don't know that I am quite satisfied. I know the public
will consider the fourth part rather tame and flat, if
not dull. And I am not sure whether I don't slightly
share this view. This is amazing. Still, I must say it
is a bit of honest work. And the effect as you finish the
last page is pretty stiff - *when you begin to think things
over*. It isn't in many books that you can see people
growing old. I read 'Une Vie' again (than which I meant
to try and go one better) and was most decidedly disappointed in it. Lacking in skill!

37. A.J.G., IN THE 'STAFFORDSHIRE SENTINEL'

11 November 1908, 3

The only thing we have to find fault with in Mr. Arnold
Bennett's new novel is the title. 'The Old Wives' Tale'
is a name which does not by any means do justice to an
exceedingly fine novel, of deep and absorbing interest
throughout. Mr. Bennett's new book contains the finest
work he has ever done, and there is little doubt that it
will be the most successful and most popular, as it is the
most fascinating, of all his novels. Mr. Bennett has
brought his most brilliant powers to bear on his new work,
and one can only marvel at the immense amount of labour
and concentration involved in the construction of a novel
of such wide scope, as well as at the broad experience
and close observation of the world essential to the presentation of so vivid a picture of human life. The book
is long, and full of the most minute details of the lives
of its characters, but it is at the same time so humorous,
so shrewd, so entertaining, and so thoroughly human in its
interest, that it is impossible to regret the length of
the story. Mr. Bennett presents to us live people, showing us the development of their characters under the
stress of circumstance, and the added experience of every
passing year - revealing the scars left by the blows that
have shaped them, with such full and intimate understanding of the subject, that one cannot but be impressed
with the reality of the story he tells. He writes with
a certain playful detachment, but there can be no doubt as
to his real sympathy with his theme. 'The Old Wives'
Tale,' with close upon six hundred pages of by no means
large print, is certainly not a book for an impatient
reader, but lovers of the classic tradition in English
fiction will find generous entertainment within its covers.
    Mr. Bennett's book covers a wide area, both of time and
place. The story begins in the Five Towns in the early
sixties, in the days when the 'Staffordshire Signal' was
'a two-penny weekly with no thought of football editions';
it passes on to the Paris of 'l'année terrible,' and gives
a vivid description of life during the siege of 1870; and
it finally returns to the Potteries of the present day,
when the word Federation has begun to agitate the public
mind, and when matters of immediate local interest are
referred to in the 'Staffordshire Day by Day' column of
the 'Signal.' At the very outset of the story the author
describes the strip of manufacturing district lying like

a blot in the north of a beautiful country:-

[Quotes Book 1, ch. 1, section 1, 'No person who lives in
the district' to 'toy with a chop on a plate'.]

Here, then, in the midst of the district, and in a part
of 'Bursley' which is easily recognisable under the thin
disguise of 'St. Luke's Square,' Mr. Bennett starts the
story of the Baines family. They were the proprietors of
the large draper's shop in the Square - and lived - as
people in the sixties were wont to do - in the house
attached to the shop. Mrs. Baines is a fine character,
and a clever study, but it is mainly with the history of
her two daughters, Constance and Sophia, that the story
is concerned. John Baines, who had had a 'stroke,' and
whose greatest interest in life was the weekly visit from
his old friend, Charles Critchlow, has long ceased to be
anything but an invalid whose life was carefully watched
over by his attentive family. The shop was managed by
Mrs. Baines and two invaluable assistants, one of whom,
Mr. Povey, afterwards entered the family by marrying
Constance, and eventually relieved Mrs. Baines entirely
of the shop. The girls are an instance of the marvellous
diversity of character so often seen in members of the
same family. From the outset it is plainly to be seen
that Constance, plain, dutiful, and unimaginative, is
foreordained to Mr. Povey and a placid domestic existence.
But Sophia, beautiful, rebellious, headstrong, and ambitious, had a different career ahead of her. Her pre-
dilection for Mr. Gerald Scales, a commercial traveller
who periodically visited the Baines' shop, was at once
the cause of a family catastrophe and her exodus from the
Five Towns. The sensational end of an elephant at Bursley
Wakes had drawn away Mrs. Baines and Constance from the
care of the paralytic:

[Quotes Book 1, ch. 4, section 1, 'On the previous night
one of the three Wombwell elephants' to 'or perhaps will
ever occur, in Bursley'.]

Sophia, left in charge, was in turn drawn into the shop
by the fascinating personality of Gerald Scales, and the
result was the disappearance from life of John Baines.
In spite of maternal stratagem, Sophia's passionate youth
prevailed, and the timely inheritance of £12,000 having
fallen to Gerald's lot, the two eloped. The first portion
of the book ends with Constance's marriage to Mr. Povey,
and the retirement of Mrs. Baines. The second portion of
the book is devoted to Constance, and her uneventful and

laborious life. Her only boy, Cyril, is described from
babyhood, through childhood and hobbledehoyhood onwards to
young manhood, with a minutia which impresses one as the
truthful record of a real life. It is all very clever,
very real, and very true. The son of the unimposing and
homely little draper is shown finally as a successful art
student who insists on leaving his mother, his home, and
the Five Towns to start a career as an artist in London.

The third - and what will be to many minds by far the
most fascinating - part of the book is devoted to Sophia,
and her chequered career. From London the eloping pair
had passed to Paris, and in Paris Sophia remained for many
years. Mr. Bennett reproduces the Paris of a bygone time
with marvellous accuracy and attention to detail. Under
Gerald's auspices Sophia was enabled to see many phases
of life in the gay city, from the sparkle of the restaurants of the Second Empire, down to the horror of a public
execution. The description of the scene round the guillo-
tine, the savage crowd assembled to gloat over the spectacle, and all the sordid details of the machinery of
justice, is one of the finest pieces of writing in the
book. Four years having sufficed to convince them both of
the calamitous folly of their marriage, and to inspire
them with mutual hatred, it did not take long to reach
the climax of separation. From the moment when Sophia
took up in Paris the life of an independent and remarkably
practical woman, the fascination of her history is re-
doubled. Only a clever woman could have so determinedly
fought her way through difficulties and dangers, with so
cool and contemptuous a disregard for the people who threw
them in her way; but it is probable that even Sophia could
not have accomplished all this without the education of
her life with Gerald Scales. At this time 'she was a
woman of commanding and slightly arrogant charm, not in
the least degree the charm of innocence and ingenuousness.
Her eyes were the eyes of one who has lost her illusions
too violently and too completely. Her gaze, coldly comprehending, implied familiarity with the abjectness of
human nature. Gerald had begun and had finished her
education. He had not ruined her, as a bad professor may
ruin a fine voice, because her moral force immeasurably
exceeded his; he had unwittingly produced a masterpiece,
but it was a tragic masterpiece.

The fourth and last portion of the book is entitled
What Life Is, and here Mr. Bennett gathers together all
the broken and tangled threads of the lives of his characters, and shows very faithfully and very clearly, if somewhat depressingly, the end of illusions and the grimness
of old age. He does not seek to palliate the appalling

passage of the years, and though he does not hide the
fact that there are compensations for the old, it is made
plain that only the young and the vigorous can tread
proudly on the neck of circumstance.

Not the least interesting part of Mr. Bennett's book
are the references to local people and affairs.
Mr. Critchlow finds in the 'Signal' a reference to Sophia,
and reads it aloud to her sister:

> 'How do those "Signal" people find out things?'
> Constance murmured.
> 'Eh, bless ye, I don't know,' said Mr. Critchlow.
> This was an untruth. Mr. Critchlow had himself
> given the information to the new editor of the
> 'Signal,' who had soon been made aware of Critchlow's
> passion for the Press, and who knew how to make use of
> it.

There are numerous portraits, the following being one
which may be readily recognised:

[Quotes the description of Dr Stirling, Book 4, ch. 3,
section 2.]

Federation looms large in the closing pages of the book,
and the interest in the subject is our apology for the
length of the following amusing extract:-

[Quotes Book 4, ch. 5, section 3, 'Meanwhile, in the
matter of Federation' to 'was to give the answer'.]

We can warmly recommend 'The Old Wives' Tale.' It is
essentially a book whose every character, down to the
humblest, bears the stamp of genuine humanity - a quality
both rare and valuable in modern fiction.

38. GILBERT CANNAN IN THE 'MANCHESTER GUARDIAN'

11 November 1908, 5

Gilbert Cannan (1884-1955), novelist and playwright, wrote
for the 'Manchester Guardian', the 'Star', and other
papers.

The second half of Mr. Arnold Bennett's new novel, 'The Old Wives' Tale' is unworthy of the first, and is in some sort a betrayal, for in its unreality the tricks and artifice of the author's method are so apparent as to send the mind in a hypercritical and irritated condition to the first half, which had been so entertaining and delightful. It is then discovered that, though Mr. Bennett has extraordinary powers of observation, some wit, a gift of irony, and a certain sense of character, he has not the power to weld his details into a convincing whole. Each detail is true enough and roundly projected, but there is a lack of cohesion, of correlation, and there is always the suspicion that the characters exist for their author but not for each other. In the first half of the book Mr. Bennett is in the familiar atmosphere of the Five Towns, and writes with such a sure hand and often with so much charity and sympathy that the destiny of Constance Baines, dull and ordinary as it is, must be followed with interest. The destiny of her sister Sophia occupies the second half of the book, and though there is nothing in the events of her life which is improbable, her whole history is impossible and uninteresting, because, we are inclined to think, it begins with a character, Gerald Scales, who is of fiction and not of life. The house of Sophia's destiny, therefore, is built upon sand and very soon falls to the ground, and though Gerald very quickly disappears (he deserts her as soon as he has come to the end of his money), he has wrecked his author's story. The book is twice the length of the ordinary novel of these days, and the tale of Constance is practically complete in itself. It is perhaps the best thing that Mr. Bennett has yet achieved. In none of his books do we remember a better character than Samuel Povey, and Critchlow, though he is near caricature, is drawn with immense cleverness. The second half has too many of those errors of taste which seem to be bred out of the influence of the French novel on the Nonconformist mind.

39. AN OLD WIVES' TALE [SIC], UNSIGNED REVIEW, 'TIMES LITERARY SUPPLEMENT'

12 November 1908, 403-4

Whether it is because a vogue for the long novel is beginning to set in again, or, as we rather surmise, because his whole heart was in his story, only Mr. Arnold

Bennett can himself reveal; but his new novel, 'An Old
Wives' Tale', runs into nearly 600 pages of small print.
How much labour, how much patience, enthusiasm, and
sublime trust that fact entails needs little demonstra-
tion. The trust was by no means ill-advised. It is a
book one reads on and on with something of the intense
absorption with which one would read the autobiography
of a old friend. It ambles from event to event, from
year to year, grandfather to all but great-grandchild,
never fading in interest and reality. Yet it is merely
the life story of an old draper's two daughters, Constance
and Sophia, born and bred in the rather sombre, ugly
Midland town of Bursley. We see them first in their girlhood, in the crinoline days, chattering, quarrelling,
weeping, rebelling, in their queer old ill-built and
beloved house over the double shop - rather plain, loving-
hearted, and obedient Constance; fine, impulsive, arrogant, and beautiful Sophia. After nearly fifty years of
their lives' vicissitudes, shocks, monotony, and irrevoc-
ableness, we at length bid goodbye to old and mangy
Fossette, Sophia's French poodle, greedily devouring her
breakfast, her mistresses dead - their last, only-
surviving and cold-blooded friend. Not often comes a book
in which every human being portrayed so quietly takes our
confidence. We follow their fortunes just as we follow
our own - childhood, love, marriage, children, the world,
death. It is, therefore, an intimate story. It is unusually outspoken. We are even occasionally tempted to
fancy that its author may just possibly have submitted
his proofs to the friendly scrutiny of an old midwife.
It has successfully survived that searching ordeal. But
then, most men and women are upwards of, if not hopelessly
over, forty, and are not to be touched, or discouraged, or
nonplussed by a looking-glass that reflects what they see,
not what they are entreated to tell life's youthful illu-
sionists they dream they see. The book is leagues distant
from the erotic; it is neither pessimistic, mor mystical,
nor fantastic. It is often the happy task of fiction or
poetry to isolate such facets of life. But this tale is
really and indeed an old wives' tale told, as it were, by
Juliet's nurse to Mercutio. She spares that intuitive and
practised youth no detail; she all but ignores his acid
commentary. Almost everybody dies. Is it not the cumulative experience of our odd days here on earth that everybody *does* die - except our blessed selves? That alone is
pure conjecture. Mr. Bennett does not even seem to chose
and see the paths his characters are to tread. Constance
and Sophia, whom we defer to so respectfully in the last
few chapters, are just such old women as life makes of the

young girls we met so enchantingly in Chapter I. How
diverse their several fortunes were! And yet, though
environment is something, character is all but all.
So cunning is fate that she colours her inevitable with
the beautiful glamour of chance. But there are other
readers who like their novels cinematographic rather than
philosophical. And to them it may be confided that
'An Old Wives' Tale' swarms with incident. It embalms
two of the most remarkable corpses to be encountered in
fiction. There is a crime worthy of Dickens, yet a crime
that would have won the heart of Nathaniel Hawthorne.
There is a most sinister guillotining. And Sophia, it may
be added, spends at least thirty years of her life in a
palpitating Paris, years, moreover, that include the
garish early seventies. This suggests, perhaps, a rather
highly-seasoned dish. It merely in fact proves how true
to experience this book is; for all these threads weave
themselves aptly and inconspicuously into these quiet,
ordinary people's lives in much the same way as that
concatenation of crime, disaster, and futility, a morning
newspaper, add to the domestic peace and seclusion of a
solitary breakfast.

40. LETTERS BETWEEN H.G. WELLS AND BENNETT

Undated mid-November and 18 November 1908

My dear Bennett,
    You know what life is. I have really wanted badly to
write you at length about 'The Old Wives' Tale' and make
you understand that it isn't simply just genial mutual
flattery and so forth that I want to send you this time.
And days slip by and all sorts of things get in the way
of that really satisfying old style letter. I think the
book a quite pre-eminent novel so that it at least doubles
your size in my estimation. It is far too big, too fine
and too restrained to get at first anything like the
recognition it is bound in the long run to bring you.
It is the best book I have seen this year - and there have
been one or two very good books - and I am certain it will
secure you the respect of all the distinguished critics
who are now consuming gripe-water and suchlike, if you
never never write another line. It is all at such a high
level that one does not know where to begin commending,

but I think the high light for me is the bakehouse
glimpse of Sam Povey. But the knowledge, the details,
the spirit! from first to last it *never* fails.
    I wish it could have gone into the 'English Review'.
Well, I go round telling everyone I meet about it - I
wish Chapman & Hall would do the same. Go on great man!
Yours ever, H.G.

My dear H.G.,
    What am I to say in reply to your remarks? Consider-
able emotion caused in this breast thereby! Also no doubt
a certain emotion in yours, as you cannot write such
letters often!
    We must strive to live up to this. That is all....
Yours ever, E.A.B.

41. EDWARD GARNETT'S REVIEW IN THE 'NATION', AND BENNETT'S
RESPONSE

21 November 1908, 314, 316, and 23 November

Edward Garnett (1868-1937) was an author and critic; he
was friend and advisor to Lawrence, Conrad, and other
authors, and literary advisor to several publishers. His
review was unsigned. For his opinion of 'Anna of the Five
Towns' as a reader for Duckworth see p. 20.

In reviewing Mr. Bennett's short stories more than a year
ago, the 'Nation' advised him to return to the matter and
method of his 'Anna of the Five Towns,' which as a
description of old-fashioned provincial life in the
Potteries is a piece of work Balzacian in its human
interest. We pointed out that when the provincial loses
touch with his local types and local atmosphere and mig-
rates to London, his artistic talent is usually frittered
away in pleasing the fourth-rate tastes of Philistia.
Mr. Bennett now responds with 'The Old Wives' Tale,'
a novel of 578 pages, which traces the fortunes of the
Baineses, a Pottery tradesman's family, from the sixties

to the present day. Both as a human document and a novel
the book would have delighted the great French natural-
ists. Most novelists are rarely quite at one with their
subject; a little above or below it, they enrich, romanticise, or impoverish it. But Mr. Bennett really is his
subject, the breath of it, intellectually, in a remarkable
way. By the miracle that befalls now and then when the
spirit of an environment attains artistically a re-birth,
and rises clamant in the spirit of a writer, the tone of
our author's judgments, standards, and tastes seems to be
the spiritual legacy of generations of level-headed, commercial Midlanders, a race obstinate and staunch of backbone, utilitarian in outlook, yet not without imagination
and romance streaking its hard vulgarity. That this old
chapel-going, money-worshipping race should, amid the mud
and soot and steam and flame of the Potteries, bring
itself up to date with big villas and costly motor-cars
and Continental travel, is typical of modern manufacturing
England, but that it should grow critical of itself and
produce Mr. Bennett, who in 'The Old Wives' Tale' unrolls
before us in epic breadth the changing fortunes of the
Bursley shopkeepers, is really a rare stroke of fortune.
The novel will repay the attention of the social historian; in it lives again not merely a generation of trades-
folk that is now dead or done for, but the undying soul
of provincialism.

The opening, as the closing, scene of the epic is laid
in St. Luke's Square, round which the shopkeeping aristocracy of Bursley in the sixties is ranged. Mr. Baines'
draper's shop is the business establishment most respected
by the burgesses of Bursley, and Mr. Baines, a bedridden
paralytic for twelve years, is still 'our honored fellow-
townsman' in his neighbors' phrase, and in Mr. Critchlow's,
his old crony, the chemist. Mr. Critchlow, a tall, thin
figure, of rasping common sense and pharmaceutical dignity, is admirably indicated; so is Mr. Povey, the inconspicuous, ambitious, efficient shop assistant, Mrs.
Baines' right-hand; and so is Mrs. Baines herself, the
comely, stout, and commanding matron, who watches her cus-
tomers, her servants, and her daughters, Constance and
Sophia, with calm brows and all-seeing eyes. Where Mr.
Bennett shows himself the artistic master of his burgesses'
atmosphere, which he must surely have absorbed in early
youth, even as Dickens before him, is in the relation
which he draws of the family life upstairs to the shop
life below and the town life outside. The old-fashioned
shopkeeper was a substantial person, narrow in outlook,
but an inheritor of honorable traditions, and in his way
a pillar of the State no less than his near relative, the

yeoman farmer. Mrs. Baines, née Syme, from the moorland
parish of Axe, and her majestic and awe-inspiring sister,
Aunt Harriet, are persons typical of the wholesome history
of generations of farming housewives.

The formidable worldly shrewdness, innate Philistinism,
amd commercial aptitude of the British middle-class is
built on such social foundations as the Baines, the Symes,
the Maddocks, the Bolderos, the Birkenshaws, and the
Scales (all families in the drama) embody, and could we
trace back their social origins we should recognise that
a larger national drama lies behind, in the transformation
of the yeoman and small farmer into the tradesman and the
modern commercial Briton. Here is the significance of
this social epic: none of the characters, in mental
refinement or manners, show any inheritance of gentle
breeding. It is a stratum of Midland trading progress
and prosperity, the inner humanity of these Pottery folk,
homely and harsh as their own Staffordshire clay, that
confined the author's horizon. The two heroines, Sophia
and Constance Baines, whose life stories our author traces
from their impulsive girlhood till their death as elderly
women finally laid on the shelf, are presented with the
good-humored familiarity of their nurse who sees through
them, or of an aunt who will 'stand no nonsense.' We
assist at the notable death-bed scene of the paralytic
Mr. Baines, when the beautiful Miss Sophia, who should be
watching in the sick-room, is flirting with the gallant
young Mr. Scales, the commercial traveller of the great
Birkenshaws, and horribly well done is this death-bed in
its actuality and hard vulgarity. Vulgarity - we use the
word advisedly, for even the masterly scenes are painted
with a harsh complacency of tone, and a brutal stress
laid on obtrusive material facts that are both a criticism and a reflection of the shopkeeping soul. The court-
ship of Sophia by the commercial Don Juan, Mr. Scales, his
plotted seduction of her in a London hotel, the shrewdness
of her resistance, his sulky acquiescence in their marriage and their honeymoon in Paris, all this is photographic in its detail, and, no doubt, fairly true to the
manners of Bursley.

Similarly we do not criticise, but follow with the tribute of our absorption the narrative of how the placid
Constance is wooed and won by the mild but energetic
assistant, Mr. Povey, of how Mrs. Baines, in defeat,
fades off the drapery horizon, of how Cyril, the son and
heir, is born, of his unpleasantly spoiled youth, and the
paternal struggles to instil into him decency. Let us
confide to the author that his epic here grows tedious,
as elsewhere where we suspect him of obvious reminiscences.

But the whole narrative holds us; it is life, life petty, commonplace, mysterious, beneath its daily mediocrity and apparent inconsequence, and we are suddenly arrested by the cynical and shattering domestic tragedy of a Bursley burgess, our highly-esteemed fellow citizen, Mr. Daniel Povey. Mrs. Daniel Povey is an irreclaimable drunkard, and in a fit of ungovernable rage her respectable husband, the confectioner, murders her. His arrest, trial, execution, and the fruitless petition and public protest of the Bursley townsmen, all this is recorded and analysed with a force and sincerity that command our applause. Mr. Bennett shows that he has studied in a good school, and the best French realists would shake him by the hand. Mr. Povey, the draper, who has thrown himself body and soul into the defence of his cousin, the confectioner, catches pneumonia, dies of his exertions, and with Constance a widow, we turn to follow, again at epic length, the fortunes of her sister, the indomitable Sophia.

In Book III. our author sketches with undeniable cleverness Sophia's life in Paris with her wastrel of a husband, and the rapid decline of the couple's fortunes. Effective though the picture is, we perceive that the vulgarity of the mental atmosphere is not that of the late sixties, but of forty years later. It is the Paris of yesterday seen through the uncompromising stare of a modern Bursleyite that is presented to us, though we are frankly entertained by the account of the siege, of Sophia's relations with the aged *cocotte*, Madame Foucault, and of the rise and glory of the Pension Frensham in the Rue Lord Byron. Mr. Bennett always interests us by his keen absorption in the hard vulgarities of the commercial atmosphere, English or French, but he is not quite himself till he brings Sophia, now a woman of sixty, back to Bursley with a fortune of many thousand pounds. From this point the narrative is masterly. The description of the aged Constance's obsession by the cares of her incubus of a house in St. Luke's Square, of her useless worries, of her sciatica, of her devotion to her hard and ungrateful son Cyril, of the two old ladies' sojourn in the Rutland Hotel, Buxton, and of Sophia's defeat, and their return to the grimy embraces of their birthplace - all this is handled with the skill of an old Dutch master. Then the wretched Gerald Scales reappears suddenly out of the void which has hidden him for thirty-six years, and dies at Mr. Boldero's, the Manchester jeweler. The death-bed scene, Sophia's dulled reflections on the waste of her life, her return to Bursley, and her own sudden death by a stroke, all this again is seen and shown us with a horrible prosaic remorselessness that could not be bettered. The closing

chapter, entitled The End of Constance, the irrevocable
end of all these human plans and projects, these matings
and meetings, these journeyings, these ambitions, and this
petty wearing away of youth, health, and strength till our
dim eyes glaze and fix in the fading light, these chapters
bring to a close what is, in its scheme and performance, a
really remarkable work. We cannot but congratulate Mr.
Bennett on his return to the field of provincial life that
is by rights his own. He knows the provincials through
and through.

Dear Edward Garnett,
     (For I suppose it is you who have written the very
masterly review of my novel in the 'Nation'.) I just want
to ask your opinion on one point. Have you read 'A Great
Man' and 'Buried Alive', two of my novels that do not deal
with the Five Towns? If so, do you consider that in doing
them I 'frittered myself away in pleasing the fourth-rate
tastes of Philistia'? I do not seek to pin you to a
phrase, but to have your opinion broadly, because I regard
your opinion as a valuable one. Personally I consider
these two books just about as fine in the ironic vein as
we are likely to meet with. I may tell you that I have
no intention of sticking exclusively to the Five Towns.
I often feel that I am short of room there. I do not
think the third part (Paris) of 'The Old Wives' Tale' is,
on the whole, anything better than a first-class tour de
force. Much of it is very good faking, but it is faking.
You are wrong in assuming that Cyril's youth contains
reminiscences, except as to stealing money. I was, however, never found out! Otherwise your review is a solid
mass of rightness....

> Believe me,
> Yours cordially,
> Arnold Bennett

42. LETTERS BETWEEN FRANK HARRIS AND BENNETT

27 and 30 November 1908

Bennett wrote to Harris on 29 October, mentioning that
'The Old Wives' Tale' was just being published, and saying,
'I really should like to know what you think of it, - and

its chances for 1958' (LAB II, 228).

My dear Arnold Bennett,
...And now, how am I to write to you? We represent the
extremes of two opposing theories of art. How you have
been able to do justice - and more than justice to me -
I am unable to imagine. I find it hard to do justice to
you. I am indignant with myself for want of generosity;
but the truth will out, I am angry with you. We owe each
other frankness - you and I - entire sincerity - that is
the measure and proof of our mutual esteem.
    I've read your three books; but of course 'The Old
Wives' Tale' is the one you would wish to be judged by.
First of all, the workmanship is astounding; finer far
than George Moore's best; finer, I think, than Hardy's
best. The style is always beyond reproach; thoughts,
emotions, incidents, all perfectly clothed. The architecture too, as Goethe called the skeleton, superbly designed
- no faults anywhere in design - no flaw. The story-
teller's unique faculty everywhere apparent - then a
masterpiece.
    Half way through the book I thought so. I cried to my
wife after reading Sophia's first adventure in Paris to
her abandonment - 'An amazing book! I must finish it'.
Then the disappointment. You've made a fine creature,
just when we are vitally interested in her and her tragic
deception and the chances of her growth she falls to the
ordinary! True to life, Yes perhaps - but not truer than
the wild chance that she should pass the open portal into
the future and become a symbol - magnificent. Half way
through the book I envied you your amazing faculty for I
thought you were going to do - what do I say? had done, a
masterpiece - then -
    If I am wrong you must forgive me. I thought you had
painted the dull conventional English life of the home-
staying, conventionally correct sister at such length to
give the contrast point, to make Sophia credible to us.
I wanted her seduced and abandoned, and then I wanted her
to take her life in her hand and go on making her body the
servant of the spirit, determined to grow, to realize all
that was in her, to get the knowledge she craved for, and
to reach the heights! I saw, too, that such a woman would
inevitably, sooner or later, come across some man big
enough to appreciate her - a man who would have money,
place, everything. The confession of such a woman to the
man who loved her and whom she loved, seemed to me enormous. Then, the marriage, and the life in a foreign

country, the great life she is born for, and then home
yearnings and a visit to her stay-at-home sister and the
contrast between mangy tabby-cat and the superb wild
animal.

And you could have done it all; your description of the
execution and Sophia's rise above her ignoble husband -
all show the true flame, and you preferred to bring her
down to dulness and make her a lodging house drudge and
quench her noble spirit in petty economies. You give her
a muck-rake instead of a soul. It is all right but it
depresses me, it disappoints me. This book seems to me
but the pedestal of the statue. I want the statue. Or
is this merely a proof of my thirst for ideal things, for
figures greater than life, carved out of some enormous
cliffside by a greater than Aeschylus. I should like to
trace gigantic ebony figures out of the night itself with
a flaming torch. I want the realism; but I want also to
see the soul conquering its surroundings, putting the
obstructions under its feet; heaping up the funeral pyre,
if you will, from which the spirit may take flight.

You must not ask me for more than I can give. I am
partly in sympathy with Ruskin's criticism when he talked
about 'the weepings of a Pentonville omnibus'. If they
live the usual Pentonville life and like-minded die the
usual Pentonville death, then, I have no use for them.
But Pentonville is as free to the night-winds and stars
as any other part of this visible globe....

Yours ever,
Frank Harris

My dear Harris,

I am not at the opposite pole to you. Because I am at
both poles. I quite agree with your fundamental criticism of 'The Old Wives' Tale'. That is to say, I quite
agree with it in certain moods. I am capable of regret-
ting that Sophia developed as she did. My original intention was to make her a magnificent courtesan. But I
altered this, after due thought. I conceive that what
she did in fact become was just as interesting & as good
as anything else. What *you* want in life and in art is
the *expensive* - I mean the spiritually expensive. I want
it too. But not much of it (I did it in 'Sacred & Profane
Love'). At bottom I regard your attitude as flavoured
with a youthful sentimentality. At bottom I am proudly
content with the Pentonville omnibus. Why not? If I
cannot take a Pentonville omnibus and show it to be fine,
then I am not a fully equipped artist. (And I *am*.)
Ruskin of course was a sublime sentimentalist. There is

nothing better in my book than the return of Constance
from the railway station after seeing Cyril off to London.
Pure Pentonville! Not even sexual passion in it! If anyone says that such material & such an event are not proper
for the very greatest possible art, I say that they are.
(I never could argue!) People may talk about ideal art,
heroic art. But let an artist get away from the *average*
truth into an ideal of his own, & whatever he creates I
will say to him: 'But I can imagine something more grand
than that. Why the devil did you stop *there*?' What you
wanted, in reading 'The Old Wives' Tale', was another book,
but not a better one. To me the difference between one
form of human life and another is insignificant. *It is all
almost equally exciting.* That is my view. Someday I shall
do another book in the expensive vein of 'Sacred & Profane
Love'. And then you will see. I shall be very much
indebted to you if you will say in 'Vanity Fair' exactly
what you think of the novel. Go for it with all your fervour. If the article is as good as your letter it will be
very good. But shove the article in at once or it will be
commercially useless. I can't send you a photo, as I
haven't one. I detest photos of myself....

> Yours ever,
> Arnold Bennett

43. FRANK HARRIS, A GREAT REALISTIC NOVEL, 'VANITY FAIR'

9 December 1908, 754

Everyone is agreed that there are two schools in novel-
writing, as, indeed, there are two schools in all the
arts, the realistic and the romantic, as they are called
to-day, and the first thing to note about them is that
classics have been written in both styles; though, for
the most part, the masterpieces have included, or shown
an amalgam of, both methods. Naturally enough, the
English have always leaned to the romantic style, prefer-
ring, as might have been expected of a nation of colo-
nisers, the novel of incident and adventure to the painting of real life and ordinary passions. Shakspere, of
course, was an extreme romantic: he never wrote a play
about his own time and country, and the main interest of
his contemporaries, the sea-struggle with the Spaniards,
appears to have scarcely touched his consciousness.

It is usual to speak of Defoe and Fielding as realists; but the theme in 'Robinson Crusoe' is purely imaginary and romantic, even if the painting is realistic; and 'Tom Jones,' though a classic, is more esteemed than read, because of its faithful rendering of sexual desire. Scott was a prince of romantics, and by reason of a smaller mind and simpler feelings, much less of a modern than Shakspere. I always put Chaucer and Scott together in my chronology. Dickens and Thackeray both belong to the romantic school, though the one by dint of humour and the other by perfection of style discover realistic tendencies. The modern English novels which are on the way to become classics are all romantic; 'The Cloister and the Hearth,' 'The Mayor of Casterbridge,' 'Lorna Doone,' all disdain the simple life of our time. Avowedly realistic novels such as 'Esther Waters,' 'The Market Place,' 'The House with the Green Shutters,' and 'Maurice Guest' are on a lower level of esteem, though not perhaps on a lower level of artistic achievement.

Just as the tendency in England is towards romanticism so the tendency of novels in France and Russia, and even in Germany, Italy and Spain, has all been towards realism, and the realistic novel on the Continent counts its victories in a dozen masterpieces. The original impulse to realism seems, however, to be spent now in both France and Russia. No one would call Marcel Prévost a realist, though his painting of sexual passion is realistic enough; and Elémir Bourges and Anatole France, the two chief masters of modern French literature, are in frank opposition to what has been known as the naturalistic school. Tolstoi, too, in these latter years, seems to keep his romantic impulses for 'Resurrection' and his other novels, while spending his realism in passionate invectives against the courts and government of his country.

I have written all this to establish the fact that realistic art is not much admired in England. Ruskin's description of George Eliot's characters as 'the sweepings of a Pentonville omnibus' has a certain attraction and spiritual significance for us. We English have gone to the ends of the earth in search of riches and adventures: we have made cities in the frozen wastes of the Klondyke, and driven exploring parties across the torrid deserts of Central Australia; it is in our blood to be impatient of ordinary life here in England, and still more impatient of the faithful painting of it. It is quite true that Pentonville is as open to the night wind and as near the stars as the valley of the Yukon or the back blocks of New South Wales; but the unknown and the extraordinary tempt us, and we are impatient of the tea-table politics

of West Ham and the tepid pastimes of Upper Tooting. Is
there anything reasonable in this, or is it only the lust
of the English blood and a permission of the will?
George Eliot tells us that, 'if one had a perfect understanding of any ordinary life, it would be like hearing
the grass grow and the squirrel's heart beat, and we
should die of the roar that lies on the other side of
silence'; but no genius has yet been found capable of
painting a realistic picture that shall stand with 'Hamlet'
or 'Antony and Cleopatra,' and although Sancho Panza may
amuse us more, we all feel that the centre of interest is
in his master, the mad knight. 'The extraordinary,' as
Goethe said, 'is what endures in art and literature.'
   The English conviction bears out the German's saying,
and teaches that we only invent art because life is not
interesting enough, that we arrange the elements of life
to make the great meanings of it clearer, to bring out
the pathos of it, or the humour of it, or the force of it,
or the desire of it, or the beauty of it.
   Of course, if we arrange and idealise too much the
picture becomes silly: 'Chill October' is too romantic;
we prefer a little homely landscape by Constable. The
exact mean between the real and the ideal is very difficult to strike, but that should be the aim, and we condemn
a novel to a certain extent by calling it realistic or
romantic, though in England to call it romantic is admit-
tedly to praise it.

'THE OLD WIVES' TALE.'

'The Old Wives' Tale,' by Mr. Arnold Bennett, is a
realistic novel of extraordinary merit. From beginning to
end the style is excellent; as simple, clear, adequate,
and rhythmic as the style of Tolstoi. The architecture,
too, of the book, as Goethe called it, the skeleton of it,
as I should prefer to call it, is astonishingly well constructed - everywhere the brain power is of the highest -
the story-telling faculty, too, is of the very finest, as
good as Thackeray's best. The product, then, must be - a
masterpiece?
   Let me describe the book before judging it. It pur-
ports to be the life history of two sisters, Constance and
Sophia, the daughters of a shopkeeper at Bursley, a manufacturing town in Staffordshire. The two sisters live for
us, each with her individual life. Constance, very affectionate and dutiful, marries the man who, after her
father's death, manages the shop, and has a son by him,
called Cyril, who has certain artistic gifts. Cyril wins

local prizes, and at length establishes himself as an
artist in London. The life of Constance is one long
devotion, first to her mother, then to her husband,
Mr. Povey, then to her gifted son, Cyril. The overflow
of her affectionate nature goes always to her brilliant
sister, Sophia. Almost the whole of the first half of
the book is taken up with this life of Constance, and we
know no novel in which ordinary English life has been
rendered with more magic. We know the shop and the town,
and Mrs. Baines and Constance and Povey and Cyril, as we
know our own family and belongings. Moreover, again and
again this knowledge of the commonplace and familiar leads
us, in Mr. Arnold Bennett's skilful hands, to passages of
exquisite pathos, or astounding description. After the
marriage and honeymoon, Constance and her husband return
home and take up their abode over the shop. The following
morning Constance watches Sam Povey dress:-

[Quotes Book 2, ch. 1, section 2, 'Constance already loved
to watch' to 'close to hers, made her dizzy'.]

   In this one page the two people are realised to perfection. And here is another page in which the mother-love
of Constance for her son Cyril, twenty years later, is
even more finely rendered. They are together in the
sitting-room. Cyril wants to sit up to finish a painting
he has begun; while Constance believes it would be better
for his health if he went to bed early.

[Quotes Book 2, ch. 6, section 2, 'At ten minutes to ten
she said' to 'the pain it gave her'.]

   Let us throw off conventions and admit the plain
truth: mother love is here more intensely realised in
its passionate affection than Shakespeare realised it
in Constance. Mr. Arnold Bennett is among the wonder
workers in English literature.
   The second half of the book deals with the life history
of the handsome elder sister Sophia. She is presented to
us as very pretty and proud: even as a girl a certain reserve strength of character is subtly indicated. She
falls in love with a young commercial traveller, of a
better class than the ordinary, called Gerald Scales: she
is won by his good looks and gentlemanliness (he is a
University man). A small fortune is left him of twelve
thousand pounds; he asks her to run away with him, and she
consents. He means to seduce and not to marry her; but
she insists on marriage, and after a little quarrel he
pays the price. They go abroad to France, and she soon

finds out that he is selfish, irresponsible, ill-tempered
and pleasure-loving. In four years the money is squan-
dered, and the ill-mated pair hate each other, or rather,
as the author says finely, 'she loathes him, and he resents her.' He leaves her at the beginning of an illness;
she faints and is taken by a journalist, who knows her, to
a house where two cocottes live. They nurse her through
her fever, and when she gets well she repays their kindness by managing the flat for them and taking care of them
through the siege of Paris in '70-71. At the end one of
them tempts her, asks her to go out and meet a man, a very
rich man, very generous. Here comes the crisis of the
book: her English instincts predominate: she will not go:
she settles down into a household drudge, saves money,
takes a lodging house, and begins to make money. With the
years she grows wealthy and is greatly esteemed in the
Quarter. Finally, growing old, she sells the boarding
house for a large sum, and returns to her sister. Her
death and the death of Constance a little later, are both
pictured with the same remorseless, kindly clearness, and
the book ends.

It is a little disappointing to me: I had expected that
the author, were it only for the sake of the contrast,
would make Sophia a magnificent courtesan, in sharp relief
to her homely sister Constance. In thinking of how he
would treat the theme I had imagined all sorts of things:
had hoped that he would show how Sophia rose superior to
her loose living, how she seized the chances offered to
her, and grew wiser and sweeter through the new experiences till she finally met some man worthy of her, who
would marry her in spite of all, and then the sisters
might meet again and contrast their experiences and views
of life.

But this was not to be. Mr. Arnold Bennett chooses to
make Sophia almost as commonplace *pot-au-feu* as Constance.
The worst of it is that he could have painted Sophia in
the great way if he had wanted to. There are scenes in
the book of the life of the courtesan in Paris better
painted than anyone else could paint them, and he could
render the soul of the woman who rises superior to circumstances, superior even to disgrace, for he has done it in
an earlier book, in 'Sacred and Profane Love,' and done it
splendidly. I think if he had done it here, this book,
'The Old Wives' Tale,' would have been the greatest novel
in English. He might say, indeed would say, that I am
asking for another book, whereas he has given us this one.
Quite true; but I want both elements in a supreme book,
both the realism and the flaming leap of the human spirit
that spurns and disdains its surroundings and reaches

ideal issues. I want the exquisitely fine, transparent
glass of realism, filled with the ruby or golden wine of
imaginative romance.
   But Mr. Arnold Bennett has decided otherwise, and all
I can say about 'The Old Wives' Tale' is that it seems
to me the best realistic novel in English; in itself a
great book, yet with a promise in it even greater than
its performance. I expect a masterpiece from Mr. Arnold
Bennett, finer than the best yet given us in this jostling
screaming time.

44. R.A. SCOTT-JAMES, IN THE 'DAILY NEWS'

29 December 1908, 3

R.A. Scott-James (1878-1959) was literary editor of the
'Daily News' at this time. He founded the 'New Weekly'
a few years later, and was somewhat bitter that Bennett
offered him nothing more than encouragement. He published
'Fifty Years of English Literature' in 1951.

Most of us who are under fifty years of age - one cannot
help assuming that writer and reader are something appreciably under that to some unthinkable, but to others trivial,
half-century - can hardly realise that there are men and
women about us who were brought up in a world so totally
unlike ours that we regard it as purely historical. Yet
Mr. Arnold Bennett has brought out this fact in a way that
will cause misgivings to the very youngest of us. He takes
us back to the most vivid memories of our childhood. He
recalls to us what England was like and what people were
like in an age when electric trams were unknown, when
bicycles were rare, when the retail trader was a person
possessed of a soul of his own, or something which might
have passed as such. He has shown us people born in one
world and growing old in another. He has presented to us
the fantastic but too terribly true panorama of certain
persons who were young and idealistic, who were middle-
aged and practical, who were old and acquiescent; of persons who were born mid-Victorians, who became later-
Victorians, who to this day survive as firm survivals
among the moderns - moderns who themselves, being

appreciably under fifty, will survive to a derelict old age among people as unlike us as we are unlike the heroes of Mrs. Ward Beecher Stowe. No one of us will attain a ripe old age without experiencing three different genera-tions in our epoch of perpetual change. The tragi-comedy of growing old is Mr. Arnold Bennett's subject.

And in treating this subject, in three-fourths of his book at any rate, the author has surpassed himself. He has given us some people, and the place in which they lived, in all the minutiae of their and its existence. He has combined the realistic modern method with the bitter, ironical, sententious method of Thackeray. I should hesi-tate to say that there is anything in the first half of this book which Thackeray would have done better. And I do not think that Thackeray ever illustrated a law of life remorselessly working itself out with such philoso-phic intentness as Mr. Bennett reveals. His mind and his perceptions are at work simultaneously. He is observant, humorous, bitter, idealistic, and grimly, playfully syn-thetical. That was the world our fathers were born in - and it was; that is what our fathers are among us to this day - and it is. 'You cannot step twice into the same river,' said Heraclitus. 'You cannot go back to the town you were born in,' Mr. Bennett means to say; and his book makes his meaning clear.

Constance and Sophia are the girls, women, widows whom we see growing up from the fifties to the latter part of the first decade of the twentieth century. When we meet them first they are young girls - fifteen and sixteen - 'rather like racehorses, quivering with delicate, sensi-tive, and luxuriant life; exquisite, enchanting proof of the circulation of the blood; innocent, artful, roguish, prim, gushing, ignorant, and miraculously wise' - at an age when, 'if one is frank, one must admit that one has nothing to learn: one has learnt simply everything in the previous six months.' These two young people are uncon-scious of 'the miraculous age which is us,' They lived in the Potteries before the Potteries had acquired that big black spot on the map which now both dignifies and degrades their existence. They lived in and around the important draper's shop in 'The Square,' under the wing of their respected parents, the once active citizen, now paralytic, Mr. Baines, and Mrs. Baines, the ruler, the dictator of the household and of the morals of all its members.

In the first stage we see Constance and Sophia subjected to this parental rule, to mid-Victorian adamant. They take castor oil when they are bidden. They do not leave the house without the sanction of Mrs. Baines. They must

not, needless to say, realise the fact that marriageable
young men are real facts. They must pay attention to the
shop, preserving a proper distance from the assistants.
They must be careful that Maggie, the servant, does not
overhear familiar conversations. They must not go into
the drawing-room except on Sunday afternoons. They must
wait upon their paralytic father with proper punctilio.
And they must be quiet and attentive when Mrs. Baines is
directing their morals. Then Mr. Baines dies, because
Sophia has been looking out of window at a dashing commercial traveller; and Mr. Bennett soliloquises:

> John Baines had belonged to the past, to the age
> when men really did think of their souls, when orators
> by phrases could move crowds to fury or to pity, when
> no one had learnt to hurry, when Demos was only turning
> in his sleep, when the sole beauty of life resided in
> its inflexible and slow dignity, when hell really had
> no bottom, and a gilt-clasped Bible really was the
> secret of England's greatness. Mid-Victorian England
> lay on that mahogany bed. Ideals had passed away with
> John Baines. It is thus that ideals die; not in the
> conventional pageantry of honoured death, but sorrily,
> ignobly, while one's head is turned.

The death of Mr. Baines is the herald, not only of his
own oblivion, but of the break-up of his own generation
as typified by Mrs. Baines. But that generation does not
give place easily; it tries to shut its ears to the knocking at the door, insistently as it knocks in the whimsical,
assertive personality of Sophia. The romantic commercial
traveller whose fault it was that Mr. Baines died a premature, though scientifically speaking a belated, death,
is the symbol of the new influence which Mrs. Baines is
too out-of-date to resist. Sophia runs away with the commercial traveller, makes him marry her, and is translated
from the Square to Paris. Poor Sophia! She is the victim
of being half a generation ahead of her times, a suffragette before it was an honour to be a martyr to the
cause. But in Constance the old influences are stronger.
She persists like a piece of old furniture which survives
the relic-hunters and the broker's men. She marries that
trusted assistant, Mr. Povey, who has such a head for
inventing tickets and labels and sign-boards, who himself
outdistances Mr. Baines as railway trains outdistance
stage coaches, and as aeroplanes will outdistance motor-
cars. The married couple actually displace Mrs. Baines,
and Constance notices her mother shortly after the honeymoon - 'Poor dear!' she thought: 'I'm afraid she's not

what she was.' 'Incredible that her mother could have
aged in less than six weeks! Constance did not allow for
the chemistry that had been going on in herself.'

And so they go on, till Mr. Povey is 'forty next birthday,' though, dear innocent soul, he scarcely notices it
as we notice it tragically in these days of quick living.
And Constance buries her mother, and becomes engrossed in
Cyril, her son, and scarcely observes how the atmosphere
in the Potteries gets blacker and blacker, and the trains
run nearer and more frequently, and the electric trams
replace the horse trams, linking up the Five Towns of the
'District.' And Mr. Povey too gets buried, and Constance's
son goes to London, and her hair grows white, and at last -
at last Sophia comes back to live with her in the old house
in the modern Potteries. And still those two old women are
living there together.

I shall not dwell upon the career of Sophia - who has
pursued her life in Paris very wisely, shrewdly, circum-
spectly, not to say commercially, thus showing how honest
bourgeois ancestry can triumph over the flightiest of
modern temperaments. Suffice it that she is now an aged
widow, a contemporary of the Crimean veterans, living to
this day in comfortable and old-maidish sobriety in the
Potteries, hardly conscious of the fact that aeroplanes
are an innovation. It is Mr. Bennett, not the Sophias,
who makes us conscious of the strange, portentous progress
of evolution; of the lapse of time; the changing mind of
man; the clinging to old habits; the desperate love of
what has been; the inevitableness of what is to come, of
what is to replace us, and put us too on the shelf among
the outworn things. Mr. Bennett has timed his book so
that we may read it profitably before the New Year. And
he has performed his task laboriously, brilliantly,
accurately, never failing in his lifelike portraiture,
grim, humorous, cynical, elflike, yet idealistic. I
regret the modernism of 'Book III.'; but this is a real
novel, a novel of life, a novel of manners, and a philosophy for the men who will live to be in, but not to
belong to, the future.

45. UNSIGNED REVIEW, 'DIAL' (CHICAGO)

1 October 1909, 236

Unhappily named and ungainly in appearance, filling nearly
six hundred pages of close typography, opening in a way
that promises to tax the reader's endurance, and concerned
from beginning to end with mean or commonplace characters,
not one of whom is tricked out with the attributes that are
commonly thought necessary to arouse sympathy and retain
interest, 'The Old Wives' Tale,' by Mr. Arnold Bennett,
is nevertheless a remarkable work of fiction, a book of
such sincerity, truthfulness, and insight as to make the
ordinary novel seem hopelessly shallow and artificial by
comparison. Coming to us unheralded in the slack season,
it proves to be the most significant novel of the summer,
and probably of a much longer period. The Staffordshire
town of Bursley, typical of the provincial life of mid-
England, is the place, and the time is the stretch of
years from the middle to the end of the nineteenth century.
The stage-setting puts before our eyes a draper's shop in
the central square of the town, and here our attention
remains fixed, save for the single shifting of the scenery
which gives us Paris for a contrast. The proprietor of
the shop is a bed-ridden paralytic; his wife is a masterful person who directs the business with the help of Mr.
Povey, the shop-assistant, and a dependency of anaemic
virgins. There are two daughters in the household,
children when the story opens, old women toward the close,
and it is with the history of their lives that the book
has to do. Constance, the elder, marries Mr. Povey, and
in due course, the parents having died, takes over the
management of the business, is widowed in middle life, and
left with an idolized son who is nowise persuaded to follow in the footsteps of his ancestors, but develops
strange modern tastes and propensities. Sophia, the
younger daughter, has a more checkered career. Unlike
her meek and self-effacing sister, she has a passionate
nature that impels her to a disastrous adventure. The
cheap charms of a commercial traveller engage her girlish
fancy; she carries on a clandestine correspondence with
him, and finally elopes. He has recently come into a
modest inheritance which seems to be boundless wealth,
and the eloping couple go to London, with Paris as their
final objective. Marriage is no part of his plan, but he
is forced into it by Sophia's obstinate refusal to go any
farther than London except with a legally constituted

husband. Several years of pleasure-seeking follow; then,
on the eve of the Franco-Prussian war, he is at the end
of his resources, and deserts his wife, who has long
since lost all her illusions. She has a long and serious
illness, through which she is nursed by a kind-hearted
creature - a woman of the half-world - whose charge she
has accidentally become. After her recovery she under-
takes the management of a *pension*, and maintains it
successfully during the months of the siege and the com-
mune. Frugality and practical good sense - the inheritance of her stock - serve her in this crisis; her affairs
prosper, she enlarges her operations, and when her health
gives way in middle age, she sells her hostelry to a syndicate, and finds herself a woman of leisure with a comfortable fortune. All this time she has been dead to
Bursley and her family, but one day the relationship is
accidentally reestablished, and she goes to England to
visit her sister, also comfortably retired from business.
The visit grows into a stay, and for some ten years the
two old women share their old home. Then Sophia learns
that her husband is not dead, but is just at the point of
ending a wretched and poverty-stricken life; she hastens
to his last refuge, and finds only his dead body. She
has thought of him only with disgust for many years, but
this shock nevertheless proves fatal. Constance, now left
alone, does not long survive, and the family is extinct,
save for her son, whom the world has not taken at his
mother's appraisal, and whose colorless existence makes
no appeal to our curiosity.

Such is the outline of a book which the author
describes as 'a novel of life.' This it is in a very
exact and human sense. Just life, real and unadorned,
a futile affair for all concerned, is what is portrayed
in its pages. It is life viewed with microscopic vision,
described with absolute fidelity, distorted by no trace of
caricature, and commented upon, as we pass from phase to
phase, with grave, sardonic, sometimes almost savage,
irony. There is not a character in the book that is
ennobled or glorified by the devices dear to the romantic
novelist; there is no alluring heroine and no conquering
hero, there is no indulgence in empty rhetoric, and there
is no apparent effort to heighten either motive or situation. Yet with all this restraint, or perhaps just
because of it, the final impression is deep and the resultant force overwhelming. As the figures pass before our
eyes, and their lives one by one gutter out, we are made
to know them better than we know most of the human beings
of our actual acquaintance. This is true not only of the
half dozen chiefly concerned, but also of the minor

figures in almost equal degree. If we were transported
by some magic carpet to mid-Victorian Bursley, we should
have the advantage over their neighbors in our intimate
acquaintance with these people. We understand them as we
understand Balzac's men and women, and the great French
novelist never shaped more authentic creations. The
coloring of this novel is by no means as drab as this or
any outline would seem to indicate. It is animated and
even vivacious, for the most part cheerful in tone and
shot through with gleams of humor. Its texture is so
finely wrought that it is not to be read by leaps and
bounds without serious loss. It extends to nearly a
quarter of a million words, and few of them are superfluous. If it be censured for defect of ideality, it
must be praised all the more for shrewdness, for accuracy
of observation, and for the deep note of human sympathy
which only the most careless of readers could miss.
Moreover, although in its essence it is impressive of the
futility of the average life, we gather this message only
in our reflective moments of semi-detachment; we do not
brood over it, any more than do the characters themselves.
To them, life is an affair of ups and downs, no doubt, but
it is also too closely packed with immediate interests to
permit of their viewing it in broad perspective. The
author will probably be charged with pessimism, but one
has only to contrast his method with that of a genuine
pessimist like Mr. Thomas Hardy to realize that the term
is hardly elastic enough to cover both cases.

46. FREDERIC TABER COOPER, IN THE 'BOOKMAN' (NEW YORK)

October 1909, 186-7

Frederic Taber Cooper (1864-1937) was an editor and author.
He wrote about Bennett at length in 'Some English Story-
Tellers', 1912 (see p. 300). In his monthly reviews of
fiction Cooper usually chose some subject with which to
link the reviews. For October he chose W. Robertson
Nicoll's remark about 'The Old Wives' Tale': 'the story
is a masterpiece, and it lacks only a touch of poetry to
put it in the very front rank'. Cooper discoursed upon
the meaning of 'touch of poetry', and thought that perhaps
it meant artificiality and dishonesty.

'The Old Wives' Tale', by Arnold Bennett, is the volume
which Dr. Nicoll singled out for the qualified phrase
which suggested the present article. Frankly, it is a
book which fully deserves all that he has said in its
favour and something more besides. Not for many months
has a piece of fiction appeared which conveyed an impression of such magnitude, such finished workmanship, and
such a fund of reserve power. There are many books which
impress one with a sense of amplitude, a sense of being
spread over a very broad canvas. It is much rarer to find,
as in the present case, a book which gives a sense of
depth as well as breadth, a book that has a wonderful,
far-reaching perspective, making you feel that you are
looking not merely upon the surface of life, but through
and beyond the surface into the deep and hidden meanings
of human existence. As in the case of all novels which
really deserve the attribute of bigness, 'The Old Wives'
Tale' achieves its effects without the aid of a spectacular background or of exceptional and exalted characters.
Indeed, it would be difficult to imagine anything more
essentially mediocre and commonplace, more uniformly dull
and grey than the whole external atmosphere of this strong
and poignant story. A small manufacturing town of middle
England, with scant sunlight struggling vainly to pierce
the veil of soft-coal smoke which perpetually overhangs it;
a central square with its five public houses; its bank, its
two chemists, its five drapers; and on the floor above the
most imposing of these drapers' shops living apartments
occupied by the family of this particular shopkeeper.
Narrow, hopelessly conservative, unspeakably bourgeois in
their attitude toward life, the Baines family, nevertheless, stand out in this story as fair average representa-
tives of the human race, sufficient exponents of the three
great mysteries of life, birth, marriage and death.
There are, of course, exceptional people in the world,
people who achieve great things, and whose names are
enrolled permanently on the honour roll of fate. But to
the great majority the sum and substance of life is,
roughly speaking, somewhat after this fashion: there is a
brief period of youthful illusion, when one forms brave
plans for great achievements, and the years which really
count all lie ahead in a glamour of rosy hope; and then,
almost before one knows how it has come about, one is old,
and the years that count all lie behind, and the sum
total of accomplishments, as one looks back, seems insignificant, and one is glad to cherish the memories of brief,
fugitive happiness snatched here and there by the way.
This is not an unfair picture of the average life of the
great struggling middle class in an overpopulated country

of the Old World. And this is precisely what Mr. Arnold
Bennett has succeeded in giving us in his 'Old Wives' Tale'
of the lives of Constance and Sophia Baines, the two
daughters of the bedridden old draper through fifty years
of hopes and hardships and disillusion. It would serve
no useful purpose to analyse the plot of this volume, for
the pattern is too intricate to be briefly summed up - it
has the multifold and wonderful intricacy of actual life.
It is enough to say that there are very few books in
English which mirror back so truly and with such a fine
sense of proportion the relative amount of joy and sorrow
that enter in to the average human life - the unconscious
selfishness of youth, the rash haste to reach forward and
grasp opportunities, the relentless encroachment of disease, the loneliness of old age, the inevitability of
death. Naturally the book is, with all its merits, a
depressing one. It leaves behind it a sense of greyness
and loneliness and personal loss, and all the more so
because it possesses that rare power of making us feel
the brotherhood of these commonplace people that fill its
pages, and so rendering their successive passing away a
personal and intimate sorrow to each one of us. Undoubtedly, a Touch of Poetry, that is to say, a strain of
romanticism, idealising the meaner traits of character,
the harsher blows of fate, would lighten the gloom and
relieve the tension, but inevitably it would have shorn
the book of its chief strength, the incomparable strength
of literal and fearless truth.

General View: 1908

J.E. Barton's article reprinted here is the first general
survey of Bennett's work that is known. It was preceded
by an article in 'Hearth and Home' (27 August 1903), one
of a series, About Our Contributors, that was more concerned with the person than with the author. The writer
of that article, E.M.E., thought that Bennett's métier
was literary criticism but did note that his 'literary
ambition is to write the best serious realistic novel he
can, and also a sensational novel which shall be a work
of art'.

---

47. J.E. BARTON, FICTION AND MR. ARNOLD BENNETT, 'NEW AGE'

3 December 1908, 110-11

Joseph Edwin Barton (1875-1959) was at this time headmaster of the Crypt School, Gloucester, and later he was
headmaster of the Bristol Grammar School. He contributed
a chapter on Thomas Hardy's poetry to an edition of Lionel
Johnson's book on Hardy in 1923. The Rising Storm of Life,
a remarkable essay of Bennett's that Barton alludes to,
was published in 'T.P.'s Weekly' (5 June 1907). It
offered an apocalytpic vision of England, present and
future. It has only recently been reprinted, in 'Sketches
for Autobiography'. The story Barton refers to is Clarice
of the Autumn Concerts, which was reprinted in 'Tales of
the Five Towns' after publication in 'T.P.'s Weekly' in
1902.

The production by Mr. Arnold Bennett of his longest and
best novel, 'The Old Wives' Tale,' would seem to justify
what hereto, so far as I am aware, has not been done - an
appreciation of his work in bulk. By this I mean, of
course, an attempt to seize his symbolic value as a
writer, to perceive what in general he 'stands for.'
Usually nothing is more futile than efforts to 'place'
contemporary writers, for the simple reason that most of
them convey no real unity of impression. The only kind
of unity which the public understands is the unity of
sheer repetition, especially in local colour. A novelist
who locates all his stories in Spain, or writes untiringly
in the Devonshire dialect, or invariably makes his crises
an excuse for seascapes, or never fails to pit his heroine
against some colossal conspiracy on the part of the
Jesuits, is certain to succeed if he perseveres. The
public gets to like him, because it likes above all things
to know what to expect.

The vast majority of novel readers resemble the fashionable lady in the 'New Republic,' who, when Mr. Luke had
recited with tender melancholy his apologue upon human
life (set out for the most part in marine metaphor)
exclaimed cordially, 'Oh, thank you, Mr. Luke; I do so
love poems about the sea.' The sea, the scented orange-
grove, the passionate milkmaid, and the escaped nun
respectively claim their definite bodies of adherents;
and the assiduous specialist in any of these 'lines' is
not only sure of his following; he is equally sure of
easy and delighted recognition from amiable gentlemen who
'do' the fiction columns with the help of about twelve
stock epithets to pigeon-hole all reasonable varieties
of the commodity they have to appraise.

Real unity of impression, what we may call intellectual
unity, is apt to escape perception in any case; in Mr.
Bennett's case particularly so, since he deliberately lays
himself out to elude the superficial taster of fiction.
Inwardly, of course, he is one and the same; but outwardly
he is quite Protean, follows up the story of a girl's soul
with the story of a sensational murder, and piles a diverting social satire on the top of both. When he is doing
none of these things, he is writing short stories in the
French manner; and volumes of advice to authors, crisp
didactics on life, drawing-room dialogues, and serious
drama continue, but hardly complete, his repertory of quick
changes. No wonder, therefore, that he finds himself the
victim of incongruous eulogies in the Press, which would
incline us to regard him now as a depictor of humble lives
(consequently suitable for home reading), now as a contriver of jollity for the tired business man, now as a

weaver of le-Queux-like plots to brighten railway travel,
now as the strenuous guide of young men's mutual improvement. Needless to say that each of these presentations
is amazingly untrue, even for Press criticism. He often
describes the strange world where flourish revival meetings and Methodist sewing parties; yet anything more alien
from the pious magazine than these novels, or less appropriate as Sabbath school awards, I cannot imagine. His
humorous works are decidedly not of an order to tickle
palates already educated by 'Three Men in a Boat.'
Detective intrigues and jewel robberies are grist to his
mill, but the mass of his readers who enjoy these incidents may be trusted to miss the significance of their
setting. Lastly, he advises how to live successfully;
but the spirit and the standpoint of his advice are wholly
antithetical to the spirit and standpoint of Doctors Todd
and Smiles. The only quality, common to all his works,
which most of the discerning reviewers have perceived is
the finished facility of his style and workmanship. His
Socialist tendencies are also known to students of the
'New Age,' for he has stated and explained them in these
columns.

Being neither a professional reviewer nor a Socialist,
but simply a quiet provincial reader who happens to have
read Mr. Bennett entire, I naturally look within myself
for some reason of his peculiar appeal to my mind, and of
the speed with which I procure each new work he produces.
I seek also some definition of his continuity as a writer,
his identity as an artist, in works so diverse, superficially speaking, as 'Anna' and 'Hugo,' 'A Great Man'
and 'The City of Pleasure,' 'Whom God hath Joined' and
'The Grand Babylon Hotel,' 'Sacred and Profane Love' and
'The Sinews of War,' the short stories and a little
essay like The Rising Storm of Life. My insatiable curiosity includes further a desire to know why, in my own
opinion, 'The Old Wives' Tale' is the ripest as well as
the biggest of Mr. Bennett's novels.

Pursuing this introspective method, I recur to my first
glimpse of Mr. Bennett's quality. I came across an
extremely short story contributed to some paper; a story
of a young woman who with good talents and training as a
pianist had settled down to the trade of provincial music-
teacher. Accidentally she was noticed, was engaged to
play at an important concert, and played. Her performance
was not a fiasco. She played well. Considerable applause.
For a moment she descried the vision of fame, dizzily
bowed her acknowledgments of the call, and was not encored.
She returned to music-teaching in her birthplace, taught
there for a few years more, then married and had children

there, and presumably (for we hear nothing further),
exists there still. What impression is caught from this
résumé I cannot guess, but the story itself I found
thrilling. Thrilling. I mean, in Hilda Wangel's sense
of that adjective. 'Vécu,' a French critic might say.
It realised for me an individual life, projected for me
a culminating moment in that life, and above all invested
that moment with a profound documentary purport. What
pleased me chiefly was a happy conjunction of restraint
in the tale with zest in the telling. Obviously the writer
had immense detachment, absolute immunity from those polar
temptations which between them account for the failure of
nearly all stories; the temptation to play providence, and
the temptation to pile on the agony. No less obviously
had he keen enjoyment in noting and recounting that sad-
dish little abstract of life. It is possible that I have
exaggerated this bit of work, have read into it my subsequent sense of Mr. Bennett's fiction as a whole. No
matter. All Mr. Bennett's stories have the one striking
attribute - a lavish vitality expended, not on sentiment
or on philosophy, but on sheer joy in contemporary life
as a spectacle. His novels and what he calls his fantasias
are equally modern in spirit. He is the most modern writer
I know; for modernity with him is not so much a matter of
reflection or argument, but the air in which his temperament naturally exists. I do not deny him reflections or
arguments; on the contrary, he reflects and argues, as a
critic, exceedingly well. But primarily he is an artist,
a poet, and I know no other absolutely modern English
novelist of whom this can be said. Such things as the
Bursley electric trams and Bursley corporation, London law
courts, and plutocratic excesses in the Riviera, are
integral and fully dissolved elements of his imaginative
experience. He feels their poetic content quite spontane-
ously. If his medium were verse instead of prose, his
work would utterly confute the Stevensonian dogma that
the term 'hatter' is impossible for emotional verse.
He would absorb and alchemize the hatter with complete
success. In other words, his emancipation from the conventions of a dying epoch is so complete that it needs
no bush. It tinges every page of his writing, without
effort or conscious process. His novels are essentially
more modern, therefore, than the novels of Mr. Wells, for
example, or the plays of Mr. Shaw. His characters neither
wriggle on an entomologist's pin, nor pirouette dialecti-
cally, as properly galvanised impersonations of Will-to-
Live are expected to do. (Let me here state that I know
all about these artist-philosophers and their contention
that artist-philosophers are the only artists who matter.

More of this anon.)   The human comedy, as presented by
writers like Mr. Wells and Mr. Shaw, is a vehicle for
certain versions of the modern gospel.   I enjoy them.
I enjoy a dance of ideas, even when they appear in fancy
dress, as men and women (or rather, as women and men).
I enjoy Mr. Wells's pert little greengrocers and wispy
little schoolmasters, who assume so suddenly a cosmic
significance as centres of universal cataclysms.   But
there are seasons when I wish to contemplate this splendid,
turbulent and exciting modern epoch with pure pleasure,
with no moral or philosophic obsession whatever; to gaze
enrapt on this world of swift transit, large hotels,
crumbling creeds, cosmopolitan culture, incredible wealth,
fierce materialism, and recrudescent superstitions, without
one single impulse to reprove it, or pity it, or put it
right.   This is where Mr. Bennett comes in, this is the
magic drop he distils for me.   I cannot for ever be
regarding mankind as a fumbling and stumbling swarm of
homuncules, struggling towards Utopia with frustrate little
sparks of intelligence to guide them.   To see men as Kipps
walking is after all a somewhat depressing and myopic
frame of mind which can only be indulged at intervals.
Mr. Bennett has deliberately chosen, for theme of his more
serious novels, that stratum of English humanity which
previously had invited three writers so diversely excellent as George Gissing, Mark Rutherford, and Mr. Wells
himself.   Austerely bitter stoicism, deadly moral earnest-
ness, and scientific pity predominate respectively in the
social studies of this trio.   Mr. Bennett, with a weapon
of style by no means inferior in range, and certainly of
lighter make, has approached the same theme in a new way.
He has started, as the genuine realist in fiction must,
by giving to his people a native setting; and this implies
that he is a romanticist as well, for it is in the native
setting - adequately seized and interpenetrating the lives
of the characters - that realism and romanticism in fiction
kiss each other.   The nocturnal furnace-fires, silhouetted
pit-wheels, and looming slag-heaps, the crude vitality of
the people and their astonishingly depraved dialect, the
hard piety and blatant irreverence, quaint local feuds,
reckless pleasures, monotonous manufacture redeemed by the
beautiful touch of art which completes it, sooty build-
ings, garish drink-palaces and liquid mud that compose the
live towns (I know them) are for Mr. Bennett the ingredients of an astounding poem.   He feels their atmosphere
intensely.   And his potters, shopkeepers, and town-
councillors are all instinct with it too.   His sympathy
with their souls is complete.   I mean his artistic sympathy.   Patronage, pity, ridicule, cynicism are therefore

totally foreign to his method. These people who were
born in Bursley or Knype (including the prosperous relations who have migrated to Oldcastle), who discuss the
local rates in the local bars, sell pottery and buy motor
cars, dress shop-windows and accumulate petty gains, are
connoisseurs of football, preserve the more fervid religious cults and associate in Bands for purposes of Hope,
all alike he takes with absolute seriousness. I mean
artistic seriousness, which as everybody ought to know is
compatible with the utmost humour and buoyancy of spirit.
Against this background, and operant in this society, he
perceives the decay of an old order and the chaotic fer-
ment of a new. Beginning with real people in a real place,
and assigning both to place and to people that primary
importance which is due to facts (visionaries please note),
Mr. Bennett can afford to see his world with modern eyes,
can fling himself with wild gusto into the turbid current
of mental, moral and material revolution without dehumanis-
ing in the least the milieu which that revolution affects.
The Five Towns and their actual existence have been
Mr. Bennett's sheet-anchor as a novelist. They have kept
him human in spite of Herbert Spencer, and solid in spite
of a somewhat reckless theoretical acquiescence in the
promptings of life-force. No doubt Mr. Bennett is a sym-
bolist as well as a realist and a romanticist. Very much
so. His Annas and Leonoras and Phyllises and Annunciatas
and Sophias and Constances have each her own suggestive
value, as well as individuality. They suggest, in various
degrees of tragedy, various phases in the emergence of new
susceptibilities and a new ethical standard. The Death of
Simon Fuge - a truly remarkable piece of work - is fine by
very virtue of the symbolic vein that qualifies the realistic vigour of its narrative. But in all these works, as
I have hinted, Mr. Bennett has got hold of flesh and blood
to begin with. In all of them the praise of life - first
function of the artist - precedes its analysis. And his
Socialism (or Radicalism, or whatever he calls it) is
likewive subjected to aesthetic laws. He can visualise a
thousand-pound motor car without dragging in the sweated
toiler - who is probably enjoying his beer round the corner. He can show us with a genial smile, a realism quite
free from acrimony, the social aspirations and improved
drawing-rooms of prospering trades-people - a topic which
the lesser artist, or the artist-philosopher, would instil
with delicate venom. The capricious millionaires, vast
shops, and cities of pleasure that populate his less
serious fictions are mostly large negations of Socialism.
London, the largest of such negations, is a fairyland in
his fantasies. His sense of modern London is unrivalled

among novelists. But he could not feel modern London as he
does if he had not felt the Five Towns. A novelist is
like Ulysses; to imbibe the miracles of the world, he must
have known his Ithaca and its tugging at the heart.
Mr. Bennett's easy control (as novelist) of that propagan-
dist instinct which doubtless he possesses, I attribute
to three things: first, to the compelling humanity of the
Five Towns, then to his enormous joy in simply looking at
life, lastly - this is a pure guess - to an intimacy with
French authors.

I have no space left to describe 'The Old Wives' Tale.'
It is the best because it is the most restrained, without
loss of vitality. It covers many years, and several whole
lives. I like the title. The story concerns young girls
who become old wives; it concerns that most entrancing,
inconsistent, garrulous, and legendary of old wives' tales,
real life. In two former novels, each admirable in its
way - 'Sacred and Profane Love' and 'Whom God Hath Joined'
- Mr. Bennett showed faint signs of getting away from his
moorings. In the one I detected a note of daring (as
reviewers call it) for daring's sake; something of the
brilliant tour de force, a trespass from his main path of
development, an adolescent impulse to shock the aged. The
other, I fancied, was just a little hard; excellently conceived and worked out, with one splendid lyrical passage
(pages 273-5), but on the whole a trifle over-French for
the warmer and softer genius of English fiction. (1) 'The
Old Wives' Tale' is a return to his proper element. It
has fuller poetic power than anything he has done. It is
on a scale more epic and architectural. The passing of
these two lives, this loss of youth, is very broadly and
powerfully handled. Here, the thwarting of happiness by
iron circumstance, which steels the strong character but
destroys its joyful possibilities. There, the slow pressure of custom on a soul more fortunate but more plastic.
And we are made to feel the flaming away of lives in
general, the resistless tide of change, with startling and
terrible episodes (as many as two executions, if you
please) projected against a background of less vivid but
not less real tragedy. Immeasurable disasters! but convincing, and robbed of some of their terror because they
proceed in detail and in due course, like life itself,
from point to point, enabling us to endure them, just as
life itself communicates to us this antidote of endurance.
The quintessence of life is surely this force, which life
alone possesses, of persuading us that to live and to feel
are in themselves immensely desirable. An artist is he
who discerns this quintessence, condenses it, and there-
with impregnates his creation. The novel, to my mind, is

pre-eminently the art-form which must rely on contemporary
scenes and contemporary emotions in achieving such a work.
How rare the achievement is I need not say. Hence my
praise of 'The Old Wives' Tale.' Useless? inactive for
the regeneration of society? My answer is that men must
feel and understand life thoroughly before they tinker
with it; that art outlines philosophy, as the Greeks are
aware, just because it roots itself in that sure ground
of instinct and emotion with which the philosopher - his
eye on the horizon - is apt to lose touch.

Note

1 The lyrical passage is in ch. 7, and begins, 'She lay
   calm on the sofa, clasping him tightly with both her
   hands'.

'The Glimpse'

7 October 1909

48. UNSIGNED REVIEW, 'ATHENAEUM'

30 October 1909, 522

We have no doubt that Mr. Bennett would, if put to the
test, claim the middle part of this novel as that which he
himself valued most. We should be unable to follow him in
that. Apparently the story was written for that second
book, which sets forth so imaginatively the glimpse which
the hero is allowed into the other world. But ordinary
readers will probably prefer the very human and remarkably
clever opening, in which a man discovers that his wife is
in love with his friend, and will regret that Mr. Bennett
did not work out his plot from that situation on a more
terrestrial level. Up to the supposed death of the narrator our interest is held firmly; but with the plunge into
a fantastic, if finely imagined land of spirits, our attention flags. Doubtless those scenes in the glimpse are
characterized by a fine power of visualization; but, after
all, they are projections in space, and do not advance the
action or emotions of the human beings in whom our interest
was engaged. And when we resume ordinary life in the last
book it is to find it unconvincing and strange, as if it
had undergone some transmogrification owing to the glimpse.
This is not a real novel; it is a *tour de force*, but there
is no denying its extreme cleverness.

49. G.H. MAIR, IN THE 'MANCHESTER GUARDIAN'

3 November 1909, 5

G.H. Mair (1887-1926) was a leader writer and literary
editor on the 'Manchester Guardian'. Later he went into
government work, and he was in the Ministry of Information
with Bennett at the end of the First World War. With this
review, Bennett was given first place for the first time
in the 'Manchester Guardian' reviews of fiction.

Mr. Arnold Bennett is so very versatile, he has shown himself a master in so many kinds of writing, that each time
a new book appears from his pen one approaches it wondering whether this also is something fresh and whether he
has again passed on and conquered at a bound some new
domain. This new-published novel, 'The Glimpse', is in a
sense a half-way house towards a fresh conquest. It is
neither new nor old. There are the qualities which shine
in some earlier novels and which we have learnt to expect
from one who has gone to school to Mr. George Moore - gone
to school, however, not slavishly, but with a liberal
independence, as a pupil of genius should. That is to say,
we have Mr. Bennett the novelist of London, the opulent,
the artistic, the luxurious, with his exquisite skill in
realising and re-creating an environment, and his delicate
and fastidious appreciation of a life which is sensuous
and always at the same time a-tingle with intellect to the
finger-tips. We get, too, his own proper qualities, distinct from those he has learned, which make his work
momentous - the insight, for instance, with which he
envisages the importance of small actions, that subtle
kind of concentration in which nothing that is trivial or
commonplace or merely instinctive is seen without seeing
also the attendant pondering of a mind which occupies
itself endlessly with the measuring of hairsbreadths and
the weighing of feathers, desperately seeking to realise
its least sensations.
    Had Mr. Bennett, then, been content to write this story
of the sudden and tragic crisis in the lives of Morrice
Loring, the wealthy musical critic, and his wife Inez as,
under the influences and with the qualities we have described, he might have written it, it would still have
been a remarkable book. But he went further than this.
The core of the novel - its title shows the weight the

author attaches to it - is made up of a vision of what lies beyond human life and human sight which came to this Morrice Loring when he, struck down by an attack of Angina pectoris brought on by the sudden knowledge of his wife's deceit, lay in a trance that looked like death. This 'Glimpse' gives Mr. Bennett the opportunity for a very wonderful and beautiful piece of writing, and it has a very striking dramatic value to the progress of the tale. Loring wakes from the trance to find that his wife had thought him dead and taken poison. All the incidents which follow - her death, the coroner's inquest (Mr. Bennett is very fond of coroners' inquests), the quietly settling life in his flat after these catastrophes were past - gain in significance and in impressiveness from what he has seen. But the vision itself is another matter. The reader of imagination demands no more of such a thing than self-consistency and that organic unity which, if written down in white heat and glowing radiantly to the writer, it should have. Instead Mr. Bennett the critic, terribly well informed in the doctrines of Theosophy and the evolutionary hypothesis, builds up coldly, piece by piece, block upon block, the fabric of a vision which is realised only externally and gains most of the effect it produces from the likenesses which it suggests to the reader of things he has already heard or read. Frankly this part of the novel is a disappointment. It is possible, however, as we have said, that this is only Mr. Bennett's half-way house to a new domain, and that next time he may do again what he did in the 'Old Wives' Tale' and launch a masterpiece. We hope he will.

'Clayhanger'

15 September 1910

50. UNSIGNED REVIEW, 'TIMES LITERARY SUPPLEMENT'

15 September 1910, 328

Towards the end of 'Clayhanger' a phrase occurs that seems
to reveal as with a flashlight the whole impulse and motive
of Mr. Arnold Bennett's prodigious novel - 'a terrific zest
for life.' For life, that is, neither tragic, comic,
romantic, nor 'realistic,' neither high nor low - though a
tint from every one of these varieties of it may be conspicuous, each in its own place - but simply the slow,
vast, creaking panorama, surrounded by which every human
creature moves in by one pigeon-hole out of eternity, and
moves out by another, a panorama crowded with detail,
heightened by a needle-sharp absorption and curiosity,
dwelt on with an enthralled delight - such is the zest by
which Mr. Bennett is possessed and enslaved. Bursley (Mr.
Bennett's unwearying _protégé_) rumbles and lumbers on from
the seventies into the eighties; strike and Sunday-school
centenary, Home Rule, the Jubilee, influenza pass it by;
summer sun and November fog colour and blot it out; its
busy, diverse men and women grow up, marry, or refrain
from marrying, grow old, die. Not one of them, except
perhaps Hilda, is striking or unusual, else than commonplace. Every third-class railway carriage every day of
the week yields just such an assortment of our fellow-
creatures as throngs 'Clayhanger.' Edwin Clayhanger himself is simply the least common multiple (_plus_ the indefin-
able but invaluable something that makes him Edwin) of
that vast regiment - the men in the street. A slow stream
of trivial events swirls on. The events are undoubtedly
trivial, the stream slow; yet we awake, when the last page

comes, stiff and cold out of the hypnotic trance in which
we have watched the tide slip by, simply because every
human being in this book has been convincingly taken
direct from life. Their moment here reveals their whole
existence. 'Clayhanger,' indeed, happens to be the first
volume of a trilogy that will be completed in 1912. This
book tells of Edwin, the next will tell of Hilda, the last
of their marriage. But the point is that Mr. Bennett, had
he the leisure of a Methuselah, could obviously promise to
weave just such another 574 pages around the most casual
and transitory of each of his characters. His is the gift
of divining the whole creature from a glimpse of one of
the least of its bones, the secret character from a gesture, a history from a line in the face - a kind of imaginative clairvoyance. And so the fascination falls on the
reader. We too are taken captive by this terrific zest
and resent the least interruption. We fidget at Mr. Bennett's ironical and philosophical intrusions, at what we
feel at times are faults of taste and feeling, at the
glance of confidence or of triumph which he occasionally
casts, not towards the gallery in which we sit, but where
sits his critical, as distinguished from his creative,
self. But all is easily forgiven in the long run. And
if love be a state of continual anxiety about any one,
then we love Edwin and perfectly understand, even share,
his passion for Hilda. If slow death can be considered
an essential part of life, then we are quite legitimately
enthralled by the horror that haunts the softening of
Darius's brain. We may hesitate for a moment over the
significance or the truth of some little detail; but
Mr. Bennett wins in the end; the mosaic grows. Like 'The
Old Wives' Tale' 'Clayhanger' is a triumphant epic of the
commonplace. Its poetry is the poetry of the sheer ordi-
nariness of ordinary things and ordinary people. Its aim
not to exalt, or essentialize, or satirize, but to present, life. And for those who share Mr. Bennett's insatiable curiosity that is to aim point blank at the
object of their most vivid enthusiasm.

51. JAMES DOUGLAS, IN THE 'STAR'

17 September 1910, 4

James Douglas (1867-1940), author, literary critic, and

editor, reviewed regularly for the 'Star', and was assistant editor.   In the 1920s he was editor of the 'Sunday Express'.

'Is the novel written out?' This question is asked by the 'Daily News,' which quotes the following passage from an article in the 'Temps': 'The subject matter of the novel, which is far from being infinite, particularly when, as in most cases, the novel is a love story, appears exhausted, worked out. What is there left to say after so many generations of great novelists?' The best answer to the French critic is to cite 'Jean Christophe,' the great novel by Romain Rolland, which is being published in fragments. Already seven volumes have been issued, containing about 60,000 words each. There are to be three more, making ten in all. Mr. Edmund Gosse describes 'Jean Christophe' as 'the noblest work of fiction of the twentieth century,' and yet the writer in the 'Temps' asks, 'what is there left to say?' The novel, like the newspaper, is eternal. So long as life lingers on the earth there will be novels, and there will be newspapers, for newspapers are made out of the raw material of life and novels are the imaginative representation of that raw material. Whatever else may be 'written out,' fiction will remain unexhausted and inexhaustible. For every generation has its own vision of its own life, and every man of genius has his own expression of it.

If we turn from French fiction to English fiction, we find evidence of the vitality of the novel. I pass over Mr. Wells, whose story, 'The New Machiavelli,' now appearing in 'The English Review,' promises to be the greatest political novel of our time. I pass over Mr. Galsworthy and Mr. Conrad, whose novels are new things in fiction. I take 'Clayhanger', by Mr. Arnold Bennett. It is as long as 'The Old Wives' Tale,' but it is twice as good. The patient realism of 'The Old Wives' Tale' was amazing, but the French episodes were not an organic part of the story, and the artistic quality of the story suffered in consequence. There was also a lack of spiritual and imaginative vision, which made the author's method seem cold and hard and photographic. But in 'Clayhanger' Mr. Bennett has suddenly grown to full stature, and at no moment of the story does he lose touch with the warmth and glow of life. In many respects, he seems to challenge comparison with 'Jean Christophe.' Towards the end of the story one comes upon this footnote:-

In the autumn of 1911 the author will publish a
novel dealing with the history of Hilda Lessways up to
the day of her marriage with Edwin. This will be followed by a novel dealing with her marriage.

These three novels will be nearly as long as 'Jean Christophe.' And yet one does not grumble, for there is no
padding in 'Clayhanger.' The theme needs the space, for
Mr. Bennett clearly aims at painting the whole business
of life, with its network of relationships and interests.
Not life in vague outline, but the real, grotesque,
pathetic, sordid, wistful, splendid, hideous, beautiful
complexity of it.

It is wonderful how rich life is if we look at it fear-
lessly. The people in 'Clayhanger' are not exaggerated
versions of observed character. They are not heightened
by caricature or romance. They grow up in one's mind as
one's friends grow. They are all ordinary people. Edwin
Clayhanger, the 'Jean Christophe' of the story, is any
young man living in any provincial town. He is different
from the young men drawn by Mr. Wells only by reason of
his temperament and environment. But Mr. Bennett winds
his way into the maze of his mind and gradually makes you
know him as if he were yourself. At times you are shocked
by the sharpness of the revelation. No doubt the intimate
characterisation of this ordinary young man is auto-
biographic - so far as intellectual and imaginative movements are concerned. His soul is a living thing, and its
pain is like a memory, its ecstacy like an experience.
There are few novels that take you so absolutely into the
inner consciousness of a human being. And it is not only
in the sexual side of the man's nature that he lives. He
lives quite as truly in his relations with his father and
his sisters. Is there any novel which depicts quite so
sincerely the terrible gulf between a father and his son?
The thing is done without any hard strokes or violent
emphasis. It has a tragically inevitable quality. One
sees the pitiless inscrutability of life in it. And never
is the note of pathos or irony forced. The truth is set
down simply in plain, bare words, and allowed to do its
work. One illustration of this is the scene in which
Mr. Shushions, the old Methodist class-leader, sheds his
'epic tear.' Another is the scene in which Darius goes
with Edwin to the bank to surrender to his son the power
of signing cheques. The book is full of such scenes, and
the cumulative effect of them is to make one shrink back
from life half in dismay and half in wonder. The sense
of entanglement that visits one now and then in a mood of
vision is ever present in the slow movement of the story.

What is this strange energy that makes men and women
stumble along these zig-zag paths towards the grave?
The Greeks called it destiny. We call it circumstance
or the life-force or the will-to-live or what-not. But
labels are nothing. The pressure is outside us as well
as inside us, and we are what life chooses to make of us.

Hilda Lessways is the riddle of the book. The story
winds round her like a lethargic river, leaving her for
years and then twisting back to her. The 'veiled period'
in George Borrow's life is the most provocative of all,
and similarly the 'veiled period' in Hilda's life in-
flames our curiosity. We want to know why she left Edwin
at the very peak and pinnacle of their passion - left him
to marry a man who turns out to be a bigamist and a convict. The mystery resembles that in Meredith's posthumous
novel, 'Celt and Saxon.' It will tax all Mr. Bennett's
powers to make Hilda's flight consistent with her love
for Clayhanger. How he is going to do it I have not the
slightest surmise. But readers of 'Clayhanger' will wait
with impatience for the unravelling of the enigma. As she
stands, Hilda is a fascinating creature. The scene in
which Clayhanger kisses her for the first time in the
little cubicle of his father's shop is a masterpiece of
emotional verisimilitude, with just the physical verity
that is necessary to make you feel like an eye-witness
of the episode. One gets this physical verity in Wells
and Conrad and George Moore. It is only an elusive touch,
but it solidifies and fixes the whole thing.

I think it is this physical verity which makes 'Clayhanger' so irresistibly human, so magnetic, so hypnotic.
The organic detail is never tiresome, for it is worked
into the story with crafty care, and it is never worked
into it for its own sake. It has the human impress on it.
It is part of the flesh and blood and soul and mind of the
people. It is their daily life. The Bursley environment
is not romantic, and yet it is so closely associated with
the people that it becomes more romantic than the stones
of Venice. Big James, the compositor, is a living human
being, and one sees him with his apron tucked round him,
as if he were physically there. The meals, the talk, the
clumsy stir of national life beyond the lives of the
Bursley folk, the blind gropings of labor - these and
a hundred other things absorb one's attention and hold
one fascinated. But the most tantalising piece of realism
in the story is Hilda. 'You needn't be afraid of me,' she
said to Clayhanger, in one of their curiously electric
meetings. If I am not mistaken, Hilda is one of those

great women who are made for men to be afraid of with the
fear that passes all understanding.

52. UNSIGNED REVIEW, 'STAFFORDSHIRE SENTINEL'

19 September 1910, 2

Mr. Arnold Bennett's new novel, 'Clayhanger,' is, as we
have already indicated, a fine piece of literature, worthy
to rank with his 'Old Wives' Tale.' Many Potteries people
may possibly find 'Clayhanger' the more interesting novel
of the two, for the story and the people it contains are
almost entirely confined to the Potteries area.
    The tale opens on 'a breezy Friday in July, 1872.'
Edwin Clayhanger, the son of a Bursley printer, had 'left
school that day,' after having passed seven years at the
Oldcastle Middle School:

[Quotes Book 1, ch. 2, section 1, 'He had received' to
'than that of the Middle School' and Book 1, ch. 1, section 2, 'Slim, gawky, untidy' to 'simplicity of those
eyes'.]

    We 'must' quote Mr. Bennett's opening references to
Newcastle and Porthill and Longport and Burslem....

[Quotes Book 1, ch. 1, section 1, 'Edwin Clayhanger stood'
to 'its sublime stupidity'.]

But the sins of the fathers must not be visited upon the
children, of course! To Edwin, as he lingers on the canal
bridge, comes a school-chum, Charlie Orgreave, at school
invariably called 'the Sunday.' The Orgreaves lived at
Bleakridge (which may perhaps be interpreted as Cobridge),
in 'one of the older residential properties of the district, Georgian, of a recognisable style, relic of the
days when manufacturers formed a class entirely apart from
their operatives.' Mr. Orgreave was an architect, and the
family was genial and cultured. Charlie Orgreave who in
later years became a doctor, had a sister Janet, a charming girl, of whom more anon.
    To return to Edwin Clayhanger, who is leaving school at
sixteen. His father is the first 'steam printer' in
Bursley, and has a book-selling and printing business,

which he has built up until it has attained substantial
proportions. Darius Clayhanger, Edwin's father, is a
remarkable man. Darius lived in Turnhill (Tunstall) when
a child, and was first taken to work by his mother, in
January, 1835. He began his career as mould-runner to a
muffin-maker, and had a cruel time of it. This enables
Mr. Bennett to introduce a telling description of the
evils of factory life in the earlier part of the Nineteenth Century - the long hours, the cruelties, the
debauchery, the truck system, and so on. These references
are probably based on what is recorded in 'When I was a
Child.' All that has passed away now. Darius's father
was 'too prominent and too independent in a strike,' and
was 'blacked by every manufacturer in the district.'
Consequently, when Darius was nine years old, the family
found themselves in a workhouse. Darius was rescued from
this slough by a Mr. Shushions, the superintendent of a
Sunday school, who got him a situation as a printer's
devil. The memory of the workhouse remained bitter in
Darius's soul; he had character, and became, as we have
seen, a master-printer, but the misery of his early days
influenced his whole life. He was a man of grim exterior,
and his children thought him a tyrant. His wife, a woman
of superior rank to himself, died young. His son, Edwin,
the 'well-educated' youth of sixteen, resented what he
thought Darius's unreasoning harshness towards him. He did
not dream that Darius had in his way a romantic tenderness
for his children. They knew nothing of the workhouse episode, and he toiled and slaved and schemed to build up a
business which would give his children a better and happier start in life than he had had and which he hoped his
son Edwin would carry from success to success, with prosperity and happiness, after him. Edwin, the boy of
'superior education' of sixteen, felt contemptuous towards
his father; and to himself used shocking language about
his father; in after years he realised fleeting glimpses
of the affection which was in his father's heart all the
time. But Darius never received any formal or real
acknowledgment of his efforts. He grew old and doddery
and the business passed to Edwin. The only reward that
Darius had was to see Edwin in the business and succeeding
in the business. Edwin announced when he left school that
he wanted to be an architect, but his father, with apparent brutality but with more tact than Edwin dreamt of,
ignored or ridiculed the idea of it, and compelled Edwin
to settle down to the printing and bookselling business
already in existence. Edwin has a poetical side, but his
father's 'commonsense' kept Edwin's nose to the grind-
stone, much to Edwin's material benefit. Fathers and sons

are often like that - the sons 'superior' and ungrateful,
yet all the time inferior in grit and foresight and of
course in experience to their coarser fathers, who are
fairly content to 'pass out' unthanked, though they may
sigh a little to themselves, when they see their sons set
on the path of fortune. So the world wags on, and fathers
go and sons take their places; there is a fine sense of
self-sacrifice at work. Mr. Bennett, though he does not
moralise about it, expounds the philosophy of it in his
minute description of the lives of the Clayhangers and
their friends. In old Darius, Mr. Bennett has created
a rugged personality whose reality is one of the most
remarkable things in the book.

The dramatis personae having been thus partly arranged,
the tale follows Edwin into his father's shop and records
his progress in the business. We make the acquaintance of
Mr. Shushions, now an old man, and like Darius, not given
sufficient credit for his earlier efforts. There is also
Big James, or more correctly James Yarlett, who used to be
a 'news comp.' on the 'Staffordshire Signal,' and is now
Darius's foreman. He 'made the fourth and heaviest member
of the celebrated Bursley Male Glee Party.' They 'sang at
dinners, free-and-easy concerts, and Martinmas tea meetings. They sang for the glory and when there was no
demand for their services, they sang to themselves for
the sake of singing. Each of them was a star in some
church or chapel choir.' Big James's rendering of The
Miller of the Dee had been renowned in the Five Towns
since 1852. There are also Clara and Maggie, Edwin's
sisters, and Mrs. Nixon, the Clayhangers' servant, and
Mrs. Hamps, Edwin's aunt, a handsome and generous woman.
Having to take a 'proof' of some job printing to Mr. Enoch
Peake, Edwin goes to the Dragon to find that gentleman,
and thus sees something of a jollity arranged by the
Bursley Mutual Burial Club, of which Mr. Peake is chairman, and incidentally he witnesses a performance by Miss
Florence Simcox, 'the champion female clog-dancer of the
Midlands,' whose 'high kick' suggests to his budding mind
that there is more to be known about the ways of the world
than even his philosophy had dreamt of. A Methodist
Sunday school centenary also occurs, and a strike in the
potting trade. There are references to the 'Blood Tub,'
and a 'Felons' dinner is described. Darius builds a new
house for himself at Bleakridge, partly prompted thereto
by Osmond Orgreave, the architect.

[Quotes Book 2, ch. 3, section 1, 'Osmond Orgreave had a
good deal' to 'steam-cars in Trafalgar Road'.]

The course of the novel develops from placidity to
romance, and from romance to tragedy. Edwin, who takes
much interest in the building of the new house, and who
falls into the way of self-culture, is manoeuvred into
a friendly visit to the Orgreaves' house, and one rather
fancies that Janet was an admirer of his. But at the
Orgreaves' house Edwin, now a young man, meets with a girl
named Hilda Lessways. At first, he does not like her,
but she is a girl of original mind; she seems 'taken with'
Edwin, and he soon comes to live upon the expectation of
seeing her. Hilda Lessways suddenly announces that she
must return to Brighton. This so stirs up Edwin that he
kisses her, and in kissing a woman for the first time is
at once transformed from a boy into a man. They confess
their love for one another, and a day or two later she
writes to him from Brighton:-

> 'Dearest', - This is my address. I love you.
> Every bit of me is absolutely yours. Write me. - H.L.'

In a very little time, however, her letters cease, and
the distracted Edwin is on the point of telegraphing to
her, when he learns from Janet Orgreave that Hilda has
married a man named Cannon at Brighton. It is a terrible
blow to him, but much to his own surprise, he settles down
to business, a bachelor, but dreaming constantly of Hilda.
His engagement to Hilda had never become known, and owing
to his shyness with the Orgreave family all he knew was
that Hilda was a friend of Janet's, that she came of a
Turnhill family, but that her life had been mostly spent
in the south of England.
  Years rolled on, and much happened in those years in
the political history of England, as Mr. Bennett recalls
to his readers. Incidentally, he mentions the interest
excited in Bursley, as elsewhere, by Mr. Gladstone's
introduction of the first Home Rule Bill, and the rush
to purchase the special edition of the 'Signal' containing
a summary of Mr. Gladstone's speech published the same
night - which is a fact, as our files testify. An election takes place in Bursley, and so on - there is a wealth
of detail of the panorama of life in Bursley as the years
roll by, and every page of the book tells. There is a
reference to 'the facade of the Sytch Pottery. It was
a long two-storey building, purest Georgian, of red brick
with very elaborate stone facings which contrasted admirably with the austere simplicity of the walls. The porch
was lofty, with a majestic flight of steps narrowing to
the doors. The ironwork of the basement railings was
unusually rich and impressive. "Ever seen another

pot-works like that?" demanded Mr. Orgreave, enthusiastically musing.' Such a building may possibly be found opposite Hilltop Chapel.

Ten years go by, and George Cannon, the child of Hilda, comes on a visit to Janet, who, however, is reticent about Hilda herself. Edwin Clayhanger and the boy become great friends. He is swinging the child to and fro:

[Quotes Book 4, ch. 2, section 5, 'But the child George' to 'But rancour against Hilda - !'.]

Mr. Bennett has a vivid understanding of human emotions, as well as an amazing knowledge of the intricacies of the lives of all sorts and conditions of people. The manner in which he brings the obscure workhouse experience of Darius in the long-distant past into the same novel with the present-day romance and tragedy of Hilda is masterly. Some people may think that Mr. Bennett is too realistic in indicating the use of 'red' and other language by some of his characters; but after all, such things 'are,' and if one striker swears, others are quite prepared to sing hymns. Mr. Bennett 'holds the mirror up to nature', or takes mental and penetrating photographs and reproduces them. They are at any rate real, and this reality is profoundly interesting.

The boy George goes away and comes back again, is seized with illness, and nearly dies from influenza. The account of the illness introduces a reference to Dr. Stirling, who had become very popular on settling in Bursley. Janet told Edwin that Hilda was now a widow, and he had gone surreptitiously to Brighton and found her in great poverty. He rendered her assistance. When George is so desperately ill, Hilda comes to Bursley for the first time since the evening ten years before when Edwin had kissed her. She now tells Edwin that she is not a widow, that her supposed husband turned out to have been married before, that Georgie was illegitimate, and that George's father had been in prison for bigamy and was now in prison for some other crime. She tells Edwin the story of her marriage - but Mr. Bennett does not pass the explanation on to his readers. The novel ends here. But in a footnote, the author says: 'In the autumn of 1911 the author will publish a novel dealing with the history of Hilda Lessways up to the day of her marriage with Edwin. This will be followed by a novel dealing with the marriage.'

Now, Hilda Lessways was a girl of strong mentality, big sympathies, deep insight, compelling femininity, daringly frank because she sought to seize the truth and to eschew

the hackneyed and mere convention. At twenty-four, she
was whole-heartedly in love with Edwin. Yet she suddenly
married a blackguard, and brought poverty and misery upon
herself and almost broke Edwin's heart. Why did it all
happen in this way? The novel 'Clayhanger' is fascinating
and irresistible; it is a splendidly graphic account of
the lives of a number of people whom we seem to know very
well through a long period of years, and after all, is it
not a common weakness of human nature to take great interest in the details of our neighbours' private lives - when
we happen to hear of them? Mr. Bennett has a marvellous
insight into the innumerable complications that go to make
up even the most seemingly hum-drum lives; and his powers
as a literary recorder reach unprecedented brilliance in
this novel. He fascinates us by the account of the lives
and loves of Edwin and Hilda so far as it has gone, and
leaves us desperate for the autumn of 1911 to come, so
that we may see the explanation of Hilda's secret.

53. T.M. YOUNG IN THE 'MANCHESTER GUARDIAN'

21 September 1910, 5

T.M. Young (1873-1946) served on the editorial staff of
the 'Manchester Guardian' from 1896 to 1913. He then
entered the Civil Service.

Mr. Arnold Bennett is a writer whose work one has hitherto
admired with anxiety and misgiving. He has shown himself
capable of making, as in 'An Old Wives' Tale,' [sic] a
contribution to the literature of our time of substance
and serious worth. On the other hand, his lapses into
triviality have been at times a severe trial of one's
faith in his ultimate achievement. It would be hard to
find a parallel case to Mr. Bennett's, to match the gap
that yawns between his best and his worst. Not even Mrs.
Browning, Mr. Kipling, or Mr. Phillpotts has given us such
astonishing contrasts, for in Mr. Bennett they cannot be
explained by a growth in grace ad power; they involve the
fundamental conceptions and intentions, the spirit and
intellectual quality of his work not less than the art of
its accomplishment, and suggest that he himself, whilst

maintaining and cherishing a serious and high purpose in
literary art, has quite consciously and wilfully jeopar-
dised his reputation by experiments of economic rather
than literary interest.

But there is no doubt about 'Clayhanger.' Here we have
Mr. Bennett at his very best, and Mr. Bennett at his best
is a very reassuring person. To borrow a phrase from a
famous series of sporting prints which might have adorned
the room in which his Bursley 'Felons' genially ate their
annual dinner, he is one of the 'Right Sort Doing the
Thing Well.' He has done it not only well but on a magnificent scale, for this novel rivals in dimensions the
world of Mr. De Morgan and the middle Victorians. It
covers nearly six hundred pages, and contains, if our
arithmetic has not failed us, no fewer than 68 chapters;
and it is with a sense of grateful wonder and appreciation
that the retrospective reader, contemplating his own
achievement, realises how easy and pleasant it was.
Wonder, we say, because in the retrospect it is a little
difficult to define the qualities that saved the story
from even occasional dullness. It is a story about dull,
commonplace people in a dull, commonplace town, and nothing happens to any of them that is at all unusual, except
that the hero is suddenly and unaccountably jilted. The
narrative is so utterly devoid of melodramatic incident
or of ingenious complication of any kind that it might be
described as the long and simple annals of the middle
class. Moreover, Mr. Bennett has none of Mr. De Morgan's
amiable and entertaining garrulity and, it must be added,
none of his droll humour. No single page of this book,
as almost any page of Mr. De Morgan's, would suggest the
amplitude of the whole. The book is long simply because
the story is told fully, and the story is told fully
because all its interest and significance lie in the fullness of its telling. This, we think, is the secret of
Mr. Bennett's true accomplishment as a novelist. He has
perceived, as Mr. Wells has perceived, the enormous
possibilities of the common type and the common lot as
material for the artist, and he has realised, perhaps
more clearly than anyone else, that in a large view of
human life the masses and proportions of experience have
a value far exceeding for most of us that of its details.
Comparisons and contrasts with Mr. Wells are inevitably
suggested, and the contrasts are only heightened by the
obvious analogies which may be traced between such a novel
as this and 'Tono-Bungay' or 'Kipps.' Mr. Bennett has
little or nothing of Mr. Wells's passionate feeling for
beauty, none of his ardent vitality, none of his hot
insurgency, and none of that brilliant genius which in

a phrase of vivid descriptive significance can conjure up
a scene, a personality, or a piece of emotional experience. Mr. Bennett convinces us by an overwhelming array
of pertinent evidence; he achieves realism by seeming to
omit nothing of significance rather than by any unerring
faculty for seizing upon and emphasising that which is
of supreme significance.

But if his method is that of conscientious industry
rather than inspiration he nevertheless achieves his end
and creates the illusion and atmosphere of actuality.
This Clayhanger family is not only alive in every branch;
its life is a part of the life of the Five Towns, profoundly influenced by the soil and social climate in which
it grew and yet essentially typical of universal human
experience. The tragic isolation of the strong, tyran-
nical father, ageing and failing in the midst of his
children, uncomprehending and uncomprehended to the last;
the almost imperceptible passing of youth and expectancy
into middle age and accepted limitations; the small and
steady accretions of alienation and disappointment; in a
word, the larger pathos of life, Mr. Bennett sees with
sympathy and reproduces with a stern, sane art. 'Clayhanger' would stand alone as a considerable achievement,
largely conceived and successfully accomplished. But it
is not to stand alone; it is only the first member of a
trilogy, for with a courage and resolution which one cannot but admire Mr. Bennett intimates at the end of this
story that its one unresolved mystery will be dealt with
in another novel to be published a year hence, and that
this will be followed by a third, of which the subject
will be Edwin Clayhanger's marriage with the inscrutable
woman. We look forward to the completion of this great
scheme with all the confidence inspired by a successful
beginning.

54. UNSIGNED REVIEW, 'ATHENAEUM'

15 October 1910, 453

At the present moment there is a school of fiction which
is frankly reactionary from romanticism. Its chief exponents here are Mr. George Moore and Mr. Bennett, though
there are others who are inclined to subscribe to the
doctrines. Mr. Wells with a high imagination can never

be wholly naturalistic. These novelists work upon a principle which is not new to fiction, but is rather a revival.
It is not so much the quantitative element in their work
as the qualitative that counts and stamps them. Thackeray,
Balzac, and others, have written at as great length, but
it would be absurd to compare those masters with modern
writers whose ideal is merely the production of effect by
the accumulation of detail. Thackeray's length is an
accident, due to the appearance of his work in magazines
or parts; the present huge volume of Mr. Bennett is
designed. In fact, it is not from Thackeray or Balzac that
this school traces its descent, but from Zola. It is a
stenographic school of fiction; it aims at reproducing
life in all its particularity; it has no reticences at its
wildest, and no selection at its mildest. It worships the
unessential, holding it to be the essential. That a man
turns a street corner may alter his whole life, but the
fact should only be recorded when it does so.

Mr. Bennett revels in the commonplaces of life. Perhaps he would prefer to call himself sociological. His
novel may claim to be that rather than psychological, for
it is concerned rather with the play of a small number of
commonplace characters on one another than with any complex *vie intime*. The psychology of Edwin Clayhanger is
excellently rendered, but it could, we think, have been
suggested, and would have been suggested, by a master of
art, in a quarter of the space. The irrelevances here
gathered may be important in the continuous connexions of
organic life, but the point is that they are unimportant
to the art of the story. In no case do they give a better
picture of the events and characters than would be gained
by artistic elimination; indeed, the prevalence of detail
clogs and obscures. Once only do we get an impressive
effect, which is in the account of the last illness of
Darius Clayhanger. But even this suffers from diffuseness
and prolixity. On p. 573 we are informed in a foot-note
that the author will publish a book dealing with the history of his heroine to the time of her marriage, and
afterwards one relating to the marriage of the hero and
heroine. This is to make life art - which it is not.

55. UNSIGNED REVIEW, 'NEW YORK TIMES'

29 October 1910, 599

In this story the author conducts you realistically to a
point where the heroine tells the hero that the man he
supposes she married long ago is serving a term in prison
for bigamy. The explanation of this piquant situation is
interrupted on the last page, and an asterisk refers to a
note informing the reader that the author will next year
publish another novel telling all about it, except what
will be told in still another. There is something
strangely disconcerting about this, and Mr. Arnold Bennett
must not be surprised that one who has followed him
through 698 pages of very uneven interest resents it.
     Conviction for bigamy has long been an accepted device
in melodrama for relieving the heroine of an error of youth,
but you hardly expect that sort of thing in a very serious
and highly superior sample of the modern novel - one at
once frankly philosophical and pretentiously literary.
The reader whose books are his friends is the more exasperated with the author of 'The Old Wives' Tale' for his
dereliction in the matter of that impertinent asterisk and
the note dependent on it, because there is much in the
story which is not tedious, much, indeed, that seems to
admit the writer to the select company of those who have
something to tell us about our fellowmen that we are not
unwilling to know and might grieve to miss. To be sure,
Mr. Bennett indulges a passion to tell in lavish detail
much else that hints would suffice to convey: to be sure,
he paints with an unction which is hardly wholesome in-
firmities of mind and body and states of disease and
decay. To be sure, it may be questioned whether his taste
in human beings is not quite as bad as his taste in the
use of asterisks.
     All these things may be granted without reserve, yet
the fact remains that the boy introduced to you on the day
of his leaving school and allowed to grow up under your
eye in one of the Five Towns of England's industrial section beside the Mersey Canal, lays hold on you as something even uncomfortably human. The most of the story is
no more than the detailed recital of this boy's relations
with a self-made father, relations which lead to hate that
is out of the ordinary. Mr. Bennett's idea is to register
the deep impressions of trivial events upon a sensitive
youth. The crises of the tale are within that youth's
bosom. In that bosom the flame of high resolve burns

incandescent as he quits school, though even to wise old
women he is only a fresh-faced gawky lad, 'the spittin'
image of his poor mother.' There smoulders the boy's
fierce impatience with the insincerities of his elders.
There is the agony which is the cause of the youth's
painful awkwardness in the face of the self-possessed
young persons of the opposite sex. There, blowing hot
and cold by turns, the silly mixture of fear and exulta-
tion in the first encounter with one of that sex who shows
a marked and - to the youth - inexplicable and miraculous
preference for himself over other youths. All these
things are conveyed with a vividness which argues a keen
recollection of the parallel periods in the writer's past
- which is apt to awaken in the reader forgotten or half-
forgotten thrills, glows and cold dull thuds of his own.
The ability to do that thing - to make the reader put
enough of his own feelings out of his own experience into
your puppet to vivify him - or her - is, of course, the
ultimate test of one's title to write fiction at all.
That test Mr. Bennett stands.

As the boy grows older - as the situation resolves
itself chiefly into a long psychological vigil, while
a strong man, self-made in a cruel school, suffers
gradual defeat and decay at the hand of nature and old
age - the narrative grows too pathological for the broad
purposes of a proper novel, though it may be of great
value to medical specialists. The father - the strong
man whose decay you watch partly through his son's eyes -
is a type not quite real and very forbidding. A little
girl child appears into whom has been breathed the queer
elfishness of a particular period of real little girlhood,
and the heroine is sufficiently queer and ardent to pique
curiosity. A vast deal of elaborate character drawing!
In other cases, it seems fairly safe to assume the characters to be much less interpretive of human nature than
expressive of the author's complacency with himself as an
interpreter. In other words, the personages seem constructed solely of what he has abstracted for the purpose
of making them, and not at all to the real persons dimly
seen and partly guessed at, as all real folk in fiction -
as in life - might seem to be.

It may be added that Mr. Bennett is cursed with a
desire of exegesis. He explains too much, even where he
sheds real light. He has a gift of word-painting, but he
puts in too many words. In short 'Clayhanger' could have
been told, and would have been told better, in 300 pages
than in 700. Yet it is confessedly only the beginning of
a trilogy dealing with the same hero and heroine.

56. WILLIAM MORTON PAYNE, IN THE 'DIAL' (CHICAGO)

16 November 1910, 381-4

William Morton Payne (1858-1919), educator and literary critic, was assistant editor of the 'Dial' from 1892 to 1915.

What Mr. Arnold Bennett calls 'the inherent and appalling sadness of existence' is the real theme of his 'Clay-hanger,' which by accident only is a story of life in the Five Towns which readers of 'The Old Wives' Tale' know so well. When we say that the new novel is quite the equal of the earlier one, possibly surpassing it in relentless realism and grim power, we say enough to indicate that it is a work of extraordinary importance. In the larger sense, it gives us an account of the social evolution of an English provincial community during the closing three decades of the nineteenth century; in the narrower and more intensely vitalized sense, it is concerned with the fortunes of one Darius Clayhanger, printer and stationer, and of his son Edwin. There are other figures, sisters, an aunt, employees, friends, and acquaintances, but these two are dominant, and with these two alone, vividly and minutely realized, typically significant, we are chiefly occupied. The tragedy of the narrative is found in the crushing influence of the older generation upon the younger; Edwin has impulses and aspirations which might have born fruit in a more favorable environment, but he is just lacking in the strength of will needed to free him from the iron tyranny of prescription. The struggle is soon over - it is a struggle that hardly gets outside the arena of his own thoughts - and he settles down to plod in his father's footsteps, take on the abhorred busi-ness, and forget that he has ever been tempted to revolt. This novel is, as we said of the earlier one, a tale of mean lives in mean surroundings, but the truth of its portrayal is so insistent that we are ready to acquiesce in the absence of most of the elements that go to make up ordinary romance. The author is so afraid of drifting into any semblance of sentimentality that he seems at times positively inhuman. His own hatred for Darius matches that of the son, and even the spectacle of the old man in his last stage of hopeless paresis can hardly wring from him a suggestion of tender sympathy. It is impossible

to describe this book in honest terms that shall make it
appear attractive, yet such is its power that we would not
spare a single page; the very trivialities with which it
mainly deals are touched with such genius that we find
them interesting against our will, and we must admit that
they are needed for the total effect of the composition.
The book is open to one serious criticism. Hilda, the
young woman whom Edwin loves, and who accepts him in one
moment only to turn from him in the next, is not a real
person in the present narrative. As some one says of her,
'She's nothing at all for about six months at a stretch,
and then she has one minute of the grand style.' We learn
why she is thus left a mystery when we read the appended
note which promises a whole novel about her next year, and
we have no doubt that we shall know her inmost nature when
that novel shall be in our hands; but it is certainly a
defect of artistry thus deliberately to evade the full
responsibilities of one work in order to keep sufficient
material for another yet to be written. Her conduct, as
we here get glimpses of it, has neither rhyme nor reason,
while her appearance and her character are so inadequately
portrayed that Edwin's infatuation is nowise accounted
for. To the present reader of Edwin's age, which means
in the early fifties, the book has a special interest in
which younger readers cannot share. Pursuant to his
larger purpose, the author has filled his narrative with
echoes from the past, which evoke in us all sorts of dim
memories. The things that were doing in the outside
world, and of which even the Five Towns got some sort of
inkling - political happenings, currents of fresh thought,
and the progress of civilization - are brought into personal relations with the Clayhanger prejudices, and thus
we read from time to time of such matters as Colenso and
the higher criticism, home rule, Gladstone and Parnell,
the Queen's Jubilee, the obstinacy of Northampton in sending Bradlaugh to Parliament, the 'prayer gauge' (here by
a curious slip attributed to Thompson instead of Tyndall),
'The Light of Asia,' and the early epidemics of influenza.
All these historical matters are deftly made to serve
their purpose in the author's work of characterization,
and at the same time to help to bring back a half-
forgotten age. There are to be two more novels in the
series - the story of Hilda, already spoken of, and a
final volume dealing with the life of Edwin and Hilda
after their long-delayed marriage.

    If we had not previously received proofs of Mr. Ben-
nett's versatility, we should wonder that the same pen
should have produced 'Clayhanger' and 'Helen with the High
Hand.' 'In the Five Towns,' he says, 'human nature is

reported to be so hard that you can break stones upon it.'
This readers of 'Clayhanger' will readily admit, but when
he adds that 'sometimes it softens, and then we have one
of our rare idylls of which we are very proud,' the assertion needs the confirmation supplied by the light-hearted
comedy of 'Helen with the High Hand.' The young woman
thus designated is the great-stepniece of James Olleren-
shaw, a bachelor of sixty, and the miserly accumulator of
miserable weekly shillings from the several hundred cottages which he owns. Owing to an ancient feud, he has not
recognized Helen's existence for the twenty-five years of
her life, but one day that designing young woman insinu-
ates herself into his life to the extent of becoming his
housekeeper without asking his permission. The shock is
twofold, for she gives him surprisingly good things to
eat, and worries the wits out of him by her reckless
expenditure. She soon has him as wax in her hands, per-
suades him, by alternate cajolery and the threat of going
away, to purchase a mansion and live in it, and in the end
he is prepared weakly to submit to her most irrational
demands. His enlarged acquaintance with feminine nature
inspires him to the audacity of loving and winning a
portly widow of the town (not without encouragement, it
must be admitted), and his evolution is complete. Meanwhile, Helen has a little love affair of her own, which
her resourceful talent enables her to bring to the desired
issue. It is capital fooling, humorously charming from
start to finish, and we are glad to have it as a pendant
to Mr. Bennett's gloomy large-scale depiction of the Five
Towns.

57. UNSIGNED REVIEW, 'NORTH AMERICAN REVIEW'

December 1910, 849-50.

The great novelist is he who takes the common experience of ordinary people and so vitalizes and interprets
it as to make us, for the moment at least, see it as
the wealth it really is.
    The difficulty is, not to lose sight of the signifi-
cance of the banal, not to find people less interesting
because they resemble one another, not to find daily
happenings any the less wonderful that they are daily
to keep always before us the marvellous quality of the
usual.

These recently published words of a charming essayist
are perfectly apposite to the work under discussion. That
Arnold Bennett is a very great writer he proved in that
remarkable novel, 'Old Wives' Tale.' 'The Glimpse,'
which followed immediately after, was disappointing and
bore marks of being a refurbished early work. With 'Clayhanger' Mr. Bennett offers us a worthy successor of 'Old
Wives' Tale.' Once more he is in the *milieu* of the Five
Towns - a locality in Staffordshire where crockery is
manufactured, a setting absolutely mediocre and undistinguished. The hero, Clayhanger, is merely a nice young
fellow who likes to read and yearns for more elegance and
refinement than his home can offer him. Without great
force or energy, he is industrious and honest; without
overwhelming abilities, he has a taste for literature and
art; without deep tenderness, he has kindly emotions and
a fund of fairness and good-will. He and his father fail
to understand each other; and the son, who is the less
self-willed of the two, is forced into a business career
which he loathes. He has two perfectly commonplace
sisters - one a domestic creature, faithful and honest,
and the other flippant and foolish. There is no glamour
of romance thrown about the situation; there are no adventures. No attempt at all is made to rectify reality.
But it is a very great novel, none the less; so great that
it throws into the shadow all the novels of the last
decade. Even 'Tono-Bungay,' full of meat and life as it
was, seems slim and unpleasant in comparison. There is
nothing unpleasant here. If one stop to analyze wherein
the greatness consists one finds it to lie in three qualities: an uncompromising and exact sense of truth, unwavering concentration of a flood of consciousness on one subject, a mastery of technique. To work backwards on these
three points, one would notice first how unobtrusively the
narrative flows. There are no tricks of technique, no
eloquent passages, no moralizings, no crises. The author
is as objective, as silent in his own person as Flaubert
himself in 'Madame Bovary.' There is no word-painting, but
language is used throughout as subordinate, as a medium,
not as an end in itself. The effect is of supreme simplicity and clarity, but the amazing thing is the amount
the author sees. The details whereby he reconstructs a
period, a place, the atmosphere of a home, a room, are
legion. Nothing escapes him. He sees everything. How so
young a man can completely set before us a mid-Victorian
drawing-room, an old-fashioned parlor in a Brighton
boarding-house, a new suburb of 1870, is a marvel and a
questioning. He cannot possibly remember these things,
but he can set them there in his pages in their habit as

they lived. Even in the same manner the political and
literary issues of the day are revived.

The second facet of Mr. Bennett's genius is his abundant
consciousness. We have pointed out that he chooses for
his subject a perfectly commonplace man in perfectly
commonplace surroundings; and of these he makes, by the
flood of knowledge and understanding and 'awareness' he
sheds upon them, an enthralling book, a book to re-read
and re-read. He so vitalizes and interprets the common
light of every day that we seem, for the moment, to understand all life from the light thrown on the typical
moment. And it is no longer commonplace; it is luminous
and wonderful and awakening that life should be like this.
And, finally, Mr. Bennett has that gift which outweighs all
romance, the sense of truth; he neither belittles facts nor
heightens effects. He looks steadily at his fact, he sees
true, he reports accurately. If this seems to be other
than great praise, it is because our sense of values needs
transvaluation. 'Clayhanger' is a very great novel.

58. UNSIGNED REVIEW, 'ATLANTIC MONTHLY'

May 1911, 662

From Arnold Bennett comes another of his realistic novels,
so long that they bid fair to be as long as life itself,
and yet are full of interest. Again a section of life in
one of the Five Towns is presented, dreary, smoky, sordid;
and against this background moves Clayhanger's lad, 'the
spitten image of his poor mother.' 'The fat old women ...
who, in child-bed and at grave-sides, had been at the very
core of life for long years,' see, when he passes, only a
fresh lad with fair hair and gawky knees and elbows, 'but
they could not see the mysterious and holy flame of desire
for self-perfecting blazing within that tousled head.'
Through seven hundred pages he holds your attention as he
slowly gives up his plans and hopes, reluctantly abandons
his own ambitions and enters his father's business, loves
a woman who unaccountably proves false, and, believing in
her throughout, wins her at the end, when life has played
with her and cast her off and she brings him only her
wrongs. It is apparently a story of slow defeat, wrought
inch by inch with terrible thoroughness, yet the last
words are, 'He braced himself to the exquisite burden of
life.'

It is a rather fine thing, the art of Arnold Bennett,
though one would not be exaggerating in saying that it
lacks selective power. He denies himself the spectacular;
here is none of the picturesque misery of the slums; here
is no vivid rendering of quick sensations, only the endless jogging on along humdrum ways. Slowly the personalities emerge, going the round of their dreary tasks, and as
you follow you have no sense of reading a book, only a
half-painful, half-pleasant feeling of sharing human experience, difficult in a thousand homely ways. The actual
uncertainty of daily life attends you. Was it, or was it
not, a pity that the boy had to give up his hope of being
an architect? You never know, any more than he did; and
the same blind forces seem to carry you forward that carry
you on in existence itself. This grim clinging to life
and the best one has found in it, though it be but a
decent habit, the fashion of stumbling blindly along the
trail of old hopes, brings to the reader at times an
almost intolerable sense of reality. Maggie, who never
suspects her own heroism; Hilda Lessways, revealed to you
chiefly through her sympathy with the old Methodist parson, whose only offense against society was that he had
forgotten to die; the father, with his hard idealism
wrought out in his stationer's business, are more real
than many personages in fiction more vividly sketched;
and the father's illness and death bring before you with
almost unendurable pathos the manifold pitifulnesses of
life. If, at times, you stop, resenting the author's
power, saying that this is a rendering of experience
without faith, without beauty, with no windows left open
for the soul; if you cry out against the intolerable
thoroughness with which the author seems to represent all
of life except the point, you realize, upon longer consideration, that this is an art of submerged ideals, and
of faiths that live on unconscious of themselves. After
all 'Clayhanger' is a story of the slow, sure shaping of
the clay in the light of a divine idea.
     Two comedies, also from the hand of this indefatigable
author, appear among the new books: 'Helen with the High
Hand,' and 'Denry the Audacious,' the former a study of
feminine, the latter, of masculine audacity, of power to
work one's will, just the quality lacking in the hero of
'Clayhanger.' 'Helen with the High Hand' has a touch of
artificial in the heroine's character, suggesting old
comedy types; and the best of the book consists in the
presentation of the old uncle, with all the minute realism
of a Dutch portrait. The second comedy is by far the
better of the two, and the account of the hero who knows
invariably how to grasp the opportunity of the moment is

amusing throughout. How, one wonders, did the Five Towns
happen to produce a type which seems American rather than
English, possessing in such marked degree the qualities
that have led here to success in business and in states-
manship? But the irony of 'Clayhanger' and 'The Old
Wives' Tale' is better than the humor of the lighter
stories.

59. MONUMENTAL REALISM, UNSIGNED REVIEW, 'NATION' (NEW
YORK)

7 December 1911, 541-2

The Arnold Bennett who has just left us after a brief but
triumphal progress from New York to Chicago, stands out as
the author of three big books. The general reading public
has probably been chiefly impressed by the bigness of
quantity. But there are enough critics who have found in
him bigness of the other kind. Mr. Bennett is a veteran
at the writing game, but his present reputation is founded
on the 'Old Wives Tale,' and the two published volumes of
his 'Clayhanger' trilogy. In these three books he has
displayed a method of minute realistic detail that is
studiously unemotional in development. His ambition, as
evidenced in his novels and as expressed in his critical
opinions of the great writers of the past, is to see life
clearly and to see it - and there comes the uncertainty
with regard to Mr. Bennett: whether it is his ambition
also to see life whole or only to see it minutely. Both
in the mere physical bulk of his latest books and in their
preoccupation with the souls of people, rather than their
acts, this Englishman has invited comparison with the
giants of an earlier age. In the opinion of more than
one enthusiastic critic, he easily takes his place with
the writers of other 'big' books, with Balzac, with
Tolstoy, and with the early eighteenth century English
realists. To decide whether he deserves the place, we
must rid ourselves of the impression which mere bulk and
a serious purpose are bound to produce, even in the professional critic. The question is whether Mr. Bennett's
subject matter, which is of every day, goes well with the
spread of his canvas, which is epic.
    Novels longer than 'Clayhanger' have been written and
will continue to be written from time to time. But it may

be said at once that the pulse of vitality must beat in them much stronger than it does in 'Clayhanger,' if they are to take their place with the literature that lives long. We cannot set any bounds to the length of a novel because we cannot see any bounds to its capacities. Because the author is at liberty to pour into the novel anything and everything - prose and poetry, drab reality and imagination, history, philosophy, criticism, anecdote, autobiography, argument, and preachment; because he can people it with any amount of emotional variety; because he can multiply incident and situation at will - for these reasons 'Tom Jones,' 'Vanity Fair,' 'War and Peace,' 'Les Misérables,' and 'Père Goriot' are possible. You can write a novel of epic length if you give it epic food, and that means a crowd. Seven hundred pages of drab analysis of a single ordinary man cannot, for all its truthfulness, make 'Clayhanger' alive, for the reason that the book simply has not bone and muscle enough to carry the fat. There are dull stretches in Balzac, in Tolstoy, and possibly in 'The Newcomes' and 'David Copperfield,' but they are the flat interludes between periods of splen-did emotion. You skip these dreary periods because you are in a hurry to get to the delectable feast. But in 'Clayhanger' there is little to skip from or to. The plain stretches on endlessly; you walk till you get tired; then you rest and walk on again. If it is psychological dissection you are after, one mood is as good as another. And therein consists one objection to the 'Clayhanger' method. The writer has attempted to do a novel of analy-sis on a scale that will tolerate only the novel of mag-nificent creativeness.

But 'Clayhanger' is true! Well, it is true in the sense that it gives us a vast succession of veracious detail. But, after all, is it the business of the artist to draw up catalogues or to create something that is single, harmonious, rounded out, whole? Artists may create in a flash or may create with patient and minute craft, but the required result is the same - a living individualized man or woman, a concrete, individualized Form. For minute craftsmanship can never be its own object, and Clayhanger's sensations in putting on a new suit or procuring the use of a study-room all to himself simply will not bear the pagefuls of analysis Mr. Bennett brings to bear upon the subject. We can readily allow pages of psychological analysis to such tremendous crises of the spirit as Dostoievsky can evoke in 'Crime and Punishment'; we can allow it even to Jean Valjean, be-cause - well, there is no other word for it - we feel that such moments are 'big,' are truly fraught with eternity;

whereas the boy Clayhanger's emotions as he leans over the bridge-railing and pitches stones into the water are not.

To the extent that Mr. Bennett in 'Clayhanger' is true to his ideal of an impassive and minute realism, his work leaves us comparatively cold. To the extent that he forgets and permits himself a dip into old-fashioned emotion, into old-fashioned dramatic situations, he has made the book real. When one has put down 'Clayhanger,' the two chapters that stand out clearest in the memory are the magnificent early chapter which describes the pitiful experiences of the infant factory-slaves of early industrial England as Edwin's father had lived them, and the chapter in which that same father dies. In both places, Mr. Bennett has been deeply moved, has written with passion and with tears, and has attained effects that are never attained, unless you are stirred by the deeper things. The matter is simple: while we are what we are, the putting on of a new suit of clothes will remain a less important thing than a death-bed, and no matter in what dazzling psychological phenomena we may dress the former event, it will still be the same. Of course, in saying this, we may be the slave of the old-fashioned romantic literature, which the new realism relegates to the scrap heap; but as a realist, Mr. Bennett must acknowledge the reality of prejudice.

Thus, one's objections to a Clayhanger trilogy in two thousand pages are based on what we take to be two fundamental errors in Mr. Bennett's method - the belief in psychological thread-spinning for its own sake and the belief that emotion has no place in the creative artist's soul. The great realists have never been ashamed to shed tears. Balzac did it over the death-bed of old Goriot, as Thackeray did over the death-bed of Col. Newcome, as Dickens did over the death-bed of Nell, as Tolstoy did over the death-bed of Prince André - a scene in which he has put enough psychological verity, one feels tempted to say, to carry an entire 'Clayhanger' - as Turgenieff did over the death-bed of Bazaroff, as Hardy over the death-bed of Jude. The 'big' books have always been written about such big things as birth and love and death.

'The Card'

23 February 1911

60. DIXON SCOTT, IN THE 'MANCHESTER GUARDIAN'

23 February 1911, 7

Dixon Scott (c. 1891-1915) was a young critic of distinction, associated particularly with A.N. Monkhouse on the
'Manchester Guardian'. He died of dysentery at Gallipoli.
This review and others were published in the posthumous
volume 'Men of Letters' in 1916. Bennett noted in his
'Journal' on 26 February 1911 that Scott's review was 'one
of the best I ever had, and no effusiveness either'.

That Mr. Bennett could have given us a better book than
this; that much of it is frankly just frivolling and more
of it almost rowdily rollicking; that though it deals once
again with those confounded Potteries it has nothing of
the dark dignity of 'Clayhanger' ; these are bound to be
some of the things our Cockney cousins will be printing
this morning as they solemnly decide that 'The Card,' like
the 'Grand Babylon Hotel' and 'How to Live on Twenty-four
Hours a Day,' is another of the things they must try to
overlook for the sake of 'The Old Wives' Tale.' There is
a crumb or two of reason on their side; 'The Card' *is* a
sort of skylarking, a 'Merry Wives of Windsor,' bearing
much the same relation to 'Clayhanger' that snap does to
responsible bridge or Cinquevalli's cue-play to Diggle's;
but to regard it as a giddy aberration, an indiscretion,
is to get a wholly wrong idea about both it and its maker.
'The Card' is genuine Bennett; it flings a happy light on
the whole fascinating Bennett problem; and indeed the

really fundamental thing to say about it, comparatively,
is not that it ought to have 'Clayhanger's' qualities, but
that 'Clayhanger' would be better if it had some of the
qualities of 'The Card.' But that is a fact not easily
seen in a London fog. The Metropolitan viewpoint in these
matters (as every day makes plainer) is inevitably as
oddly askew as London itself is on the map; the Londoner
sees life, England's life, at an angle, foreshortened,
as from a stage-box; instead of taking to it gradually,
breast-on, from the primitive beach, every step an adventure, he nips into it aslant, deep water at once, from the
door of his sophisticated bathing-van - a solid half of
experience irrecoverably missed. And thus, as a consequence, the provinces are always for him a kind of vague
hinterland, protoplasmic and grey, an illimitable East End
somewhere at the back of the shires; and even if he
doesn't actually ask wearily, with Mr. Walkley, 'What *are*
the Five Towns anyway?' he does feel that the proper tone
to speak of the provinces artistically is a sort of Gissing greyness, as who should talk of Soup Kitchens and the
Submerged. A Pottery 'Il Penseroso' he can understand,
but not a Pottery 'L'Allegro.' In 'Clayhanger,' where
spades were called spades, he thought he detected the
sombreness - did indeed (positively!) praise that sanguine
and romantic book for its unflinching austerity. But in
'The Card,' where, though spades are still trumps, the
game goes undisguisedly *allegretto*, he suspects mere unreality and loud farce. 'What's he done? What great
Cause has he ever been identified with?' asks a virtuous
old Councillor indignantly on the last page of the book.
He is speaking of Denry Machin, the card, the man who
bluffs his way to funds and favours by dint of cheek and
mother-wit. It might be Mr. William Archer solemnly re-
proving the author. And the stout, sensible Staffordshire
reply, on which the curtain comes down, 'He's identified
with the great cause of cheering us all up,' is perhaps
one that, as a defence of Mr. Bennett, only a born provincial can properly understand.

For it is probably true that to enjoy 'The Card' completely you must be lucky enough to be born a little
nearer to the centre of things than London. To appreciate
Mr. Bennett's art, a purely provincial product, to see all
that it stands for and all that it is bringing us, you too
must be a provincial - seeing London, as a consequence, a
third storey, not a basement and first cause. It is the
half-dazed tripper, fresh through the portals of Euston,
at whom the cool Cockney smiles, who is the real connoisseur of London, the expert in its life and lore; and Mr.
Bennett has never lost that primitive relish for the

spectacle of Piccadilly and the Strand. Harrod's (see his 'Hugo') is as wonderful to him as the Bagdad bazaars; the Savoy (see 'The Grand Babylon Hotel') far more thrilling than the Palace of the Doges. And they are romantic (this is the great point) not because he is bedazzled by them, but because his shrewd provincial eyes are fresh and strong enough to see them in their quiddity - as elaborate engines 'functioning' ingeniously, draining England so neatly of its succulent tit-bits, plucking waiters from the Alps, inhaling and expelling human bodies. Even those of his readers who would blush to be caught reading 'Hugo' must have seen how assiduously he resolves things to their structural elements, beginning one book, 'The Old Wives' Tale,' with a reference to parallels of latitude and another with an adjusting side-glance at the solar system. It is because life is so mechanical that he finds it so romantic. To such a man, seeing the structure from cellarage to cowls, aware (like Edwin Clayhanger) of the hot-water pipes hidden in the walls, the smallest item in a Pottery parlour fairly twinkles with picturesque possibilities - every street, every shop, presents a forest of fascinating levers, - and there is no higher happiness in life than to pull this and that, learn their cute combinations, master the art of *savoir-faire*. As a result, all his novels are practical demonstrations of that art; his characters, less or more, are virtuosi in life - learning 'How to Live on Twenty-four Hours a Day.' And just as in 'Clayhanger' we got Edwin fingering levers and rods rather falteringly - sometimes setting things in motion unconsciously, like the country cousin, new to hotel-tricks, who stepped into a snug waiting-room, pulled the bell-rope, and found himself shooting skywards in a lift, - so, too, in 'The Card' we have Denry Machin tugging and experimenting audaciously, using the actual apparatus of contemporary Potterydom to provide him with money and mansions and as many adventures and victories as were ever carved out with a sword.

It is the gayest exposition. Nothing is ever done 'off' on Mr. Bennett's stage; we see exactly what Denry does and how he does it; how (for instance) fishing a scrap of chocolate out of a glass of lemonade and perceiving its precise relation to Llandudno he converts it into a cool five hundred pounds. *Toujours l'audace!* Like a madcap chauffeur, Mr. Bennett loves to rush himself and his characters into tight corners, trusting to the crush of the crisis to squeeze out the brilliant solution; and he is never floored. One would like to make a list of these escapades and blithe improvisations, and show how much their effect of reality, of eminent feasibility, is

due to the driver's adroitness as well as his daring, to
Mr. Bennett's cool eye for relative and ultimate values.
But a point perhaps better worth making is the fact that
it is the very furiosity of the fun, the element of fan-
tasy and extravagance, that gives the last touch of truth
to the tale as a picture of reality. 'Every life is a
series of coincidences. Nothing happens that is not
rooted in coincidence' - thus the *raisonneur* in 'The
Card.' Now the danger that dogs Mr. Bennett's more sober
achievements, built up with such Euclidean logic, tracing
causes with such exquisite clarity, is that they may fail
to convey the sense of the fantastic element in life, the
untamed force that pounds through the fabric so incal-
culably, dishevelling and exalting the neat systems. Two
and two make five in real life; in 'Clayhanger' perhaps
they too often add neatly up to four. It is this Gothic
element in things that makes such a jolly gargoyle as
'The Grand Babylon Hotel' a more faithful symbol of reality than some much sterner stuff; and it is this heightened irrational strain that one wants to see swaggering
through the cool symmetry of 'Clayhanger' like organ-music
throbbing through a church. Artists of another type
(Mr. Henry James, for instance) can give us the equivalent
in the form of coloured metaphors and vaulted imagery and
the evocative music of words. Mr. Bennett, who has no
turn for oratory and stained-glass window work, can give
it us supremely well in the shape of a stalking impersonal
plot. This is what one means by saying that 'Clayhanger'
might borrow a trick or two from 'The Card.' Its author's
masterpiece will be a blend of *savoir-faire* papers and
shockers and 'Clayhangers' - a thrifty utilisation that
appeals to the provincial mind. And of course, since two-
thirds of it are still unborn, that masterpiece may prove
to be 'Clayhanger' itself.

61. UNSIGNED REVIEW, 'TIMES LITERARY SUPPLEMENT'

2 March 1911, 88

In his really big novels, 'The Old Wives' Tale' and
'Clayhanger,' for instance, Mr. Arnold Bennett's confident
admirers feel that he is writing not only for themselves,
but for posterity. Taste may change, of course, and these
rigorously bioscopic presentations may give place to a

form of literature not quite so firmly attached to life's
exacting apron-strings. But even if taste does change,
and so radically, it is only Mr. Bennett's masterpieces
that would die of neglect. He writes another kind of
book, such as 'The Card', in his spare time, as it were.
And here life is slightly, dexterously distorted.
Coincidence plucks softly at the strings. By hook or by
crook we are going to be kept very lively and agog. 'The
Card,' indeed, is a kind of fairy-tale - a fairy tale told
in terms of the Five Towns. Denry (a maternal variant of
Edward Henry) is the only character that much matters,
though Nellie and Ruth Earp are trustworthy reserves.
He is the Dick Whittington of the story; Bursley is his
London Town, and the last chapter leaves him fabulously
wealthy but unspoilt, its unprecedentedly youthful and
immensely popular Mayor - identified, as one of his
friends assured his chagrined rival, Councillor Barlow,
'with the great cause of cheering us up.' There must be
thousands of Denries in England who never will be mayors
simply because they restrict their careers to their day-
dreams. They will be enormously 'cheered up' by the
adventures of their prototype. This particular Denry has
a daemon, and every tide in his career this daemon
inspires him to take precisely at the flood. At sixteen,
for instance, he finds himself dancing in his 'church
boots' with the extravagantly aristocratic Iris, Countess
of Chell, at the Mayor's ball, a privilege entirely due
to instant obedience to the counsels of this inward self.
Over and over again, with the promptitude of a 'corner-
man,' he inquires 'Do *you*?' just at the moment when any
other form of articulateness would have landed him in confusion. He is constantly *in extremis*, never nonplussed.
He is double-natured; canny and cautious by instinct,
daring and resourceful by inspiration; mean-spirited and
unscrupulous, with casual bursts of a really heroic fineness of feeling; rather a cute and horrid young man on the
whole, whom it is yet impossible to resist. Mr. Bennett
even in his spare time, even when he is merely a markedly
clever imitator of himself, is an artist. Otherwise, her
widowhood's conventional term of mourning over, Bursley
would have undoubtedly taken its beloved Iris and its
record Mayor even closer to its bosom.

62. REVIEW SIGNED N.H.W., 'T.P.'S WEEKLY'

17 March 1911, 327

Had not one to laugh over the portraiture of Denry Machin
in Mr. Arnold Bennett's new novel, 'The Card', one must
surely weep. It is almost whimsically satirical, but, as
in all effective satire, it has a strong element of truth.
Far as a novel can preach, 'The Card' preaches 'If you
want to make any success in life it is best done through
cheek - always cheek. Be not over scrupulous as to means,
provided they can be used so as not to be found out; cul-
tivate a thick skin and learn to exploit both the virtues
and the faults of your neighbour.' Let it be admitted
that the incidents which carry along this very up-to-date
gospel are often purest farce; still underlying all is a
certain vein of grim satirical truth and a subtly-conveyed
admiration on the part of the author for the Denrys of
life. At a very early age Denry Machin was described by
his intimates as 'a card,' and the definition is admirable. I do not know what the Cockney meaning of 'card'
would convey, but I know the word is used in Ireland in
a sense that absolutely fits in with the 'Five Towns'
application - a card is a man pleasant and devil-may-care,
but with a certain shrewdness and keenness that enable him
to get the better of his duller neighbours. The 'Card' in
his wildest extravagances never forgets number one; in
fact, the cult of number one is the beginning and end of
his pleasant existence.
     Denry Machin first saw the light in surroundings and
circumstances that rarely in the case of limited intelligence lead to greatness. His mother lived in a small
house in Brougham Street, Bursley, for which she paid four
shillings and sixpence a week rent. For occupation she
combined the art of the needle with the art of the wash-
tub. She made up ladies' own materials in their own
homes; but such was her skill in lathering flannels and
handling fine laces that, as our author puts it, 'often
when she came to sew she remained to wash.' Now, those
who know the habits of the inhabitants of the 'Five Towns'
(and who to-day does not?) will understand that the income
brought in from the dual efforts of Mrs. Machin was not a
very large one. Denry consequently had to look out for
himself at a very early age. Luckily, at twelve, he was
saved from the necessity of manual labour by winning a
Board School scholarship. Being neither industrious nor
intelligent, he had gained his place by fraud. His success

gives Mr. Bennett an opportunity for expounding a bit of school ethics: 'Of course it was dishonest. Yes, but I will not agree that Denry was uncommonly vicious. Every schoolboy is dishonest by adult standard. If I knew an honest schoolboy I would begin to count my silver spoons as he grew up. All is fair between schoolboys and masters.' The value seems taken from this bit of didacticism by Denry the man remaining as dishonest as Denry the boy. But, then, is not Mr. Bennett's satire that we recognise no dishonesty where there is success?

To act as clerk to a local solicitor for some years bounded the ambitions of Denry. Then came the Countess. Here is a delicious description which may surely be used to earmark someone in even a very limited acquaintance with ladies of title:

> The Countess of Chell was born of poor but picturesque parents, and she could put her finger on her great-grandfather's grandfather. Her mother gained her livelihood and her daughter's by allowing herself to be seen a great deal with humbler but richer people's daughters. The Countess was brought up to matrimony. She was aimed and timed to hit a given mark at a given moment. She succeeded. She married the Earl of Chell. She also married about twenty thousand acres in England, about a fifth of Scotland, a house in Piccadilly, seven country seats (including Sneyd), a steam yacht, and five hundred thousand pounds' worth of shares in the Midland Railway. She was young and pretty. She had travelled in China and written a book about China. She sang at charity concerts and acted in private theatricals. She sketched from nature. She was one of the great hostesses of London. And she had not the slightest tendency to stoutness. All this did not satisfy her. She was ambitious. She wanted to be taken seriously.

The social progress of the Five Towns became the hobby of the Countess, and she opened the campaign with a ball to the inhabitants. To this ball Denry got admission under false pretences. The Countess danced with him; he made the Countess laugh; he was the success of the evening. All Five Towns was agog next day with the story of the washwoman's son who had made a Countess laugh. It began to shake its united head and declare there must be something in the fellow. And Denry agreed with Five Towns. He was also inclined to think he was a 'devil of a smart fellow,' and he resolved henceforth to live up to the belief. For on the road to success true self analysis would be a very serious stumbling block.

Denry lost his situation as a result of the manoeuvre by which he got to the ball; but what for another would be a misfortune was for him but a stepping-stone to becoming rent collector. And from that day he never looked back. We follow eyes wide with amused amazement his adventures, knowing he will turn up a trump every time. Once when in love he nearly came a cropper; sex dazzlement clouded his usual good judgment, and Ruth Earp is so finely drawn by the author that we forgive Denry his slight swaying on the path of common sense. Ruth was very refined - did she not teach dancing? Does he marry Ruth? That is a question readers must find out for themselves. They must follow Denry from one piece of bluff to another; they may try to analyse the proportion of true business acumen that went to the support of his self-confidence; but they will find that the tiny streak of real work that Mr. Bennett allows in his character comes out in his relations with his women folk - be it mother, sweetheart, or wife. Here is a scene with his mother, who insists on remaining in her four and sixpenny cottage no matter what his income is. He finds her sitting up late, cold and coughing:

> 'Look here, mother,' said he, 'you must have a doctor.'
> 'I shall have no doctor.'
> 'You've got influenza, and it's a very tricky business, influenza is; you never know where you are with it.'
> 'Ye can call it influenza if ye like,' said Mrs. Machin. 'There was no influenza in my young days. We called a cold a cold.'
> 'Well,' said Denry, 'you aren't well, are you?'
> 'I never said I was,' she answered, grimly.
> 'No,' said Denry, with that triumphant ring of one who is about to devastate an enemy. 'And you never will be in this rotten old cottage.'
> 'This was reckoned a very good class of house when your father and I came into it; and it's always been kept in repair. It was good enough for me. I don't see myself flitting; but some folks have gotten so grand. As for health, old Reuben next door is ninety-one. How many people over ninety are there in those gimcrack houses up by that Park, I should like to know?'

Later, with his sweetheart, we get even a pleasanter glimpse of Denry. Perhaps it is as well to leave him

at such a moment.   It makes us reconciled to the fine
irony that makes him happy in his choice of a wife,
respected and admired by his fellow-townsmen, and with
as much money as can make him play the general benefactor.
And all because he was a 'Card,' not troubled with a conscience or a great regard for the wherefores of getting
money as long as he got it.   A most enjoyable book, and
a striking proof of Mr. Bennett's remarkable versatility.

63. A.J.G., IN THE 'STAFFORDSHIRE SENTINEL'

24 March 1911, 4

In spite of its title, Mr. Bennett's new book has nothing
to do with gambling - though its hero often enough juggled
with the chances of Fortune.   It deals with the type of
individual who is generally described in the north country
as a 'caution;' and by the time the book is finished most
people will have come to the conclusion that the author
himself is something of a 'caution.'
    'The Card' is very funny - probably the funniest thing
Mr. Bennett has ever written, a book which is bound to be
read to an accompaniment of smiles, chuckles, and open
laughter.   The peculiar quality of its humour does not
make it any the less attractive.   Its popularity is
already assured, for, though quite a new book, the second
edition is just issued.   Mr. Bennett has given his
imagination full play, and the result is a series of
improbable incidents and wild adventures which in some
instances border on the farcical.   Those who class Mr.
Bennett as one of the realists of present-day fiction may
be surprised to find that he could imagine so many
improbabilities, and yet possess the art which gives them
for the moment the semblance of actual happenings.   The
book is full of contrasts.   One is caught up in a whirl-
wind of mad impossibilities, which are yet full of laughter, and suddenly brought to a standstill against some
little fact of everyday life - some little homely incident
whose sheer truthfulness is something of a shock after a
long tale of absurdities.
    The background the author has chosen for his tale is
the 'Five Towns' of some ten to twenty years ago.   In the
course of the story some of the characters move to
Llandudno, and again to Switzerland, but the Potteries

still remains the natural field of their activities.
There is a certain amount of portraiture, and some amusement may be derived from recognising - or imagining that
one recognises - some of the originals. It is at any rate
fairly obvious that a few of the characters have been
built on living foundations. The hero himself is a native
of 'Bursley,' and being named Edward Henry Machin, his
mother, as the author observes, 'saved a certain amount
of time every day by addressing her son as "Denry,"
instead of Edward Henry,' Denry and Denry's mother are
wondrous characters. One of the most prominent features
of the hero's career is his unswerving love for and devotion to his narrow-minded, obstinate, grim, but excellent
mother. Denry rose from a humble cottage at 4s. 6d. a
week to be the owner of the most remarkable house in
Bursley. And this is how he did it.

By sheer audacity of thought and action he won a
scholarship from the Board School to the Endowed School
at the age of twelve. At sixteen he left school to become shorthand clerk to Mr. Duncalf, a solicitor, who was
also Town Clerk of Bursley. Things went uneventfully for
some years until existence was transformed by a chance
meeting with the Countess of Chell, the great lady of the
neighbourhood - beautiful, gracious, and democratic. By
devious ways he acquired an invitation to the municipal
ball, a dress suit, and a dance with the Countess -
springing at a bound into notoriety as a man of consequence and power. Bursley and the general world became
an oyster, and Denry felt that his business was to find
the means of opening it. Nothing damped by his dismissal
from Mr. Duncalf's, his natural resourcefulness suggested
a new and profitable way of business, and Denry captured
Mr. Duncalf's rent collection business, and became a
moneylender on a small scale, to the poor occupants of
poor cottages. This led to the ownership of some of the
cottages, and, as a property owner, Denry was elected to
'the most sparkling fellowship of the Five Towns' - the
Sports Club at Hillport. Denry's first visit to the club,
with all the consciousness of his humble origin hanging
round his neck, is one of the most humorous things in the
book.

About this time Denry developed his acquaintance with
a guileful young woman of spendthrift habits - Ruth Earp,
a dancing mistress. The acquaintance ripened so rapidly
under the influence of a midnight adventure in a pantech-
nicon van (and here surely Mr. Bennett reaches the high
water mark of farcical improbability) that Denry found
himself duly engaged. The next act in the comedy of this
engagement takes place at Llandudno, the Mecca of engaged

couples from the Five Towns. There Ruth's confidence in
her lover as a man of means first flattered, then surprised, next alarmed, and finally terrified him. Never
had he come across such spending capacity, and Denry's
mind misgave him. A diversion occurred in the shape of
a storm and a wreck, of which Denry wrote a glowing
account for the 'Staffordshire Signal.' But not even the
storm could avert the impending catastrophe of a broken
engagement, which was brought about by the utterance of
a single word. The scene on Llandudno Station is all the
more wonderful because it is so simple, so homely, and
so perfectly natural.

Denry was sacrcely broken-hearted when he was left
alone at Llandudno to pursue a great idea and a great
scheme. He purchased the life-boat which had gone out
to the wreck, installed the ex-owner as coxswain, and
the wrecked Norwegians as crew, and instituted a series
of hourly trips to the wreck, for the sum of 2s. 6d.,
return fare. All Llandudno responded to the bait, and
at the end of the first day Denry was fairly afloat on
the sea of financial success. For weeks people indulged
in the lifeboat trips, and their originator was pocketing
an income far beyond his wildest dreams. He began to
prove himself singularly fertile in ideas, and everyone
of them was successful. Photographs of the lifeboat and
its passengers sold like wildfire; then followed a mysterious 'Chocolate Remedy' for sea-sickness, which was
on sale from Morecambe to Barmouth; 'rocket fetes' were
organised, and altogether Denry, in his own phrase,
'wakened up' Llandudno, and filled his pockets.

Denry's schemes and ambitions did not end here. He
established the 'Five Towns Universal Thrift Club,' and
by a complicated arrangement between himself, the working
people, and the shopkeepers, he managed to please everybody, and make money. Interspersed with all these money-
making schemes, there are many frolics, in which Denry,
his mule, and the Countess of Chell all figure largely,
and Denry proved himself, more and more convincingly,
the 'card' of the district. His next step was a battle
with his mother over the removal from the cottage of his
birth to a remarkable mansion, fitted with every known
and unknown labour-saving contrivance. Merely to read
of the wonders of that house will gladden any ambitious
housewife's heart. All through the book there are continual references to the 'Signal,' and in connection with
this is described the only scheme in which Denry did not
score in a financial sense. A rival to the 'Signal' came
to an inglorious end, after a brief, if exciting career.
The 'Signal,' it is said, 'went on its august way, blind

to sensational hoardings,' and apparently oblivious of
any attempted rivalry. But the warfare between the
'Signal' boys and the rival boys is rich in incident and
in fun, and Mr. Bennett, with his inside knowledge of
newspaper life, seems to have written these chapters 'con
amore.' At the end of it all, Denry 'had had too disconcerting a glimpse of the rigours and perils of journalism
to wish to continue in it ... and the "Signal," subsequently often referred to as "The Old Lady," resumed its
monopolistic sway over the opinions of a quarter of a million of people, and has never since been attacked.'

The next scheme Denry embarked upon was the securing
of a wife, and this he carried out in the same wildly
impulsive but highly successful way common to the rest
of his ideas. Incidentally Ruth Earp gets rather badly
treated, and yet there is a sneaking impression that she
really deserved all she got. The honeymoon in Switzerland, as an impression of fashionable hotel life, is
clever and amusing, but it has little real connection
with the main theme of the story. Still there are many
people who will enjoy a realistic description of how other
people travel and amuse themselves in the Alps. Tobog-
gans, skis, and luge-dances, cotillions, and flirtations,
all the accessories of wintering in the Alps, are graphically and humorously described, and Denry is, of course,
one of the central figures.

The story ends with Denry's attainment of the 'supreme
honour' possible to him as a successful man - the mayor-
alty of his native town of Bursley. These things were,
obviously, before the days of Federation. The last
sentences are illuminating:-

'A little group of Councillors were discussing
Denry.
'What a card!' said one, laughing joyously. 'He's
a rare 'un, no mistake.'
'Of course, this'll make him more popular than
ever,' said another. 'We've never had a man to touch
him for that.'
'And yet,' demanded Councillor Barlow, 'what's he
done? Has he ever done a day's work in his life?
What great cause is he identified with?'
'He's identified,' said the first speaker, 'with
the great cause of cheering us all up.'

And speaking from personal experience, that is exactly
what Denry's history may be warranted to do.

'Hilda Lessways'

21 September 1911

64. UNSIGNED REVIEW, 'TIMES LITERARY SUPPLEMENT'

21 September 1911, 340

'Hilda Lessways' proves one thing at least beyond all possible dispute - Mr. Arnold Bennett's confidence in his
insight and comprehension. This would be clear even were
that confidence justified much less completely in its outcome than it is. For though 'Hilda Lessways' may not
actually break new ground in fiction it is undoubtedly
suggestive of possibilities never hitherto so deliberately confronted. It suggests that the novelist of the
future may conceivably be the maker of only one book,
the master of one definite set of circumstances seen from
all possible points of view, over and over again freshly
treated *via* the consciousness, as it were, of each of its
several characters. The thought at first sight may be
little short of shocking. Yet with Mr. Bennett for its
pioneer it is even fascinating. We foresee our children
living not merely rich, extravagant, outlandish, complex,
tragic fragments of other people's lives as communicated
in fiction, but lucidly yet intricately multiplying their
whole experience and survey. And this for the reason that
'Hilda Lessways' is not simply a sequel, nor an appendix,
nor even a commentary on 'Clayhanger,' but very largely
'Clayhanger' in renewed and unanticipated yet unsurprising
terms. If 'Clayhanger' was the partial warp of a chosen
piece of life's fabric, this is its partial woof. What
gave that book its key, or rather what was its instrument,
was Clayhanger's almost startlingly ordinary, perfectly
intelligible personality. There, events rather than their
master or victim kept us vividly interested. Here, all

but one sole mind and heart - their thoughts, passions,
feelings - hold us captive. Impulsive, enigmatic,
irresistibly arresting, Hilda awakened in the reader
of 'Clayhanger' a curiosity that has easily survived a
a year of waiting and expectation. Now, over much the
same ground, but also over its gaps and intervals, Mr.
Bennett conducts us again, and though we certainly know
Hilda more surely and intimately than we did in 'Clayhanger,' still at the conclusion of its successor she
leaves us unsatisfied. Still enigmatical and elusive
and intensely absorbing, she cries *au revoir*, and we
close the book, filled again with an anxious impatience
to skip the year that must divide us from that 'later
history' which is to complete an extraordinary trilogy.
Such, moreover, is Mr. Bennett's instinctive grasp and
penetration and gift of writing that we would gladly
resign ourselves to a whole series of novels dealing
with the same theme, but entitled 'George Cannon,' 'Sarah
Gailey,' 'Osmond Orgreave,' and even, though here we just
hesitate, 'Florrie.'

In some respects 'Hilda Lessways' is a more skilful
piece of art than 'Clayhanger.' It is less diffuse, less
incidental, a little less pathological, a more definitely
complete thing. Here and there the grasp falters. Here
and there this spy on life intrudes in person, is not only
the master of his characters, but cannot conceal his elation in the fact. At times Mr. Bennett slips into a style
not absolutely his own, or is content to sweep his reader
on in a rush of telling phrases, and to let Hilda see
more clearly and feel with a more conscious complexity
than we are convinced Hilda could. Taste, too, is occasionally at fault. Many passages on the other hand are
flawless - the tender, reticent, imaginative description,
for instance, of poor Sarah's impotent attempt at suicide
or (at the other extreme) of the congested and revolting
moment of Louisa's rebellion over Florrie's 'sheets.'
But the most vital feature of the book is the peculiar
analysis of Hilda's love for George Cannon. She is only
twenty-one. Her innocent infatuation for this man has
resulted in a tragic neglect of her dying mother. A nervous breakdown follows. In this condition she becomes,
according to Mr. Bennett, 'the last intelligent victim
of a malady which has now almost passed away from the
civilized earth; she existed in the chill and stricken
desolation of incommutable doom.' That malady is the
conviction of sin. From this conviction and haunting,
helpless sense of shame as regards a lover who so far as
she is aware loves her honestly and marries her as openly
as circumstances permit, Hilda never recovers. Mr. Bennett,

that is, makes this young girl consciously guilty of a
moral obliquity not only ignored in the Decalogue but
undreamed of by Mrs. Grundy. We cannot question the
subtlety with which this problem in psychology is treated.
But here again Mr. Bennett seems to be presenting possibilities and threatening us with a peril never before
quite so precisely suggested.

65. T.M. YOUNG, IN THE 'MANCHESTER GUARDIAN'

21 September 1911, 4

'Clayhanger,' the first member of Mr. Bennett's great trilogy, left us with one unanswered riddle hanging out, like
a tangled bight of slack rope from its neatly coiled and
stowed running gear. When everybody and everything else
had been squared up, sorted out, and told off in the
author's peculiarly conscientious and workmanlike fashion,
Hilda Lessways remained standing as a huge note of interrogation at the very end of the story. We had no more
knowledge of her than was vouchsafed to Edwin Clayhanger
himself, and no more inkling than he why, within a few
days of their obviously sincere and beautiful discovery
of their love for one another, she should have jilted him
with no more circumstance than a note to her friend Janet
Orgreave: 'I am now married to George Cannon. The marriage is not quite public, but I tell you before anybody,
and you might tell Edwin Clayhanger.' That was, in
effect, the end of 'Clayhanger,' for what followed after
a lapse of years was really the beginning of another
story, which is to form the third member of the trilogy.
It did nothing to clear up the mystery enshrouding Hilda
and her conduct.
    'Hilda Lessways,' published to-day, is the answer to
the riddle, the unravelling of the mystery, and we may say
at once that, whether it be read as a self-contained novel
or as a supplement (it is not a sequel) to 'Clayhanger,'
it is a story of profound and absorbing interest. As a
study of character and temperament, of the queer illogical
springs of conduct and of varieties of emotional experience, it transcends mere accomplishment and rises to the
height of imaginative genius. We do not remember any
woman of man's creation about whom we learn so much from
her creator, and so much that seems to be inevitably and

incontrovertibly true, as Mr. Bennett tells us about his
heroine. Most of the great heroines of fiction are great
for us largely because we are allowed to see them roman-
tically, to share (more or less, according to our imaginative capacity) in clothing them with humanity, to invest
them with our own dearest illusions; these are the heroines with whom the susceptible reader falls in love, and
he falls in love with them often in proportion to the
cunning reticence of their literary creator. One does
not fall in love with Hilda Lessways, for that is incompatible with full knowledge and understanding; but one
sees her from within, comprehends and accounts for her,
and understands her compelling attraction for Cannon and
for Clayhanger, neither of whom, by the way, understood
her in the least. 'Hilda Lessways' will probably arouse
in many women readers, and perhaps in some men too, a hostile feeling of the same kind, though not quite so intense,
as was excited by poor little Ann Veronica. If so, it
will be partly due to the fact that Hilda is very far
indeed from being a typical woman (if indeed there be any
such creature), and partly to the fact that in certain
particulars Mr. Bennett's presentation of her is more candid and intimate than some of us may care for. It will be
said, no doubt, with more or less impatience and with undeniable truth, that she is a 'man's idea of a woman,' and
it will be strenuously denied that women are like that.
This kind of criticism often means no more than that women
do not wish to be represented in the character which they
condemn, and do not like it to be admired. With such con-
siderations, of course, the serious novelist has nothing
to do. He conceives and creates a personality, admirable
or despicable, commonplace or abnormal, and is only concerned that it shall come alive under his hands. And
Hilda does come alive; of that there can be no doubt.
She lived, indeed, in 'Clayhanger' an inscrutable romantic
creature; here she is stripped of her vesture of mystery
and moves before us an authentic being of spirit and clay.
She might be presented as a figure of poetry and romance
in Crashaw's lines -

Oh thou undaunted daughter of desires!
By all thy dower of lights and fires:
By all the eagle in thee, all the dove:
By all thy lives and deaths of love:
By thy large draughts of intellectual day
And by thy thirsts of love more large than they:
By all thy brim-filled bowls of fierce desire ...

and we may believe that Mr. Bennett's imagination so

envisaged her before he began to pull her to pieces and
reassemble her for us, like the excellent mechanic that
he is, to show us exactly of what human stuff such visions
are made, and how they can live in the Potteries and in
Brighton boarding-houses and become part of the lives of
our Cannons and Clayhangers.

Of the technical craftsmanship that has gone to the
making of this novel and to the dovetailing of it in with
the already published and therefore unalterable story of
'Clayhanger' it would be difficult to speak too highly.
For the first 180 pages 'Hilda Lessways' pursues an
individual although converging course; for the next three
chapters it deals with events already narrated in 'Clayhanger,' though from a different point of view, scenes
and even dialogue being common to the two narratives; and
then, after an interval in which Hilda's story resumes its
separate way, we have six chapters at the end that are
simply the other side of 'Clayhanger.' It is almost
incredible that two novels which have so much material in
common should nevertheless possess such an absolute individuality that the effect of reading one is an immediate
desire to refer to the other for new light on the situations described by both. Mr. Bennett's method is hardly
comparable with that of 'The Ring and the Book,' for his
characters do not tell their own story, neither is the
essence of his treatment a different interpreting of a
common body of facts. There is practically no interpretation, no commentary; merely a sober narrative and an
intimate record in each story of the thoughts and feelings
of one person, and one only. It is by the strictest
adherence to the plan of seeing nothing, telling nothing,
knowing nothing (for the time) that the central figure of
his story does not see, hear, feel, think, or do that Mr.
Bennett has achieved this masterpiece of construction.
It is by the same means that he has contrived to make the
whole crucial history of Hilda's fateful relationship with
Cannon entirely credible. We know Cannon only as she
knew him, see him only as she saw him; the facts of the
story are nearly all against him, and he could easily be
presented as a mean scoundrel; but although he did her a
terrible injury, he was not a scoundrel to her nor is he
a scoundrel to us. His way of parting from her was, as
she recognised, 'drastic but magnificent,' and in the
light of this story her own withdrawal from Edwin Clayhanger deserves the same epithets. Such magnanimous
cruelties are true to human nature: for women can be
almost infinitely cruel if they themselves suffer enough
by it.

In 'Hilda Lessways' Mr. Bennett's writing is never far

below his best. It is a model of plain, tight, straight-
forward narrative, equally remote from pedantry and
sloppiness. He has a singularly direct and sure way of
creating a particular atmosphere. What could be better,
within its compass, than this: 'The great silent thorough-
fare, Trafalgar Road, whose gas-lamps reigned in the nocturnal silence that the last steam tramcar had left in its
wake'? It is no accident, the part that gas-lighting
plays in Mr. Bennett's scenes, and especially in his
interiors: - '"Hilda, do turn down that there gas a bit,"
said Mrs. Lessways sharply; "It's fizzing." With a nervous exaggeration of solicitude Hilda sprang to the gas-
jet.' And again, in the final scene between Hilda and
Cannon, when he confesses his felony to her - surely an
admirable example of Mr. Bennett's power to present a
vivid picture in simple words and at the same time to
create a suspense leading up to tragedy:-

[Quotes Book 5, ch. 2, sections 2 and 3, 'Then she heard
a sob' to 'and face the situation!']

Mr. Bennett is not a poet and he does not seek to
create beauty; rather indeed he seems, as a writer, to
distrust and eschew it. There is, at any rate, little
superficial beauty in these 400 pages. But beauty breaks
in upon the story, albeit in a fitful gleam, when Clayhanger and Hilda discover their hearts to one another.
We are left waiting now for the final instalment of this
history, the novel that is to tell of their life together,
and we await it with a high expectancy. It will not, of
course, be romantic, but may we not hope that there will
be left in this fine middle-aged pair of faithful lovers
enough of 'the invincible vague hope of youth and the
irresponsible consciousness of power' to flame up and
irradiate with beauty their (hitherto) 'starless souls'?
May we hope, too, that Mr. Bennett will allow them to
live in a house supplied with electric light?

66. UNSIGNED REVIEW, 'ATHENAEUM'

21 September 1911, 352

In 'Hilda Lessways' Mr. Arnold Bennett set himself a task
of more than ordinary difficulty. He was to produce a

work which, set side by side with 'Clayhanger,' should
not suffer in comparison; and he was to afford due and
sufficient explanation of the life and being of a woman
whose actions and personality had both, in 'Clayhanger,'
been left enigmatic. Laying the book down, we feel with
regret that he can hardly be said to have accomplished
this double task with entire success. We had looked forward to seeing a character of 'force and mystery' unfolded
before us; and we have to confess that we find Hilda Lessways weak and rather blatantly ordinary. She is a wayward,
introspective, egotistic girl, whose imagination first,
and whose senses afterwards, are captivated by George
Cannon, a handsome, able, and very vulgar rogue, somewhat
perilously like many another rogue who appears in novels
not by Mr. Arnold Bennett. Her development, in so far as
any takes place, is purely sexual, though, of course, she
herself does not recognize this. We are not quarrelling
with her on that score: we would only maintain that neither in life, nor assuredly in novels, is this anything
extraordinary. One of the chapters is entitled Sin, and
depicts Hilda's remorse for having failed to hasten in
time to her mother's death-bed. In the course of it we
are informed that 'the malady [i.e., the remorse] alone
was proof that she had a profoundly religious nature.'
Nothing could be less true: Hilda shows nowhere any real
sense of compulsion or attraction from the invisible.
Her whole life, alike on its selfish and on its compas-
sionate side, lies wholly within the compass of things
visible and terrestrial.

The impression she makes of weakness may be due in part
to some over-emphasizing of her relations with Cannon. In
regard to him she is the feminine - fascinated, subdued,
surrendered. She performs one or two startling but childish actions; she perseveringly learns shorthand before any
other girl of the Five Towns had ever thought of doing so,
and then works hard and stubbornly with it as an 'editorial secretary'; and also she sticks very pluckily to an
old friend of her mother's, a gloomy and suffering spinster, through the miseries of keeping a sordid boarding-
house. But even so she does not exactly show force; for
the most part she is only carrying out, with more or less
energy and determination, plans which are not her own -
nay, of which she disapproves.

The regularity with which - sitting at table with her
friends, or walking out of doors - she inhales the acrid
savour of life, and finds herself steeped in adventure,
not only becomes in the end monotonous, but strikes us
also as a mood characteristic of a later stage of life
than the early twenties.

Like 'Clayhanger,' the present book shows us the world
almost entirely from the angle at which the principal
figure stands. This method tends to risk everything on
the success of that figure; and accordingly the other
characters here have more or less suffered. Nevertheless
they are, on the whole, more real, convincing, and human
than Hilda, even if we see only one aspect of their humanity. Mr. Bennett excels in depicting the poignancies of
bodily disease, and the grimness of circumstance which so
often surrounds it. Sarah Gailey - with all her incapable
capacity, her unhappiness, her neuritis - really lives.
In contact with her, Hilda too becomes more alive, albeit
at a degree of vitality lower than that which Mr. Arnold
Bennett elsewhere aims at conferring upon her. It might
perhaps be maintained that in general Mr. Bennett works
with most security in portraying the moods and actions
incident to low vitality - whether this be a temporary
or a permanent condition.

67. UNSIGNED REVIEW, 'NATION' (NEW YORK)

5 October 1911, 315-16

That rather surprising promise of the note on the last
page of 'Clayhanger' that the story of Clayhanger and
Hilda was to be developed in two succeeding novels, is
already half-fulfilled. The mysterious Hilda, whom we
saw in the earlier narrative only through the baffled
eyes of Edwin Clayhanger, is here expounded in full.
Only Mr. Bennett would have done just this thing. You
recall how in 'The Old Wives' Tale' different parts of
the chronicle are recorded from different points of view.
Always there is a virtual interlocutor, the centre of a
peculiar world, which impinges upon or overlaps scores of
other worlds, but is never concentric with them. To such
a world the reader was introduced in 'Clayhanger.' The
son of the Bursley printer does not tell his own story,
but in telling it for him Mr. Bennett sticks so closely
to his point of view that Clayhanger Senior and the
Orgreaves, and Hilda, and the whole Five Towns world,
seem to exist only in their relation to this young man.
He is not a brilliant young man. His life is tame enough
in outward incident, and even when the humdrum is broken
by some emergency, he does not always come up to the

scratch. He prevents the wreck of the printing office, to
be sure, but he is woefully lacking in the matter of the
luckless Mr. Shushions. Hilda, it will be recalled, is
the champion on that occasion.

But Clayhanger's insignificance is no more clearly
proved by his tameness than Hilda's significance by her
erratic way. Our interest in him through those seven
hundred pages is sufficient proof that he is not merely
a commonplace person. It is true that, since we share
Clayhanger's ignorance of her true character and motive,
Hilda is the more challenging figure throughout the earlier story. The present narrative is not a sequel, but
a complement. Much of the old ground is covered, many
of the same incidents are recorded. Nevertheless, the
scene has definitely shifted. We are now adventuring
in another world, a world of which Hilda Lessways is the
centre, and in which Clayhanger has a merely contingent
place. As we have said, only Mr. Bennett would have been
likely to do just this thing in this way. If Mr. De
Morgan, say, had been moved to retell a story of his from
a different point of view, he could hardly have resisted
the temptation to cross-allusion and reminder. Mr. Bennett nowhere hints by a word or a gesture that the earlier
narrative exists. And he is bold enough, in several instances, to reproduce the dialogue of 'Clayhanger' word
for word, or with the slightest omissions. So in describing from Hilda's point of view the striking incident of
her nocturnal interview with Edwin on the darkling porch
of the Clayhangers' new house, we listen to the same
words, but we listen through Hilda's ears. And, of
course, the angle of description changes.

There is something very 'convincing' in this complemen-
tary method. It leaves no doubt that the writer is absolutely in the confidence of his characters. And there is
an odd charm in the double approach of the same scenes and
the same incidents. The family group of the Orgreaves is
the same in both pictures, but with differences in coloring and arrangement. Poor old Mr. Shushions, whose 'sole
crime against society was that he had forgotten to die,'
is a less disgustful and more pathetic figure in the
woman's eyes than in the man's.

If Mr. Bennett has an obsession, if there is a really
morbid streak in the texture of his fancy, it shows itself
in the insistent delineation of types of age and decay.
That was what chiefly distressed many sensitive readers
in 'The Old Wives' Tale'; and the dissolution of the elder
Clayhanger was unsparingly rehearsed, in all its slow and
dreary stages. Wasting and helpless age is again figured
in 'Hilda Lessways.' Sarah Gailey, to be sure, is not

much past middle life; but when we are first introduced
to her, she has fought her fight and set foot upon the
downward road of years. The attempt at suicide which
Hilda frustrates is a less disheartening proof of her
hopelessness and uselessness than the story of prolonged
invalidism which follows. At that moment, indeed, poor
Sarah Gailey attains her highest power of self-expression.
Hilda does not judge her adversely: 'She had a feeling
that she ought to apologize profoundly to Sarah Gailey
for all that Sarah must have suffered. And as she heard
the ceaseless, cruel play of the water amid the dark
jungle of ironwork under the pier, and the soft creepings
of the foam-curves behind, and the vague stirrings of the
night-wind round about - these phenomena combined mysteri-
ously with the immensity of the dome above and with the
baffling strangeness of the town, and with the grandeur of
the beaten woman by her side; and communicated to Hilda a
thrill that was divine in its unexampled poignancy.' Hilda
is always being thrilled. That harsh and angular manner
which so puzzled Clayhanger did not actually repel him,
because of the obscurely felt presence of extreme sensibility beneath it. We learn all about it now from the
inside: how the world enchanted the vivid nature, how
an experience beckoned, how the least promising incident
might be invested with romance by her eager fancy. And
here, of course, we find the key to her strange desertion
of Clayhanger, in the first hour of their triumphant love.
It is all perfectly natural and inevitable, since Hilda
is what she is. The narrative brings us only to that
moment of renunciation, which seems to Clayhanger a moment
of betrayal. That is, it brings us only half-way through
'Clayhanger,' reckoning the length of the record, and far
from half-way in point of time. Mr. Bennett has, after
all, fallen considerably short of his promise to print
a novel this year 'dealing with the history of Hilda Lessways up to the day of her marriage with Edwin.' It is
perhaps as well that this change of plan has been made.
We have surely a clear enough notion as to what those
sordid and heart-breaking years in the Brighton boarding-
house must have been to the dauntless Hilda. But we are
glad of the assurance of a note appended to the present
volume that the later history of Edwin and Hilda is to
form the theme of another novel. May fate have permitted
them happiness: it is certain that Mr. Bennett can have
had nothing to do with it!

68. AN ENGLISHWOMAN'S HOME, A NEWS ITEM, 'MORNING LEADER'

11 October 1911, 7

On the preceding day in the 'Morning Leader' appeared a
news story entitled A Vast Sloppy Steamy Greasy Social
Horror. The title came from Book 1, chapter 4, section 2,
of 'Hilda Lessways', and the story quoted at some length
the passage in which the phrase occurs. The passage describes the prospective drudgery of the new servant
Florrie and the oppressive domesticity of the life of
Mrs Lessways, particularly in its emphasis on cleanliness.
The writer of the story said: 'Mr. Bennett has written
this of a home in the Potteries, but it is only too true
of many homes elsewhere. A home should be something more
than a place to be kept clean, and a wife something better
than a forewoman over her domestics.'

Are our homes as bad as they are painted? Mr. Arnold
Bennett's scathing picture of an Englishwoman's home,
published on this page yesterday, was located in the
Staffordshire Potteries; but the Potteries people do not
admit its truth to life as a generalisation.
    There is one man who can say what he likes of the
Potteries and Potteries people with impunity, and that
man is Mr. Arnold Bennett, says our Hanley correspondent.
Everyone reads his books, the public libraries can never
satisfy the demand for them, and everyone admires the
writer, but his latest description of Potteries domestic
life as a 'vast sloppy, steamy, greasy, social horror' had
passed unnoticed until yesterday's article in the 'Morning
Leader.' Of course, the indictment is much too sweeping
is the general verdict. That view was fully endorsed by
Miss Garnett, of Fenton House, who is head of a band of
ladies of independent means who devote their whole time
to work among the poor and church duties generally. 'I
have been in the homes of all classes of Potteries
people,' said Miss Garnett, 'and you may take it from me
that Mr. Arnold Bennett is much too sweeping. His description may be that of an industrial home - it probably is:
but it is the exception, not the rule. Potteries people
generally rise very early in the morning, and the average
housewife gets a good many of her household duties done
before she sends the children off to school. In most
Potteries homes,' added Miss Garnett, 'everything is very

neat when the afternoon arrives.

'As happens elsewhere, the Potteries housewife is not
at home to visitors on Mondays and Tuesdays. These are
washing and ironing days, but the womenfolk find plenty
of time for enjoyment. The theatres, the music hall, and
especially concerts, are generally well patronised, and
the average Potteries housewife is no more a slave to
domestic duties than she is to amusement. I go into all
houses at all hours,' added Miss Garnett, 'and it is the
rarest thing for me to find things upside down. Mr. Arnold
Bennett's description of the duties of the new servant
engaged by Mrs. Lessways is very amusing, but by one who
knows the working girls of the Potteries, it cannot be
regarded in the least seriously. Potteries girls much
prefer work on a pot bank to domestic service at its best,
but drudgery of the type indicated by the distinguished
novelist would not be performed by the average independent
girl more than once.'

Miss Garnett states further that she has the greatest
difficulty in persuading girls to go into service,
although one girl for whom she found a situation is now
head housemaid in one of the palaces. 'With the demand
for girl labor in the staple industry of the Potteries,
no one will allow herself to become a dehumanised drudge
in domestic service. It must be remembered that the proportion of actual residents in the Potteries who keep servants is comparatively small. Many people have temporary
assistance, such as charwomen on washing days, but in one
parish there are less than half a dozen houses which employ domestic servants.'

Miss Garnett summed up the general opinion in the district when she remarked, 'It really is not fair to apply
Mr. Arnold Bennett's description to Potteries housewives
generally.'

Nor were the charges made against English home management taken more seriously by Miss M.M. Dalglish, secretary
of the Metropolitan Association for Befriending Young Servants, who was seen in London by a 'Morning Leader'
representative.

Miss Dalglish, whose association makes a point of
seeing how servants are treated, thinks Mr. Arnold
Bennett's picture very exaggerated indeed - a typical
masculine exaggeration in fact.

'We find, on the whole,' she said yesterday, 'that
mistresses are considerate and kind. The drudge imagined
by Mr. Bennett is very rare. Of course, there will always
be a few mistresses who dislike nothing so much as seeing
the servant sitting still for a moment, but they are the
exception rather than the rule. There is such a demand

for servants nowadays that mistresses are obliged to treat them well. If not, the servant simply goes to another situation.

'The general health of servants would compare very favorably with the health of workers in shop or factory. The hours are doubtless long compared with those of other workers, but the employment is varied, and there are intervals of rest. Service also provides a good training for the girl's future home when she marries. Mr. Bennett must be mistaken in thinking the "dehumanised drudge" anything but very exceptional. Servants are in too independent a position to become drudges.

'I agree that there are a good many homes where the mistress and daughters have not enough interests outside domestic matters, and so cause a certain amount of un- necessary confusion, but it is difficult to believe that Mr. Bennett is serious in writing of domestic work as "a vast, sloppy, steamy, greasy, social horror." A good deal of work must, of course, be done, but I can't agree that there is anything like the "hidden shame" that seems so thoroughly to have got on Mr. Bennett's nerves.'

69. UNSIGNED REVIEW, 'SPECTATOR'

14 October 1911, 602

Mr. Arnold Bennett has invented an alternative to the sequel, and, though we may acquiesce in its adoption by so gifted a writer as he is, we cannot contemplate its general introduction without some misgiving. This inven- tion is what may be called the parallel novel. In 'Clay- hanger' we had a large section of the life-history of a certain Edwin Clayhanger, in which a good deal of space was devoted to his relations with Hilda Lessways, cul- minating in an engagement suddenly and inexplicably broken off. But 'Hilda Lessways' does not only give us with great minuteness of detail the distressing circum- stances which induced Hilda to incur the charge of jilting her lover; it goes back on her tracks, and where the orbits of the two characters intersect each other repeats the scenes and even the conversations that have already occurred in 'Clayhanger'. This might at first sight be considered a labour-saving appliance, but it is really nothing of the kind. The point of view is entirely

changed, the interpretation of the situation by Hilda is
quite different from that of Edwin.   This method is open
to criticism, but it is employed with remarkable ingenuity
and it is thoroughly typical of the curiously absorbing
interest that Mr. Arnold Bennett shows in his characters.
Such an interest, as novel readers hardly need to be
reminded, is no guarantee of a similar attitude on their
part.   The enthusiasm of the creator is not always infec-
tious: it sometimes only provokes irritation; and in these
pages, as in those of 'Clayhanger', we find it difficult
to share Mr. Bennett's enthusiasm for 'the largeness,
prodigality, and culture,' the 'facile yet aristocratic
unceremoniousness' of the Orgreaves.   Anything less aristocratic it would be hard to conceive than this kindly,
comfortable family circle, of which the dominant note is
humanity tempered by facetiousness.   But though we cannot
take the elegance of the Orgreaves as seriously as Mr.
Bennett does, the essential truth of the portraiture is
undeniable.   Mr. Bennett has the Trollopian gift of
engaging our sympathy with thoroughly ordinary, commonplace, undistinguished, third-rate people and investing
them with qualities which excite curiosity and even
fascination.   He has no illusions about his characters,
but he is curiously free from anything like animosity
towards them, even whey they represent views to which
he is diametrically opposed.   He has Trollope's copious-
ness without his laxity of phrase, but his style never
transcends the level of efficiency.   It lacks distinction,
terseness, grace, audacity, and never gives one that
almost physical thrill which Miss Martin and Miss Somer-
ville almost alone amongst living novelists have the power
to excite.   He treats of the great facts of life strenuously rather than nobly.   Death is too closely linked with
disease, old age with infirmity, and love with sexual passion.   His indulgence in realistic details is none the
less odious for never being irrelevant.   Yet with all this
insistence on the material side of life Mr. Bennett cannot
escape from the need of idealization.   We have spoken of
his characters as commonplace people, but the statement
needs reservation.   Hilda Lessways is neither refined nor
fastidious, but she is credited with 'mystery and force'
and with an untutored but sound literary instinct which
enables her to appreciate the magic of Hugo, Crashaw, and
Tennyson.   George Cannon, the flash attorney who capti-
vates Hilda by his florid masculinity and dashing enterprise, is half-French by origin and wholly complex in his
combination of egotism and considerateness.   In both these
figures on a coarse-grained basis there is engrafted a
strain of the unusual.   For all its photographic

accumulation of details the picture is no more a faithful
transcript of life than some cinematographic pictures in
which the illusion is complete, though the facts of life
are distorted.

Speaking for ourselves, however, we have no serious
ground for quarrel with Mr. Bennett for his lapses from
the canon of probability. It is precisely this discontent
with a drab environment, this struggle after self-
assertion and self-enfranchisement, which lends attractiveness to his principal characters. Mr. Bennett is
neither a supreme artist nor a remorseless realist, but
with all reserves he has qualities which place him in the
forefront of living novelists. If we do not feel on closing the pages of 'Hilda Lessways' that we want to read it
again as soon as possible - perhaps the greatest tribute
to the wizardry of the story teller - at least we look forward with eagerness to the next instalment of his encyclo-
paedic tragi-comedy of the Five Towns.

70. UNSIGNED REVIEW, 'ENGLISH REVIEW'

November 1911, 731

'Hilda Lessways' is unquestionably a feat, a brilliant
achievement in our literature. And yet one is not satisfied. The critic, not the professional critic necessarily,
but any cultured man who has read, and especially Flaubert and the French school, knows this book to be a
remarkable work, an advance, he feels almost inclined to
to say, on 'Clayhanger' or on the 'Old Wives' Tales'
[sic], which placed Mr. Bennett in the forefront of living
European writers. The man is immense. In point of sheer
observation, revelation of character, fictional interpretation, and, above all, in the objective attitude
towards his art, Mr. Bennett stands on this work supreme
in English literature. His technique is consummate. His
detail and paring work, his dramatic sense, his subtlety,
his penetration, his *cocasseries* of humour - these things
fill one with wonder. But this is what needs to be said.
Despite the notable book that 'Hilda Lessways' is, despite
the literary architectonics of this epochal trilogy, 'The
Card', one of Mr. Bennett's throw-offs, a little freak
book of fun, remains the best thing he has yet done, the
most satisfactory, nay, even from the higher standard of

judgment, the most vital. Vital because the most human.
Mr. Bennett was plainly interested (personally) in 'The
Card'. The young man appealed to him. There were other
people, too, in the book that appealed to him. There was
chien in those people, colour, rhythm, in short the book
was more subjective than his higher work, it was consequently less closely knit, as said the writer to himself, 'Hey, my lad, this ain't my top-notch work, I'll
let go for a lark.' Let go, he did. Away flew the
Flaubert objectivity of method. Away flew the chisel,
and for once in a way the pen flew away with Mr. Bennett.
Note the movement in 'The Card', the humour, the raciness
of expression, the warmth, the little revelatory autobiographical touches. Now, in 'Hilda', Mr. Bennett is on
his mettle, steeled to his method, and the *chien* disappears, the warmth vanishes, these people are bared to
the skin - that is his genius - but they have the nudity
of the line of Thorwaldsen. In 'Hilda', Mr. Bennett set
out to explain the woman, the cause of her strange jilting
of young Clayhanger. *La femme* - it was thus passion that
must be the *leit-motif*. Yet there is little passion in
the book. Not enough. We do not quite understand her
yielding to the indomitable Mr. Cannon; we do not even
know when she does yield. The heart - the heart which
has reasons which reason does not know - is not rendered
to us. Extraordinary as it all is - the Orgreave gallery
is one of the finest character studies in our literature -
one misses the feeling of the flesh. Almost we doubt this
Hilda. We should, we really should, have liked to have
learnt more about Mr. Cannon's methods of conquest. Perhaps this is meticulous criticism. Yet somehow we feel
that we are right; we wanted to plumb the soul of this
girl. But there is no note of ecstacy - the *enfant trom-*
peur of love is applied rather than felt. Compare that
with the poignant introspective writing of Madame Willy's
'Vagabonde'. Something of that we should have wished for
in 'Hilda' - that is the danger of objectivity in art -
it misses the soul. No other writer could have written
this 'Hilda Lessways', to be sure. Mr. Bennett now takes
his place at the very summit of his art. And yet it
leaves us wondering: wondering to what height he will
eventually attain, wondering, too, whether Mr. Bennett
is an artist as distinct from the craftsman who is obviously what is called a genius.

71. WILLIAM MORTON PAYNE, IN THE 'DIAL' (CHICAGO)

1 December 1911, 471

The chief artistic defect of Mr. Arnold Bennett's 'Clayhanger,' as we pointed out at the time of that book's
appearance, was its failure to account for Hilda's mysterious conduct in deserting Edwin just after they had
exchanged the pledges of their mutual love. A brief note
informed the latter that the writer was married to one
George Cannon, whose name was thus first brought to our
attention, and the later accounts of Hilda's life as the
keeper of a lodging-house in Brighton gave us to understand that her husband had been a criminal and had left
her to look after herself. We were informed at the close
that a second novel would clear up the mystery, dovetailing the experiences of Edwin and Hilda. Mr. Bennett has
now kept his promise by writing 'Hilda Lessways,' from
which we learn that the heroine had been infatuated with
George Cannon from her early girlhood, that she had been
secretly married to him, and that it was just after her
discovery that her husband had another wife still living
that she had yielded to Edwin's suit. This is a little
puzzling, for Edwin Clayhanger had never heard the name
of George Cannon, although the latter had lived for many
years in the neighborhood, and had become rather notorious
in more ways than one. So the mystery turns out to have
been nothing more than a tricky device on the part of the
author to keep the interest in suspense, and necessitate
the writing of a second book by way of explanation. Of
this second book, we are bound to say that, while it
solves the original puzzle, it does so in a rather commonplace fashion, and by no means gives us a counterpart of
'Clayhanger' either in psychological penetration or in
sympathetic delineation. This 'Ring-and-the-Book' method
of telling the same story from the view points of different observers is not justifiable unless each new version
comes to us as a fresh and vital creation. Mr. Bennett
has flagged upon the second 'lap,' and his 'Hilda Lessways' is distinctly disappointing. It makes the impression of a task perfunctorily performed, and is stretched
out to the desired length by a forcing process in which
resort is had to a great deal of insignificant material.
Particularly, it carries beyond all reasonable bounds the
device of accompanying the act and the spoken word by a
statement of the unuttered thought. We should say that
nearly one-half of Hilda's words here printed within

inverted commas were not spoken at all, but were only the
thoughts that flitted across her consciousness. This sort
of thing may be psychologically effective if it is done
sparingly, but something should be left to the imagination, and the stuff becomes mere padding as the author
here makes use of it. We should still think 'Hilda
Lessways' a novel of remarkable power were he not compelled to match it all the time with the extraordinarily
high standard of achievement set up by its two great predecessors; it simply falls far short of meeting the test
when that inevitable comparison is made. There is yet to
be a third novel in completion of the series, and that,
we trust, will reveal once more the conscientious artistry
and the high creative faculty that proved so overwhelming
in 'Clayhanger' and 'The Old Wives' Tale.'

General Views: 1910–12

By 1910 Bennett stood in the front rank of contemporary
English novelists. In 1911 he made his much publicised
trip to America, and by the end of 1911 he was as famous
there as in England. By 1912 he was doubly notorious as
co-author of the internationally successful play 'Milestones'. One easy measure of his public reputation was
his income, which in 1912 amounted to as much as all he
had earned in the preceding twenty-two years. Another
measure was the frequent reference to him in the popular
press. From this time forward until his death, his views,
his tastes, his presence at public functions, his physical
appearance, and his health were presumed to be matters of
general interest. All this was abetted and sustained by
his remarkable production of work of many sorts for many
sorts of people.

The three pieces reprinted here represent the more
serious discussion of him and his work in his first years
of fame. Early in 1910 there was a piece on him in the
'Glasgow Herald' (12 February). Ostensibly concerned with
his humour, it offered general comments on his work, saying mainly that his realism was not grey like Gissing's
but humorous and tender. There was 'an Arnold Bennett
number' of the 'Bookman' (March 1911), with a general
article by F.G. Bettany that Bennett in a 'Journal' entry
(7 March) described as 'pretty good'. It was reprinted
in the American 'Living Age' (April 1911). H. Hamilton
Fyfe published two articles on him, in the 'Daily Mail'
(25 October 1911) and in the 'London Magazine' (October
1912). Fyfe was acquainted with Bennett at the turn of
the century, and the articles offered an interesting perspective on Bennett the man. Max Beerbohm in his 'Christmas Garland', 1912, parodied his style. The 'Star' (20
July 1912) glanced lightly over his life and work. The
'Manchester Guardian' (9 November 1912) defended him

299

against the charge of pot-boiling. For a couple of items
on him in America in 1911 see p. 65. There were other
items there in the 'Review of Reviews' (April 1911),
'Current Literature' (May and June 1911), and 'Book News
Monthly' (May 1911), where he was called 'a new master of
English fiction' and 'the British Balzac'. After his
American trip, 'Current Literature' offered a full-page
photograph of him, with the caption, More Talked About
Than Shaw (January 1912). 'Good Housekeeping' (February
1912) printed his views on books and women. More importantly, in the 'Atlantic Monthly' (January 1912), H.G.
Wells wrote at length on The Contemporary Novel, and said
briefly that Bennett was 'quite the greatest of our contemporary English novelists', singling out 'The Old Wives'
Tale' and 'Clayhanger' as the prime examples of his
genius. And Frederic Taber Cooper (see headnote to No.
46), in 'Some English Story-Tellers', 1912, said that 'the
ugly fact remains that Mr. Bennett ... for more than a
decade deliberately prostituted a talent that approaches
close to the borderline of genius'; nevertheless Cooper
thought that Bennett might do even bigger things than 'The
Old Wives' Tale' and 'Clayhanger'.

---

72. THE GREY NOVEL, 'NATION'

10 December 1910, 436-7

Bennett wrote in his 'Journal' on 12 December 1910 that
this was 'the most striking article on me that has yet
been written'.

It seems already a reminiscence, veiled in the dim mists
of youth, that we, who are living to-day, engaged in hot
controversy over the merits of Zola and the Realists.
We clutch the table to assure ourselves of tangible fact,
or run to the mirror to make certain of our own identity
at the recollection of that distant dispute. For to-day
it is with an effort that we remember that Zola was ever
called a Realist at all. He was, indeed, a plodding student of facts which the story-teller is wont to resign
without envy or curiosity to the economist, the social
reformer, or the pathologist. He had a conscience which
a statistician or a nursery governess might have coveted.

He had a zest in work which was much more French than his style. But the spirit of the Realist was not in him. He sought the lurid and the outrageous. He had a naïve delight in gross crimes and strange sins which would better have become a Greek tragedian, or an Elizabethan dramatist. There was, for him, a House of Atreus in every French provincial town. A miracle, a war, a revolution, the death of a drunkard by spontaneous combustion, an illicit love within the limits of affinity prescribed by Canon Law - are these the themes of realism? To be a Realist, it is not enough that one should write in prose. Wordsworth could manage it in a lyric. Nor does it suffice to study the slums and shops and mines and hospitals, which the conventional romantic has usually neglected. Hugo could dip into the underworld. Dostoieffsky could rummage in garrets, and both of them were princes of romance. 'Verily,' said the Caliph, 'this is a wonderful occurrence, and worthy to be recorded in a book.' So long as that is our motto, we are still in the climate of Bagdad, and all we write is an Arabian tale. Romance is the search for the black tulip and the Holy Grail, but it is no less romance when it hunts for the two-headed chicken and the bearded woman. It is the delight in the exceptional, it is the impulse to fill our books with remarkable occurrences. It is the instinct that what is interesting is the thing that does not happen every day. It is the spirit which the halfpenny journalist shares with Dumas and Walter Scott.

We have at last among us a true and notable realist, and the strange thing is that the world has received him with a cordial welcome, yet without controversy and without a sense of the greatness and uniqueness of his achievement. When Arnold Bennett wrote 'The Old Wives' Tale,' the discerning critic had no hesitation in placing him among the masters, and ranking his novel among the real books of our generation. It was life without drawing-rooms. It was story-telling without conventions. Above all, it gave what is rarest in the novel of any literature - a sense of the massive continuity of human existence. Here was no hasty episode, no brief romance, no distilled essence of a single life. It was a history that marched with steady steps over the decades and the generations. In the background was the peculiar hard clay of a pottery town. One watched its red brick growing black with the years. Railways invaded its customs and its isolation; it evolved by slow changes from its mid-Victorian slowness to the brisk modernity of motor-cars. The tale centred round a drapery store, and three generations came and went as it developed new methods of business. The story had its brief love episodes, which fitted themselves within its framework, subordinate to all the

crowded variety of life. It was a conscious and complete
revolt against the individualism of romance. Whole libraries are filled with the records of the brave attempt
which young men and women make to achieve in passion an
individuality which passion itself destroys. But here was
a novel which saw life on an epic scale. Tolstoy, indeed,
had produced the same sense of vast interactions in 'War
and Peace.' That, too, is a novel with a whole society
for its hero. But Arnold Bennett had been content to dispense with any great historic motive. His hero was not
an empire at war, but a hum-drum pottery town at peace.
Yet, with his grey material and his smoky background, he
gave the same sense of marching generations and continuous life. Other novelists have attempted to describe this
same lower middle-class life. Dickens delved in it for
humor and pathos. Mr. Wells has used it once and again to
illustrate a Fabian criticism of our whole social system.
But here was a chronicle from within, which took the existence of the chapel and the shop at its own valuation,
followed its fortunes with an entire seriousness, made of
it neither a cosmic tragedy nor a critical comedy, and was
content to tell us how life used two young girls with
marked, though by no means exceptional, temperaments.
The triumph of the book is that its texture is woven for the
most part of incidents which are the habitual daily happenings of a class which leads the least varied existence in
the most tedious of all environments. Yet the realisation
is so vivid, the character-drawing so sure, the fitting of
cause and effect so nice, the sense of a broad current of
human life on which these unimportant persons are slowly
borne along so impressive and so over-mastering, that the
book achieves the interest of a great historical study.
    'The Old Wives' Tale' was not, however, an austere
example of realism. It did not wholly disdain the 'wonderful occurrence' which the Arabian Caliph would have coun-
selled his chronicler to set down in a book. It varies
the habitual life which it seeks to represent, and relieves the monotony of the pottery town with much that is
exotic, and a little that is far from being typical or
diurnal. There is a murder, for example, superbly conceived indeed, and with a rare and intimate psychology.
It is a murder which seems inevitable, and it leaves the
murderer with no blood upon his hands. There is also a
long episode in the siege of Paris, a masterly fragment,
that almost shocks by its wilful refusal to employ the
conventional romantic material which such a theme suggests.
It is the siege without glory or tragedy, the siege as the
little shopkeeper and the mistress of a pension saw it,
a problem in domestic economy. A further book on the same

great scale has proved Mr. Bennett's ability to dispense
even with these sparing borrowings from romance. 'Clayhanger' is not, perhaps, so absorbing a tale, but it is
an even more interesting literary adventure. One never
quits the pottery town. One never stirs from the shop,
save to migrate to a suburban villa as the fortunes of
the shop expand. The temperaments of the chief persons
are even less exceptional. The happenings are even less
abnormal - the jilting of a young man by a young woman,
the slow death of an old man by softening of the brain,
the return of the young woman after many years, and the
reward of the young man's sulky fidelity. It happens
every day. One could believe that nothing else happens,
so inevitable is it all. There is hardly a character who
escapes commonplace, unless it be the mysterious young
woman, and her, for very shame, the author keeps in the
background. The story is nothing but the biography of a
young man of moderate vitality, deficient in self-
assertiveness, with refined tastes, and domestic instincts,
who grows to manhood in a printer's shop, under the dominion of a rather oppressive, self-made father. One
hardly knows what most to admire in the book - the mastery
of the descriptive passages, which present the old-world
pottery and the old-world workhouse of the hungry 'forties,
the bitter, truthful pen which draws the Sunday-school
jubilee and the strike, the affectionate portraiture that
sketches some of the minor characters, the strong, rough
sculpture that hews out old Clayhanger for us the almost
autobiographical and introspective intimacy with which we
learn to know his son. But it is in no one detail that the
book is great. It is great because it makes important and
absorbing and intelligible the common life of common people
in a common town.

It is by reason of their curiously selfless quality
that these novels of Mr. Bennett's are unique. Other
writers we have had, who turned with a transient and
fallible realism of method to similar themes. George
Douglas left behind him the one book in our language which
has an almost Russian sharpness and passion of vision.
But 'The House with the Green Shutters' is an emotional
outbreak. It is a furious dissection of the Lowland Scot
by a Lowland Scot. It is a great shout of anger, in which
the author seems to be avenging the less typical Scot of
all the ages upon the rampant and combative persons of the
more typical Scots who have dominated them. Gissing
worked in the same grey material, but nearly always with
the stimulus of a rancor against the accidents of life,
which gives his books a harsh vitality, while it robs them
of objectivity. But Mr. Bennett, sensitive though he is,

and neither pitiless nor cold, has achieved the calmness
of a scientific treatise. He neither praises nor blames.
He is content to understand. His characters are intensely
individual. They are typical only in the sense that they
are never persons of unusual genius or rare sensibility.
They are not the literary or artistic temperaments whom
the second-class novelist paints by preference, because
he must always project himself upon his canvas. The defect of his work is, indeed, that he has suppressed himself so completely that his books hardly retain an emotional unity. They express no attitude towards life,
still less a view of life. One can more readily guess
what manner of man he is from a brilliant *jeu d'esprit*
like 'Buried Alive,' than from one of these elaborate
novels, into which he has packed all the maturity of his
experience, and all the labor of his artistic ambition.
They are disembodied experience, a chronicle without an
author. Here at least is realism. It is not the crude
flinging down of masses of fact. It is the urbane
arrangement of facts. It is the setting forth of the
whole process of normal life as a notable intellect has
seen it, an intellect that is big enough to have lost
interest in itself. These ultimately are the men and
women who matter. These in the last resort are the
nation. You find them dull? You ask for ideas? But
these are the people for whom the absorbing business of
living is enough. They move from generation to generation. They are the changing town. They are sons and
fathers, and their continuity beneath its slight external
variations is human life. It is only the pessimism of
other-worldliness which can find the spectacle uninteresting.

73. W.D. HOWELLS, EDITOR'S EASY CHAIR, 'HARPER'S'

March 1911, 633-6

William Dean Howells (1837-1920) was dean of American
critics and novelists. The errors of fact and lack of
knowledge in his article reflect the circumstance that
American critics had come upon Bennett in a hurry.
Bennett wrote a cordial response to the article (see LAB
II, 273-4), recalling that twenty-six years earlier he as
a youth in the Five Towns had read in 'Harper's' a story

by Howells called The Mouse-Trap. A.N. Monkhouse in the
'Manchester Guardian' (25 March 1911) took note of the
Howells article, saying that everyone knew there were two
Arnold Bennetts and that it was to be hoped 'that in "The
Card" the author of "The Old Wives' Tale" has finally
written down the author of "The Ghost"'. Howells wrote
again on Bennett in March 1912.

One of the slighter trials of the adventurer in the
uncharted seas of literature is to have tardier navigators
hailing him under their laggard sails, or the smoke-stacks
of their twin-screw, turbine, separate-tabled, thirty-
thousand tonner, and bellowing through their trumpets,
so that all the waste may hear, the insulting question
whether he has ever sighted such and such islands or
sojourned on the shores of such and such continents:
islands where he has loitered whole summers away, continents where he has already founded colonies of enthusiastic settlers. Probably the most vexing thing in the whole
experience of Columbus was having Vespucius ask him
whether he had happened to notice a new hemisphere on his
way to India; though it could have been no such trial as
having people come to you with books of Mr. Arnold Bennett,
and urging you to read 'The Old Wives' Tale,' as if the
places and persons of it were entirely novel to you half
a dozen years after you had read 'The Grim Smile of the
Five Towns.' Still, it shall not spoil our pleasure in
speaking of Mr. Bennett, now, when everybody else knows
him or knows about him.
     Perhaps they do not know all about him. Perhaps they
do not know, even if they know that he began writing fiction in partnership with Mr. Eden Phillpotts, that he
united his own with that other uncommonly sincere and
original talent in writing romances as ungenuine as any
we happen to think of at the moment. Yet one ought to
distinguish, one ought to say that the joint output of
the firm was brilliantly ungenuine, though perhaps it was
the worse for being so. It may have deceived them as to
its real nature so, and kept them the later from finding
their true selves.

     'Lights that do mislead the morn'

are fires more fatally ineffectual for good than none.
But Mr. Bennett seems to have trusted longer to their
will-o'-the-wisps than Mr. Phillpotts. The generation
of his real and true work is partially 'A Man from the

North.' 1898; 'Anna of the Five Towns,' 1902' ; 'Whom God
Hath Joined,' 1906; 'The Grim Smile of the Five Towns,'
1907; 'The Old Wives' Tale,' 1908; 'Clayhanger,' 1910.
The generation of his romantic novels, since he left writing them together with Mr. Phillpotts, is partially 'The
Great Babylon Hotel,' 1902; 'Buried Alive,' 1904; 'The
Gates of Wrath,' 1908; 'Hugo,' 'The Glimpse,' 'The Ghost,'
fantasticalities of dates not precisely ascertainable by
us, but evidently coeval with the contrasting realities
cited. There are two or three of his books which we have
not read, and which we cannot classify, but apparently he
has found a comfort, or a relaxation, or an indemnifica-
tion in writing a bad book after writing a good one. It
is very curious; it cannot be from a wavering ideal; for
no man could have seen the truth about life so clearly as
Mr. Bennett, with any after doubt of its unique value; and
yet we have him from time to time indulging himself in the
pleasure of painting it falsely.

As far as we have noted, his former partner, since
their dissolution, has not yielded to the same sort of
temptation. Alike in their truer work they have preferred the spacious limit; they have tended to the gigantic, the one in height, the other in breadth; and they
have tended alike to the epical in motive, to the massive
in form. The mass of Mr. Bennett is wrought over with
close detail, which detracts nothing from its largeness,
though in his latest work he has carried largeness to the
verge of immensity, without apparently reflecting that
immensity may be carrying largeness too far. If he does
not break under it himself, his reader may; though it is
only honest to say that we are not that sort of reader.
In fact, 'Clayhanger' has left us wishing that there were
more of it, and eager, or at least impatient, for the two
other parts which are to complete the trilogy promised;
an enemy might say threatened; but we are no enemy, and
we rather admire the naïve courage of the author in giving
so brave a warning, especially at a moment when the reader
may be doubting whether he can stand any more of Hilda.
For ourselves we will say that we can stand a great deal
more of Hilda, and that we should like very much to know
how or why, having just engaged herself to Clayhanger, she
should immediately marry another man. We should like to
have the author's explanation. We are sure that it will
be interesting, that it will be convincing, even if it is
not satisfactory. That is his peculiar property: to be
convincing if not satisfactory, and always to be interesting. We would not spare the least of his details, and as
we have suggested, his mass is a mass of details, not only
superficially but integrally.

If it shall be demanded how, since he is a mass of
details, his work can also be epical, we will say that the
central motive of his fiction - that is, his good fiction -
is the collective life of those Five Towns and that his
fiction revolves round this, falling back into it by a
force as of gravitation, when it seems finally thrown off
from it.   It is epical, not with the epicality of the
Odyssey, but of the Iliad, and its hero is a population
of Achaian homogeneity; yet it is not Homeric so much as
it is Tolstoyan, and its form, its symmetry, its beauty
is spiritual rather than plastic.   For this sort of epical
grandeur, which we find in high degree in Mr. Bennett's
true fiction, the supreme Russian gave once for all the
formula when he said, 'The truth shall be my hero,' and
it was not necessary for the Englishman, when he took the
Five Towns for his theme, to declare that he was going to
act upon it; you could not read a dozen paragraphs of his
book without seeing what he meant to do, what he was
already about.   Tolstoy's inspiration was his sense of the
essential value of every human being, who in any scheme of
art must be as distinctly recognized as every other,
whether prominently shown or not.   Something must be said
or done to let you into the meaning of every soul in the
story; none could be passed over as insignificant; each
presence contributed to the collective effect, and must
be proportionately recognized.   Life may seem to consist
of a few vast figures, of a few dramatic actions; and the
representation of life may reflect this appearance; but
for the artist there can be no seeming except as the
result of being, and his design, in fiction at least, must
be so Pre-Raphaelite that the reader can always see the
being within the seeming.   The nakedness of humanity under
its clothes must be sensible to the painter or he will not
be able to render the figure, even if apparently it is no
more part of the drama than a table or a chair; really, it
can never help being part of the drama.

We do not say that the perception of this is always
evident in what Mr. Bennett does, or the consciousness
of it; but we do say that without it, latent or patent,
his work would lack mastery, the mastery which we feel
in it.   He has by means of it made his Five Towns, just
wherever or whatever they are, as actually facts of the
English map as if their names could be found in the gazet-
teer.   The towns are so actual, in fact, that we have
found their like in our own country, and when reading the
'Grim Smile' of them, we were always thinking of certain
American places.   Of course one always does something of
this sort in reading a book that convinces, but here was
a book that studied unexpected traits of English life

and commended them so strongly to our credence that we
accepted them for American, for New England, for Connecti-
cut. Afterward in reading more of the author's work, say
'The Old Wives' Tale' and 'Clayhanger,' we were aware of
psychical differences in those manufacturing-town, middle-
class English people from our own, which we wish we could
define better than we shall probably be able to do. Like
our own they are mostly conscientious, whether still sunk
in their original Dissent, or emancipated by the Agnostic
motions of modern science; they are of a like Puritan conscience with our own New-Englanders; they feel, beyond the
help of priest or parson, their personal responsibility
for wrong-doing. But it appears that they accept Nature
rather more on her own terms and realize that human nature
is a part of her. They do not prize respectability
less; they prize it rather more; but they do not stretch
accountability so far as our Puritanized wrong-doers; they
know when to stop atoning, when to submit, and, without
any such obsolete phrasing, leave the rest to God. Those
conscientious, manufacturing-town, middle-class English
outlive their expiation; they serve their terms; but with
our corresponding penitents the punishment seems a life
sentence.

Of the sort of vital detail in which the author abounds
it would be only too easy to multiply instances, but we
will take only one, one so luminous, so comprehensive,
that it seems to us the most dramatic incident, like, say,
a murder, or an elopement, or a failure in business, could
not be more so, or so much so, in so little space. When
Sophia, in 'The Old Wives' Tale,' after her long sojourn
in Paris, had come back to her sister in one of the Five
Towns, and they were both elderly, ailing women, they were
sitting one night waiting for supper. 'The door opened
and the servant came in to lay the supper. Her nose was
high, her gaze cruel, radiant, and conquering. She was
a pretty and an impudent girl of about twenty-three. She
knew she was torturing her old and infirm mistresses. She
did not care. She did it purposely.... Her gestures as
she laid the table were very graceful, in the pert style.
She dropped forks into their appointed places with disdain; she made slightly too much noise; when she turned
she manoeuvred her swelling hips as though for the benefit
of a soldier in a handsome uniform.'

Here is not only a wonderful bit of detail, a pinch of
mother earth precious beyond rubies, but a cosmical implication in which a universe of circumstance and condition
and character is conveyed. Here is not only a lesson in
art beyond the learning of any but the few honest men and
women presently writing fiction, but an illustration of

the truth which commonplace detail alone can give. It is
at once intensely realistic and insurpassably imaginative,
as the realistic always and alone is; but more than anything, it is interesting and poignantly pertinent to the
affair in hand, which is not to ascertain or establish the
excellence of Mr. Arnold Bennett's work, but to put the
reader upon the train of a psychological inquiry often,
not to say constantly, engaging the curiosity of the Easy
Chair, and moving it to speculation which it has had no
great difficulty in keeping trivial, at least in appearance. We mean the question of that several self, which
each of us is sensible of in his own entity, without much
blushing, or, in fact, anything but a pleasing amaze, but
which he perceives in others with stern reprobation as
involving a measure of moral turpitude.

We have already noted not only the wide disparity, but
the absolute difference of nature in the two varieties of
Mr. Arnold Bennett's fiction, parallel in time and apparently of like deliberate intention. So far as our knowledge of it goes, and we do not say it goes the whole way
or quite inclusively, every alternate book of his is ungenuine in material, false in make, and valueless in
result, so far as any staying power with the reader is
concerned. We can think of but one such story which
seems to summon a measure of reality to the help of its
structural hollowness; in 'A Great Man' there is something
like human comedy in the unhuman farce; a good deal of
living detail in the persons and situations from time to
time forces your faith in the general scheme of make-
believe. It is an amusing book; it is good farce; but it
is essentially farce, and things do not happen in it, but
are made to happen. For the rest, we may safely say, the
author's different books are as unlike as so many peas:
peas out of the pod, and peas out of the can; you have but
to taste, and you know instantly which is which.

It is not less than wonderful, the difference in the
product which is apparently always green peas; we use the
figure respectfully and for its convenience, and not in
any slight of a writer whose serious performance no one
can pass us in prizing and praising. Since Tolstoy is
gone, and Björnson is gone, and Flaubert, and Zola, and
the Goncourts, and Frank Norris, and all the early natural-
ists are gone, and we have no more books from Perez Galdós
or Palacio Valdés, there is no writer living in whose
reality we can promise ourselves greater joy than Mr.
Bennett. For one thing, we can instantly know it from
his unreality; we lose no time in doubt; the note of
truth or the note of untruth is struck with the first
word; in one case we can securely lend our whole soul

to listening to the end; in the other, we can shut the
book, quite safe from losing anything.

But again the question is not so much aesthetical or
ethical (the one always involves the other) as psychological. Apparently there are two selves of the one
novelist who are simultaneously writing fiction entirely
opposed in theory and practice. Can there, outside of the
haunts of the Advertising Muse, be any possible comparison
between 'The Gates of Wrath,' say, and 'The Old Wives'
Tale,' say? If we are right in holding that there can be
none, then is not it within the force of hypnotic suggestion to constrain the self of Mr. Bennett writing such
books as 'The Gates of Wrath' to write such books as 'The
Old Wives' Tale,' and to do this invariably? The self
which we here propose to constrain may reply that it
addresses an entirely different public which does not care
for 'Old Wives' Tales,' but wants 'Gates of Wrath,' and
continually more of them. To any such argument we should
return that a public of this sort is profitably negligible;
and in our contention we believe we shall have the earnest
and eager support of that self of Mr. Bennett's which
writes only, and can write only, 'The Old Wives' Tales,'
and the like, and to which we are now looking impatiently
for the two remaining parts of the 'Clayhanger' trilogy.

Of course there is always the chance that there may be
two Mr. Arnold Bennetts, rather than two selves of one.
Or it may be that there is a pseudo-Mr. Arnold Bennett who
is abusing the name of a master to foist his prentice
inventions upon the public. In this case we hardly know
what to suggest in the way of remedy. It would be difficult to bring such a matter into court, or if it could be
got there it might result in giving an undesirable extension to the publicity of the prentice work. Otherwise, we
should hope that something in the nature of an injunction
might be made to apply to the practices of the pseudo-Mr.
Arnold Bennett, which are clearly *contra bonos mores*.
After all, however, it may be best simply to let the
genuine author write the ungenuine down. He is unquestionably competent to do so, or at least there is no
author now living who is more competent. It is scarcely
the moment, here at the foot of our fourth page, to state
his qualifications in full, but we may say that the genuine Mr. Arnold Bennett writes with a directness which is
full of admirable consciousness. Slowly, carefully, distinctly, he accumulates the evidence of situation and
character, and then sets them forth so steadily, so
clearly, that your mind never misgives you as to their
credibility. In the long stretches of time covered by the
action, the persons of the drama grow up from childhood to

youth, from youth to age, and when they die it is no more theatrically than when the immense majority of the race daily attests its mortality. More important than all this, it is shown how each seed of character bringeth forth fruit of its kind, and does not turn into some other kind because of the weather, the drought, the frost, the tempest; no nature is changed in a single night from black to white, or the reverse. We do not allege instances because the books are all instance, but what is certain, without any such trouble, is that here once more, and in the years that we might have feared would be years of famine, we have a harvest of fiction, such as has not been surpassed in any former season, and the field of it is so wide that no one of wholesome appetite need hunger. Whether the reaper shall finally stand out against the sky as vast as the reapers of other days, does not matter. Probably he will not. Along with other kinds of heroes, the author-hero has probably gone forever. At least, in the interest of literature, we hope so.

74. WILLIAM MAAS, MR. ARNOLD BENNETT, 'DAILY CHRONICLE'

30 June 1911, 4

William Maas is not otherwise known.

Zola wrote a novel the title of which was rendered by an English translator 'How Jolly Life Is.' One would not have gathered this from a general acquaintanceship with his books. Mr. Arnold Bennett has not yet written a book with a title 'How Interesting Life Is,' but it is one that might suitably stand for his 'collected works' - novels, fantasies, frolics, and belles lettres.

Life, of course, is interesting to every writer, otherwise he would not, or could not, write about it. But life is not interesting to all writers for the same reason. For example, to Mr. H.G. Wells life is interesting in so far as it comes up to or falls short of the new world of his imagination, which he burns to substitute for the present imperfect one. That is why life is not accepted by Mr. Wells, but questioned, criticised, rebelled against. To Mr. Shaw, again, it is the ideas concerning life that constitute matter of absorbing interest. He is not interested so much in humanity as in the ideas that govern (or mislead) humanity. An idealess creature, a witling, is not for Mr. Shaw a subject for portrayal or speculation, but a reason for bombarding a town council with questions as to why such an unemployable is allowed to exist within the precincts of an intelligent municipality. It is the prevailing ideas of life that Mr. Shaw is perpetually overhauling.

To Mr. Arnold Bennett life is interesting as an extraordinary experience. It is the most interesting thing that ever happened to him. A pageant of delight, a phenomenon to be for ever curious about, and a miracle for endless reflection. It interests him not as a spectator, but as a participator; only occasionally as a virtuoso. He is insatiably curious about it. Possessing in an eminent degree what is called an experiencing nature, he absorbs life at every pore, and brings it forth, vivid and glowing, from the crucible of his ardent mind. He brings nothing to life and takes nothing from it, but imparts a radiancy, a vitalising quality to all that his experience seizes on. He makes you surprised that life is such a lively matter. Life just as it is. Mr. Bennett does not protest that one aspect of life is more interesting than another. All life that he experiences is equally interesting - equally phenomenal and miraculous.

He will take you into a common-place locality situate in the Five Towns, introduce you to common-place people doing common-place things in a common-place way, and yet you are interested. Not because you are persuaded that these common-place people are not really common-place. Mr. Bennett's lasses and geese are not represented as queens and swans, but because the impact of an intensely interested mind on such scenes has generated the necessary heat to inform them with life. The interest is communicated, and it is a truth Mr. Bennett helps us to realise that any and every phase of life is interesting to us if it is served up, so to speak, alive and kicking.

It is a psychological truism that a work of art inevitably communicates the condition in which it is produced. What is written easily will be read easily; the work of a thoughtful man will be read thoughtfully; what is pleasant to write will be pleasant to read; and thus it is the passionate interest with which Mr. Bennett portrays life that endues his work with the power to make life equally interesting to others.

Many people imagine that Mr. Bennett has made a deliberate choice of the material of the best-known of his novels; that he has given us an insight into life in the

Five Towns because it seemed new ground to break, and
nobody had done it before him. This is not the case.
Every novelist worth considering writes at first hand,
and only out of his own experience. His material is his
life, and Mr. Bennett has only written of the life that
went on around him. It happened to be life in the Five
Towns. Had it been life anywhere else, Mr. Bennett would
have described it with equal zest and fidelity. He has
a consummate gift for accurately describing what he sees.
It is the distinguishing feature of his work. Drawing
always from the model, as it were, he takes nothing on
trust, but scrutinises everything that comes within his
experience, and records it with almost scientific exact-
ness. Mr. Bennett describes, we should say, rather than
expresses; is curious about things rather than filled with
wonder at them. He makes you see people as they are, and
as you could have seen them for yourself if you had been
as interested in them. But Mr. Bennett is something more
than an infallible draughtsman. He draws not only with
accuracy, but with great tenderness and sympathy; with a
relish and sprite-like humour. Eschewing sentimentality
as a mist more than anything else responsible for distort-
ing the true outlines of life, Mr. Bennett exhibits a fine
feeling for life; his sympathies are always on the side of
humanity.

Not all Mr. Bennett's books are concerned with the Five
Towns. Circumstances presently led him elsewhere, and
enlarged the ambit of his experience. The first twenty-
one or two years of his life were spent in Hanley, where
he was born, and where as a youngster of 18 he entered
into the world of print through the portals of the local
paper. These first contributions did not meet the un-
qualified praise of the provincial editor. They were
sketches of life in the Five Towns, and were provocative
of such difficulties as might have been anticipated between a contributor who presented life as it was and an
editor who demanded life as, in the opinion of his readers,
it ought to be.

It is amusing to think that Mr. Bennett was pigeon-
holed for the law. His father, a practising solicitor,
looked to his son to carry on the legal traditions of the
family. With this intent Mr. Bennett came to London, and
under cover of a solicitor's clerkship in Lincoln's-inn-
fields began to form literary tastes; not with any vault-
ing ambition, but in obedience to a natural lust for knowing about such things. The law was not an engaging mistress; the wooing was desultory and lukewarm, and when the
first examination occurred she administered her rebuke by
ploughing the philanderer in every single subject.

Mr. Bennett speaks of the few years that followed as
idle ones. It appears to us no disparagement. Indolence -
what Sir Thomas Browne called supinity - is a fault to be
reprobated. But idleness which means no more than a lack
of appreciation of the false doctrine of 'getting on' has
provided the artist with his hours of insight. Beauty
owes nothing to the world's busy men. We apprehend a
danger in commending idleness in a general way. It is a
privileged state for certain kinds of temperament. For
these it is a blessed necessity, a period of second birth,
the renaissance of those finer, deeper, and surer parts
of our nature that come to maturity only in hours of idleness. Often enough it marks the time when we begin to
feel much about a matter, which we can only do, as
Matthew Arnold says, 'by dwelling upon it, by staying our
thoughts upon it, by having it perpetually in our mind.'
Instinctively our nature gravitates towards its like, the
seeds of our being germinate and make root in an element
congenial to its growth.

With Mr. Bennett it was a time of big projects, valiant
resolves, vast enterprises; he was 'for whole volumes in
folio.' A boy's dreams seldom come true till he awakens
in manhood. Then he begins to interweave the threads that
his fancy had chosen - for no purpose save that they were
pleasing. So we believe it was with Mr. Bennett. He discovered a taste for the fine arts; began to 'feel much'
about music, literature, painting, sculpture, architecture; not as the relaxations of a dilettante, but as
definite expressions of human life. He absorbed them,
got them into his system, so that life now is incomplete
without them. The effect is very marked on his writings.
When Mr. Bennett delineates a character associated with
one of the arts, it is shown to be something more than a
subject for quasi-clever commentary. You feel that his
interest in such matters is a live interest, not an
affected embellishment. He has 'stayed his thoughts'
on these things, and got to know the true from the false.
It is really quite remarkable how even the best of novelists ordinarily treat intellectual matters as something
apart from and exceptional to life. Their characters are
invariably top-weighted with their culture. It never
quite fits them. They wear their ready-made intellectual
outfit with a braggart or a self-conscious air. They are
artistic without being artists, poetical but not poets,
literary with no feeling or faculty for literature. Their
taste and instinct is uniformly erroneous and untrust-
worthy, and the truth is told when it is confessed that
these things are ordinarily not part of the life of the
gentleman behind the pen. This is where Mr. Bennett

has the advantage of them. So much for idleness.

Equally valuable, we believe, was the loneliness that attended Mr. Bennett during these first years in London. It is not a portion one would willingly choose, and many a lad from the Midlands and the North has felt the unrelieved gloom shroud his soul as, friendless and unregarded, he has paced out the hours of desolation that are the lot of a stranger in London. His appetite for society whetted by the gala of life about him, he nurses his hunger with menace or despair. But the society of others denied him, he haply makes a valuable acquaintance, one people more fortunately situated never make - he makes friends with himself, turns his eyes inwards, and, getting to know something of himself, takes the first step towards getting to know something of others.

It will be encouraging to those about to write a novel to know that Mr. Bennett, after accomplishing a certain amount of miscellaneous journalism, approached the task of writing his first novel, 'A Man from the North,' with a good deal of diffidence. Acquaintances persuaded him that 'he had it in him,' though he protested he had no gift for novel writing. Their persuasions luckily prevailed, and were amply justified. The usual travail accompanied the first-born, but it came into the world alive, and was presently frocked by Mr. Lane. It is now in its fourteenth year, and ready for a new suit.

'The Regent'

4 September 1913

75. DIXON SCOTT, IN THE 'MANCHESTER GUARDIAN'

4 September 1913, 5

No dactyllic disquisitions this morning, at any rate - for
this morning sees Mr. Arnold Bennett playing Cards again;
and the rapid snap, whirr, and snick with which he cuts,
deals, and then goes off, irrepressibly trumping trick
after trick, is a process quite conspicuously unconnected
with prosody. Not, indeed, that that itself isn't a circumstance possessing a certain amount of significance. In
fact, to be quite fair to it, it really fits like a key
straight into the book's winning qualities. For the rum
mental law that makes our Ruskins and Swinburnes - our
supreme lovers and masters of richly orchestrated words -
practically post-deaf to every other kind of music (Ruskin
couldn't tell Auld Lang Syne from Annie Laurie, and Swin-
burne was nearly as bad) seems to have a corollary which
provides that men like Mr. Shaw and Mr. Bennett (rapt
adorers of St. Cecilia, devotees of grand opera) shall
possess, by way of set-off, the musicians bump of mathe-
matics, and so, when they come to write, shall cling
always to the logical - playing words like chessmen, never
like keys, - arranging them in rational rows, stripped
brightly bare of all the illusive, incalculable, eminently
unreasonable aids of melody and cadence. Of course, their
work has its beauty, but it is architectural, not oral;
it is all explicit, male, classical, never feminine or
fugitive; it says all it means, despises implications,
never tries to beglamour us with spells or shifting
gleams; its very visions are passed on to us as observations. Mr. Bennett's circumstantial statements! And his

marks of exclamation! And his geometrical progressions of
conjunctions! It is the writing of a man who has discovered the romance of the reasonable, the wild excitement
of watching logic track and pounce. But it is also the
work of a man who likes pure music so much that he has
a contempt for the bastard verbal kinds. Mr. Shaw's
favourite recreation is playing a pianola. Anyone could
guess it from his way of holding his pen. And a performance on a pianisto is the first thing Denry Machin gives
us when the curtain rises on this continuation of 'The
Card.' We might have known it before the curtain went up.
With nothing more to go upon than Mr. Bennett's way of
dealing out his sentences, both Denry and pianisto could
be predicated.

And there can be no doubt about it that it is this
inevitability of Denry that explains why we are all bearing up so uncomplainingly beneath Miss Hilda Lessways'
persistent non-appearance and receiving Mr. Machin's
attempts to entertain us in her stead with such splendid
good-humour. For Hilda's indisposition has a deep and
dark reality; there is a special sense in which she is
far less fully vitalised than the Card. For behind the
latter is the whole vigour of his author's personality –
not simply, as in her case, a dramatically diverted vein
of it, fed by imaginative sympathy. Mr. Bennett's own
genius is not only masculine, it is of the Card's particular kind; and the result is that the latter lives with a
gusto and reality that fairly plays all the other characters off the boards. Compare his capacities with even
those of Edwin Clayhanger. Edwin's distinctive gift, we
are told, was a dim proclivity towards draughtsmanship.
Very well: we accept it; we take the author's word; but
it is merely a statement, untested – we never see any
samples of his powers. But Denry's special idiosyncrasy
is simply solid mother-wit – and the book does what he is
praised for while we watch. There is absolutely no deception. We are not merely assured that Denry got into a
hole, and that he then turned it into a gold mine. There
is the pitfall – there goes Denry into it, – and there in
due course authentic nuggets appear, golden ideas and
precious tips which you may pick up off the page and
pocket for your own private use after the performance.
Suppose you wanted to design a theatre far more sensibly
and satisfactorily than any other theatre in the world,
how would you set about it? What practical rules would
you observe? 'The Regent' fully explains. Suppose you
longed to crush, impress, overwhelm, and generally reduce
to a psychological jelly some complacent whipper-snapper
of a bounding Metropolitan, and suppose you had nothing

to do it with but a common gas-jet, five minutes, and the
contents of your pockets, how would you set about *that*?
Read 'The Regent,' page 55. Is it a valet you want to
prove a hero to? See 'The Regent, ' page 81. How to Deal
with Domineering Lawyers - 'The Regent,' page 179. How to
Deal with Dogbite - 'The Regent,' page 173. How to Cure
Nettle-rash - no, that is suppressed. How to Deal with
Dukes - 'The Regent,' page 175. How to Lay Corner-stones
in an Absolutely Unprecedented Way, How to Extricate Yourself from an Entanglement with a Radiant Actress-Heiress
with the Minimum of Trouble, Tears, and Treachery, How to
Cure Dyspepsia, How to Take a Theatre Call - how, in fact,
to Live on 24 Hours a Day and successfully Work the Human
Machine - see 'The Regent,' pages 1-319. And all the pre-
scriptions are genuine. Not a single solution is faked.
The methods are perfectly sound. These are not the pre-
arranged demonstrations of your Sherlock Holmes type of
hero, marvellously retracing the steps his author has just
taken. Every problem comes as fresh to the writer as to
the reader; its elements are all shown in advance, and
then they are honestly adhered to; the success depends
entirely on the Card's native shrewdness - never on the
exercise of the divine right of authorship. It is a
series of displays of pure, unaided common sense.

And the reason of this genuineness is simply that
Denry's great gift is actually a bit of Mr. Bennett showing through. The picture has been given verisimilitude
by the excellent device of the artist fitting his own
face into a hole in the canvas from behind, above the
painted body. That dodge alone is pure Denry and enough
to betray the identity: none but a man with more gumption
than most writers are blest with would have seen how to
turn his own life to such account. 'The Regent' is almost
a *roman* à *clef*, so freshly does it serve up Mr. Bennett's
last experiences. Sir John Pilgrim will be recognised;
so will Miss Rose Euclid; Denry's eyes are his maker's.
Mr. Bennett has just been to New York; Denry goes there
too. 'I like New York irrevocably,' said the former
when he landed there; 'This is my sort of place,'
announces Denry. The coincidence is nothing: it is the
canny economy that is unmistakable. All very well for
Mr. Bennett to assure us that the Card was 'utterly indifferent to aesthetic beauty,' that his 'passion for
literature was frail,' and that the work of art he most
admired was an oil-painting of a ruined castle, 'in whose
tower was a clock, which clock was a realistic timepiece
whose figures moved and told the hour.' These things do
not deceive us. Little though it may appear to resemble
it, that oil-painting is really a red-herring.

And if anybody asks sceptically why, if all this is
thus, Mr. Bennett doesn't devote this conquering gift of
savoir-faire to pulling off the great golden coups in
reality instead of simply explaining how they could be
done, the answer is easy. He does. Read his autobiography, 'The Truth About an Author'; remember the
straight road he has trod; remark how it is set with
gilded 'Milestones.' Denry Machin came up from the
Potteries and took theatrical London by storm; it is
merely because Mr. Bennett has already done the same.
Denry Machin built a theatre, which he called 'The
Regent,' that proved one of the most effective and
profitable and intelligent undertakings of the year.
Mr. Bennett has written a book with exactly the same
title which is now going to do precisely the same.

'The Price of Love'

1 October 1914

76. A.N. MONKHOUSE, IN THE 'MANCHESTER GUARDIAN'

1 October 1914, 3

Mr. Bennett recalls his old citizen who returned from
London saying, 'I *like* Bursley'; he likes the houses and
the furniture as well as the people, and, thinking about
him in terms of this time, we may try to imagine what a
bombardment of the Five Towns would be to him. He is a
well-proportioned man, and his affection does not blind
him nor blur the fine efficiency of this record. All
manner of common relations between common people are
raised to the power of humanity, and a series of events
by no means exalted becomes extraordinarily interesting.
It is a story of two thieves of whom one is an honest man
astray and the other a slippery fellow, and it has a
strange dramatic turn when the honest man confesses to
the admiration of the other's wife. But Mr. Bennett is
not satisfied, of course, with a mere situation like this,
and, almost protestingly, we see the wife's return of sympathy and affection for her base and cowardly husband.
She has the capacity – attributed to women and common to
many of us – of putting things aside, and she is not
strong in moral repulsions. We see that to such a woman
criminality is a formal thing that only existed as a force
to influence her while the personal relations involved in
it were fresh and hot. Mr. Bennett suggests, indeed, 'an
everlasting vigil,' but we should take it, on the whole,
that this is to prevent inconveniences. She accepts her
husband, she pays the price of love, and we can see that
she will charm others into accepting him too. It is an
uneven comradeship, and perhaps we must not ask how long

it would endure. For she is capable of seeing things, and
when they are starkly without glamour the price to pay
will be very heavy.

Mr. Bennett does it all beautifully, and his wit does
not merely link things whimsically; it takes their shape
and makes us know them better. He knows a great deal
about life, and knows it sanely and kindly and shrewdly.
The spirit of adventure may turn inward to his own mind,
but his people do not betray him; they are not clever with
his cleverness nor wise with his wisdom. He makes them
true to our knowledge of them, and yet they can give us
exquisite surprises. Mrs. Tambs 'could feed four children
a day on sevenpence, and rise calmly to her feet after
having been knocked down by one stroke of a fist. She
could go without food, sleep, and love, and yet thrive.'
We seem to know her, and yet she is truly astonishing
when Mr. Batchgrew would have disturbed her mistress and
'with swiftness she darted up the steps and inserted a
large fat, wet hand between raised knocker and its bed.
It was the sublime gesture of a martyr, and her large
brown eyes gazed submissively yet firmly at Mr. Batchgrew
with the look of a martyr.' And we can relish not merely
Batchgrew but Mr. Bennett's joy in him. 'He felt that he
was invulnerable at all points and sure of a magnificent
obituary;... when he supervened into an environment he had
always the air of an animal on a voyage of profitable discovery. His nose was an adventurous, sniffing nose, a
true nose.' And the boorish Julian 'was averse even from
shaking hands, and when he did shake hands he produced a
carpenter's vice, crushed flesh and bone together, and
flung the intruding pulp away.' Yet Mr. Bennett relents
ironically to say that girls 'quarrelled over him in
secret as the Prince Charming of those parts.' Such are
the standards of the Five Towns, which can provide such
splendid material for one who is, among other things, a
bit of a modern Dickens.

77. UNSIGNED REVIEW, 'ATHENAEUM'

3 October 1914, 328

The first hundred pages of this novel contain features
rare indeed in the work of Mr. Arnold Bennett - chief
of them the dependence upon coincidences which more than

once makes the narrative appear far-fetched and unreal.
Not that even the opening chapters lack altogether the
quality characteristic of the author. In particular they
lay the foundation of an admirable and original study of
an old woman, for which the various component elements –
conspicuous among them is a determination not to be or
to be regarded as 'behind the times' – have been chosen
and combined with care, skill, and success.

In the young man who figures as a hero of sorts we
get the record of shrewd observation; and we noticed
Mr. Bennett's discriminating appreciation of a certain
ridiculous affectation of secrecy about their movements
which many young men seem to think confers distinction
on them. Nevertheless, the plot of the theft of bank-
notes as unfolded in these early chapters is thin, and
the book throughout contains lapses from verisimilitude
which seem to us to betoken either hurried or immature
work. If this is not a recently written book, then of
course the former is indicated; if our second thought
has aught of truth in it, then we are trying it by a
severer standard than we should have used if publication
had more closely followed execution.

The whole as an analysis of self-justification on the
part of a man morally invertebrate is a sterling piece
of work, but the author's incisive flashes of humour occur
in it more rarely than usual.

The action throughout is laid within the Five Towns
which the author has made famous, though little beyond
dialect betrays the fact. The human traits displayed
are as common as, unhappily, the kinema, the selection
of which as an entertainment is so typical of the kind
of youth here limned by Mr. Bennett. Who, for instance,
the world over does not know the man who never seems 'able
to decide whether a cigarette was something to smoke or
something to eat'? or, again, better (or worse) still,
the messenger whose

> destiny was never to inspire respect or trust, nor to
> live regularly (save conceivably in prison), nor to
> do any honest daily labour. And if he did not know
> this, he felt it. All his movements were those of an
> outcast who both feared and execrated the organism
> that was rejecting him?

We intend high praise to the author's heroine in declaring her to be the antithesis to that splendid embodiment
of self-reliance 'Helen of the High Hand.' That is also
to declare her to be a far less unusual type, though
beneath her outward calmness beat a suppliant heart whose

secrets no one could have laid bare with a finer and surer touch than Mr. Arnold Bennett. But then, in spite of our few words of criticism, we should have credited no one else with being the author of these 350 pages.

78. A.J.G., IN THE 'STAFFORDSHIRE SENTINEL'

2 November 1914, 3

In addition to this review, the 'Sentinel' reprinted, on 1 October, the review in the 'Times Literary Supplement'.

Mr. Bennett's new novel, 'The Price of Love,' is not yet the third volume of the trilogy which began with 'Clayhanger' and continued with 'Hilda Lessways.' The fortunes of Edwin Clayhanger and Hilda Lessways are still a subject of curiosity and expectation, In the meantime Mr. Bennett has published another tale of the Five Towns, serious in its conception and moral, but brightened with the author's accustomed flashes of humour and shrewd observation.

The heroine is one of those women who, firm and self-reliant in all affairs but that of love, are as clay in the hands of the man upon whom they set their affections. Rachel Louisa Fleckring appears on the first page as the useful, attractive, and thoroughly competent 'lady-help' of an old lady of Bursley. Mrs. Maldon is a cleverly-drawn character. She, and her house, and her precise habits, commonplace though they may be, are invested with a surprising interest. The atmosphere of 'cosiness' and well-being is conveyed from the printed page with undoubted art. Upon the quiet feiminine household is thrust the aggressive personality of Councillor Batchgrew, and here again is a type in the delineation of which Mr. Bennett excels. In 'Helen with the High Hand' and others of his books we have grown familiar with one product of the Five Towns - the hard headed, domineering, money-making old man who is yet liable to succumb at unexpected moments to feminine wiles. Mr. Batchgrew brings Mrs. Maldon the proceeds of some of her property, amounting to nine hundred and sixty-five pounds, and leaves the roll of notes with her for the night.

Out of the old lady's would-be careful hiding of the

notes grows the plot of the story, and all the suspicion
and misery which the theft of money entails. That, however, is not of so much account as the analysis of the
character of one man - the morally invertebrate hero of
the story. The opening of his career gives the key to his
future:-

[Quotes ch. 2, section 1, 'At the age of eighteen, Louis
Fores' to 'exposure and a jury'.]

From the Bank Louis Fores proceeds to the offices of
two successive firms of manufacturers, where in the most
gentlemanly and elegant manner possible, he continues his
petty depradations. Finally comes the temptation of his
aunt's money, and the working out of this part of the plot
is too good to be read anywhere except in the novel itself.
The book excels in the insight with which it depicts the
eternal self-justification of a morally weak man. Yet
this weak man, as often happens, secures the love and
devotion of a woman his direct antithisis. Rachel loves
him blindly to begin with, and afterwards with her eyes
open, but nevertheless with the protective, sheltering,
and even humble love which some women feel for some men.
It is all summed up in the last pages, which record
Rachel's reflections.

[Quotes the last two paragraphs.]

Apart from the main interest of the love match which
has an acute financial side to it, there are all the illuminating glimpses of life in the plain little streets and
plain little houses of the Five Towns which Mr. Bennett's
admirers enjoy. To shop in Bursley on a Saturday night
under Mr. Bennett's guidance, to see the joys of the
Cinema through his observant eye, and to study domesticity
with the aid of his sagacious understanding are excursions
and adventures full of surprising revelations. 'The Price
of Love' is a tale which invests the commonplace with an
intense and ever tragic interest. The dialect and the
surroundings are only to be found in the Five Towns, but
the human traits so ably laid bare are, unhappily, to be
found the world over.

'These Twain'

14 January 1916

79. A.N. MONKHOUSE, A GREAT NOVEL, 'MANCHESTER GUARDIAN'

14 January 1916, 12

This third story of Mr. Bennett's great trilogy may be
read without reference to the other two, but it gains by
our consciousness of the whole design and of the fuller
life of the characters; to realise the beauty of Janet
Orgreave, for instance, it is necessary to know her in
the earlier books. In 'Clayhanger' and 'Hilda Lessways'
we learnt to know a man and a woman, but our knowledge
was incomplete because the most vital relation was un-
explored. So here we have a story of modern love, not
pushed to any tragical extreme, but with elements of
romance and tragedy that belong to common life. The Hilda
of 'Clayhanger' was extraordinarily romantic, and her
strong and passionate nature is not crippled either by the
grim struggles of her early womanhood or by a comfortable
marriage. Mr. Bennett begins this third phase with the
most admirable episode of the house-warming, in which
Edwin and Hilda seem to have reached a kind of perfection.
They are safe, and Hilda now is passionately in love with
safety. She loves her husband, and always her pride and
affection underlie her revolts against his enterprise.

> She trusted him profoundly; and yet she had constant
> misgivings, which weakened or temporarily destroyed
> her confidence. She would treat a statement from him
> with almost hostile caution, and accept blindly the
> very same statement from a stranger. Her habit was
> to assume that in any encounter between him and a
> stranger he would be worsted. She was afraid for him.

> She felt that she could protect him better than he
> could protect himself against any danger whatever.

She plays strongly for the lead, and, cunning though she
is, Edwin is irritably aware of it. This middle-class
life of the Five Towns is very safe, but the moment you
begin to live away from its customs and conventions it
becomes dangerous, or at least irksome. It is a life that
by itself is inarticulate, and it has commonly been
described scornfully and therefore untruthfully; Mr.
Bennett can see all that is wrong with it, and yet he
penetrates to all sorts of beauties and humanities. Edwin
represents what is good in this society, but he is of it
and Hilda is not, and the story resolves itself into a
tremendous and secret struggle between them. Mr. Bennett
has never done anything more truthful and profound than
this, nor anything more absorbing. Edwin, of course, has
something of the natural man's tyranny, and in their disagreements his language and conduct are commonly much
harsher than his thoughts. And yet he is moved to say
to himself, 'She is the bitterest enemy I have,' and we
perceive with dismay the enormous and disproportionate
share of mere resentments in the world. The deep, persistent opposition of husband and wife never leads to complete estrangement, for affection and custom are too
strong. He finds her full of subtle untruth, but life
without her is inconceivable: 'This woman will kill me,
but without her I shouldn't be interested enough to live.'
So he says, and when in the alternations of the struggle
he prevails, it is her turn to say, 'I submit, and yet I
shall never submit.' The disagreements in themselves may
be trifling but they are reinforced by the woman's passion
and the man's strength. Generally Hilda gets her way, and
generally it is the wise way, for his inertia is great.
And yet she is an exasperating woman, and his grievances
are real. But Edwin makes his great discovery, which is
something more than the formula of the beaten husband: 'To
yield to a just claim was not meritorious.... To reconcile oneself to injustice was the master achievement.'
He is big enough and strong enough to find meaning and support in this, though there are times when he feels how much
easier would be devotion or sacrifice than to accomplish a
pacific smile.
    The story is simple, and yet it is strange. Mr. Bennett
gathers an immense amount of life which most of us care-
lessly let slip; he is continually unveiling the bare,
illuminating truth where we have been accustomed to some
sort of striking convention. It is a resolute and serene
facing of life's issues, and the particular life has in it

something very solid and assured; the map of Europe may be
rolled up, but we cannot believe in the destruction of
Duck Bank. Mr. Bennett has to his hand precisely the kind
of society for his design, but we must not regard this as
just a happy accident, and Hilda herself is not of the
Fine Towns. A woman of finer breeding might have been
less provocative, and perhaps not less alive, and yet her
lack of compliant manners makes her sincerities profoundly
satisfying. When she enters the room with Janet, who has
lost the parents that were her closest hold on life, Mr.
Bennett tells us that Hilda looked 'fierce and protective,'
and the phrase is a striking one; it tells us something
characteristic and fine about her. But when we read a
little further and of her abandoned friend, 'like an old
woman in the shell of a young one,' it becomes greatly
imaginative; it is an epitome of the scene's emotion.
Every man who reads the book will be affected by Hilda
in the kind though not in the degree that she affects her
husband, and every man will see himself in Edwin. If,
then, we are asked whether this is the story of any wife
to any husband the answer must be Yes and No. These are
individuals, and in self-defence we note the differences
from ourselves. Perhaps the experience is sometimes edifying rather than exhilarating, and there may be some danger
that Mr. Bennett will make us overconscious. He is sensitive to the significance of every action and of every word;
beside the actual speech of the character is set the inner
meaning, and in this intricate network of motives and
appearances no thread is lost. There are some great episodes in the book, such as the death and the funeral of
that abominable - or saintly - old woman Auntie Hamps; and
all these characters - the Benbows, the Orgreaves, and the
rest - whom we knew in the other books continue to be very
much alive here. There is no failure among them, and Mr.
Bennett passes with easy mastery from one environment to
another. It is all in the Five Towns, and even in one of
them, but the households of the Clayhangers, of the Benbows, and of Maggie and Auntie Hamps are precisely and
significantly differentiated. And he appreciates them
all; he is a creator without impious doubts of his creatures, and if there is a touch of irony or a flash of
scorn it is to help in their characterisation. He has
succeeded in what was, perhaps, the most difficult task;
Tertius Ingpen, the friend, is charmingly done, and,
though Edwin has a mood in which, turning from married
life, 'he saw the existence of males, with its rationality
and its dependableness, its simplicity, its directness,
its honesty, as something ideal,' it is Ingpen whose
placid existence helps to reconcile him to the perpetual

adventure of that impulsive intriguer Hilda. Mr. Bennett's
books have never lacked vitality, but in 'These Twain'
there is a strangeness of intimate life that he has hardly
achieved before. In detail and in design it is greatly
successful. It has not every quality of every sort of fiction, and for this it may be blamed, but it is a deep and
wise study of life faithfully and beautifully presented.
Mr. Bennett's trilogy is one of the representative works
of our time.

80. FREDERICK WATSON, IN THE 'LIVERPOOL DAILY POST'

14 January 1916, 7

Frederick Watson (1885-1935) edited the 'Cripple' for many
years, a journal concerned with crippled children. He was
a contributor to the general press.

There is nothing slipshod in a modern trilogy. It is not
the mere feat of writing three books about the same people,
though that is arduous enough. Even less is it achieved
by neatly cutting one enormous manuscript into three handy
portions - a kind of compromise for mental incontinence.
Such a performance would fall into a trilogy, but would be
received by publisher and public alike with austerity.
Moreover, if Mr. Bennett allowed over four years to elapse
between the second and third volume general paralysis
would set in. That kind of trilogy might be more artistic - but it would be intolerable. At the same time, the
assurance that any or all the books of the series can be
read separately - that is to say, without dependence upon
what has gone before - carries with it certain elements
of danger. The difference between 'Clayhanger' and 'Sherlock Holmes' is simply a matter of treatment. In 'Clayhanger' a character - timid, egotistic, and temperamental -
is produced by a cumulative process as a building is
raised from the lowest foundation. In 'Sherlock Holmes,'
each chapter depends upon an arrangement or a climax of
a purely dramatic or melodramatic nature. The psychology
of Holmes is secondary and is revealed by action; the
personality of Clayhanger is of the first importance and
is betrayed by introspection.

In that sense, to regard the three books of the trilogy as one might regard three separate adventures of Holmes may be a commercial asset - it is surely impossible from a critical or artistic standpoint. Whatever their qualities as separate achievements, as a trilogy they must stand or fall together.

II.

In 1910 'Clayhanger' was published, to be followed in 1911 by 'Hilda Lessways.' In these books the two central characters, reared under the same blighting atmosphere of the Five Towns, touched and parted. Unfortunately, however, the two books were by no means coterminous and less interdependent than they might have been. 'These Twain,' the concluding volume, marks the terminus of the 'Clayhanger' and 'Hilda Lessways.' It might, in that sense, have been called 'Marriage,' or, though a harder word, 'Compromise,' for throughout the narrative occur and reoccur, like the harsh striking of a clock that will never cease altogether while it runs at all, the clashing of sheer masculine obstinacy and obtuseness with feminine irresponsibility - the tedious adjustment of one personality upon another that must either produce equilibrium or divorce.

Edwin Clayhanger, in Hilda's eyes a youth of mystic glamour, sees her as a strange, elusive creature, quite unfathomable. This much did we gather in the two earlier books. It was after considerable turmoil that these two married, and at such a favourable juncture many an author would have washed his hands of the whole business and retired under a noisy cascade of wedding bells.

No so Mr. Bennett. The magic words 'hero' and 'heroine' are unknown to him. There is something more than relentless in 'These Twain' - there is that pitiless note of futility that sat by the deathbed of Darius Clayhanger - that walked with Sarah Gailey in 'Hilda Lessways' like a shadow. It haunts every scene, every character, and it slackens its pace, as it were, with relish at the end of poor Aunt Hamps, watching by the bedclothes, setting out in the hearse to the graveyard. That melancholy delight in distressful sickness and the death of elderly persons is a weakness in Mr. Bennett. That life leads to such scenes is a commonplace, but the ineffectiveness of existence is infinitely more tragic than the actual falling of the curtain. In Mr. Bennett's masterpiece, 'The Old Wives' Tales' [sic], the coming of death was foreshadowed from the opening pages. Where life hardly flows the mere

cessation of breathing has beyond that no artistic significance.

III.

'These Twain,' coming so long after its companion volumes, might be expected to conclude the trilogy upon a
note if not of hope at least of permanence. In Clayhanger
and Hilda Lessways were drawn by Mr. Bennett's master hand
two baffling, egotistic characters. In 'These Twain' any
illusions regarding them are rent aside. But in the
rather commonplace young man and the difficult young woman
that remain, are there not still depths that may leap out
at some dark or tragic hour? Of that Mr. Bennett is probably well aware. Or, to put it another way, one would
expect after reading three books concerned with two
characters to be able to say, 'That reminds me of Edwin
Clayhanger,' or 'How like Hilda Lessways that is' - just
as one says quite loosely, but still with sincerity, 'A
regular Sairey Gamp,' or 'He's a Sam Weller if ever there
was one.' I would not care to be so emphatic about Hilda
Lessways as that. It may be that industrialism has
crushed character, and the finest art portrays human life
in neutral colours. But bidding farewell to Edwin Clayhanger and Hilda Lessways in a country house which Edwin
loathes but has been forced to buy, with George, Hilda's
odious illegitimate son, leaving them thus upon the ebb
tide of a silly wrangle, childless, dissatisfied - one may
be forgiven some disappointment that after a vigil of four
years Mr. Bennett has cast us such scanty crumbs of con-
solation.

'Life,' said Stevenson, 'is monstrous, infinite,
illogical, abrupt, and poignant; a work of art, in comparison, is neat, finite, self-contained, rational, glowing, and emasculate.' In that sense 'These Twain' is
nearer life than art. But beside 'These Twain' must stand
'Clayhanger' and 'Hilda Lessways.' They may be read
separately - they must be judged together. One must not
condemn a trilogy such as this by an old-fashioned desire
for completion where in life there is only change, or by
the lack of happiness where, in human experience, monotony
is the counterpart of maturity. Mr. Bennett has never
drawn, so far as I can recollect, a happy woman, or a man
who was not moved by common and brutal things. Which may
be true to his experience of the Five Towns. The trilogy
is incomplete in the sense that 'The Old Wives' Tale' was
on the surface an aimless and formless chronicle. It is
simply the artistic difference between a masterpiece which

marches indomitably onward and a narrative that hesitates,
or slips back from entirety.

In the development of the central characters of 'These
Twain' there is no evidence of the maturity that stands so
often as a buttress between marriage and divorce. Hilda
at forty is still as irrational, headstrong, and perverse;
Edwin is still egotistic and, like so many of Mr. Bennett's
characters, altogether lost to humour. Not merely is
'These Twain' independent of the two earlier books in
substance and in development, but it floats apart with
hardly a binding cable. It drifts uncontrollably away
to an unknown haven.

But as the work of a master hand, restrained, ironic,
irresistible, it serves to remind us once again that in
Mr. Bennett English literature discovered with the 'Old
Wives' Tale' in 1908 a writer of unquestionable genius.

81. SIDNEY DARK, BOILED MUTTON WITHOUT CAPER SAUCE, 'DAILY
EXPRESS'

14 January 1916, 4

Sidney Dark (1874-1927) was on the staff of the 'Daily
Express' for many years. Bennett wrote to Lord Beaverbrook in 1919: 'Your Sidney Dark is a terrible fellow.
He always was. I have known his work for twenty years
or so, and it was invariably incompetent' (LAB III, 93).

'These Twain' is the sequel to 'Clayhanger' and 'Hilda
Lessways.' In it Mr. Bennett brings the story of Edwin
Clayhanger to an abrupt conclusion. There is no obvious
reason why the annals of the Clayhanger family should not
be continued in another 'great trilogy of novels.'
Certainly Edwin and his wife are well over forty when
Mr. Bennett leaves them. but life has not really lost all
its savour and adventure when forty has been passed.

Perhaps (it is a bold suggestion) Mr. Bennett has grown
a little bored with the Clayhanger family. If he has, I
can understand and sympathise.

Mr. Bennett's record of middle-class life in the
Potteries is, with a certain definite limitation, admirable and almost great. His knowledge of his characters

is comprehensive. His appreciation of action motives is
extremely acute, and, since he is a born story-teller, he
is constantly aware of the drama that exists hidden in the
daily doings of every man and every woman.

Real people are always interesting, and the Clayhangers
and their friends and relations are certainly real. They
would, however, be infinitely more interesting if Mr. Bennett had some knowledge of the one great essential fact
that 'there is a divinity that shapes our ends, rough-hew
them as we may.'

The Bennett world is a world without God, which means
that it is an unreal world, as false and as complete a
sham as a stage scene with its canvas trees and its
painted landscapes. All his characters, the sympathetic
and the antipathetic alike, are eagerly seeking mean ends
which they hardly understand, almost without the aspirations, the fears, and the dreams that are the mark of
humanity and separate us from the beasts of the field.

Edwin and Hilda are married. They live together for
years with a comparatively small amount of bickering and
quarrelling. They are, we are assured, in love with each
other, and this is Mr. Bennett's exalted idea of what love
means to a woman:-

> The fact was that she had married him for the look in
> his eyes. It was a sad look, and beyond that it could
> not be described. Also a little, she had married him
> for his bright, untidy hair and for that short, oblique
> shake of the head which, with him, meant a greeting or
> an affirmative. She had not married him for his senti-
> ment nor for his goodness of heart. Some points in him
> she did not like. He had a tendency to colds, and she
> hated him when he had a cold.

It is many years since I read anything so preposterous.
Mr. Bennett's theory that love can turn to hatred when the
loved one begins to sneeze suggests terrible prospects of
unhappiness. Of course the idea is not original. Mr. Shaw
years ago dilated on the horror of the man with a cough,
but Mr. Shaw knows as much about human love as a porcupine
knows of the differential calculus. Mr. Bennett, too, in
the passage I have quoted, vividly demonstrates his absolute ignorance of the meaning of that human love which has
been, is, and must always be the link between the individual man and his Creator.

The basic idea of 'These Twain' is that Hilda is in
love with her husband, but when it is analysed this love
is nothing but the baldest physical attraction. She is
continually yearning to kiss Edwin and throw her arms
round his neck. She is never once ready to surrender a

single ambition, a single plan, or a single prejudice to please her husband.

Edwin rebels naturally and properly against this abominable affection. Then in the last chapter he makes a great discovery:-

> Then there flashed into his mind complete the great discovery of all his career.... Injustice was a tremendous actuality. It had to be faced and accepted.... To reconcile oneself to injustice was the master achievement.... He was awed, thrilled, by the realisation.

The one thing that no man can possibly reconcile himself to is justice. Were justice supreme in the world life would be unendurable. The gift of Christianity to man is the possibility of escaping the penalties of our sins. 'An eye for an eye and a tooth for a tooth' is justice. Were it generally adopted the earth would be populated by the blind and the toothless. The idea that man yearns for justice is one of those absurd fallacies only possible among hardheaded people born in the Potteries and cursed with what Mr. Bennett calls a 'damnable grim detachment' from the realities.

Narrowness of vision and understanding is Mr. Arnold Bennett's outstanding characteristic. His limitation does not prevent him writing admirable novels, for what he sees, he sees clearly and his powers as a narrator are supreme. It does, however, render him entirely futile as a philosopher.

The hard materialism so obvious in 'These Twain' is equally obvious in Mr. Bennett's voluminous articles on the war. He has never escaped from the Black Country. Perhaps the greatest achievement of his career was to live in Paris and to remain unaffected and uninfluenced by the broad, tolerant humanitarian spirit of France. Mr. Bennett records almost with satisfaction that the people of his native Five Towns lack manners. As a writer (I know nothing of him personally) he is curiously mannerless.

He describes life in its bitter, beautiless phrases, and shouts at you: 'This is life, whether you like it or not.' Mr. H.G. Wells, who in his best work has also described clearly and vividly the mean days of mean people, always suggests that he regrets the lack of sunshine.

Dickens found sunshine in back kitchens. Mr. Wells can't find it, but he wishes it were there. Mr. Bennett is quite certain it can never be there, and he is likely to be very rude to you if you suggest that he is wrong.

I cannot imagine Mr. Bennett ever really enjoying

himself. I should say that his idea of a rollicking afternoon would be to have tea with Mr. Philip Snowden and to discuss with him the iniquities of Mr. Henry Chaplin.

Men are as their diets. Mr. Shaw always suggests lentils to me. Mr. Bennett is always associated in my mind with boiled mutton without the caper sauce.

82. UNSIGNED REVIEW, 'TIMES LITERARY SUPPLEMENT'

20 January 1916, 29

Mr. Arnold Bennett here completes the story begun in 'Clayhanger' and continued in 'Hilda Lessways.' We have seen Edwin Clayhanger grow from boy to man, and we have seen Hilda Lessways grow from girl to woman, along the perilous path of marriage (as she believed it to be) with the bigamist George Cannon, and the times of adversity when she kept a boarding-house at Brighton. And now Clayhanger has won the woman he had always loved, and Hilda has won her man, with his wealth and his respectable position as the leading printer in his particular part of the 'Five Towns.' These twain are married, and the question becomes, What are they going to make of marriage, of each other, of life?

Readers of the previous novels will know their Edwin Clayhanger, gentle, orderly, firm, and just a little romantic; and they will declare him to be an almost ideal husband for a sensible woman. They will know their Hilda Lessways, impulsive, courageous, rather wilful, and will regard her as a woman worth winning, and worth waiting for as many years as faithful Edwin waited for her. Neither of them is very young now, or foolish. They have tried the world, and the world has tried them. They have means, ambition, and a mental cultivation and a social sense to some degree in advance of their friends and neighbours - in advance of Auntie Hamps, for instance, who in this volume dies, 'magnificent,' cruel, devoted, and hypocritical to the last, or of Edwin's sister Clara and her vulgar husband Albert Benbow. The Clayhangers will 'get on,' we may be sure. The time has come for the Orgreaves to go down. That delightful family is scattered and for the most part degraded. But it is time for Edwin and Hilda to come up in the world.

And that they do. Edwin's business grows. Ambitious

Hilda makes something as near a country gentleman of him
as he is capable of becoming. They leave Darius Clayhanger's commodious and well-appointed town house for
a house in the country; they set up a horse. In all that
kind of thing Mr. Bennett, as you might expect, is very
good to these children of his. But for the rest - the
enormous rest; for love, and life, and the joint and
separate growth of a man and a woman in the generous
possibilities of human nature? Well, no student of
Mr. Bennett's work will expect too much of him in these
regards. His is not a 'romantic' mind; it is not a sanguine mind; it is not a mind of any sort of faith or
enthusiasm. At the same time, perhaps not many readers
will expect anything so entirely middle-class as Mr.
Bennett here gives them. The novel is middle-class, not
so much because the Clayhangers are thoroughly middle-
class people in a thoroughly middle-class setting, but
because Mr. Bennett's view of marriage is intellectually and spiritually middle-class. Mr. Arthur Symons
in a fine and famous sonnet has told us of the hatred of
sex for sex. There is nothing middle-class about that.
Spread over 500 and more pages by Mr. Bennett, and
expressed by means of Edwin Clayhanger and his wife,
the idea assumes a very different quality. But the idea
is there - the irreconcilable enmity of man and woman.
Edwin and Hilda are not friends; they are enemies. They
are joined together by two things only, physical passion
and a community of worldly interest. And of these the
former is the only bond to which Mr. Bennett allows much
power; for, if it came to separation, each could fight
for his hand alone. Married life is a 'long, passionate
struggle' between enemies. *Faute de mieux* and under the
influence of passion, each decides to see the best and to
make the best of what there is in the other. That, no
doubt, is something, considering that Hilda is reckless,
a little spiteful, and meaner in her methods than a woman
need be, and that Clayhanger is annoyingly 'set,' precise,
and pernickety. But of friendship, of intimate communion,
of joint and interdependent growth towards completeness
and the high freedom of love in action, there is not a
hint. It is all as depressing as the atmosphere of the
Five Towns and as constricted as a prison-yard.
    Within its mean and forbidding limits, the novel is
consummately efficient. In the years of work that preceded its formation Mr. Bennett has acquired a mastery
of such material as he has learned that he can handle with
effect. He makes things and people absolutely 'real.'
So far as may be, he is just; what he is able to see in
human nature he sees minutely and in due relation. He

knows how, without 'pressing,' to get the last ounce of
effect; and there are scenes in this novel - the death
of Auntie Hamps, the visit of Hilda to Princeton gaol,
where George Cannon was a convict, the discovery by Edwin
of a woman in the rooms of his bachelor friend Tertius
Ingpen - which compel warm admiration. What he understands Mr. Bennett understands so thoroughly and can so
lively express that the limits to his understanding seem
all the more to be deplored.

83. A DUEL OF SEX, UNSIGNED REVIEW, 'NATION'

22 January 1916, 616, 618

In the story of Edwin Clayhanger's relations with his
wife, Hilda, after he has ensconced her triumphantly in
his model super-comfortable villa residence in Bleakridge,
the Bursley suburb, Mr. Arnold Bennett has perforce been
led to a study of the most baffling phenomena known to
man. Edwin is now thirty-six, the owner of the leading
printing-business in the town, the head of the family, a
prosperous, respected citizen. He has his own ideas about
everything, and about the future, too. So has Hilda. It
is obvious to even a primitive intelligence that, since
the man is both obstinate and accustomed to getting his
way, and since the woman is wilful and means to get hers,
their happiness in the future depends on the strength of
her fascination, on her management of him, and on his good
sense. As the story develops we discover that two of these
factors hold firm against the friction of the conjugal
yoke. Hilda is always a mysterious, enchanting, and delicious creature, in his eyes, though deceptive and unscrupulous and inexcusable in her disregard of her husband's
wishes, and Edwin's good sense in the end always prevails
over his harsh male obstinacy. But it is undeniable from
Edwin's account - and the story of their marital conflict
for much the greater part is the record of his sensations
and reflections - that Hilda manages him badly. She has
all a woman's arbitrariness and unfairness; she has excessive, exasperating confidence in her own powers, and so
she coolly sets aside everything that conflicts with her
own plans. She is narrow in her views, and, worst of all,
she will interfere in affairs that are not in her province,
as in her husband's business plans.

This is the burden of Edwin Clayhanger's complaint:
you can't argue with this woman; you can't make her see
reason; she sets everything aside with an obstinate gesture, and goes and does it again, to your face or behind
your back, because she will have her own way. But, of
course, the conscious bitterness of Edwin's masculine
indictment of feminine illogicality and capricious injustice is all mixed up and smothered more or less in the
honey of his love. The question, therefore, for women
to decide is whether Hilda did not show much more art
in her management of her husband and his shortcomings
than he himself was aware of. If she had been more ready
to respect and abide by his decisions, would he not have
become more self-satisfied, more dominating and opinion-
ated, and more immovable in the groove of his predilec-
tions? By her very ruthlessness in imposing her will upon
him, by the mysterious incomprehensibility of her impulses,
Hilda does, in fact, sharpen her husband's spiritual perceptions and widen his complacent Bleakridge horizon. But
is this to be set to Hilda's credit? The question cannot
be answered, because Mr. Bennett tells us ten times more
about what passes in the man's mind and heart than in the
woman's. Perhaps this is wise of him, for when Hilda
speaks her mind, as she does on a few occasions, and notably in the last six pages, one wonders whether her creator also is not a little baffled by her. Of course, this
is Mr. Bennett's cleverness to put an interrogation mark
after many of her actions and to leave it uncertain as to
what exactly she recognized beyond the entire reasonable-
ness of her own point of view. It is clever of Mr. Bennett
to give us only fitful, evanescent glimpses into the depth
of her love for her husband, for, of course, the answer
lies there - how much of Hilda's heart is not monopolized
by her absorption in getting her way? A man's question
that demands the verdict of clever women, one that most
women will answer with a shrug of the shoulders, when they
have decided as to what in their own case would be the
value of Edwin's husbandly pride and infatuation.

To separate the calyx from the enclosing petals is a
clumsy tribute to a piece of art, but Edwin Clayhanger's
growing consciousness of masculine simplicity, directness,
honesty, and fair-mindedness, in contrast to the incalculable forces of feminine instinct, is a challenge to both
sexes. That some readers will see Hilda through the
mirage of her husband's unappeasable passion, while others
will scrutinize her coldly, in the light of her calculated
ends, is proof of the living complexity of the portrait.
The story of the marriage, however, is not to be separated
from the story of the household in Trafalgar Road and the

tissue of its intimate relations with the whole clan of
the Clayhangers' relatives, friends, and acquaintances.
We are again immersed in the thick, harsh atmosphere of
Bursley *Kultur*, and we struggle again against the ritual
of the stern Victorian deities worshipped by Auntie Hamps,
the Benbows, Mr. Peartree the Wesleyan minister, Mr.
Breeze the bank manager, and the Town Council, and we
turn for relief to the rival ritual of the few free
spirits of Bleakridge, such as the Orgreave family, with
their 'musical evenings.' Mr. Bennett's power over us
has never been more assured.

In any case, Mr. Bennett's illuminating humor, his
intense veracity, his sardonic, whole-hearted absorption
in the constructed impulses of his Bursley types, have
never shown to more advantage. Take the jet-clad figure
of Auntie Hamps, for example, with her 'gorgeous and sustained hypocrisy,' she becomes in our author's hands the
final, impressive symbol of the Victorian age, in all its
terrific conventionality, its solid virtues, and shameless
meanness. The scene of her deathbed, surrounded by her
nephews and nieces and the flock of their children, though
not so pitiless as the notable deathbed scene in 'Old
Wives' Tales' [sic], is most masterly. Or take the episode of 'The Orgreave Calamity,' the break up and bankruptcy of the Orgreave household, and the hurried, passing
acceptance of the tragedy by the circle of intimates, with
their special interest in the attendant scandal, all this
is very cunningly reflected from the mirror of life.
Mr. Bennett's craftsmanship, by the way, is always seen
at its best when the fates break into a tragic scene with
a fresh unforeseen stroke in another quarter. Very crafty
is the arrest of Edwin's musings at his night watch beside
the dying figure of Auntie Hamps, by the knocking at the
front door, and by Albert Benbow's arrival with the news
of Ingpen's fatal accident. This is a sudden shake to the
spiritual kaleidoscope, which rearranges all the patterns
of Edwin's perceptions into a scheme of new significance.
The artistic development of the whole marriage story is
also exceedingly artful, a great deal happening suddenly,
at times, to reveal and bring to fruition passionate feelings in Edwin and Hilda that might otherwise have smoul-
dered in obscurity for years. If some people fancy there
is 'a lack of continuity' about this treatment, and that
the story is too episodic in arrangement, this merely sig-
nifies that the growing subtlety of Mr. Bennett's art has
escaped them.

84. FRANCIS HACKETT, HUSBAND AND WIFE, 'NEW REPUBLIC'

4 December 1915, 125-6

Francis Hackett (1883-1962) was an Irish-American author
and critic. He reviewed 'The Old Wives' Tale' for a
Chicago paper in 1910, and Bennett liked the review very
much. In the 1920s he and Bennett became friends, and
Bennett gave him advice on novel-writing. 'These Twain'
was published in America in December 1915.

Where Arnold Bennett achieves greatness in his conscientious fiction is in his resolute fidelity to common human
beings as they are. In one American novel, 'The Rise of
Silas Lapham,' there was a full anticipation of his method
and spirit, but it is difficult to find anywhere else
another complete example. Greatnesses of a different
order, greatnesses which cannot be compared, are to be
found in Mr. Bennett's contemporaries, but he above the
rest has mastered the art of preserving in fiction the
color, the tone, the flavor, the odor, the surface, of
provincial urban usualness. Such usualness has been
approached in varying moods by numerous English and American novelists. Moore and Gissing have attempted it.
Frank Norris and Henry Fuller and Edith Wharton have come
at it. It has been part of the problem of every modern
bourgeois novel. But no one has succeeded as well as
Arnold Bennett in giving it comprehension and proportion.
What it is, this routine bourgeois life, most of us know
only too well. It is immensely that familiarity which
breeds disregard. But so powerful and miraculous is art
that as soon as this life is presented to us by one to
whom it has appealed, presented with acute and exquisite
fidelity, it becomes poignant and beautiful. No matter
how the thing in itself may estrange us, no matter how
we may despise and rage at its conditions, we are enabled
by the artist to come into full understanding of it, and
we are grateful to the core of our being for the honesty
that retained every tedium, every banality, every inadequacy, for our understanding. To give the sanction of art
to the nobility of human nature is precious, but it is no
more precious than to bring into the sanction of art the
unremitted commonplace. For it proves that there is no
such thing as commonplace, that where there is truth there
must be beauty.

And in his account of the married life of Edwin Clayhanger and Hilda Lessways Mr. Bennett has adhered to the
veracity that implies beauty. No one who read 'Clayhanger'
or 'Hilda Lessways' could suppose that the truth of their
marriage would be romantic. It is not romantic. It is,
in the conventional sense, desperately unromantic and dis-
illusioning. But it is full of an assuaging comprehension
and an illimitable tenderness. To be tender over unusual-
ness is possible to almost every imagination. Women who
tritely accept tuberculosis in negro tenements can weep
with Stevenson over the lepers. Men who are bored to death
by the hardships of scrubwomen can blaze with sympathy for
a prostitute. Sedentary people of every description are
exalted at the thought of war. But it needs genuine imagination to remain responsive in despite of repetition and
custom, and this imagination Mr. Bennett possesses. The
younger novelists strive as a rule to present situations
that are complicated by some piquant irregularity - an
illicit lover or two, a brilliant youth horridly addicted
to heroin, a millionaire disciple of the I.W.W., and other
exciting exhibitions of the orchid in Kansas. But the
material that Mr. Bennett takes is the material of dis-
regarded and unsensational lives, showing by the aid of
his devoted imagination the depths in the stuff of which
those apparently ordered lives are made.

To those who met Clayhanger and Hilda Lessways before,
the task of depicting their union seemed formidable. Hilda
Lessways was an inexplicable creature, and in marriage she
was bound in some degree to be explicated. The limitations
of Edwin, on the other hand, presaged an attitude as husband which could hardly fail to impede that swinging step.
And then there was the child. Could Mr. Bennett domesti-
cate Hilda in the Five Towns without losing her magic?
Could he sustain without wearying us the patient chronicle
of confined and dutiful lives? For some, perhaps, the
answer will not be favorable to Mr. Bennett. Admitting,
as all must admit, the incomparable resources of his intimacy, the triumphant fertility of his invention, there will
be readers to miss in Mrs. Edwin Clayhanger the impetuosity
and glamour of the girl whom Edwin loved from afar. These
readers will question whether Hilda is the same Hilda.
They will believe that somewhere, somehow, Mr. Bennett's
divination has faltered. For my own part, I am not sure.
The flagrance which permitted Hilda to deviate from Edwin
without a word - that flagrance which he was once so
falsely represented as accepting entire - seems to disappear into her character unelucidated, and with it some
of her salience. She began as mountain torrent. The
sweep of her personality in marriage is the sweep of a

channelled stream. That a woman of such brilliant and
dashing gesture should so subside, that she should attune
herself so readily to a marriage so signally without ultimate confidence, is a great deal to concede. That there
should be so few attempts at ultimate confidence is, perhaps, too much to concede, especially as the marriage is
rather unwittingly concentrated on the standpoint of the
man. But the change seems to me for the most part greatly
credible. Hilda's taming, her acquiescence, seems to me
very much 'like life.'

[Quotes Book 1, ch. 7, section 1, 'The fact was that she
had married him' to 'in her pride she thought'.]

So far from knowing Hilda's mind about himself, Edwin
goes through a long and harrowing process of what is
euphemistically known as 'adjustment.' And the complemen-
tary process is necessitated for Hilda not so much on
account of her ignorance of Edwin's processes, though that
is profound, as on account of the exactions of her contrary will. Judged by some marriages, this conflict may
seem unusual. There are persons who inform you that never
in their married life have they heard a cross word. But,
outside such feastings on angel-cake, sharply and touch-
ingly typical is the Clayhangers' alternation between
sacrament and sacrilege. Not by words do the Clayhangers
reach comprehension. Hilda is curiously more ready to
surrender her body than to surrender her mind. She never
foregoes a hard consciousness, 'it's each for himself in
marriage, after all.' But apart from this rather unusual
articulation of the warfare that is marriage, she and
Edwin represent with extraordinary accuracy the permuta-
tions of allied but rival purposes - purposes which can
no more be made identical than the weather which favors
oats can be made identical with the weather which favors
corn.
   One thing I miss in Hilda - her sexual consciousness
outside marriage. One thing I vainly expected in Edwin -
jealousy. Even of the resurrected George Cannon he is
not apprehensively jealous, merely fiercely instinctive
that Hilda shall not see him. One thing I wondered about -
that Hilda and Edwin did not have a child. One thing I
disliked - that Hilda 'padded' about her bedroom. But
that last is the pathos of things as they are.
   If Hilda and Edwin were not set in the community of the
Five Towns, the provincial England of 1892, the peculiar
richness and thickness of their veracity would be infinitely less powerful. But Mr. Bennett has revived with
mastery our sense of that community, and restored it to

us in new significance because his perception and his
charity are more mature. The death of Auntie Hamps alone
appeared to me a lapse in artistic intuition. It was too
reminiscent of unforgettable reflections in 'The Old Wives
Tale.'

Whether Hilda proves less liberating than one expected,
or Edwin more frustrated, 'These Twain' completes with
great success a drama for which many must have trembled.
There are things about 'These Twain' that seem fuzzy -
the delineation of Tertius Ingpen, for one, and the business capacity of Edwin. But on the whole there is a power
and security of characterization that is incontrovertible,
and an amplitude of incident so natural and so significant
that the sense of life never departs. Whether one regards
the amusingly accurate idiom of young George, the picture
of Trafalgar Road or of Dartmoor, the flashes of anger or
of passion, 'These Twain' is the product of a searching
and just susceptibility to the tone and movement of life.

The gratitude that is due to any real artist is great,
but the gratitude due to an artist who adheres to life in
its common motivation seems to me exceptional. The very
sensitiveness that makes a man an artist tends to confine
him to those situations which engage and indulge his
sensitiveness. Because the world of gross and urgent
action, of common necessity, is hostile to the spectator,
the spectator easily becomes hostile in return. But Mr.
Bennett is a spectator who has retained a beautiful sympathy for motivations and susceptibilities alien to the
artistic type. He has transcended interest in 'ideas'
and purposes to spread human nature before us. It is a
triumph of disciplined fictive imagination, a triumph both
of artist and man.

'The Lion's Share'

14 September 1916

85. REBECCA WEST, THE GIRL WHO LEFT HOME, 'DAILY NEWS AND LEADER'

14 September 1916, 4

Rebecca West (1892–   ) and Bennett apparently never liked each other, although in later years she wrote of him with seeming affection in 'The Strange Necessity', 1928, and in her little pamphlet 'Arnold Bennett Himself', 1931. The woman question was a particularly vexing one for her in her relationship with H.G. Wells, and Bennett's devotion to Mrs Wells possibly had something to do with the dislike.

Sir Walter Scott, it may be remembered, divided his works into those in which he used the big bow-wow, and his lesser works. Well, in 'The Lion's Share,' which is published to-day, Mr. Arnold Bennett has not exercised his big bow-wow; that large, sombre, Five-Towns animal has lain curled up at his feet while he has drowsily recalled the odd and jolly and dangerous things one used to do before the war, and put them at the disposal of Audrey, the discontented, snub-nosed girl who was imprisoned by an exacting father in a beautiful but dreary Essex home. It is now the fashion in many intellectual circles to despise Mr. Bennett, as it is the fashion to despise all authors who have performed the crude act of publishing anything. But it is interesting to notice that because he has worked so hard at the craft of writing, at the art of investing the dreams of a not wild imagination with beauty, he cannot help but achieve good writing and beauty even in a book written

without much devotion and with a light intention. For
there is very great beauty in those early chapters which
show Audrey, the lovely vessel of the lovely draught of
youth, at once unhappy and radiant, against the background
of the shallow estuary of Mozewater and its many wonders –
'red barges beating miraculously up the shallow puddles
to Moze Quay, equinoctial spring-tides when the estuary
was a tremendous ocean covered with foam and the sea wall
felt the light lash of spray; thunderstorms in autumn
gathering over the yellow melancholy of death-like sunsets, wild birds crying across miles of uncovered mud at
early morning and duck-hunters crouching in punts behind
a waving screen of delicate grasses to wing them, and the
mysterious shapes of steamers and warships in the offing
beyond the Sand....'

Audrey's father, Mr. Moze, was not a nice man; the only
occasion on which he had been known to laugh was when the
cat fell out of the bathroom window on to the lawn roller.
Yet in her relations with him Audrey, like so many of the
figures erected lately by novelists to prove the fine
rebellious quality of the Younger Generation, like Ann
Veronica or any of the disgruntled families that inhabit
the gloom of the Repertory Theatre, leaves us unconvinced
of her splendour. Since in real life clever people can
usually get the upper hand of stupid people, it seems a
little odd that the only victory Audrey and Ann Veronica
could score over their respectively demented and imbecile
parents was to run away. One will never really believe
in the alleged magnificence of the Younger Generation till
one reads a book about the Daughter who Stayed at Home and
the father who, in consequence, started at the sound of
her voice as at the crack of a whip.

But Audrey never really runs away, for on the day of
her flight her father is killed in a motor accident when
on his way to a meeting of an Anti-Romanist society.
('His connection with the society had originated in a
quarrel between himself and a Catholic priest from Ipswich,
who had instituted a boys' summer camp on the banks of
Mozewater near the village of Moze. Until that quarrel,
the exceeding noxiousness of the Papal doctrine had not
clearly presented itself to Mr. Moze. In such strange
ways may an ideal come to birth.') And thereafter the
book is, as has been said, just a drowsy evocation of all
the odd and jolly and dangerous things that could be done
before the war. Innocently assuming the name and dress of
a widow, so that she can have more freedom, she goes to
France. Driving through Paris by night, she thrills at
the sight of the Boulevards, where 'throngs of promenaders
moved under theatrical trees that waved their pale emerald

against the velvet sky.' She dances at the ball in the
studio of the magnificent M. Dauphin, who tells her with
the solemnity of the perfect snob that he counts among his
friends 'more than two-thirds of the subscribers to Covent
Garden Opera.' She falls in with Rosamund, the calm
tyrant at the head of that 'family trio whose Christian
names were three sweet symphonies,' and is introduced
to the Suffrage Movement; its sweet and steadfast, though
schoolgirlish, comradeship, its delicious adventures all
over the country, at the centre of the whirling joy-wheel
in the exhibition, while the pursuing policemen were for
ever cast off from the run by centrifugal force, at the
home of the Spatts (perhaps the most cultured family in
Frinton-on-Sea); and its appalling discoveries, such as
the punishment cells in Holloway. And there appears, to
try to lure her away from Feminism, Madame Piriac, who
is a vast and cruel satire of that type of woman whom one
was always afraid Mr. Bennett really liked, an elegant
Frenchwoman, who pretends to know all sorts of tremendous
secrets about life, but who has probably no profounder
secret than that she uses Hinde's curlers. 'Unless you
use your youth and your freedom and your money for some
individual you will never be content,' she tells Audrey.

It is the whole point of the book that Audrey proves
them both wrong. She picks up a violinist of genius, with
large timorous eyes, and in spite of the fact that so far
as one can learn from Mr. Bennett's description, he was,
to use the American phrase, nothing to write home about,
she falls in love with him. She makes a way for him
through the brutally absurd musical world; she sees to it
that he has a concert in the Salle Xavier. ('Wagner, at
Venice, had once threatened Xavier with a stick, and also
Xavier had twice run away with great exponents of the rôle
of Isolde. His competence as a connoisseur of Wagner's
music, and of the proper methods of rendering Wagner's
music, could therefore not be questioned, and it was not
questioned.') She marries him tempestuously, and leads
him off to tour those German cities whose approval is
necessary before he can have a London success. But that
is not all she does. 'I want,' she cries to Rosamund,
'to have a husband and a house and a family, and a cause
too. That'll be just about everything, won't it? And
if you imagine I can't look after all of them at once,
all I can say is I don't agree with you.... Supposing
I had all these things. I fancy I could have a tiff
with my husband and make it up, play with my children,
alter a dress, change the furniture, tackle the servants,
and go out to a meeting and perhaps have a difficulty
with the police all in one day. Only if I did get into

trouble with the police I should pay the fine - you see.
The police aren't going to have me altogether. Nobody.
Nobody, man or woman, is going to be able to boast that
he's got me altogether.' She wants, in fact, the lion's
share of life. One greatly admires Mr. Bennett for making
his small but spirited contribution to the theory of
feminism so excellent and rich a story of adventure.

86. UNSIGNED REVIEW, 'SPECTATOR'

11 November 1916, 588-9

According to the publishers' announcement, Mr. Arnold
Bennett's new novel is a blend of the realism of his Five
Towns stories with the more genial manner of 'The Card'
and its sequel. This is in a sense true; the method is
more circumstantial than that adopted in his earlier sensational romances; there is a rough resemblance between
'the Card' and Audrey Moze, the central figure of 'The
Lion's Share,' in that both were of the type of 'climbers,'
and after the funeral episodes of the opening chapters we
emerge into an atmosphere which is mainly that of comedy.
None the less there are essential differences between this
story and the chronicles of 'the Card.' He made his way
to success and affluence by his ability, while Audrey's
path was smoothed by circumstance. She started higher up
in the social ladder and inherited a fortune. What marks
her out from her kind was her audacity and lack of scruple
in availing herself of her opportunities - in breaking free
from the traditions and restrictions which had fenced her
round in the lifetime of her parents. 'The Lion's Share'
is not merely an example of what has been called the
'emancipation novel'; it is a satire - detached and
unimpassioned after Mr. Bennett's wont - on various aspects
of modern feminism, in which special prominence is given to
the suffragist movement. On this subject Mr. Bennett may
claim to speak from a certain amount of inside knowledge,
seeing that for several years he was editorially connected
with 'Woman,' a periodical which bore the somewhat enigmatical motto of 'Forward but not too fast.' That, however, was in the 'nineties.' What Mr. Bennett's views are
on the suffrage question now we do not know, but certainly
his portraiture of its modern hierophants is the reverse
of flattering. As for Audrey herself, who was for a while

caught up in the vortex of militancy but speedily extri-
cated herself, though she continued to subscribe to the
cause, she reminds us not a little of the fifth, seventh,
and eighth species of women as classified by Simonides –
those which were made respectively out of the sea, out of
cats, and out of mares with flowing tails. The sea-woman –
we quote from Addison's essay – was all mutability, the
cat-woman was addicted to thefts, cheats, and pilferings,
and the woman who resembled the mare with a flowing tail
'was never broke to any servile toil and labour' and
passed her time in self-adornment. Indeed it would not
be difficult to find modern instances for nearly all the
unflattering things said of women by the ancients in the
pages of this story, beginning with the cynical maxim,
'Believe no woman even when she tells you the truth.'
There are times when one grew positively fond of 'the
Card,' because of his detached contemplation of his own
career, and the mingled pride and amusement which he feels
in his upward progress. After all, he was the architect
of his fortunes, and Audrey was not. She is not altogether
destitute of a sense of her absurdity, but she is more selfish, more self-protective, and less genial. And what is
true of her is true of nearly every other character in the
book. They are amusing, vivacious, sardonic, interesting,
but there is not one that appeals to the affections of the
reader. The story is romantic in regard to incident, but
ruthlessly unromantic in its treatment of character and in
its deliberate avoidance of all hero-worship. And as with
the characters, so with the view of life which is here
presented. Mr. Bennett gives us a really brilliant picture
of the gaiety and levity of Parisian life in pre-war times
– the life of the big hotels, the restaurants, the studios,
the boulevards – but of the great soul of France that lay
beneath all this froth and phosphorescence there is not a
trace. Mr. Bennett may fairly answer that to have dwelt
upon this aspect of the spirit of France would have been
out of keeping with the scope and aim of his story; all
the same we cannot but regret the omission in a book published to-day, though we admit that it is a book in which
there is little room for high ideals or austere aspirations. The point of view throughout is one in which the
comforts, amenities, and luxuries of life are almost con-
tinuously insisted upon. Mr. Bennett has never been more
frankly materialist, or perhaps it would be fairer to say
more concerned to show that happiness depends on the command of money. In describing the 'seemly Georgian residence' which was Audrey's home he observes: 'Its dormers
and fine chimneys glowed amid the dark bare trees, and they
alone would have captivated a Londoner possessing those

precious attributes, fortunately ever spreading among the
enlightened middle-classes, a motor-car, a cultured taste
in architecture, and a desire to enter the squirearchy.'
There may be some underlying irony here, but the resultant
impression of the story as a whole does not support such
an interpretation. As an entertainment it is less consis-
tently exhilarating than some of Mr. Bennett's comedies,
possibly because of the exasperating quality of the central figure, but there are many enjoyable and thoroughly
humorous passages, none better perhaps than Miss Ingate's
account of her early adventures in art:-

[Quotes towards end of ch. 9, 'Well, it was like this' to
'to be any good'.]

Miss Ingate is a very minutely drawn portrait of the venturesome spinster of middle age; her candour is diverting,
and in many ways she is a 'good fellow'; but even here Mr.
Bennett is careful to discount our sympathy in advance by
telling us at the very outset that though she had a great
eye for snobbishness in others, she was not free from it
herself. When we spoke above of Mr. Bennett's method
being unimpassioned, an exception ought to have been made
of the scene - perhaps the most remarkable in the book -
in which Audrey declines the proposal of the suffragist
leader, 'Rosamund,' that she should devote herself, body
and soul, to militancy. This is a 'straight talk' of
woman to woman with a vengeance, in which Audrey formu-
lates the gospel of self-expression with a passionate
egotism.

General Views: 1913–16

In these years appeared the first book on Bennett, F.J.
Harvey Darton's 'Arnold Bennett', issued in 1915 and again,
revised slightly, in 1924. The book occasioned a review of
Bennett's life and work by Holbrook Jackson in 'T.P.'s
Weekly' (1 May), with a large portrait of Bennett on the
cover of the magazine. Jackson thought that Bennett's
realism was closer to Hardy's than to Gissing's. Darton's
book was formally reviewed in the 'Daily News' (8 May),
where Bennett was called 'the most significant novelist of
the present day'. Bennett himself thought that Darton's
book was deplorable. He catalogued miscellaneous errors
in it in a letter to John Squire (LAB II, 364-5), and he
reported some years later that Darton had once stopped
him on the street and apologised for the book. R.A. Scott-
James (see headnote to No. 44) surveyed his work at length
in 'Personality in Literature' in 1913. Henry James, in
the first of two articles on The Younger Generation in the
'Times Literary Supplement' (19 March and 2 April 1914),
gave attention to Bennett's technique (see p. 351 for
details). The material reappeared in 'Notes on Novelists'
later in the year. Two interviews with Bennett were published in 1914, Mr. Arnold Bennett on the Modern Novel, on
the Call of the Stage, 'Daily News and Leader' (30 July,
written entirely by Bennett), and The Most Read Novelist,
the 'Star' (3 August). In America the 'New Republic' (11
January 1915) reflected upon Bennett's socialism in conjunction with the views on the artist's responsibility to
the public expressed in 'The Author's Craft'. A long article by George Bronson-Howard, Arnold Bennett as Melodramatist, 'Bookman' (New York, May 1915), reviewed Bennett's
sensational fiction. An article in the 'Metropolitan' (New
York, September 1915) discussed the universality of the
Five Towns. The posthumous volume of Dixon Scott's 'Men
of Letters', 1916, reprinted his reviews of 'The Card',

'The Regent', and 'Those United States'. J.W. Cunliffe in the 'Independent' (21 February 1916) discussed the universality of Arnold Bennett's Provincialism. W.G. Murdoch discussed Bennett's style in a small piece in the 'Quarterly Notebook' (December 1916).

---

87. STUART PRATT SHERMAN, THE REALISM OF ARNOLD BENNETT, 'NATION' (NEW YORK)

23 December 1915, 741-4

Stuart Pratt Sherman (1881-1927) was a distinguished American critic. Bennett described this article to George Doran as 'extremely fine' and added that 'on the whole I regard it as the best article I have seen on the subject'. There were responses to the article on 6 January 1916, a reply by Sherman on 20 January, and further responses on 3 and 10 February.

In a discussion of Mr. Dreiser's work, recently printed in these pages, I offered a protest against the confusion which results from calling all novelists who deal with contemporary life realists; and I proposed, as a means of making useful distinctions among them, a scrutiny of the bundle of general ideas which constitutes for each his 'working philosophy,' and which, as I maintained, necessarily underlies the artistic representation of each and in considerable measure determines its form. Having proposed to distinguish Mr. Dreiser as a naturalist on the basis of his theory of animal behavior, I felt the need of supplementing my argument by exhibiting the relationship, in some conspicuous exemplar, between genuine realism and a respectable theory of human conduct.

I.

Arnold Bennett at once appeared in at least one respect to be the most promising candidate for the position. His works, to be sure, are of very unequal value, for, frankly writing to live, he has diversified the production of masterpieces by the production of potboilers. But all sorts of good judges unite in declaring that his best

novels - 'The Old Wives' Tale,' 'Clayhanger,' 'Hilda Lessways,' and the newly published 'These Twain,' completing
the Clayhanger trilogy - produce upon them an unprecedented impression of reality. These books, we are told,
challenge and endure a comparison not with literature, but
with life itself. Their 'transcript' of Five Towns society
is so detailed, so nearly complete, and so accurate that
it may be used by the student of human nature with almost
the same confidence that he places in his own first-hand
observations. I was glad to find general agreement on
this point, for it relieved me of the task of justifying
my own conviction that Mr. Bennett is a realist.

The only objection that I saw to the choice of Mr. Bennett as the contemporary realist was that the very critics
who praise the reality of his representations insist
rather sternly that he has no 'philosophy of life,' that
he does not interpret his facts, that his value resides
wholly in the energetic integrity of his transcript. Mr.
Darton, who has just written a book about him, and who is
himself a novelist, says: 'In the Five Towns novels there
is no ideal. There is no criticism. There is no tradition or philosophy of society. There is nothing but life
as the people described live it and see it and feel it.'
This is highly interesting, if true. If true, it effectively disposes of my contention that an artist cannot
observe without a theory. If true, it should suggest to
the younger realistic writers who are looking to Mr. Bennett as their master the wisdom of making all haste to get
rid of their ideas.

Mr. Darton's assertion that Arnold Bennett's work has
no value save that of mere representation was anticipated
by Mr. Henry James in his discussion of the 'new novel'
in 1914, and was by him extended to an entire group of the
younger writers, of which he specified Mr. Bennett and Mr.
Wells as the leaders. The distinguishing characteristic
of the group, according to Mr. James, is 'saturation.'
By this he means, as I take it, that all these novelists,
and to a high degree their leaders, are masters of the
materials of their art. They know with extraordinary completeness and detail *what* they are talking about. When
they have made us see what they have seen, they yield us
no further satisfaction. They squeeze the sponge or, as
Mr. James puts it, the 'orange'; this gives us an 'expression of life.' Expectant but disappointed criticism cries:
'Yes, yes - but is this all? These are the circumstances
of the interest - we see, we see; but where is the interest itself, where and what is its centre, and how are we
to measure it in relation to that?'

I cannot follow a critic who finds Wells and Bennett

alike in their dominant value, and, what is far more
interesting, neither can Mr. Wells! Stung to the quick
of his celestial mind by the polite implication that he
is only a thoroughly immersed sponge, he has retorted in
his semi-pseudonymous 'Boon,' 1915, with a scathing criticism and a 'take-off' on Mr. James, whom he links with
Mr. George Moore by virtue of their sterile aestheticizing.
That is *their* dominant 'value' - their central 'interest.'
His own central interest, as he reasserts with more than
customary vehemence and formlessness, is the expression
of his yearning for a life of divine efficiency and divine
ecstasy. He has a theory of conduct which has developed
out of that romantic yearning; and his representations of
life in fiction are experimental illustrations of that
theory. It is quite absurd to charge an author with 'mere
representation,' who almost invariably bursts the outlines
of his hero, disrupts his narrative in mid-career, shat-
ters the illusion of reality, and buries all the characters under the avalanche of his own personal dreams and
desires. Mr. Wells, in brief, cherishes a 'philosophy of
life' which makes it impossible for him to write a realistic novel. He is dedicated to romance. His high calling is to write pseudo-scientific fantasies and fairy
tales of contemporary society.

Mr. Wells in 'Boon' incidentally repudiates yoke-
fellowship with the novelist of the Five Towns in a passage which gives us the key to Mr. Bennett's philosophical
position. Mr. Bennett is there recorded as a 'derelict,'
an 'imperfectly developed,' an 'aborted' great man surviving from the old times: 'Would have made a Great Victorian
and had a crowd of satellite helpers. Now no one will
ever treasure his old hats and pipes.' This is both amusing and instructive. Mr. Wells does not call a man a Victorian without malice aforethought. If I may be pardoned
a violent expression, Mr. Wells would like to slay all the
Victorians; better still, he would like to believe that
they are all dead. What he objects to in that generation
is not the 'mere representation' of the novelists; it is
the accursed philosophy of life which underlies their
representations. Mr. Bennett rises up to prove, alas,
that this philosophy is not dead yet. His solid realistic
novels protest against Mr. Wells's fairy tales. His vision
of life protests against Mr. Wells's vision of life. 'The
Old Wives' Tale' makes 'The Research Magnificent' look like
child's play. Put 'These Twain' beside 'Marriage,' and
instantly the art of the latter seems flimsy and incon-
dite, and its informing ideas fantastic. And one may perhaps just note in passing that beside any one of Mr. Bennett's novels, Mr. Dreiser's 'Genius' instantly appears to

be a 'barbaric yawp.' An author whose work thus judges,
so to speak, another work with which it is brought into
contact, has a potent critical value meriting examination.

II.

The popular impression that Mr. Bennett has no general
ideas is easily explained by the fact that he does not
attempt, as Mr. Wells does, to break down the boundaries
between the literary *genres*, and to make the novel serve
at the same time as a narrative of events and as a philosophical dissertation. Respecting the personalities of
his *dramatis personae*, wishing to preserve the sharpness
of their outlines in their own atmosphere, he does not
impute to them his ideas nor set them to discussing them.
With a restraint unusual among English novelists, he refrains from 'editorial' comment upon his 'news.' When he
wishes to set forth his ideas, he writes a book of popular
philosophy: 'Mental Efficiency,' 'The Feast of St. Friend,'
'The Plain Man and his Wife.' If these books were as well
known to the American public as the novels are, we should
hear no more in this country about Mr. Bennett's lack of
ideas. On the contrary, all our women's clubs would be
debating, in their eager, simple-hearted fashion, The
Philosophy of Arnold Bennett.
    Mr. Darton, more sophisticated than our fellow-
countrywomen, says in effect that the philosophy of Mr.
Bennett is not worth discussing. The works named above
have been advertised in England, he tells us, as containing 'big, strong, vital thinking.' But, he continues,
'"big, strong, vital thinking" is just what these remarkable little books do not contain. They contain the com-
pletest common-sense, expressed with astonishing simplicity
and directness, and based upon unimpeachable honesty of
outlook. They are a guide to efficiency, to self-help,
to practical idealism, to alertness of intelligence, to
sinewy culture, to every high quality which every crass
Briton has always thought the crass Briton does not show.
The United Kingdom is ... almost overstocked with agencies
for the purpose, from the physical energies of Mr. Sandow
to the benevolent writings of the late Lord Avebury....
They are quite perfect lay sermons. But' - and this is the
damning word - 'they are not original.' I perfectly agree
that Mr. Bennett's general ideas are not 'original,' and
commend his judgment in not tying up his art to anything
so transitory as a 'new' philosophy. I object to the
implication, in which Mr. Wells will rejoice, that because
they are old they are dead or deficient in strength and

vitality. I will not stand upon the word 'big,' a term
which should be reserved for the use of advertising managers and radical reformers. But I cannot reconcile Mr.
Darton's description of these books as guides to every
high quality needed by the crass Briton with his assertion
that there is no criticism in the Five Towns novels,
except on what seems to be the untenable assumption that
Mr. Bennett, the popular novelist, and Mr. Bennett, the
popular philosopher, are distinct and non-communicating
beings.

The beginning of wisdom, according to this philosophy,
which runs counter to our current naturalism, is the
recognition of a fundamental duality in human experience.
Mr. Bennett presumes not God to scan, but looking into
himself as a microcosm, reports that the universe consists
of a power-to-control, which is the quintessence of man,
and of a power-to-be-controlled, which is nature. The
zest, the object, and the compensation of existence lie
in the possibility of extending the dominion of the human
over the natural power. 'For me,' he says, 'spiritual
content (I will not use the word "happiness," which implies
too much) springs from no mental or physical facts. It
springs from the spiritual fact that there is something
higher in man than the mind, and that something can control the mind. Call that something the soul, or what you
will. My sense of security amid the collisions of existence lies in the firm consciousness that just as my body
is the servant of my mind, so is my mind the servant of
me. An unruly servant, but a servant - and possibly getting less unruly every day! Often have I said to that
restive brain: "Now, O mind, sole means of communication
between the *me* and all external phenomena, you are not a
free agent; you are subordinate; you are nothing but a
piece of machinery; and obey me you shall."'

The responsibility for extending the dominion of man
over his own nature, and, indirectly, over his remoter
circumstances, Mr. Bennett, in opposition to our popular
sociological doctors, places primarily upon the individual.
While Mr. Wells, for example, urges us to cast our burdens
and our sins upon society, and goes about beating up
enthusiasm for schemes to improve the 'mind of the race'
by leagues of Samurai and legislative enactments, Mr.
Bennett fixes his eye upon plain John Smith, and says:
'I am convinced that we have already too many societies
for the furtherance of our ends. To my mind, most societies with a moral aim are merely clumsy machines for doing
simple jobs with a maximum of friction, expense, and
inefficiency. I should define the majority of these
societies as a group of persons each of whom expects the

others to do something very wonderful. Why create a society in order to help you perform some act which nobody can perform but yourself?' Arnold Bennett says disappointingly little about that 'big' idea, 'the mind of the race.' And whenever he contemplates that impressive and admired abstraction, 'the backbone of the nation,' it resolves itself under his realistic gaze into the by-him-no-less-admired but certainly less generally impressive spinal columns of John Smith and other homely vertebrates.

In dealing with the relations of John Smith to Mrs. Smith, the Victorian Bennett feels obliged to say, in opposition to those who hold out for these plain people the prospect of a life of freedom and sustained ecstasy to be attained by upsetting the established social and economic order, that the ideas of freedom and ecstasy are romantic will-o'-the-wisps. In the recent 'evolution' of society he perceives rapid changes for the better in living conditions and a gradual amelioration of manners and tastes, but no significant alteration in the elements of human nature. 'Passionate love,' he insists, 'does not mean happiness; it means excitement, apprehension, and continually renewed desires.' 'Luxury,' he adds, 'according to the universal experience of those who have had it, has no connection whatever with happiness.' 'Happiness as it is dreamed of cannot possibly exist save for short periods of self-deception which are followed by terrible periods of reaction. Real practicable happiness is due primarily not to any kind of environment, but to an inward state of mind. Real happiness consists, first, in an acceptance of the fact that discontent is a condition of life, and, secondly, in an honest endeavor to adjust conduct to an ideal.'

It must infuriate an advocate of moral revolution and loose fluent sensuality, like Mr. Wells, to hear Mr. Bennett, bracketed with him as a leader of the new school, asserting that 'the great principles, spiritual and moral, remain intact.' It must perplex an apologist for moral anarchy and strident self-assertion like Mr. Dreiser to find a fellow-realist declaring that 'after all the shattering discoveries of science and conclusions of philosophy, mankind has still to live with dignity amid hostile nature,' and that mankind can succeed in this tremendous feat only 'by the exercise of faith and of that mutual good-will which is based on sincerity and charity.' But what must distress them both beyond measure is this able craftsman's exposition of the relation of moral conventions to artistic form. 'What form is in art, conventions are in life.... No art that is not planned in form is worth consideration, and no life that is not planned in

conventions can ever be satisfactory.... The full beauty
of an activity is never brought out until it is subjected
to discipline and strict ordering and nice balancing.
A life without petty artificiality would be the life of
a tiger in the forest.... Laws and rules, forms and
ceremonies, are good in themselves, from a merely aesthetic point of view, apart from their social value and
necessity.'

These are the ideas of a man who has taken his stand
against Mr. Wells's Utopia on the one hand and against
Mr. Dreiser's jungle on the other. As old as civilized
society, they have the conservative complexion of all
traditional and enduring things. They are not worth
discussing if they are not challenged. Like fire and
water, they do not appear vital till they are denied.
Ordinarily a novelist has not needed consciously to concern himself with them, unless he has intended to trample
them under foot. But in the face of the present naturalistic invasion, when humanistic ideas are in the trenches,
fighting for existence, a novelist who paints men in preference to tigers, supermen, or scientific angels, has
interestingly taken sides.

III.

The general theme of Mr. Bennett's masterpieces,
determined by the central interest of his philosophy,
is the development of character in relation to a society
which is also developing. He has no foolishly simple
mechanical formula for expressing the nature of the relation between the individual and the social process. He
has rather a sense that this relationship involves an
interplay of forces of fascinating and inexplicable complexity.

His sense of the marvellous intricacy of his theme
explains his elaborate presentation of the community life
in which his principal figures have their being. He is
bent upon bringing before the eye of the reader every
scrap of evidence that may be conceived of as relevant
to the 'case.' The reader who believes that character
is determined mainly by inherited physiological traits
finds in the Five Towns novels a physiological account
of three successive generations. The reader who holds
that education is the significant factor is abundantly
supplied with the educational history of father and children and grandchildren. The reader who lays stress upon
a changing environment and the pressure of the hour sees
how from decade to decade and from year to year the hero

or heroine is housed and clothed and fed and occupied and
amused; and wrought upon by parents and children and relatives and friends and servants and strangers; and subjected
to the influences of social customs and business and politics and religion and art and books and newspapers trans-
mitting to the thick local atmosphere the pressure of the
world outside. The reader who looks for the main currents
of the nineteenth century in the Five Towns discovers the
Clayhanger family and their neighbors developing in relation to the democratic movement, the industrial revolution,
the decay of dogmatic theology, the extension of scientific
thought and invention, the organization of labor, and the
diffusion of aesthetic consciousness. One's first impression before this spectacle is of admiration at the
unrelenting artistic energy which keeps this presented
community life whole and steady yet perceptibly in motion
through a long span of time.

One's second impression is of admiration at the force
of composition which keeps the principal figures from
being 'swamped' in the life of the community. They are
immersed in it and dyed in it and warped and battered and
grooved by it; yet they are never made to appear as its
impotent creatures; somehow they are made to emerge above
their 'environment' as its creators and preservers - its
plain, grim, but enduring heroes. The secret of this
'somehow' is that Mr. Bennett implicitly recognizes as
an artist what he explicitly declares as a popular philosopher, namely, the existence in the individual of something deeper than the body, deeper than the mind - an
ultimately responsible, independent, spiritual self, with
the power to control, in some measure, its circumstances.
In his preface to 'The Old Wives' Tale' he tells us that
the originating impulse of that work was a conviction that
a 'heart-rending novel' might be written to express 'the
extreme pathos in the fact that every stout, ageing woman
was once a young girl with the unique charm of youth in her
form and movements and in her mind.' The theme as he
states it is only the threadbare platitude of Cavalier
poetry - the deciduousness of physical beauty; and its
pathos is only skin deep. But the theme as he develops
it is the spiritual truth sung by the Puritan - 'only a
sweet and virtuous soul, like seasoned timber, never
gives'; and its pathos is indeed heart-rending. Constance
and Sophia, the two heroines of 'The Old Wives' Tale,'
appeal to tragic compassion not because they were young
and fair and have grown old and grotesque, but because
they hungered for love and life yet have quietly and
proudly starved in their respectability rather than touch
a morsel of forbidden food. After a considerable course

of reading in the 'temperamental' novels of the naturalistic school, one begins to feel that the resisting power of
formed character has vanished from the earth. I shall not
soon forget the sigh of relief that I uttered when I came
upon a certain passage in the story of Sophia's resistance
to the various invitations of Parisian sensuality. The
poor girl in her loneliness craving for sympathy and affection finds her physical and mental self responding involun-
tarily to the ardent wooing of the kindly Chirac. '"My
dear friend," he urges with undaunted confidence, "you must
know that I love you." She shook her head impatiently, *all
the time wondering what it was that prevented her from
slipping into his arms.*' She does not slip into his arms;
and one rejoices - not because one's moral sense is gratified, but simply because one is pleased to find occasionally a novelist who recognizes an inhibited impulse, in
the sexual connection, as among the interesting 'facts of
life.' Though the self of a person with the power of
inhibiting impulses may have no definite circumference,
it has a defined centre, about which the framework of
character may be built. Mr. Bennett portrays persons with
various powers of inhibition, but his heroes have, or
achieve, character. The interest of his story centres
in the deliberate acts of rational beings, who are conscious, like Hilda Lessways, of their miraculous power
to 'create all their future by a single gesture'; and
so the rich mass of his observations becomes a coherent
illustration of human responsibility.

The Clayhanger trilogy, triumphantly completed by the
publication of 'These Twain,' expresses with the moving
force of dramatic representation the ideas more simply
exposed in 'The Plain Man and His Wife.' The first volume
has for its theme the development of the character of
Edwin Clayhanger from the eager formlessness of his boyhood
to the steadiness, honesty, application, efficiency, solidity, tolerance, justice, and self-control of his manhood.
The theme of the second volume is the development of the
character of Hilda Lessways from the innocent, ignorant
rebelliousness and rapturousness of girlhood, through a
brief ill-advised matrimonial adventure, to the vibrant,
hopeful, open-eyed egoism and rather grim determination
of early womanhood. The theme of the third volume is the
further development of this 'dynamic' and that 'static'
character through the difficult and at times almost baffling process of adapting themselves to living together as
man and wife. Taken together, the three novels constitute
an impressive criticism of Mr. Wells's theory of the life
of sustained ecstasy and, if you please, of Mr. Dreiser's
theory of the life of ruthless animality.

It is clear that Mr. Bennett has attempted to present
in the completed trilogy an adequate account of the fiery
conflict, with typical antagonists, of the Eternal-
Feminine with the Eternal-Masculine. If you are a man,
you will writhe, or you ought to writhe, at the exposure
in Edwin of your own obstinate conviction that you think
straight and that your wife does not, and at the exposure
of your hot fits of indignation at her shifty evasions of
your flawless argument. If you are a woman, you will
blush, or you ought to blush, at the exposure in Hilda
of your own illogicality and your willingness to gain
ends - commendable no doubt - by perfectly unscrupulous
means. Hilda respects and loves her husband deeply, but
she is irritated by his colds, by his little set habits,
by the deliberateness of his temper, and by the inarticu-
lateness of his appreciation of her. Edwin loves his wife
and feels the charm and force of her personality; but he
distrusts her intellect and cannot entirely approve of her
morality. He is exasperated by her interference in his
business. He keenly resents the injustice in which she
involves him through acts inspired by her ambition for him
and by her passionate and jealous devotion to the advancement of their own family interests. She develops social
aspirations in which he does not share, and a desire for
a style of living which promises him increased burdens
with no added satisfactions. Their common effort seems
to multiply luxuries and superficial refinements without
in the least sweetening or deepening or strengthening their
spiritual intercourse. He tells himself in a moment of
intense self-commiseration that the great complex edifice
of his business, 'with its dirt, noise, crudity, strain,
and eternal effort,' exists solely that Hilda may exist
'in her elegance, her disturbing femininity, her restricted
and deep affections, her irrational capriciousness, and her
strange, brusque common-sense.' He asks himself in poignant self-pity, 'Where do I come in?' After repeated scenes
of domestic tension he walks out of his house and home with
hot brain and twitching nerves. He mutters to himself:
'She won't alter her ways - and I shan't stand them.'
In what he takes for ultimate despair, he says to himself,
'as millions of men and women have said to themselves, with
awestruck calm: "My marriage was a mistake."'
But as this plain, average man wanders aimlessly through
the streets of the Five Towns with tumult in his breast,
confronting the ruin of his private universe, he has an
experience comparable in character and significance with
that of Thomas Carlyle when in sultry Leith Walk he authen-
tically took the Devil by the nose. When his brain cools
and his nerves stop twitching and his formed character

returns to its equilibrium, he has first a flashing intuition into a method by which he can reconcile himself to
his 'universe.' 'It was banal; it was commonplace, it was
what everyone knew. Yet it was the great discovery of his
career. If Hilda had not been unjust in the assertion of
her own individuality, there could be no merit in yielding
to her.... He was objecting to injustice as a child
objects to rain on a holiday. Injustice was a tremendous
actuality! It had to be faced and accepted. (He himself
was unjust. At any rate, he intellectually conceived that
he must be, though honestly he could remember no instance
of injustice on his part.) To reconcile one's self to
injustice was the master achievement.... He yielded on
the canal-bridge. And in yielding, it seemed to him that
he was victorious.' He has found content by accepting
discontent as a condition of life, and by honestly endea-
voring to adapt his conduct to an ideal. In his recognition of the need of a more flexible intelligence and a
stiffer backbone he embodies at once the principle of progress and the principle of conservation. He is the hero
of his generation, not victorious but conquering. He
cannot stand like Benham in 'The Research Magnificent,'
and say, 'I am Man. The Thought of the world.' But he
might stand, if he had the habit of attitudinizing, and
say, 'I am a man. A vertebral unit in the backbone of
the nation.'

One cannot plan a life in conventions without cutting
out of it many wayward desires and 'beautiful impulses.'
The young lions and lionesses of radicalism are forcing
the question upon us whether one can plan a life in beautiful impulses and wayward desires without cutting out the
plan. Mr. Bennett answers in the negative, and votes for
preserving the plan. I do not undertake to speak critically of his philosophy. I only observe that it seems to
support an altogether decent theory of human conduct. And
this in turn underlies an artistic representation of life
remarkable for its fulness, its energy, its gusto, its
pathos, its play of tragic and comic lights, its dramatic
clashes, its catastrophes, and its reconciliations - in
short, for its adequacy. I fear that my reasoning will
not make much impression upon the young, for the young,
as Mr. Randolph Bourne tells us, are in love with life;
and to accept conventions is to reject life. The young
will still turn to Mr. Wells, 'for he,' says one Rebecca
West, of London - penning for the 'New Republic' perhaps
the most delicious sentence in modern criticism - 'for he
has inspired the young to demand clear thinking and intellectual passion from the governing classes, instead of the
sexual regularity which was their one virtue and which,

he has hinted, is merely part of a general slothfulness
and disinclination for adventure.' As I sadly take my
obscure place in the rear of the 'cretinous butlers' who
do not like Mr. Wells,' I summon my Christian charity to
declare that much shall be forgiven a champion of Mr.
Wells, whose critical arrows go singing, like this sentence of Rebecca West's, straight to the heart of laughter.

88. DOROTHEA PRICE HUGHES, THE NOVELS OF MR. ARNOLD
BENNETT AND WESLEYAN METHODISM, 'CONTEMPORARY REVIEW'

November 1916, 602-10

Dorothea Price Hughes was active in Wesleyan councils.
She was a lecturer and journalist, and wrote 'The Life
of Hugh Price Hughes'.

The novels of Mr. Arnold Bennett are not only acknowledged
masterpieces but are among the most widely read books of
our day. Their author's choice of subject, and his treatment of that subject, are both full of significance. He
is determined to face the facts of modern democracy as he
sees them, and finds his inspiration in the grimy thorough-
fares and suburban residences of a great manufacturing
centre, 'The Five Towns.' He does not regale his readers
with stories of princesses and diplomats and aristocratic
adventurers, for he knows, as Whitman knew, that their tale
has often been told before and in the best way, and that
the tale of the milliner, the draper, and the adventurous
clerk has seldom been told as it should be. He strips it
of all make-believe and sentimentality, showing milliners
and clerks as they act and speak in everyday life, not
melodrama, and revealing those grim social facts which do
much to explain their lives. His stern realism is the
more impressive because he is an artist. To find and
express beauty is a craving of his nature, and he discovers
it often in unlikely places where it is hidden from lesser
artists. He has the French love of the apt word and the
fitting phrase; and in an age when novelists are careless
about form and methods of presentment, he gives pleasure
by providing marvels of technique.
      Merely to indicate his sensibilities and achievement

would require a space which the present article does not
permit. But could full acknowledgment be paid to them,
a further question would still arise, a question surely
which must finally be asked of every novelist. How far
does he truly represent humanity? Do his portraits of the
men and women of commercial England convince us by their
truth, revealing human nature to us as we see it in ourselves and recognise it in others? The writer's aim in
this article is to answer the above question by considering Mr. Bennett's treatment of a portion of the life of
commercial England, 'Wesleyan Methodism,' partly because
the writer knows something of Wesleyan Methodism, and
partly because a novelist's treatment of a subject as
vital as the creed and religious expression of a people,
throws light on other aspects of his treatment.

Wesleyan Methodism is a form of religion that is either
liked or disliked, loved or hated. People who know something of it or have been brought up in it, seldom feel
neutral towards it as they do towards less pronounced
forms of religious life and belief. Mr. Bennett certainly
does not feel neutral; he hates it. Even if he did not go
out of his way to say so, we should discern this hatred
after reading his first description of a Methodist official or of any ceremonial in which Methodists take part.
We scarcely need the following admissions concerning
Edwin Clayhanger:-

> It was at the sessions of the Bible Class that Edwin,
> while silently perfecting himself in the art of profan-
> ity and blasphemy, had in secret fury envenomed his
> instinctive mild objection to the dogma, the ritual,
> and the spirit of conventional Christianity, especially
> as exemplified in Wesleyan Methodism. He had left Mr.
> Peartree's Bible class a convinced anti-religionist, a
> hater and despiser of all that the Wesleyan Chapel and
> Mr. Peartree stood for. He deliberately was not impar-
> tial, and he took a horrid pleasure in being unfair.
> He knew well that Methodism had produced many fine
> characters, and played a part in the moral development
> of the race; but he would not listen to his own know-
> ledge. Nothing could extenuate for him the noxiousness
> of Methodism.

Wesleyan Methodism in its origin was a challenge to men
and women, and even its most conventional forms continue
to make large claims on the allegiance of individuals. It
is not merely that members are expected to devote large
portions of their time and money to the service of their
Church, but they are deprived often of social status

and the opportunities that belong to it. Their religion
is that of trading and artisan England, not of professional and upper class England, and it is this rather
than any theological peculiarity which condemns it in the
eyes of a large number of English people. It is associated in their minds with shop-assistants and agricultural
labourers and the association is a right one. These were
the people who joyfully received the Gospel that Methodism
had to preach, and so long as that Gospel continues there
will be shop-assistants and agricultural labourers among
the honoured members of a Methodist Society.

Quite naturally therefore Mr. Bennett gives Wesleyan
Methodists a prominent place in his picture of a democratic community. When his hero and heroine profess any
religion at all it is that of the Wesleyan Methodists,
the traditional religion of traders and artisans. Even
when they are antagonistic to its claims like Edwin Clayhanger, they are not absolved from a lifelong contest with
it. The fact that Clayhanger refuses to become District
Treasurer of the Additional Chapels Fund does not end the
struggle. Methodism is always on the outskirts of his
life, a portentous and immovable presence, challenging
and irritating him. But the majority of Mr. Bennett's
characters do not criticise their Methodism or even contest it. They accept it magnificently as it is, attending
its services and filling its offices, convinced that their
form of worship is the best possible, and that all others
are inferior to it. Their Methodism indeed has become
part of the local clan life of the district, separating
them from the other clans.

This assumption, like many others that appear unreasonable, had its origin in the past. The Methodist Societies
of a hundred years ago lived apart from the world around
them, partly because they professed aims and experienced
joys which were not shared by most of their neighbours,
and partly because those neighbours despised Methodists
and eschewed their society. The tale of these early
Methodists, their joys and sorrows, privations and heroism, though known to a few, is still unknown to the majority of their fellow-countrymen, and this ignorance is not
surprising; it is the fate of most religious heroes.

But Mr. Bennett is naturally concerned with the great
grandchildren of early Methodists, and sternly ignores the
shades of heroic ancestors. He brings his searchlights to
play on the aims and motives of persons who use phrases
and sing hymns which imply supernatural standards of conduct on the part of those who utter them. So the question
that forces itself on the mind of his readers is this. In
what do the people of the Wesleyan Methodist clan really

differ from those of other clans? Are their vital interests and occupations different from those of other human
beings?

Now the vital interests of human life as pictured by
Mr. Bennett are twofold, the passion for making money and
the sex passion. The supreme aim of a man's life, he
shows, is and should be to make money. By his ability
to do this he wins both his own self-respect and the esteem
of those around him. When he is a superior order of man
like Clayhanger or the Card, he longs to perfect his
talents or to embark on adventures, but always with the
prospect of money at the end of the labour and the adventure. A labour indeed and an adventure that did not hold
out this prospect would not be worth the undertaking; for
the ultimate value of every activity in the Five Towns of
commercial England is its equivalent in cash. In no other
British novel, surely, is the all pervading money value so
predominant; and the Methodist clan, as pictured by Mr.
Bennett, forms no exception to the rule. Its members are
equally dominated by the passion for money getting and the
prime necessity for seeing all things in their cash equi-
valents: Methodists who are loyal to their Church and
devoted to its welfare, bring their monetary values into
its affairs and councils. Occasionally the master passion
of their lives breaks all restraint, and we have pictures
like that of Ephraim Tellwright, the Methodist miser, and
the wretched Sunday-school superintendent who commits
suicide in his clutches.

But athwart this passion for hard cash gleams the
attraction and the passion of sex. The hero on his quest
has to meet the heroine on hers. Now the women characters
of Mr. Bennett are exceedingly interesting, and quite the
most significant in his portrait gallery. They merit
examination not only because many of them profess the religion of Methodism, and are therefore relevant to the purpose of this article, but because ordinary women have
seldom received the dispassionate and minute treatment
of Mr. Bennett. Ordinary women, as a rule, do not interest
the male novelist except in so far as they touch the lives
and meet the needs of the men around them. But Mr. Bennett's heroines have a history apart from the heroes. Many
of them have to earn their own living, and, contrary to
established opinion, take a distinct pleasure in doing so.
Into the struggle and adventure for cash they enter, often
with much of the zest of the hero, keeping their own coun-
sel and hardening their hearts, as he does. Should marriage relieve them from bearing the brunt of the battle,
they still participate in it, because they, too, need
money to spend or to save, and always acquiesce in those

methods which seem likely to obtain it.

Heroines like Leonora, who neither toil nor spin, are careful to bestow their favours on men of means; and when the hero keeps a shop his wife can actively share in the business. She becomes then, in a true sense, the life-long partner of her husband. The ecstasy of their early married life fades into a memory of the past, but neither differences of temperament nor of point of view can dissolve the golden link which makes their financial interests one.

The sex passion therefore does not seriously clash with the hero's financial prospects, as the heroine either shares his passion or is imbued from her youth with an immense respect for cash values; and the heroines who profess Wesleyan Methodism form no exception to the rule. Methodism cannot deliver Anna Tellwright from the sway of a miserly father or prevent her from carrying out his merciless precepts. As an heiress she is a financial asset to the man who loves her, but beyond that cardinal fact she has no influence on his business methods and no interest in the human beings whom he employs, and that is the case with most wives of wealthy men in the Five Towns. Even if they were not there, their busband's business would go on just the same, as that business is a prime necessity and an end in itself.

But there are other sides of men's lives which they do affect very much. No other English novelist has devoted so much care and attention to the middle-class woman in her home.* The Card, as well as Edwin Clayhanger, knows on opening his own front door, that he is entering a realm which he no longer controls. Yet his wife is the reverse of assertive, and is the very opposite of Clayhanger's masterful wife. As a girl she was a sweet, clinging creature who evoked the sympathy and the chivalrous instinct of the man who married her. But as wife and mother she has become a woman of power. Most of the women who preside over the domestic realm are in Mr. Bennett's eye women of power, and their power often is in inverse proportion to their ability to use it.

What pictures of powerful and incompetent mothers he gives in those professing Methodists, Mrs. Baines and her daughter Constance. Constance can never say 'No' to her only son, who disregards in consequence all her wishes; and when her husband throws himself into the cause of a fellow-citizen she impedes him to the best of her power, because she cannot understand why he should imperil his health and personal ease for one who does not belong to the family circle. The four walls which had always confined her, draw closer about her as she grows old, until

she becomes a prisoner within them. Yet the four walls
are merely the shell of what was once a home, and she has
both the means and the opportunity to procure change of
scene as well as domestic improvement. But she clings to
the shell and knows no life outside its senseless routine,
yet she is a member of the Wesleyan Communion, and on the
day before her death the minister pays her a visit. The
religion that he represents, however, is powerless either
to comfort her heart or to enlarge and beautify her life.

Religion also is unable to curb and guide the powers
of women like Auntie Hamps and Aunt Harriet, against whom
the novelist bears a special grudge, and who work havoc
in households which are not theirs. The fact that such
persons profess to 'lean hard' on certain tenets of their
religion increases their repulsiveness. They 'lean hard'
on the unfortunate young people whom they crush and misunderstand, and worship heathen gods, the conventions and
prejudices of people who are ignorant and well-to-do.

Through sheer observation of the facts, therefore, Mr.
Bennett has depicted a certain equality between men and
women. Women have disabilities and limitations imposed
upon them, but they also have special privileges and
powers. The hunger for money and the desires of sex
belong to them as well as to men, and religion cannot
deliver either men or women from excess in these cravings
or atone for any lack in their satisfaction.† Both hero
and heroine are in bondage to the master passions, and
from their heart at times goes up a cry for deliverance.
Anna Tellwright at the Revival Service prays in vain for
a power that will lift her above herself, and in so doing
is typical of the novelist's better characters. But the
religion which they profess has no power to deliver or
heal. It is part of their everyday life, an inseparable
adjunct of it, like the streets of the Five Towns and the
furniture of their best parlours, but it has no concern
with the most absorbing things in their lives, money and
sex.

Mr. Bennett cannot conceive of Methodism as a positive
power delivering men and women in the hour of their Destiny; he does perceive it as a force that is able to
restrain them. Sophia Baines is not saved in the hour
of her Destiny, but when she has taken the fatal step,
the inherited instincts of Methodist forbears prevent
her from sinking into the mire. With a passion that
surprises herself as much as the reader, she retains her
purity and self-respect in the world of Paris, driving
hard bargains with the sinners around her. In the Siege
of Paris she makes a corner in provisions, and when it is
over runs a boarding-house famous for its first-rate

management and unimpeached respectability. She takes a
grim pleasure in her own business acumen, but she lives
joyless and self-centred, a splendid icicle in the glittering life of Paris. Yet she is full of glorious capacity
for joy - joy that her pride and youthful sin make for
ever impossible.††

Methodism, therefore, in the Five Towns restrains the
actions of certain people and finds employment for a
smaller number. But it is quite exceptional for men and
women to take joy in their religion. That it is possible
to experience true delight in its service or anything
approaching poetic rapture, never occurs to them. Its
officials are either creatures of routine or apostles
of gloom. Yet it is the ecstasy, the emotional excess
of Methodism that distinguishes it from other forms of
religious life. In temper often it has been Catholic
and Southern rather than Protestant and British, for which
reason it has never quite won the approval of many sober,
clear-headed people. There were terrors in early Methodism, but the terrors had corresponding joys, though these
unfortunately have attracted less attention, just as the
joys of Dante's 'Purgatorio' and 'Paradiso' have been
overshadowed by the more sensational horrors of his
'Inferno.'

In Mr. Bennett's picture of the people called Methodists there is only the terror, the terror not of a distant theological hell but of a judgment here and now on
the sins and frailties of men:-

> It is strange how Fate persists in justifying the
> harsh generalisations of Puritan morals, of the morals
> in which Constance had been brought up by her stern
> parents. Sophia had sinned. It was therefore inevit-
> able that she should suffer. An adventure such as she
> had in wicked and capricious pride undertaken with
> Gerald Scales, could not conclude otherwise than it had
> concluded. It could have brought nothing but evil.
> ('Old Wives' Tale.')

This view of human life might be described as an obsession
with him. Not only does he frequently reiterate it but it
is stamped on every tale that he tells. When the sinner
himself is unable to pay the full penalty, his child or
some other innocent person does it in his stead. On the
pure soul of Annunciata falls the burden and guilt of her
father's sin. She atones for that which the previous
habits and dulled consciences of her parents do not permit
them to expiate. Even in those cases where his men and
women seem to evade all those penalties which they should

rightly incur, we feel that their fate is only postponed.
Leonora has extraordinary luck and secures perhaps a
temporary respite, but she no more than anybody else will
evade judgment or obtain peace of mind and the satisfaction of her cravings.

Such, then, is the picture that the novelist paints of
Methodist people in commercial England, and no truthful
person can deny the accuracy of his portraiture. What he
has seen he has faithfully reproduced, and Methodists who
do not blind their eyes to the facts, know that he has
seen a good deal. He sees money values dominating the
councils of that Church just as they dominate other councils of men, and he observes men and women conducting
their love affairs like their business transactions, in
watertight compartments which deny their own hymns. He
sees routine and triviality in places where they need not
exist and in the sheltered homes of well-to-do people he
perceives beautiful young life, rich in promise of power
and joy, but doomed by parental selfishness and its own
frailty to incur terrors of judgment in the future.
Sombre and gloomy as the picture is, it is scarcely a
surprising one. No careful observer of modern Methodism
could fail to perceive what Mr. Bennett has so brilliantly
depicted.

But what is astonishing is that which the novelist has
not seen. He only sees the rich people sitting in the
front pews and those clients who sit behind them. There
are Methodist heroes and heroines of whom he knows nothing;
who lack indeed the instinct for cash values but are alive
with other instincts. For every parody of Methodism pictured by Mr. Bennett it is easy to name a dozen persons
who are a credit to it. But the dozen are often unknown
people who do not proclaim their own virtues, though they
are to be found everywhere, even in the chapels of the
Five Towns. There are unselfish dressmakers and shop-
assistants, cheery carpenters and men of business, into
the secret of whose lives Mr. Bennett has never seen, for
they are outside the glittering circle in which cash
values and the sex passion reign supreme. Even to that
circle surely he is often unfair. Its men and women
cherish aspirations and perform kindly acts which have
escaped his observation. There are wealthy men who know
how to be generous and really attractive women who can be
unselfish. In the chapel of the Five Towns sit quiet men
and women - ministers' wives, chapel keepers, and obscure
Sunday-school teachers - who could tell tales of the
congregation that he cannot. For every sin and longing
after sin they could cite a good deed (forgotten perhaps
by the doer) and tell tales that would break the heart

of how sinful men longed and strove after righteousness.

The people who really know seldom write. As a writer himself, Mr. Walter Bagehot once put it: 'The worst of people who write is that they know so little.' But the art of expression when it is understood and perfected, is such a wonderful thing that it is easy to credit the masters of it with a knowledge they do not possess. Mr. Bennett can see religion as a restraining force in the lives of sinful human beings and, on certain emotional occasions, as an unlovely demand for repentance and righteousness. What he cannot perceive is that Methodism, or any other religion, should provide the poetry and passionate inner secret of a life. Religion to him is never a vital, creative thing that causes the heart to sing. He does not see that the religion which he despises has provided more than revival meetings and popular preachers and prohibitions; it has provided the inner poetry of lives, and that is the real power of Methodism, or any other religion – its poetry. Into the lives of toiling and struggling men and women a secret joy has entered, a passion which lifts them above the world. Bit by bit it has illumined and moulded other passions, delivering them from egoism.

The writer recollects a carpenter to whom it was said: 'I believe you are a Methodist?' Instantly his face was transformed, as he dropped his tools out of sheer delight. 'I am, Mum. Our circuit is ——,and our minister the Rev. ——,is a fine fellow.' Then he began relating the trials and victories of his church, while his face shone like that of a poet declaiming his own verse.

On another occasion the writer used to visit an old lady, who was not only an intense Methodist, but one whose religion had opened her heart and mind to the needs and interests of the world around her. Of education in the ordinary sense she had had none, but she read her newspaper daily, after her chapter in the Bible, and gleaned from them and other sources an amount of information that was sometimes disconcerting to her listener. She was a working woman, and had had a family of sons and daughters to bring up, but she knew more of the public life of England than most women of the leisured middle-class. Religion by cleansing her heart had illuminated her brain; and the same phenomenon has been seen again and again in the towns and villages of England. Men who would otherwise be loafing over the village bar have been so quickened by their study of the Bible and the institutions of their church, that they take an intelligent interest in human life. As class leaders and local preachers they have been trained not only to study and to express themselves, but to guide the lives of others and to manage the affairs of a community.

The position which Methodism accords to her laity, while insisting on certain ministerial privileges, is very remarkable, and has done more to uplift and educate influential groups of working men than many a direct educational agency. The Methodist church has penetrated behind counters and into back parlours which were hermetically sealed against the ordinary avenues of culture. Indeed, like the author of the Epistle to the Hebrews, the writer feels powerless to indicate the number of those who have lived and died in a faith that taught them to view the everyday world in the light of a vaster, unseen world. By such men and women surely rather than by its hypocrites and backsliders Methodism should be judged, - even in the Five Towns.

Yet Mr. Bennett's portraits, like the distorted and grotesque figures seen in dreams, have a haunting quality; for they reveal with a grimness equal to that of any mediaeval or early Methodist preacher, the fate of men and women who are impenitent egoists, chained to self and its desires. Their bodies are well fed and comfortably housed in a corner of commercial England, but their state of mind often recalls those visions of a Hell where men lie imprisoned in burning tombs, and chase along arid plains banners which elude and mirages that fade. In their hearts, as in that Hell, the worm dieth not and the fire is not quenched.

Notes

*Imagine Rudyard Kipling or Sir Conan Doyle or Rider Haggard or any other typical British novelist devoting the pages which Mr. Bennett does, to detailed descriptions of household life and domestic management.

†In the sins of sex he regards men and women as equally guilty. Other novelists often try to account for and condone such sins, either from the man's point of view or the woman's; but Mr. Bennett sternly refuses to do this. The moral sensibilities of the governess Mademoiselle Renée are as deadened and perverted as those of her employer, and the novelist makes no attempt to excuse the sin of either.

††Part of Mr. Bennett's power consists in making us feel this. The capacities of many heroes and heroines of fiction do not impress us. When they miss joy we do not feel that they have missed much, because their joy, like themselves, would lack zest and colour and be of a mild watery description. But it is the reverse with his

characters, who are full of wonderful vitality and never cease craving for and demanding their birthright.

'The Pretty Lady'

28 March 1918

89. A.S. WALLACE IN THE 'MANCHESTER GUARDIAN'

28 March 1918, 3

A.S. Wallace succeeded A.N. Monkhouse as literary editor
of the 'Manchester Guardian'. He served on the paper for
many years, retiring in 1941.

The framework on which Mr. Bennett hangs his book is the
attachment of a wealthy bachelor of fifty to a Parisian
courtesan who comes to London as a refugee from Ostend in
1914. The note of light-hearted cynicism struck at the
opening of this episode, in the promenade of a famous
music-hall, is sustained throughout, and is dominant in
all the selected glimpses he gives of London in the first
three years of war. As these glimpses succeed one another
the impression emerges of the whole as a social satire
which draws its force not from indictment or open irony
but from a positively zestful preoccupation with the
selfishness, futility, hysteria, and vice which war
stresses in a great capital. That astonishing power
of Mr. Bennett's to build up swiftly and vividly a whole
character or scene by the use of a few significant details,
and to reach out confidently for the unlikely and audacious
but quite perfect phrase, is here lavished on describing
the *ménage* and mentality of a courtesan, the vaporous discussions of a war charity committee manned by 'society
women' and snobs, the hectic excitements of the night club,
the platitudes of the club proper, the obsession of titled
amateurs with barefoot dancing in the interests of the

372

wounded, and the views of prostitutes about the increasing restrictions on the 'gay life.' Sometimes the satire is almost intolerable, as when the chairman of the Lechford War Hospitals Committee replies 'with calm self-control' to a vote of condolence on the loss of his son at the front:

'Yes, and if I had ten sons I would willingly give them all - for the cause.' And his firm, hard glance appeared to challenge any member of the committee to assert that this profession of parental and patriotic generosity of heart was not utterly sincere. However, nobody had the air of doubting that if the chairman had had ten sons, or as many sons as Solomon, he would have sacrificed them all with the most admirable and eager heroism.

Sometimes the constant raillery is laid aside to allow full view of such a gem-like picture as that of the funeral of Lord Roberts in the Abbey; or it fails, as it must, in the face of a Zeppelin raid, when the 'pretty lady' is carried home to her flat in a faint and our comfortable bachelor finds a child's severed arm come hurtling at him over the house-tops. But these breaks in the pattern of the book serve only to strengthen the general design.

And what of human nature does it give us to set beside, not Edwin Clayhanger or Mrs. Gerald Scales - for it makes no pretence to be of the genre or scope of the books that framed their portraits, - but, let us say, of the people in 'The Card' or 'The Regent'? A couple of brilliant neurotic society women, one of whom is killed in an air raid while the other is left contemplating suicide, are drawn, or rather overdrawn, with tremendous skill. The slack sentimentalist of fifty whose love affair is the main theme is chiefly useful as the means through which we see the phases of London life that the author would show us. Of them all, doubtless by design, it is the courtesan, Christine, who stands out as real, demanding more than mere admiration of the cleverness spent in sketching her. Her consuming hope that some day she will be 'put among her own furniture' by a reliable elderly lover, her mystic belief that she is appointed to be the godmother of a shattered artillery officer who stumbles into her flat from the trenches - 'In playing the slave to him she had the fierce French illusion of killing Germans,' - her expansion in the sunshine of domesticity when a brief security comes to her, her final disappearance, through a miserable misunderstanding, into a void

blacker than that from which she emerged – these, despite
an analysis of the stratagems and devices of her professional career that is Maupassant-like in its ruthlessness,
give her a humanity that shines in contrast with the rest
of this world of humbug and hysteria.

In its breathlessly clever use of words the book is
perhaps the most brilliant Mr. Bennett has given us, but
after this frenzied excursion into life high and gay it
would be just splendidly restful to be back again in the
Five Towns.

90. JAMES DOUGLAS, IN THE 'STAR'

5 April 1918, 4

When Bennett died in 1931, Douglas wrote an appreciation
of him in the 'Sunday Express' (29 March) entitled My
Friend Arnold Bennett. He recalled there how he had
slated 'The Pretty Lady' and how the very next day he had
run into Bennett at the Reform Club. Bennett came up to
him in the smoking room:

> Smiling mischievously at me he took his cigar case out
> of his breast pocket, and gave me a cigar.
> 'James', he said, 'I forgive you'. As I lighted the
> cigar of truce, I retorted: 'Arnold, is this a pardon
> or a punishment?' How he laughed!... He bore no
> malice. He possessed the divine gift of forgiveness.

Mr. Arnold Bennett apologises for his new novel, 'The
Pretty Lady' by prefacing it with this quotation from that
master of irony, Samuel Butler: 'Virtue has never yet been
adequately represented by any who have had any claim to be
considered virtuous. It is the subvicious who best understand virtue. Let the virtuous stick to describing vice –
which they can do well enough.' I decline to express any
opinion as to whether 'The Pretty Lady' proves the truth
of Butler's paradox. It is a description of vice, realistic in details, sentimental in treatment. The sentiment
is meant to drape the realism and make it palatable to the
British palate. As it is false sentiment, it has no claim
to be palliated on the ground that it is artistic. The

relations between Christine and 'G.J.' are disagreeable, not merely because they are illicit, but because they are varnished over with artificial romance.

If this book had been written and published before the war, it might have been reprieved as a brilliantly hard study of decadent London life. But the war forces the critic to set up a severe standard of aim and intention for art as well as for other forms of national energy. No artist has any right to fall below that standard of aim and intention. If he does so deliberately, he is not a good citizen. It is his duty to ennoble his readers and to inspire them with ideals which will make them better fit to do their part in the national struggle. If he sets out to amuse them, he must amuse them harmlessly and helpfully. Subjected to these tests, it must be said that Mr. Bennett has done his country an ill turn by writing this book in mid-war. In the first place, he has painted a meretriciously false portrait of a courtesan, using all his literary skill to romanticise and sentimentalise her dreadful trade. He has falsified the facts of life in order to excuse and extenuate his minute presentation of ugly details. The book is a medley of false realism and false romance, and artistically it is a complete failure.

Its hardness of heart is repulsive, and although its desperate strivings after softness of heart may be evidence of the author's consciousness of his failure as an artist, they do not in any way persuade me to condone the theme of its treatment. He tries hard to secure sympathy for Christine and her despicable parasite, and he goes so far as to call in a sham religiosity to assist him. It is a futile attempt, and it breaks down ludicrously over and over again. I know that it may be said that it is all objectively dramatic, and that one has no right to confuse the self-deception of an author's characters with the self-deception of the author. But the thing goes deeper than that. Mr. Bennett represents certain spiritual states and moral emotions in certain people who are manifestly incapable of experiencing them. His human nature is as false as his observation of their environment is unpleasant.

When Rossetti wrote 'Jenny' he wrought pity in the minds of his readers, but I find no such effect in Mr. Bennett's handling of the same theme. He does not move his readers to pity Christine or 'G.J.' or Lady Queenie or Concepcion. To my mind the lack of moral unity in the book is its gravest fault. One might forgive that if there were in it the whip of the satirist, but I cannot

believe in a satirist who sentimentalises odiously
successful degenerates. I hardly care to say what I think
of Lady Queenie and Concepcion, because one cannot analyse
poison gas. One can only smell it and clap on one's gas-
mask.

The pen has its victories as well as the sword, and
every English pen ought to be a clean, shining weapon.
Our novelists ought to write for the young citizens of
both sexes who are in sore need of mental and moral sus-
tenance. The war has given them a thousand high themes.
Why on earth should they go nosing about our metropolitan
drains? Why should they lavish their literary cunning
upon cesspools? The land is full of unimaginable hero-
isms. Our boys are being martyred by the million. Hearts
are being lacerated by incalculable sorrows. This is no
time to regale our hurt minds with glimpses of the nether
world. We are not in the mood for idylls of the promenade
and pastorals of the pavement.

91. W.L. COURTNEY, IN THE 'DAILY TELEGRAPH'

5 April 1918, 3

W.L. Courtney (1850-1928) reviewed for the 'Daily Telegraph' and for other journals for many years.

Mr. Arnold Bennett owes no small measure of his popularity
to his vivid appreciation of what is topical and up-to-
date. He is remarkably clever; he possesses a keen
journalistic instinct; he has ample resource and a quick
divining mind; he is admirably responsive to all the
interests of the time; he can draw characters which live
and write conversations which really reveal. A sympathetic observation we hardly expect from him: he rarely
yields to mere sentiment, and never to mere sentimentality;
there is a hard, metallic glitter about his style and his
mode of construction, which is triumphantly effective just
in proportion as it fails to win our regard. We admire,
but do not cherish; applaud but do not always take his
books to our hearts. He has a dozen ways of gaining our
attention, and whatever he may exhibit patently to our

gaze, we are convinced that he has a great deal more in
reserve. Admirably equipped as a raconteur, he seems to
be something more than the teller of stories; he is the
august impersonator of a particular period, he is the
twentieth century incarnate, giving us the very form and
pressure of our time. We can imagine that to anyone who
asks what is the twentieth century, almost without thinking we should answer, 'Mr. Arnold Bennett.'

His latest novel is called 'The Pretty Lady.' The
title gives the story away. It is a close and penetrating
study of a fille de joie, intimately and intensely French,
in her relations with a selfish, superior, capable
Englishman, who is 50 years of age, and has an abundance
of matured experience of life. But it is more than that.
It is equally a study, and a very brilliant one, of London
society - the smartest set, bien entendu - and their behaviour in times of war. Hence it is excessively topical;
it boldly grapples with what some novelists have found an
encumbrance, a problem at once annoying and insuperable,
the dreadful reality of the titanic European struggle.
One of the principal personages of the story is killed by
a piece of shrapnel, because she insists on going to the
roof of her house to see a Zeppelin; and there is a vivid
sketch of what happens in London streets during an air
raid, which would be hard to beat in its poignant intensity. And, indeed, there is more in the novel even than
the moral and social effects of war. There are two portraits - quite apart from Christine, the pretty lady -
admirably drawn, one a society type of a selfish aristocratic war-worker, Lady Queenie Paulle; the other a more
complex character, more difficult to understand, and perhaps not quite so successful in its delineation, Concepcion
Iquist, afterwards Mrs. Carlos Smith.

I imagine that his characters ran away with Mr. Arnold
Bennett, as characters have a way of doing with their
creators. Every novelist will tell you that A and B and C
would insist on going their own path, despite the careful
guiding hand of their anxious parent, and launched themselves into all sorts of unforeseen complications, thus
causing endless trouble by their perversity. Do you suppose that G.T. Hoape (why so ugly a name?), the man of 50,
originally intended to marry Concepcion after poor Carlos
Smith got himself killed in the war? Not a bit of it. He
was very afraid of Concepcion, and knew that he could have
been quite happy living with Christine in their 'nid
d'amour.' Why, too, did Queenie stupidly allow herself
to become the victim of an idiotic bit of shrapnel so

comparatively early in the story? She was, I feel sure,
intended for better things - to marry G.T. Hoape perhaps,
and to learn the higher ethics from the lips of that
intelligent but slightly pedantic moralist. And Christine,
too, dainty, attractive, good-hearted, 'pretty lady. -'
But that is another story, which requires a paragraph to
itself.

We must not suppose for a moment that Christine is
intended to point a moral or adorn a tale. Nevertheless
she does serve this purpose, whether with or without Mr.
Bennett's consent. For she is the heroine of the book,
and on her our interest and to a large extent our sympathy
are concentrated. The author is a realist, and therefore
we have none of the theatrical limelight which illumines
the figure of the 'Dame aux Camellias.' But by subtle
touches here and there she is made for us both real and
human - a wicked little sinner and yet indubitably charming. Of course, she has temperament - all the women in
the novel have temperament. And quite in the proper moral
way she is made to suffer - not, indeed, for her delin-
quencies, but for a curious element in her of super-
stitious mysticism. Just because she has an immense
reverence for 'the Virgin of the VII. dolours' and of a
supposed task of healing committed to her charge by Heaven
itself, she loses her lover, who thinks her no better than
a wanton. Poor Christine! She is a victim of the perversity of Fate. G.J. has not much imagination, but he
might - if the author of his being had been a sentimentalist - have given her another chance. How all this comes
about I must leave the reader to discover for himself.
I can safely promise him that in the perusal of the book
he will not often have a dull moment. It is all very
clever, more than a little cynical, and tremendously up-
to-date.

92. UNSIGNED REVIEW, 'STAFFORDSHIRE SENTINEL'

24 April 1918, 2

See p. 81 for an excerpt from the 'Sunday Chronicle'
review to which this review alludes.

We have read Mr. Arnold Bennett's new novel, 'The Pretty
Lady,' with all the more care because of the slashing
attack upon it that recently appeared in the 'Sunday
Chronicle' - an attack based upon its sexual references
and its supposed offence to Roman Catholics. We have had
no opportunity of ascertaining what Roman Catholics really
think about it; but the passages referred to describe the
spiritual comfort which a prostitute curiously derives
from praying before the Lady of the VII. Dolours. The
episode assists to reveal the unusual personality (according to Mr. Bennett) of this French prostitute, Christine,
the daughter of a French courtesan who tried to secure an
innocent life for her daughter, but being unable to make
her independent, initiated her into the 'profession' so
that she might practise it to the best advantage. While
the novel seems open to considerable criticism, not so
much from the point of view of workmanship, as from that
of the higher qualities of literature, we come to the conclusion that the 'Sunday Chronicle' article was more sensational than sound, and that it failed to grasp Mr.
Bennett's point of view.

   Christine had gone from Paris to Ostend upon an adventure; she escapes from Ostend when the Germans enter,
and comes to practise her 'profession' in London, carefully investing her savings in French securities. While
leading a life of constant promiscuity, her journeyings
being limited between her flat and certain theatre promen-
ades (what does the L.C.C. say about this?), Christine
falls in love with a stodgy and priggish bachelor of
fifty, who moves in fashionable society, and who becomes
enamoured of her; and after she has for some time shared
his attentions with others, he places her 'amongst her
own furniture,' as the French phrase has it, and at this
moment abandons her.

   This Mr. Hoape, commonly called 'G.J.' by his friends,
is for reasons not obvious an object of affection to two
society ladies, one of whom gets killed in an air raid,
leaving the other practically to make an offer of marriage
to 'G.J.,' which he accepts. It is not clear that he
would have broken with Christine, the lady of the promen-
ades; but he does Christine a grave injustice, by placing
a hasty and the worst and a terrible misinterpretation
upon an action of hers without seeking any explanation,
and, though she awaits him, he is never going back.

   Christine, according to Mr. Bennett, has, though
practising her 'profession' deliberately (impelled thereto
partly by the necessity of living and partly by temperament), always scorned the ordinary street-walker, and has
retained an air, appearance, and disposition of refinement.

Most people would say it couldn't be; but Mr. Bennett,
with his photographic and microscopic faculty of observation, would probably insist that Christine is a reality.

Truth to tell, we found this novel rather difficult to
read, and had to stick at it by force of will. There are
'realisms' about Christine which repel by their flagrancy
and crudity, and oblige us to say that it is in some
respects a dangerous book; but these 'purple patches' are
not numerous and are but incidental to the novel as a whole.
The novel is certainly far below the plane of Gustave
Flaubert or Thomas Hardy; and though it contains a great
deal about the War, it is rather of the Times Weekly' and
'Annual Register' order, and it can scarcely be regarded
as a 'War novel,' or a society novel, in the sense that
'Vanity Fair' is a novel of the Waterloo period. There
are what may be called journalistic summaries of the War,
and there are minute descriptions of several sorts of
London houses; but Mr. Bennett's passion for detailed
descriptions is almost a vice, and extraordinarily clever
as they are, they are scarcely inspired. For that reason,
perhaps the realisms about Christine may fail to do much
harm, though young and sensitive people should not read
it. Nor can we regard it as a fair picture of general
London life in War-time. The glimpses of this sort of
thing are vague, and 'G.J.' and his two 'respectable'
lady-friends, whose temperaments are so irritating and
unrestful compared with Christine's tact, are something
of freaks. Perhaps as becomes so constant a contributor
to the 'Daily News,' Mr. Bennett doesn't intend to give
London society credit for much sincerity, unless it be
allied with stupidity. He has had a great opportunity,
and has, perhaps deliberately, thrown it away, and thus
gives us not another 'Old Wives' Tale,' but a novel which
on the whole we class with the 'pot-boilers' with which he
interludes his more serious work. We hope we do Mr. Bennett no injustice in this; and would ask if the Foreword
is part of the joke. But whatever classification the
novel belongs to, it is clever. Mr. Bennett is the cleverest of English contemporary novelists, as an artist in
words; but that does not give him the first prize.

One of the realities of the book is the soldier who
believed in charms - and so many people do; and the reference to charms and mysterious voices must, we suppose, be
taken as a further piling up of photographic descriptiveness. We expect that Mr. Bennett, an industrious literary
artist, has a profound and healthy-minded contempt, or it
may be a contemptuous compassion, for people who favour
visions and charms; and has dragged in these references
as a characteristic of the times and a sop to the credu-
lous.

Written with less photographic descriptiveness, and a
higher purpose and a larger vision, the novel might have
become distinguished. Looking back upon the novel, it
mostly fades away into the problem of the character of
Christine; and if Mr. Bennett after all intended it mainly
as a character-study of Christine, he has been conspicuously successful. It is a revolting theme; and yet human
nature is so curious and complex that there is an inter-
mittent wonder as to whether there may not after all be a
Christine here and there. Mr. Wells, in 'Marriage,' has
effectively discussed the question of the multiplicity of
people sometimes found under one hat; and looked at as
pure art, for the purpose of illustrating Christine's
character, the 'purple patches,' which are undoubtedly
very skilful, become less offensive. The corollary is
that Christine is very badly used by G.J., and that it is
dreadful to speculate upon what further degradations there
might be in store for Christine. Does she become a saint
or a devil? And there are other alternatives. Does Mr.
Bennett contemplate a sequel; or is the novel so 'up-to-
date,' that 'time does not permit'? The last lingering
feeling about the novel, the concluding sentences of which
are almost poignant, is a feeling of anxiety about the
fate of Christine. So Mr. Bennett must have made her very
much alive and endowed his creation with human vividness.
He has the knack of visualising the women he writes about.
In most of his novels, as we long ago remarked, and continue to think, the women he introduces have more definite
actuality than the men.

93. FRANCIS HACKETT, IN THE 'NEW REPUBLIC'

15 June 1918, 210-11

In Mr. Arnold Bennett, it is convenient to say, there are
two seams of personality. From the more difficult seam he
has extracted his masterpieces. In those few volumes, subdued yet rich and varied, he has exhibited a power of
keeping his sensations inside the frame of permanent human
relationships and sympathies. He has taken the commonest
of themes - brothers and sisters, fathers and mothers,
aunts and uncles - and to them he has given full yet
beautifully measured consideration, thronging his account
of them with that plenitude of detail which is never

successful unless penetrated with emotion. In regard
to everything that concerns those domiciliary themes
Mr. Bennett has been master. If one thinks of them
as material to be matured, few gestations have been
so perfect as his gestation of the philistine Five Towns.

But there is another Mr. Bennett, a Mr. Bennett whose
capacity for sensation singularly outruns his capacity for
emotion, a cheaper and more vivacious Mr. Bennett who has
left the Philistia that nourished him to strut in Paris
and London. This second Mr. Bennett is a much more flashing person, but where in the Five Towns he was truly a man
of the world, in the world he is essentially a man of the
Five Towns. This is not his intention. All aware inside
of the deficiencies that are native to philistine England
and to himself, Mr. Bennett's pride requires a high attitude, and he quickly affects the airs of what he considers
'connoiseurship' and fastidiousness, and he takes the vengeance of ostentation on the world that reproves his
uneasiness. This gaucherie is only important because it
deranges Mr. Bennett's sympathies. Where he is thoroughly
at home an extraordinary degree of sympathy emanates from
him. Where he is not sure of himself, his vanity and
self-consciousness impede him, and he becomes extremely
anxious to show that he is 'initiated' and 'understands
life.' The real man, the Wordsworthian Englishman in him,
is only accessible when experience has mellowed him and
assured him that he is in no way absurd.

In 'The Pretty Lady' Mr. Bennett is more assured about
London than heretofore, but on the whole it is rather a
bad assurance. There are frequent passages so finished
and lustrous that Mr. Wells in all his glory has scarcely
excelled them, but the totality of the book is inferior.
The brightness of the surface, however, is stabbing. How
is a novelist to give prompt effectiveness to the moral
chaos of the war? Mr. Bennett understands England well
enough to know that nothing could so instantaneously mark
a change in the whole tone of life as the installment of a
prostitute at the centre of interest, so quite coolly and
deliberately he focusses the British institution of the
music-hall promenade, and from that market of sexuality he
takes a French cocotte and he places her at the heart of
his story. The significance of this choice is its definite relation to the war. The leave-train from the front
brings the drunken officer to her, and it is she who
dresses the officer hurriedly to rush him back to France.
Her neighbor is a 'Russian' cocotte just back from the
Irish rebellion - the discarded companion of a member of
the Irish administration, now linked up with a colonel.
The 'night clubs' attract others, youths back from Suvla

and elderly men home for a week-end, men who have done
their duty by their relatives and are now 'on the loose.'
Mr. Bennett's frankness about fornication, the Londoner's
acceptance of unlimited fornication as the concomitant of
war, is enough in itself to upset the pieties of the old
order; but in addition to this disclosure of 'the pretty
lady' as a much-needed consolatrix there are the personages of Lady Queenie Paulle and Concepcion Iquist, 'super-
celebrated' pursuers of sensation up to and beyond the
ordinary limits. The shadows cast by the monde and the
demi-monde interlace and entangle in this novel. The link
to its three conspicuous women is a well-off bachelor of
nearly fifty. A sensible, substantial Englishman, he is
romantic enough to give himself to war-work once the
implications of the war reach him; and he is matter-of-
fact enough to accept from the French girl, Christine,
the voluptuous girlishness that his fifty-year nature
enjoys.

By letting down the barriers of respectability, Mr.
Bennett is enabled to represent in full measure the torrent of his sensations from the war. To him the war is
more than a political exigency. It is something that has
come out of the lairs of human nature - a force stronger
than all the civilized restraints from which it has
plunged forward, slavering and panting. 'The war was
growing,' his hero reflects, 'or the sense of its measure-
less scope was growing. It had sprung, not out of this
crime or that, but out of the secret invisble roots of
humanity, and it was widening to the limits of evolution
itself. It transcended judgment. It defied conclusions
and rendered equally impossible both hope and despair....
The supreme lesson of the war was its revelation of what
human nature actually was.' This is a candor quite different from the candor of statesmen, and by taking three
women on the edges of class - the cocotte, the spoiled and
reckless aristocratic girl, the adventurous masculine
woman with starved emotions - Mr. Bennett adds to the
revelation, shows how tremendously the war has registered
on personal conduct, and on no conduct so illustrative as
sex-conduct.

Up to a certain point it is done brilliantly. The
material that the war has poured in on Mr. Bennett he has
manipulated with amazing skill. It is not merely that he
narrates a conversation at the club with a new muscular-
ity, or describes a state funeral or an air-raid or an
inquest with superlative economy and force. He gives also
a most vigorous and sardonic version of the vulgar
fashionableness of war-work, the 'vicious foolery of
government departments,' the bathos of war-benefits and

pageants and bazaars, the hysterical efficiency of women's
contribution to making munitions, on the Clyde. There
are, in addition, bits of humanity such as the officer
giving the prostitute his mascot, the kind of naïveté that
is so revelatory. Mr. Bennett is munificent in 'The
Pretty Lady,' and his terseness was never so effective.

But interesting as it is to every one to read about
prostitution, I do not think that Christine's fate really
engaged Mr. Bennett. He says, in effect, 'See! I know
the inmost secrets of this young thing. I read her like
a book.' All too visibly he licks his chops in the
delight of possessing such insight. Her Catholicism, in
particular, he rejoices to reveal. But just as he calls
the Blessed Virgin a 'goddess' and so misses the essence
of devotion to the *Mother* of God, so he exhibits a pretentious smartness in much of his account of women throughout. 'Lady Queenie Paulle entered rather hurriedly, filling the room with a distinguished scent.... Lady Queenie
obviously had what is called "race."' Discernments like
these remind one of The Duchess. Christine's mysticism
and Lady Queenie's 'race' are part of Mr. Bennett's paraphernalia. His real purpose is to project the sensations
that the war had loaded on him, not to develop or reveal
these characters.

The inept ending of 'The Pretty Lady' discloses the
poverty on this side of Mr. Bennett's inspiration. He has
found little in Queenie or Christine or Concepcion or
G.J. Hoape, but admirable puppets for his present game.
The game, however, is a thrilling one. It is to preserve
the sensations of 1914-1917. And if Mr. Bennett had not
himself shown the artistic superiority of possessing personalities rather than sensations, his novel might be
warmly praised.

'The Roll-Call'

16 January 1919

94. A.N. MONKHOUSE, IN THE 'MANCHESTER GUARDIAN'

16 January 1919, 6

One would suppose that Mr. Bennett might have some influence in the selection of a 'dust cover' for his novel, and that which enfolds 'The Roll-call' suggests that he is not very serious this time. The design is rather clever, very hideous, and wildly unsuitable, and we may resent, too, the assertion, in a prominent advertisement, that 'can a man love two women is the theme of this novel.' It is nothing of the kind, though George Cannon does transfer his affections from a good, humble girl to an enchantress who is not a bad sort after all. George Cannon, it will be remembered, is Hilda Lessway's son, and we have glimpses of the Clayhangers and a slight, depressing one of the charming Janet Orgreave as a dry spinster. Obviously, then, this is a serious book, for Mr. Bennett could not tamper with his masterpieces even in a sequel, but it is not great in the 'Clayhanger' kind nor in the 'These Twain' kind. It is, of course, a good novel, but, strange to say, not a highly distinguished one; it is the work of Mr. Bennett's accomplishment, but not of his inspiration or of a fresh vision. In this frivolous London environment we miss the solidity of the Five Towns, and it appears that the people have more of mood than of character. And yet Mr. Bennett does give to them real values and not sham ones. It is the true fairy tale in which the charwoman may flash upon us as a princess and dingy, disreputable London may become an enchanted garden. Mr. Bennett comes from the Five Towns, and he is no more to be put down by London than was his Card. He will even show

385

you what a grand place it is, after all, and quite cheer
you up about it. And with that awful tolerance of the
artist he will give you brilliant pictures of its deprav-
tiy. He is a bit of a gossip, but he can be inspired to
turn and rend. There is, for instance, a fine and salu-
tary passage on a typical performance of musical comedy,
which describes the uneasiness of the hero under 'the
extraordinary juxtaposition of respectability and a ribald
sexual display.'

George Cannon is the young man adventuring who wants,
among other things, 'when the time came, to be finely
vicious,' and acknowledges to himself his need of luxury.
Yet he is capable of devotion, and perhaps Mr. Bennett
only means that all young men hanker after vice and
luxury. The desertion of the poor girl is not wholly
base, and if we seem to detect any harshness in relations,
we may expect that they will soon be humanised and ration-
alised. Even the glittering Lois is subdued by the enigmatic, and positively takes her place in the family scheme.
Mr. Bennett likes success, and Cannon has that in sufficiency till the war breaks out, and we leave him learning fast the ways of our strange military machine. This
account of the early experiences of an officer in the
Royal Artillery is excellent, but it is episodical; it
effaces other impressions, and one does not retain any
clear idea of the whole. Naturally the book is full of
close and witty descriptions, and if we are sometimes
dashed by the notion that Mr. Bennett has no difficulty
in ranging us all he is yet uncannily adept in perceiving
the significance of little variations. He is immensely
learned on woman and the marital relation, immensely
competent in presenting the aspects of things, and his
merits as an entertainer are prodigious. In mere read-
ableness the book is a masterpiece.

95. FRANCIS HACKETT, IN THE 'NEW REPUBLIC'

8 February 1919, 60-1

A profound inferiority seems to infect this novel by
Arnold Bennett - inferiority, that is to say, to his own
finer creations. It is not less skillful than the Clayhanger series. On the whole it is near the head of his
list for knowing craftsmanship. Nor is its subject-matter

less significant. Mr. Bennett's triumph so far has always
been to reveal significance in the supposedly dull and
mean-spirited bourgeoisie; and George Edwin Cannon, his
new preoccupation, is bourgeois to the bone. The
inferiority, if such it is, springs from a lack of serious
insight into the London variety of that middle-class life
about which the earlier Mr. Bennett was so inspired. The
London variety is piquant and exciting to Mr. Bennett but
it is not second-nature to him to write about it - and Mr.
Bennett has the kind of emotional slowness that needs
immense security before it can expand. 'The Roll-Call,'
it need hardly be said, is inescapably interesting. It is
sharply colored in detail and adroitly plotted out as a
whole. But for all its distinction, for all its flashi-
ness and appositeness, it is meagre in just those psychological and emotional certitudes that Mr. Bennett's preoccupation with the bourgeoisie leads one to expect.

'The Roll-Call' really marks Mr. Bennett's conquest by
London. Loudly as he once boasted that he'd show up the
provincialism of the great city, he has ended by succumb-
ing to its power and actually acquiring its most vulgar
point of view. The big northern municipalities survive
for him. They continually heave their bulk above the
horizon of 'The Roll-Call,' panting with energy and prosperity. But they are no longer seen as the centre of a
vital tradition, they are seen as the raw material for
George Edwin Cannon's architectural adventure. He is to
carve his career out of them in the form of gigantesque
town halls. It is in this mood of the unscrutinized ambitious, the ambitious mounting on the shoulders of London,
that Mr. Bennett interprets the capital. No longer, as he
once thought, is London the sophisticated and pretentious
and worldly elder brother of the strong, gruff, kindly
northern towns. It is instead a subtle and sinewy master
of all the arts and purposes to which humanity is heir.
It is, indeed, worldly, but it is impregnable in the very
civilization to which its contemporaries aspire. When
Hilda and Alderman Edwin Clayhanger come to town they come
as definite outsiders. They are estimable human beings
but, Mr. Bennett confesses it, they are jay.

This shift in emphasis brings into high relief the most
difficult of all social themes, metropolitan specialization and metropolitan concentration on success. Mr. Bennett had no longer on his hands a homogeneous group to be
carefully and patiently evaluated. He is no longer writing out of deep-dyed intimacies and warm associations.
The person on his hands is an ambitious solitary youth,
Hilda Lessway's son come up to town, and that youth is the
creature of a large and strenuous game which subordinates

personal relations and restricts personal emotions and
enslaves every adherent but the heroic. It is this
specialization that handicaps Mr. Bennett.

He succeeds in placing George Edwin Cannon as the
egoistic apprentice and later the rising public architect
of his time. He also successfully includes with that
portrait the evolution of the provincial into a smart
and successful Londoner, father of three expensive children and husband of an expensive modern London wife. In
addition to this compact portraiture he brilliantly depicts for his metropolitan reader the new bourgeois London in which such a youth disports himself - the bachelor
club, the ostentatious restaurant, the box at a musical
comedy, the motor. And he precedes this with the grub
stage of the youth - his Chelsea rooming house, the popular concert, the evening party of beer and brawn, the
Thames excursion boat. This diversified life, tipped
in with a most accomplished hand, is rounded up by the
coming of war in 1914 and Mr. Bennett completes the
audacity of exhibiting the minutiae of an architect's
office by closely detailing the experiences of the architect as a green lieutenant in the royal artillery during
the training period prior to France. But the emotional
and psychological values of this experience - Mr. Bennett
repeatedly fails to focus them. Seen critically and per-
ceptively, the career of metropolitan specialization is
not an end in itself. It is merely a variation on the
provincial life and the man who wins in it without observ-
ing the democratic obligations natural to the Five Towns
gets nowhere in particular in the end. But the emphatic
vulgarity in every turn and twist of George Cannon's
advancement does not arrest Mr. Bennett. He accepts the
'career' at its face value. He is content with the exciting chase into which the youth is plunged.

Mr. Bennett does a great deal to whoop up that chase.
By leaving out Cannon's self-interrogation, and by making
as vivid and tense as possible each one of his selected
experiences, an effect of speed and vim is created which
goes far to suggest reality. Then the chase itself, the
pursuit of the great architectural prize offered by a
northern municipality, keeps the reader alert and interested in the youth's success.

Mr. Bennett lays his colors on thick. Cannon meets
Marguerite and at once phrases it as 'a vast romantic
adventure, staggering and enchanting.' Later the girl
becomes to him 'a cushion. The divinest down cushion!
That was what she was. She was more. She defended a man
against himself. She restored him to perfection. Her
affectionate faith was a magical inspiration to him; it

was, really, the greatest force in the world.' The terrific, the stupendous, the mighty, the exquisite and the prodigious bang against each other on Mr. Bennett's pages and stupefy the reader like noise. 'The exquisite activity of creating town-halls for mighty municipalities' becomes pure reverberation after the phrase: 'A manservant entered with a priceless collection of bon-bons.' But this hyperbole, which seeks to hide Mr. Bennett's deficiency in feeling, does not destroy the competent history of Cannon's effort to win the great competition, and his marital capture by the sophisticated Lois who incited him to compete.

The genuine feeling in 'The Roll-Call' is not inspired by people at all. Mr. Bennett gives something of his beloved Alice Challice to Marguerite and something of the hero of 'Buried Alive' to the man who marries her. (Marguerite is 'the down cushion' discarded by young Cannon). Aboundingly salient are the portraits of Mr. Enwright, the brilliant hypochondriac architect, and of Mr. Haim, the acrid father of Marguerite, who marries the charwoman and who regains his daughter by losing his wife. But more than a perception of salience, genuine absorption is needed to permeate a creation with beauty, and the chief beauty in 'The Roll-Call' is in the descriptive etchings that enrich the book.

[Quotes Pt 1, ch. 1, section 3, 'Mr. Haim exhibited first' to 'over the back thereof', and Pt 1, ch. 7, section 4, 'Although the day was Saturday' to 'Nobody had disembarked'.]

Such descriptions, perfectly unforced and beautifully possessed, are found at every turn throughout 'The Roll-Call.' They give witness to Mr. Bennett's living joy in his art.

But they do not redeem 'The Roll-Call's' singularly charmless and inadequate sense of life. What, after all, is George Edwin Cannon like? Mr. Bennett may triumphantly say, like 'life.' But indeed he is like life patronized and averaged and flattened, life bluntly and coldly perceived. Mr. Bennett's enquiry is conducted with a sharp headlight up to the point where Cannon begins to be differentiated. Beyond that point Cannon is imperceptible and impalpable. He wants to stand at the head of his profession. He has ambition. He is susceptible to persons of the opposite sex. He conceives of them as vaguely 'mysterious' and in some way eluctable, though he is grimly satisfied when on 'crucial' occasions he prevails over his wife.

But so far as Marguerite is concerned or his colleagues

or his friends, he is without rapport or imaginative experience. Beyond his architecture and his career the world is a place in which to be amused and keep fit and pay his wife's bills. When the war comes, indeed, he declines to take the tip of Sir Isaac Davids. Sir Isaac Davids' 'realism,' uttered in a 'thick, rich voice,' leaves him unconvinced. 'Damn it,' he asks himself after a sleepless night, 'Am I an Englishman or am I not?' Being the son of George Cannon, the answer is, not quite an Englishman. But Mr. Bennett forgets his hero's ancestry. 'Like most Englishmen,' murmurs Mr. Bennett, 'he was much more an Englishman than he ever suspected.' He was also much more a tribal animal. Even in this crisis, his feelings have no marked personal accent. He enlists and stands up to his destiny, but he is still the imperfectly differentiated successful man.

The enlistment, to tell the truth, is a novelistic alibi. It is an escape from dealing candidly and fully with the impoverished existence of this London philistine. Beyond his career as an architect there is his career as a man and this Mr. Bennett leaves like a statue still in the mud. What special definition of Cannon should the reader ask for, outside the establishment of an average that Mr. Bennett may be believed to aim at amusedly? Only a clear definition of that average's spiritual inadequacy. To represent the complacent average without marking this failure is to leave the representation superficial. Such superficiality was not to be found in Mr. Bennett's human estimates of the Five Towns. It is to be found in the bright sterility of these estimates made in the glaring lights of London.

96. UNSIGNED REVIEW, 'STAFFORDSHIRE SENTINEL'

12 February 1919, 2

We have recently read Mr. Arnold Bennett's new novel, 'The Roll-Call,' and did so with irresistible interest and very great pleasure. We regard it (apart from the classic 'Old Wives' Tale') as Mr. Bennett's best piece of work. There is a maturity about it that there is no mistaking. It is not merely clever; it is brilliant and profound. He dives below exterior superficialities, and shows us the souls of people. Mr. Bennett was always extraordinarily

able in arraying the characteristics and the activities of
his characters; but in this novel he has not only picked
their brains, but probed their souls, and set up a perspective of life, which is so apt to be started with vivid
emotions or high ambitions, or both, and then later to encounter dangerous and heartbreaking shoals.

Mr. Bennett sees life 'larger' than he used to do; it
is not merely a cold-blooded development, but rather a
maturing of his powers of observation, analysis, and expression, and perhaps or probably a natural and 'unconscious' rather than a calculated development. The study
of George Edwin Cannon, the callow but polished and ambitious young architect, who goes from the Five Towns to be
articled to a firm of architects in London, where during
the next fifteen years or so he has adventures and
successes and buffetings, is a literary and human masterpiece. It seems too intimate to be only 'observed.' It
is alert and vivid, full of moods and speculations. It
is real. The story of the American lady may be a little
fanciful, and novelists 'must' have a framework; but
nearly all the people in the novel are 'alive,' and we
found both the 'story' and the 'people' so interesting,
that we could not rest until we had ploughed through the
book, and then longed for the continuation in some future
novel. Even the American lady may be real; the longer we
live, the more we learn of the ramifications of human
nature and of society.

'The Roll-Call' is the fourth novel of a series based
in the Potteries, though each novel is of course complete
in itself. The first was 'Clayhanger,' in which we were
introduced to old Darius Clayhanger, a Burslem printer,
and his son Edwin, who wanted to be an architect, because
their friends the Orgreaves were an architectural family.
'Clayhanger' is an essential part of any 'history' of
Burslem and neighbourhood, because it contains so many
actual people and so much 'local colour,' only very thinly
disguised. In the second volume, 'Hilda Lessways,' the
troubled youth is recounted of the woman whom Edwin Clayhanger ultimately married, after she had been deluded into
a false marriage with one Cannon and had had a child, whom
Edwin Clayhanger adopted. The third volume, 'These Twain,'
deals with the married career of the couple and their
growing prosperity. The fourth and present volume, 'The
Roll-Call,' relates primarily to Hilda Lessways' child,
George Edwin Cannon, as he prefers to call himself when
he becomes a man and learns about his origins. Hilda
Lessways and her husband Edwin Clayhanger appear to have
had no children of their own, but both of them were very
indulgent and devoted to the boy. It is a point in

psychology that Edwin Clayhanger took to the boy from his
earliest years because he was the child of the woman he
(Edwin) loved, even though there was another father.
Mr. Bennett seems to be quite 'modernist,' by the way, in
accepting the woman as the main stream of life.

We have looked through the four volumes again to see if
we could catch Mr. Bennett out in any anachronisms, but we
finally gave up the chase, and came to the conclusion that
his four generations are all in order. Certainly in one
of the earlier novels he appears to have described a local
Parliamentary election in advance of its time, but that is
a license permitted to a novelist. Otherwise, from old
Darius, the Burslem printer, down to the fourth generation
in London, there is a wonderful chronology, covering about
a century, and the 'procession' of life, with its ups and
downs, its passings away and its family changes and
developments, is brilliantly depicted. The first volume
tremendously arrested our interest eight or nine years
ago; the intermediate volumes raised some doubts as to how
far the vitality of the series could be maintained; the
end of the fourth volume leaves us gasping for more, and
with a renewed respect for the whole four, which are a
splendid proof of Mr. Bennett's genius, and increasingly
demonstrate the fertility and resource of his innate as
well as cultivated powers as a writer, the instrument
of his masterly faculty of observation and insight and
of a gift of understanding which should carry Mr. Bennett
to much greater fame yet, and ever still worthier. It is
becoming clearer that North Staffordshire has produced a
novelist who stands in the very front rank of English
writers, and who has secured a permanent place in English
literature, in which he has enshrined the soul of our
well-beloved Potteries.

97. H.W. BOYNTON, NOVELS OF CHARACTER AND ATMOSPHERE,
'BOOKMAN' (NEW YORK)

March 1919, 50-1

H.W. Boynton (born 1869) was author of a number of books
on American and English literary figures.

Most novelists have a recognizable constituency or following. Thousands of readers look for and religiously accept any book by Conrad or Galsworthy or Wells, as if the man's work were all of a piece, and any item of it could safely be taken as a Conrad or a Laura Jean Libby, in the collector's phrase. Witness the current large sale of 'Joan and Peter', certainly very dull and perfunctory as a story of anything but Mr. Wells's latest mental adventure - which is all that at heart any Wellsian expects of his master. But the case of Bennett is different. There are several Bennetts, each with his following; and these followings are not especially friendly to each other. There is the following of the sober ironist of 'The Old Wives' Tale' and the 'Clayhanger' series, and there is the following of the whimsical humorist of 'Denry the Audacious' and 'Anna of the Five Towns'. I know people who adore 'Hilda Lessways' and have no use for 'Buried Alive'; and the other way round. And I know other people (in fact, I am one of them) who adore both of these Bennetts and have comparatively little interest in certain other Bennetts who now and then make themselves heard in the flies or the cellarage. I may as well own that for me the real Bennett, or the best Bennett, is the one who permits himself to exist and to be heard again in 'The Roll-Call'. Here, for one thing, he is at home, with his own people, the breed of the Five Towns - transplanted to London, it is true, but the same people for all that. We know where they get the sturdiness and canniness to make headway against the hostility or indifference of London. We know where they get their accents, their carriage, and their very features. For these are our own people also, some of them at least, Orgreaves and Clayhangers whom we know better than we know our neighbors, thanks to their kinsman and interpreter. I for one feel in this story of Hilda Lessways's son a kind of spontaneity and finality, a rightness approaching infallibility, in insight and expression, such as I felt in 'Clayhanger' and 'Hilda Lessways', and somehow could not feel in 'These Twain', where Mr. Bennett's cleverness seemed at times too busy at its own game.

In outline, the story is a good deal like the recent 'Housemates' of J.D. Beresford: the young fellow coming up from the provinces to the experiences of a London lodging-house and a London architect's office. Mr. Beresford, we know, was trained in architecture, and a practising architect for some years; but where did Mr. Bennett get his minute knowledge of that profession? 'Who's Who' has him busy at the law till, at about twenty-five, he became an editor.... You recall that Clayhanger's neighbor Orgreave was an architect; his son John is a member of the London

firm to which young George Cannon is attached. George and
his stepfather Clayhanger are excellent friends, but on
setting out to have a try at the world for himself, George
elects to use the name of that amiable bigamist who has
given him being, if not legally a name. George, in fact,
is 'an extremely independent, tossing sprig', with a good
and sensitive mind, and a will to make the most of himself.
Enwright, the head of the firm, is a man of big tastes and
sane methods, and young George is happy in the discipular
relation. He himself has a touch of genius to apply to
his store of learning; so that presently, impelled by the
chance remark of a pretty girl, he goes in and wins single-
handed one of the great competitions of the time. But
this is only important to us for its influence on his
character, and that is rather luckily modified by his failure to follow up this first huge stroke. Ten years later
we find him married to the rather shallow, conventional
girl who, in a way, incited that stroke; and settled down,
with a child or two, to domesticity, pecuniary responsibility, and no great prospects or even security for the
future. However, he has landed another big job and has
got another well hooked when 'the roll-call' reaches him.
He cuts loose from everything (at the moment when a third
daughter is being produced for - or against - him), and
we part from him as a new-fledged lieutenant of artillery,
thrilling with the composite sense of escape, bondage, and
consecration of the man who has of his own free will
'joined up'. Those who prefer Bennett the ironist, the
sober (not solemn) interpreter, to Bennett the amusing
commentator or Bennett the clever manipulator, will find
their meat in this further and perhaps final record in
the Clayhanger series.

   One quality that demarks Mr. Bennett rather strikingly
from his contemporaries is that he is not statedly *against*
anything. He is an ironist, not a satirist; a chronicler,
not a prophet or even a protestant. Messrs. Shaw, Wells,
Galsworthy, and most of their juniors and disciples are
'antis' primarily - anti-Victorian, anti-middle class,
anti-matrimonial. Down with respectability, down with
cant, down with convention - and up with anything you
choose. In contrast with this species of inverted Victor-
ianism, Mr. Bennett's mellow ironic method has the human
largeness we constrain ourselves to call Elizabethan (O
Mark Twain, and Lewis Carroll, and Meredith, and all other
hearty souls that went your way unhampered in that 'Victorian' world!). If there is any idea or moral in 'The Roll-
Call' it is the simple one that from peril of surfeit and
smooth ways the shock of war has rescued many an one for
the better, whatever may have happened to him thereafter.

We don't know whether George Cannon comes out of the war
alive, we don't even know how he came through his first
action; and in a sense it doesn't matter.

'Mr. Prohack'

27 April 1922

98. MR. ARNOLD BENNETT'S EXPERIMENT, UNSIGNED REVIEW,
'DAILY MAIL'

26 April 1922, 5

Mr. Arnold Bennett's novel 'Mr. Prohack,' which is being
published this week, is not exactly new; it appeared
recently as a serial, and those who read it in instalments
found that it was not exactly a story. It is rather a
series of episodes illustrating the author's interest in
finance, which shone out strongly also in his latest play
'A Love Match.'
     The book is likely to be a great success, for it is
great fun. Not for a long time has Mr. Bennett's humour
played so searchingly and brilliantly over the surface of
life to-day as it is lived by those who are able to spend
profusely. He drops a fortune into the lap of a Treasury
official whose household have just begun to feel the pinch
of Peace conditions and he shows in elaborate detail how a
fortune can be spent upon making existence more luxurious,
more ostentatious, and more entertaining.
     Mr. Prohack himself treats the change in his condition
as a joke. He enjoys learning to be a busy idle man,
riding in a luxurious motor-car, buying his wife a £5,000
pearl necklace, turning £80,000 into nearly a quarter of a
million by a deal in Rumanian oil. But he is never
dazzled by his wealth. He has always taken a humorous
view of life and his humour does not desert him. This
gives the book an agreeably satiric flavour and saves the
reader from being oppressed by the atmosphere of money.
     It is Mrs. Prohack who throws herself with complete
zest into the pleasure of spending without stint. She is

pathetically unable to understand why her daughter, type
of the intelligent girl of the period, takes so little
interest in the possibilities opened out before her.
Sissie is an engaging young woman, her father's daughter.
Charlie, the son, finds he has the money touch, lives
resplendently, as a financier should, at the Grand Babylon
Hotel; and seems likely, after a bankruptcy or two, to end
up much richer than his papa.

What Mr. Bennett means by it all is not very clear.   Is
it to be read as a satire or merely as a diverting picture
of the way the rich live?   Diverting it certainly is.
Even when the freshness of the invention wears off, there
are still so many flashes of wit and shrewd observation,
so many incisive sketches of character, so much boisterous
good humour that it remains attractive to the end.   One
feels that the author enjoyed writing it, enjoyed experimenting with a new technique of novel-writing, enjoyed
gloating over a yacht which cost £700 a month in wages
alone and a house in Manchester-square.

Those who 'want a story' will be disappointed, but 'Mr.
Prohack' will amuse many whom stories often bore.   Only
two slips from the vivid verisimilitude which marks the
book are to be noted.   Chauffeurs of to-day do not pick
their teeth with forks at table, nor do Treasury officials,
when they are indisposed, complain of feeling 'queer.'

99. REVIEW SIGNED F.S., 'MANCHESTER GUARDIAN'

27 April 1922, 5

Although Mr. Bennett's humorous sympathy is to be found in
most of his books, even in the most serious of them, 'Mr.
Prohack' represents that humorous sympathy in its more
marked form; and for this reason claims a place beside
'The Card,' 'A Great Man,' and 'Buried Alive.'   In their
way, these three books are among the very best that Mr.
Bennett has written, and although 'Mr. Prohack' is more
sophisticated than its delightful predecessors it is definitely in key with them.   It has, perhaps, nothing quite
as startlingly ludicrous as Denry Machin's 'Rothschild!'
but it is the product of the same assured, rich, knowing
comic sense as these other books.   Nothing could be more
characteristic, for example, or more mischievous, than the
frank talk between Mr. Prohack and his daughter upon the

subject of a suitor for the latter. Mr. Prohack is sublimely wise. His daughter heartily accepts his advice,
and responds with suitable compliments. It is only after
the compliments have duly impressed the reader that Mr.
Prohack realises that he has been asleep all the time.
The scene, in fact, is an illumination of that cynical
slang phrase of the day, 'And then you woke up!'

   This note of mischief is sustained throughout the book.
For the first two or three pages one is doubtful whether
Mr. Bennett has quite recaptured his old spontaneity; and
there is a slight air of forced freshness in some of the
opening sparrings between Mr. Prohack and his wife. Mr.
Bennett's habit of using, or making his characters use,
humorous exaggerations of phrase makes them appear at
times unduly self-conscious in the domestic circle. But
once one accepts this idiom one finds that Mr. Bennett's
hero is not only 'trying to be funny' in the manner of
Pooh Bah, but that he brings to the study of life much of
Mr. Bennett's own shrewd and witty insight. Indeed, to
some readers Mr. Prohack will appear a riper and more
delightful product than Denry Machin. He has the same
marvelling innocence in the face of splendour, and the
same miraculous good fortune with his investments. He too
is entirely baffled by the astounding mysteriousness of
all women, but particularly those who are closest to him.
He makes discoveries about himself every minute, as Denry
did. And yet he is a different man, living in a different
world, mentally alive to many things as to which Denry
must have remained ignorant until his death. This greater
intellectual quality gives Mr. Prohack a new richness.
He is still capable, as Denry always was, of the *mot*. He
has essentially the mind and outlook of the wit. But he
understands more, and it is this fact which makes his comments upon the modern world of such interest and significance. Mr. Prohack has been a Treasury official for many
years, and he suddenly inherits a hundred thousand pounds.
He thus does what all men dream of doing. He immediately
bursts into a spending campaign, after nearly tripling
his wealth by a lucky gamble. But the point to be emphasised is that he is all the time living supremely in the
real world. He and his family and friends are the only
fantastic people in it. The rest of the world is there,
actually in progress, behind them. This book is about
real things, in spite of its humorous character. It is a
criticism of our time, not the less searching because it
is also great fun, because it is oblique, teasing, ironic,
humane, fantastic.

   Mr. Bennett's chief contributions to the novel are
unquestionably 'The Old Wives' Tale' and the Clayhanger

trilogy, but his service to modern literature will be
inadequately recognised if we underrate, because they are
humorous, his lighter novels.   In these, thrown off so
easily, as it seems, can be found the essential Mr.
Bennett, who is not to be replaced by any other writer,
but whose deep and absorbed interest in everything relating
to human beings is that of a humorist.   It is one thing to
be a wit, which Mr. Bennett certainly is, in company with
other writers.   It is another, and a rarer thing, to bring
humour to the contemplation of life.   Mr. Bennett has
always done that.   He has brought humour to the contemplation of himself, and to those fantastic persons who are
projected in his lighter books.   That is his quality.
Naïvely astonished at their own cleverness all these cards
may be; but nobody could be more amused at them than they
are at themselves.   The same thing is true of Mr. Prohack.
He may take everybody else in.   He never takes himself in.
He is a marvellous wise idiot, with an antic love of fun
and unscrupulous resource, dominated by his sense of decency and his benign attitude of disrespect for the whole
world.   If he had been invented in a past era of English
letters he would now be a saying.   As it is, his lapses
from perfect taste will no doubt distress some of our most
refined readers, while the majority of people will content
themselves with being as amused by this book as they have
been by any book published since 'The Regent.'   For a few,
and we must number ourselves among them, the book will
seem to be more than another 'Regent.'   In its pictures of
Mr. Prohack, his wife, his son, his daughter, it is highly
diverting, wise, and full of humorous sympathy.   But it
also pictures for us something of the form and pressure of
the time, and for that reason it is, and should be, a not
negligible document.   At any rate, it is a pleasure to
welcome Mr. Bennett back to the novel, and that 'Mr. Prohack' should be an addition to his definitely humorous
works will no doubt bring the greatest pleasure to the
greatest number, which is a state much to be commended.

100. 'AFFABLE HAWK', IN THE 'NEW STATESMAN'

29 April 1922, 96

'Affable Hawk' was the pseudonym of Desmond MacCarthy
(1877-1952), who was literary editor of the 'New Statesman'

at this time. Later he founded 'Life and Letters' with
some help from Bennett. Bennett spoke well of him as a
critic on several occasions, and wrote to Frank Swinnerton
in 1924, 'He has much taste (except for the stage) & he is
one of the best talkers I ever heard' (LAB III, 211).

In dealing with a new book a reviewer should first describe it in a few plain sentences much as though he were
in a witness-box and his readers were a common jury;
afterwards he may discuss it in a manner most interesting
to himself; and then, if he really is a critic, what he
says should prove interesting to those whom Mr. Arnold
Bennett, discoursing upon the making and destroying of
literary reputations, once called 'the passionate few.'
On the wrapper of Mr. Bennett's new novel the publisher
has printed a general description, which with some reservations and expansions will serve well enough: 'Mr. Arnold
Bennett's new novel may be described as a cross between
his humorous works and his fantasias, with an added strain
of seriousness. It is a cheerful and amusing story, with
some sensational events in it and much social satire.'
This curt, cool description suggests, then, that this
novel has, on the one hand, something in common with 'The
Card,' or with 'A Great Man,' that less-known story which
a literary Baedeker ought to star, and, on the other,
with, say, 'The Grand Babylon Hotel.' Certainly, 'Mr.
Prohack' the book, and Mr. Prohack the hero of it, are
both respectively germain to 'The Card' and Denry; but the
kinship of this new novel with such works as 'The Grand
Babylon Hotel' is too trifling for notice. The essence
of a fantasia is a high-spirited defiance of probability,
and here there is no such defiance. There is plenty of
genial exaggeration, occasionally too pronounced considering its relation to a realistic background, and, of
course - for Mr. Bennett is the author - there is,
throughout, in the descriptions of houses, clubs, hotels,
Turkish baths, shops, clothes, ornaments, furniture,
yachts, motors, dining, dancing, and the making and spending of money, an immense, unflagging gusto. But despite
this gusto the book itself is far from being inspired by
high spirits or optimism. Our attention is drawn to 'an
added strain of seriousness' in it. True: 'Mr. Prohack'
entertained me, and also left a residuum for reflection.
The wrapper describes it as a 'cheerful, amusing story.'
'Amusing' it certainly is; but 'cheerful'? That query
raises a delicate and difficult point for 'the passionate
few.' At first 'Mr. Prohack' seems a very ordinary book,

but it is really a queer one, especially exciting to
critics as indicating where 'the cheerful, amusing,' not
to say often garish, surface of Mr. Bennett's picture of
the lives of the wealthy is apt to crack, and reveal -
what? Disillusionment with the pleasures, possessions,
immunities and powers money can procure? No; something
else which I will try to suggest.

The peculiarity of Mr. Bennett's social satire is that
it is accompanied by a profound temperamental sympathy
with whatever excites it. To satirise effectively anybody or anything it is necessary to feel some sympathy,
otherwise you cannot strike straight and hard; but in
Mr. Bennett's case there is an overplus of sympathy, conscious and unconscious, which confuses the result. Thus
when you have finished 'Mr. Prohack' you find yourself in
doubt whether the book is intended as a general picture of
futility or of attainment. Was the sudden good fortune of
the Prohack family after all a Timon's feast, a matter of
warm water under silver dish-covers? It looks rather like
it. Yet a doubt remains. With his intellect Mr. Bennett
constantly assents to the proposition that the solid
happiness of possessing £20,000 a year and a son who is
a financial magnate can be easily exaggerated; yet his
temperament keeps shouting enthusiastically as he tells
the story of the Prohacks, in a tone very far from that
of an ironic host, 'Lap, lucky dogs, lap!' The voice of
his temperament is louder. Hence the reader's confused
impression at the close of a book, which does nevertheless
contain 'much social satire,' and satire particularly
directed at the getting and spending of money. The book
closes with a description of a magnificent yacht on which
young Prohack takes tea at long intervals, and (almost in
the spirit of 'Bouvard and Pécuchet') with Mr. Prohack
taking up work to make more money which he does not want.

Some weeks ago there appeared in this paper, in a
criticism of 'The Love Match,' a protest against what
seemed to the writer an undue preoccupation on Mr. Bennett's part with money, and the prestige value of costly
possessions. Being myself at one with this critic, my
heart sank, therefore, when the first thirty pages of 'Mr.
Prohack' showed that its theme was to be the introduction
of a family belonging to 'the new poor' into the category
of 'the new rich.' Money again! I sighed. Not that I was
above sympathising with this hard-worked Treasury official,
the father of a grown-up son and daughter, when having
first discovered that his salary was hopelessly insufficient to meet the increased cost of living, he suddenly

inherited over £100,000, which was soon increased to a
quarter of a million; on the contrary I sympathised with
Mr. Prohack's compressed elation as he went home with his
delicious secret only too personally. What made my artistic heart sink was the fear that Mr. Bennett was going
merely to play up to this too wistful fellow-feeling –
'Oh, if that could only happen to me!' – instead of
addressing his book to that detached percipient in me,
who rather incongruously answers to my name, has an
address, a bank book and relations. However, as will have
been gathered from the above paragraphs, I soon began to
be reassured.

The character of Mr. Prohack is endearing and original.
There is a touch of the middle-aged pierrot about this
conscientous civil servant, who so suddenly finds himself
one of the idle rich. It is a point of honour with him
never to be above his good fortune, and he never feels
more sensible than when he thrills with gratitude at
having been excused the duty of inching and pinching, and
succeeds in enjoying his riches like a child. Qualms of
irrational shame at his fortune he promptly represses; he
is a very social creature and he does not hold with Marcus
Aurelius. But, nevertheless, he is constantly shocked by
the habits of expense his income thrusts upon him, and
bored and harassed by obligatory gaieties, and the fuss
and vulgarity in which the position of being a paragraphed,
photographed 'swell' involve his family. His idleness,
even the immunities of his position, irk him terribly;
like an over-washed and combed pet dog he misses the
stimulus of fleas. If his heart were not perpetually
playing a tender domestic tune, he would wish himself back
in the old routine, but his marriage is a refuge from
serious botherations. Mr. Bennett introduces him to us as
'the terror of departments,' an official of iron determination. This is a mistake. We never catch sight of one
trait which suggests it, while the temper of his mind (the
wisdom of his relations with his children is only that of
Mother Cary's with her chickens) is a whimsical, half-
ironical patience. Like 'Denry' he has the gift of un-
reflecting promptness, and a parvenu's reverence for the
real tip-top thing; he is continually gratified by his
success in concealing the fact that he is too much impressed. One elderly masterful woman of the world is so
bewitched by him that she leaves the country, knowing her
infatuation hopeless. If I understood the type Lady
Massulam is meant to be, this is absurd. Mr. Bennett has
showered honours a little too thick on his modest hero.
He is credited with a disturbing faculty of seeing things

baldly as they are; he also sees them with a beglamoured
eye. It is this double and conflicting vision in Mr. Bennett which makes this novel queer, as well as vivid and
extremely honest.

101. UNSIGNED REVIEW, 'PUNCH'

3 May 1922, 359

I have read 'Mr. Prohack' from end to end, looking for
the 'social satire' promised on the wrapper, but I am
bound to say I found Mr. Arnold Bennett's latest novel
about as satirical as a store catalogue. A store catalogue is an excellent documentary foundation for social
satire; and so is 'Mr. Prohack'. But just as there must
be a large number of estimable people who do not see the
ludicrous or contemptible side of a fat annual circular
largely devoted to patent boot-trees, self-adjusting
chairs and electro-plated siphon stands, so there must be
a large proportion of Mr. Bennett's readers who will
accompany Mr. Prohack from his obscure but still more
creditable job in the Treasury, and his obscurer but still
more creditable home behind Hyde Park Gardens, to the
effortless acquisition of a quarter of a million pounds
and a mansion in Manchester Square, with no sensations
whatever beyond a reverent envy. They will put up as
placidly as he did himself with the increasing infantility
of his wife, the hugely magnified competence of his daughter, the vindictive speculativeness of his son and the
whole accurately-listed train of wasters and charlatans
who attend his ill-starred rise into the limelight of the
New Rich. And they will be as grateful to Mr. Bennett as
the crow that perches on a scarecrow is to the farmer who
put it there. But why 'satire'?

102. JAMES DOUGLAS, THE OLD LOVERS' TALE, 'SUNDAY EXPRESS'

14 May 1922, 5

I seldom read serials, but I read 'Mr. Prohack' as it was
doled out morning by morning in the 'Westminster Gazette.'
It went very well with my bacon and eggs. It became a
habit, and I was sorry when it was all eaten. But I ate
it all over again when it came out in its coloured jacket.
That is to say, I have eagerly read it twice over, which
is the acid test of a novel.

Mr. Prohack is what Mr. Walkley would call the epony-
mous hero of the tale. He might even call him the epony-
mous husband, for although Mr. Prohack is forty-six, he
is incurably and incorrigibly in love with his plump,
girlish, middle-aged wife. This is rare in novels,
although it is common in life. The miracle of marriage
could not be worked for forty or fifty years in hundreds
of thousands of homes if it were not common. Mr. Bennett
divines the romance of this common miracle, and gathers it
fresh like manna with the dew on it. Do not imagine that
he is a hard, cynical, callous realist, who hates and
despises human nature. He is nothing of the sort. He is
a wistful, tender, gentle sentimentalist, who knows that
there is far more love than vinegar in the veins of ordinary men and women. He builds the fairy palace of romance
upon the concrete foundations of realism. Life as he sees
it is pulsating and palpitating with romantic energy. He
bewitches you with the strange surprises and caprices of
the heart. He compels you to love his grey, drab, ordinary, commonplace people because there is a fairy magic in
them that melts you and moves you. It is the workaday
magic of life.

Mr. Prohack is a Treasury official. He is known as
'the terror of the departments.' But this tiger of economy, who has saved for his country hundreds of millions
during the war, cannot make both ends of his salary meet.
He is hard up. His wife cannot pinch and scrape him out
of his poverty. Like millions of other wives, she is
baffled and beaten by penury. Suddenly he learns that he
is a rich man. He comes into a fortune of one hundred
thousand pounds. Ten thousand pounds a year! Many years
ago he had lent £100 to a fellow called Angmering. This
fellow had become a war profiteer, and on his deathbed he
left Mr. Prohack a third of his ill-gotten wealth. This

tale describes the amazing consequences of this freak of
fate. It shows you the effect produced by it upon the
lives of Mr. and Mrs. Prohack, on the life of their son,
Charlie, and on the life of their daughter, Cissie. No
novelist since Balzac has treated money more lovingly and
more cunningly than Mr. Bennett. He knows that love and
money are the master keys of modern romance. With these
two keys he unlocks every door in the modern heart. In
this tale he carries the key of love in one hand and the
key of money in the other, and with them he lets you into
all sorts of magical chambers and Aladdin's caves and
enchanted corridors and castles in the air.

I have been brought up to believe that money hardens
the heart and sours the character. Mr. Prohack convinces
me that money is the fairy that transforms misery into
joy, selfishness into generosity, folly into wisdom. Take
the case of Charlie. He is a young warrior who had
returned from the war full of magnificent and austere
ideals. He had expected to help in the common task of
making heaven in about a fortnight. He was disappointed,
as hundreds of thousands of young warriors were disappointed. He grew bitter and cynical and melancholy.
Mr. Prohack with a wave of his magic wand transfigures the
young warrior. Charlie has heard of 'an affair at Glasgow.' Three hundred is needed. As far as Charlie is concerned, it might be three thousand. 'I expect I could let
you have three hundred,' says Mr. Prohack. 'You couldn't!'
'I expect I could.' Mr. Prohack 'had never felt so akin
to a god. It seemed to him that he was engaged in the act
of creating a future, yea, a man. Charlie's face changed.
He had been dead. He was now suddenly alive.' Charlie
catches the night-train to Glasgow and ... well, you just
read the story of Charlie's magical dealings with money.
The romance of it all! Don't tell me that money is the
root of all evil. It is also the root of all good.

Then there is Cissie, the adorable Cissie and her
dancing concern, and her secret sudden marriage to her
ridiculous Ozzie, and the dinner in her flatlet, and the
champagne, and the caviare and the pâté de foie gras. But
why should I waste my panegyrics on the minor characters
when I have Mr. Prohack and his absurd, crafty conspirator
of a wife to glorify? Really, I cannot tell you whether
I am more in love with Mr. Prohack or Mrs. Prohack, with
the inimitable Arthur or with the incomparable Eve. Her
name is Marian, but he calls her Eve, and she is everything that a woman, a wife, and a mother ought to be. How
on earth did Mr. Bennett discover the secret of the

tenderness which he has lavished upon this middle-aged
pair of married lovers? Who taught him the tricks that
enable him to steal their hearts out of their prosaic
bodies, and show us their heavenly systole and diastole?
I suppose it was the shy muse of romance who is always
hiding round all the corners of realism. All I know is
that genius has a way with it, and that there is a bit of
Barrie even in our cool, polished, worldly wise Bennett.
At any rate, I catch myself sniffing and swallowing and
smiling to myself over these little intimate bedroom and
boudoir revelations and disclosures.

   Sentiment and satire! Wistfulness and wisdom! It is
a queer mixture. Perhaps Mr. Bennett is an armour-plated
humanist. Perhaps his heart is a thousand times softer
than his head. I don't care. All I know is that I can
never have enough of Mr. Prohack's domestic whimsies and
humours and Mrs. Prohack's innocent arts and crafts. I
catch myself hankering after the dream of a world in which
all thin, grey-haired husbands are desperately in love with
with all plump, grey-haired wives. I know some of them,
and the world must be full of them. They never carry
their unbroken hearts into the courts or the newspapers.
They are, maybe, unconscious of the romance that breathes
over their ancient Edens. But, bless your soul, they will
all delight in this old lovers' tale. For there is a Prohack inside every city and suburban husband and an Eve
inside every city and suburban wife. Don't you wish you
could make love to your middle-aged wife like Mr. Prohack?
And doesn't your middle-aged wife wish you could? And the
fairy joke of it all is that you can, and probably do,
although neither of you knows it!

'Lilian'

19 October 1922

103. S.P.B. MAIS, MR. BENNETT WRITES ANOTHER 'PRETTY
LADY', AND MR. BENNETT DEFENDS 'LILIAN', 'DAILY EXPRESS'

19 October 1922, 6; and 20 October (also 21), 6

S.P.B. Mais (1885-1975) was a journalist, novelist, and
lecturer in English literature. In his 'Chronicle of
English Literature' in 1936 he wrote appreciatively of
Bennett but added that he takes 'an equal delight in the
coarse and the ugly and the vulgar, which has put off
certain readers'.

Mr. Arnold Bennett cannot be a good critic of his own
work or he would scarcely have produced so inadequate
a successor to 'Mr. Prohack' as 'Lilian', published
to-day.
   Mr. Prohack was a Dickensian character, richly humorous
and (what is rarer) humorously rich. Lilian is merely a
designing minx. Lilian is a twenty-three-year-old
chestnut-haired typist, whose unambitious father (pro-
fessionally an art master) left her penniless but ambitious. Her employer, Mr. Grig, ran a typewriting office,
in spite of the fact that Winchester and Cambridge had
been responsible for his early years. It was a peculiar
kind of office; it kept open all night. This gave Mr.
Grig his opportunity to tell Lilian that she was beautiful.
   Unfortunately there is a Miss Grig, a sister of Mr.
Grig, whose personality is revealed by Mr. Bennett in the
words, 'she was one of those women who, for the performance

of the morning and the evening rites, trebly secure themselves by locks and bolts and blinds from the slightest
chance of a chance of the peril of the world's gaze.'
Isabel Grig adores her brother; she is quick to realise
that Mr. Grig is telling Lilian that she is beautiful, so
Lilian is dismissed.

She spends all her savings in a frock which she wears
at a dinner with Mr. Grig; the frock, her beauty, and the
good dinner drive Mr. Grig to enunciate his grey-haired
philosophy: 'The woman runs risks, but nothing to the
risks she'd run in marriage. And if the thing dies out
in her ... she's free as air to start again - a woman
wants making. Only a man can make a woman. She has to
be formed.'

There is a great deal of it.... It is good of Mr. Bennett to tell us what those elderly roués say (on the
films) to those foolish young butterflies whom they set
out to seduce. Lilian, of course, succumbs. She is,
remember, ambitious.

We next find her sumptuously décolleté in a sumptuous
hotel in the south of France, where fortunes are made by
foreigners who have 'discovered that the English don't
want to be prim any more.' Mr. Grig is being good to
Lilian, and Lilian is being good to Mr. Grig. She takes
him out in the cold night air, and he gets pneumonia.
She tells him that she is going to have a child. He
decides to marry her, and, having married her, dies.

She returns to run the typewriting office on the money
Mr. Grig left her. This book has Mr. Arnold Bennett's
name on the cover. That alone will sell it. The contents
have the merit of brevity and little else. Do the rosy
raptures of chemin de fer, private yachts, and other con-
comitants of 'vice' still attract novel readers? For my
part I prefer 'Ouida.'

It is a great pity. Surely Mr. Bennett need no longer
write 'pot-boilers.' Oh for a touch of the vanished hand
that wrote 'The Old Wives' Tale.'

To the Editor of the 'Daily Express.'

Sir, - 'S.P.B.M.' calls my novel 'Lilian' a pot-boiler.
The 'Oxford Dictionary' definition of pot-boiler is: 'A
work of art or literature done merely to make a living.'
That is to say, the writer of a pot-boiler has venally
contrived something for a purely commercial end, and
solely for money.

Nearly all writers write for money. Shakespeare did.
But the serious writers do not write solely for money.
Serious writers produce the best work they can, and hope

to make a living out of it.

Literary critics seem to have fallen into quite a habit of describing as a pot-boiler any novel which they do not like. They have not the least right to do so, and in doing so they presume upon the indifference of authors. Such a description is undoubtedly libellous. Not that I should ever dream of bringing a libel action! But some day some critic with more cheek than prudence will find himself in trouble.

If 'S.P.B.M.' knew the literary world as he should, he would know that the writing of a novel like 'Lilian' involves a considerable financial sacrifice to its author, in the matter of serial rights alone. It would have been easy for me to write a novel twice as remunerative as 'Lilian.' Only I wanted to write 'Lilian.'

This letter is not concerned with purely literary verdicts. I am not prepared to deny that 'S.P.B.M.' is the greatest critic of the age, or that I am the meanest of novelists.

Yours truly, Arnold Bennett

'Riceyman Steps'

25 October 1923

104. JAMES DOUGLAS, THE MISER AND THE MAID, 'SUNDAY
EXPRESS'

28 October 1923, 7

In an article on Romeo and Juliet in the Slums, 'Daily
Express', 12 December 1929, Douglas recalled the love
scene between Elsie and Joe as his favourite love scene
in fiction. Again on 27 January 1935 he was put in mind
of Elsie by a newspaper story of an overworked servant
girl.

Mr. Arnold Bennett has recreated himself by a colossal and
tremendous effort of the imagination. He has gone apart
into a lonely wilderness and prayed for his soul and found
it. The name of the wilderness is London, and the oasis
by which he knelt down in ardent humility and austere
reverence is Clerkenwell. Clerkenwell! My Clerkenwell!
Your Clerkenwell! Everybody's Clerkenwell! The titanic
genius which hewed 'The Old Wives' Tale' out of the grey
romance of the Five Towns has hewn 'Riceyman Steps' out of
the grey romance of London Town. I took up the story at
five o'clock in the afternoon of last Friday after a hard
day's work. I was tired. I read with one eye, for the
other was out of action owing to an abrasion of the cornea
caused by a puff of grit blown out of a street watchman's
brazier. The type is clear, but not large, and I was
reading against time. One hundred and thirty thousand
words. Whew! I read till one in the morning, at the rate
of sixteen thousand words an hour, or about two hundred

and fifty words a minute. I dog's-eared hundreds of pages.
And I did not yawn once. Every page, yea, every sentence,
produced its aesthetic reaction. It was a terrific and
tremendous spiritual experience. I had lived an age in
eight hours.

Mr. Bennett is a great artist. He has put into this
astounding novel all his astounding powers of pity and
tenderness and compassion and love and understanding. He
has not hardened his heart against our divine human nature.
He has not despised our spirit. He has not sneered at our
childishness. He has not scoffed at our stupidity. He
has searched for the thing in us that is more wonderful
than all the things outside us - our small, mean, petty,
glorious, magnificent, murky soul. And he has found the
soul of man in three ordinary, commonplace, foolish,
ignorant, silly creatures - a marvellous man and two marvellous women. Mr. Earlforward, Violet, and Elsie are
beings so violently alive that you cease to be yourself as
you live through their passions and sensations. Your consciousness of your own ego is swept away by the rush and
sweep of their joys and sorrows. 'Heavens!' you say, 'I
am that queer man; I am that queer woman; I am that queer
girl.' And you know that the illusion is caused by the
fact that human nature is always in unison with human
nature, and that you are capable of being an Earlforward,
a Violet, or an Elsie.

Mr. Earlforward is a miser, but he is not a monster.
He is a man. Nearly all the misers in literature are mon-
sters. This miser is a poor, kind, pitiable being who
crucifies himself on the cross of avarice.

The amazing aspect of him is that you are forced to
love him, not because he is a miser, but because he is a
human being. And yet there never was a more merciless or
pitiless miser. Here is the whole anatomy of miserdom,
etched delicately and minutely in scene after scene, episode after episode. The soul of the miser is seen like an
anatomical chart, with every muscle and nerve radiating
from the spine and the brain. The power of the passion is
frightful. It ravages the whole man. Mr. Earlforward is
as tragic as King Lear, and he shakes you and shocks you
like King Lear.

The realism of the story is staggering. No artist has
ever painted a background more vividly than this dingy
book-seller's shop and its dingy environment. The whole
thing stings and tingles and vibrates so passionately that
you are steeped in its noise, its colour, its smell, its
movement. Clerkenwell saturates you. And it is not mere
cataloguery, if I may coin the word. It is life - magical, romantic, hazardous, dangerous life, all trembling

and shivering in a mystery of beauty and charm in its
grime and squalor and decay. This is the pure, sheer
genius of imaginative divination. It is the poetry of
common existence and ordinary dailiness.

The miser's wedding gift is a safe. Horrible! But not
more horrible than the life they lead after the honeymoon.
They starve themselves. They starve Elsie, their
'general.' Violet, after vain rebellions, surrenders to
the miser's way of life. And Elsie, that miracle and pro-
digy of drudges, serves the miser and his wife with un-
faltering devotion. I admit that I wept over Elsie and
her lover, Joe. She is only a London slut. She is only
one of those slaves who scrub and toil for meagre fare and
meagre wages. But she is more lovable and more adorable
than any chocolate-box heroine. Mr. Bennett has, with one
slash of his sword, destroyed the whole hateful legend of
the 'slavey' and the 'skivvy'. He has made the drudge
divine. And he has not sentimentalised or romanticised
her. He has simply set her down as she dreams. Her devotion to Joe is heartbreaking. Her watch for his return is
inexpressibly tragic. Her nursing of him is indescribably
sublime. The dying miser in one room and the fever-
stricken lover in another and Elsie ministering to both -
what a revelation of Elsie's soul! I own that I worship
Elsie. She is a creature far too bright and good for
human nature's daily food. But the world is full of
Elsies and the world is not worthy of them. And that is
the grace and glory of this superbly romantic tale. It
canonises and haloes the common life of the common folk.
It transmutes and transfigures the love and loyalty and
tenderness that lurk in the simple human hearts of simple,
ordinary beings. It reveals the undying romance of the
drab and the dull and the prosaic. In fine, it vindicates
life against all the cynicisms of all the cynics and all
the pessimisms of all the pessimists. I congratulate Mr.
Bennett. He has never written and he never will write a
tale more splendidly magnificent in its pity and its tenderness. He loves us as we are, and we are grateful.

105. A.S. WALLACE, MR. BENNETT AT HIS BEST, 'MANCHESTER
GUARDIAN'

2 November 1923, 7

Mr. Bennett's admirers have been waiting for such a
reassertion of his powers as this. It is in the direct
succession of the half-dozen books he has given us in the
last twenty-five years that we may fairly expect to live.
We would not put Henry and Violet Earlforward and their
maid Elsie on quite the same plane with the sisters in
'The Old Wives' Tale' nor with Clayhanger and Hilda. They
are not, for one thing, thrown on so vast a canvas. Mr.
Bennett gives us only a year of their lives, and as their
background, not a continent nor a whole country, but a
corner merely of a shabby London district. Yet we have
the same rare and satisfying sense with the Earlforwards
as with the others, of knowing them intimately - better
far than many of us know the people nearest to us - and of
knowing, too, that in their every thought and deed they
are of the durable stuff and texture of humanity. Beside
them the war-shocked neurotics and spoiled society pets
of Mr. Bennett's recent moods draw back to a respectful
distance.

In outline the novel has a simplicity and strength that
are classic. Nothing complicates or disturbs the steady,
inevitable submission of the two chief characters to their
destiny. Mr. Bennett's theme, the tyranny and triumph of
overmastering meanness, might easily in other hands have
been intolerably sordid and depressing. One is thankful
for the sanity, the compassion, and the humour with which
Mr. Bennett treats it. His Henry Earlforward has no kinship with the talon-fingered, malignant miser of melodrama. The evidences of his dominating passion are almost
comic in detail. As a mere incident it would be a matter
for mirth that this quiet, pleasant, middle-aged bookseller should give the widow he marries a safe as a wedding
present, should courteously prove to her how eminently
reasonable it is to purchase her second wedding ring from
the proceeds of the sale of the first, and should prefer
to sham ill in order to go home early on their one day of
honeymoon rather than face up to paying for tea on the top
of other frivolities at Madame Tussaud's. And surely
there is no cause for tears in the fact that, loving him
passionately and having an answering streak of prudence,
if no worse, in her own nature, she should humour him
from the start at every turn of their daily life, yielding

now in the matter of lighting a fire, now in that of
eggs for tea? Yet as the full strength of Henry's passion
is, almost whimsically, revealed by this little circumstance or that, and as its grip closes more and more
firmly on his wife, it is clear that no escape is possible
for them. Violet has moments, too late, when virtual
starvation has brought illness on them, of furious rebellion. Her sense of proportion is never destroyed so
wholly as her husband's, and she makes at times a tremendous effort to break the spell that has enmeshed them. It
is useless. When at last she escapes it is to hospital,
where weakness caused by months of routine privation
denies her the strength to survive an operation that
might have saved her. Henry, gently but appallingly consistent to the end, quietly defiant of doctors and physic,
of warmth and of food, scarcely outlives her. His death,
marooned by his passion among his ledgers, is memorable in
fiction.

These two victims of a dreadful obsession need, if they
are to be thrown into bold relief, a strong contrasting
figure. For this Elsie the maid serves. She overflows
with human kindness, with loyalty, with generosity. She
is as essential a part of the frowsy Clerkenwell shop as
its litter of dusty books or its carefully-watched meat
safe where every scrap is kept for future use, but she
colours the texture of its life with pure gold. Elsie
calling in the doctor on her own responsibility, working
ceaselessly on a beggarly wage, suffering the torture of
the damned through hunger, stealing raw bacon in the
night and scourged with repentance on the morrow; Elsie
hoping against hope for the return of her lover - a down-
at-heels, ex-soldier liable to fits whom she has banished
for his own good and who comes back to her straight from
gaol and weak with malaria; Elsie at the last, in charge
of the sinister shop and house, with her master, yellow as
his parchment and thin as a lath, dying in the best bedroom and her lover delirious in the attic - it is Elsie
with her great heart that sharpens the edge of our compassion for the doomed couple with whom she lives.

The Clerkenwell background, of shabby streets, decrepit
squares of congested tenements and an ugly roaring high-
way, is filled in with a confident selection of significant detail that seems as effortless in its ease as it
is graphic in its result.

106. UNSIGNED REVIEW, 'PUNCH'

7 November 1923, 455

'I'll show you,' Mr. Arnold Bennett seems to say in an
unwritten preface to his new novel, 'whether my hand has
lost its cunning or no. I'll push aside all my 'Denrys',
'Lilians' and 'Prohacks', and bring on some of my ordinary
obscure common folk. Nor shall they be of the Five Towns,
but I'll take a drab forgotten island of Camberwell and
make a place thereon for a middle-aged second-hand bookseller whose first early passion for hoarding money fights
with and overcomes his late-flowering passion for a woman,
also middle-aged if still handsome and vivacious. And you
shall see into their most secret thoughts and understand
and pity them. And within a year I'll kill them both of
under-nourishment. My real heroine shall be a charwoman -
solid, loyal, not uncomely, slow of thought and speech,
infinitely charitable, splendidly sane. Oh, yes, and I'll
give my book a title that won't of itself sell two copies
- 'Riceyman Steps'; and you'll see it will be a winner.
I'll make it all not just merely credible but inevitable,
and so close-knit that the perceptive reader, for whom
(after myself, of course) I here write, will not care or
dare to skip a word. Believe me it will be one of the
very best pieces of work I've ever done.' And I thoroughly
agree. Mr. Bennett, when serious, is never the romantic.
But still less is he the mere photographer of the crude
and squalid; and never really a cynic. Elsie, the charwoman, is a beautifully tender piece of work. All through
one is drawn to one's fellows, a little more persuaded of
the truth of the plausible doctrine of compensations, and,
above all, if one has any feeling for technique, entranced
to watch a superb craftsman's hand at work. Certainly the
best Bennett since 'The Old Wives' Tale'.

107. GERALD GOULD, IN THE 'SATURDAY REVIEW'

10 November 1923, 525

Gerald Gould (1885-1936) was on the staff of the 'Daily
Herald' for a number of years. He was a poet and essayist.

Has Mr. Arnold Bennett 'come back'? That is the speculation which sets the fingers of his admirers trembling as
they open each new book he publishes. For, it is certain,
he was once a champion.

His admirers? We are all that. It is precisely because we are so bound to admire 'The Old Wives' Tale' and
'Clayhanger' and 'Whom God Hath Joined,' that we cannot
but deplore 'The Lion's Share' and 'The Roll-Call' and
'Lilian.' They are well enough. But they are utterly
unworthy of the great Mr. Bennett. The last-named work,
indeed, was so frankly trivial that we began to give up
hope. Mr. Bennett, it appeared, had for all practical
purposes retired from the ring. He was willing every now
and then to box an exhibition match, just to flutter the
fans; but as for handing more of what a famous sporting
journalist has called 'the bye-bye medicine' to the grim
enemy against whom all our champions battle for immortality - well, there seemed no longer any question of that.
'Riceyman Steps' re-opens the question. It is a serious,
a solid piece of work. It has almost all the old Bennett
dexterity of manipulation, it has even flashes of the old
Bennett poetry - as in the picture of Elsie, the starved
maid-of-all-work, for whom 'kindness had a quality which
justified it for its own sake, whatever the consequences
of it might be.' It is so good that our excitement over
what its author will give us next becomes a positive
fever. It may be - it *may* be - that Mr. Bennett is coming
back after all. But I cannot think that he has come.

For one thing, his theme is artificial - it looks as if
he had said to himself, firmly, that he would take
Clerkenwell, and cancer, and the lust of greed, and, in
short, the most obvious and flamboyant triumphs of the
devil, and compel them to witness to the unquenchable
nobility of the human heart, and, in short, to the glory
of God. No harm in that, if he did compel them: but does
he? A middle-aged bookseller, with a dirty shop and a
sweated charwoman, marries a widow: one of the links between them is that they sweat the same charwoman. He is
a miser. They install the charwoman as a general servant -
now not only sweated, but kept so short of food that she
is irresistibly compelled to steal and eat raw bacon in
the night. Within a year, both the miser and his wife are
dead, the one of cancer and the other of collapse after an
operation for a fibroid growth. Possible, no doubt - but
wholly lacking in that august inevitability which it might
have derived from a different treatment. We ought to feel:
'This happened. How sad!' (for humanity naturally feels
a sadness in the death of even the most repulsive people).
All that I personally am able to feel is: 'Mr. Bennett

says that life is like that, whereas in fact it is not
particularly like that.' There is the limiting note
of generalization throughout.

There, I think, is the weakness which Mr. Bennett,
'mewing his mighty youth,' will have to shake off if he
is ever to return to the firm earth and bright skies of
reality. He is too knowing, too much the showman. Above
all, there are constantly those fatal generalizations
about women:

> The lie, invented on the instant, succeeded per-
> fectly. And Elsie, the honestest soul in Clerkenwell,
> gave it the support of her silence in the great cause
> of women against men.

What is this great cause? Meaningless, absolutely
meaningless! - yet presented with the air of one who is,
so to speak, telling you! A hundred pages later we find:
'The deep-rooted suspiciousness which separates in some
degree every woman from every other woman....' Nor do we
have to wait long for the assertion that 'nearly every
man' is capable, on occasion, of being 'as irrational as
a woman.' The extraordinary thing about such sayings is
their ingenuousness. The world is half peopled with
women: one cannot live anywhere save on a desert island
without meeting them, and realizing that they are as infinitely individual and various as the other sex (how, for
that matter, could they not be?); yet grave gentlemen go
on and on laying down the law about them as if they were
an abstraction in a library. However, I prefer Mr. Bennett saying what is patently nonsensical to Mr. Bennett
saying what is perfectly obvious - and then ejaculating
'Strange!' as if he had by sleight of hand discovered to
us the secrets of our mysterious, terrific prison-house.
And lastly, if Mr. Bennett has envisaged his own creations
at all, why, after repeatedly insisting that his miser
wears a beard, does he make him wonder, after a few days'
illness, to find stubble on his cheek, and ask himself:
'How long was it since he had shaved?' All the same, Mr.
Bennett is indubitably a great man; and if I pick holes in
him, it is not without reverence.

108. ROSE MACAULAY, IN THE 'NATION AND ATHENAEUM'

10 November 1923, 248

Rose Macaulay (1881–1958), distinguished novelist and
essayist, won the James Tait Black Prize - which Bennett
himself won with 'Riceyman Steps' - with her 'The Towers
of Trebizond' in 1956. Her review of Bennett followed
reviews of works by Padraic Colum, Jack London, and others.

... How sharp a contrast, nearly every way, is Mr. Arnold
Bennett's 'Riceyman Steps'! Mr. Bennett has no literary
graces, no bland elegance of style; it is not in these
that his charm lies. He writes without rhythm and without
beauty. The persons he writes about are depressingly
stupid, ugly, and unlovable. But, at any rate, there they
are, alive and solid, actual people in an actual world;
and how much this is! Mr. Bennett moves us, and, I think,
means to move us, to no sympathy with his creatures; their
cancers, their fibroid growths, their underfeeding, their
gluttony, their affections, he presents with the cool,
skilled detachment of the artist or the surgeon, but with,
in addition, humour that almost endears them to us after
all. 'Riceyman Steps' is a very brilliant book; in it Mr.
Bennett has got quite away from millionaires and the
vulgar rich, and returned to the vulgar poor, setting them
against a sordid background in Clerkenwell. His miserly
bookseller, his vulgar, affectionate wife, and their
kindly, loyal, greedy, starved servant girl, are all
superbly alive. The book is not perfect in form; it has
its tediums; it is long-drawn; in parts it drags; the
situations are repeated. But it is full of admirable
scenes strongly imagined, wittily expressed: the bookseller and his lady out on a day's pleasuring, shadowed by
the man's passion for parsimony; the servant in the kitchen yielding to the temptation of the steak; Riceyman
Square on a Sunday morning. The shrewd, sharp realism of
these and other passages shows Mr. Bennett at his best.
He meant, presumably, to draw a truthful and amusing picture of a small and distressed group of people against an
unlovely background of Clerkenwell streets; and he has
brilliantly succeeded. 'Riceyman Steps' is very certainly
the best novel he has written for a long time.

109. J.B. PRIESTLEY, ARNOLD BENNETT AT LAST, 'SPECTATOR'

10 November 1923, 704

J.B. Priestley (1894-) was in 1923 at the beginning of
his long and distinguished literary career. For his
general article on Bennett see No. 112.

It was the engaging habit of Edward Henry Machin, otherwise Denry the Card, to make up his mind, when things were
at their worst, 'to teach 'em a thing or two.' Mr. Bennett apparently made up his mind to teach us a thing or
two, and he has succeeded. Weary of novels that were as
smart as new paint but might have been written by one of
the waiters of the Grand Babylon Hotel, bored or exasperated by pocket philosophies that gave us the commercial
correspondence-school view of life, we have thought of Mr.
Bennett as a writer whose best work was over and done with
long ago; we have openly talked as if he were a spent
force in contemporary letters. We withdraw unreservedly.
'Riceyman Steps,' this new novel of his, is the peer of
'The Old Wives' Tale' and 'Clayhanger,' and if it has not
the panoramic sweep of the earlier stories, it is even
better constructed. We have often seen references to Mr.
Bennett's 'deadening objectivity'; but here, while there
is still the objectivity (for the author has not changed
his naturalistic methods), only a person who really wanted
confectionery instead of literature would discover anything deadening.
    The scene is laid in the dismal region of Clerkenwell,
and all the action passes there, with the exception of a
brief honeymoon trip to a teashop in Oxford Street and
Madame Tussaud's. Needless to say the sights, sounds
and smells of Clerkenwell are touched in with a master
hand. The characters are few and the story itself quite
simple. A middle-aged second-hand bookseller, Earlforward by name, falls in love, in his own fashion, with a
widow who keeps a shop across the way. The two get married and take into their house, as maid, a girl named
Elsie who has acted as charwoman for them. Elsie is a
war-widow who has a lover in the person of Joe, a shell-
shocked ex-soldier. Owing to insufficient nourishment
(Mr. Bennett talks of cancer, which seems unlikely), both
Earlforward and his wife are taken ill; she is removed to
a hospital and dies there after an operation; he remains

at home, refusing medical attention, under the care of
Elsie. The latter, a bewildered, unsophisticated creature, whose fine instinctive actions are magnificently
described, has also her lover, Joe, suffering from
malaria, upon her hands. In the end, Earlfoward himself
dies; Joe recovers, and he and Elsie go into the service
of the local practitioner, Dr. Raste. These are the
facts. The further facts are that Earlforward is a
miser; his wife only one degree better; Elsie steals
scraps of food; Joe is little more than an idiot. Here,
it is obvious, there is a glorious opportunity for that
deadening objectivity. And yet there is none.

Mr. Bennett, with infinite cunning, while seeming to
show us Clerkenwell and introduce to us, rather casually,
a few people who live there, while appearing to add one
remembered fact to another in the easiest fashion, is
really allowing us to peep into the minds, the hearts,
the souls of his principal figures. We know how it would
all look from the outside, how it would read in, say, a
newspaper report, and, thanks to our author's command of
the method he has made his own, we do seem to be looking
at it from the outside; and yet we are inside the characters, we are living with them in every moment, and we are
compelled to sympathize with them, and what seems of awful
significance to them assumes a like significance for us,
so that it is only when our author looses his hold that
this is Clerkenwell as we think we know it, that these are
misers as we have heard them commonly described, and so on
and so forth. This is the great triumph of the book. We
doubt if Mr. Bennett even remembers the passage (for,
ironically enough, we may be certain that he long ago
decided that Stevenson was beneath his notice), but there
is one part of Stevenson's delightful essay on the romantic attitude to life, 'The Lantern-Bearers,' in which,
defending his thesis that there is a poet in the centre
of every man's mind, he singles out the unpleasant figure
of Dancer, the miser, and shows what might be made even of
him if one worked from the centre outwards. Mr. Bennett
has actually done this with Earlforward, who should be
detestable, with all his ghastly economies, but whom we
actually like, in spite of the fact that there is not a
single sentimental flourish in Mr. Bennett's description
of him and his actions. His wife is a silly, mean, little
creature, but she is also a woman, moving doubtfully between Clerkenwell and Eternity, and we follow her breathlessly, glad when she is glad (perhaps because she has won
a battle over the lighting of a fire or a piece of cheese)
and miserable when she is miserable. Even better than the
Earlforwards is the figure that seems to us the corner-

stone of the whole erection, the figure of Elsie, with
her appetite and paltry thefts, her huge loyalties and
unspoken passions, her little ill-spelt letter from her
lover which she carries about until it is coming to
pieces, her terrible last weeks in the house, when her
master is lying ill on one floor, her lover (unknown to
her master) lying ill on another floor, her mistress
dying in hospital, when she is called upon to endure a
kind of awful siege and is raised into a heroic figure,
as simple human creatures so often are, by the sudden
pressure of circumstance. But it is in the actual conduct
of the narrative, the actual scenes that are introduced
so easily and naturally before our eyes, without any
appearance of undue haste, and yet with every little
piece of description or dialogue adding precisely its
quota to the general picture, that Mr. Bennett's genius
is to be discovered; and such scenes must be left to the
reader himself, for they cannot be adequately epitomized.
The story is not, of course, entirely without flaws.
Thus, for example, Mr. Bennett's account of Earlforward
in the opening chapters does not altogether square with
the later description of his actions and with our later
idea of him, and it looks as if he were just a little too
eager to obtain our sympathy before showing us the whole
Earlforward. Again, the casual mention towards the end
of the book of the fact that Elsie is a war-widow on a
full pension seems very belated; it hardly appears possible that such a fact would have escaped the Earlforwards, with their nose for money. But these are
trifles when compared with the massive achievement of the
book, which makes most of our recent triumphs in fiction
seem rather paltry affairs. Mr. Bennett, by denying himself every romantic aid, by frankly accepting the ugly and
commonplace and transfiguring it, has justified his
method even to those who have always disliked the method;
and he has triumphed over his critics in the only way that
such critics, if they are devoted to their profession,
will be glad to recognize; he has at last written a book
that does not shake our faith in his genius but makes us
passionately and delightedly reaffirm it.

110. RAYMOND MORTIMER, IN THE 'NEW STATESMAN'

10 November 1923, 148

Raymond Mortimer (1895-1980) was for many years literary critic for the 'Sunday Times'. The three revues mentioned at the beginning of Mortimer's remarks are Aldous Huxley's 'Antic Hay', Rose Macaulay's 'Told by an Idiot', and Carl Van Vechten's 'The Blind Bow-Boy'.

By the side of these three revues, 'Riceyman Steps' seems a very compact and solid affair. It is the most serious novel Mr. Bennett has written for a long while, well planned and carefully written, without the least surrender to popular taste. Caviare to the general, then, very probably; but hardly that *caviare frais* which the gourmet likes best. Mr. Bennett is the *Balzac de nos jours*, and in no book has this ambition (surely conscious, for is he not a French scholar?) been more clear than in his new novel. The miserly bookseller, the middle-aged and comfortably-off widow who is rash enough to marry him, the patient, servant girl - they are all figures from 'La Comédie Humaine.' (Particularly good, by the way, is the treatment of the girl's feelings towards her mistress.) And then the passionate interest in things, the elaborate inventories, and the continual preoccupation with money - Mr. Bennett challenges comparison at every turn. If the result, in spite of all his skill and honesty, is rather dreary, it is, I think, not only because he lacks the terrific impetus of Balzac's imagination, but because he lives eighty years later. The conditions of life in Clerkenwell which he so exactly describes are not essentially unlike some that Balzac wrote about. But the mind of the reader has changed, and so has that of the author. Careful realisation of possible human beings has ceased in itself to be interesting, and the qualities that still attract us to the 'Comédie Humaine' are not those which contributed most to its original success. It may be agreeable to think of works of art as existing outside of time, but actually they must be considered in relation to a variable factor - the mind of the spectator or reader. 'Riceyman Steps' leaves one with the highest opinion of Mr. Bennett's literary character, and it successfully achieves its end, but it is old-fashioned. And the serious artist cannot afford to neglect fashion.

(The word 'zeitgeist' sounds more impressive, but it is not so pretty.) Balzac does not seem démodé because we appreciate his fidelity to his period. He expresses everything which is in his mind. Mr. Bennett does not. Many of our established novelists write dull books because they are dull people. Mr. Bennett is remarkably alert. Artists, again, are sometimes born out of date, and one can conceive of a contemporary who should rival Balzac on his own ground because by some anomaly he felt like him. But Mr. Bennett is proud to be a modern, and is always quick to recognise new forms and new sensibilities. No one wants him to adopt a method foreign to him, but he is here most competently making something too old-fangled for satisfactory self-expression. Mr. Bennett's earlier books succeeded, as is the way of good writers' first works, by reason of the freshness and energy behind them. The example of all his predecessors goes to show that having reached the age when his position is established, he must rely on qualities which at first he could afford to neglect. One of these is a greater delicacy of style, and another, more important, is a completer rendering of what is significant and, may I add, novel, in his experience of life.

111. FILSON YOUNG, MR. BENNETT STOPS BOILING THE POT, 'NEW YORK TIMES BOOK REVIEW'

18 November 1923, 7

Filson Young (1876-1938) wrote a number of books concerned with travel and communication. In his later years he was an adviser to the BBC.

The two books that are certain to be most talked about here in the next few weeks are Arnold Bennett's 'Riceyman Steps' and Winston Churchill's second book on the war, 'The World Crisis, 1915'. Both should have a special interest for American readers, because Arnold Bennett is at once probably the most prolific and the best known of contemporary English front-rank novelists, and because Winston Churchill is not only the foremost figure in the English political world, but half American.

I confess that I looked forward without much hope to
another book by Arnold Bennett.   Until I read it I had
regarded him as one of England's war losses.   That great
interruption and deflection deprived us of more than
blood and treasure.   It quenched infinitely more spiritual
and creative fire than it kindled, and more than one
English writer whom it found entering on his best and
ripest period was so damaged by it that his career may
be said to have ended in 1914.   Nothing that Arnold Bennett has written since had been in my mind at all comparable with the great series of novels which he wrote round
the Staffordshire pottery towns.   He had, so to speak,
fallen at a critical moment in his career, and it was not
likely that he would rise again.

Well, that, I am glad to say, was a mistake.   In the
new novel he comes back to the method he employed in his
earlier works, and with the manner he has also recovered
something of the spirit that made 'The Old Wives' Tale'
a true masterpiece of universal comedy and pathos.   This
new book is in plan as simple as a book could be; it is
just a study of a year or two in the lives of two miserly
people and their servant girl in a highly characteristic
quarter of London.   I wish the book and its spirit could
be really appreciated by some of the younger school of
novelists: it would be a wonderful lesson to them in
treatment. For the few characters in the book are all
sordid, not to say squalid, and the opportunities for
plunging into a kind of realism that is popular with
writers of the moment - the realism of the catalogue and
the photograph - are unlimited.   But the book is full of
an atmosphere of spiritual charm and even beauty.   I will
not say that it is free from sentimentality, because it is
not.   But it is not the worst kind of sentimentality,
because it is not used to gild over the squalor with a
coat of sham refinement: but rather to lay bare, like a
polish or a varnish, the true grain of beauty and heroism
that lies in the apparently sordid material.   To read a
book like this by an author who has meant so much to one
in the past is like welcoming an old friend who has come
back from the dead.

General Views: 1924

From 1917 until his death in 1931 Bennett was the subject
of a number of general articles and studies. It seems
fair to say that none of this material advanced understanding beyond the level of the essays in the 'New Age'
and the 'Nation' in 1908 and 1910. Critics often praised
Bennett's technical virtuosity or his psychological insight, but no one made a move to discuss either in much
detail. This was due in part to the character of criticism of the time, which usually practised appreciation
and review rather than close scrutiny; but it must also
have been due to a certain transparent quality of his
work that seemed to make analysis supererogatory. All
was plain and readable, and what more was there to do
than to describe and admire, describe and scorn, or
describe and select? (No matter that there was often
extreme contradiction about what was worthy of praise
or scorn.) Perhaps in all the years from 1908 to 1931
the two most narrowly focused articles were those by
Stuart Pratt Sherman and Dorothea Price Hughes (Nos 87
and 88), which undertook in individual ways to describe
limits to Bennett's realism, but even these articles
seemed to do little more than to illuminate the obvious.
The later years saw the publication of the second book
on Bennett, L.G. Johnson's 'Arnold Bennett of the Five
Towns', 1924, which elicited from Bennett an appreciative
letter (LAB III, 233). In the same year or earlier,
George Doran issued a booklet called 'Arnold Bennett,
Appreciations', with pieces by H.T. Follett, J.W. Cunliffe,
and others. An earlier form of the booklet, called
'Arnold Bennett, An Introduction', contained material
going back to 1911. Also in these later years appeared
the first known English thesis on Bennett, The Work of
Arnold Bennett as a Novelist, by Amphilis Carter, for a
master's degree at Birmingham in 1927. Bennett wrote to

Miss Carter to say that 'of course I cannot be a good
judge of any work on this particular subject; but I must
say that I find it very interesting indeed, and certainly
the best work on that subject that I have yet come across'
(SOT). For a list of material on Bennett in these years
see the Appendix.

---

112. J.B. PRIESTLEY, MR. ARNOLD BENNETT, 'LONDON MERCURY'

February 1924, 394-406

Bennett wrote to Priestley about the article, 'I did not
agree with all of it; but at any rate I thought it very
able and I agree heartily with all the praise; also I
thought that some of the animadversions were rather good'
(LAB III, 224). In his 'Journal' on 16 February 1924
Bennett expressed annoyance with Priestley's strictures
on technique: 'a bit thick', he thought. Priestley's
essay was reprinted in his 'Figures in Modern Literature'
later in the year.

There are more than fifty volumes now in the 'List of
Works to date,' that faces the title page of every book
by Mr. Bennett, and at the very sight of this monstrous
bibliography, a kind of despair falls upon the critic who
would try to estimate such an author. Nor is there any
way out of it; the list must be faced resolutely, man-
fully, or the criticism will suffer. It will not do to
treat Mr. Bennett as the author of only three books
instead of fifty-three; we cannot write at length about
'The Old Wives' Tale,' 'Clayhanger' and, let us say,
'Riceyman Steps,' and then condemn all our author's other
works, his fantasias, short stories, plays, pocket philosophies and books of travel and chit-chat, to the pulping
machines with one wave of the hand. Many of these works
may cut a better figure in their author's ledger accounts
than they ever will in the literary histories of our time,
but they are there and cannot be rightly ignored, for the
real Mr. Bennett is not the writer of this or that book
but is to be found somewhere behind all these books, perhaps buried beneath them but buried alive. Moreover, it
is dangerous to dismiss whole rows of these less important
volumes, because Mr. Bennett, being amazingly unequal, can
suddenly fall to writing well in unexpected places just as

he can fall to writing badly. As examples of the craft
of writing, the actual business of setting down a number
of facts and impressions in words, as distinct from the
wider art of creation in literature, he has probably given
us nothing better than the first few sketches in 'Paris
Nights,' which was called a 'bold, brilliant, exciting
book' when it first came out but has not, I imagine,
attracted much attention recently; so that, to take only
this one example, Mr. Bennett cannot be fairly judged
without his 'Paris Nights.' It is clear that to be seen
distinctly he must be seen against the background of his
complete works, good, bad and indifferent; many people
only know the author of 'The Human Machine' or 'How To
Make The Best of Life,' some others only know the author
of 'The Old Wives' Tale' or 'Clayhanger,' but both authors
must be the subjects of any critical estimate of Mr.
Arnold Bennett. The only danger there is in such a
thorough examination, when space is limited, is that the
mere bulk of work prevents close detailed criticism, with
its eye on the individual book, its insistence upon chapter and verse, and inevitably encourages that loose easy
generalising mode of criticism of which Mr. Bennett so
far has had, perhaps, more than his fair share. This
danger, however, is the least of many, and if Mr. Bennett
has to suffer yet a few more easy generalisations, he must
remember that he himself has been generalising no less
easily and loosely throughout some half a hundred volumes.
   These volumes are the work of a trinity of authors.
The first, the most prolific and easily the best known,
is the omniscient Mr. Bennett, the connoisseur, the tip-
ster of life and the arts, the man who can put you wise,
who can tell you a thing or two, who has made a stir in
the big city and is now 'in the swim,' 'in the movement'
(his favourite phrases - see works *passim*), a terrible
fellow who knows more about life than even the head
waiter of the Grand Babylon Hotel. He has been everywhere
and knows everything; he is curious and knowledgeable
about cities, books, railway trains, soup, water-colours,
frocks and skirts, and the Parisian Theatre; he is a lover
of experts and probably wishes to become the expert of
experts. In all this intense curiosity about every side
of the life of his own time there is a zest, gusto, infec-
tious enthusiasm, that is entirely admirable. At a time
when so many clever persons are trying, in one way or
another, to escape from life, to pretend that the real
world is not there, we have here a very clever man who
cannot have too much of it, a realist who discovers as
much delight in a fact as some of his fellow authors do
in an idea, and has the power to communicate something of

that delight. Whatever else he may be, this Mr. Bennett
is certainly a great journalist. Yet the result of this
intense curiosity, this unflagging zest for things, is an
attitude that is knowing rather than wise. There are too
many limitations. Whole sides of life and states of
mind, and these by no means the least important, some of
them perhaps the most important, seem to mean nothing to
him; he knows his world like the great journalist he is,
but it is still the journalist's world, the world of the
evening papers and not that of the poets, the saints and
mystics, the great philosophers and historians; the voice
is always that of an oracle, brimmed with certainties, but
it is too often the oracle of the smoke-room. The section
of his work which, with something like blasphemy, he
cheerfully labels Belles-Lettres is nothing less than an
epic of the cocksure. In his so-called Pocket Philosophies, or at least in some of them, he combines the vulgarity of the early Utilitarians (whose detachment perhaps
modified it) with the equal vulgarity of a typical smart
young materialist of the Eighties, whose dying whispers
can be caught in Mr. Bennett's favourite metaphors, his
talk about the Human Machine and so forth. Many sensitive
readers, after learning from our author how to make the
best of life, must have come to the conclusion that life
was not worth making the best of, so sadly had it been
vulgarised.   So, too, his criticism, though there are
delightful elements in it, is too often merely the cheerful impudence of a clever man who is not making a critical
effort and is too interested either in attacking or
following literary fashions to be capable of such an
effort. It is this Mr. Bennett who is responsible for the
miscellaneous books, who contributes a paragraph on every
other page in the lighter novels, does his share of the
dialogue in the plays, and even finds his way into the
more serious novels. Unfortunately for him and fortunately for us, however, his work, except that in the
pocket philosophies, is usually brought to nothing because
there is someone at hand to give the game away, to reveal
the fact that the writer is not really a bored encyclo-
paedic guide to the life of wealth and taste but is really
a dazed enthusiast, a kind of wondering poet from the provinces, staggered at the way he is 'getting on.' You have
only to open the first book to hand of Mr. Bennett's to
see how frankly the game is given away: 'Then it suddenly
occurred to me that if I had gambled with louis instead
of five-franc pieces I should have made 200 francs - 200
francs in rather over an hour! Oh, luxury! Oh, being-in-
the swim! Oh, smartness! Oh, gilded and delicious sin!'
That is not the first Mr. Bennett at all; it is the second,

chanting his happy litany.

This second Mr. Bennett is simpler, more naive and enthusiastic, and altogether more engaging than the first; and he is nearer by a thousand leagues to the soul of literature, for he has one quality that is an essential ingredient of great romance - a sense of wonder. True, it is very limited; not only is the past closed to it, that living past which has been woven into the fabric of tradition and has secured for our delight the fragrance, colour and bloom of centuries, but much else that does not glitter on the surface of things is hidden from it too; and yet even this limitation is our gain, for it means that our author is lost in wonder at things that most other authors have ceased to wonder at, so that in his own fashion he has created a new kind of poetry. He is Wonder in a billycock, Romance with an excursion ticket to London, as mazed and dizzy at the sight of Harrods or the Savoy Hotel as Mr. de la Mare is with his dream of Arabia or Mr. Turner with his vision of the Andes; he comes to a metropolitan hotel as Childe Harold came to the Dark Tower. The advantages of being a provincial, one who has long been acquainted with the solid realities of life as they are to be discovered in small industrial towns, where the solid realities are most starkly displayed, and who is now zestful and ripe for the magnificent frivolities, the splendid mummeries, of London, these advantages were never better illustrated. In novel after novel, particularly those of the lighter kind, it is this Mr. Bennett, with his fresh vision, his humour and high spirits, who carries off the situation; he has only to take us all into a big hotel or restaurant or the Turkish Baths, and the trick is done and we are all excited, interested or amused again, all stepping out of King's Cross or St. Pancras still grasping the return half of our tickets, trying to look like persons who know what is what and are not to be trifled with, great city or no great city, but inwardly out-gasping and gaping stout Cortez himself. He does it time after time; Denry's whole existence, as we know him in 'The Card' and 'The Regent,' is one long excited climb; Priam Farll and his lady go trotting about the town and we are thrilled anew with them; Mr. Prohack quits his office to be one of the idle rich and has some wonderful sensations in the West End; and so on and so forth; the situation never palls on the writer and we catch something of his zest. He is the rhapsodist of gigantic hotels and restaurants, White Cities, fashionable theatres and clubs, Turkish Baths, two thousand pound motor cars, pianolas, exclusive tailors, labour-saving devices, everything that is modern, expensive, luxurious, and not to be found in

the Five Towns, or at least, in the Five Towns when Mr.
Bennett lived there.   Practically all his lighter stories,
most of which he certainly enjoyed writing, are stories of
wealth and luxury; they are crowded with millionaires who
live in suites at colossal hotels, and are, in reality, a
kind of fairy story that Mr. Bennett, seeing relaxation
after the austerities of naturalistic fiction, is telling
to himself, an old dream that comes back to his mind every
time he sits down to write an easy idle tale.   There is a
fairy tale somewhere in every creative artist, and Mr.
Bennett's is an up-to-date medley of millionaires whose
hotel bills are twenty-five to fifty pounds a day, magnificently expensive and charming women of the world,
experts, from medical to sartorial, ready at any moment
to dance attendance and charge astounding fees, a full
chorus of chefs, waiters, chauffeurs and flunkeys; and
in the midst of it all some half-sophisticated, half-
simple soul, busy fulfilling old dreams and pinching himself to discover if he is yet awake; while in the background, the symbol of the luxurious life, the heaven of
all climbers and Cards and Human Machines and men who
live on twenty-four hours a day, there looms and blazes
against the night sky - the Grand Babylon Hotel.   If Mr.
Bennett should ever become a legend and his work come to
be regarded as a number of folk tales (and stranger things
have happened), about one-third of his works will be
grouped together as the Grand Babylon Hotel Cycle and
attempts will no doubt be made to determine its religious
significance.   Meanwhile, the significance for us of these
comedies of high life and high jinks that are played,
without regard to expense, on carpets five inches thick,
lies in the fact that in them the dreams and aspirations,
the romantic possibilities of what had hitherto appeared
to be the least promising class in the kingdom, the
middle-aged members of the middle-class, have been seized
upon and pressed into service as they never have before,
for the possible instruction of a few sociologists and the
delight of all good novel readers.   Finally, the secret of
these romantic comedies of middle-age by a middle-aged
novelist, the secret of their somewhat naive charm, is
that at heart they are simply boyish; this second Mr. Bennett is nothing more (nor less) than a brilliant and
delightful youth, not quite out of his teens, who has out-
grown his tin soldiers and treasure islands only to make
the Grand Babylon Hotel, golden, shining, the centre of
his dreams and summit of his aspirations.

    But even though another ten stories should be added to
it, the Grand Babylon Hotel cannot entirely blot out the
night sky and the strange stars, and not all the hosts of

porters and page boys can prevent Change and Death from
forcing their way into its velvet, gilded lounge; in
short, there is a great deal more in life, and in the
art that would pretend to grapple with life, than was
ever dreamed of in the philosophy of the second Mr. Bennett. But there is yet another Mr. Bennett, the third
and last, who has made the largest contribution to the
major works but who is yet less distinct than the others
and can hardly be described, without grave injustice, in
a few lines. He does not glide over the surface of things
as the other two do; he has not their almost metallic
optimism; indeed, all his brave epicurean gestures cannot
prevent us from noticing that he is at heart troubled and
somewhat pitiful, sceptical, but, despite his fine show of
indifference, not coolly sceptical, but disturbed, leaning
ever towards pessimism. He it is who has written so many
passages like the following, which comes from that little
encounter between Carlotta and old Lord Alcar in 'Sacred
and Profane Love':

> '...Only the fool and the very young expect happi-
> ness. The wise merely hope to be interested, at least
> not to be bored, in their passage through the world.
> Nothing is so interesting as love and grief and the one
> involves the other. Ah! would I not do the same again!'
> He spoke gravely, wistfully, and vehemently, as if
> employing the last spark of divine fire that was left
> in his decrepit frame. This undaunted confession of
> faith which had survived twenty years of inactive medi-
> tation, this banner waved by an expiring arm in the
> face of the eternity that mocks at the transience of
> human things, filled me with admiration....

He it was - to go from an early book to one of the most
recent - who wrote the title (but nothing else) of the
last volume of philosophy for the million that the first,
omniscient, Mr. Bennett gave us; the title is 'How to Make
the Best of Life,' which has a strange ring, suggesting
that the writer, so apparently cheerful, so cocksure,
believes in his heart of hearts that life is a bad business - but (and we can see him yawning and shrugging) he
can give the young readers a few tips that might ease
their gradual descent into the grave. He it was, too,
who devised that fine melancholy thing, 'The Old Wives'
Tale,' which has two suffering heroines, Constance and
Sophia Baines, and three conquering heroes, Time, Mutability and Death. The shadows of these three are over 'Clayhanger' too, and here again we cannot fail to notice how,
in selecting and arranging his material, he has chosen to

emphasize the passing of the old, the coming of the new,
change and decay. Here, we feel life, which may be something more than sound and fury, may be coloured with passion, shot through with beauty, brought into harmony for
an hour or so by love, is still a tale told by an idiot,
the silliest, saddest old wife. Many critics have seen
in this Mr. Bennett a sociologist, mainly because sociology in the guise of fiction has been fashionable and Mr.
Bennett happens to have worked closely over large canvasses and has been inspired more by the character of a
whole region than by a few individuals; but actually,
though he has sometimes taken over a few sociological
tricks from his friend, Mr. Wells, he is no sociologist.
Like Mr. Wells, he is fond of emphasising the fact that
times change, and passages like this are common:

> John Baines had belonged to the past, to the age
> when men really did think of their souls, when orators
> by phrases could move crowds to fury or to pity, when
> no one had learnt to hurry, when Demos was only turning
> in his sleep, when the sole beauty of life resided in
> its inflexible and slow dignity, when hell really had
> no bottom and a gilt-clasped Bible really was the
> secret of England's greatness. Mid-Victorian England
> lay sleeping on that mahogany bed. Ideals had passed
> away with John Baines. It is thus that ideals die;
> not in the conventional pageantry of honoured death,
> but sorrily, ignobly, while one's head is turned....

and he will often show a whole countryside moving from one
era to another, but unlike Mr. Wells (with his laboratory
and lecture-room manner), he does not describe growth and
development, movement towards a certain end, so much as
simply change itself, the social kaleidoscope. As for his
pessimism, his vaguely uneasy scepticism, that is always
liable to show itself when the easy mental attitudes of
the omniscient and the wondering Mr. Bennett can no longer
be maintained, it is rather felt everywhere, like an
atmosphere, than definitely encountered; but it is certainly there, and it is this that makes so many persons,
men and women, who do not ask for barley-sugar from
literature, who can relish their Hardy, Meredith, Conrad,
indifferent or even antagonistic to Mr. Bennett's finest
work; and even the rest of us must have caught ourselves
and our friends more often heartily praising such work
than returning to it for another reading. Mr. Bennett's
literary methods, as distinct from his attitude of mind,
have, of course, their influence here, and they will be
noticed below; but it is worth remarking that this third

Mr. Bennett, like the two others though in a less degree, has still some unfortunate limitations; we feel a want of values, and notice a certain insensitiveness to the finer shades of feeling, the more subtle traits of character, the more poetical and mystical states of mind. He deliberately makes all his figures smaller than himself so that he can see round them rather than enter into them. He is something more than an ironical spectator; he is frequently moved both by a generous enthusiasm and by pity, and he can often strike out a gushing spring of romance and beauty from what would appear barren rock. There is, for example, one chapter in 'Clayhanger,' a chapter that may possibly make a stronger appeal to North country readers than to others, which describes how the young Clayhanger, in search of a customer of his father's attends a Free-and-Easy at the local tavern and there dis- covers the art of clog-dancing as understood by Florence Simcox:

> Her style was not that of a male clog-dancer, but it was indubitably clog-dancing, full of marvels to the connoisseur, and to the profane naught but a highly complicated series of wooden noises. Florence's face began to perspire. Then the concertina ceased playing – so that an undistracted attention might be given to the supremely difficult final figure of the dance.
> And thus was rendered back to the people in the charming form of beauty that which the instincts of the artist had taken from the sordid ugliness of the people. The clog, the very emblem of the servitude and the squalor of brutalised populations, was changed, on the light feet of this favourite, into the medium of grace. Few of these men but at some time of their lives had worn the clog, had clattered in it through winter's slush, and through the freezing darkness before dawn, to the manufactory and the mill and the mine, whence after a day of labour under discipline more than mili- tary, they had clattered back to their little candle- lighted homes. One of the slatterns behind the door actually stood in clogs to watch the dancer. The clog meant everything that was harsh, foul and desolating; it summoned images of misery and disgust. Yet on those feet that had never worn it seriously, it became the magic instrument of pleasure, waking dulled wits and forgotten aspirations, putting upon everybody an enchantment....

But if we turn back to the fifty-odd volumes, the Bennett canon, we may choose to see them not as the work

of three different authors but as the work of one author
who has been played upon by three different sets of influences corresponding to the three divisions into which his
life, during its most formative period, very easily falls.
There is, first, his childhood, education and early manhood in the Five Towns. From 1867 to the beginning of the
'Nineties, young E.A. Bennett, brisk as a bee, was unconsciously hiving facts and impressions, scenes and characters for the day when Arnold Bennett, already a smart
journalist with a story or two to his credit, should seek
a new element for his fiction and suddenly pluck out these
fat golden honeycombs. Mr. Bennett created the Five Towns
but only after they had created him. It must not be
thought, though, that he owes his success to the interest
and appeal of his chosen 'locality' - as some smaller
writers do - for the result would have been just the same
had he been born and bred in Lancashire or the West Riding,
on the Tyne or the Clyde. He was made by the Five Towns
only because they stuffed his head with material to which
he had only (it is a big 'only') to apply his later dexterity and craft to transform into magnificent fiction;
and this material was so plentiful, his early memories
crowded so thick and fast upon him, that his work, willy-
nilly, took on that fullness and richness which is one of
the glories of English fiction. There was a time when Mr.
Bennett, under French influences, was probably all in
favour of thin, rigid, brittle narratives, of the kind
that are quite wrongly regarded as masterpieces of technique, and so was all against such fullness and richness,
such lively and crowded canvasses, but fortunately there
was a divinity that shaped his ends and that divinity was
the Five Towns, 'smouldering and glittering' in his
memory. His real mastery and his real popularity began
with the Five Towns stories, and, with the exception of
his latest novel, 'Riceyman Steps,' all his best work is
linked up with his birthplace. It must not be forgotten,
too, that his early popularity was due in part to the fact
that he had what we might call a 'locality' reference that
helped the ordinary reader to remember his name and work;
he was the Arnold Bennett who wrote amusing stories about
the Five Towns. At first, in his volumes of short tales,
like the 'Grim Smile of the Five Towns,' and such things
as 'Helen with the High Hand,' he had a tendency to act
the showman instead of the plain chronicler; in the middle
of a story he would beat a big drum and invite the reader
to walk up, walk up, to see the strange characteristics of
the Five Towns. This trick, however, in its most aggressive form, he soon dropped and there is little of it after
1908. He shares with his sturdy fellow-townsmen, whom he

has described with such gusto, many leading traits, not the least of which is a robust sense of humour that, if it lacks subtlety, has at least few blind spots. Like them, too, he is always steadily aware of the grim realities, the unpleasant facts of existence; he knows the provincial and industrial tragi-comedy.

The second period is that of his early years in London, when he was engaged in journalism and ingenious pot-boiling of various kinds. He became a very successful journalist, and has remained one ever since; most of his lighter novels, whatever else they may be, are certainly good journalism, and so too are many of his plays; their style and manner are often those of the short articles on the leader page of a newspaper, and their topics are frequently the topics of the moment, though not so ephemeral in interest that the novels cannot be read or the plays performed after the lapse of a few years. Such a novel as 'Mr. Prohack,' for example, has only a slight story, but is such excellent journalism that it could have been split into fragments, with only a few changes, and published in this periodical and that magazine as sketches of the times. During this period he edited a popular paper for women, and it is often claimed that this experience, obviously a very valuable one, initiated him into all the secrets of feminine psychology; he was admitted behind the scenes and has stayed there ever since. Certainly no modern novelist (if we may believe women themselves) can touch in the details of a woman's life so lightly and surely; but a good deal more than a few years' acquaintance with popular journalism for women is needed to make a man the father of great daughters in literature, and if there is an advantage in knowing some feminine characteristics, as it were, off by heart, such easy knowledge is also not without danger to a creative artist, as we shall presently see. What such popular journalism did do was to give him a thorough understanding and appreciation of the topics, the situations, incidents and characters that have the firmest hold upon the popular imaginations; and this understanding enabled him to lead the monster gently by the nose, and taught him not to fly in its face. His journalism gave him ideas, not purely literary ideas, but ideas of every description, and no novelist of our time has had more; with him, as the late Dixon Scott once pointed out, there is no deception; he not only tells us exactly what his characters can do, but he actually shows us how they do it; when he introduces into a novel a new kind of house or an ideal theatre he gives us an exact description of the labour-saving devices in the house and the interior arrangements of the theatre; when he tells us

how Denry made a fortune and a reputation as a wit and
joker, a Card, we see exactly how it was done, we are
given the schemes, the wit and jokes, until we realise
that the writer himself is a Card too, and that we might
all set up as Cards if we studied the life of Denry with
sufficient care. Further, it taught him that the great
sin in writing is to be dull, and since then he has been
many things, exasperating, irritating, intolerable, but
never dull; even when he was working under the influence
of the bleakest naturalistic theory of the art of fiction,
he was never dull, but always bright, alert, efficient, if
nothing else. But while he learned to see the dramatic
situation, and the equally dramatic 'problem' in his
miscellaneous writing, and to make his style snappy and
perky and button-holing, in all but his very best pieces
of work we see the trail of the newspaper and the bright
weekly all over his situations and his style, and in the
latter we too often hear the click and rattle of efficient
mechanism that is functioning freely (the metaphor and the
several words that compose it are all favourites of Mr.
Bennett's) rather than the music of an instrument, finely
tuned and delicately handled. Even in his best things he
never achieves a really fine style. He has written a good
deal about prose style, but it is very doubtful if he
realises what is involved in a great prose style. He, in
common with many other writers on the subject, appears to
think that style is simply the accurate expression of the
writer's matter or thought. But style, in the purely
literary sense of the term, has a three-fold function:
it expresses the thought by a logical arrangement of sym-
bols; it contrives to intensify emotion by its undertones
and overtones, suggestion and association of all kinds;
and further it gives pleasure of itself merely as an
arrangement, a pattern, a decoration. Most of us think
ourselves fortunate if we succeed in making our style
fulfil the first part of its function, and Mr. Bennett,
like Mr. Wells, but unlike Mr. Hardy or Mr. Conrad, is no
more successful. He sometimes comes near to a personal
style by making use of certain tricks, the chief of which
is a succession of short exclamatory sentences that begin
with a panting conjunction and end with a gasping mark of
exclamation; but such tricks are far from being pleasant.
Indeed, had there not been another set of influences at
work, Mr. Bennett might have declined altogether into a
writer of bright melodramas and amusing clap-trap
articles. 'When one looks back,' he has written, 'one
sees that certain threads run through one's life, making
a sort of pattern in it. These threads and the nature
of the pattern are not perceived until long after the

events constituting them. I now see that there has been a
French thread through my life.' This last set of influences, in short, is the result of his early interest in
French, chiefly modern French, literature (at a time when
his acquaintance with our own literature was only slight),
and of an equal interest in French life that finally led
to his living in France for nearly ten years.

It is obvious that an impressionable man of letters
cannot prefer a foreign literature (and one entirely alien
in its outlook and manner) and suffer a voluntary exile
for so long without some considerable change taking place
in his point of view and his methods of work. Only a long
and close study, based on something more than an outside
knowledge of Mr. Bennett's work, could assess the value
of such influences, but we may reasonably permit ourselves
a few guesses. In the first place, France developed and
sustained his literary conscience; Mr. Bennett may have
boiled the pot but he has at least boiled it properly and
not taken money for leaving it luke-warm; never at his
worst has he fallen into the disgraceful slovenliness that
spoils so much of Mr. Wells's later work; and at his best,
though he may not reach the last subtleties of construction or the ultimate felicities of style, he has shown a
fine conscientious craftsmanship and has done all that a
man can consciously do to bring his work near to perfection. Further, contact with French life and thought has,
I imagine, sharpened his sense of the dramatic and given to
to his handling of any dramatic situation a certain lightness and crispness. He is not by nature a dramatist at
all because his finest work demands that background to the
action which only a novelist can touch in; and the people
of his plays are not so solid as the persons in his novels
mainly because he sees them as a novelist sees them; but
nevertheless he has contrived to write a number of
successful and entertaining plays simply because he has
good ideas, original but not too original (think of 'Milestones,' 'What the Public Wants' and 'The Title'), and
because he has, too, this light but sure dramatic touch.
So far, this literary apostasy has brought nothing but
gain; but actually there have been serious losses. Mr.
Bennett, who, unlike many novelists, has always been something of a literary theorist, began writing novels at a
time when he was a fervent admirer of Mr. George Moore,
Maupassant and the French naturalistic school. He was a
great advocate of 'technique,' which really meant nothing
more than a suppression of the narrator and a deliberate
simplicity in the narrative, the action, the background.
Later, in 'The Author's Craft,' which is easily the best
of the short talks and is really a very sensible and lucid

discussion of some very difficult subjects, he admitted
that his earlier attitude towards the novel was mistaken:

> With the single exception of Turgenev, the great
> novelists of the world, according to my own standards,
> have either ignored technique or have failed to under-
> stand it. What an error to suppose that the finest
> foreign novels show a better sense of form than the
> finest English novels!

What an error, indeed! The fact is, of course, that the
art of fiction as practised by the great novelists *is*
technique, and any other 'technique' is either some
inferior method or a mere catch-phrase of the pontifical
critic. But Mr. Bennett began with such admirations, and
in following the wrong masters did violence to his own
genius. He himself is essentially a Romantic with certain
ironical, sceptical twists in his mind; and his early
ideas of what a serious novel should be seem to me to have
been definitely harmful because they have made him divide
his work in a fashion that has hindered his development as
a great novelist. To put it shortly, the second Mr. Bennett has never settled down to work in harmony with the
third Mr. Bennett; we have had all the rich comedy, the
fantastic romance of the commonplace, the high spirits on
one side, and the writer's magnificent sense of a social
background, his wide sweep, his feeling for obscure and
only half-articulate tragedy, his grave pity, on the
other side; 'The Card' is a fine tale and 'Clayhanger' is
a finer, but we might have had, and might still have, a
story that was both the Card and Clayhanger and therefore
something more, which would have been unquestionably one
of the greatest works of our time. The naturalistic and
realistic elements in his work have always been sadly
over-emphasized by critics. He is essentially one of our
English Romantics, whose feeling for romance is so strong
that he can find it where most persons would never even
dream of looking for it; indeed, this may be said to be
his great contribution to the English Novel. Practically
all his more serious novels are simply romantic obstacle
races, almost romantic conjuring tricks; for he carefully
puts away all the usual trappings, shows us the most
commonplace people in the dingiest and dreariest setting,
takes off his coat and rolls up his sleeves, and proceeds
to evolve romance. One of his first serious novels,
'Leonora,' shows us that it is possible for a woman
verging on middle-age, the mother of grown-up daughters,
suddenly to become the victim of a consuming romantic
passion. Mr. Bennett himself, I imagine, must be

surprised when he learns that he is regarded, as he so
often is regarded, as one of the enemies of romance, only
anxious to destroy the illusion by holding out for his
readers' inspection the wigs and grease-paint and paste-
board castles of this life, a writer who stands chuckling
with Time himself over the crumbling ruin of so many
little lives. It is true, as we have seen, that he is
aware, and by no means blithely aware, of the ironies of
existence in such a world, and that behind his superficial
convictions, his downright opinions on art and Bollinger
1911 and barbers, there lurks a mournful scepticism, but
actually this only makes him more passionately attached
to the romance, the dumb poetry, the hidden agonies and
exultations of commonplace persons. He has made full use
of the simple fact that however dull and prosaic a man
may appear to others, however tedious his life may seem,
to himself his life is always exciting, amazing, and he
himself a daily miracle; and in three out of every four of
Mr. Bennett's stories, it will be found that the most
piquant effects have been obtained simply by a continual
contrast of what he might call the 'the outside' and the
'inside' views of a person's motives, actions, character.
If, as I imagine, his readers so often mistake his intentions, no doubt the fault is largely his and is the result
of some flaw in his art; but it is easy to see what has
happened, for while the reader (of the more important
novels) has naturally seen the story progressing in a forward direction, as it travels from the first chapter to
the last, Mr. Bennett himself has seen the story backward,
as it were, has first conceived the final situation and
then worked out the rest of the tale in the light of that.
The difference is important. Thus, in 'The Old Wives'
Tale' the reader sees the history of one of Time's innumerable conquests, the decline and fall of feminine
grace and beauty, the eternal cruel process by which two
exquisite girls, things of wonder, are slowly transformed
into two helpless old women; but the author, while he sees
all this too, really begins with a vision of two lonely
old women, harmless creatures in a provincial town who
would excite no comment beyond perhaps a pitying remark,
and then realises that behind them, even them, there is an
epic, the play of gigantic instincts, a series of strange
tragi-comedies that have been secretly enacted in commonplace shops, houses and hotels. We see the two old women
and 'nothing more'; but he sees the whole story, typical
and yet marvellous, and that is his triumph. That he conceived the story in 'The Old Wives' Tale' backwards is
made plain in his preface to the later edition, and there
can be little doubt that the same thing happened with the

later tales. In the Clayhanger trilogy, he probably began
with a mental picture of a seemingly commonplace married
couple, middle-aged, middle-class, prosperous, contented,
apparently prosaic. But behind them he saw, reeling back
into the middle years of last century, the histories of
Edwin Clayhanger and Hilda Lessways, and he knew that the
middle-aged ease of 'These Twain' was nothing less than a
port in some Fortunate Isles that the pair had only
reached after incredible adventures on the high seas of
youthful life. Again, he probably saw that magnificent
novel, 'Riceyman Steps,' from the angle of those contents-
bills noted in the last chapter, Mysterious Death of a
Miser in Clerkenwell, Midnight Tragedy in King's Cross
Road and the rest, and actually we ought to have such
newspaper summaries of the story somewhere at the back of
our minds when we are reading it, so that we are conscious
of the piquant, or, rather, in this instance, moving contrast already noticed, the contrast here between 'a sordid
affair in Clerkenwell' involving one of the seediest parts
of London, two misers, a simple charwoman who steals
scraps of bacon, and her semi-idiotic lover, the contrast
between this and the actual story as we come to know it
from within, a story that has in it humanity and the
world, love and death, strange loyalties and fantastic
bravery, and that odd nobility and even beauty, which a
ruling passion, no matter how ignoble it may appear,
(which was reviewed at length in these pages two months
ago), though it lacks the epic fullness of the two great
Five Towns stories and is more limited in its scope, is
undoubtedly Mr. Bennett's greatest achievement as a pure
craftsman, and is perhaps the best example of his disguised romantic method, of the romance that fights its way
through reality when all the gates of easy appeal have
been barred.

But in none of these works has the complete Mr. Bennett
appeared; something that crackles and blazes so delightfully in the lighter novels has been rigidly excluded from
them, and for this exclusion, this deliberate limitation,
we may perhaps thank those early views of the novel,
largely learned under French influence, that have already
been noticed. That influence, too, is partly responsible
for a certain characteristic that is at once a virtue and
a great fault in Mr. Bennett as a novelist. This is a
generalising tendency which can be seen in everything he
touches but which is most easily observed in his treatment
of love. He is, above all our other novelists, the novelist of middle-aged love; time after time, he has, for
example, shown us with much humour, dramatic effect, and
truth, the way in which apparently bored, condescending

or amused husbands, who pride themselves on a lack of sentiment, conceal in their bosoms an immense admiration, genuine passion and solid respect for their wives; no living novelist is better able to handle the general realities of sexual relations. But - and here he seems to me very French - the relations always remain too general; it is always, or nearly always (for Hilda Lessways and Clayhanger perhaps provide an exception) a man and The Sex; we are not shown the peculiar, the unique relation between two individuals, a certain man and a certain woman, but we are simply shown 'an affair' in progress; the situation is touched off very cleverly, but it is merely typical, an approximation, excellent indeed for brisk articles on married life or light comedies but beneath the level, the highly individualised level, of great fiction; everywhere the emphasis is laid on what might be called the constant factors in sexual life, love and marriage as they appear to a psychologist and not as they should appear to an artist; his men may be finely individualised but they are not individualised in their sexual relations, and as for his women, they are too often simply *La Femme*, and no sooner do they make their appearance than we hear, coming faintly down the wind, the vast and endless generalisations of the Boulevards. This is not the least but it is the last of the many limitations that must be noticed, however ungrateful it may seem, in any account of one of the most prolific, entertaining and (within certain limits) conscientious writers of our time. When Denry the Card was chosen as Mayor, one of his rivals, with the solemnity of a literary critic, asked what Denry had done, 'what cause was he identified with,' and this devil's advocate was crushed by the reply that Denry was identified 'with the great cause of cheering us all up.' Mr. Bennett, in his lighter work, in which he has sketched so inimitably the urban comedy of the twentieth century, is identified with the same great cause and is, indeed, a Denry of letters. In his more ambitious novels, he has done something more worth while than even playing the Card, for he has taken ugly places in ugly epochs and by dint of rare understanding and noble labour has transformed their chronicles into art; has set a whole host of seemingly commonplace persons, the people of well nigh a whole countryside, marching down the years in that great procession which is headed by Hamlet and Falstaff, Uncle Toby and Cleopatra, Becky Sharp and Squire Western, Mr. Pickwick and the Wife of Bath.

113. VIRGINIA WOOLF, CHARACTER IN FICTION, 'CRITERION'

July 1924, 409-30

In 1924 Virginia Woolf (1882-1941) was on the verge of
publishing her best works, 'Mrs. Dalloway' in 1925 and
'To the Lighthouse' in 1927. She represented the high-
brows of literature in the 1920, and to her and to some
of her friends Bennett represented the old guard - and
an old guard with too much influence. Bennett himself
was generally sympathetic to young authors, and he was
personally helpful to a number of them (see LAB *passim*
for a few details on Lawrence and Eliot), but he was a
frank critic and enjoyed controversy, and he said unpleasant things about young and old. He was perhaps less
taken with Virginia Woolf than with any other of the
important young writers of the 1920s, and in 'Cassell's
Magazine' on 23 March 1923, in an article called Is the
Novel Decaying?, he had some unkind things to say. He
began with the assertion that 'the foundation of good
fiction is character-creating, and nothing else', and
then he turned to 'Jacob's Room': 'I have seldom read
a cleverer book... It is packed and bursting with originality, and it is exquisitely written. But the characters
do not vitally survive in the mind because the author has
been obsessed by details of originality and cleverness.'
There was comment on the article by 'Affable Hawk'
(Desmond MacCarthy) in the 'New Statesman' (31 March).
Virginia Woolf replied in the autumn. Her essay,
entitled Mr. Bennett and Mrs. Brown, was published in
America on 17 November and in England in the 'Nation and
Athenaeum' on 1 December, where it elicited much comment,
some of it defending Bennett. She revised it for a talk
for the Cambridge Heretics, and then gave it to T.S. Eliot
for the 'Criterion'. It was published later in the year
as a Hogarth Press pamphlet as 'Mr. Bennett and Mrs.
Brown'.

It was not an original attack, and discussions of it in
recent years have agreed that it was ill-considered and
that it attacked Bennett on Woolf's own weakest point.
But in its time it was a signpost for the young, and since
then it has commonly been offered as a key document of the
revolution in life and literature in the twentieth century. It was doubtless the most influential and damaging
piece of criticism of Bennett that ever appeared.

The reaction against Bennett may be said to have begun
with his first novels and essays. He aroused notable
antagonism as well as sympathy and admiration. As he

became commercially successful and famous, the antagonism grew. In her review of 'The Lion's Share' in 1916 (No. 85), Rebecca West remarked that 'it is now the fashion in many intellectual circles to despise Mr. Bennett'. The most famous exhibition of the fashion prior to Virginia Woolf's essay came with Ezra Pound's depiction of him as the yacht-owning Mr Nixon in 'Hugh Selwyn Mauberley' in 1920. Pound made an incidental attack on Bennett in 1919, remarking in a review that Wyndham Lewis's 'Tarr' did not have the click of Mr. Bennett's cash-register finish'. When Pound reprinted his 1919 remarks in 'Literary Essays' in 1954 he added as a footnote: 'E.P. rather modified his view of part of Bennett's writing when he finally got round to reading "An Old Wives' Tale" [sic].' The history and substance of the Bennett-Woolf argument have been discussed by Philip Rahv, Mrs. Woolf and Mrs. Brown, in his 'Image and Idea', 1949; Irving Kreutz, Mr Bennett and Mrs. Woolf, 'Modern Fiction Studies' (Summer 1962); Hepburn, Realism vs. Character, in 'The Art of Arnold Bennett', 1963; Paul Goetsch, A Source of Mr. Bennett and Mrs. Brown, 'English Literature in Transition', vol. 7, 1964; Louis Tillier, 'Arnold Bennett et ses romans réalistes', 1967; and Samuel Hynes, The Whole Contention Between Mr. Bennett and Mrs. Woolf, 'Novel' (Autumn 1967). See also, 'Virginia Woolf, The Critical Heritage', 1975, edited by Robin Majumdar and Allen McLaurin, for a summary account and for the 1923 version of Woolf's article. None of these commentators point out that in the years before 1924 reviewers of Bennett's novels very often expressed admiration for his psychological subtlety. The Clayhanger trilogy was especially praised. Mrs Woolf's view contradicted a longstanding opinion in certain quarters.

It seems to me possible, perhaps desirable, that I may be the only person in this room who has committed the folly of writing, trying to write, or failing to write, a novel. And when I asked myself, as your invitation to speak to you about modern fiction made me ask myself, what demon whispered in my ear and urged me to my doom, a little figure rose before me - the figure of a man, or of a woman, who said, 'My name is Brown. Catch me if you can.'

Most novelists have the same experience. Some Brown, Smith, or Jones comes before them and says in the most seductive and charming way in the world, 'Come and catch me if you can.' And so, led on by this will-o'-the-wisp, they flounder through volume after volume, spending the best years of their lives in the pursuit, and receiving

for the most part very little cash in exchange. Few catch
the phantom; most have to be content with a scrap of her
dress or a wisp of her hair.

My belief that men and women write novels because they
are lured on to create some character which has thus imposed itself upon them has the sanction of Mr. Arnold Bennett. In an article from which I will quote he says: 'The
foundation of good fiction is character-creating and nothing else.... Style counts; plot counts; originality of
outlook counts. But none of these counts anything like so
much as the convincingness of the characters. If the
characters are real the novel will have a chance; if they
are not, oblivion will be its portion....' And he goes on
to draw the conclusion that we have no young novelists of
first-rate importance at the present moment, because they
are unable to create characters that are real, true, and
convincing.

These are the questions that I want with greater bold-
ness than discretion to discuss to-night. I want to make
out what we mean when we talk about 'character' in fiction; to say something about the question of reality which
Mr. Bennett raises; and to suggest some reasons why the
younger novelists fail to create characters, if, as Mr.
Bennett asserts, it is true that fail they do. This will
lead me, I am well aware, to make some very sweeping and
some very vague assertions. For the question is an extremely difficult one. Think how little we know about
character - think how little we know about art. But to
make a clearance before I begin, I will suggest that we
range Edwardians and Georgians into two camps: Mr. Wells,
Mr. Bennett, and Mr. Galsworthy I will call the Edwardians; Mr. Forster, Mr. Lawrence, Mr. Strachey, Mr. Joyce,
and Mr. Eliot I will call the Georgians. And if I speak
in the first person, with intolerable egotism, I will ask
you to excuse me. I do not want to attribute to the world
at large the opinions of one solitary, ill-informed, and
misguided individual.

My first assertion is one that I think you will grant -
that every one in this room is a judge of character.
Indeed it would be impossible to live for a year without
disaster unless one practised character-reading and had
some skill in the art. Our marriages, our friendships
depend on it; our business largely depends on it; every
day questions arise which can only be solved by its help.
And now I will hazard a second assertion, which is more
disputable perhaps, to the effect that on or about December 1910 human character changed.

I am not saying that one went out, as one might into a
garden, and there saw that a rose had flowered, or that a

hen had laid an egg. The change was not sudden and definite like that. But a change there was, nevertheless;
and, since one must be arbitrary, let us date it about the
year 1910. The first signs of it are recorded in the
books of Samuel Butler, in 'The Way of All Flesh' in particular; the plays of Bernard Shaw continue to record it.
In life one can see the change, if I may use a homely
illustration, in the character of one's cook. The Victorian cook lived like a leviathan in the lower depths,
formidable, silent, obscure, inscrutable; the Georgian
cook is a creature of sunshine and fresh air; in and out
of the drawing-room, now to borrow the 'Daily Herald',
now to ask advice about a hat. Do you ask for more solemn
instances of the power of the human race to change? Read
the 'Agamemnon,' and see whether, in process of time, your
sympathies are not almost entirely with Clytemnestra. Or
consider the married life of the Carlyles, and bewail the
waste, the futility, for him and for her, of the horrible
domestic tradition which made it seemly for a woman of
genius to spend her time chasing beetles, scouring sauce-
pans, instead of writing books. All human relations have
shifted - those between masters and servants, husbands and
wives, parents and children. And when human relations
change there is at the same time a change in religion,
conduct, politics, and literature. Let us agree to place
one of these changes about the year 1910.

I have said that people have to acquire a good deal of
skill in character-reading if they are to live a single
year of life without disaster. But it is the art of the
young. In middle age and in old age the art is practised
mostly for its uses, and friendships and other adventures
and experiments in the art of reading character are
seldom made. But novelists differ from the rest of the
world because they do not cease to be interested in
character when they have learnt enough about it for practical purposes. They go a step further; they feel that
there is something permanently interesting in character
in itself. When all the practical business of life has
been discharged, there is something about people which
continues to seem to them of overwhelming importance, in
spite of the fact that it has no bearing whatever upon
their happiness, comfort, or income. The study of character becomes to them an absorbing pursuit; to impart
character an obsession. And thus I find it very difficult
to explain what novelists mean when they talk about
character, what the impulse is that urges them so powerfully every now and then to embody their view in writing.

So, if you will allow me, instead of analysing and
abstracting I will tell you a simple story which, however

pointless, has the merit of being true, of a journey from
Richmond to Waterloo in the hope that I may show you what
I mean by character in itself; that you may realise the
different aspects it can wear and the hideous perils that
beset you directly you try to describe it in words.

One night some weeks ago, then, I was late for the
train and jumped into the first carriage I came to. As
I sat down I had the strange and uncomfortable feeling
that I was interrupting a conversation between two people
who were already sitting there. Not that they were young
or happy. Far from it. They were both elderly, the
woman over sixty, the man well over forty. They were
sitting opposite each other and the man, who had been
leaning over and talking emphatically to judge by his
attitude and the flush on his face, sat back and became
silent. I had disturbed him, and he was annoyed. The
elderly lady, however, whom I will call Mrs. Brown, seemed
rather relieved. She was one of those clean, threadbare
old ladies whose extreme tidiness - everything buttoned,
fastened, tied together, mended and brushed up, suggests
more extreme poverty than rags and dirt. There was something pinched about her - a look of suffering, of apprehension, and, in addition, she was extremely small. Her
feet, in their clean little boots, scarcely touched the
floor. I felt that she had nobody to support her; that
she had to make up her mind for herself; that, having
been deserted, or left a widow, years ago, she had led
an anxious, harried life, bringing up an only son, perhaps, who, as likely as not, was by this time beginning
to go to the bad. All this shot through my mind as I sat
down, being uncomfortable, like most people, at travelling with fellow passengers unless I have somehow or
other accounted for them. Then I looked at the man. He
was no relation of Mrs. Brown's I felt sure; he was of a
bigger, burlier, less refined type. He was a man of
business I imagined, very likely a respectable corn-
chandler from the North, dressed in good blue serge with
a pocket-knife and a silk handkerchief, and a stout
leather bag. Obviously, however, he had an unpleasant
business to settle with Mrs. Brown; a secret, perhaps
sinister business, which they did not intend to discuss
in my presence.

'Yes, the Crofts have had very bad luck with their
servants,' Mr. Smith (as I will call him) said in a
considering way, going back to some earlier topic, with a
view to keeping up appearances.

'Ah, poor people,' said Mrs. Brown, a trifle con-
descendingly. 'My grandmother had a maid who came when
she was fifteen and stayed till she was eighty' (this was

said with a kind of hurt and agressive pride to impress
us both perhaps).

'One doesn't often come across that sort of thing nowadays,' said Mr. Smith in conciliatory tones.

Then they were silent.

'It's odd they don't start a golf club there - I should
have thought one of the young fellows would,' said Mr.
Smith, for the silence obviously made him uneasy.

Mrs. Brown hardly took the trouble to answer.

'What changes they're making in this part of the
world,' said Mr. Smith looking out of the window, and
looking furtively at me as he did so.

It was plain, from Mrs. Brown's silence, from the
uneasy affability with which Mr. Smith spoke, that he had
some power over her which he was exerting disagreeably.
It might have been her son's downfall, or some painful
episode in her past life, or her daughter's. Perhaps she
was going to London to sign some document to make over
some property. Obviously against her will she was in Mr.
Smith's hands. I was beginning to feel a great deal of
pity for her, when she said, suddenly and inconsequently,

'Can you tell me if an oak-tree dies when the leaves
have been eaten for two years in succession by caterpillars?'

She spoke quite brightly, and rather precisely, in a
cultivated, inquisitive voice.

Mr. Smith was startled, but relieved to have a safe
topic of conversation given him. He told her a great deal
very quickly about plagues of insects. He told her that
he had a brother who kept a fruit farm in Kent. He told
her what fruit farmers do every year in Kent, and so on,
and so on. While he talked a very odd thing happened.
Mrs. Brown took out her little white handkerchief and
began to dab her eyes. She was crying. But she went on
listening quite composedly to what he was saying, and he
went on talking, a little louder, a little angrily, as
if he had seen her cry often before; as if it were a painful habit. At last it got on his nerves. He stopped
abruptly, looked out of the window, then leant towards
her as he had been doing when I got in, and said in a
bullying, menacing way, as if he would not stand any more
nonsense,

'So about that matter we were discussing. It'll be all
right? George will be there on Tuesday?'

'We shan't be late,' said Mrs. Brown, gathering herself
together with superb dignity.

Mr. Smith said nothing. He got up, buttoned his coat,
reached his bag down, and jumped out of the train before
it had stopped at Clapham Junction. He had got what he

wanted but he was ashamed of himself; he was glad to get
out of the old lady's sight.

Mrs. Brown and I were left alone together. She sat in
her corner opposite, very clean, very small, rather queer,
and suffering intensely. The impression she made was
overwhelming. It came pouring out like a draught, like a
smell of burning. What was it composed of - that overwhelming and peculiar impression? Myriads of irrelevant
and incongruous ideas crowd into one's head on such
occasions; one sees the person, one sees Mrs. Brown, in
the centre of all sorts of different scenes. I thought of
her in a seaside house, among queer ornaments: sea-
urchins, models of ships in glass cases. Her husband's
medals were on the mantelpiece. She popped in and out of
the room, perching on the edges of chairs, picking meals
out of saucers, indulging in long, silent stares. The
caterpillars and the oak-trees seemed to imply all that.
And then, into this fantastic and secluded life, in broke
Mr. Smith. I saw him blowing in, so to speak, on a windy
day. He banged, he slammed. His dripping umbrella made
a pool in the hall. They sat closeted together.

And then Mrs. Brown faced the dreadful revelation. She
took her heroic decision. Early, before dawn, she packed
her bag and carried it herself to the station. She would
not let Smith touch it. She was wounded in her pride,
unmoored from her anchorage; she came of gentlefolks who
kept servants - but details could wait. The important
thing was to realise her character, to steep oneself in
her atmosphere. I had no time to explain why I felt it
somewhat tragic, heroic, yet with a dash of the flighty,
and fantastic, before the train stopped, and I watched
her disappear, carrying her bag, into the vast blazing
station. She looked very small, very tenacious; at once
very frail and very heroic. And I have never seen her
again, and I shall never know what became of her.

The story ends without any point to it. But I have not
told you this anecdote to illustrate either my own ingenuity or the pleasure of travelling from Richmond to Waterloo. What I want you to see in it is this. Here is a
character imposing itself upon another person. Here is
Mrs. Brown making someone begin almost automatically to
write a novel about her. I believe that all novels begin
with an old lady in the corner opposite. I believe that
all novels, that is to say, deal with character, and that
it is to express character - not to preach doctrines, sing
songs, or celebrate the glories of the British Empire,
that the form of the novel, so clumsy, verbose, and un-
dramatic, so rich, elastic, and alive, has been evolved.
To express character, I have said; but you will at once

reflect that the very widest interpretation can be put
upon those words. For example, old Mrs. Brown's character
will strike you very differently according to the age and
country in which you happen to be born. It would be easy
enough to write three different versions of that incident
in the train, an English, a French, and a Russian. The
English writer would make the old lady into a 'character';
he would bring out her oddities and mannerisms; her buttons and wrinkles; her ribbons and warts. Her personality
would dominate the book. A French writer would rub out
all that, he would sacrifice the individual Mrs. Brown to
give a more general view of human nature; to make a more
abstract, proportioned, and harmonious whole. The Russian
would pierce through the flesh; would reveal the soul -
the soul alone wandering out into the Waterloo Road,
asking of life some tremendous question which would sound
on and on in our ears after the book was finished. And
then there is the writer's temperament to be considered.
You see one thing in character, and I another. You say it
means this, and I that. And when it comes to writing each
makes a further selection on principles of his own. Thus
Mrs. Brown can be treated in an infinite variety of ways,
according to the age, country and temperament of the
writer.

But now I must recall what Mr. Arnold Bennett says. He
says that it is only if the characters are real that the
novel has any chance of surviving. Otherwise, die it
must. But I ask myself, what is reality? And who are the
judges of reality? A character may be real to Mr. Bennett
and quite unreal to me. For instance, in this article
he says that Dr. Watson in 'Sherlock Holmes' is real to
him: to me Dr. Watson is a sack, stuffed with straw, a
dummy, a figure of fun. And so it is with character after
character - in book after book. There is nothing that
people differ about more than the reality of characters,
especially in contemporary books. But if you take a
larger view I think that Mr. Bennett is perfectly right.
If, that is, you think of the novels which seem to you
great novels - 'War and Peace.' 'Vanity Fair,' 'Tristram
Shandy,' 'Madame Bovary,' 'Pride and Prejudice,'
'The Mayor of Casterbridge,' 'Villette' - if you think of
these books, you do at once think of some character who
has seemed to you so real (I do not by that mean so lifelike) that it has the power to make you think not merely
of it itself, but of all sorts of things through its
eyes - of religion, of love, of war, of peace, of family
life, of balls in county towns, of sunsets, moonrises, the
immortality of the soul. There is hardly any subject of
human experience that is left out of 'War and Peace' it

seems to me. And in all these novels all these great
novelists have brought us to see whatever they wish us to
see through some character. Otherwise, they would not be
novelists; but poets, historians, or pamphleteers.

But now let us examine what Mr. Bennett went on to
say - he said that there was no great novelist among the
Georgian writers because they cannot create characters who
are real, true, and convincing. And there I cannot agree.
There are reasons, excuses, possibilities which I think
put a different colour upon the case. It seems so to me
at least, but I am well aware that this is a matter about
which I am likely to be prejudiced, sanguine, and near-
sighted. I will put my view before you in the hope that
you will make it impartial, judicial, and broad-minded.
Why, then, is it so hard for novelists at present to
create characters which seem real, not only to Mr. Bennett, but to the world at large? Why, when October comes
round, do the publishers always fail to supply us with
a masterpiece?

Surely one reason is that the men and women who began
writing novels in 1910 or thereabouts had this great difficulty to face - that there was no English novelist living from whom they could learn their business. Mr. Conrad
is a Pole; which sets him apart, and makes him, however
admirable, not very helpful. Mr. Hardy has written no
novel since 1895. The most prominent and successful
novelists in the year 1910 were, I suppose, Mr. Wells,
Mr. Bennett, and Mr. Galsworthy. Now it seems to me that
to go to these men and ask them to teach you how to write
a novel - how to create characters that are real - is
precisely like going to a bootmaker and asking him to
teach you how to make a watch. Do not let me give you
the impression that I do not admire and enjoy their books.
They seem to me of great value, and indeed of great necessity. There are seasons when it is more important to
have books than to have watches. To drop metaphor, I
think that after the creative activity of the Victorian
age it was quite necessary not only for literature but for
life, that someone should write the books that Mr. Wells,
Mr. Bennett, and Mr. Galsworthy have written. Yet what
odd books they are! Sometimes I wonder if we are right to
call them books at all. For they leave one with so
strange a feeling of incompleteness and dissatisfaction.
In order to complete them it seems necessary to do something - to join a society, or, more desperately, to write
a cheque. That done, the restlessness is laid, the book
finished; it can be put upon the shelf, and need never be
read again. But with the work of other novelists it is
different. 'Tristram Shandy' or 'Pride and Prejudice' is

complete in itself: it is self-contained; it leaves one
with no desire to do anything, except indeed to read the
book again, and to understand it better. The difference
perhaps is that both Sterne and Jane Austen were interested in things in themselves; in character in itself;
in the book in itself. Therefore everything was inside
the book, nothing outside. But the Edwardians were never
interested in character in itself; or in the book in
itself. They were interested in something outside. Their
books, then, were incomplete as books, and required that
the reader should finish them, actively and practically,
for himself.

Perhaps we can make this clearer if we take the liberty
of imagining a little party in the railway carriage –
Mr. Wells, Mr. Galsworthy, Mr. Bennett are travelling to
Waterloo with Mrs. Brown. Mrs. Brown, I have said, was
poorly dressed and very small. She had an anxious,
harassed look. I doubt whether she was what you call an
educated woman. Seizing upon all these symptoms of the
unsatisfactory condition of our primary schools with a
rapidity to which I can do no justice, Mr. Wells would
instantly project upon the window-pane a vision of a
better, breezier, jollier, happier, more adventurous
and gallant world, where these musty railway carriages
and fusty old women do not exist; where miraculous barges
bring tropical fruit to Camberwell by eight o'clock in the
morning; where there are public nurseries, fountains, and
libraries, dining-rooms, drawing-rooms, and marriages;
where every citizen is generous and candid, manly and magalgo-
nificent, and rather like Mr. Wells himself. But nobody
is in the least like Mrs. Brown. There are no Mrs. Browns
in Utopia. Indeed I do not think that Mr. Wells, in his
passion to make her what she ought to be, would waste a
thought upon her as she is. And what would Mr. Galsworthy
see? Can we doubt that the walls of Doulton's factory
would take his fancy? There are women in that factory
who make twenty-five dozen earthenware pots every day.
There are mothers in the Mile End Road who depend upon the
farthings which those women earn. But there are employers
in Surrey who are even now smoking rich cigars while the
nightingale sings. Burning with indignation, stuffed with
information, arraigning civilisation, Mr. Galsworthy would
only see in Mrs. Brown a pot broken on the wheel and
thrown into the corner.

Mr. Bennett, alone of the Edwardians, would keep his
eyes on the carriage. He, indeed, would observe every
detail with immense care. He would notice the advertisements; the pictures of Swanage and Portsmouth; the way in
which the cushion bulged between the buttons; how Mrs.

Brown wore a brooch which had cost three-and-ten-three at
Whitworth's bazaar, and had mended both gloves - indeed
the thumb of the left-hand glove had been replaced.   And
he would observe, at length, how this was the non-stop
train from Windsor, which calls at Richmond for the convenience of middle-class residents, who can afford to go
to the theatre but have not reached the social rank which
can afford motor-cars, though it is true, there are
occasions (he would tell us what), when they hire them
from a company (he would tell us which).   And so he would
gradually sidle sedately towards Mrs. Brown and would
remark how she had been left a little copyhold, not freehold, property at Datchet, which, however, was mortgaged
to Mr. Bungay the solicitor - but why should I presume to
invent Mr. Bennett?   Does not Mr. Bennett write novels
himself?   I will open the first book that chance puts in
my way - 'Hilda Lessways.'   Let us see how he makes us
feel that Hilda is real, true, and convincing, as a novelist should.   She shut the door in a soft, controlled way,
which showed the constraint of her relations with her
mother.   She was fond of reading 'Maud', she was endowed
with the power to feel intensely.   So far, so good; in his
leisurely, surefooted way Mr. Bennett is trying in these
first pages, where every touch is important, to show us
the kind of girl she was.
     But then he begins to describe, not Hilda Lessways, but
the view from her bedroom window, the excuse being that
Mr. Skellorn, the man who collects rents, is coming along
that way.   Mr. Bennett proceeds:

> The bailiwick of Turnhill lay behind her; and all
> the murky district of the Five Towns, of which Turn-
> hill is the northern outpost, lay to the south.   At
> the foot of Chatterley Wood the canal wound in large
> curves on its way towards the undefiled plains of
> Cheshire and the sea.   On the canal-side, exactly
> opposite to Hilda's window, was a flour-mill, that
> sometimes made nearly as much smoke as the kilns and
> the chimneys closing the prospect on either hand.   From
> the flour mill a bricked path, which separated a con-
> siderable row of new cottages from their appurtenant
> gardens, led straight into Lessways Street, in front of
> Mrs. Lessways' house.   By that path Mr. Skellorn should
> have arrived, for he inhabited the farthest of the cot-
> tages.

One line of insight would have done more than all those
lines of description; but let them pass as the necessary
drudgery of the novelist.   And now - where is Hilda?   Alas.

Hilda is still looking out of the window. Passionate and
dissatisfied as she was, she was a girl with an eye for
houses. She often compared this old Mr. Skellorn with the
villas she saw from her bedroom window. Therefore the
villas must be described. Mr. Bennett proceeds:

> The row was called Freehold Villas: a consciously proud
> name in a district where much of the land was copyhold
> and could only change owners subject to the payment of
> 'fines,' and to the feudal consent of a 'court' pre-
> sided over by the agent of a lord of the manor. Most
> of the dwellings were owned by their occupiers, who,
> each an absolute monarch of the soil, niggled in his
> sooty garden of an evening amid the litter of drying
> shirts and towels. Freehold Villas symbolised the
> final triumph of Victorian economics, the apotheosis
> of the prudent and industrious artisan. It corres-
> ponded with a Building Society Secretary's dream of
> paradise. And indeed it was a very real achievement.
> Nevertheless, Hilda's irrational contempt would not
> admit this.

Heaven be praised, we cry! At last we are coming to
Hilda herself. But not so fast. Hilda may have been
this, that, and the other; but Hilda not only looked at
houses, and thought of houses; Hilda lived in a house.
And what sort of a house did Hilda live in? Mr. Bennett
proceeds:

> It was one of the two middle houses of a detached
> terrace of four houses built by her grandfather Less-
> ways, the teapot manufacturer; it was the chief of the
> four, obviously the habitation of the proprietor of the
> terrace. One of the corner houses comprised a grocer's
> shop, and this house had been robbed of its just pro-
> portion of garden so that the seigneurial garden-plot
> might be triflingly larger than the other. The terrace
> was not a terrace of cottages, but of houses rated at
> from twenty-six to thirty-six pounds a year; beyond the
> means of artisans and petty insurance agents and rent-
> collectors. And further, it was well built, generously
> built; and its architecture, though debased, showed
> some faint traces of Georgian amenity. It was admit-
> tedly the best row of houses in that newly settled
> quarter of the town. In coming to it out of Freehold
> Villas Mr. Skellorn obviously came to something
> superior, wider, more liberal. Suddenly Hilda heard
> her mother's voice....

But we cannot hear her mother's voice, or Hilda's voice: we can only hear Mr. Bennett's voice telling us facts about rents and freeholds and copyholds and fines. What can Mr. Bennett be about? I have formed my own opinion of what Mr. Bennett is about - he is trying to make us imagine for him; he is trying to hypnotise us into the belief that, because he has made a house, there must be a person living there. With all his powers of observation, which are marvellous, with all his sympathy and humanity, which are great, Mr. Bennett has never once looked at Mrs. Brown in her corner. There she sits in the corner of the carriage - that carriage which is travelling, not from Richmond to Waterloo, but from one age of English literature to the next, for Mrs. Brown is eternal, Mrs. Brown is human nature, Mrs. Brown changes only on the surface, it is the novelists who get in and out - there she sits and not one of the Edwardian writers has so much as looked at her. They have looked very powerfully, searchingly, and sympathetically out of the window; at factories, at Utopias, even at the decoration and upholstery of the carriage; but never at her, never at life, never at human nature. And so they have developed a technique of novel-writing which suits their purpose; they have made tools and established conventions which do their business. But those tools are not our tools, and that business is not our business. For us those conventions are ruin, those tools are death.

You may well complain of the vagueness of my language. What is a convention, a tool, you may ask, and what do you mean by saying that Mr. Bennett's and Mr. Wells's and Mr. Galsworthy's conventions are the wrong conventions for the Georgian's? The question is difficult: I will attempt a short cut. A convention in writing is not much different from a convention in manners. Both in life and in literature it is necessary to have some means of bridging the gulf between the hostess and her unknown guest on the one hand, the writer and his unknown reader on the other. The hostess bethinks her of the weather, for generations of hostesses have established the fact that this is a subject of universal interest in which we all believe. She begins by saying that we are having a wretched May, and, having thus got into touch with her unknown guest, proceeds to matters of greater interest. So it is in literature. The writer must get into touch with his reader by putting before him something which he recognises, which therefore stimulates his imagination, and makes him willing to co-operate in the far more difficult business of intimacy. And it is of the highest importance that this common meeting-place should be reached easily, almost

instinctively, in the dark, with one's eyes shut. Here
is Mr. Bennett making use of this common ground in the
passage which I have quoted. The problem before him was
to make us believe in the reality of Hilda Lessways. So
he began, being an Edwardian, by describing accurately
and minutely the sort of house Hilda lived in, and the
sort of house she saw from the window. House property
was the common ground from which the Edwardians found it
easy to proceed to intimacy. Indirect as it seems to us,
the convention worked admirably, and thousands of Hilda
Lessways were launched upon the world by this means.
For that age and generation, the convention was a good
one.

But now, if you will allow me to pull my own anecdote
to pieces, you will see how keenly I felt the lack of a
convention, and how serious a matter it is when the tools
of one generation are useless for the next. The incident
had made a great impression on me. But how was I to
transmit it to you? All I could do was to report as
accurately as I could what was said, to describe in detail
what was worn, to say, despairingly, that all sorts of
scenes rushed into my mind, to proceed to tumble them out
pell-mell, and to describe this vivid, this overmastering
impression by likening it to a draught or a smell of burning. To tell you the truth I was also strongly tempted
to manufacture a three-volume novel about the old lady's
son, and his adventures crossing the Atlantic, and her
daughter, and how she kept a millinery shop in Westminster, the past life of Smith himself, and his house at
Sheffield, though such stories seem to me the most dreary,
irrelevant, and humbugging affairs in the world.

But if I had done that I should have escaped the
appalling effort of saying what I meant. And to have got
at what I meant, I should have had to go back and back and
back to experiment with one thing and another; to try this
sentence and that, referring each word to my vision,
matching it as exactly as possible, and knowing that somehow I had to find a common ground between us, a convention
which would not seem to you too odd, unreal, and far-
fetched to believe in. I admit that I shirked that arduous undertaking. I let my Mrs. Brown slip through my
fingers. I have told you nothing whatever about her. But
that is partly the great Edwardians' fault. I asked them -
they are my elders and betters - How shall I begin to
describe this woman's character? And they said, 'Begin
by saying that her father kept a shop in Harrogate.
Ascertain the rent. Ascertain the wages of shop assistants in the year 1878. Discover what her mother died of.
Describe cancer. Describe calico. Describe - ' But I

cried, 'Stop! Stop!' And I regret to say that I threw
that ugly, that clumsy, that incongruous tool out of the
window, for I knew that if I began describing the cancer
and the calico, my Mrs. Brown, that vision to which I
cling though I know no way of imparting it to you, would
have been dulled and tarnished and vanished for ever.

That is what I mean by saying that the Edwardian tools
are the wrong ones for us to use. They have laid an
enormous stress upon the fabric of things. They have
given us a house in the hope that we may be able to deduce
the human beings who live there. To give them their due,
they have made that house much better worth living in.
But if you hold that novels are in the first place about
people, and only in the second about the houses they live
in, that is the wrong way to set about it. Therefore, you
see, the Georgian writer had to begin by throwing away the
method that was in use at the moment. He was left alone
there facing Mrs. Brown without any method of conveying
her to the reader. But that is inaccurate. A writer is
never alone. There is always the public with him - if not
on the same seat, at least in the compartment next door.
Now the public is a strange travelling companion. In
England it is a very suggestible and docile creature,
which, once you get it to attend, will believe implicitly
what it is told for a certain number of years. If you say
to the public with sufficient conviction, 'All women have
tails, and all men humps,' it will actually learn to see
women with tails and men with humps, and will think it
very revolutionary and probably improper if you say
'Nonsense. Monkeys have tails and camels humps. But men
and women have brains, and they have hearts; they think
and feel,' - that will seem to it a bad joke, and an improper into the bargain.

But to return. Here is the British public sitting by
the writer's side and saying in its vast and unanimous
way, 'Old women have houses. They have fathers. They
have incomes. They have servants. They have hot water
bottles. That is how we know that they are old women.
Mr. Wells and Mr. Bennett and Mr. Galsworthy have always
taught us that this is the way to recognise them. But
now with your Mrs. Brown - how are we to believe in her?
We do not even know whether her villa was called Albert
or Balmoral; what she paid for her gloves; or whether her
mother died of cancer or of consumption. How can she be
alive? No; she is a mere figment of your imagination.'

And old women of course ought to be made of freehold
villas and copyhold estates, not of imagination.

The Georgian novelist, therefore, was in an awkward
predicament. There was Mrs. Brown protesting that she

was different, quite different, from what people made out, and luring the novelist to her rescue by the most fascinating if fleeting glimpse of her charms; there were the Edwardians handing out tools appropriate to house building and house breaking; and there was the British public asseverating that they must see the hot water bottle first. Meanwhile the train was rushing to that station where we must all get out.

Such, I think, was the predicament in which the young Georgians found themselves about the year 1910. Many of them - I am thinking of Mr. Forster and Mr. Lawrence in particular - spoilt their early work because, instead of throwing away those tools, they tried to use them. They tried to compromise. They tried to combine their own direct sense of the oddity and significance of some character with Mr. Galsworthy's knowledge of the Factory Acts, and Mr. Bennett's knowledge of the Five Towns. They tried it, but they had too keen, too overpowering a sense of Mrs. Brown and her peculiarities to go on trying it much longer. Something had to be done. At whatever cost of life, limb, and damage to valuable property Mrs. Brown must be rescued, expressed, and set in her high relations to the world before the train stopped and she disappeared for ever. And so the smashing and the crashing began. Thus it is that we hear all round us, in poems and essays, the sound of breaking and falling, crashing and destruction. It is the prevailing sound of the Georgian age - rather a melancholy one if you think what melodious days there have been in the past, if you think of Shakespeare and Milton and Keats or even of Jane Austen and Thackeray and Dickens; if you think of the language, and the heights to which it can soar when free, and see the same eagle captive, bald, and croaking.

In view of these facts, with these sounds in my ears and these fancies in my brain, I am not going to deny that Mr. Bennett has some reason when he complains that our Georgian writers are unable to make us believe that our characters are real. I am forced to agree that they do not pour out three immortal masterpieces with Victorian regularity every autumn. But instead of being gloomy, I am sanguine. For this state of things is, I think, inevitable whenever from hoar old age or callow youth the convention ceases to be a means of communication between writer and reader, and becomes instead an obstacle and an impediment. At the present moment we are suffering, not from decay, but from having no code of manners which writers and readers accept as a prelude to the more exciting intercourse of friendship. The literary convention of the time is so artificial - you have to talk about the

weather and nothing but the weather throughout the entire
visit - that, naturally, the feeble are tempted to outrage, and the strong are led to destroy the very foundations and rules of literary society. Signs of this are
everywhere apparent. Grammar is violated; syntax dis-
integrated, as a boy staying with an aunt for the week-end
rolls in the geranium bed out of sheer desperation as the
solemnities of the sabbath wear on. The more adult
writers do not, of course, indulge in such wanton exhibitions of spleen. Their sincerity is desperate, and their
courage tremendous; it is only that they do not know which
to use, a fork or their fingers. Thus, if you read Mr.
Joyce and Mr. Eliot you will be struck by the indecency of
the one, and the obscurity of the other. Mr. Joyce's
indecency in 'Ulysses' seems to me the conscious and calculated indecency of a desperate man who feels that in
order to breathe he must break the windows. At moments,
when the window is broken, he is magnificent. But what
a waste of energy! And, after all, how dull indecency is,
when it is not the overflowing of a super-abundant energy
or savagery, but the determined and public-spirited act of
a man who needs fresh air! Again, with the obscurity of
Mr. Eliot. I think that Mr. Eliot has written some of the
loveliest lines in modern poetry. But how intolerant he
is of the old usages and politenesses of society - respect
for the weak, consideration for the dull! As I sun myself
upon the intense and ravishing beauty of one of his lines,
and reflect that I must make a dizzy and dangerous leap to
the next, and so on from line to line, like an acrobat
flying precariously from bar to bar, I cry out, I confess,
for the old decorums, and envy the indolence of my ancestors who, instead of spinning madly through mid-air,
dreamt quietly in the shade with a book. Again, in Mr.
Strachey's books, 'Eminent Victorians' and 'Queen
Victoria,' the effort and strain of writing against the
grain and current of the times is visible too. It is much
less visible, of course, for not only is he dealing with
facts which are stubborn things, but he has fabricated,
chiefly from eighteenth-century material, a very discreet
code of manners of his own, which allows him to sit at
table with the highest in the land and to say a great many
things under cover of that exquisite apparel which, had
they gone naked, would have been chased by the men-
servants from the room. Still, if you compare 'Eminent
Victorians' with some of Lord Macaulay's essays, though
you will feel that Lord Macaulay is always wrong, and Mr.
Strachey always right, you will also feel a body, a sweep,
a richness in Lord Macaulay's essays which show that his
age was behind him; for all his strength went straight

into his work; none was used for purposes of concealment
or of conversion. But Mr. Strachey has had to open our
eyes before he made us see; he has had to search out and
sew together a very artful manner of speech; and the
effort, beautifully though it is concealed, has robbed his
work of some of the force that should have gone into it,
and limited his scope.

For these reasons, then, we must reconcile ourselves
to a season of failures and fragments. We must reflect
that where so much strength is spent on finding a way of
telling the truth the truth itself is bound to reach us
in rather an exhausted and chaotic condition. Ulysses,
Queen Victoria, Mr. Prufrock - to give Mrs. Brown some of
the names she has made famous lately - is a little pale
and dishevelled by the time her rescuers reach her. And
it is the sound of their axes that we hear - a vigorous
and stimulating sound in my ears - unless of course you
wish to sleep, when, in the bounty of his concern, Providence has provided a host of writers anxious and able
to satisfy your needs.

Thus I have tried, at tedious length, I fear, to
answer some of the questions which I began by asking.
I have given an account of some of the difficulties which
in my view beset the Georgian writer in all his forms.
I have sought to excuse him. May I end by venturing to
remind you of the duties and responsibilities that are
yours as partners in this business of writing books, as
companions in the railway carriage, as fellow travellers
with Mrs. Brown? For she is just as visible to you who
remain silent as to us who tell stories about her. In
the course of your daily life this past week you have had
far stranger and more interesting experiences than the
one I have tried to describe. You have overheard scraps
of talk that filled you with amazement. You have gone to
bed at night bewildered by the complexity of your feelings. In one day thousands of ideas have coursed through
your brains; thousands of emotions have met, collided, and
disappeared in astonishing disorder. Nevertheless, you
allow the writers to palm off upon you a version of all
this, an image of Mrs. Brown, which has no likeness to
that surprising apparition whatsoever. In your modesty
you seem to consider that writers are of different blood
and bone from yourselves; that they know more of Mrs.
Brown than you do. Never was there a more fatal mistake.
It is this division between reader and writer, this humility on your part, these professional airs and graces on
ours, that corrupt and emasculate the books which should
be the healthy offspring of a close and equal alliance
between us. Hence spring those sleek smooth novels,

those portentous and ridiculous biographies, that milk
and watery criticism, those poems melodiously celebrating
the innocence of roses and sheep which pass so plausibly
for literature at the present time.

Your part is to insist that writers shall come down off
their plinths and pedestals, and describe beautifully if
possible, truthfully at any rate, our Mrs. Brown. You
should insist that she is an old lady of unlimited capacity and infinite variety; capable of appearing in any
place; wearing any dress; saying anything and doing
heaven knows what. But the things she says and the things
she does and her eyes and her nose and her speech and her
silence have an overwhelming fascination, for she is, of
course, the spirit we live by, life itself.

But do not expect just at present a complete and satisfactory presentment of her. Tolerate the spasmodic, the
obscure, the fragmentary, the failure. Your help is
invoked in a good cause. For I will make one final and
surpassingly rash prediction - we are trembling on the
verge of one of the great ages of English literature.
But it can only be reached if we are determined never,
never to desert Mrs. Brown.

'Lord Raingo'

7 October 1926

114. A.N. MONKHOUSE, IN THE 'MANCHESTER GUARDIAN'

7 October 1926, 7

When you get a new novel by Mr. Bennett you want to know
whether it is in the great manner, so finely recaptured
in 'Riceyman Steps,' or whether it is only one of his
admirable inferiorities. Here, at least, are quantity,
a fluent ease, precision, and dazzling efficiency, with
much of high quality if not enough of Mr. Bennett's best.
It is a war novel, and Raingo is a famous and unscrupulous millionaire with a wife, a mistress, and much handsome, tarnished paraphernalia. Manchester folk will be
alive to the *roman à clef* when they read that Raingo was
a boy in Eccles (not, one understands, in its fashionable
part), and that Clyth, the Prime Minister, was one of his
companions there. And when Clyth appoints his friend to
the Ministry of Records, which seems to be the euphemism
for Bribery Department, the two hobnob together very much
in the manner of the old cronies in 'Hindle Wakes,' the
remarkable difference being that Houghton's people are
really friends while Mr. Bennett's are treacherously
intent on personal advantage. To many it may appear that
the intimate pictures of the life in Downing Street and
the whole scheme of winning the war by intrigue and press
cuttings make something of a fairy tale, if a sinister
one. Mr. Bennett contrives to give the impression of
knowing everything, taking everything into account, and
yet we can't quite believe him. He shows us the great
people with their masks on and off, grandiose and intimate; a War Cabinet which seems like a family affair in
which every man's hand is against his brother and nobody

says what he thinks. It is the seamy side of politics,
and you may choose whether to take what Mr. Bennett says
as surmise or revelation, platitude or indiscretion. When
he writes of the Five Towns we know that it is true.

Here, then, is a war, conceived by so many in terms of
idealism, conducted by cynics. The Prime Minister 'had no
scruples, no sense of justice or of decency, no loyalties,'
and his followers appear to be like him. You may ask how
it could possibly be so; how there could be such a curious
absence of just men with the simple desire to do right.
The answer seems to be that they all had megalomania, that
Raingo's lust for power corresponded with some like obsession in all his colleagues. Some residue of sanity
remains, for these are not men to make fools of themselves, and they must act with efficiency or they will
be supplanted. Mr. Bennett is cunning in getting at the
weaknesses of human nature, and he suggests that these
politicians have lost touch with the realities of war
because they are possessed and overwhelmed by the fierce
conflict among themselves. They may not be perfectly conscious of it, but they are selfishly intent on their own
doings, from the Prime Minister to the Labour member of
the War Cabinet - a kind of able, egotistical buffoon, -
and they turn occasionally to shout platitudes at the
admiring public.

It is not a noble world; it is not even a tolerable
one. Mr. Bennett is satirical, he is ironical, and sometimes you might think that he is joking. Doubtless there
is an infusion of the artist's contempt for the man of
affairs, but he does not sound the note of indignation;
he is not charitable but he is indulgent. And always his
hero Raingo is making his contacts with life; he is the
opposite of austere, continually returning to humanity.
He has two lives - the public, flamboyant, glorious one
and the secret, sinful, human one. This contrast is the
theme of the book, and the later chapters are concerned
with Raingo's illness and death. Here, in this slow,
intense struggle for life, Mr. Bennett holds us, as he has
done so many times before, and Raingo captures our sympathies; he is a man like ourselves and no longer the
phantasmal politician. Another issue to the story was
possible, and Mr. Bennett's avoidance of it is notable.
There is nothing more striking than the return of Raingo's
son from the war, broken in health and crudely contemptuous of all the pomp and circumstance at home. The contrast is perhaps too obvious, and Mr. Bennett preferred
not to develop it nor even to strengthen it. Perhaps this
was an austere choice, but the ineffective use of the boy
as part of the machinery of the story, with a little

corner of happy ending for him, is rather disconcerting.

It is a book that will arouse vexation, scorn, approval both boisterous and secret, and perhaps some edifying reflection. Mr. Bennett may convince us that we have many ignoble impulses but hardly that public life is entirely controlled by them. We should like to take it that this is the illusion of Raingo's point of view, but Mr. Bennett gives no ground for that.

115. J. ST LOE STRACHEY, IN THE 'SPECTATOR'

9 October 1926, 593

John St Loe Strachey (1860-1927) edited and owned the 'Spectator' for many years.

The first point of criticism to be made about Mr. Arnold Bennett's novel is its amazing competence. There is not a flaw in the novelist's technique. We may like or dislike his general attitude towards our beehive and its tireless, angry, agitated workers, and their ineffable littleness and miserable impotence in the vastness of time and space. We may hunger to hear more of the soul, and of man's unconquerable mind, and less of the material and sordid side of life. Granted, however, the limitations of the attempt, the book is a masterpiece. What the author sets out to do, that he accomplishes. No one who knows anything of the difficulty of smooth, selective, and yet comprehensive, narration, the difficulty of not describing too many things, and of not treating them too minutely; the difficulty of letting the flow of the story be neither jerky, nor rapid, nor slow, nor erratic, but even, both in pace and volume, can possibly refuse high praise to Mr. Arnold Bennett's methods of presentment.

His character drawing is as successful as is his narration. Rather, it is an appropriate part of the narration, for a lucid relativity is everywhere apparent. No person, no incident, no description appears without a definite purpose, and also without being duly related to the novel as a whole. There are no persons or happenings or animadversions or epigrammatic assertions which 'hang loose' on the story.

Though a touching, if squalid, love story is super-
imposed, 'Lord Raingo' is first, last, and all the time
a political novel - as much so as Disraeli's 'Sybil' on
the one side, or Trollope's 'Phineas Finn' on the other.
Yet it has neither the grand air of the first, nor the
innocence and intimacy of the other. I am not going to
tell the story, even in bare outline. That would not be
fair to the book, to its author, or to the reader. All
I shall say is that it provides a realistic record of the
men who ruled us, cajoled us, manoeuvred us, hoodwinked
us at home and abroad, during the last two years of the
War. Their apologists have, in effect, already told us
that they had to practise a brutal economy of truth and
to act like Clapham Chathams and Wandsworth Walpoles *for
our good!* Probably the predominant partners in the Coalition were quite sincere in thinking their pinchbeck
Machiavellism justified by necessity. Whether it was
really a point of salvation to endure profiteers gladly,
and to 'monkey' on so huge a scale with the old standards
of truth and honour, will, however, have to be judged at
the Bar of History some fifty years hence. The decision
will, I daresay, be 'Not guilty, but never do it again,
because it was dangerous, enervating, and unnecessary.'
In any case, Mr. Arnold Bennett is no conscious satirist.
He is not out to castigate, but to paint what he holds to
have happened. He shows us the men who felt sure they were
were winning the War - men clothed in a little brief
authority, scampering and scuttling about Parliament and
Whitehall, and playing their fantastic pranks before the
high heaven of the nation's self-sacrifice and noble bold-
ness. Yet as here represented they are not tragic, or,
again, satanic figures, but only, as Melbourne said,
'damned vain.' Sly, suspicious, and jealous they are, but
all the time pathetically willing to place their own dishonour upon the country's altar as a sacrifice. That this
is, on the whole, a true picture, I do not doubt. They
gave what they had to give, like the poor patriotic demi-
mondaine in Maupassant's story of the war of 1870. It
must also be noted that Mr. Arnold Bennett has not written
a book of personalities. You cannot fit the caps of any
living men on his puppets' heads. They are all given
characteristics that belong to none of the War Ministers.
For example, the Prime Minister is a Roman Catholic of
Lancashire-Irish origin!

Lord Raingo, the millionaire, who is suddenly given a
Ministry and a Peerage, and who has an uncanny power of
'boosting' causes and men and things, including himself,
is in his soul an epitome of the new Political War Lord.

He was not without thought of his country and its

welfare, was not a cruel, or inhuman, or coldly selfish
man, but he only knew one way of playing the game of life,
and it was not - well, shall I say? - the way of the 'perfect gentle knight.' Lord Raingo was in the Ministry,
though not in the Cabinet; but we see him speaking in the
Lords, in the Prime Minister's room, at a Press Banquet,
and a Cabinet luncheon. That last is a powerful picture.
We get glimpses that scare us, like the revels seen through
the door of 'some strange house of idols at its rites.'
We watch displayed the spites, the follies, the petty
treacheries, the personal hates and perfidies; the deter-
minations to put a spoke into a rival's wheels be the consequences what they may, the cant, the corruption and the
jealousies! They all boil together like the oils in a
witch's cauldron.

Jealousy is the ruling passion in the scene. It per-
vades the whole story. It and its blind, malevolent companion, Suspicion, cloud the mind of Lord Raingo throughout the book. The 'hero' - never was the word more
abused - is haunted by the thought that his mistress is
betraying him. Jealousy dogs him in his official life.
He inspires it in others and feels it himself. He neither
trusts nor is trusted. Mr. Bennett's treatment of his
side-shows calls for unbounded admiration. Besides the
personal jealousies, we get an unforgettable picture of
Departmental jealousies - the blind and bitter hatred of
one office for another. As vivid is the study of the
Club attitude towards a great national crisis - the nagg-
ing of disillusioned, wearied, cat-like old men. Then
come illustrations, closely studied, of some of the most
cynical aphorisms preserved among our political arcana.
Take as an example that saying of the Victorian Prime
Minister, 'There are no friendships at the top.' We see
a dozen proofs of this. Take next the 'desperate saying'
of Halifax that the dependence of a great man on a greater
is a degree of subservience of which ordinary people can
form no conception. Whether Mr. Bennett has studied the
political aphorisms of the greater Trimmer I do not know;
but, at any rate, he has reached a similar conclusion.
The attitude of the superb Lord Ockleford towards his colleagues is an equal mixture of superficial courtesy and
fundamental superciliousness. Towards the Prime Minister
it is abject.

Halifax's comment that 'the art of Politics is a very
coarse one' is indirectly insisted on throughout the novel.
Again, the biblical tag which Bacon rolled under his
tongue, 'the heart of kings (i.e., ruling men) is unsearch-
able,' is borne out by the study of the Prime Minister.
Lord Raingo thought he knew his old Eccles friend through

and through. Yet once a member of his Government, he
finds out what the Hebrew critic meant. We also see
exposed the true reason why modern Ministers cling to
office so foolishly and often in circumstances of such
deep humiliation. To give up the procession of Red Boxes
through their rooms and the knowledge that they *know*,
while others are ignorant, is a sacrifice they cannot
make. We see also how close a Trade Union is formed by
the holders of Ministerial office and 'nearby' men.
Finally, we are called to note that curious antagonism
which always arises between active and ambitious newspaper proprietors and Prime Ministers. 'The hand that
fed him' is always, think the Proprietors, being bitten
by the head of the Administration!

The book ends with a most vivid and moving picture of
a deathbed. Never has the scenic side of that dread drama
been more closely or more successfully studied. The parts
of patient, near relations, doctors, small and great,
nurses, and servants are admirably portrayed. There is
much detail, but not too much. For example, Lord Raingo
is worried by his constant slipping down into his bed, but
is, of course, unconscious of the fact having any significance. We wonder whether Mr. Bennett, who has evidently
studied what old-fashioned doctors called 'the Agony,'
extended his researches to Hippocrates. If he did, he
would find that 'the position of the patient in bed' is
noted by the observant Greek as of prime import in prog-
nosis.

Though to the unrolling of the 'scene' that awaits us
all is given so much space, no one who reads intelligently
will say that the story of the illness is unduly pro-
tracted. The artistry is *of its kind*, perfect and appropriate.

It is not for what the book says, but for what it leaves
unsaid, unsuggested, unthought, that I feel bound to express censure and regret. Aristotle was surely right when
he demanded a catharsis from the Tragedian. If by a work
of art you awaken the emotions of pity and terror, you
must salve them or allay them also. If not, they will
haunt the mind, not quiet it. In Lord Raingo's tragedy
we have much to perturb, but nothing to purify or to calm.
Spirits are touched, but not finely or to fine issues. We
are awakened and yet devitalized. The book, in spite of
its temperateness, unsensationalism, and negation of
rhetoric, never for a moment inspires. Rather, it bids us
despair - for ourselves and for all mankind. From such a
conclusion every pulse and nerve in the human frame
revolts. And that revolt is not mechanical, material,
meaningless. It is a sign, a proof that our existence is

something more than 'a tale told by an idiot signifying nothing'; - the worst of practical jokes, played on an unconscious automaton, by a chemical process working in the illimitable inane!

116. C.E.M. JOAD, IN THE 'DAILY HERALD'

13 October 1926, 9

C.E.M. Joad (1891-1953) was a voluminous writer on philo-sophical subjects.

That you can always propagate a propaganda if you have the proper geese is one of the fundamental axioms of those who rule. For its successful application two things are required, unscrupulousness in the propagators, and gulli-bility in the geese; and its result is vanity in the former and folly in the latter.

Propaganda touched its greatest heights and produced its maximum effect in this country during the last two years of the great war, and Arnold Bennett's new book is a brilliantly vivid and unforgettable account of the way in which it was done. It is first and foremost a political novel on the grand scale; there has been nothing like it since Disraeli's 'Sybil' and Trollope's 'Phineas Finn.'

It is the story of the sudden appointment to the Ministry of Records of Sam Raingo, a self-made million-aire; of his playing for and successful capture of a peerage; of his love for his mistress Delphine and his exasperated toleration of his wife Adela; of his successful boosting of stunts and management of men; of his relations with and jealousies of the other members of the Cabinet; and, finally, and in great detail, of his illness and death.

The tale is told with a self-confidence and assurance, with a mastery of the narrator's art so complete as to seem effortless, in which more than in any other quality lies the secret of Mr. Bennett's reputation as one of our greatest novelists. Mr. Bennett succeeds in investing with a sort of glamour the most trivial conversations, the most insignificant incidents, with the result that 'Lord Raingo' is always above everything, even in its smallest details, absorbingly interesting; you simply cannot stop reading it.

Because of his breathless interest in the smallest
details of the lives of the great, an interest which
amounts almost to excitement, I have often seen it said
that Mr. Bennett's attitude to life is that of the
incurable provincial, who, having seen the sights of
London and had a glimpse or two of high life, has never
been able to forget the experience.

His hands, it is alleged, have been uplifted ever since
in a gesture of perpetual wonder and admiration of the
ways of the great; he is one sustained exclamation mark.
This criticism seems to be unjust. Mr. Bennett has described with just the same gusto the economies and mean-
nesses of the miser of 'Riceyman Steps,' invested in the
'Old Wives' Tales' [sic] with the same glamour the extrac-
tion of Povey's tooth.

But in making all life exciting he does sometimes seem
to be devoid of a sense of values. He is so interested
in telling us exactly what it is that happens that he
omits altogether the function of comment. He describes
base things without indignation, noble things without
elevation.

He exhibits for us in this book the follies, treacheries, jealousies, ambitions and personal hates of the men
in high places; he presents us with a Prime Minister who
at the most serious crisis of the war can say, 'There are
no public worries; there are only private worries,' and
justifies a base action by informing us 'that there are
no friendships at the top'; he shows us the limitless
duplicity practised upon the public by men in authority,
yet never for a moment does he allow a note of indignation
to creep into his flowing, easy style.

I have, indeed, an uncomfortable suspicion that admiration of their dexterities is the chief emotion inspired in
him by these great men. It is this absence of moral standards, this acquiescence in whatever happens, that somehow
prevents me believing Mr. Bennett's novels will win a
permanent place in our hearts. They are masterly achievements rather than great books.

117. UNSIGNED REVIEW, 'TIMES LITERARY SUPPLEMENT'

14 October 1926, 694

Mr. Arnold Bennett's latest novel, 'Lord Raingo,' complete

in eighty-seven instalments neatly cut and labelled, is
an entertaining but rather farcical utilization of
material collected during the war.   Samuel Raingo, a rich
man of fifty-five, who for one reason and another has been
losing his grip on life during the war, is suddenly
revived, some time in 1918, by a telegraphic invitation
to breakfast with the Prime Minister, Andrew Clyth.
Raingo had been in the House of Commons formerly, but had
been disgusted that the Prime Minister, an old boyhood's
friend of his from Eccles, had given him nothing, 'not
even a chairmanship of committees.' (Parliamentarians,
by the way, will be as amused at this little piece of
inaccuracy as they will be mystified by the procedure,
later on, where the Prime Minister gets the second reading
of a man-power Bill in a debate of about two hours'
length, but needs three divisions to get it; moreover, the
omniscient Mr. Bennett seems unaware that the traffic in
Bridge-street is held up, not only for Prime Ministers,
but for all members of Parliament, not out of obsequious-
ness, but under the authority of a sessional order.)
Andrew Clyth is in a difficulty, he needs a Minister of
Records, a stubborn but able director of propaganda who
will also efficiently control the Secret Service money.
Raingo bluffs and gets a peerage as the price of his consent. He assumes office, takes his seat, and kisses
hands; he takes stock of his department, works hard, makes
enemies and overreaches himself; he gets a rap over the
knuckles, but is restored to glory at a banquet to over-
seas editors who make him into a kind of hero - we did not
grasp exactly why. This is Lord Raingo's apogee, from
which he shoots rapidly downwards into bed and dies of
pneumonia in about 140 pages.

Mr. Bennett is nothing if not racy and descriptive.
Breakfast at 10, Downing-street, where the Prime Minister,
a consummate actor with long silvery hair, tries his arts
in vain upon the canny Raingo; a lunch of select spirits
from the War Cabinet, who tease one another like quarrel-
some children; the House of Commons, the House of Lords,
the Privy Council, the interior of the Ministry of
Information - of Records we mean - these are but light
tasks for this agile pen. His caricatures of Ministers
are broad and uproarious, Tom Hogarth, 'bald, blonde, and
challenging,' Sid Jenkin, the kindly but immensely self-
important Labour Minister, the pompous Earl of Ockleford,
and the lugubrious Chancellor of the Exchequer all back-
bite and quarrel together in the best low-comedy manner.
However, the only part of the book that is nearly worthy
of its author is the exhaustive study of the fatal illness, nurses, doctors, surgeons, temperatures, lies and

fears, which ends the career of poor Lord Raingo, who was allowed to see far too many visitors. But, when we remember the pneumonia of Mr. Povey in 'The Old Wives' Tale,' short and undistinguished like Povey himself, the expansive and expensive detail of Lord Raingo's sick bed seems a little tawdry.

118. LEONARD WOOLF, IN THE 'NATION AND ATHENAEUM'

16 October 1926, 86

Leonard Woolf (1880-1969) was in these years literary editor of the 'Nation and Athenaeum'.

Mr. Bennett's new novel 'Lord Raingo' has had the kind of pre-natal boom which modern stunt journalism has made possible. Whether it does much good to Mr. Bennett, the reading public, or to literature may be questioned, unless good be measured by copies sold or circulation. At any rate, when I took my dog to a vet. on the day after the publication of the book, the vet. told me that his daughter had told him that there was a portrait of Mr. Lloyd George done to the 't' in 'Lord Raingo.' Such is the power of advertisement and of the evening papers. And I could confirm the word of the daughter of the veterinary surgeon, having read the book and recognized the portraits, not only of Mr. Lloyd George, but of Mr. Churchill, Lord Curzon, Mr. Bonar Law, Mr. J.H. [D.A.] Thomas, and even of some of the lesser fry who, in political waters, swim around the great whales. It was significant, I thought, that the daughter of the veterinary surgeon was more interested in the fact that an ex-Prime Minister had been done to the 't' than that the hero of the book was Lord Rhondda - in the roman à clef it is not the novel but the key which matters, and the key to an ex-Prime Minister is more interesting than that to an ex-Minister of Food.

Mr. Bennett is one of three leading novelists, and his book must be judged by the standards of literature as well as by those of 'Who's Who.' But the 'Evening Standard,' if not the book itself, makes it difficult to get away from the 'Who's Who' atmosphere. The hero of the book, Lord

Raingo, is unmistakably the late Lord Rhondda. Innumerable other characters are unmistakable portraits of well-
known, and less well-known, people, some living, some dead.
And not only are the characters of these real people used
by Mr. Bennett, but often the circumstances of their lives
and their small personal peculiarities. I differ from a
good many of my colleagues in thinking that there is nothing against Mr. Bennett because he has 'lifted' real
people out of life into his novel. Many great novelists
have done the same. In the greatest novel ever written,
'War and Peace,' Tolstoi went so far as to give some of
his characters the same Christian names as those of the
real people from whom they were unmistakably drawn. And
I cannot see why the characters of well-known politicians
should be in any way sacrosanct; if it is right for a
novelist to use his grandmother for one of his characters,
why should he not be allowed also to use his friend the
Prime Minister for another? The test of a novelist is not
whether he has put 'real' people into his book, but what
use he has made of them when he has got them there.

The novelist who, like Mr. Bennett, has chosen very
well-known people for his models runs a risk. He runs the
risk of increasing his circulation and reducing his literary reputation. He knows that a large number of people
will not read the book as a novel, but will concentrate
their entire attention upon the question whether the portrait is 'like' or fair or justifiable, and, on a still
lower level, upon the question, who is who. Mr. Bennett
has not escaped the danger and the penalty. It is a pity,
for his reputation, that he ever wrote this novel. It is
not a good novel; in parts it is worse than anything which
he has written, though in other parts he shows what very
great gifts as a novel writer he still has. What makes
the book so bad is that it wobbles in its innermost inside, and therefore, of course, Mr. Bennett wobbles too.
The wobble is so big and so persistent that, in mid-
passage, the reader with a feeble stomach may easily be
overcome with a kind of literary mal-de-mer. The book
begins like a photograph, or rather like a photograph
which has been coloured to look like an oleograph. This
oleographic photograph is of political London in the
middle of the war. Even here the skill with which certain
effects are obtained is very considerable, because to a
casual or hasty reader it will not even be apparent. It
is also sometimes extremely amusing; the chapter, for instance, in which the Prime Minister and the new Lord Raingo
share the broth is superb. But already the wobble is
apparent. The whole thing starts as if it were to be a

brilliant political satire, the characters being photographic dummies. The crudity of these characters' psychology would not matter very much if the intention of satire
and caricature had been maintained. But there seems to be
no consistency either in the intention or in the characters themselves. Even dummies, photographs, and caricatures should have some stability or they become merely
vague shapes in a kaleidoscope. Raingo himself is a
psychological kaleidoscope. He begins almost an imbecile,
as far as intelligence is concerned, and his character
seems to be limited by a childish pleasure in the prospect
of being a lord. By the middle of the book he has become
a man of immense intelligence and perspicacity and of great
psychological subtlety. The caricature of Lord Rhondda has
developed into a real character of whom Mr. Bennett, the
novelist, is obviously the father. But the development is
never explained, and the gap between Mr. Raingo of the
book's beginning and Lord Raingo who can beat the Prime
Minister at his own clever game is never filled in. Mr.
Bennett himself is conscious of the difficulty, for he
appears half-heartedly to offer the explanation that Mr.
Raingo had practically retired from all active business
when the book opens.

   The mysterious change of Raingo from childish imbecility
to subtlety and intelligence is only a particular instance
of the book's fatal wobble. One does not ask for more
psychological consistency in the characters of a novel than
in those of real life, and Heaven knows the human soul whom
we meet going about its affairs in the actual world aston-
ishes one often enough by its capacity for instabiltiy.
But the mystery of Lord Raingo is due, not to the eternal
wobble of the human soul, but to the wobble in Mr. Bennett's craftsmanship. Lord Raingo is an imbecile when Mr.
Bennett is a caricaturist; he is Lord Rhondda when Mr.
Bennett is a grim realist; he is a subtle and intelligent
character when Mr. Bennett is a novelist. Up to page 269
Mr. Bennett never decided which he wanted to be, and the
book, the characters, and the reader see-saw helplessly
on a kind of triple see-saw which only Mr. Bennett could
have so ingeniously invented. On page 269, however, he
decided finally to be a novelist. But by that time it was
too late. The illness and death of Lord Raingo, which
occupy the last 140 pages of the book, have nothing to do
with what has gone before. They form an episode which
could have been written only by a novelist of great skill,
but it is an episode which is both out of proportion and
out of relation to the remainder of the book. It is, in
fact, the end of a novel which Mr. Bennett has never
written.

119. UNSIGNED REVIEW, 'PUNCH'

20 October 1926, 446

My first thought on turning over the four-hundredth page
of 'Lord Raingo' was that, in this masterly merciless
book, Mr. Arnold Bennett has returned to his best form;
my second, that it will make angry and disillusioned men,
of whom there are plenty, angrier and more disillusioned.
Here is a novel, conceived in the grand manner and technically of so perfect a craftsmanship as to be beyond
criticism. 'Lord Raingo' will probably become a classic.
Learned professors of a hundred years hence will take it
down lovingly from their shelves and browse over this picture of Whitehall under the microscope in the Great European War. We, however, are still in the year 1926,
getting, it is true, a clearer perspective of the War as
time rolls on, but even now, many of us, sore and puzzled
from the aftermath. And so, for all its wit, for all its
drama (and no one can tell a tale more thrillingly than
Mr. Bennett when he chooses), the book leaves one with a
feeling of savage despair for the sanity and safety of the
human race. In a world of sacrifice, humility and courage, can it be that there was so much cynicism and chicanery in Downing Street, so furious a jealousy between the
various Ministries in Whitehall? It can. The book has
the stamp of bitter truth. It is idle to pretend that
because Andy Clyth, Prime Minister, is represented as
'tall' and 'Lancashire-Irish' we are dealing with fiction.
In so far as the politics of the book are concerned, we
are dealing with real personages, and those who enjoy the
game of fitting caps to heads will have the time of their
lives. But the game is too easy. Who, for instance,
could mistake Sid Jenkin or Tom Hogarth? Certainly not
Sid Jenkin, who will be the first to appreciate his portrait. Only Mr. Bennett's hero, Lord Raingo, remains outside, aloof, mysterious, and a great piece of writing.
A type rather than an individual. Lovers of Mr. Bennett's
earlier work cannot fail to enjoy him, for what else is
he, after all, but our old friend 'The Card' plunged into
Affairs. 'Lord Raingo' is a great and courageous novel,
but it will disturb the sensitive reader almost beyond
endurance.

120. EDWARD SHANKS, IN THE 'LONDON MERCURY'

November 1926, 97-8

Edward Shanks (1892-1953), author and critic, was on the
staff of the 'London Mercury' in its first years.

If the answer to that question still interests anybody,
I think I can say who is the original of Lord Raingo. It
is Mr. Bennett himself - or a part of him, a part of that
part which has previously served for souls to the Card and
similar characters. Let us suppose Mr. Bennett coming to
London not to write novels but simply to make money, Mr.
Bennett, that is to say, with a mind of the same cast but
with gifts and sensibilities severely limited in range, and
you have Lord Raingo in fairly clear outline. He is only
a millionaire with apparently a narrower range of interests
than Mr. Bennett would as a rule find tolerable in his
principal character, but he is at heart a Card and it is
his cardishness that delights his creator. The essence of
the Card is cunning in action, naïvety in enjoyment of the
fruits of action. Raingo plays the Prime Minister like an
experienced angler, but his internal ejaculation, 'And
I've got the title without paying a cent for it,' is in a
schoolboy key, as is every official exploit of his from
then on.
    All this is good fun and bears no doubt some relation
to life, but it is not the most important part of the book.
The last third of it, describing Lord Raingo's last illness
and death, is on an almost immeasurably higher level than
the rest and ranks in brilliance with anything Mr. Bennett
has done in this line - not forgetting the illness of Mr.
Earlforward and the marvellous convalescence in 'The
Glimpse'. Just why Mr. Bennett should have this inclina-
tion towards the sick-room it is not easy to say. But
he has it, and in the sick-room his penetrative and
descriptive powers are often at their best. Here he
reaches his climax in a terrifying passage when Raingo,
after making an effort to work so as to convince himself
that he is recovering, suddenly abandons it:

    'All right, isn't it, Sir Arthur, this working a
bit?' Geoffrey asked.
    'Certainly! Certainly! If he feels like it. And
doesn't overdo it.'

Sam detected the insincerity in the benevolent tones as infallibly as though he had been the reader of all hearts. He could almost see Sir Arthur winking at Geoffrey, almost hear him whispering: 'Doesn't matter much what he does now. Let him follow his fancy.' So morbid and sensitive was his imagination!

Yet by another act of imagination he ignored all that, and went on pretending to work, and treated the important doctor as perfectly non-existent. Then he grew tired of the sham and continued it hopelessly - with the dogged, feeble, pathetic hopelessness of a boat's crew pounding and sweating in the wake of winners who are passing the post. And then he pushed all the papers away with a disillusioned sigh. The pretence was at an end. He did not care, now, who knew it had been a pretence. Let them all think what they chose.

The nurse brought him food. He took a spoonful, then pushed the basin away as he had pushed the papers away, and some of the contents were spilt on the bed. He groaned, and slid weakly down the incline of the pillows toward the interior of the bed and became an emaciated, unshaven, panting sick man with fright and despair in his eyes.

That one passage was surely better worth doing than the most intricate and revelatory *roman à clef* ever written.

121. EXCHANGES BETWEEN LORD BIRKENHEAD AND BENNETT IN THE 'DAILY MAIL'

23-30 November 1926

Lord Birkenhead (F.E. Smith, 1872-1920) was a distinguished statesman, lawyer, and biographer. One of his recently published books was 'Famous Trials'.

[1. Trifling with Reputations, 'Daily Mail', 23 November 1926, 8. The article was an interview with Birkenhead, in which he spoke first about the recent publication of scandal-mongering memoirs and then turned to the novels of Bennett and Wells.]

...Asked whether he thought novelists were justified in introducing real persons into fiction, Lord Birkenhead said that this practice also seemed to him an objectionable one.

'When Mr. Arnold Bennett wrote a novel called "Lord Raingo," it was widely stated - and he did not contradict it - that the principal character was modelled on a member of the Coalition Government. In fact, the work was vulgarly advertised upon this basis.

'What right,' asked Lord Birkenhead, 'has Mr. Arnold Bennett, whose public services, as apart from his literary merits, are unlikely to be celebrated in song or story, to suggest that his imaginary puppet was modelled from an actual statesman?

'Mr. H.G. Wells has committed the same offence by a different but equally well-advertised method.... Yet, such is his prestige as an immaginative novelist - to which I for one subscribe - that he now arrogates to himself the right to disparage the work of the men who have done things, when things had to be done, through the lips of a man who has found literature (without responsibility) a very lucrative calling.... I make my profound objection to the reproduction in books of private, or alleged private, conversations, to the dissemination of lying slanders about living and dead statesmen, and to the overweening conceit of novelists, puffed out by the advertisements of the publishers of their imaginative efforts, as arbiters of public men's actions and characters.'

[2. Bennett, letter dated 23 November, addressed to the editor. It appeared on 24 November, 9, following editorial discussion of Real People in Fiction.]

Sir, - In his interview with your representative printed to-day, Lord Birkenhead said:

> When Mr. Arnold Bennett wrote a novel called 'Lord Raingo' it was widely stated - and he did not contradict it - that the principal character was modelled on a member of the Coalition Government. What right has Mr. Arnold Bennett to suggest that his imaginary puppet was modelled from an actual statesman?

The answer to this question is that I never suggested such a thing. The character of my Lord Raingo was modelled on no statesman, and is the result of no attempt at portraiture.

I have said so in private ten thousand times, but it is

not my custom to deny misstatements about my books in
public. If it was, I should have to give my life to the
business.

As regards the deceased statesman whom doubtless Lord
Birkenhead has in mind, I may say that I never had the
slightest acquaintance with him.

It is apparent from his concluding remarks that the
author of 'Famous Trials' was for some undisclosed reason
getting a bit cross. His emotion led him to the use of
certain vituperative clichés. The vituperation one can
excuse and enjoy; but the clichés will afflict the
lettered.

Arnold Bennett

[3. Bennett, Trifling with Reputations, 'Daily Mail', 25
November, 8.]

Is a novelist entitled to deal exhaustively and critically
with modern politics?

It is conceivable that some people, and in particular
those who adorn St. Stephen's - or make of St. Stephen's
a circus - may reply that he is not entitled to deal with
modern politics. It may well be urged that the statesmen
who during the last twenty years by their wisdom and
energy have brought Britain to her present height of prestige and prosperity should be secure against the irrever-
ent pens which make such havoc among all other sections
of society.

It may well be urged that the freedom of the Press
should have limits and that it should not extend beyond
the top of Whitehall. That is an argumentative position
which any man is entitled to take, and to hold - until he
is thrown out of it by the force of reason or ridicule.

But if a novelist is indeed entitled to deal with
modern politics, then in order to obtain verisimilitude
he must devise, for some of his personages, individuals
who bear some resemblance to individuals in real life.
Statesmen are so well known to the reading public; they
have such opportunities (which they do not often neglect)
of vulgarly advertising themselves and stamping themselves
on the collective memory, that there is absolutely no way
of getting away from them.

Say that a novelist needs a War Prime Minister for his
plot. If he drew a Prime Minister with the attributes of
the Governor of the Bank of England or the Archbishop of
Canterbury or George Robey he would certainly and justly
be accused of failure to convince, though such attributes

might accurately fit into the political character. He is bound to draw a Prime Minister who is somehow like a Prime Minister, and since there is only one Prime Minister at a time he must draw a Prime Minister who is somehow like, or reminiscent of, *the* Prime Minister. And so on.

This may be inconvenient for great statesmen, but it is one of the inevitable penalties of their unique greatness - part of the price which they must pay for having an unparalleled time.

Of course, the political novelist who respects himself will use tact. His minor figures, sketched in lightly and with tolerance, may approximate to actuality or to a mixture of actualities; but he will take care in his major figure (if a statesman) not to draw any sort of portrait of a statesman living or recently dead; and as to episodes, he will employ only such matters - for instance keeping a mistress or suffering a fatal illness - as are the commonplaces of political life.

And if any statesman stands up and protests: 'This novelist's hero keeps a mistress - the scribbler has no right to make a portrait of me,' the sufficient answer is that the statesman is flattering himself.

For the rest, the method which I have outlined has been the practice of reputable novelists for generations, and the pages of the most admired novels in literature are studded with examples of it.

Lord Birkenhead in these columns on Tuesday last bitterly complained because the 'imaginative novelist'(*sic*) 'now arrogates to himself the right to disparage the work of men who have done things.' Tut-tut!

The case of Mr. Wells lies apart from the above general theory. Mr. Wells permits his hero to name living statesmen and to make remarks about them. But why not? Statesmen pass half their days in being rude to one another. Anonymous journalists indulge themselves daily in harsh criticism of the saviours of society. Why should novelists, though their brains are obviously inferior to those of statesmen, if not of journalists, be debarred from the same joyous pastime? At any rate, Mr. Wells's hero never equalled the contumelious candour with which Lord Birkenhead has treated two novelists whom he names by name.

[4. Lord Birkenhead, letter dated 26 November, addressed to the editor. It appeared on 29 November, 8. He turns to Bennett after discussing another aspect of his views.]

...If his statement published in 'The Daily Mail' on November 21 is well founded, I certainly owe him an apology. But not being by nature a specially apologetic man I must require that a few points should be made plain.

Mr. Bennett says in very definite language: 'The character of Lord Raingo was modelled upon no statesman, and is the result of no attempt at portraiture.'

With the greatest possible respect for Mr. Bennett I find it necessary to make it quite plain that I do not accept his assurance.

I cannot directly prove him wrong – as otherwise I very easily could – because to do so would be to repeat the offence. I am therefore driven from the stronger points of the argument to the weaker. But these are quite strong enough.

A great firm of publishers, Messrs. Cassell, published Mr. Bennett's novel. A great newspaper, the 'Evening Standard', purchased the serial rights. Another great newspaper – not without close association with the 'Evening Standard' – the 'Daily Express' gave much attention to the preliminary boomings of this story 'in which the character of Lord Raingo was modelled upon no statesman' but which were recommended to the purchasing public in very different terms.

Messrs. Cassell's say: 'Set in the period of the late war this story centres round a number of Cabinet Ministers and other prominent politicians, Samuel Raingo (a millionaire, afterwards made a Peer) being the principal figure.'

This recommendation by his publishers was not, one may suppose, without pecuniary advantage to Mr. Bennett. It was not, at any rate, contradicted by him.

The 'Evening Standard' in an editorial article said (and they should have known for they were Mr. Bennett's employers):

> A leading reviewer who has read the novel has declared that the central character may easily be identified. Mr. Bennett has refused to express agreement or disagreement.

It is, of course, evident that Mr. Bennett's refusal can have had no relation to the extreme and obvious book-puffing advantage of this kind of talk.

But, making all kinds of allowances for the delicacy which leads him, as he tells us, to ignore public criticism, I am a little puzzled how I am to explain the silence of our sensitive novelist in view of the statement which occurred in the 'Daily Express' of September 13 – the Monday before Mr. Bennett's publication. I quote it in full:

The book is the story of the life of an ex-Cabinet
Minister holding office during the later years of the
war. The woman in the case was well known at one time
in the popular dining rooms and the fashionable dancing
clubs which she visited nearly every night.

It is perhaps permissible to ask Mr. Bennett the
following questions in relation to this statement appearing in an important organ to which he is a regular contributor:

1. Did he see it when it appeared?
2. If he did, knowing it to be untrue, why did he
not contradict it?
3. Did he perhaps think that this kind of scandalous
suggestion about his forthcoming book (for he has told
us now that it was scandalous) would increase its
circulation; and did this consideration lead him to
remain silent?
4. How could he on any other conceivable view as a
conscientious artist have remained silent?

And, indeed, in this connection I must refer to the
article in the 'Daily Express', dated September 14, which
I (respecting that paper as I do) know that its managers
would not and could not have published without warrant:

Mr. Bennett has actually taken the life of a Cabinet
Minister who held office during the later years of the
war. He has cast an actual life which has only been
known to a few persons into the mould of a novel.

Was this true or was it false?
Was Mr. Bennett accurate in his statement of November
24 to the 'Daily Mail', or were his publisher, the
'Evening Standard', and the 'Daily Express' right? *Non
mihi tantas componere lites*. Either Mr. Bennett or all
his journalistic sponsors and puffers deceived us. Which,
which, which?
And in the meantime I note no sign that Mr. Arnold
Bennett proposes to write a novel about Mr. Wells or Mr.
Wells about Mr. Bennett. Why not? They are obviously
so much more omniscient than we are, and so much more
prepared to embrace their portion of civic responsibility.
For instance, why do they not contest a democratic constituency and show us how to govern England instead of
making money by demonstrating our incompetency?

[5. Bennett, Statesmen in Fiction, 'Daily Mail', 30 November, 8. Bennett wrote this article as a letter of reply to Birkenhead's letter published on the 29th. But the 'Daily Mail' telephoned to ask for a second article before he posted the letter, 'so I crossed out the Sir, and Yours truly, and called it an article and charged £60 for it' ('Journal', 29 November).]

I said in my letter to the Editor of the 'Daily Mail', published on Tuesday:

> The character of Lord Raingo was modelled upon no statesman and is the result of no attempt at portraiture.

And I will now say further that so far as I know there is in the whole of my novel only one unusual incident which is related to fact.

Lord Birkenhead replies: 'I do not accept his assurance.'

Possibly not. It would be inconvenient for Lord Birkenhead to do so. With characteristic impulsiveness he got himself into an impossible position, and to refuse to accept my assurance was his only way out of it.

The controversy ought properly to end here. But Lord Birkenhead goes on to make more misstatements and also to ask me several plain questions. I will stretch a point to answer his questions and to correct his misstatements.

He says: 'I cannot directly prove him wrong - as otherwise I very easily could - because to do so would be to repeat his offence.'

This is not so. He could not prove me wrong. Even if both of us were at liberty to mention names and to write freely, he could not prove me wrong; but I could prove myself right.

He says:

> Messrs. Cassell's say: 'Set in the period of the late war, this story centres round a number of Cabinet Ministers and other prominent politicians, Samuel Raingo (a millionaire, afterwards made a peer) being the principal figure.'

This statement as to my novel is perfectly accurate. My novel is chiefly about a number of Cabinet Ministers and about one in particular. How else should the novel have been described? As a story about tinkers?

He says further:

The 'Evening Standard' in an editorial article said
(and they should have known, for they were Mr. Bennett's employers): 'A leading reviewer who has read
the novel has declared that the central character may
easily be identified. Mr. Bennett has refused to
express agreement or disagreement.'

'A leading reviewer' may well have made the remark
attributed to him.

I may point out in passing that the 'Evening Standard'
were not my 'employers,' any more than Lord Birkenhead
would be the employer of the department store from whom
he might buy a safety razor. Lord Birkenhead should
really give attention to the meaning of words. Nor, even,
did I sell 'Lord Raingo' to the 'Evening Standard'. Until
the 'Evening Standard' had decided to buy the serial
rights of the novel I was unaware that the serial rights
(which I had sold long before to a great firm of magazine
publishers) were in the market.

Lord Birkenhead quotes further a statement from the
'Daily Express':

The book is the story of the life of an ex-Cabinet
Minister holding office during the late years of the
war. The woman in the case was well known at one time
in the popular dining-rooms and the fashionable dancing
clubs, which she visited nearly every night.

And as to this, he invites me to answer four questions:
(1) Did he see it when it appeared?
The answer is Yes.
(2) If he did, knowing it to be untrue, why did he not
contradict it?
The answer is that Lord Birkenhead should read again my
previous letter.
(3) Did he perhaps think that this kind of scandalous
suggestion about his forthcoming book (for he has told us
now that it was scandalous) would increase its circulation; and did this consideraton lead him to remain silent?
The answer is No. (Incidentally, I have not said that
the suggestion was scandalous.)
(4) How could he on any other conceivable view as a
conscientious artist have remained silent?
The answer is that my duties as a conscientious artist
are confined to my work in my book. It is not my business, and I should conceive it as an impertinence, to
attempt to teach the conductors of some of the most brilliant newspapers in this country how they ought to run

those newspapers and how they ought to deal with their own goods.

I am glad to note that in his second communication Lord Birkenhead has thought well to modify the polemical excesses of his first. Only my warm personal regard for him induced me to answer his first communication at all. I must, however, animadvert upon his continuing innuendoes about pecuniary advantage. The *tu quoque* to the author of 'Famous Trials' and of numberless journalistic articles would be too easy; and might be too devastating. The imputation of unworthy motives rarely helps an argument and nearly always weakens it.

[On 1 December Bennett wrote in his 'Journal': 'When I opened the "Daily Mail" this morning I found that Birkenhead had made no further answer to me; so the incident is now, I suppose, closed. The press has been very generally in my favour. I had prepared some heavy artillery to kill him if he had continued the fight.' The heavy artillery presumably included the fact that before he was first interviewed by the 'Daily Mail' Birkenhead had asked Max Beaverbrook whether Raingo was a portrait of himself, Birkenhead! Some weeks prior to publication, Frank Swinnerton said in the 'Bookman' (New York), in his Simon Pure column, that Beaverbrook was the original for Raingo, a statement that Bennett asked him to recall. In later years Swinnerton said that the portrait was basically of Bennett himself, an opinion that was in accord with the general view on such matters expressed by Bennett in connection with 'The Card' (see p. 60). For discussion of the material from Lord Rhondda's life used by Bennett, see Louis Tillier, 'Studies in the Sources of Arnold Bennett's Novels', 1969. See also the Introduction above, p. 99. Bennett had a few more words to say on the matter in his Explanation to the 'Savour of Life'. The last word belonged to Winston Churchill, to whom Tom Hogarth in the novel bore resemblance. He and Bennett met at the Other Club a couple of days after Bennett had fired the last shot in the battle. Churchill said, 'Receive the congratulations of Tom Hogarth' ('Journal', 2 December).]

'Accident'

10 January 1929

122. DESMOND MacCARTHY, IN THE 'SUNDAY TIMES'

13 January 1929, 6

'The Finest Badger,' 'Pure Badger,' 'Badger'; 'New-laid
Eggs,' 'Fresh Eggs,' 'Eggs'; men seeking shaving-brushes,
women who keep house, are familiar with these distinctions;
readers also are aware that in the book-market 'Finest
Bennett,' 'Pure Bennett' and 'Bennett' are on sale.
Indeed, these grades in his work are so distinct that some
have jumped to the conclusion that he writes pot-boilers.
He does not. What I believe to be the true explanation
I shall divulge, but let me first slap on to his latest
novel the proper label; 'Accident' is 'Pure Bennett.'
    It is not only written with care but constructed with
care. The novel has a shape. The method of narration is
strictly consistent; everything is felt through one temperament and seen by one percipient. And not only that,
his changing moods reveal new things in the characters
with whom, through him, we become acquainted; as our understanding of Mr. Alan Frith-Walter himself (prosperous
engineer, well-preserved, over fifty) increases, so, too,
does our insight into his travelling companions.
    He is on his way from London to Genoa to join his wife,
travelling in a sleeper on the Paris-Rome Express; and, of
course, we are not permitted to forget for long together
either details of the way in which the rich travel, or the
marvels or the short-comings of modern luxury and organisation. The novel, with the exception of the closing
scenes, is an account of his journey.
    Frith-Walter's leading instinct is to forget himself
and live imaginatively in others. When there is conflict

between two of them he is convinced by each in turn; then reconverted to admiration where he had criticised and to contempt where he had admired. He cannot resent for a moment the hurried snappishness of a waiter without remembering the next that the man can probably love a woman or play with a child; nor can he bend over a fried sole without (alas!) reflecting with amazement that it has been pulled from the sea by a fisherman and conveyed by a long chain of intermediaries to his plate. It strikes him as astonishing that for £300 he should be able to purchase the efficient devotion of his secretary (who bears the name of Miss Office), and that while the passengers at Victoria Station are bound for the ends of the earth the porters should remain behind. There is, in short, in the compass of his wonder, not to speak of the occasonal naivety of it, something foreign to the mental make-up of those who play themselves important parts in organising civilisation.

Frith-Walter's moods vary largely with the degree to which he assimilates occasional sips from Wordsworth's 'Prelude' - his pocket flask, his spiritual pick-me-up, or to which he is worried by the utterly unforeseen presence on the train of his newly married daughter-in-law.

'Pearl' is running away from her husband to her mother, because 'Jack' has resolved to stand as a Labour M.P.; to her an exasperating folly, a humiliating treachery to his class. At once Frith-Walter, who barely knows her, is impressed by her finish and aplomb; then he is distressed by her egotism and hardness; next amazed at her poise, her resolute good sense and kindness. In the middle of the night, at Aix-les-Bains, 'Jack,' who has flown from Newcastle, boards the express. Surely, thinks his father, this leap of impetuous passion will close a gulf which argument has failed to bridge between them. But 'Pearl' remains cold and collected; and Frith-Walter's sympathies continue to be tossed to and fro between the two tense young creatures. Sometimes he thinks of their separation as a ghastly family calamity; sometimes he divines in their uncompromising antagonism a noble tragedy worth even that cost.

The final solution is as indecisive as Frith-Walter's responses have been to the situation itself; 'Jack' renounces his resolve out of his passion for 'Pearl,' and 'Pearl,' rather than he should weakly give up a political career for a woman, chooses to stick to him. The percipient felt both relief and regret at 'Jack's' surrender; after 'Pearl's,' that he will always be worried by life; he resolves to go on reading Wordsworth. The conclusion is limp and inconclusive. What was Mr. Bennett's idea?

Surely it has escaped him? There was something there,
something which urged him to write the book, and is
glimpsed in it here and there by the reader. Would,
after all, a tragic parting of lovers have been best?
Passion in conviction, or passion between man and woman;
which should win in a life worth living? The solid house
overlooking the bay - comfort, harmony, commonsense, all
that house stands for - or the dark welter of instinctive
life beyond, which should be man's choice if he is to
live? The idea which prompted him to write had surely
something to do with these questions - with an adjustment
between claims of commonsense and the tragic view of life.
And it escaped him! Most of Mr. Bennett's recent work has
had neither the support of an entirely robust hedonism,
nor of the romantic tragic sense which lit and trans-
figured murky pages of 'The Old Wives' Tale.'

The novel is of all literary forms the one in which
success is rarest; and it can be, if successful, the most
artistic of all forms, precisely because its aesthetic equilibrium lies deep within it and is independent of all rules:
coherence so complicated can only be achieved by the
intellect and heart of an author working together better
than he knows. Mr. Bennett has been stimulated by these
problems; but he has no solution. Neither, it is true,
have we; but it is for the artist to discover one, though
on an intellectual level he may not even recognise that
he has done so. Mr. Bennett has chosen an alternative,
always open to so efficient a craftsman, that of presenting us merely with a plausible fragment of experience
broken off from life. The surface work is deft and
finished; the outward shape of his book good, but there
is no deep informing spirit within it. This story is
haunted by the ghost of an unembodied solution. That
'accident,' too, which the reader anticipates so
impatiently is really unimportant; the principal characters are neither the worse nor the better for it. Its
importance, if any, is in connection with an old man and
his wife, who are also travelling on the train. These two
are extraordinarily well sketched; he has never drawn a
more memorable minor character than Mrs. Lucass, the 'hag-
beauty,' or in fewer strokes suggested a more profound
pain-happiness relation between man and wife.

The 'hag-beauty' first strikes Frith-Walter as the most
hysterical shrew who ever humiliated a helpless husband in
public. On the boat he scrapes acquaintance with old Mr.
Lucass, and discovers to his surprise that he speaks of her
with wistful devotion. Later, on board the train, he has
tea with the 'hag-beauty' herself while her extenuated

husband is lying down, and to his still greater amazement
discovers in her a daemonic and indomitable intensity of
life and loyalty which compels his admiration. The indication of the 'hell-paradise' in which these two old
people live *vis à vis*, halcyon and stormy as young love
and jealousy, conceivably owes something to suggestions
from the works of Mr. D.H. Lawrence; but, as might be
expected, in Mr. Bennett's hands, the comic aspect of such
a sex-relation does not escape our notice. Rumour of an
accident on another line has thrown the 'hag-beauty' into
a state of frantic nerves. When the train stops by chance
at a deserted wayside station she escapes from it, her
wretched husband following her. One scene I shall certainly take away with me out of this book: the picture of
a dark, windy, puddled platform with a grotesque woman on
it, turning her back obstinately to the train, and an old
beaten man trying to placate her; both marooned together
in the dead of night.

His attitude to this extraordinary but convincing old
couple and their world, where the ugly is indistinguishable from the beautiful and the stress of pain from the
exhilaration of pleasure, is characteristic of a strain
in him which his choice of subjects has often rendered
inoperative. It is one to which he has owed his most
signal achievements. Thanks to it his studies of 'the
Potteries' were more than excellent photographs of the
provinces. He responds to the surface of life like an
auctioneer, to success like a parvenue, but to courageous
blind vitality - like a poet. Look again at 'The Matador
of the Five Towns'; that response has made it one of the
best of English short stories.

Mr. Bennett was born an indiscriminate lover of life,
and to be in love with life, even blindly, is far better
than to be put out of temper with it in comparison with
an ideal indistinctly apprehended. It is astonishing how
easy it is to persuade people that the world is unworthy
of them: they are flattered. But in the end they are more
grateful to one who makes them feel that it is they who
are not up to the world. It is this sense which, without
tricking things out in fancy colours, he has brought them:
he has often succeeded in lending to commonplace characters
something of the hero in a most unheroic world. This love
of life implies, of course, that he is not - indeed,
emphatically, he is not - a writer who distinguishes un-
erringly between what is more and what is less worth while.
We are not indebted to him for a finer and more precise
scale of values. He is too indiscriminate in his response
to life for that. He does not judge the aims of his
characters; indeed, he hardly judges at all. He *accepts* -

and presents a picture.

Whether the aim of his characters is to get on, to
become efficient, to be rich, to get the better of someone
else, to marry, or just to struggle somehow along, we get
from Mr. Bennett no criticism of these aims as ends. We
do not see them in the light of any outside standard,
moral or aesthetic, but from *within*, as they appear to the
person actually pursuing them. The character in question
may be narrow and vulgar, and may be inferred to have the
foggiest notions of what is really worth while in life;
nevertheless, it is his or her estimate of the value of
what is striven for which Mr. Bennett, thanks to an extraordinary directness of sympathy, communicates - and makes
the criterion. And mention of his sympathy brings one to
another of his qualities which is remarkable, and contributes in a measure to making his books so popular: his
astonishing lack of author's egotism in portraying character. This makes him so fair all round.

He is one of the most objective and least egotistic of
writers. Compare him for a moment with Mr. Wells in this
respect. It is natural to compare them because both men
in their novels have performed for us the service of
reflecting the modern world in a way which shows us, and
will show the historian, what changes are, and have been,
going on. One feels as one reads Mr. Wells's books that
his perceptions have always been sharpened by the way the
confusion of the existing social order has impinged upon
himself, has baffled, tortured, and amused him. His fiction is autobiography in disguise, doctored and altered
often beyond recognition as fact, but in spirit autobiography. So, too, his thinking has the air of always
having been prompted by his own predicaments at the
moment, however disinterestedly it may have been afterwards pursued. Thanks to being such a bundle of conflicting sensibilities, reactions and passions, to being so
human - to use a familiar tag - this reflection of a
personal response to life has been rich in results. Mr.
Wells has shown us things worth seeing because he is so
personal; Mr. Bennett because he has forgotten himself.
Compared with Mr. Wells, he is an 'eye' without an intellect behind it. What is, however, behind that eye is a
sympathy which enables him to find ordinary characters as
interesting as they are to *themselves*.

I said at the beginning of this article that I would
give my own explanation of the marked unevenness in Mr.
Bennett's work; lack of space now compels me to use metaphor. You know those little electric motors which can be
affixed to sailing boats and drive them along when the
wind drops. They have spoilt sailing, though they are

exceedingly convenient. Arnold Bennett is an artist who
was born (unfortunately for us, yes, and for him, too)
with such an attachment. He can move rapidly in any
direction without waiting for the breath of inspiration;
he can make progress without tacking. He has been cursed
with an irrelevant and impartial efficiency. He can write
a readable article on anything from Proust to the 'three-
piece' dress; he can make 'a job' of any theme though he
has only a craftsman's interest in it; and the result has
been that he has been unable to distinguish easily between
what he can do and what he can do *best*. He confuses in
himself the conscientiousness of the craftsman with that
of the artist. The result would always be respectworthy
in one from whom we could receive nothing better; but
often the artist's heart isn't in it,

> And the high gods know in a minute
> That it isn't the genuine thing.

123.   REVIEW SIGNED H.B., 'MANCHESTER GUARDIAN'

18 January 1929, 7

There exist short stories by Mr. Bennett of superlative
excellence and to these, even to The Death of Simon Fuge,
might have been added another were 'Accident' (in matter
a short story) not expanded, by our author's indulgence in
his foible of conveying information to posterity, into the
form of a shortish novel. We can well envisage the
encyclopaedist of 200 years hence citing 'Accident'
amongst his authorities for the article on European travel.
'Clocks, enormous clocks everywhere! Their long hands
showed four minutes to seventeen, and then simultaneously
the hands jumped and showed three minutes to seventeen.
'Here' - in the Gare de Lyon - 'time did not fly; it
leaped like a grasshopper, from minute to minute, under an
impulse of electricity generated miles away in some huge
throbbing interior of whirring wheels, furnaces, boilers,
and greasy pale mannikins.' So is it all described, the
Pullmans of the Southern Railway, the halt in mid-Kent
when 'five hours elapsed, which the Pullman clock naughtily
measured as five minutes,' the boat crossing, the Paris
train, and the Rome express - richly, freshly, illuminat-
ingly, and too informingly described. But the question for

the contemporary reader is what, if any, character does
'Accident' create to hang on the line in its author's
grand gallery of portraits? We hold that the point is not
a territorial one, that the genius of Mr. Bennett is not
delimited by the boundaries of the Five Towns, but that
the points are sex and social status. Women of the middle
and lower classes inspire him to profundity, men of the
millionairish class to whimsicality. It is not a case of
the Five Towns novels and the rest, for in association
with the preposterous caprices of rich men, or with the
noble caprice of the painter who tired of his identity,
Mr. Bennett has created women worth their places on the
line beside Constance and Sophia, Hilda, Anna and Elsie.
Such a woman was Harriet Perkins in 'The Strange Vanguard,'
and such another we hoped to encounter in 'Accident.'
We failed to find her, and 'Accident' secures a place, but
a good place, amongst the left-handed works of its invariably dexterous author.

   Alan Frith-Walter, if prosperous, is less than a
millionaire, and Mr. Bennett is less than inspired about
him, with the result that there is, this time, no high
clash between some vagary of a wealth-intoxicated man and
the sagacious sanity of an earth-treading woman, but,
instead, there are the passive wonderings of an unself-
centred man in his fifties confronted by the problem of
his son who proposes on five thousand a year to stand as
a Labour candidate, and of Pearl, Jack's wife, to whom the
boy's resolve is outrageous treachery. That problem,
ultimately solved by Jack's surrender to Pearl, capped by
Pearl's surrender to Jack, discloses itself gradually to
the humanly worried Alan, and if the railway accident,
beautifully described, has little relevance to the story,
the full facts about Pearl and Jack come to light through
a series of travel accidents positively exciting by sheer
inventiveness. There is tough hammer-and-tongs argument
between Jack and Pearl about the incongruities of a rich
man in the Labour party and the possibilities of his
better serving Labour from without: good stuff and explicit where, had it come in a short story, it might have
been better stuff and implicit. Incidentally there are
Mr. Bennett's waiters; Mr. and Mrs. Lucass, who definitely
belong on the line in the annexe to his major portrait
gallery; the development of Pearl under Alan's eyes from
stranger to being, charmingly, his daughter-in-law; and
Alan finding in 'The Prelude' and in his determination to
read more Wordsworth antidotes against a son gone Red in
politics. It is Pearl's book, and she isn't one of Mr.
Bennett's significants; but how magical in his unfailing
capacity to wonder is even the palest Bennett hero, how

good is this graceful shapely novel! A minor Bennett is
the work of a master.

124. CYRIL CONNOLLY, IN THE 'NEW STATESMAN'

19 January 1929, 470-1

Cyril Connolly (1903-74) was one of the major critics of
the past half-century who spoke against Bennett. He
referred to Bennett once as a 'cart-horse of letters'.

The explanation of the apparent vagaries of Mr. Bennett
appears to be that he does not write potboilers, but that
he conscientiously produces three grades of work - writing
good novels for those who like literature, novels for
those who read fiction, and books like 'The Strange Vanguard' for those who read anything. Certainly, no one can
expect Mr. Bennett to go on producing 'The Old Wives'
Tale', but there ought to be some sub-title - diversions
of a novelist - recreations of a man of letters - which
should enable the reader to classify these later works with
the corresponding frolics of leisured headmasters,
journalising clerics, or poetical gaolbirds. Imagine Mr.
Yeats producing three grades of poetry, or Mr. John three
qualities of painting, and the absurdity of the apologia
for Mr. Bennett becomes apparent. For Mr. Bennett is in
a responsible position. He is one of the very few famous
novelists of the last generation who have not entirely
lost the respect of youth. This is partly because he has
resisted the sclerosis of the imagination which drives
elderly novelists into the last Tory refuges of English
society, so that while Mr. Galsworthy and Mr. Walpole are
borne down the stream of time, humped anxiously on slabs
of property like Eskimo dogs marooned by the thaw on
crumbling pack-ice, Mr. Bennett is appreciating Proust and
Joyce, and even inducing other people to do so too.
Again, Mr. Bennett does not write about himself. His
novels are not self-dramatisations; they are not axe-
grinders, and do not date like the propaganda of Wells or
the satire of Galsworthy. Lastly, Mr. Bennett has an
aesthetic sense; his books are for those - or could be -
who like writing as much as those who like reading, and the

praise of authors is ultimately more gratifying than a
vast popularity with scientists, stockbrokers, or American
culture fans. With all these advantages, Mr. Bennett
might become a very powerful influence in contemporary
literature. A drastic critical operation could curtail
his Siamese liaison with Mr. Galsworthy if only he could
write for a public as intelligent as himself. Mr. Wells
and Mr. Shaw, the remaining evangelists, have always been
pamphleteers rather than literary artists; Mr. George
Moore is an artist and nothing else. The new generation,
suspicious of mere technique, is equally unmoved by mere
propaganda; it finds in writers like Proust a blend of
style with a personal philosophy of life which other
generations discovered in Flaubert or Dr. Johnson. Mr.
Bennett has - if he left off telling the man in the street
what he calls 'the difference between a book and a bath
bun' - the profound experience of life and the capacity to
generalise from it in artistic form which nearly all his
theorising contemporaries lack; but, instead of being a
pilot, he is a populariser, and when he might show a
tragic and intelligent perception of the beauty of life
and the value of art, he writes 'Accident' instead.

It is also urged that Mr. Bennett's excessive love of
life is the explanation of his often mediocre comments on
it. But just as the love of wit is no justification for
a profusion of bad puns, so there is something peculiarly
irritating about Mr. Bennett's gourmand affection for
existence in general. To love life is to have the curiosity to search for the occasions when life is lovable, and
the enterprise to create them. Human life is, after all,
a picture-puzzle with half the pieces missing: to love it
is to love it where it makes sense, and to make sense of
it is the selective principle of all art. Mr. Bennett
does not select in his carefully graded C3 novels; he
gives full rein to his own preoccupation with male vanity
and material success, and to his reader's desire for a
happy ending.

Yet 'Accident' is a curious book. I cannot imagine a
C3 reader extracting any pleasure from it. It is a study
in family intimacy - an English attempt, perhaps, to
destroy the Wilder-Westcott round-up of this intangible
relation into high-class American best-sellers. Alan,
rich elderly business man, takes the Rome express to join
his wife at Genoa. Pearl, ultra-modern daughter-in-law,
is also on the train, fleeing from her husband because he
has decided to stand Labour. Jack, son and husband,
catches the train by aeroplane at Aix, just in time for
the catastrophe. All end up at Genoa in Elaine, the
mother's, suite, and Jack abandons Labour only to be

restored to it by the chivalrous Pearl, who will not let
him change. Alan and Elaine are left marvelling at the
heroism of the younger generation. The other characters
are the Rome express itself and a pair of elderly lovers
who live in the hell-heaven dear to Mr. D.H. Lawrence
(*nec tecum possum vivere nec sine te* is still the para-
doxical rabbit in the hat of all 'intimacy' exploiters).
It is odd, incidentally, how our three underdog writers,
Mr. Lawrence, Mr. Bennett, and Mr. Michael Arlen, all
attribute to their supermen the same qualities of mystery,
cruelty, omnipotence, and instinctive knowledge of behaviour, so that the English aristocrat is indistinguishable
from the continental head-waiter and the Mexican Indian
from the little brown man of the sleeping cars. The dis-
comfort of the rich, of course, remains a central feature,
being as much an obsession and a mystery with Mr. Bennett
as was to former theologians the prosperity of the
wicked.

Yet the book, despite the innumerable inconveniences of
the *train de luxe* (the chief comic character, clowning its
way from the Channel to the Mediterranean), is seriously
written and shows an admirably unity. The action takes
place in forty-eight hours. It accelerates gently from
the start, and the four characters in the drama (to which
the old love-hating couple form a curtain-raiser) appear
one by one in the perfect classical tradition of a French
tragedy. After the large canvases and loose chronology
of modern novels this conformity is very soothing.

But the chief defect of 'Accident' is Mr. Bennett's
hero. Readers of novels are a naive class. Unless they
are very definitely told otherwise, they regard the central figure of a book as a hero, as the author's ideal of
what a man should be. Thus, the hero who slowly turns out
to be a rogue without any indication of the author's dis-
approval is a set piece that may easily missfire. But Mr.
Bennett's hero is a colossal bore. In the case of the
hero-bore one must try and discover if the hero is meant
to be a figure of fun, if the novel is helped by the
reader looking at the characters through a lens of ennui
('Bouvard et Pécuchet' is an example of this) or if the
author genuinely stands godfather to his hero's opinions,
unaware that he has sponsored a mooncalf. Let us get Alan
clear. He is rich, vain, elderly, and successful. He
loves his wife, he is proud of his son, admires his
daughter-in-law. These three grades of affection Mr.
Bennett absolutely understands. But Alan has brought 'The
Prelude' with him. His two chief qualities are a capacity
for easy generalisation, for simple philosophising on his
surroundings, and an elastic tolerance which enables him

to see the good in everyone. In fact, he veers like a
weathercock to every situation, so that in this way he is
very deliberately a barometer which the author has installed to register the fluctuations in the quarrel between Jack and Pearl. But the barometer-hero is a
failure, for the reader is bored by his reaction and
finally loses interest in the quarrel altogether.

But he must feel sorry also for Pearl; her youthfulness was somehow pathetic; he must not be hard on her;
he wanted to soften everybody, and he must soften himself; his resentment against Jack was illogical...
The waiter snatched up their soup cups as though they
had been in unlawful possession of them. Not a nice
sympathetic waiter. But probably he was exasperated
by the everlasting journeyings between Paris and the
frontier, and the contacts of the close kitchen, and
the pricks of discipline, and the short, shaking nights,
and the absence of home life. In love, somewhere! or
a wife, somewhere! No doubt he could smile on a girl
or spoil a child, as well as anyone. Alan tried to
think well of the waiter. The fish arrived, one fish,
one complete animal per person. Sailors had fished the
animal now on his plate out of the wild winter sea.
A flushed, perspiring cook had bent over it in the
terrible heat of the stuffy kitchen. Wonderful! The
wonder ought to kill all uncharitableness...

Happy-go-lucky kind of person, Jack! But that was
only his youthfulness. Youth did not calculate, plan,
weigh pros and cons carefully. It took chances. The
chances had favoured Jack. Wonderful thing, youth!
The lad had decided in an instant what he would do;
and he had done it, successfully. Earlier in the day
he had been in Newcastle. Newcastle, another world, a
million miles off. Then in the sky. Then in the suburbs of Paris. Then in the sky again, and over moun-
tains. And lo! he was here, in the same train as
Pearl! Marvellous!

Well, it is a long rest. Feel no more. It's the
moment you feel. Must be damned unpleasant. Can't
believe it at first. Mistake it must be: someone else.
Try the house opposite. Wait. I wanted to. I haven't
yet. Then darkened death chamber. Light they want,
whispering round you. Would you like to see a priest.
Then rambling and wandering. Delirium, all you did all
your life. The death struggle. His sleep is not
natural. Press his lower eyelid. Watching is his nose

pointed is his jaw sinking are the soles of his feet
yellow. Bam! expires.

The last quotation is from 'Ulysses'. It shows both
the origin of Alan's thought process and a like obsession
with the reality of the obvious. But Bloom is a comic
character, his mind is a second hand jumble of cheap
superstition and cheaper science, and it is meant to be.
Alan with the same flabby tolerance, the same penny in
the slot reactions to the commonplace, the same cheap
emotions, the spurious and tipsy nobility of sentiment to
which he jacks himself up by the leverage of 'The Prelude', is apparently meant to be a fine and uncorrupted
modern man. Nothing is more second-rate than the easy
tolerance bred from laziness, timidity and facile sympathy, except possibly the capacity to excrete cheap
platitudes from everyday events at the rate at which
green grass passes down a goose's gullet, and Mr. Bennett's hero, for all his occasional moments of paternity,
is far inferior to the millionaires and maîtres d'hôtel of
his minor novels. The mind of Alan Frith-Walter, seedy
as the bottom of a bird cage, is not the vehicle which can
bring home to the reader so truthful and painstaking a
study of the beauty of personal relations.
Again, the author has missed the real beauty, the lyric
wail of modern travel; only once, in the description of a
night halt in a wet station, does he really catch it, and
for all the effectiveness of his description, there is
nothing to equal the poetry of trains of Mr. Larbaud, or
Laforgue's

> O qu'ils sont pittoresques les trains manqués
> qu'ils sont à bientôt - à bientôt
> les bateaux
> du bout de la jetée.

Yet all the way through one is struck by sentences of
admirable crispness, by an accuracy of observation, and
an economy of style that are unrivalled; the book is
strewn with phrases that are intimations of the author's
immortality, but intimations and nothing more. 'Accident'
ought certainly to be read. It is a serious book, and an
entertaining one; only the author's ability to do better
makes the critic severe. Anyone fond of trains, of turning Labour, of the family, should read it, and anyone fond
of reading should find it, though poor in content, how
objective in treatment, how delightfully classical in
form!

'Imperial Palace'

9 October 1930

125. H.G. WELLS, IN A LETTER TO BENNETT

7 October 1930

Arnold you are a dear. You are the best friend I've ever
had. This may colour my vision. I don't think it does.
We are also contemporary writers and that alone ought to
keep us clear headed about each other. But this big book
of yours seems to me a really great book. I've read it
with much the same surprise and delight that I felt about
'The Old Wives' Tale'. It's amazingly complete. It's
your complete conquest of a world you've raided time after
time - not always to my satisfaction. It's an immense
picture of a social phase and there is not a character in
it that isn't freshly observed true to type and individual - so far as I can check you. Gracie I thought began
a little too splendid but that comes all right in the en-
semble. I agree with the thesis of the increasing 'secon-
dariness' of women. I've tried that myself in 'Clissold'
and 'The Secret Places of the Heart'. The women won't
like you....

Yours ever, H.G.

126. IVOR BROWN, IN THE 'MANCHESTER GUARDIAN'

9 October 1930, 7

Ivor Brown (1891-1974) was leader writer and drama critic
for the 'Manchester Guardian' from 1919 to 1935. Later he
was editor of the 'Observer'. Bennett was especially
pleased with his review.

Here is a bigger and better Babylon. To compose on the
grand scale is not a novelty for Mr. Bennett. He reverts
to grandeur of layout and is no mean follower of the bulky
fashion. He does it with ease. You may say that his
survey of changing fortunes and domestic economy in the
super-Babylonian hotel could be shortened; a floor
manageress might be dropped here, an assistant chief of
cuisine might vanish there. But you cannot say that Mr.
Bennett has abandoned his theme in pursuit of length for
length's sake, or thrown in a hamper of red herrings and
fresh hares to stock the Babylonian larder. If we go to
see Smithfield at dawn, it is not for the sake of essay-
writing. It is because Smithfield is the right scene
for a strange occurrence. Others, panting after longitude
in the contemporary fashion, may throw in their descriptive articles, running from Zoo to Limehouse in search of
picturesque padding. Mr. Bennett never loses breath or
energy. The Imperial Palace Hotel is his wash-pot, and,
if his shot is occasionally cast over Europe, that is only
because hotel-mergers make the Imperial Palace the first
link of a cosmopolitan chain.
    Mr. Bennett remains as interested as ever in human
organisation. He admits and he describes the disorganis-
ing power of human affection and human passion. The
conversation between Miss Gracie Savott and Mr. Evelyn
Orcham on the conflict between women and work is one of
the best things in the book. But sex is kept in the
second place as a factor in the story. What excites
the larger commentary is the amazing amount of arrangement
which goes into the distinctive social phenomena of our
time - department stores, luxury hotels, and so on.
Whether the immensity of this work is properly expended
is another question. Mr. Bennett permits himself an
occasional ironic reflection, but he does not dogmatise
on the ethics of society. He describes with detail and
with a sustained excitement the human skill and all the

personal loyalties, conflicts, skirmishes, and sacrifices
which are bubbling away beneath the great containing
vessel of luxury like the gas-jets beneath a majestic
geyser.   That he has the eye and sympathy for such a
scrutiny we know.   Now they are employed on a more searching examination than before.   This is no fantasia.   It is
sociology shot with romance.

The central figure is Evelyn Orcham, organiser.   He
found the Imperial Palace ordinary; he made it unique.   To
this masterly panjandrum comes Sir Henry Savott, a millionaire whose hobby is merging.   Savott wanders about
the world seeking what he may combine.   He might have
carried a label when voyaging among the owners of hotels
and film studios - 'Stop me and sell one.'   He picks on
Orcham as the obvious monarch of a League of Luxury
Hotels, and the merging of the Imperial Palace with its
less notable rivals abroad is the main part of the story.
Sir Henry's daughter Gracie also singles out Orcham as
unique.   She is the rich society girl of our time, with a
touch of the Elizabethan in her blood.   She can write as
well as race; memoirs and motor-cars mingle among her pur-
suits.   She reads the Bible and Shakespeare, selects
Orcham, and then rejects him.   She must be exclusively
adored, and he, after all, has given his heart to hotels;
she could never own it all.   For Orcham remains the enigmatic Violet Powler, a girl from Kennington with a considerable and equal power of disturbing men and organising
chambermaids.   She is prepared to marry Orcham; she will
not devour him.

But this book is not to be subtitled La Vie Amoureuse
d'Evelyn Orcham.   It is a picture of power, of which feminine power is the lesser if the more picturesque fraction.
The Imperial Palace is power.   Are not its bowels manned
by the pick of ex-navymen, working the engines that warm
and cool and wash and cook for the world's greatest?   Is
not the whole gigantic affair, half-cushion and half-
kitchen, sustained on its pinnacle of excellence by
relentless loyalties and disciplines and drudgeries?   No
patron must ever be regarded as wrong.   Hideous doctrine,
demanding human sacrifice, and yet, under Orcham's control, making the Imperial Palace no longer an inn but a
counter in high finance.   Mr. Bennett might have worked
the irony of this considerably harder; he is content to
suggest it.   But here is the panorama as he can particularly paint it.   There is none of them, from director to
page, who does not live as a unit while functioning in
the great machine of service which pours out its champagne, caviare, gala nights, and dividends.   Mr. Bennett
is the complete courier.   'This floor for engine-rooms,

printing works, audit department. Next for glass, china,
staff dining-room.' We are given the inside view of the
wage-earning as of the ambitions and desires and loves
that make the infinite complexity of the organisation.
The author has gone to great lengths, and he has left no
pantry door unopened. Yet, while the tale is long, the
style is terse; perhaps the omission of verbs for impressionistic purposes is overdone. The weight of the book
and the size of the print are to some extent deterrent.
It is the greater compliment, therefore, to Mr. Bennett to
say that six hundred and thirty pages still inclined one
to press the bells of the Imperial Palace Hotel and to
make new demands of its impeccable service.

127. SYLVIA LYND, IN THE 'NEWS CHRONICLE'

9 October 1930, 4

Sylvia Lynd (1888-1952) was a poet and novelist.

Decidedly an unheavenly world this of Mr. Bennett's; but
what an interesting one! If all the graces and most of
the virtues have failed to find a lodging in 'Imperial
Palace,' there is all the more room for comedy and knowledge and wisdom. This is simply an amazing book. An
encyclopaedia not only of hotel keeping but of human
nature, of manners and customs and character. It is one
of the best books that Mr. Bennett has written. It over-
awes by the immensity of its detail, it fascinates by the
diabolical shrewdness of its perceptions. It is full of
tolerant humour and the unceasing delight in the energies
of civilisation that is characteristic of Mr. Bennett.
     There is an elation about 'Imperial Palace' which
infects the reader. Mr. Bennett's hero - or secondary hero
we should say rather, since his real hero is the hotel
itself - has, we feel, a good deal in common with Mr. Bennett when we read:

     Could any private preoccupation, could any hidden
     fatigue, impair his activity? To ask was to answer.
     Nothing could disconcert, embarrass, hamper, frustrate
     his activity.... It was in the moments which made the

heaviest demand upon his varied faculties that he
lived most keenly.

Mr. Bennett has lived keenly while writing this book,
we feel - as a result, we read it with a zest that amounts
to excitement.
For what Mr. Bennett satisfies here is the desire for
knowledge, the inquisitiveness that is the ruling passion
of all save the dull. To arouse and satisfy curiosity at
a strike, that is the function of 'Imperial Palace.' I
was wholly unaware, till I began it, that I had any particular wish to know how the organisation of a big hotel
is carried on. Certainly I had no desire to visit Smithfield Market in the small hours or a model laundry at
Kennington in the afternoon. But before I had read two
paragraphs I was all agog to see them, setting off as
obediently in Mr. Bennett's company as if I were being
taken to a First Night or a Rugby International.
With him board meetings contain no boredom and base-
ments cease to be base. I felt the delay over the return
of those three frilled shirts as the directors of the
'Imperial Palace' felt it, their guest departing without
his promised shirts, 'disillusioned, wounded.' I rejoiced
in the nice revelation of human frailty that is to be
found in the passage which describes Violet Powler, pro-
moted from the laundry at Kennington to the position of
one of the housekeepers at the Imperial Palace, as

humorously surprised to discover herself highly critical of the laundry work. She admitted defects which,
if they had been brought to her notice by the laundry
staff, she would never have admitted in the laundry.

Mr. Bennett's actual story - the loves of Evelyn
Orcham, first for Gracie, a not impossible though highly
improbable she, the daughter of a millionaire, and next
for Violet Powler, whose 'tranquil benevolence and commonsense' compelled him 'to enlarge the definition of feminine beauty in order to make room for her in it,' though
admirably full of surprises, are less interesting than
this creation of a world in which a hotel director is king
and in which meat and wine, chefs and boilers, chambermaids and psychological jugglery are balanced in a sort of
solar system.
Mr. Bennett's hotel is not, perhaps, as big as the universe, but it seems very nearly as elaborate. He has
given us a gloriously copious, rich and humorous book in
which the most timid can be on familiar terms with head
waiters and reception clerks, can own private suites and

order Krug 1919, and treat civilisation as a vast doll's-
house in which work is fun and all the sinister trickery
of commerce child's play.

128. FRANK SWINNERTON, IN THE 'EVENING NEWS'

10 October 1930, 8

Frank Swinnerton (1884-), prolific novelist, essayist,
and critic, was Bennett's best friend. They met in 1911.
In his recent book on Bennett, 'Arnold Bennett, A Last
Word', 1978, Mr Swinnerton says that he and Bennett
agreed not to review each other's books, and that he
acquiesced reluctantly to his editor's desire that he
review 'Imperial Palace'. Bennett, says Mr Swinnerton,
'was not altogether satisfied with what I said'.
Swinnerton's obituary of Bennett is reprinted below,
No. 135.

Just over thirty years ago it was a part of my job as an
office boy to trudge round London delivering to various
addresses free copies of a not very successful religious
weekly. An office boy is a window gazer. Thus it happens
that I can claim in some sense to have been 'in' at the
beginning of Mr. Arnold Bennett's career as a popular
novelist, for one day I saw, in the window of 'The Golden
Penny' (a journal of that time) the announcement that this
week's issue contained the opening chapters of a great new
serial entitled 'The Grand Babylon Hotel.'
    'The Grand Babylon Hotel' was not Mr. Bennett's first
novel, but it was the first to take the eye of the public.
It was a success. And, although it had been written as a
sensational serial story, it was a work very characteristic of its author.
    Mr. Bennett has always been a lover of the grand; he
has an inexhaustible interest in our modern Babylon; and
the luxury hotel has always been his plaything. It is not
at all surprising that he should have written, thirty
years or so later, an entire novel about another Babylon
hotel, about millionaires, about beautiful women, and
about members of the hotel staff. 'Imperial Palace' is
such a book.

Hotels have appealed in the past more to dramatists than
to novelists as scenes for the action of their characters.
The reason is clear. One can bring together in an hotel
the most unlikely neighbours; one can concentrate the
activities of all these people, with unending complication;
one can allow oneself every improbability.

To the dramatist, therefore, and especially to the
writer of comedy or farce, an hotel provides a practicable
scene of the first order. It has been otherwise with the
novelist, who is very free to move hither and thither,
carrying all his characters with him, and who need only
group them in the same spot when he chooses to do so.

For this reason it becomes a coincidence that while Mr.
Bennett writes 'Imperial Palace,' Madame Vicki Baum, in
the same period of time, hands us, in 'Grand Hotel,'
another book, the principal scenes of which are laid in
what might well have been one of the subsidiary hotels of
the Orcham group described in 'Imperial Palace.'

But the two books are not comparable. Madame Baum uses
her hotel merely as a scene. She tells in the slickest
possible manner the tale of a decayed dancer, a dying man
who is seeing life in his last weeks, an adventurer, a
business man, and a living suicide, all of whom are at the
Grand Hotel in Berlin for a few hectic days.

Her book glances at the hotel staff, but in effect the
hotel is no more than a device. As a device it is extraordinarily well handled. The book has pace, vividness,
and a kind of flickering illusion that keeps the reader
alert and entertained from the beginning to the end. It
will be deservedly successful.

In Mr. Bennett's book the hotel is more than the scene
in which odd people encounter one another. It is, so to
speak, at this point that 'Imperial Palace' parts company
with 'The Grand Babylon Hotel.' In Mr. Bennett's old book,
it will be remembered, a millionaire bought the hotel because Jules, the celebrated head-waiter, refused to serve
him with filleted steak for two and a bottle of beer.
That was the beginning of trouble for the millionaire.

But in 'Imperial Palace' the hotel itself is by way of
being the chief character in the book. It is not so in
the end, because Mr. Bennett provides a human romance; but
for the first several hundred pages it dominates everything - a fascinating world in little.

We are shown its brilliance by night and day; we descend
to its kitchens and its engine department; we enter its
suites, meet its managers, chambermaids, housekeepers, and
the shareholders in the company; we visit its laundry, are
told of its profits, its breakages, of staff loyalty and

staff jealousies; we discover many of those intricate
problems of policy and supply of which, but for this book,
we should never have dreamed.

In fact, ingeniously instructed as the story proceeds,
we learn as much as we are ever likely to know of the life,
public and secret, of a great luxury hotel set up in the
heart of London.

I have said that all these details are ingeniously woven
into the story. Up to a point they are the story; and
those to whom detail is abhorrent must forgo any hope of
enjoying 'Imperial Palace.' The book makes its effect by
means of close and significant detail. It is as detailed
as Mr. Bennett's 'Clayhanger.'

It is slow moving; the descriptions, spiced with those
exclamatory adjectives which Mr. Bennett uses as effectively as did Alexandre Dumas, are long and unhurried;
there are more than six hundred closely printed pages of
larger size than those of an ordinary novel.

To me this detail is almost unceasingly interesting.
I noticed, in reading, only one or two pages where my
curiosity faded. As long as the book is concerned with
the Imperial Palace, and with the employees of the Imperial
Palace, it has the quality of Mr. Bennett's work at its
best, or very nearly at its best.

The hero is Evelyn Orcham, an organiser of great talent,
who has manoeuvred the Imperial Palace into first place
among the luxury hotels of the world. For Evelyn, the
management of such an hotel is not a duty; it is a romance.
He is devoted to his job. It is his life.

Quite early in the book (he is a widower) he makes up
his mind that a wife is a liability, and not an asset; and
he resolves that he will never marry again. A wife would
come between him and the hotel. Therefore there must be no
wife. Such is his passion.

But no sooner has he made his resolve than Gracie,
daughter of the rich baronet who schemes a gigantic hotel
merger (to include the Imperial Palace), arrives. Gracie
is one of these impulsive, bad-mannered young women who
lead men by their noses, change their minds with their
clothes, are wonderfully fascinating, and so are distur-
bers of all hotel managers and all good resolutions.

Gracie, to my mind, nearly ruins 'Imperial Palace.' She
never says an interesting thing, and Evelyn's ecstatic
comments upon her charm and her intellect leave me cold.
Also, the episode in which, by painfully crude means, she
seduces him, is related at disproportionate length. It is

an episode only; it has no consequences for Evelyn (other
than passing anger) or the Imperial Palace; and, unless I
am wrong, it is inferior in quality to the rest of the
book. More positively, it reduces our respect for Evelyn,
who is not in love with Gracie, but is helpless and fatu-
ous before her attack.

If Gracie is a liability to the book, Violet is a distinct asset. Violet, in fact, is superb. The chapter in
which she and Evelyn talk 'unofficially' (it is called
Powder and Rouge) is the work of a master. It is packed
with character, with insight, with humour.

For Violet, once staff-manageress at the laundry, is
introduced into the hotel itself as floor-housekeeper.
She becomes head housekeeper. She is, to 'Imperial
Palace,' what the heroine of 'Buried Alive' is to that
book. She is calm; she is confident and competent; but
she is a woman.

She is one of the successes of this book, and she contributes to its ultimate success. For when Gracie is
gone, and when the book, having lost momentum, having lost
its own particular magic, is still, as it were, reeling,
it is Violet who gradually brings it round.

That it is brought round there is no doubt at all. It
ends triumphantly, and one reads the final chapters with
emotion and delight. As we look back through the pages,
after so long a journey, we are conscious of the extent to
which illusion has been imposed, so that for the time the
fortunes of these characters have seemed more important to
us than our own affairs.

The hotel and its staff have been all about us. We
have lived in and with them, seeing through their eyes,
feeling with their hearts. And, owing to Mr. Bennett's
own special convention, which enables him to show, with
humour, the outward (and perhaps terrifying) aspect of a
person, and at the same time to show, with even greater
humour, the less obvious and much less self-assured inner
feelings and perceptions of the same person, all these
characters are three-dimensional. They live. They
breathe. They suffer. We accept them as welcome additions to our authentic acquaintance.

If it be now asked whether 'Imperial Palace' is a great
book, I shall reply with deliberate evasiveness that it
has many of the qualities which in the past have been
regarded as giving greatness to a book. It has that large
humanity which for me is an essential of any great novel.
It has extraordinary verisimilitude. It has a sincerity,
an integrity, such as will always entitle Mr. Bennett's
best work to our admiration. And it is interesting with

the interestingness that arises from sincerity, humanity
and verisimilitude.

But whether it is a great book I cannot say.   I think it
is not, because I cannot now see it as an organic whole,
because the episode which might have been passionate is
meagre and tiresome, and because big business (even the
merging of luxury hotels) seems to me as a theme to be
grandiose, but neither beautiful nor romantic.
    'Imperial Palace' is a long and impressive work.   It
has many passages of both beauty and romance.   It held me
engrossed, hour after hour, as I read its crowded pages.
Why bother about greatness?   For to-day it is enough that
the book is quite obviously from the hand that wrote 'The
Old Wives' Tale' and 'Clayhanger.'   It is also quite
obviously from the hand that wrote 'The Card' and 'Buried
Alive.'   And I feel sure that the author of 'The Grand
Babylon Hotel' had some share in planning the spectacle.
Why not?

129.   DESMOND MacCARTHY, MARRY YOUR HOUSE-KEEPER,
'SUNDAY TIMES'

12 October 1930, 6

If sub-titles were still the fashion, the heading at the
top of this column would, I think, be suitable for this
story.   Marry Your Housekeeper, or, There's No Place for
Passion, strikes me as the upshot of Mr. Bennett's gigantic novel, and as the conclusion to which he comes - perhaps with a certain reluctance.   It is a flat conclusion,
but, of course, Mr. Bennett knows that.   Has he not often
shown us before that it is the prosaic which is really
romantic?   Is it not his 'message,' so to speak, to the
age that there is nothing more fascinating than efficiency?
True, he has shown us other things, which, for my part, I
think more important, but he has urged nothing upon us more
often or emphatically than that.
    The deepest fault I have to find with this novel is
that, though he has placed his hero between the Practical
and Profane Love (like Garrick in Reynolds's picture be-
twixt the Muses of Comedy and Tragedy), nevertheless his
hero's choice of the Practical in this case does not make
its due effect.   At the end of the book Violet Powler,

first a sub-supervisor in the Imperial Palace Hotel
laundry, then a matron of its eighth floor, and lastly
the Matron of all its matrons, proves to be the final
choice of Evelyn Orcham, its director; while he, before
we reach the 630th page, is also directing (how Mr. Bennett adores hugeness!) nine other of the great hotels of
Europe. But Orcham's feeling for her is not, as critics
say, 'done.' In the decisive scenes the relation between
them fails to glow; I should describe that relation rather
as a gradual and damp adhesion. But please, when I say
that, do not think that I suppose the *coup de foudre* to be
the only symptom of love or the one most worth describing.
Perhaps the most thrilling love-stories of all describe
love slowly dawning, and the steps by which lovers discover each other - 'Villette,' for example. But here it
is a case of a crescendo of esteem rather than of love.

Of course, Mr. Bennett knows how to set about what he
wants to do. Powler is first presented to us as nice and
plain, and as her employer becomes more aware of her marvellous reliability her inconspicuous charms expand.
Powler is a spot on which the eye of the great panjandrum
of the Imperial Palace rests with increasing satisfaction;
she is all right. Powler, in the words of Heine's song,
may be said to be, for him, *Die Ruh*; but, alas! the
accompaniment of Schubert's music is never even faintly
heard. And unless it is the case that the hearts of born
organisers are merely thermometers for registering a
mounting appreciation of efficiency (which I doubt), it
must be said that Mr. Bennett has failed to make her transformation in her lover's thoughts from 'Powler' into
'Violet' convincing.

And this is not a defect which affects part of the book;
it destroys the balance of the whole. For the contrasting
episode of Profane Love, the Orcham-Gracie relation, is so
excellently done that it eclipses the Orcham-Violet relation, which was nevertheless meant to eclipse *it*. I hazard
this assertion because clearly Mr. Bennett never meant to
leave us with the impression that Orcham was a butter-
fingers who lets what matters in life slip through his
fingers. Orcham's creator upholds his choice; it ought,
therefore, to have been more impressive. On the other
hand, I do not think Mr. Bennett has ever 'done' anything
more vivid than Gracie herself, Gracie's behaviour to
Evelyn Orcham, and Evelyn's behaviour to her. I have
traced this pair twice through the whole novel, the second
time with increased admiration. Pages 371 to 496 are very
good, and Gracie's farewell letter and his reply round
them well. It is extraordinary what subtle completeness
of presentation has been achieved by sheer honesty of

narration. The striking thing about Arnold Bennett is
that plain integrity of mind. His respect and affection
for Orcham is of the kind that would compel any other
author to have made him cut a finer figure as a lover, or
turned Gracie a vamp.

But I can imagine Mr. Bennett, should these lines catch
his eye, saying 'What nonsense you talk! Destroyed the
balance! I didn't mean to write a love story or a double
love story. My subject was a great hotel. A superb
and marvellous triumph of organisation! It was a subject
worth treating, because one of the distinctive notes of
modern civilisation is, as I make one of the characters
say, the prodigious development of "the luxury hotel."
What I tried to do was to show what faculties are required
to run one. To do this properly I had to go into the
details of every department that contributes to the
astounding result. You are evidently a little inclined
to jeer at the length of my book, but my object could
only be attained by piling up detail. I had to show my
organiser *at work*. On the human side, what I wanted to
exhibit was the life of a man in relation to an unusually
complicated job, and one, too, to which he is profoundly
and rightly attached. Of course, since such a person must
be a man, and not an automaton, I had also to show his
emotional life. The most serious rival of a man's work
is normally his relations with women. I had, therefore,
to go into those in his case, but they were not my theme.'
(For the moment, in imagination, I stand rebuked.) It *is*
true that Mr. Bennett, in writing 'Imperial Palace,' has
aimed at what Zola aimed in such books as 'Au Bonheur des
Dames' or 'Germinal.' It is also true that his main subject is 'a luxury-hotel,' but before I try to judge the
book from that point of view and defend myself I must make
a confession.

It is sometimes a critic's duty to talk about himself,
though by no means as often as might be inferred from
reading some critics. It is so when he is far from thinking a subject as attractive as it is to the author he is
criticising. For instance, if he is reviewing a book,
say, about a seminary, and is personally affected by a
priest, as many people are said to be affected by the presence of a cat, he should reveal that fact early. Now
there is much in Mr. Bennett's past works, let alone this
last one, which almost excuses us for believing that the
modern 'luxury-hotel' is his spiritual home, so often and
so fervently has he dwelt upon its amazing costliness and
convenience, and so invariably is he impressed by everything in modern life it summarises and represents. Yet
there are people who prefer lodgings. I am one of them.

To me the 'luxury-hotel' is awful. Nor is this the sour
estimate of one of the bitter excluded poor; I have
entered them frequently - at the expense of others. But
it is only the company of friends that makes these places
endurable to me. When undistracted by talk, or when un-
concentrated upon a plate (thank goodness, the food is
almost always excellent!), my genial spirits droop.
Misanthropy descends upon me as I watch the crowd munching
to music.

From those lounges of gilt and mirrors, from those
drawing rooms and writing-rooms done up in 'styles,' there
is no escape for the imagination, except in the direction
of banking accounts and thrusting snobbery; there is not
an object on which the eye can rest which does not proclaim Pretentiousness as the key to the art of living,
and all the more insistently when the object itself happens to be also 'refined.' 'Imperial Palace' could,
therefore, have hardly found a less sympathetic reader.
You wonder perhaps how in that case I can even tolerate
Mr. Bennett, let alone admire him as I do. Well, I said
the presence of a friend makes even a 'luxury-hotel'
tolerable to me, and Mr. Bennett's humanity and integrity
are like companions to me. Of course, I grin as I read
over the ease with which he is impressed, not only by
luxury, but by what he thinks astounding instances of
'poise' in people which are nothing of the kind; but I
forgive him for being taken in for the sake of his superb
plain humanity. I may have to wait and wade through a
lot before it comes, but soomer or later a wave of it
always breaks over me.

The fact is, much of what Mr. Bennett has done in this
novel is more suitably accomplished in those advertisement
pamphlets which describe the latest liner or hotel, and
are profusely illustrated with photographs of the dining,
writing, and lounging rooms, of the bar, the hair-
dresser's, the gymnasium, the kitchen, the Royal suite,
the average bedroom, etc., etc.; pamphlets which also give
you the company's figures and statistics of its cutlery,
linen, furniture, and expenditure in every department.
What was wanted for an artist's purpose was not an inventory of parts, but, what Mr. Bennett can do well, a
general impression, a feeling of a whole. Then he could
show (and now we are getting to something more interesting) the relation of the man who runs this whole to his
own creation. Here is another technical problem for the
novelist. Unfortunately, the qualities which make a good
organiser and manager, though they have to be exercised
in constantly varying directions, are simple and monotonous. If he shows him exercising them in handling every

type of employee, high and low, it becomes boring. Mr.
Bennett has illustrated the same qualities in Orcham many
more times than was necessary for his purpose as a novelist. He does each one well, but he is so swept on by his
own surface efficiency as a writer that he cannot, apparently, help doing it again and again and again.

If only he were lazy, what a much better artist he
would be! He would then sometimes 'be still,' and so
discover what, as an artist, he is aware of, but, all too
dimly, where the deepest possibilities of his themes lie.
In this case the deepest centre is the relation between
Orcham's working life and his emotional life; to this the
whole hotel is a mere circumference - or it ought to be.
Mr. Bennett, though those who read him superficially may
not perceive it, is well aware that there are worlds with
a different set of values from those of the practical
world he delights to glorify, and to which he pins his
faith. Of the religious world he knows nothing, of the
artist's world, oddly enough, very little; but he does
understand the world of passion. It is present in this
book in the shape of Gracie. Orcham is pulled into it,
but passion makes nonsense of the world in which he lives
and moves and has his being. Arnold Bennett is extraordinarily fair to Gracie; she is not a vamp. She represents an ideal which requires perhaps more courage and
sincerity to live by than his work exacts, but it implies
a totally different sense of proportion.

The tragi-comic bewilderment of the sensible man in
love asking himself at every violent turn of a scarify-
ingly intimate relation, 'Is this woman a liability or an
asset?' with varying answers according to her willingness
to adapt herself to him, could not have been better done.
Gracie who is far more quick than he is, soon discovers
he *cannot* live in a love-world and breaks with him; and
Orcham, after a pang of humiliation - for he knows there
is something splendid in what he has missed - goes back
to his proper place. Is, then, a concentration on the
practical incompatible with a life of emotion? No, says
Mr. Bennett, and gives him Violet Powler.

You see, then, how it might injure a novel which was a
deep investigation into life and more than a description
of hotel-management, if that part were inadequately done.
If Mr. Bennett disclaims having aimed at more than
description, his critic must reply, 'Then you have not
used your finest gifts in this book.'

130. HAROLD NICOLSON, IN THE 'DAILY EXPRESS'

16 October 1930, 6

Harold Nicolson (1886-1968), diplomatist, author, and
critic, served briefly at this time on the staff of the
'Daily Express'. He reviewed Arthur Balfour's autobiography before turning to Bennett.

...Then there is Mr. Arnold Bennett and his fat novel.
I can say what I like about Mr. Bennett, as he is beyond
criticism. I admire his work so much that I do not care
if I hurt his feelings.
  For his last novel, I fear, is not a success.
  I should wish, had I the space, to probe the curious
problem why Mr. Bennett has a passion for hotels. They
release some inhibition in him which I should like, out
of human curiosity, to define.
  Mr. Bennett is sensitive to luxury, book-keeping, and
power. Somewhere in Mr. Bennett there must lurk a love
of lavish administration, a love of organised extravagance, the pleasure-pain of profitable wastage. He is
deeply stirred by the picture of Lucullus with an account
book, of Petronius with a steel safe, or Trimalchio even
in galoshes. In this book his 'pang has found a voice.'
  I felt when I had finished it as if I had been conducted over the Royal Mint to the accompaniment of champagne and Rimsky Korsakoff. I felt as if, on pile carpets, I had explored the intricacies of a biscuit factory.
I felt that I knew all about hotels, and floor order-
slips, and the 'dry teas' of the housekeepers.
  But I am bothered if I know why Mr. Bennett should have
cast his Blue Book in the shape of a romance.
  For 'Imperial Palace' reminds me of a super wireless
set disguised as a bergère sofa. The technical side is
so detailed and so informative that the romantic side
strikes one as elaborately useless.
  I am prepared to admit that Evelyn Orcham was a
Napoleon; but I am not prepared to admit that such compelling personalities select as their mistresses the
Amazons of Brooklands. They respond to the feminine, not
to the male. Mr. Orcham, I admit, reverts in the end to
type, but it takes him a good 500 pages to do so.
  Nor can I accept Sir Henry Savott as a successful portrait of a plutocrat. It may be that I was disconcerted

by my inability to share Mr. Bennett's enthusiasm about
an hotel. But it may also be that the psychological
ineptitudes (I repeat the expression defiantly - '*psychological ineptitudes*') of this book really are beyond
endurance.

I hoped against hope that Mr. Bennett's theme would be
the tiresome manner in which women interfere with work.
Almost, but not quite, that *was* his theme. And no one
could do it better than Mr. Bennett.

131. V.S. PRITCHETT, IN THE 'SPECTATOR'

18 October 1930, 553-4

V.S. Pritchett (1900-), distinguished author and critic,
wrote a perceptive, brief review of Bennett in his 'The
Living Novel', 1947.

Like the child in the legend of St. Nicholas, Mr. Bennett
has dreamed he was in paradise, though all the time he was
in pickle. By paradise Mr. Bennett understands, of
course, the super, de luxe, grand Babylon hotel, all-
British, all-talking, all-everything. And by pickle I
mean that period of documentation which Mr. Bennett passes
through before serving himself up. Documentation he has
very rightly been dinning into us for years until, it
seems to me, in this book, he has made the capacity for
information more important than the capacity for experience. In 'Imperial Palace' documentation attains its
apotheosis. It is strange, however, that Mr. Bennett, who
has been dinning Balzac into us as well, should not have
paid attention to the warning in 'Le Chef D'Oeuvre
Inconnu', about the painter who painted and painted and
painted until there was nothing on the canvas. Documentation, pickling oneself in facts, has its similar snares.

The Imperial Palace is the kind of hotel whose directors are gods, whose managers are archangels, whose myriad
head-waiters and staff are the choir of cherubim and sera-
phim. Such an hotel, like the department store, is an
agglomeration peculiarly symptomatic of our time, and Mr.
Bennett believes in it, likes it, worships it, and knows
more about it than anyone else. He can tell you exactly

what goes on, from what happens when you order a soufflé,
to the reactions of the hotel laundry when you complain
about your frilled evening shirts. In these things Mr.
Bennett is sublimely knowing. The central figure of the
book is not Evelyn Orcham, the super business man who
directs the hotel, who is its creator, and whom romantic
and illicit love fails finally to seduce from his creation; but the Imperial Palace, the hotel itself. This is
a curious reversal of *rôles*. The overwhelming tendency is
for every character and episode to illustrate some phase
of hotel organization, and not for this to illuminate some
phase in the development of character. And you have
to be mightily interested in *de luxe* hotels rather than in
people to go so far with Mr. Bennett. Yet Evelyn Orcham's
affair *outside* the hotel with Gracie Savott, the daughter
of one of his directors, is nothing like as good and convincing - though, being out of the hotel, it is much more
refreshing - as his affair with the sober, dutiful Violet
Powler, who is creeping up the ranks of the business.
Mr. Bennett has always made a point of deifying the banal
and ordinary, and Violet Powler is his triumphant justification. This is the dull woman made beautiful, passionate, perfect, a character made to grow and deepen before
our eyes, with masterly skill. The guests of the hotel
de luxe have frequently been drawn by Mr. Bennett; now he
has 'done' the staff, and, indeed, at the Imperial Palace
one has perhaps perversely the impression that there are
hardly any guests. There is a great deal that is absolutely first class in this book, but one needs to be a
very old patron of the management not to find pages and
pages of it terribly dull.

132. J.E.S. ARROWSMITH, IN THE 'LONDON MERCURY'

November 1930, 82-3

J.E.S. Arrowsmith is not otherwise known.

'Imperial Palace: or the hotel keeper's complete guide...'.
This sub-title was not appended by Mr. Arnold Bennett, but
it should have been; and the most important word in it
would have been the word 'complete.' For not only is this

astonishing novel a perfect guide to the working of a
modern 'luxury hotel' (Mr. Bennett's phrase), it is also
a most useful guide for the proprietor to the conduct of
his personal life, and his feelings in general. Nothing
is left out that the proprietor could possibly come up
against - from the squabbles of his 'floor-housekeepers'
to a threatened miscarriage to one of his guests. Evelyn
Orcham, the owner of the Imperial Palace, deals with them
all. He is, in the words of an old song, 'here, there,
everywhere, all over the spot'; he knows everything that
is going on from the moment it is, however remotely, in
the air. He 'savours' everything: it is all a keenly
'sensed' romance to him. He is as instantly 'intrigued'
by every movement of the corporate body over which he
rules, as he is by every delicate susceptibility of the
personal body which he himself inhabits.... But isn't it
all, really, happening in Mr. Bennett's head? Could an
ordinary, active man ever stand the racket of living in
such a state of high-tuned sensibility? Indulging his
rich imagination, in the quietude of his own study, Mr.
Bennett can allow himself to taste the flavour of each
incident of a day in the fullest, or most hum-drum of
lives, but can he, fairly, endow his puppets with the
necessary detachment to live each moment, in the flesh, at
the high-pressure that these moments can be thought of in
the mind? In short can one vibrate to every small aspect
of an event while one is actually living through it? This
is what Evelyn Orcham does. While living the most occupied of lives, he yet lives faster still in his brain, and
still remains about as well-preserved and set-up a man as
could be found. And as for Gracie - ! She should be a
broken wreck in about five years at the pace she goes on!

Gracie Savott is the daughter of the millionaire financier who is scheming to bring off a great 'deal' by
negotiating a merger between the Imperial Palace hotel and
various other hotels on the continent in which he is
interested. Mr. Bennett has here arranged for himself
one of the most riotous of his 'happy hunting grounds.' He
can spend and spend and spend, vicariously! Here money is
water to be spilt about regardless. And in doing this Mr.
Bennett is a master. The luxury of his 'luxury hotels,'
and the luxurious life of this young lady give him all the
rope even he can want. And after this he has still this
amazing young woman's feelings in which he luxuriates with
an intenser freedom still. Gracie is, indeed, one of Mr.
Bennett's major creations. She is at one and the same
time incredible and fascinating. She could be: but never
for one moment can one believe that she has been. She may
be: for Nature is said to copy Art; but it will be a

curious adventure (as it was for Evelyn) for the people
who meet her. Evelyn is, frankly, beaten by her. Her
utter disregard of rules, her seriousness, her caprice,
her daring, her flashing understanding, intoxicate and
undo him. But she sees through the effect of her own
devices. She sees that she has only succeeded in seducing
him, and not in creating love for her - as she wants to be
loved - in him. So she pitilessly throws him over. He
relapses, not seriously hurt, into the arms of the steady
Violet - one of his housekeepers.

On the detailed working of the hotel the guide-book is
unexceptionable. From the engines - underground -
through the kitchens, the dining rooms, to the suites of
apartments up to the eighth floor, we are taken in turns;
not to mention those necessary adjuncts to an hotel - the
Laundry and Smithfield. And each visit is a little picture in itself. Of the characters required to fill in
the numerous and varied scenes allotted to them it can be
said that each is compacted from reality, is firmly and
truly drawn satisfying and interesting in itself. Mr.
Bennett is equally at home in imagining them as he is in
a luxury hotel. Altogether it is a fascinating book; a
little overloaded by a wealth of descriptions; but why
quarrel with descriptions so entertaining? The writing is
in Mr. Bennett's best form. Forceful, nervous, high-
tensioned stuff; not beautiful and shapely (sentences
without verbs have long been Mr. Bennett's special prero-
gative) but always so infused with vitality that never a
paragraph flags. This is the biggest thing that Mr. Bennett has done since 'Riceyman Steps.'

General Views: 1931

With Bennett's death on 27 March there was a general out-
pouring of comment. His death itself occasioned front-
page stories in London papers, and in Stoke-on-Trent it
was a banner headline, 'ARNOLD BENNETT - NOVELIST OF THE
FIVE TOWNS' - rather in contrast to the slight attention
given there to his novels during the preceding decade.
Two days later in Stoke-on-Trent he still had one half of
the headline news: 'Battleship in Collision'/'Mr. Arnold
Bennett'. Aside from the appreciations reprinted below,
there were notable appreciations and reviews by James
Douglas in the 'Daily Express' (28 March) and the 'Sunday
Express' (29 March), Edward Shanks and Viscount Castle-
rosse in the 'Evening Standard' (28 March), Lord Beaver-
brook in the 'Sunday Express' (29 March), Ivor Brown in
the 'Week-end Review' (4 April), Richard Jennings in the
'Spectator' (4 April), Robert Ellis Roberts and another
in the 'New Statesman' (4 April) and Roberts again in the
'Nineteenth Century and After' (May), John Squire in the
'Observer' (5 April), the 'New Republic' (8 April),
Dorothy van Doren in the 'Nation' (New York, 15 April),
M. Lanoire in the 'Revue de Paris' (1 May), Francis
Hackett in the 'Saturday Review of Literature' (2 May),
M. St Claire Byrne in the 'National Review' (May),
Geoffrey West in the 'Adelphi' (May), André Gide in 'La
Nouvelle Revue Française' (May); and Stephen Gwynn in the
Fortnightly' (May).

133. 'MANCHESTER GUARDIAN', WITH A PORTRAIT ABOVE

28 March 1931, 14

Enoch Arnold Bennett (whose death is announced on another
page) was born on May 27, 1867, at Hanley, where his
father practised as a solicitor. He was educated at
Newcastle-under-Lyme and entered his father's office, but
subsequently worked in a London solicitor's office. In
1891 he won a twenty-guinea prize given by 'Tit-Bits,'
and in 1893 he became assistant editor of 'Woman.' In
1896 he became editor, but he resigned the post in 1900
in order to devote himself to literature. His first book,
'A Man from the North,' was published in 1898, when he
was over thirty. From 1900 onwards, he spent much of his
time in France, and it is remarkable that a good deal of
his earlier work was written there. He knew his Paris
well, and if he knew the Five Towns better his books on
them are not merely in terms of the Five Towns.

'The Grand Babylon Hotel' and 'Anna of the Five Towns'
were both published in 1902, and they may be taken as some
indication of two lines of development. 'Whom God Hath
Joined' (1906) shows Bennett seriously at work. And then
in 1908 he published 'The Old Wives' Tale.'

There may be a difference of opinion sometimes as to
the immediate cause of a famous writer's reputation; there
can be no doubt that Arnold Bennett made the conspicuous
advance with the publication of 'The Old Wives' Tale,' a
story of an extraordinarily fine design. He had done
admirable work, he had made a name as a novelist, and even
as the historian or expositor of an industrial area, but
this story of Sophia and Constance, daughters of a Bursley
tradesman, raised him to the class of those who count in
English fiction. It was so free from flamboyancy, from
the traditions of romance, that many were reluctant to
admit Bennett as one of the elect. Yet the truth of his
picture, its comprehensiveness, the serenity and simplicity of his approach to phases of life which he knew so
well, have converted all but the eccentric or supercilious. He belongs to the great line of our novelists, and
he has revealed a deeply interesting phase of English
life. Such observation as his has its creative element.
It has been said that 'the map of Europe may be rolled up,
but we cannot believe in the destruction of Duck Bank.'

Bennett is one of the few who could write adequately on
more than one plane, and his 'Clayhanger' (1910) was
clearly in his great manner. With a fine confidence he

announced this as the first volume of a trilogy; the second part of this, admirable as it was, disappointed the expectations of some who had acclaimed the earlier one. And then there was a considerable and unexplained delay. Bennett has often been accused of writing himself out, and several times his admirers have awaited the next masterpiece with some anxiety. Various books intervened, but at last the third part of the Clayhanger group appeared, and with brilliant success. It suffered, perhaps, from the reproach of some critics who found in it a departure from the manner of its two predecessors. It is, perhaps, more of a modern novel than these; the long duel between husband and wife is not pushed to a tragical extreme, but they are modern lovers, and the pride and affection which keeps them safe has yet its element of the precarious. It is a strong and subtle study, and Bennett has done nothing finer than the secret struggle between them. Their deep, persistent opposition - she is not of the Five Towns - never leads to complete estrangement, but Edwin can say to himself 'She is the bitterest enemy I have' and, again, 'This woman will kill me, but without her I shouldn't be interested enough to live.' And it is for her to say 'I submit and yet I shall never submit.' Bennett's books have never lacked vitality, but in 'These Twain' there is a strangeness of intimate life that he had hardly achieved before.

Between 'These Twain' and 'Riceyman Steps,' which will be generally accepted as one of the masterpieces, there was a considerable output of secondary work. Bennett has never permitted himself to be overwhelmed by the sense of his own capacities, and he has always been ready to let absolute best yield to the best for the occasion. Again we were assured that his days of first-rate work were over, and again he emerged triumphantly from the obscurities. 'Riceyman Steps' is first rate; perhaps a sympathetic exploration would find among his earlier books material of a quality that should not be ranked lower, but here we have the complete and almost impeccable work of art. At his best Bennett is fine in episode (he is said to object to episode in the novel despite his own successful use of it) and in character, satisfying in design. If in his ventures beyond the Five Towns we are not always perfectly sure of him, he does constantly return to humanity - unless, indeed, the point is an extravagant excursion beyond it.

For Bennett's accomplishment is remarkable for the multiplicity of what may be called his side-lines. His plays can hardly be ranked among these, for he was a considerable dramatist, though they are far inferior to his

novels. It has been suggested, indeed, that his competence, his 'sense of the theatre,' did not give his originality full play there. Perhaps the best of his plays
is 'The Great Adventure,' a version of his highly diverting story 'Buried Alive.' It is a real comedy and gave
excellent acting opportunities. 'What the Public Wants'
is a capital satirical comedy, and 'Milestones,' written
in collaboration with Mr. Edward Knoblock, had a great and
deserved popular success. A revival of interest in Bennett's plays generally should be due, and our repertory
theatres might lead the way.

Bennett has written some score of novels, innumerable
short stories, a dozen or so of what have been called
'pocket philosophies,' and another dozen or thereabouts of
miscellaneous volumes. He has commonly reprinted his critical articles, and he has been one of the most voluminous
of reviewers. From the old days when he contributed a
weekly article to the 'New Age' he has given shrewd and
frank opinions upon hundreds of new books; he is the sort
of man who would naturally keep up with things. Perhaps
he would hardly be ranked as a great critic, but he has
always been one - to a superlative degree- who knows what
he is talking about. He is not one to suffer fools
gladly, but in various books he has offered valuable
guidance to ignorance and innocence. Indeed, it would
appear that he never touched anything without becoming
an authority upon it.

Recent publications have revealed Bennett as an expert
on hotel management, and, if we are not mistaken, his
activities have included a directorship of the Savoy
Hotel (as well as of the 'New Statesman'). It is understood that he knew how to order a dinner, and from the
days of 'The Grand Babylon Hotel' onwards the hotel has
always held interest and significance for him. That
famous story - and perhaps with it might be classed two
extravaganzas in which, long ago, he collaborated with Mr.
Eden Phillpotts - is typical of one of those talents which
might be conceived as a setting to his genius. 'The Card'
and 'The Regent' are on another plane; they must be differentiated from his more fantastical excursions, though
they will not rank with his best.

Arnold Bennett has gone about the world noticing
things, and he has been respectful to what he saw, but not
over-awed by it. He has sympathised but not sentimentalised: he has an imagination which has worked, not among
elves and dragons, but in the domestic circle. He found
the world a mass of detail and did something to reduce it
to order. He always knew what he was doing. He could
write down, or at least he could write differently, but

there was no mental abasement, and he could always take
his place again. He was a patient man doing his best to
sort out the truth and to make a great design of it. He
liked to do things well, and he wrote a beautiful hand.
He used to earn about threepence an hour by writing, and
presently he was paid two shillings a word. He was
successful and deserved success. He was an adventurer
and a conqueror. You can hardly be lyrical about Arnold
Bennett, but you may regard him with deep admiration. You
may feel with him sometimes that kindness is an asset for
a novelist. He does not display a passion for humanity,
but, in forms that will endure, he shows his understanding, sympathy, and faith.

134. ARNOLD BENNETT, MASTER OF HIS CRAFT, 'STAFFORDSHIRE SENTINEL'

28 March 1931, 3

By the untimely passing of Mr. Arnold Bennett, Staffordshire has lost one of the greatest of her sons; for, in
a very different sphere, he may well rank in lasting fame
and achievement with the great Josiah Wedgwood himself.

He was not only a national literary figure, for he was
read in many countries. In the United States he was probably more highly appraised than in this country - the
American sales of his books were very great indeed - and,
on the Continent, to mention that one came from Arnold
Bennett's Five Towns was more surely provocative of interest than to observe one came from England's ceramic
centre. Many were the Americans and others who came to
the Potteries, just to seek out the places of the novels,
like visitors who make pilgrimage to Hardy's Wessex.

There was indeed some relationship - nevertheless with
marked contrasts - between Hardy's and Bennett's literary
art. There was a similar truth of characterisation and a
working out of destiny through all the stages of life, but
without Hardy's fatalism and pessimism. Bennett, on the
contrary, was an optimist amid sombre surroundings; and,
at will, could turn to fantastic melodrama or to highly
amusing satire and even farce, as in the hilarious adventures of 'The Card.' But Hardy was of the soil, truly
rural, and showed us life in the open-air spaces or on the
Dorset heaths.

Bennett generally chose life indoors - in a Victorian middle-class house of the Five Towns or in the gilded luxury of a *de luxe* hotel. He described with photographic detail the places and things about his people, their simple, every-day acts, and he analysed their reasons and their promptings; but with a sure hand he built up their characters, so that the picture of them and their foibles became indelibly impressed - such as Clayhanger, in the novel of that name; the two sisters, in 'The Old Wives' Tale'; and the miser-bookseller and the girl Elsie in 'Riceyman Steps.'

His serious books were long - some ran to 500 or 600 pages - and often, when we had finished one, we wondered why our interest had been maintained through every line; for much of the description had been of small and commonplace things and events. We might not be able to explain why, but the steadily maintained interest was an incontrovertible fact.

There was genius brought to the task. He was no mere photographer; he was an artist. Yet, contrary to ordinary artistic experience, he was the most methodical and businesslike man it would be possible to discover. He organised and ordered his work, as a manufacturer might do his output - the product of the orderly mind, influenced by early legal training.

He had few early advantages, except the reasonably good education of the provincial middle-class boy. Thereafter he fended for himself. He set out to be a successful author. It is said he planned to write six books - two to pay, two for fun, and two for fame. That must have been the most modest of his ambitions; for he succeeded overwhelmingly beyond. Whatever he wrote them for - most of them paid, many of them won fame, and not a few amused tens of thousands, as well as providing fun for the author. There never was a man who so accurately and successfully ordered his career. He said, 'I will be a successful author,' and he was.

Remarkably wide were his writings - forthright journalism, characterised by sound commonsense; literary, musical and artistic criticism; novels which were a panorama of life; plays, two of which, 'Milestones' and 'The Great Adventure,' were immense successes; and essays on many subjects, some of them partly autobiographical.

Arnold Bennett's death, at 63, in the ripeness and fullness of his powers, was premature; but he could hardly have surpassed his *chef d'oeuvres* of middle life. Nevertheless, his recent novel of *de luxe* hotel life, 'Imperial Palace,' was monumental within its own department.

His was a life of unremitting industry and a long tale

of great literary work accomplished. His first modest
contribution was to the 'Sentinel' - the 'Signal' of his
books - and, after a short legal career, he turned to
journalism. He never ceased to be a journalist. He was
thirty before he published his first novel; but ten years
later he was famous. His success has grown steadily in
strength, and his reputation has never fluctuated from the
upward trend. He was a master craftsman.

135. FRANK SWINNERTON, ARNOLD BENNETT, AN APPRECIATION,
'EVENING NEWS'

28 March 1931, 8

Before Bennett died, Swinnerton was asked by the 'Evening
News' to write an appreciation of him, and this is what
Swinnerton wrote. He wrote of him on a number of other
occasions, notably in 'Background with Chorus', 1956,
'The Bookman's London', 1951, 'The Georgian Scene', 1934,
'Swinnerton, An Autobiography', 1936, 'Tokefield Papers,
Old and New', 1949, and 'Arnold Bennett, A Last Word',
1978.

Arnold Bennett was the best, the kindest, the most generous, and the greatest man with whom I have ever come into
close contact. He had great sagacity, great simplicity,
a good deal of most lovable vanity; and he was astound-
ingly modest. The better one knew him the more one loved
him, and the more impressive his quality as a man became.
    All his friends will agree with me as to his character,
even if they deny greatness to his literary work. And
all will agree that to a powerful personality, in which
resoluteness, integrity, and a love of plain speaking had
their obvious place, he united a charm at once mischievous
and benign which many of his readers must have missed.
    Strangers often formed very different opinions from
these. They were sometimes a little frightened by his
reputation. They misconstrued his abruptness of manner.
They found him assertive and inflexible. And they believed the legend that he was a man who had mapped out
his life with the sole object of amassing money. Many of
them resented his success. But I do not know anybody who

was indifferent to him.

Let me try to give some notion of what Arnold Bennett looked like. He was stoutly built and about five feet nine or ten inches in height. He held himself very erect and his shoulders very rigid, so that his body had no natural swing as he walked, but rather swayed stiffly from side to side. He always walked slowly and with great seriousness.

His brow was square and rose straight from eyes that looked tired, because of rather heavy eyelids, to the small flourish of hair which latterly replaced the famous coif made fun of by caricaturists. His cheeks were clear and showed a faint colour. His mouth was irregular and his upper teeth were also irregular.

The eyes, once the first impression of tiredness had passed, were a warm brown, and smiled. Bennett was a master of the wink. When some effusive stranger button-holed him to express admiration, Bennett was at all times courteous; but, if he caught a friendly eye beyond his enthusiast, one of those heavy lids would irresistibly quiver.

In repose his expression, I should have said, represented calm melancholy. But his smile was very sweet, and the aura of kindness which surrounded him was such that he was extremely popular with children. Odd as it may seem to some, he could converse with children very effectively. But he was a shy and sensitive man, who normally talked little.

When I first knew him, he once referred to Mr. H.G. Wells's unlimited brilliance as a conversationalist by saying briefly: 'He talks, you know. I can't do that.' And in those days he could not, or did not, talk. When pressed for an opinion by guests at his own table, he would often jerk his head in my direction, and say '*He'll* tell you.'

One day I said to him: 'I talk too much.' He said: 'Yes, but from politeness.' It was politeness that caused Bennett to talk more freely in later years. He did not really enjoy talking. But he talked to entertain his guests, to 'make things go,' and he did this very well, though sometimes with exaggeration of his own mannerisms.

And I am here reminded to mention a fact which explains much about Bennett which has puzzled and irritated his less sympathetic readers. I have said that he was exceptionally shy and sensitive. He stammered. It was not a slight stammer; but when he was at all agitated the stammer became a complete inhibition of speech.

So strong was his will that he always persisted in fighting the stammer until he could pronounce the word he

had in mind. Hence his abruptness, which communicated
itself to his writing, and gave that writing an air of
dogmatism.

He would say, if his opinion were challenged: 'I can't
argue.' It was often thought that he disdained argument.
This was not the case. He argued with his intimates; but
with his intimates he rarely stammered, unless he had
something painful to tell them.

His voice was rather harsh, and gave the impression of
being high-pitched. His manner was, to friends, genial.
Very often, one would catch sight of him from a little
distance, seated, very carefully smoking a cigarette.
Probably making a note in a tiny notebook which he always
carried. His expression would be grave.

But as one approached he would look up. 'Hello, boss,'
he would say, saluting with a finger to his forelock.
Or, if one had a surname which he liked to pronounce, but
which offered difficulties to his tongue, he would *say* the
first letters with mock ceremoniousness - as 'Well, Mister
S-W-I-innerton.' Comparatively few people, except in company, called him 'Arnold.' To innumerable friends, old
and young, he was 'A.B.' It was as if they used a diminu-
tive.

And his friends really were innumerable. They were
absolutely sure of his interest and his integrity. They
went to him with all sorts of petitions, troubles, confes-
sions. He listened to them at length; then he gave his
advice. He corresponded with them - hundreds of them. He
was always ready to help them, and did so, with money,
encouragement, and sympathy.

Sometimes he would refer to one of them as 'he.'
'That chap,' he would say. A pause. A jerk of the head.
Then: 'He has to be *helped*.' And he *was* helped. Once,
when I had received an appeal, and had shown him the
letter, he said (though he did not know the applicant):
'What are you going to send? I should like to do the
same!' And out popped one of the odd cheques which he
always carried for emergencies.

He came, as is well known, from Staffordshire; and I
think his first interest in myself (otherwise a literary
interest) arose from the fact that mine is a Staffordshire
name. He was born a Methodist. And in spite of the fact
that intellectually he was an agnostic he remained essentially a Methodist (and a Midlander) all his life.

The sneers of some people (who had not learned courtesy
in the course of an otherwise elaborate curriculum) at
his 'provincialism' had no truth so far as his intellect
and his imagination were concerned. He was provincial in
the sense that the Provinces, the backbone of England, are

provincial. He also retained certain provincialisms of
speech and pronunciation (I only mean in such words as
'bath' or 'ask,' in which he used the light 'a,' and
such phrases as his favourite 'We shall look a bit soft').

He was easily impressed by magnificence or by a display
of knowledge. I think he could at times be caught by the
second-rate. But only for a time, for his judgment was in
constant repair, and his scrutiny was very unsentimental.
Otherwise, when he was thought 'provincial,' he was often
just humorous. As for example when he moved into a house
where the panels of all the doors had been decorated by a
former tenant with mirrors. At my first visit to this
house I said, 'Oh, Lord! I couldn't stand all this
looking-glass!' He replied, blandly, 'I was born for it!'

He dressed with great care. His shirts were always
superfine. Once, when he dined in company with a very
great personage, the personage broke a long silence by
saying: 'Mr. Bennett; do you mind if I ask you something?'
Bennett agreed to be asked something. 'Do you mind telling me where you get your shirts?'

It was a great moment. I can imagine the wave of
Bennett's hand - for he used, deliberately, a good deal of
not always graceful gesture - as he responded. That was
what I meant in referring to his lovable vanity. He could
be, and was, teased endlessly as to his clothes; but he
did give them a great deal of thought. As a consequence
he was always described by 'The Tailor and Cutter' as 'the
best-dressed author in London.'

What interested him most of all, however, was not
clothes. Nor was it talk. He had a really passionate
interest in human nature; and a really passionate love of
the fine arts. You had only to look at his beautiful and
sensitive hands (of which I never knew him to be conscious)
to realise a delicacy for which his manner might not have
prepared you; only to be in his company during the performance of music or before pictures, to realise that power
he had of yielding himself completely to beauty.

He was not a systematic critic, but was purely intuitive. As a result, some of the opinions he expressed on
particular artists or particular works were erratic. The
elegant often shivered at his judgments. On the whole,
however, these judgments (unless they were roundly stated,
when it was wise to suspect them) wore well, and will wear
well.

He was a little bitten with the desire to be up to date.
Not in private. Some of his friends used to tease him
about his pronouncements. He was always ready for such
gibes; and equal to them. And at the end of a bout of
opposed statements either the opinions did not seem so

eccentric, or Bennett would remark: 'Well, there may be
something in what you say.' Immediately afterwards,
recovering himself, he would add: 'But not much.' He
would never yield to argument; but he would listen to it
'with due respect.'

Not always, though. Several years ago, the date of
Marie Lloyd's birth became a subject of dispute between
us. I said she was born in 1870. Bennett said I was
wrong; that she must have been born much earlier. I
insisted. He said: 'We'll soon settle it. I've got all
the reference books in my study.' He disappeared. Ten
minutes later, he returned. 'Extraordinary!' said he.
'I've looked in a dozen books. And they're ALL wrong!'

But he was laughing as he spoke. His downrightness -
when not due to his stammer - was largely an innocent
pose. He was also, as I have said (the remark may have
caused some rubbing of eyes), an excessively modest man.
He never spoke of his own books, though often of the
number of words he had written that day. He accepted
printed criticism (though it was sometimes violent) better
than any other author I have ever known. His response to
private praise, when he took it seriously, was one of surprise and pleasure.

Indeed, as a proof of his modesty, I recall that once,
when somebody not myself had repeated quite reasonable
praise of his work, he meditatively said: 'Well, it's odd,
but I can't see it!' This was the truth. In public he
always pretended to be delighted with his own performance.

His greatest vanity was that he was a man-of-the-world.
He was never a man-of-the-world. He had not the pulpy
sentimentality veneered with cynicism that is characteristic of that species. He was, on the contrary, once he
went outside his own shrewd, practical genius, simple
almost to naïveté.

He had the loving heart of a good man, plus the
sensitiveness of the artist, the efficient mind of the
practical thinker, the timidity of the stammerer, the
determination of the midlander, the rigor of the moralist,
and the generosity of greatness. I think he was a great
writer, but he was a greater man.

As for his personality, it is not without significance
that he came from the same county as Doctor Johnson. It
was his habit to say that 'nine out of every ten people
improve on acquaintance,' and the more one knew Arnold
Bennett the more one marvelled at the sympathy, the
patience, the large tolerance, and the essential sweetness
and simplicity which were the sources of his strength and
of the affection of his friends.

136. DESMOND MacCARTHY, IN THE 'WEEK-END REVIEW'

4 April 1931, 504-5

This article was part of a broadcast talk on Bennett given
by Desmond MacCarthy on 30 March.

Bennett was born into a restless investigating age, an
age which was digging at the roots of motives. He was
forced to go deeper into human nature, and thus in his
finest work, 'The Old Wives' Tale', 'Clayhanger' and its
sequels, and in many chapters scattered up and down his
novels we also apprehend human beings not merely in relation to a social system but in relation to the forces
which control human life beneath the surface. This
requires a more penetrating kind of imagination.
    Compare Bennett for one moment with a living novelist
whose name with his was often mentioned in the same
breath: Mr. Wells. Bennett and Wells, Wells and Bennett -
we thought of them as two great twin-brethren, who by
means of fiction illuminated our times. They both show
the changes which are going on before our eyes, but one
feels when one reads Mr. Wells's books that his perceptions have always been sharpened by the way in which the
confusion of the existing order has impinged upon *himself*,
has baffled, tortured and amused *him*. His fiction is
autobiography in disguise, doctored and altered often
beyond recognition, but in spirit at any rate autobiography; just as his abstract thinking has the air of
always having been prompted by the exigencies of his own
predicament at any particular moment, however disinterestedly it may have been pursued. Thanks to being such a
bundle of conflicting sensibilities, reactions and passions - so 'human', to use a tag - this reflexion of a
personal response to life has been extraordinarily rich
in results: Mr. Wells has shown us things worth seeing
because he is *personal*. But Bennett showed them so well
because he forgot himself. Compared with Mr. Wells he was
an 'eye' without a character behind it. What was, however, behind that eye was a curiously complete sympathy
which enabled him to find ordinary characters as interesting as they are to themselves. The characters in Mr.
Wells's novels, when they are not projections of himself,
are as interesting as they are to Mr. Wells - that is to
say interesting in a very different sort of way.

Bennett's method is what we call the objective method. Now it is easier to see the greatness of an author in work which obviously depends upon the author himself for its charm, excitement and power. In Bennett's finest work we forget him, and it was only on second thoughts that we saw that to present character and events so impartially required rare qualities - intellectual disinterestedness and selfless sympathy. These things are very rare indeed.

Bennett showed the same detachment towards his critics as towards his characters. If you were a critic you would know that this is a magnanimity which is very rare. I always knew that if I were stating a genuine opinion about one of Bennett's books or plays, and not merely trying to be amusing and clever at his expense, even if I then wrote the most disparaging things about it, he would not only forgive me, but respect me for it. He was sublimely free from touchiness, and since he was by no means a confident man, deep inside, that gives the measure of his natural generosity of mind.

As a critic I used often to fall foul of his descriptions of luxury hotels, expensive shops, baths, clothes, ornaments, yachts, motors, etc. - his apparently too great delight in the garish surface of wealthy life. That gusto struck me as too uncritical and indiscriminate. Yet I was bound to admit that this surface was apt to crack and reveal - what? Disillusionment with pleasures, possessions and all that money can buy? No. Satire? Not exactly - something less positive than that. The peculiarity of his satire was that it was accompanied by a temperamental sympathy with whatever excited it. To satirise effectively anybody or anything certainly some sympathy is necessary; otherwise the satirist cannot strike straight and hard. But in his case there was an overplus of sympathy, conscious and unconscious, which confused the result.

I remember when I had finished 'Mr. Prohack' I found myself in doubt whether the book was intended as a picture of futility or attainment. Was the sudden good fortune of the Prohack family after all a Timon's feast, a matter of warm water under silver dish-covers? It looked rather like it. Yet a doubt remained. With his intellect Bennett constantly assented to the proposition that the solid happiness of possessing £20,000 a year and a son who is a financial magnate could be easily exaggerated; yet his temperament kept shouting enthusiastically as he told the story of the Prohacks, in a tone very far from that of an ironic host: 'Lap, lucky dogs, lap!' The voice of his temperament was louder than that of his intellect. Hence the reader's confused impression at the close of books about the rich which nevertheless did contain much social

satire, and satire particularly directed against the getting and spending of money. That particular story closes
with a description of a magnificent yacht on which young
Prohack never sails, but takes tea at intervals, and
(almost in the spirit of 'Bouvard and Pecuchet') with Mr.
Prohack, from sheer boredom, taking up routine work again
to make more money which he does not want.

  The truth is that though Arnold Bennett's material was,
especially in his most serious novels, extremely unromantic, his attitude towards it was romantic. The essence of
all romanticism is to make individual feeling the sole
test of the value of the ends pursued. The state of emotion which is called 'passion' between men and women is an
intensely romantic one, and everybody knows that the overwhelming value it attributes to the object is out of all
proportion to fact. Now, all Bennett's characters were
passionate after their ends; he took their own views of
the value of what they aimed at. There was no criticism
from outside of their desires in his books. When he was
at his greatest, he faced the tragedy of men and women
whose impulses and desires had glorified disproportionately
and eagerly one thing after another. He brought them up
against death and the injuries of time. It was this tragedy that made 'The Old Wives' Tale' so fine a book, and
his pathos often, as in 'Raingo' and in many an episode,
grim and large and impressive.

Select Bibliography

Aside from the modest material in the 'Book Review Digest'
and the 'Annual Bibliography of English Language and
Literature' there has been no systematic listing of Bennett
reviews. I have used the 'Digest' as my guide for American
reviews, but I have by no means reported on every review
that is mentioned there. My introductory material does
mention or allude to virtually every English review known
to me, but literally thousands of reviews could be added
from journals and newspapers familiar and obscure. Louis
Tillier, 'Arnold Bennett et ses romans réalistes', 1967,
and Margaret Locherbie-Goff, 'La Jeunesse d'Arnold Bennett', 1939, provided additional information. For general
bibliographies on Bennett, see Tillier, Hepburn's 'The
Art of Arnold Bennett', 1963, and the fourth volume of the
revised edition of the 'Cambridge Bibliography of English
Literature'. (See also the following pages for material
published on Bennett during his life.) For Bennett's own
writings see Norman Emery, 'Arnold Bennett, A Bibliography', Stoke-on-Trent, 1967, and Anita Miller, 'Arnold
Bennett, An Annotated Bibliography', New York, 1977. Mrs
Miller's work is mainly concerned with periodical publications.

Appendix

General Bibliography on Bennett, 1903–March 1931

All substantial general items referred to or reprinted elsewhere in this text are listed here, along with other items. I have excluded reviews and most items of slight size. A more extensive list appears in Louis Tillier, 'Arnold Bennett et ses romans réalistes'. A large mass of material in American newspapers reporting on Bennett's visit there in 1911 has never been listed.

1903 E.M.E., About Our Contributors, 'Hearth and Home' (27 August).

1908 BARTON, J.E., Fiction and Mr. Bennett, 'New Age' (3 December).

1910 A.M.T., The Humour of Arnold Bennett, 'Glasgow Herald' (12 February).
The Grey Novel, 'Nation' (10 December).

1911 BETTANY, F.G., Arnold Bennett, An Appreciation, 'Bookman' (March).
HOWELLS, W.D., Editor's Easy Chair, 'Harper's' (March).
MAAS, WILLIAM, Literary Portraits, 'Daily Chronicle' (30 June).
FYFE, H. HAMILTON, The Business Man in Literature, 'Daily Mail' (25 October).
A Tribute to Arnold Bennett, 'Harper's Weekly' (16 December).

1912 WELLS, H.G., The Contemporary Novel, 'Atlantic Monthly' (January).
HOWELLS, W.D., Editor's Easy Chair, 'Harper's' (March).
The Five Towns Man, 'Star' (20 July).
FYFE, H. HAMILTON, Arnold Bennett, 'London Magazine' (October).

ASTOR, LENOX, Bibliographies of Younger Reputations, 'Bookman' (New York, November).
COOPER, FREDERIC TABER, 'Some English Story-Tellers', London.
BEERBOHM, MAX, 'A Christmas Garland', London.

1913 ROZ, FIRMIN, Mr. Arnold Bennett, 'Revue des deux mondes' (15 Octobre).
SCOTT-JAMES, R.A., 'Personality in Literature', London.

1914 JAMES, HENRY, The Younger Generation, 'Times Literary Supplement' (19 March).
CLASSEN, E. The Novels of Arnold Bennett, 'Germanisch-romanische Monatsschrift', 6.

1915 Art and Popularity, 'New Republic' (16 January).
JACKSON, HOLBROOK, Arnold Bennett, 'T.P.'s Weekly' (1 May).
DAVRAY, HENRY, Le Romancier des cinq villes, 'Revue de Paris' (15 Mai).
BRONSON-HOWARD, GEORGE, Arnold Bennett as Melodramatist, 'Bookman' (New York, October).
Arnold Bennett - The Five Towns, 'Metropolitan Magazine' (September).
DARTON, F.J. HARVEY, 'Arnold Bennett', London.
SHERMAN, STUART P., The Realism of Arnold Bennett, 'Nation' (23 December), followed by correspondence on 6 and 20 January and 3 and 10 February. Reprinted in his 'On Contemporary Literature', 1917.

1916 CUNLIFFE, J.W., Arnold Bennett's Provincialism, 'Independent' (21 February).
HUGHES, DOROTHEA PRICE, The Novels of Mr. Arnold Bennett and Wesleyan Methodism, 'Contemporary Review' (November).
MURDOCH, W.G., The Art of Arnold Bennett, 'Quarterly Notebook' (December).
SCOTT, DIXON, The Commonsense of Mr. Arnold Bennett, in his 'Men of Letters'.

1919 RAYMOND, E.T., Mr. Arnold Bennett, 'Outlook' (13 December).

1920 GOLDRING, DOUGLAS, The Gordon Selfridge of English Letters, in his 'Reputations', London.
COX, SIDNEY HAYES, Romance in Arnold Bennett, 'Sewanee Review' (July).

1921 PHELPS, WILLIAM LYON, Arnold Bennett, Maker of Many Plays, 'New York Times Book Review' (23 January).

SHANKS, EDWARD, Reflections on the Recent History of
the English Novel, 'London Mercury' (June).
NEWTON, A. EDWARD, Twenty-Five Hours a Day, 'Atlantic
Monthly' (August).
HIND, C.L., 'Authors and I', London.
MENCKEN, H.L., Arnold Bennett, 'Prejudices, First
Series', London.

1922 MOULT, THOMAS, Arnold Bennett, 'Bookman' (June).
PRIEUR, J., Woman in the Chief Works of Arnold
Bennett, thesis, University of Paris (Sorbonne,
June).
COBLEY, W.D., Arnold Bennett, 'Papers of the Manches-
ter Library Literary Club'.
ERVINE, ST JOHN, 'Some Impressions of My Elders',
London.

1923 JUDSON, A.C., 'Arnold Bennett and the Five Towns,
'Texas Review' (January).
LITTLE, P., Books and Things, 'New Republic' (28
March).
WOOLF, VIRGINIA, Mr. Bennett and Mrs. Brown, 'New
York Evening Post' (17 November), 'Nation and Athen-
aeum' (1 December), revised for the 'Criterion'
(July 1924) and as a pamphlet (1924).
GUEDALLA, PHILIP, The Levity of Mr. Arnold Bennett,
'Vanity Fair' (November).
ADCOCK, A. ST JOHN, 'Gods of Modern Grub Street',
London.
CHESTERTON, G.K., The Mercy of Arnold Bennett, in his
'Fancies versus Fads', London.
WALPOLE, HUGH, Arnold Bennett, A Pen Portrait,
'Outlook and Independent'.

1924 HOFFMAN, RICHARD, Proportion and Incident in Joseph
Conrad and Arnold Bennett, 'Sewanee Review' (January).
DOWNS, BRIAN, Arnold Bennett, 'North American Review'
(January).
PRIESTLEY, J.B., Mr. Arnold Bennett, 'London Mercury'
(February), reprinted in his 'Figures in Modern
Literature', 1924.
'PURE, SIMON', (FRANK SWINNERTON), The Writing of
Novels, 'Bookman' (New York, March).
DARTON, F.J. HARVEY, The Man Who Saw His Own Future,
'T.P.'s and Cassell's Weekly' (29 March).
FOLLETT, H.T. and others, 'Arnold Bennett, Apprecia-
tions', also 'Arnold Bennett, An Introduction', New
York. These pamphlets issued by George Doran bear
no date; material in the second goes back to 1911;

each was probably issued at various times in various forms.
'Complete Catalogue of the Library of John Quinn', vol. 1, New York.
JOHNSON, L.G., 'ARNOLD BENNETT OF THE FIVE TOWNS', London.

1925 DUTTON, GEORGE B., Arnold Bennett, Showman, 'Sewanee Review' (January).
MUIR, EDWIN, Scrutinies IV: Bennett, 'Calendar of Modern Letters' (June).
Mayoral Dinner at Stoke ..., Criticism of Mr. Arnold Bennett, 'Staffordshire Sentinel' (11 December; see also the 'Manchester Guardian' of same date; both are small items.)
BENNETT, MRS ARNOLD, 'Arnold Bennett', London.
FRIERSON, WILLIAM C., 'L'Influence de naturalisme français sur les romanciers anglais de 1885 à 1900', Paris.
PRIESTLEY, J.B., 'English Journal', 14.

1926 Contemporary English Writers, 'Staffordshire Sentinel' (23 December; a small item).
DREW, ELIZABETH, 'The Modern Novel', London.
AAS, L., 'Arnold Bennett', Copenhagen.

1927 BEAVERBROOK, LORD, Arnold Bennett as I Know Him, 'Sunday Express' (29 May).
FORSTER, E.M., 'Aspects of the Novel', London.
CARTER, AMPHILIS, The Work of Arnold Bennett as a Novelist, M.A. thesis, University of Birmingham.

1928 The Wells and Bennett Novel, 'Times Literary Supplement' (23 August).
CROSS, WILBUR, Arnold Bennett of the Five Towns, 'Yale Review' (December).
WEST, REBECCA, Uncle Bennett, in her 'The Strange Necessity', London.

1929 DARK, SIDNEY, Arnold Bennett, 'T.P.'s and Cassell's Weekly' (9 March).
LYND, ROBERT, Arnold Bennett, 'John O'London's Weekly' (13 July).
BEARDMORE, F.G., miscellaneous articles on Bennett and the Five Towns, 'Sunday Chronicle' (3 and 10 February, 23 and 30 June, 22 December, and other dates).
FABES, GILBERT, 'Modern First Editions', 3 vols, London, 1929-32.

1930 BOUTELL, H.S., Modern English First Editions, 'Pub-
     lishers' Weekly' (15 March).
     BANNERJEE, SRIKUMAR and NATH, C.B., 'Complete Study
     of The Admirable Crichton, Milestones, The Great
     Adventure', Shahani.
     GLAYMAN, ROSE, Recent Judith Drama and Its Analogues,
     thesis, University of Pennsylvania.

1931 LASKI, HAROLD, Arnold Bennett, 'Daily Herald' (14
     March.

See pp. 63, 299-300; and 349-50 for a few small items; also
p. 515 for a list of appreciations and reviews published
upon Bennett's death.

Index

The index is divided into three parts: I Individual works by Bennett: II Periodicals and publishers, book and press associations; III General index.

I INDIVIDUAL WORKS BY BENNETT

II   PERIODICALS AND PUBLISHERS, BOOK AND PRESS ASSOCIATIONS

III   GENERAL INDEX

THE CRITICAL HERITAGE SERIES

GENERAL EDITOR: B. C. SOUTHAM

Volumes published and forthcoming